THE EPIC OF NEW YORK CITY

THE EPIC OF
New York City

Edward Robb Ellis

DRAWINGS BY JEANYEE WONG

OLD TOWN BOOKS

New York

The author is grateful to the Macmillan Company for permission to quote from *J. Pierpont Morgan: An Intimate Portrait* by Herbert L. Satterlee.

This edition published by Old Town Books
a division of Marboro Books Corporation,
by arrangement with Edward Robb Ellis
1990 Old Town Books

ISBN 0-88029-516-3

Printed in the United States of America

M 9 8 7 6 5 4 3 2 1

To the Memory of My Beloved Wife
RUTH KRAUS ELLIS

World history is city history.
   —OSWALD SPENGLER

Those who do not remember the past
are condemned to relive it.
   —GEORGE SANTAYANA

Preface

———◆◀◆▶◆———

THIS is a narrative history of New York City.

Some readers may complain about its length. I could remind them that a six-volume New York history runs to more than 4,700 pages, and another four-volume work contains more than 2,500 pages. While I worked on this book, my most painful problem was deciding what to omit. In selecting my data, I kept asking myself three questions: Is it true? Is it significant? Is it interesting?

Other readers may lament that I left out such and such a person, place, event, or institution. For every omission they might cite, I could adduce many they forgot. Instead of trying to include every date and happening, thus producing a chronicle or encyclopedia, I chose to focus on particular episodes and people.

Above all, I have tried to tell a story. In narrative form, this book attempts to trace the evolution of New York City and reveal its organic relationship to the rest of the United States and all the world. Scores of smaller books describe special areas or events in the city's history. I wanted to show the big picture.

The Epic of New York City is as accurate as I could make it. Nonetheless, I agree with Tai T'ung, who produced a history of Chinese writing in the thirteenth century and said, "Were I to await perfection, my book would never be finished."

Many kind people helped me. I owe especial gratitude to my literary agent, Lurton Blassingame; my editor, William Poole; and my friend, Tom McCormack. I give thanks to my neighbor, Joseph

7

Nathan Kane, author of many excellent reference books. I fondly remember the help I got from my favorite book dealers, Stephen Seskin, David Mendoza, and Edward A. Gradijan.

Listed alphabetically, here are the names of others who aided me: Joseph Alvarez, Walter Arm, Mrs. MacKeen Bacon, David Balch, Sheldon J. Binn, Mrs. Kathryn Ellis Burton, Mrs. Archibald Campbell, Edward Corsi, Anne Cronin, Steven David, Frank Doyle, Emerson Dye, Dr. Sol Goldschmidt, John Hastings, Dr. Lionel Heiden, Herbert Kamm, Mrs. Ruth Kimball, Yvette Klein, John La Corte, William Longgood, Victor Mangual, Paul Manning, Loring McMillen, L. Porter Moore, William J. Numeroff, Dorothy L. Omansky, Gardner Osborn, Selma Seskin Pezaro, Karl Pretshold, Mrs. Lauretta Ravenna, Werner Renberg, William E. Robinson, Henry Senber, Lou Shainmark, Maggie Thomas, Edward Tatum Wallace, Jack Waugh, Gertrude Weiner, Lucy Wind, Cecilia Winkler, Hall Wright, and William Zeckendorf.

I owe most of all to my wife, Ruth Kraus Ellis, who did not live to see this book in print. She shared my enthusiasm, sustained me in moments of depression, cared for my creature comforts to conserve my energy, and was the most efficient and willing assistant any writer could have. For all these reasons, plus the fact that she was born on Manhattan, I call this the book of Ruth.

EDWARD ROBB ELLIS

Contents

CONTENTS &» 10

Chapter 1

MANHATTAN IS DISCOVERED

WHITE men saw Manhattan for the first time in April, 1524. There were fifty of them, and they crossed the Atlantic in a ship commanded by Giovanni da Verrazano, an Italian explorer working for the king of France. He murmured to his mate, the mate barked an order, and the sailors turned to with a will. Chains rattled as the anchor sloshed through the wind-dimpled water and gurgled down, down, down. Now their 100-ton vessel, the *Dauphine*, came to rest just south of the present Verrazano-Narrows Bridge in the Lower Bay of what is now New York City.

She lay silent after the creaking and rasping of her long voyage. Crew members looked up from their chores and gazed toward the shore. A breeze flicking his beard, Verrazano stood straddle-legged on deck to peer eagerly across the diced waters of the bay. Lovely was the land, and sweet its smell. In springtime, New York's air sparkles like champagne, and Verrazano's nostrils tingled. Upon his mind he etched each detail.

It was, he thought, "a pleasant place." On both sides of his ship there rose "steep little hills." Those off starboard were Brooklyn Heights; those off the port bow lay in New Jersey. Dead ahead and to the north the explorer saw "a most beautiful stream," now called the Upper Bay. Spooning into it was the Hudson River, which he described as "an exceeding great stream of water." To the right of the Hudson lay the forested hill-humped island of Manhattan.

Gliding into view came thirty canoes filled with dusky feather-clad natives, who stroked with muscular rhythm from one shore to another, staring at the strange ship. Verrazano ordered one of his boats lowered, climbed in, and told his oarsmen to row toward the mile-wide Narrows connecting the Lower and Upper Bays like the neck of a gigantic hourglass. Some Indians, the explorer later wrote, "came toward us very cheerfully, making a great show of admiration, showing us where we might come to land most safely with our boat." He had proceeded only about half a mile when the wind freshened, the water coarsened, and a storm slashed in from the Atlantic.

Afraid that the *Dauphine* might be swiveled on her anchor line and scragged on the shore, Verrazano yelled to his men to turn around the rowboat and pull back to the mother ship. The Indians shouted their disappointment in a strange tongue as he climbed a bucking ladder onto the deck of the *Dauphine*. Then, weighing anchor, Verrazano tacked out into the tumbling open sea, "greatly regretting to leave this region which seemed so commodious and delightful."

This Italian adventurer never set foot in New York. However, he and his crew were the first Europeans to see the spot where the world's most dynamic city was to grow. Verrazano might have waited for a calm day to sail up into the Hudson, but he had no sister ship to help him if he got into trouble. Besides, he decided this river was not the Northwest Passage, not the all-water route around the northern coast of North America to the eastern (Pacific) ocean. This search, begun toward the close of the fifteenth century, was to continue for 400 years.

When these white men discovered the site of New York City that year of 1524, Jerusalem was more than 3,000 years old, Athens was at least 2,500 years old, Rome's history went back more than 2,270 years, Paris had existed about 1,550 years, London could count more than 1,460 birthdays, and Berlin was a village 217 years old.

Verrazano piloted the *Dauphine* out into the scudding waters of the Atlantic and then went below to jot down his impressions of this new land. It was "not without some riches," he wrote, "all the hills showing mineral matter in them." No gold or silver of any consequence ever was found at New York City, but the place later yielded precious and semiprecious stones, such as opals, garnets, and amethysts. In fact, 99 species and 170 varieties were discovered in Manhattan, a record perhaps never exceeded on the site of any other great American city.

Verrazano named the Upper Bay the Gulf of Santa Margherita for the sister of Francis I, king of France, his employer. He called the Hudson River the Vendôme in honor of the Duke of Vendôme, a French prince. To the metropolitan area of New York he gave the name Angoulême, the title held by Francis when he was heir presumptive to the French throne. On July 8, 1524, Verrazano sat safely at dockside in Dieppe, France, expanding his diary into a long and historic letter to his royal employer.

The first chapter in the history of New York City is really a chapter in the history of Europe. All America, for that matter, became a bloody arena, in which Europeans fought out their ancient rivalries. With Verrazano's appearance in the bay of New York the four chief contestants to claims on America had entered the historic picture. In 1497 John Cabot had discovered North America for the English, although they were slow to press their claim. The next year Christopher Columbus had discovered South America for the Spanish during his third voyage. In 1500 the Portuguese had explored the coast of the New World. The French had been so busy waging religious wars and trying to conquer Italy that they had made a late start in this western thrust.

Earlier, during the Crusades (1095-1291), Europeans first became interested in overseas expansion. As warriors and priests penetrated the fringe of the Orient, they found civilizations whose wealth and luxury far surpassed their own rude standards of living. Europeans were delighted by Oriental perfumes and dyes, rugs and silks, glass and porcelain, pearls and cotton. They doted on the exotic spices, which gave a better taste to their own monotonous diet. All these strange and wonderful wares whetted their appetite for trade. Land routes developed through central Asia to the east. Sea routes opened through the Isthmus of Suez, the Red Sea, and the Persian Gulf. Arab merchants and Italian capitalists fattened on this commerce.

Down through the years Ottoman Turks had swept out of Asia Minor to subdue vast reaches of territory, conquer Constantinople, and overrun the trade routes. As a result, these sea paths became less attractive to other nations. Then Portuguese ships sailed *east* and found a saltwater route to India around the tip of Africa. Columbus sailed *west* and later died still believing he had reached the Orient. The Portuguese and Spanish followed up their explorations with colonization, the Portuguese establishing posts in Brazil, while the Spanish founded colonies in Florida and Mexico. Now, as a result of Verrazano's voyage, the French claimed part of the Western Hemisphere, as did the English, the Spaniards, and the Portuguese.

In 1493, to avert a quarrel over land claims, Pope Alexander VI drew an imaginary north-south line through the western part of the Atlantic Ocean and the eastern part of South America. Thus, he divided the New World, giving the Spanish all land west of this line and the Portuguese all land to the east. But the king of Portugal protested, so Spain agreed to push the line of demarcation a little farther west, thus granting Portugal what today is Brazil. This high-handed division of the New World ignored the aspirations of other European nations. To date Holland had not claimed any portion of this new continent, but now she cast covetous eyes westward. England, Holland, and France looked on in envy as the wealth of the Indies poured into the coffers of Spain.

Francis I, king of France, was at war with Charles I, king of Spain. Francis scorned the Pope's line of demarcation and cared nothing about the later agreement between the Spanish and Portuguese kings. He said to Charles, "Your majesty and the king of Portugal have divided the world between you, offering no part of it to me. Show me, I pray you, the will of our father Adam so that I may see if he has really made you his universal heir."

Then Francis summoned Giovanni da Verrazano. Born about 1480 near Florence, Italy, Verrazano already was in the French maritime service and had a reputation as a tough sea dog. In those days the king of one country often hired a navigator who was a citizen of another nation. Verrazano was the first explorer officially sent out from France. Publicly, he sought a Northwest Passage to the Orient. His real purpose was to stake out a claim by France to all America north of Mexico. On January 17, 1524, Verrazano sailed from the archipelago of Madeira. In March he made his first landfall near the site of the modern city of Wilmington, North Carolina, and then followed the Atlantic seaboard to New York Harbor. Afterward, in 1527, Verrazano embarked for Brazil, where he was killed and probably eaten by native Caribs.

Francis I gave the name of New France to the North American territory discovered by Verrazano but did not immediately do anything to consolidate his claim. Charles of Spain acted faster. In 1525, the year after Verrazano touched at New York, the Spanish king sent a Portuguese navigator to explore the eastern shores of America. This man was a Negro, named Estéban Gómez. He reached the site of New York on January 17, 1526. Because this was the feast day of St. Anthony, Gómez named the Hudson River the San Antonio. Ice floes drifting downriver discouraged Gómez from pushing up into the interior. In 1526 Verrazano was killed in the West Indies, the Mogul empire was founded in India, and William Tyndale's translation of the bible became the dominant one. That was two years after Guatemala City was founded by Pedro de Alvarado and one year after Francisco Pizarro explored Peru.

The third European explorer to see New York Bay and the one whose influence lasted the longest was Henry Hudson. An experienced English navigator, he was making his third transatlantic trip, this time for the Dutch. With the Portuguese trying to monopolize the sea route around Africa, the Dutch East India Company wanted Hudson to find the elusive Northwest Passage to the Orient. He commanded the *Half Moon*, an eighty-ton flat-bottomed yacht, or galliot, mounting square sails upon two masts. His ship was smaller and his sailors less numerous than those under Verrazano. Hudson's crew of twenty consisted of English and Dutch seamen inclined to quarrel with one another. The second mate, an Englishman named Robert Juet, kept the ship's log—our prime source of information about this significant voyage.

The morning of September 2, 1609, the *Half Moon* nosed into the Lower Bay of New York. Fog muffled the shore. Within a few hours, though, the rising sun cleared the mist. Gingerly steering northeast by north, Hudson and his men suddenly saw the land. The Upper

Bay appeared to them as "a great lake of water." Pouring into this lake—really a bay—was "a great stream," the river that took Hudson's name. At 5 P.M. that day they anchored. Gazing northward from the motionless ship, they could see the high hills of Manhattan. Hudson's mate wrote that "this is a very good land to fall with and a pleasant land to see."

Henry Hudson was a careful mariner. For days he hovered about the Lower Bay, sending crew members out in boats to take soundings. Curious Indians appeared, and Hudson let some of them climb aboard the *Half Moon*. They "seemed very glad of our coming," the mate noted. The Indians, who wore deerskins and copper ornaments, held out tobacco leaves, which Hudson's men bought with beads and knives.

The fourth day after the ship anchored, the captain again dispatched a party of five men in a boat to reconnoiter. Bored with shipboard life, these seamen were delighted to see flowers and grass and agreed that "very sweet smells come from them." By then, however, some Indians had changed their attitude toward the strange palefaces. Warriors in two canoes attacked this one-boat expedition, and in the fight that followed an Englishman, named John Colman, was killed by an arrow shot into his throat. He was the first European to die on the shore of New York.

On September 11, 1609, nine days after anchoring, Hudson sailed the *Half Moon* through the Narrows, the strait separating Staten Island and Brooklyn, and voyaged up into the river afterward named for him. He and his men were awed by the majesty of the Jersey Palisades, stretching 25 miles along the western shore and reaching in places a height of more than 500 feet. Hudson took soundings as he advanced. Bearing past mountains, skirting bends, and sometimes undergoing adventures with river Indians, he finally reached the site of the current city of Albany. He remained there four days, sending his boats 25 miles farther north, to no avail. This was, after all, only a river, not the fabled Northwest Passage. Disappointed, Hudson turned around and sailed back down the waterway.

On October 4, 1609, he left New York, never to return. However, Hudson had landed here; this neither Verrazano nor Gómez had done before him. Furthermore, the *Half Moon* was the first ship ever to leave New York directly for Europe. Hudson landed at Dartmouth, but English authorities kept him—an English citizen—from taking his vessel back to her home port of Amsterdam, Holland. Dutch seamen sailed her there the following year. By then Hudson's report of his voyage and discoveries had reached his employers.

Although the Indians at New York City usually wore deerskins, upriver natives were clad in pelts of beaver and otter. Besides reporting this to the Dutch East India Company, Hudson had sent along furs as proof. Company directors were not impressed. They had ordered Hudson to find a passage to India, and he had failed. However, when word of Hudson's findings leaked out, a group of Amsterdam merchants, more imaginative than the company officials, decided they had hit on a new source of revenue.

The Dutch bought furs from Russia. In those days, when houses were scantily heated, furs were worn in Europe both indoors and out by men and women alike, so they were a desirable commodity. But the Russian emperor laid a duty on furs exported from his country. What's more, the Dutch had to pay him in gold and other European currency. Hudson, however, got pelts of equal quality from the New World Indians for beads, knives, and hatchets. Instead of trading with Russia, the crafty Amsterdam merchants made up their minds to do business with the gullible savages in a land where duties and customshouses were unknown.

In 1610 a brisk fur trade began between the Dutch and Indians. Dutch navigators and traders sailed again and again for the New World. There they entered the Connecticut River, pushed northeastward along the New England coast, cruised southward as far as Cape May, New Jersey, and advanced up the Delaware River to the mouth of the Schuylkill River. To this strip of the Atlantic seaboard, from New Jersey to Maine, they gave the name of New Netherland.

Hendrick Christiaensen glimpsed the Lower Bay of New York while sailing in a heavily laden ship from the West Indies to Holland. Upon returning to his homeland, he urged his friend Adriaen Block to charter a small vessel and head for Manhattan to engage in this expanding fur trade. Here in the New World the two men loaded their ship with pelts and persuaded a couple of Indians to return to Holland with them. Exhibited from place to place, the aborigines created a sensation. Block wrote a long account of the riches in furs to be found across the seas.

Several wealthy Amsterdam merchants now formed a partnership and outfitted two ships, placing Christiaensen in charge of the *For-*

tune and Block in charge of the *Tiger*. These mariners sailed for New Netherland early in 1613. Three months later the merchants dispatched a third vessel, under Cornelis Jacobsen May. After passing Manhattan, Christiaensen continued upriver to the present site of Albany, where he built the first Dutch stronghold in America. This stockade, thirty-six feet long by twenty-six feet wide, he named Fort Nassau in honor of the stadholder of the Dutch republic, Maurice, Count of Nassau.

While Christiaensen wintered near Albany, Block remained in the vicinity of New York City. Block's ship, the *Tiger*, caught fire in the harbor and was destroyed. Indians fed Block and his crew throughout the rest of the winter. In the spring of 1614, Block put his men to work building a new ship, the first ever constructed at New York. He named this sixteen-ton yacht the *Onrust*, meaning restless, trouble, or strife. Loosely translated, the ship's name has come down to us as the *Restless*.

Then Block became the first white man to sail up the East River and stagger through Hellegat, now known as Hell Gate, the narrow and treacherous channel between Wards Island and Queens County. Emerging in Long Island Sound, Block was astonished at this "beautiful inland sea." Captain May, for his part, nosed along the southern shore of Long Island, proving that it was indeed an island.

Some years before, Robert Juet, Hudson's second mate, apparently was the first white man to write down the name Manhattan. In the Dutch, French, and English writings of colonial times, Manhattan was spelled almost fifty different ways. Historians disagree about the origin of the word. Some say the Indians who hunted and fished on the island called themselves the Manhattans. Others say they did not apply the name to themselves but called the place Manhattan. Still others claim it was the Dutch, not the Indians, who first used the name Manhattan. However, one thing is certain: The Indians who camped on Manhattan Island were of Algonquin stock. The word "Algonquin" pertains to a linguistic group of North American Indians. When the white men came to this continent, it was peopled with only about 800,000 to 1,000,000 Indians. Most lived along the Atlantic seaboard between New York and Boston.

Socially, the Indians were grouped into families, clans, subtribes, tribes, and confederations of tribes. The Indians who hunted and fished on Manhattan, in the Bronx, and in Westchester County belonged to the Wappinger Confederacy. The Indians who lived on

Staten Island and Long Island belonged to the Delaware Confederacy. A Delaware subtribe, called the Canarsie, occupied Brooklyn.

Linguistically, there was much confusion. The Indians of North America spoke from 500 to 1,000 different languages, or more than all the languages spoken by Europeans. Unable to communicate verbally, some resorted to sign language. Although the various branches of the Algonquins spoke a language fundamentally the same, each tribe had its own dialect. The tribes that used the lower part of Manhattan had trouble understanding members of the tribe that frequented the upper reaches of the island. Some of the Indians on Manhattan had a war cry that sounded like this: *Woach, woach, ha, ha, hach, woach!*

The various Algonquin tribes were hostile toward one another. Their common enemy, the Iroquois, lived in the upper Hudson Valley. North-south Indian trails generally were known as warpaths because the Indians spread out across America in east to west strips, and north to south travel brought rival tribesmen into contact with one another. East to west paths were called paths of peace. Manhattan was laced by several paths, but the principal one was a warpath stretching from the Battery northward to what is now City Hall Park. Such was the origin of Broadway.

Manhattan's twenty-two square miles was a happy hunting ground. For game the Indians had their choice of whitetail deer, beavers, red foxes, gray foxes, black bears, gray wolves, mountain lions, bobcats, minks, weasels, chipmunks, ducks, geese, and wild turkeys—to name just a few. A bountiful supply of fish flashed through the waters swirling among the more than fifty islands within the present city limits of New York. The place was a crossroads for migratory birds, flying southward in the fall and northward in the spring.

All the area now embraced by New York City consisted of one vast forest. There were white oaks and red oaks, walnut trees and chestnut trees, maples and cedars, white pines and pitch pines, Norway spruces and yellow pines. At the base of the trees, huddled in tangled confusion, were grapevines and ferns, blackberry bushes and raspberry bushes, strawberries and mulberries.

Manhattan lay on a latitude more than 700 miles south of London, more than 500 miles south of Paris, and about 70 miles south of Rome. Because of its geographical position, plus the tempering influence of the Atlantic, New York's climate was relatively mild, although the difference between summer and winter was striking. Oc-

tober was the finest month of the year. In both spring and autumn
the air took on the quality of champagne; this helps explain why
Manhattan's inhabitants crackle with energy.

The island of Manhattan was bordered on the south by the
Upper Bay, on the west by the Hudson River, on the north by the
Harlem River, and on the east by the East River. The Hudson, one
of the most noble rivers in America, formed in the Adirondack
Mountains of upper New York State and flowed 315 miles to the
Battery, at the lower tip of Manhattan. It was a mile wide at the
Riverdale section of the Bronx. The Hudson was a tidal river, salt
water flowing as far north as Albany. It also included a deep submarine canyon, extending from its mouth at the Battery 200 miles
seaward. The East River was not a real river but a saltwater estuary,
or tidal strait, that stretched between the Upper Bay and the eastern
end of Long Island Sound, 16 miles to the northeast. When the
first white men reached here, the Harlem River was not a continuous
waterway linking the Hudson and East rivers. A traveler could ford
the Harlem River at low tide by jumping from rocks to reefs at
Spuyten Duyvil. Subsequent dredging and the construction of a
channel made it possible for ships to travel between the Hudson and
East rivers via the Harlem River.

The lordly Hudson River emptied into a huge hourglass harbor to
create the largest and best natural port in the United States and one
of the few perfect harbors in the entire world. Except for bitterly
cold days, the port of New York was free of ice and had far fewer
fogs than those shrouding the harbor of San Francisco.

Such was the region toward which the Dutch turned in great ex-
pectation. The first half of the seventeenth century was the golden
age of the Netherlands, even though at first the Dutch provinces
struggled to free themselves from Spain. Holland's commerce expanded as never before. The Dutch were the Yankees of their day,
shrewd, hardheaded, industrious, and ingenious. Forced to find their
own way to the Orient, in a surprisingly short time they disputed
command of the Indies with the Portuguese and then displaced them.

So many Dutch companies traded with the Far East that at last the
Dutch government, called the States General of the United Netherlands, found it necessary to merge all of them into one vast corporation. This was the Universal East India Company, chartered in 1602.
It was a fabulous success. Four years after its organization it declared a dividend of 75 percent. By 1620 its original shareholders

had realized a 425 percent profit on their investment. Under the terms of its charter, for 21 years the East India Company was to be the only Dutch firm with the right to trade to the east of the Cape of Good Hope and sail its ships through the Strait of Magellan. The corporation became one of the chief organs of Dutch imperialism. It was this company that had sent Henry Hudson to America in 1609, hoping he would discover a shorter route to India.

In that same year of 1609 a twelve-year truce was concluded between the confederated states of the Netherlands and Spain. "At this moment," said the French historian Taine, "Holland on the sea and in the world was what England was in the time of Napoleon." This is to say, it was a great maritime and imperialistic power.

With trade to and from the Orient running smoothly under the direction of one colossal company, the Dutch now organized another group to guide commerce between Holland and America—or New Netherland. This was the United New Netherland Company, formed by thirteen merchants of Amsterdam and Hoorn and chartered in 1614. (In the same year, when the name New Netherland formally was applied to a portion of the New World, the name New England was given to the territory lying north of it.) For three years directors of the new corporation were to enjoy exclusive rights to make trading voyages to the region between Virginia and Canada. At the end of this period, however, the States General refused to renew the charter, and the American trade was thrown open to all Dutchmen.

The result was competition and confusion. This endangered the national interest, for the English chafed at the growing traffic of Dutch ships on the Hudson River. At last the English instructed their minister at The Hague, Holland's capital, to remind the Dutch government of England's claims in the New World. Under these pressures the Dutch government granted a charter on June 3, 1621, to a group of merchants, who had organized the Dutch West India Company.

These businessmen hoped to regulate and protect the trade carried on by the Dutch in both America and Africa. They intended to set up colonies on each of the two continents and their nearby islands. Frankly patterned after the Dutch East India Company, the new firm was divided into five branches, or chambers—one for each of the five Dutch cities. Of these, the Amsterdam chamber won the most power because it contributed the most money—four-ninths of the total investment. So it was this chamber that controlled New Netherland. However, the company's nineteen directors, who governed the far-flung affairs of the entire firm, regarded New Netherland as something of a stepchild. They were intent on trying to capture Brazil from the Portuguese and colonizing Guiana and the West Indies.

The West India Company got the exclusive right to trade on American and African shores, just as the East India Company alone could send ships to Asia. Never before in history, perhaps, had any private corporation been invested with such enormous powers. In fact, it became so influential that it almost constituted a government within the government. This was to have·tremendous bearing on the affairs of the city soon to be planted in the New World.

And most of the first colonists sent here by the Dutch were French-speaking people.

Chapter 2

FIRST SETTLERS ARRIVE

THEY came in a great ship. There were 110 men, women, and children, representing thirty families, and they arrived in the *New Netherland*, a vessel of unusual size for that age. The *Mayflower*, which had brought the Pilgrims to Plymouth three years earlier, was a ship of only 180 tons. The *New Netherland* displaced 260 tons. It took the Dutch emigrants almost two months to make the trip, for they sailed a roundabout course from Amsterdam past the Canary Islands and the West Indies to Manhattan. And although the passengers didn't know it, they escaped an English man-of-war that had been ordered to sink them.

These first Dutch colonists reached here about the middle of

May, 1623. The Dutch West India Company had been incorporated in 1621, but the directors needed time to perfect their organization, find and outfit a ship, and round up people willing to head into the wilderness. Not many Dutchmen cared to leave home. However, a group of aliens living in Holland agreed to move to the New World.

They were French-speaking refugees from the Spanish Netherlands, known today as southern Belgium. As Protestants, they had fled to Holland to escape persecution from Spanish Catholics. In 1623 these Walloons had asked the English for permission to emigrate to Virginia but disliked the terms offered them. Already uprooted from their homeland and not yet having sunk new roots in Holland, they decided to make a third start in life.

The man who brought them to America was the same Cornelis Jacobsen May who had explored Long Island. He had been named the first director of New Netherland after it had been declared a Dutch province in 1623.

The Walloons sailed under orders known as Provisional Regulations for Colonists. For two years they were to be furnished with clothing and other supplies from company storehouses at reasonable prices, and they could pay on the installment plan. They were permitted to indulge in trade only if they sold their wares to company agents. They were forbidden to engage in any handicraft. Holland didn't want its emigrants to become independent of the homeland. The Walloons promised to stay six years wherever the company put them.

Captain May distributed them widely in order to occupy as much territory as possible. He sent two families and six men to the Hartford River, thus occupying a part of what is now Connecticut; dispatched two other families and eight men to the Delaware River, to settle in New Jersey and Delaware; left eight men on the site of New York City; and sent the rest of the colonists up the Hudson River to Albany. There they found that Christiaensen's stockade had been ruined by a spring freshet. The newcomers built another stronghold, named Fort Orange in honor of the ruling house of Holland. This was the first permanent Dutch settlement in the New World.

The Walloons left on the site of New York City decided that they could best protect themselves by clustering on Governors Island, 500 yards off the southern tip of Manhattan. This isle was covered with walnut, chestnut, and shellbark trees. The Indians called it Pagganack, or Pecanuc, meaning a place where nut trees grew. The Dutch colonists called it Nut Island. Three months later these first settlers were joined by forty-five more Walloons, who had traveled here in three ships.

These vessels were the *Orange Tree*, the *Eagle*, and the *Love*. They were escorted by an armed yacht provided by the Dutch government, which had learned of the abortive attempt by the English to sink the *New Netherland*. The latest colonists brought household furniture and farming tools. Two of the ships carried 103 head of livestock— cattle, horses, hogs, and sheep. Only 2 or 3 of the animals died during the voyage. The survivors disembarked on Nut Island; they might have got lost in the forests of Manhattan if they had landed there. Soon it became difficult to water the livestock on Nut Island, so they had to be transferred to Manhattan. Now the first permanent buildings rose on the site of New York City.

Conceived mainly as a trading post to which Indians and other trappers and traders could bring their furs, the colony flourished at first. In 1624 it exported to Holland 4,000 beaverskins and the pelts of 700 otters. These were worth 27,125 guilders, or a little more than the value of merchandise sent to the colony by the company. Although 20 head of cattle died from feeding on poisonous weeds, the rest multiplied.

After the expiration of Director May's one-year term he was replaced by Willem Verhulst. Before long Verhulst's colonial council found him guilty of mismanagement, and the company summoned him back to Holland. His successor was Peter Minuit, a middle-aged man whose hair was flecked with gray. Black-eyed and husky Minuit arrived on May 4, 1626. Coarse and self-willed, he had the brawn, brains, and drive needed to rule the rude outpost. The company elevated Minuit from director to director general and vested all legislative, executive, and judicial powers in him.

Minuit's first official act was to buy Manhattan from the Indians. On May 6, 1626, he convened the principal chiefs of nearby tribes on the site of Bowling Green, broke open sea chests, and gave them 60 guilders' worth of cloth, beads, hatchets, and other trinkets. The redskins had no conception of individual or tribal ownership of land. They lived a communal life in hamlets, hunting, fishing and feasting together. The Indians understood that they would yield from time to time such portions of the island as the palefaces might need.

They never expected to be driven completely off it. So for 60 guilders (equal to about 40 modern dollars) the Dutch got the use of 14,000 acres of rich and timbered land.

This southernmost niche of New Netherland was given the name of New Amsterdam for the chamber of the Dutch West India Company which mainly controlled its affairs. At first the colonists settled principally along the East River because its shore was better protected from the prevailing southwesterly winds than the banks of the Hudson were. Besides, much of the west side of Manhattan was occupied by a cemetery, a company farm and orchard, and a couple of country estates owned by two rich Dutchmen. In the summer of 1626, Minuit ordered the erection of thirty houses, mostly one-story cabins with straw roofs and wooden chimneys. Each contained a sleeping bench, or *slaap-banck,* recessed into one wall.

The company had sent along a military engineer with specific orders about locating farms, erecting public buildings, and constructing a fort. This was supposed to be five-sided and a thousand feet in diameter. The tip of Manhattan was so narrow, though, that a smaller, square stronghold was put up. The shores on both sides of Manhattan, from the Battery to what is now midtown, stood one to four blocks farther inland than at present. For example, Pearl Street on the southeastern tip of the island was then the strand or waterfront. It got its name from the pearly shells left there by tides. The Dutch, masters at landfill work, later extended the shores by making solid ground of tidal areas. Pearl Street today is separated from the East River by Water Street, Front Street, and South Street.

Public buildings arose on designated spots. Private dwellings, however, were situated helter-skelter by colonists who squatted wherever they chose. This explains the irregularity of streets which even today characterizes lower Manhattan. Before streets were laid out, two formed by common consent. One was Pearl Street along the East River. The other, farther west, followed a ridge northward through the company's farms and fields. Originally it had been an Indian trail. The Dutch named it Heere Straat, or High Street. We know it as Broadway. It was then much wider than it is now.

Minuit's engineer staked out a north-south road, called the Bowery because 12 farms, or *bouweries,* had been laid out near it—6 on one side, 6 on the other. The first 2 farms were 80 rods wide; the others, only 55 rods wide. The company created for itself a farm of 120 acres.

A dozen smaller farms, along with some cows, were given to the colonists.

The arrival of other passenger-laden ships increased the population to nearly 200 persons. Although Peter Minuit was the ultimate on-the-spot authority, public morality was supervised by Jan Lempou, the schout. His office embraced the functions of sheriff, public prose-cutor, and defense counselor. Unfortunately, Lempou wasn't present when a certain tragedy occurred.

Thus far the Dutch had experienced no trouble with the Indians, except for habitual thievery. But one day in 1626 an Indian brave and his twelve-year-old nephew walked from Westchester County down toward the company warehouse at the tip of Manhattan. They had beaverskins to trade with the Dutch. Their route took them past the Kolk "Whirlpool," or Collect, a small spring-fed pond just north of what is now Foley Square. Three workmen were plowing and clearing the edge of this pond. The Dutchmen killed the brave and stole his wares. Seemingly, neither the governor nor the schout heard about this until years later. The Indian lad, who escaped, never forgot his uncle's murder and swore to avenge himself on the palefaces.

Other Indians became troublesome near Albany at Fort Orange, killing several Dutch. Minuit ordered the surviving upstate colonists down to Fort Amsterdam for safety. He also closed Fort Nassau, which the Dutch had built on the Delaware River, and brought its inhabitants here. The newcomers increased New Amsterdam's population to about 300.

The spring of 1628 marked the arrival from Holland of Jonas Michaelius, the first regular minister to function here. His church continues today as the Collegiate Reformed Dutch Church of New York. The first and only schoolmaster the Dutch colony ever had was Adam Roelandsen. Each student paid him two beaverskins a year. Roelandsen must have been disagreeable, for practically nobody liked him. Failing as a schoolmaster or being forced to supplement his income, he took in washing.

This doesn't necessarily mean that he bent over a tub with soapy hands. The Dutch let dirty linen accumulate for six months and only then sent it out to be washed. The laundries were big establishments run by men. Perhaps the schoolmaster owned or managed such a place. This custom of semiannual washings explains why the dowry of every well-to-do Dutch girl included vast quantities of linen.

Agriculture prospered. Although the governor was less interested in farming than in the fur trade, he decided to erect mills to grind meal. Besides windmills, the Dutch put up horse mills—that is, powered by horses. Some mills were used to saw logs. The Indians were terrified by the long arms and big teeth of the windmills, which really were dangerous. A common epitaph of millers was "killed in his mill."

Minuit wrote to Governor William Bradford of the Plymouth colony to the northeast, suggesting that the Dutch and English enter into trade relations. At first Bradford hesitated, warning the Dutch not to encroach on his territory, but Minuit persisted and thus inaugurated regular coastwise traffic between New Amsterdam and Plymouth.

Much farther south, in Brazil, the Dutch West India Company was conquering, colonizing and profiting. By 1629 the company had more than 100 ships warring on pirates and the merchant ships of other nations. On the firm's payroll were 15,000 seamen and soldiers, who in the single year 1629 used up more than 100,000 pounds of gunpowder.

To establish a supply base for their expanding merchant marine, to promote the colonization of New Netherland, and to help make it self-sufficient, company directors decided to attract more settlers by giving away vast tracts of land. This was the genesis of the patroon system that played such an important role in the history of New York State; Manhattan itself was exempted. The company's plan was embodied in a Charter of Freedoms and Exemptions, confirmed by the Dutch government on June 7, 1629.

Each patron, or patroon, had to promise to transport and settle at least fifty adult colonists on a given territory within four years. In return, the government would give the patroon an estate, fronting sixteen miles along navigable rivers and extending inland as far as settlement would permit. He was expected to pay the Indians for the land, but sophisticated Dutchmen knew that this meant nothing more than a few trinkets.

This was indeed a tempting offer. Each estate could be held as a "perpetual fief in inheritance," with the fruits, plants, minerals, rivers, and springs included. Soon five patroonships were parceled out along the Hudson, Connecticut, and Delaware rivers. Who got them? Directors of the Dutch West India Company. Thus, most of the land, commerce, and government of New Netherland fell into the hands of a few greedy merchants. Little was left for independent colonists.

One of the oldest, richest, and craftiest of the company directors was an Amsterdam diamond and pearl merchant, named Kiliaen Van Rensselaer. In 1630 his agents bought from the Indians a tract of land, 24 miles long and 48 miles wide, on both sides of the Hudson River far north of New Amsterdam. This was an area even greater than his charter had cited, but his purchases were confirmed. Altogether, Van Rennselaer's feudal estate comprised 700,000 acres, which included the present counties of Albany and Rensselaer, a part of Columbia County, and even a strip in Massachusetts. What did he pay for this domain? Knives, axes, wampum, and duffel (a strong shaggy cloth).

Van Rensselaer never lived on his baronial estate. He didn't even visit it. Through an able director he managed its affairs from overseas. After he died, some of his sons arrived from Holland, settled on the property, became lords of the manor, and wrangled with their hired help.

Another patroon, also a director of the Dutch West India Company, was Michael Paauw. He was given Staten Island and the part of New Jersey that now includes Hoboken and Jersey City. This estate he named Pavonia by translating into Latin his own name, which is Dutch for peacock. Still another patroon received a large slice of land near the Narrows in New York Harbor.

In 1630 the first Dutch pioneers arrived at Rensselaerswyck up the Hudson, Boston was founded by English settlers, and a map printed in Holland showed for the first time the names of Manhattan, New Amsterdam, and the North (Hudson) River. That was the year the people of New Amsterdam marveled at an enormous ship built under their very noses.

Until then only a few sloops and shallops, all small and shallow, had been constructed here. But now two visiting Belgian shipbuilders were so impressed by the colony's fine timber and the town's magnificent harbor that they wanted to make a vessel of unusual proportions. Peter Minuit not only encouraged them but also gave them company funds. Using a horse-powered mill to saw timber into logs and logs into planks, the Belgians built a ship they named the *New Netherland*. Huge for that age, she displaced either 600 or 800 tons and bristled with 30 cannons.

When the *New Netherland* reached Holland, most Dutchmen praised her magnitude, workmanship, and beautiful timber. This sentiment was not shared by company directors or government officials. Even before completion, the ship proved more expensive than planned, and because of her size, she was costly to operate. When the construction bill reached company directors, they were outraged. Stockholders also groused because they had to help pay for her. Their complaints were echoed in newspapers, which accused the company of extravagance. The government agreed. Two hundred years passed before another ship of comparable size was built in America.

The case of the *New Netherland,* together with growing complaints about the patroons, produced a government investigation. The patroons were accused of greater interest in the forbidden Indian trade than in colonizing and cultivating their land. They smuggled furs because this paid a quicker return than farming. Peter Minuit, who had ratified the purchase of Indian land by the patroons, was charged with acting in their interests. The government ordered the company to recall him.

Leaving New Netherland in the hands of a council, Minuit sailed for Holland in 1632. A storm drove his ship into Plymouth, England, where he was detained on a charge of illegal trading in the domains of the king of England, Charles I. His detention resulted in a spirited correspondence between England and Holland. The question was, Who owned the territory Minuit had governed?

Dutch statesmen claimed that the Dutch had discovered the Hudson River in 1609, that some had returned in 1610, that a trading charter had been granted in 1614, that a fort had been maintained there until the formation of the Dutch West India Company in 1621, and that the company had sent colonists, who had occupied the land ever since 1623. The Dutch stressed their purchase of the land from the Indians, the original owners.

The English had to cudgel their brains to answer these arguments, for in 1580 Queen Elizabeth had proclaimed that mere discovery of a wild country did not give title to it. Discovery had to be followed by occupation. The Dutch knew, all Europe knew, that from Cabot's discovery in 1497 to the settlement of Jamestown in 1607—altogether 110 years—the English had not colonized any part of the New World. Still, the English replied to the Dutch that they held prior claims based on Cabot's discovery and on subsequent patents issued by King James I. They denied that the Indians were the bona fide owners of the land. Even if they were, the English argued, they still couldn't issue a legal title unless all tribes entered into a joint bargain with the purchaser. They flatly denied the jurisdiction of the Dutch government or the Dutch West India Company over New Netherland. However, they agreed to let the Dutch stay there if they submitted to English rule. Otherwise, the Dutch would not be permitted "to encroach up a colony of such importance as New England."

Worried by this legalistic wrangle, the Dutch decided to strengthen their position by instituting certain reforms. For one thing, the government reduced the size of future patroonships. Of the five original patroonships, four had failed, and only Rensselaerswyck flourished. The failures were due to problems of transportation and communication between the patroonships and the homeland, a lack of cooperation from the company, Indian troubles, tenant unrest, and the ban against trading in furs or engaging in manufacture.

Peter Minuit was succeeded as director general of New Netherland by Bastiaen Jansen Kroll. This displeased Kiliaen Van Rensselaer, who began pulling strings backstage. He wangled the appointment of one of his relatives—a nephew or cousin. This was a moonfaced clerk, named Wouter Van Twiller. By replacing Kroll with Van Twiller, the company made a stupid concession to the wily Van Rensselaer. To be sure, Van Twiller had visited New Netherland twice, but merely to supervise the shipment of cattle to Rensselaerswyck. The five years before he became overlord of this Dutch colony, Van Twiller was nothing more than a clerk in the company's warehouse in Amsterdam. Short and stout, he wore his sandy hair close-cropped and had small blue eyes set deep in his fat face.

In the full panoply of power, the new governor arrived here in March,1633, attended by 104 soldiers, wearing steel corsets and leather jackets and carrying half-pikes and wheel-lock muskets. This was the first military force ever to land on the site of New York City. Also among Van Twiller's shipmates was a new minister, a dominie named Everardus Bogardus.

By the time Van Twiller got here, five stone warehouses had been completed and were in use by the company. However, Fort Amsterdam wasn't finished. The new Dutch director general ordered the colonists to work faster, and within two years the fort was ready. Inside it Van Twiller built himself a brick house, certainly the best private dwelling in the province. The soldiers were quartered in a barracks, also built within the fort. Its main gate faced north and opened onto The Parade, now Bowling Green.

Also erected during Van Twiller's regime were the first church building on the site of 39 Pearl Street; a bakery at the corner of Pearl and State streets; a house for the local midwife; a goat pen; a huge shed for building ships; and a house, barn, boathouse, and brewery on farm No. 1, south of the present Stuyvesant Square and east of the Bowery. One sawmill was constructed on this farm; another, on the fort's southeastern bastion; and a third, on Governors Island.

Now the Dutch began growing tobacco in soil so rich that it didn't need fertilizer. The fine New Amsterdam tobacco brought prices as high as the Virginia variety and was much in demand in Holland. The present site of the United Nations headquarters was once a tobacco plantation.

During the early years of Van Twiller's administration many strides were made in trade. More and more furs were exported to Holland. New Amsterdam reaped the benefit of this commerce, for it was granted a monopoly, known as staple right. This meant that every fur-laden ship sailing down the Hudson from the hinterland, up the Atlantic seaboard from the south, or down from Newfoundland had to stop to pay a toll here before crossing the ocean. Sea captains unable to pay the fee had to unload their cargo on the shore and sell it then and there. New Amsterdam prospered accordingly.

Van Twiller didn't neglect his own interests. He became the richest landowner in and around Manhattan, persuading the Indians to sell him Governors Island, Ward's Island, and Welfare Island. At that time Nut Island was renamed Governors Island. Van Twiller also obtained an interest in 15,000 acres of rich Long Island farmland.

Although his holdings fattened, the company farm didn't produce much. Moreover, despite the growing traffic in furs, the company directors in Holland weren't satisfied. The colony's annual exports more than doubled between 1624 and 1635 but barely paid a profit on the firm's investment. Even when the fur trade hit a peak of 85,000 pelts a year, this did not compare favorably with the company's lucrative operations in Brazil, on the high seas, or elsewhere. For example, in just one year Dutch raider ships captured 17 Spanish galleons carrying loot worth 12,000,000 guilders.

Van Twiller's indifference to the public welfare irritated the intelligent men of the colony. Bogardus, a bold minister, wrote him several letters on the subject. This resulted in a feud between the governor and the pastor. Once the dominie called Van Twiller a "child of the devil" to his face and declared that if he did not behave he would give him "such a shake from the pulpit" the next Sunday as would make him tremble like a bowl of jelly.

After the governor had lost the respect of all the colonists and his weaknesses had been reported to company headquarters in Holland, he was dismissed from office. That was in the fall of 1637. Despite his disgrace, tippling potbellied Van Twiller didn't flee to the homeland but remained to enjoy the earthly rewards he had piled up for himself.

One spring day in the following year a Dutch man-of-war anchored in the East River roadstead under the guns of Fort Amsterdam and lowered a boat. Into the boat climbed a fussy little man not quite forty years old. He was rowed to a small floating dock at Pearl Street, where he scrambled ashore. Local leaders had gathered to welcome their new director general, Willem Kieft, but they gave him a restrained greeting because of the soiled reputation that had preceded his arrival. Rumor had it that Kieft was venal.

Vain and ferocious, Kieft began riding roughshod over everyone, winning the nickname Willem the Testy. He was appalled at how Van Twiller had let things run down. Kieft wrote to Holland:

> The fort is open at every side except the stone point. The guns are dismounted. The houses and public buildings are all out of repair. The magazine for the merchandise has disappeared. Every vessel in the harbor is falling to pieces. Only one windmill is in operation. The farms of the company are without tenants and thrown into commons (being used by anybody and everybody). The cattle are all sold or on the plantations of Van Twiller.

Because of harsh commercial and maritime regulations imposed by various colonies, smuggling was rife. Cargo-laden sloops sneaked from New Amsterdam to Plymouth to Virginia. Negro slaves bootlegged furs for tobacco. Company directors complained that "several persons" kept the best furs for themselves and sold inferior pelts for shipment to Holland. In defiance of the law, guns were sold to Indians, who paid twenty beaverskins for one musket. Every fourth building in town was a liquor store. In 1640 Kieft erected on Staten Island the first private distillery in the history of America.

Kieft decided to make some reforms, which he announced by means of posters tacked onto trees, barns, and fences. The sale of guns or gunpowder to Indians was prohibited on pain of death. Illegal traffic in furs was banned. Tobacco was taxed. No one could leave Manhattan without a passport. When the church bell rang at 9 P.M., everybody had to go to bed. No sailor could stay ashore after sundown. A seaman who pulled a knife on a shipmate was ordered to throw himself three times from the top of his ship into the water.

Although Kieft's restless gray eyes missed nothing, he was such a dunderhead that he foolishly tried to tax the Indians. He insisted that their presence caused the company to spend too much money on fortifications. The peaceable redskins were astonished at this order to pay the Dutch a tribute of furs, corn, or wampum. Because European coins were scarce here, even the Dutch used wampum as money. Kieft warned the Indians: "If there be any tribe that will not willingly contribute, we shall induce them to do so by most suitable means."

Kieft next decided to build a stone church inside the walls of the fort. Hoping to get the people to pay part of the cost, he resorted to trickery. A Dutch girl married a surgeon. The governor, of course, was invited to attend the wedding party. After three or four rounds of drinks Kieft took out a piece of paper and announced that he was ready to accept pledges for construction of the new church. Many giddy guests pledged generous sums. When they sobered up the next day, however, they vowed that this just wasn't the proper way to get donations for a house of worship. The company had to pay the workmen.

Besides internal problems, the governor concerned himself with affairs outside the colony. Potential dangers loomed almost everywhere he looked. To the north, mainly above the St. Lawrence River, lay New France. To the northeast was New England, the numbers of its colonies and population growing. Virginia lay to the south. In addition to watching these rivals, Kieft watched apprehensively what was happening in New Sweden, to the southwest.

Peter Minuit was so angered at being dismissed by the Dutch West India Company that he offered his services to the Swedish government. A colonizing agency, called the New Sweden Company, had been organized in 1626, but because of wars and the death of the Swedish king, no expedition had been launched at that time. In 1638, the year that Kieft came to New Netherland, Peter Minuit led fifty Swedish and Dutch colonists to the Delaware River, built a fort near present-day Wilmington, Delaware, and named it Fort Christina in honor of the young Swedish queen.

Sweden's claim to this territory was based on purchase from the Indians, whereas Holland's claim was based on Hudson's discovery. Kieft wrote a letter of protest to Minuit, who did not bother to reply but went on strengthening his fort. Kieft then asked the Dutch West India Company for instructions. Not caring to precipitate a war with Sweden, the directors ignored the matter for the time being.

In addition to the Delaware situation, Kieft faced perils in Connecticut and on Long Island. The English were arriving in America much faster than the Dutch. They began to push down from Massachusetts into Connecticut, spilling over onto the eastern end of Long Island. Soon the English settlers far outnumbered all the New Netherland Dutch. The migration of the English was strong because it was organized under Church auspices. The Dutch migration was weaker because it consisted of unorganized individuals under the thumb of the profit-seeking Dutch West India Company.

In 1623 the Dutch had started building Fort Good Hope on the present site of Hartford, Connecticut, but they hadn't bothered to complete it. Now, with the English overrunning the area, the Dutch finished the fort. Onto a big tree they nailed the arms of the Dutch government, only to have some Englishmen tear it down and substitute an insulting picture.

Kieft next turned his attention to the problem of smuggling within New Netherland. When he was unable to quash this lawlessness, the Amsterdam chamber finally decided that it might as well waive its shaky monopoly of the fur trade. In 1639 the fur traffic was "thrown free and open to everybody." All the merchants of Holland and those of friendly nations were invited to send to New Netherland any merchandise they wished and to buy pelts there. However, duties of 10 percent on imports and 15 percent on exports were imposed. In addition, both imports and exports had to be carried in ships belonging to the Dutch West India Company. This measure did encourage immigration.

Colonization was also stimulated by change in the patroonship system. Now anyone willing and able to transport himself and only 5 grown persons to New Netherland was to be given 200 acres of land. Earlier, 50 colonists had been necessary, and much larger estates had been handed out. By this time Michael Paauw had failed to make a go of his Staten Island estate, called Pavonia, so the Amsterdam directors bought back the property. They then changed the name of the isle to Staten Island in honor of the States General, or government, of Holland.

Farmers of modest means sailed from Holland to take advantage of the liberalized land policy. Laborers came from New England, where the theocratic government was growing oppressive. Arriving from Virginia were English-born convicts who had been sent there to work as plantation laborers and were glad to escape when their enforced servitude ended. Slaves were imported from Brazil in greater numbers.

To take care of this increased population, Kieft bought more land from the Indians. By 1640 almost all the area within the present limits of New York City was in Dutch hands. The governor also secured a big tract of land north of the city in what is now Westchester County. Portions of this property soon were deeded away to enterprising settlers. One was a Danish Lutheran, named Jonas Bronck, who received a grant of real estate north of the Harlem River in the present county of the Bronx. In 1642 town lots were distributed along the newly formed streets of Manhattan. The next year eighteen different languages were spoken in New Amsterdam, the city being international in character almost from the start.

As trade increased, Governor Kieft tired of entertaining visitors in his own home. With the approval of the people he erected a five-story tavern on the low ground at 71-73 Pearl Street, then the head of Coenties Slip. Built of stone, oak timber, and lime made from oyster shells, it was for years the most famous structure in town, and in 1653 it became the first City Hall.

Hanover Square in lower Manhattan was now a public common, or park, and early in 1641 people meeting there talked excitedly about the big news. Some Negro slaves owned by the company had killed another slave near the fort. Nine Negroes were captured, but no one knew which had struck the fatal blow. To make the culprit confess, all were threatened with torture; whereupon all nine declared themselves equally guilty. Perhaps they reasoned they wouldn't be put to death en masse, since laborers were needed in the growing town. The prisoners were then ordered to draw lots. The one who lost was to be hanged so that just one able-bodied man would be taken from the community. In this deadly lottery the loser was Manuel Gerrit, an enormous fellow called the Giant.

On the day set for the execution the entire populace turned out to watch, together with some blank-faced black-eyed Indians, curious about the ways of the white men. A ladder was angled against one wall of the fort. The Giant was forced to climb to the top. He was so heavy that two ropes were used to hang him. After they were placed around his neck, the ladder was jerked away. Both ropes broke. Gerrit fell to the ground, bellowing in pain, writhing, and clutching at his throat. At this piteous sight women shrieked. Men turned to the governor and begged him to let the prisoner go. But Willem the Testy told the hangman to prepare stronger ropes. At last so many voices were raised in behalf of the wretched slave that Kieft yielded to public pressure. Gerrit was freed after he had promised to behave himself in the future and not to go around helping people murder other people.

About this time the Indians posed a problem that couldn't be disposed of so easily as Gerrit. They were angry because Kieft was trying to tax them. Then too, the white men's cattle strayed onto their unfenced land and trampled their corn. The redskins sometimes protected their crops by killing the cattle, and this led to reprisals. One incident followed another. A band of Raritan Indians attacked a Staten Island plantation and slew four white men. Kieft promptly offered a reward for the head of any Raritan brought to the fort.

One summer day in 1641 a wheelwright, named Claes Smit, was busy in his lonely house on the East River far above New Amsterdam at what is now West Forty-fifth Street. An Indian appeared and asked to buy a piece of coarse cloth. When the unsuspecting Dutchman turned to get it, the redskin seized an ax and killed him. The murderer was the same Indian who, as a lad of twelve, had seen his uncle killed by Dutchmen near the Collect. Sixteen years later, a grown man, he got his revenge.

This Indian belonged to a Westchester tribe living at the site of Yonkers. Kieft sent word to the tribal chief demanding that the killer be delivered into the hands of the white men. The sachem refused. Kieft then threatened to wipe out the entire tribe, but the colonists were reluctant to launch a bloody war. Compromising, Kieft suggested that the townspeople elect twelve of their best men to confer with him on this issue. Thus, for the first time the colonists won a measure of self-government. The Twelve Men, as they were called, agreed that the murderer must be surrendered, but they wouldn't consent to a war just then because necessary preparations hadn't been made.

The following winter, however, the Twelve Men told the governor that they would approve an expedition against the Westchester tribe if the settlers were granted certain reforms. Enraged, Kieft dissolved the group. Then, acting on his own, he sent eighty soldiers toward Yonkers, carefully refraining from leading them himself. The expedition was a fiasco. The guide lost his way, the commanding officer lost his temper, and the soldiers marched back to the fort without even sighting the Indian village. Redskins saw the soldiers, though, and were so frightened by the show of force that they offered to give up the murderer. Somehow this was never done, but a peace treaty between the Dutch and the Westchester Indians was signed in the home of Jonas Bronck.

There were other Indian problems. Although Kieft had been successful in preventing the sale of guns to Algonquins in and around Manhattan, Dutch traders upriver freely bartered muskets to the Iroquois. The Algonquins and the Iroquois were deadly enemies. Armed with superior weapons, the Iroquois of the upper Hudson Valley descended on the Westchester and River tribes near New Amsterdam and demanded tribute. A thousand terrified Algonquins fled in midwinter to Manhattan and the vicinity of Jersey City. They begged the Dutch for protection, but the shortsighted Kieft snorted that he would make the Indians "wipe their chops!"

By his orders two detachments of soldiers filed out of the fort. One group marched to nearby Corlaer's Hook in Manhattan on the East River, where the Vladeck Houses now stand, and slaughtered forty Indian refugees. The second and larger detachment crossed the Hudson, proceeded to the site of Jersey City, and attacked in the dark. The engagement that night of February 25-26, 1643, is known as the Pavonia Massacre. Dutch soldiers fell on the unsuspecting Indians, murdering and mutilating about eighty men, women, and children. Then the uniformed butchers marched back to Fort Amsterdam in triumph, carrying the severed heads of some of their victims. Kieft was so delighted that he congratulated and decorated the men.

Eleven Algonquin tribes rose in wrath and war paint, took up hatchets, and did their ferocious best to wipe the white man off the face of the earth. The Dutch were unprepared for war. There was only about half a pound of gunpowder per colonist, and Kieft hadn't even bothered to warn outlying settlers that he planned to massacre the Indians. Peaceful Dutch farmers were surprised in their fields by the attacking redskins. Their cattle were killed; their homes, destroyed;

their women and children, cut down or carried into captivity. The sturdy Dutch put up a good fight, but scores were felled with tomahawks buried in their skulls. Those lucky enough to escape the first onslaught fled from their farms to the fort. Many abandoned the colony itself and sailed for Holland on the first available ships.

The fate of the entire Dutch province hung in the balance. From the Raritan River, in New Jersey, to the Connecticut River, in Connecticut, the Indians ravaged the countryside, burning, killing, and scalping. Long Island, Westchester, and Manhattan were laid waste. Soon only three farms on Manhattan and two on Staten Island remained untouched. Settlers could find safety nowhere except near Fort Amsterdam, and even there conditions were desperate.

The Indians had a combined force of about 1,500 warriors. All Manhattan male colonists were enrolled as soldiers, but no more than 200 were capable of bearing arms. About 50 or 60 Englishmen were pressed into service to prevent them from leaving the colony. Dutchmen denounced Kieft for provoking this pointless war, and he almost collapsed in terror. He tried unsuccessfully to pin the blame on his advisers. In desperation he begged the people to elect another representative body. They chose the Eight Men.

Because the fort was utterly defenseless, the Dutch erected a palisade along the present Wall Street—although this was not the one that gave the street its name. Food was so scarce that the colonists faced starvation. They appealed for help to the English at the colony of New Haven, only to be told, "We are not satisfied that your war with the Indians is just." The Amsterdam chamber of the Dutch West India Company was angry because Kieft had been ordered to avoid an open break with the natives; it too was slow in sending aid.

Fortunately for the Dutch, the Indians seemed unable to mount an unremitting siege on the fort but limited themselves to hit-and-run raids. The Dutch also were lucky enough to find an able leader. An Englishman, named Captain John Underhill, arrived here at the critical moment. Underhill was an expert Indian fighter, who had taken part in the war against the Pequot tribe in Connecticut. He brought fifty English soldiers and settlers to New Amsterdam, was guaranteed payment for his services, and then decided to strike the enemy an annihilating blow.

The biggest Indian stronghold was a village in the rugged country north of Stamford, Connecticut. Captain Underhill embarked from Manhattan in 3 yachts, which carried his own small force and the

130 to 150 Dutch soldiers finally sent here from Holland. The combined body landed at Greenwich, marched a full day, and then fell on the Indian settlement one winter's night. Before daybreak the battle was over. That ghastly night of the full moon 8 Indians escaped; the snow was reddened by the bloody corpses of 700 tribesmen. Underhill's small army lost only 15 men.

After this overwhelming victory, Dutch forces sallied forth from Fort Amsterdam, invaded Westchester County, and killed 500 more redskins. The Indians sued for peace, and a treaty was signed on August 29, 1645.

During this Indian war the Dutch colonists had lost much and suffered greatly. They blamed everything on Governor Kieft; both private individuals and the Eight Men complained about him to Holland. Kieft was summoned home to defend himself against charges of blundering and cowardice. On the return voyage the ship was sunk, and Kieft drowned. Then a grizzled warrior with a wooden leg stumped onto the scene.

Chapter 3

PETER STUYVESANT TAKES COMMAND

PETER STUYVESANT sat. The town elders stood. He kept his hat on. They took theirs off. It was a long time before he even condescended to notice them. This ominous scene took place on May 27, 1647, when Stuyvesant was inaugurated as the new director general of New Netherland.

At last, in a room tight with tension, he spoke: "I shall govern you as a father his children, for the advantage of the chartered West India Company, and these burghers, and this land." Everyone noted the sequence of values. When Stuyvesant added that "every man should have justice done him," the tension broke, and the people clapped until their palms reddened. Nonetheless, one observer reflected sourly

41

that the new governor was behaving like the czar of Russia. Some in the group analyzed the name Stuyvesant, a compound of the Dutch word *stuyven,* meaning to stir up, and the English *sand.* Would their new overlord stir up the sand, kick up dust?

Curious eyes scanned the face and figure of Peter Stuyvesant. Long locks of hair dangled on both sides of his swarthy cheeks. Frown lines cut deep into the bridge of his hawklike nose. He was clean-shaven and stubborn-chinned. For a fifty-five-year-old man he was well preserved. His sturdy soldier's body, a little above medium height, had weathered many a campaign. Faultlessly dressed in the height of Dutch fashion, Peter Stuyvesant wore a wide collar that spread over his velvet jacket like a white water lily. Ornamental slits in his jacket sleeves revealed full puffed shirtsleeves underneath. His copious breeches were fastened to his hose at the knees by handsome scarves, tied into knots. A cloth rose decorated his shoe.

His left shoe. His only shoe. Peter Stuyvesant had lost his right leg. The people of New Amsterdam sneaked glances at that wooden leg bound in silver bands. In time to come they were to hear the rat-a-tat-tat of his artificial limb when Peg Leg Peter became angry. A few even learned how he had lost his leg.

Born in Holland and the son of a minister, Stuyvesant had gone through college and then hired himself out as a soldier for the militant Dutch West India Company. His quick mind, strong character, and personal magnetism lifted him to the governorship of the island of Curaçao. During a raid against the Portuguese of nearby St. Martin Island he was wounded so badly that he was invalided back to Holland, where his right leg was amputated. He was complimented for his courage but censured for his misjudgment in launching the attack.

While convalescing, Stuyvesant was nursed by his sister, Annake, of whom he was extremely fond. Eleven years older than Peter, she was tall, rather unattractive, but as determined in her own quiet way as her stormy brother. Peter and Annake married a brother and sister. He took to wife the lovely Judith Bayard, by whom he had two sons. Annake wed Samuel Bayard. The Bayards were descended from eminent Huguenots, who had fled from France to Holland to escape persecution.

Mrs. Stuyvesant was a beautiful blonde, with a voice as sweet as her husband's was harsh. She enjoyed music and dressed herself in the height of French fashion. Besides speaking French and Dutch fluently, she acquired a good command of the English language after her arrival here. Peter was a master of Latin but spoke English halt-ingly.

Soon after the Stuyvesants had landed in New Amsterdam, Annake's husband died in Holland. Deciding to join her brother, she sailed from the homeland with her three sons and their tutor. This scholar proved to be so unscholarly that the widow took over the education of her children. In the New World she met and married one of the colony's officials, Nicholas Verlett.

Peter Stuyvesant had been ordered to put New Netherland on a paying basis. Conditions were troubled: trade faltering, smuggling widespread, money lacking, morals murky, and reforms needed. To help him govern the colony, Stuyvesant appointed a five-man council, but this was a mere gesture. He ran the whole show. One of his first problems was how to impose taxes—not to levy tribute on the Indians, as the foolish Kieft had tried to do. No, Stuyvesant would have to tax the white colonists themselves, even though for two centuries Dutchmen had declared that taxation without representation was tyranny.

With company approval, Stuyvesant decided to grant the colonists the appearance of representation and then tap their tills. He ordered the people to elect eighteen of their "most notable, reasonable, honest and respectable" men. When this was done, he himself chose half of the eighteen to serve as an advisory board. The function of these Nine Men was *to assist, when called on,* in providing for the general welfare. The history of Stuyvesant's seventeen-year rule is that of a struggle between him and the people, who wanted a truly popular government.

Taxes were imposed, but it was difficult to collect them. Kieft's blunders and greed left the colonists with little respect for any repre-sentative of the company. Kieft had not departed immediately on his ill-starred voyage to Holland after his dismissal as director general. In fact, during Stuyvesant's inauguration the deposed governor stood beside his successor and even insisted on saying a few words. Kieft thanked the people for their fidelity, wished them happiness, and bade them farewell. From the audience there arose murmurs: "We're glad your reign is over," and "Good riddance!"

Then someone suggested that Kieft should be voted the conven-tional thanks for his official conduct. Two men said bluntly that they had no reason to thank him and would not do so. One of them was named Kuyter. The other was Melyn. Both had lost much in the Indian war provoked by Kieft. By this time everyone knew the gruesome details of the Pavonia Massacre. Dutch soldiers had snatched Indian children from their mothers' breasts and hacked the infants to death. Other sucklings had been bound to boards, tortured, and then murdered. Still other Indian children had been thrown into the river by the cruel Dutchmen.

During the confrontation between Kieft on the one hand and Kuyter and Melyn on the other, these gory matters were not mentioned. Nevertheless, as Stuyvesant heard his predecessor defied and humiliated, the scowl lines deepened in his stern face. But Kuyter and Melyn were not content to let it go at that. After Stuyvesant's inauguration, after he had begun his work of reconstruction and reform, these two stubborn Dutchmen urged that an investigation be held to determine the cause of the late Indian war. They suggested that colonists should testify, evidence be compiled, and a report about Kieft's conduct be sent to Holland.

Stuyvesant now appointed a commission to pass on the propriety of such an inquiry. However, the moment it assembled, he blasted Kuyter and Melyn, calling them "two malignant fellows" and "disturbers of the peace." A company man to the core, Stuyvesant sided with Kieft from the very start. Trumped-up charges were brought against Kuyter and Melyn. They were accused of slandering and threatening the former governor. Then they were arrested on charges of rebellion and sedition and brought to trial almost immediately.

The trial, which lasted several days, stirred up wild excitement throughout the town. Taking no chances, Stuyvesant himself mounted the bench to sit as judge. No one was surprised at the verdict: guilty. Melyn was banished from New Netherland for 7 years and fined 300 guilders. Kuyter was exiled for 3 years and fined 150 guilders. Glaring at Melyn, Peg Leg Peter roared, "If I thought there were any danger of your trying an appeal, I would hang you this minute to the tallest tree on the island!"

Soon afterward, Kieft sailed for Holland with his fortune, which his enemies estimated to be 400,000 guilders. He took Kuyter and Melyn with him as prisoners. As has been noted, the ship never reached its destination, being wrecked on a rock off the coast of Wales. When it appeared that all aboard would perish, the conscience-stricken Kieft went to his prisoners and stammered, "Friends, I—I—have done you wrong! Can you—forgive me?" Kieft and 80 passengers were drowned. Kuyter, Melyn, and 18 other persons were saved.

After many adventures Kuyter and Melyn made their way to Holland, to the capital at The Hague, and there they appealed to the Dutch government despite Stuyvesant's threats. The States General usually showed more concern for the welfare of Dutch colonists than did the Dutch West India Company. The Dutch government suspended sentence on Kuyter and Melyn and granted them the right to return to New Netherland under safe-conduct passes. Kuyter tarried in Holland, probably to manage the case should Stuyvesant press it, while Melyn sailed again for New Amsterdam, where he was welcomed as a hero. All this was a blow to Peter Stuyvesant.

His reforms and other changes resulted in many *firsts* in the city's history, including the following:

In 1648 the first pier was built on the East River.

In 1652 the first Latin school was established, and the first law against fast driving was passed.

In 1653 the first prison was built inside the fort; the first poorhouse was erected at 21-23 Beaver Street; the City Tavern became the first City Hall; a night watch was created; and the first price-fixing occurred.

In 1654 the canal on Broad Street was rebuilt.

In 1655 the first lottery was held.

In 1656 the first city survey showed 120 houses and 1,000 inhabitants; the first broker went into business; and the first market was established at Whitehall and Pearl streets.

In 1657 Jacques Cortelyou became the first commuter by traveling daily between his Long Island home and Manhattan.

In 1658 the first coroner's inquest was held.

In 1659 the first hospital was erected on Bridge Street.

In 1660 the first post office was opened, and the first city directory was published.

In 1661 the first unemployment relief went into effect, and the first law against loan sharks was passed.

In 1663 the city experienced its first recorded earthquake.

Laws were hard to enforce and taxes difficult to collect because many colonists had become lawless. It was obvious to the people that the company preferred its profits to their prosperity. Racially, culturally, and religiously, the inhabitants of New Netherland were a mixed breed, taking pleasure where they found it, unlike the homogeneous and Puritanical New Englanders. Although Dutchmen were most numerous and Dutch influences generally prevailed, the influx of Englishmen, Frenchmen, and other nationals brought several cultures into jostling and creative juxtaposition.

Most people realized that Peter Stuyvesant was doing his energetic best to maintain order and develop the province, but they resented his high-handed methods and denial of democracy. In their minds suspicion grew like a cancer, They had a right to be suspicious, for without the knowledge of Stuyvesant his secretary was pocketing part of the tax revenues. Besides, the people asked themselves, why should they pay a tariff in New Netherland when no tariff was imposed in New England? What was wrong with smuggling goods back and forth among the colonies? So even though Stuyvesant used two Dutch men-of-war as revenue cutters, he still was unable to stamp out all illicit trade. At last the public learned of the graft taken by Stuyvesant's secretary; he committed suicide rather than stand trial.

Peg Leg Peter, who liked his glass of schnapps now and then, agonized over the general drunkenness and constant knife fighting in the streets. Beer was the preferred drink, but other favorites included brandy, gin, and rum. In summertime wine was cooled with ice, while in winter it was served mulled—heated, sweetened, and spiced. There were too many taverns for so small a town. These places were packed with roistering men, who drank heavily, enjoyed companionship, played chess, shot dice, stroked billiard cues, dealt cards, and doted on games of chance.

A favorite outdoor sport was called pulling the goose or riding the goose. A bird's head was greased, the fowl was hung by its feet from a rope stretched over a road, and then the contestants rode underneath at a gallop and tried to grab it. Stuyvesant forbade servants to ride the goose, but this only increased the game's popularity. The goose continued to hang high.

The Dutch introduced bowling into America. They rolled balls at nine pins set up on the lawn of Bowling Green. Autumn brought turkey shooting, and in Stuyvesant's time partridges were brought down from the air over the fort itself. In winter everyone skated and went sleighing. When the weather was warm, pantalooned Dutch youths rowed apple-cheeked maidens to picnic on Oyster Island, known today as Ellis Island.

Then too, the Dutch colonists were more addicted to holidays and festivals than the thin-lipped Puritans of New England were. On New

Year's Day courtesy calls were made from home to home, Dutch girls in manifold petticoats and other finery awaiting the arrival of eligible young men. Twelfth Night, which fell a few days after New Year's, was always gay. Housewives baked Twelfth Night cakes with a gilded bean hidden inside, and the lucky person who found the bean became King of Misrule for the evening. Children jumped over lighted candles. Singing, bedecked in costumes, all would be led about the room by three men disguised as the Three Wise Men, while a fourth carried a light suggesting the star of Bethlehem.

On St. Valentine's Day, which the Dutch called *Vrouwen-dagh,* maidens frolicked about the streets, striking young men with knotted cords. At Easter time the children painted Easter eggs. The seventh Sunday after Easter was called Whitsuntide, or White Sunday. Houses were decorated festively, games were played, and servants were allowed to act up a bit. On May Day houses bloomed with garlands of flowers, and people danced on the green around a Maypole. Ardent swains pulled blushing girls onto "kissing bridges," while thoughtless young men placed scarecrows on the roofs of houses inhabited by unmarried girls.

Like the Pilgrims, the Dutch set aside a certain day for Thanksgiving, but it did not fall on the same date each year and was not celebrated annually. For example, on August 12, 1654, Stuyvesant ordered a Thanksgiving because peace had been reached between Holland and England. Men and women danced around a huge bonfire and guzzled free beer provided by the city fathers. The beer bill that day came to fifty-eight guilders, or enough for everyone to get tipsy.

November 10 marked St. Martin's Eve, and that night and the following day the Dutch staged parties all over town. Dinner always featured roast goose. After the flesh had been devoured, the fowl's breastbone was examined. If it was hard, this foretold a severe winter; if soft, a mild one.

St. Nicholas' Eve was celebrated on December 5. This minor saint from the fourth century A.D. was the secular deity of the Dutch. Supposedly he came down the chimney on the eve of his birthday, which fell on December 6. Excited children piled up hay for his horses. The walls were hung with three oranges symbolizing the three gold dowries St. Nicholas had allegedly given to three poor but deserving sisters. It was said, too, that the saint had once saved a sailor from drowning, so salt-soaked rough-weather gear dangled in the room.

Another display consisted of birch rods meant for boys and girls who had been naughty. Christmas itself was observed quietly.

When times were good, the Dutch feasted on venison, turkey, partridge, quail, tripe, fish, oysters, mussels, crabs, corn mush and milk, headcheese, sausage, bologna, peas, cole slaw, waffles, and oily cakes something like our modern doughnut. They drank from small teacups, nibbling a lump of sugar after each sip.

This high living ended temporarily in 1650-51, when a harsh winter sent food prices soaring. The cruel cold inflicted much suffering on the colonists. Householders kept logs blazing in fireplaces lined with picture tiles, but in other rooms ink froze in pens. Most afflicted were the slaves called humble men, who carried buckets of filth from backyard privies and dumped them into the rivers. Despite the scarcity of food and rising prices, Stuyvesant provisioned company ships bound for Curaçao. This aroused the indignation of the Nine Men, who accused the governor of "wanton imprudence."

Streets were few, crooked, muddy, and overrun with livestock and fowl. During all the time the Dutch occupied New Amsterdam, the city never extended farther north than Wall Street, 550 yards from the tip of lower Manhattan. Men drove wagons so fast that Stuyvesant ordered them to walk beside their vehicles and hold the horses' reins. The first street to be paved was Brouwer, or Brewer, Street, named for its many breweries. Today it is known as Stone Street. It runs in a northeasterly direction from Whitehall Street to Hanover Square. In 1657 the first half, from Whitehall Street to Broad Street, was laid with cobblestones. These formed more sidewalk than pavement, for an open gutter was left in the center of the street. Benjamin Franklin, a resident of more sophisticated Philadelphia, later said that he could identify a New Yorker by his awkward gait when he walked on Philadelphia's smooth paving—"like a parrot upon a mahogany table."

Pearl Street, the oldest street in town, was lined with dwellings. Battery Place, bounding Battery Park on the north, was a much wider street than it is today and took the name of Marcktveldt because of cattle fairs held there. Outside town, four blocks north of Wall Street, Maagde Paatje, or Maidens' Path, began at Broadway and twisted to the southeast along the curve of a stream. Dutch girls who couldn't afford to send their clothes to a laundry washed their linen in the stream. Today the path is called Maiden Lane.

The Dutch never built log cabins, which were introduced into America by the Swedes in the Delaware Valley. The first houses erected in New Amsterdam were one-story wood structures containing two rooms. In Stuyvesant's time some houses were made of brick and stone. In 1628 kilns had been established here. They produced small yellow and black bricks, called Holland bricks to distinguish them from the larger English variety. The northern part of Manhattan provided an abundance of stone. Slowly the colonists began putting up two-story houses, whose second floors overhung the first floors.

A distinctive feature of Dutch architecture—one that lasted well into the brownstone era—was the high stoop at the front of the house. In Holland the first floors were raised high above the street, for in that *nether* land a hole in a dike could flood the land around a man's house. In America the Dutch built a steep flight of steps to the front doors. In warm weather the stoop served as the family gathering place, pipe-smoking men keeping their eyes on their neighbors' weathercocks, mothers shelling peas, and children shouting across the narrow streets.

Most front doors were ornamented with huge brass knockers shaped like a dog's or lion's head, and these had to be polished every day. Doors were large, and windows were small. Window glass was imported from Holland. Doors had an upper and a lower half. The lower half was usually kept shut so that a housewife could lean on it to gossip with a neighbor, yet keep pigs and hens out of her kitchen.

The houses had comfortable, if narrow, interiors, the low ceilings pierced by exposed wooden beams, alcoves, and window seats set into the whitewashed walls. Bare floors were scrubbed rigorously and then sprinkled with fine sand, which was broom-stroked into fantastic patterns. Furniture was plain and heavy and was made mostly of oak, maple, or nutwood. The Dutch lacked sofas, couches, or lounges. Their best chairs were made of Russian leather studded with brass nails.

Dutch matrons prided themselves on their recessed *slaap-bancks,* huge Holland beds, and massive sideboards and cupboards. Pewter mugs and copper vessels were set around racks holding a generous supply of long-stemmed pipes. China was rare. Most spoons and forks were carved from wood, although the well-to-do had silverware used only for parties. Glassware was almost completely unknown, punch being drunk in turns by guests from a huge bowl, and beer from a tankard of silver. The rich possessed mirrors; one wealthy man owned seventy. Pictures were plentiful but wretched—mostly engravings of Dutch cities and naval engagements. Window curtains were made of flowered chintz.

Clocks were scarce, time being kept mainly by sundials and hourglasses. Hardworking men arose with the first crow of the cock, breakfasted at dawn, labored through the morning, dined heartily at noon, resumed work, and then quit early in the afternoon to play. Every house contained spinning wheels, and looms became common. Behind most houses flower gardens were laid out in symmetrical designs, together with a vegetable garden and an orchard. Weather permitting, the Dutch liked to eat outdoors in summerhouses.

Houses cost from $200 to $1,000 and rented for $14 a year. From 1658 through 1661 living costs and wages were as follows: Beer sold at $4 a barrel, a sailor earned $8 a month, a horse was worth $112, the city bell ringer was paid $20 a year, the first Latin teacher earned $100 annually, lots near Hanover Square sold for $50 each, an ox brought $48, herrings sold at $3.60 per keg, and one beaverskin was worth $2.40.

A seafaring people, the Dutch enjoyed the water. Along Pearl Street small shipyards produced 1-masted sloops and 2-masted ketches. A 28-foot canoe cost $11, while a North River sloop or yacht was worth $560 or more.

Yacht, by the way, is a Dutch word. So are sloop, skipper, cookie, and cruller. A Dutch dozen or baker's dozen, meaning thirteen cookies or cakes, originated at a Dutch bakery in Albany, the term spreading to New Amsterdam. To the English a Dutch bargain meant a one-sided deal. Dutch comfort meant that conditions could be worse. Dutch courage signified booze bravery. To talk like a Dutch uncle meant to speak the truth gently but plainly.

Slaves were brought here from the West Indies and South America, but no New Netherland ship ever sailed on a slave-trading expedition to Africa. In 1654 the price of one slave was about $280. A law of 1658 forbade the whipping of Negro slaves without permission of the city magistrates; they enjoyed fairly humane treatment and were granted certain personal rights. Some were freed after long and faithful service and allowed to buy land in their own names. Peter Stuyvesant himself kept thirty to fifty slaves, his favorite being Old Mingo, who entertained him by playing the fiddle.

Despite the relative leniency with which slaves were treated, white lawbreakers suffered severely. They were branded, lashed, tortured on the rack, and dipped into water while strapped in a ducking stool. However, the Dutch never put witches to death, as was done in New England, and householders who erected wood chimneys, instead of the brick ones ordered by the governor, were merely fined.

Money obtained from the fines was sent to Holland to buy fire ladders and leather buckets for the town's eight-man fire department. Local craftsmen later produced leather buckets, whose sides were decorated by Evert Duyckinck, an artist who founded a dynasty of New Netherland painters. At last the city owned 250 leather buckets, which had to be kept filled. In winter, though, the water in them froze solidly. So did well water. The first fireman arriving on the scene had to jump down into the nearest well to chop away the surface ice with an ax. At night the community was more or less protected by a rattle watch, or rotating roster of policemen who called out the hour and shook rattles to warn thieves that they were approaching.

Manhattan abounded in rock springs that gushed pure water. The water supply did not become a problem until after the end of Dutch rule, when the population greatly increased. Burghers obtained water from springs and private wells until 1658; then the first public well was dug.

At first Peter Stuyvesant lived at 1 State Street. Later he bought land from the Dutch West India Company for a country estate, where he could spend the summer months. This consisted of an area roughly bounded by Sixth to Sixteenth Streets, the East River, and Third Avenue. Stuyvesant had brought fruit trees from Holland, and he planted an orchard with his own hands. On what is now the northeast corner of Third Avenue and Thirteenth Street he set out a peach tree that flourished for a century, after which the branches decayed and fell off. Everyone thought the old *pere-bloome* had died. Then, all by itself, it revived, greened again, and put out new shoots. Poems and articles were written about Peter Stuyvesant's doughty pear tree. When it was 220 years old, it was destroyed in 1867, after two vehicles had collided at the corner.

Stuyvesant's farm stood in the center of Bowery Village. The east-west streets were named for male members of his family, together with his title—Peter, Nicholas, William, Stuyvesant, and Governor. The north-south streets were styled after the family's female members—Judith, Eliza, and Margaret. The only surviving street is the short reach of Stuyvesant Street, preserved to keep open the approach to St. Marks-in-the-Bouwerie, a church begun in 1660 as a Dutch chapel on Stuyvesant's farm.

He obtained downtown property on the East River at the foot of Whitehall Street, where he put up a handsome stone mansion. Gardens flanked the mansion on three sides, and a velvety lawn extended to the water's edge. There the governor's private barge was docked at a landing reached by cut stone steps. This imposing residence was called White Hall, and Whitehall Street was later named for it.

The first dwelling on Manhattan north of Wall Street was erected before Stuyvesant's time in Greenwich Village. Governor Peter Minuit had set aside in perpetuity four farms for the company. Minuit's greedy successor, Wouter Van Twiller, grabbed the property for himself and founded a tobacco plantation. Then he put up a farmhouse that became the nucleus of a hamlet, known as Bossen Bouwerie, or the Farm in the Woods.

Still farther north on the island, along the Hudson River from about 14th to 135th streets, there stretched an area called Bloemendael, or Vale of the Flowers. At 125th Street a ravine, called the Widow David's Meadow sloped westward to the Hudson. Bloomingdale Village developed in the vicinity of 100th Street and the Hudson River.

About 1637 a Dutchman, named Hendrick De Forest, became the first white man to settle in what is now known as Harlem. Other colonists soon built there, but Indians ravaged the area so repeatedly that by the time Stuyvesant arrived here, all had deserted their farms. In 1658 Stuyvesant decided to improve this northeastern end of Manhattan "for the promotion of agriculture and as a place of amusement for the citizens of New Amsterdam." He promised that when twenty-five families settled there, he would provide them with a ferry to Long Island and a minister of their own.

Taking his word for it, the first settlers broke ground on August 14, 1658, near the foot of 125th Street and the Harlem River. Apparently Stuyvesant named the community New Haarlem for the town of Haarlem in Holland. The new hamlet lay eleven miles from New Amsterdam, the exact distance between Amsterdam and Haarlem in the old country. Along an old Indian path the governor carved a road connecting the two Manhattan communities. By horseback the trip each way took three hours. Dutchmen, French Protestants (Huguenots), Danes, Swedes, and Germans later developed rich farms in Haarlem, which ultimately dropped one *a* from its name.

The present five boroughs of New York City resulted from the coalescence of many individual hamlets, villages, towns, and cities. On Long Island the Dutch settled the western part, while the English gathered in communities farther east. The present boroughs of Brooklyn and Queens are located on the western end of Long Island.

Brooklyn got its start in 1634, when the Dutch founded Midwout, or Middle Woods, in the 't Vlacke Bos, or Wooded Plain. Later 't Vlacke Bos was anglicized to Flatbush. Today it lies in central Brooklyn. By 1652 this hamlet had received a patent of township from Stuyvesant, and two years afterward the original Flatbush Reformed Protestant Church was erected at Flatbush and Church avenues under the governor's direction. He raised a stockade around it as protection from Indians.

In 1636 William Adriaense Bennett and Jacques Bentyn bought 930 acres of land from a Mohawk chief, named Gouwane, in the southeastern part of Brooklyn now called Gowanus. The purchase included the area known today as Red Hook. There are two theories on why the Dutch called it Roode Hoeck: Either it described the color of the soil, or the area was covered with ripe cranberries.

In 1637 a Walloon, named Joris De Rapelje, purchased 335 acres near an East River inlet, later the Brooklyn Navy Yard. Because of him the Dutch called it Waelenbogt, or Walloon Bay. This term later was corrupted to Wallabout Bay. In 1638 the Dutch West India Company bought land east of the bay and founded a hamlet called Boswijck, or Bushwick. The Greenpoint section of Brooklyn was part of the original purchase of Bushwick.

Gowanus and Wallabout Bay were absorbed in 1646 by the village of Breuckelen, or Broken Land, named for a village in Holland of similar topography. This village had been started about four years earlier at the present intersection of Fulton and Smith streets. Breuckelen was granted a municipal form of government on November 26, 1646, or four years earlier than New Amsterdam itself. The name evolved from Breuckelen to Brockland to Brocklin to Brookline and finally to Brooklyn.

South of Flatbush another place, called Gravesend, was established in 1643 by Lady Deborah Moody, a cultured and tough-fibered Englishwoman. With the consent of the Dutch she bought the property from the Canarsie Indians for one blanket, one kettle, some wampum, three guns, and three pounds of gunpowder. Her colony included Coney Island, which the Indians called Narrioch. Born in England,

Lady Moody had left her homeland because she had been denied freedom of conscience, had removed to New England, where she had encountered further intolerance, and had then made her way to the more liberal New Netherland. Until her death in 1659 she was an active leader in her community. Even the testy Stuyvesant sought her opinion from time to time.

In 1652 Cornelis Van Werckhoven of the Dutch West India Company heard that the English were claiming some Dutch possessions on Long Island. He went there, inspected land in what is now west Brooklyn, decided to establish a colony, and went back to Holland to recruit settlers. Upon returning to Long Island, he bought property from the Indians between Bay Ridge and Gravesend, paying them in shirts, shoes, stockings, knives, combs and scissors. Then he erected a house and mill. In 1657 his town took the name of New Utrecht, for his native city in Holland.

The borough of Queens was first settled by the Dutch in about 1635. Colonization began at Flushing Bay, a shallow inlet of the East River in the northern section of Queens. Mespat, now Maspeth, was founded in 1642 at the head of Newtown Creek. The next year brought the establishment of Vlissingen, or Flushing, located in northern Queens and named for a town in Holland. It received its formal charter in 1645.

Between Maspeth and Flushing the town of Middleburg was created in 1652 by English Puritans under Dutch auspices, but after conflict between the Dutch and English the name was changed to New Town or, as we know it, Newtown. It embraced the southwestern half of present-day Queens County.

Shortly after the founding of New Amsterdam a Dutchman, named Jorissen, bought property at Hunter's Point in middle Queens near the mouth of Newtown Creek in present-day Long Island City. Many fine farms soon sprang up in the area.

About 1645 other Hollanders paid the Matinecock Indians an ax for every 50 acres of land in the northern section of Queens now called Whitestone. It took its name from a big white rock at an East River landing. Another part of northern Queens, Astoria, was settled in 1654 by William Hallett, who obtained a patent of 1,500 acres from the Dutch West India Company and the Indians. For the next 150 years this property belonged to his family.

English settlers, in 1650, founded a settlement, called Rustdorp, in middle Queens and were given a charter the same year by Stuyvesant. Soon the name was changed to Jamaica, for the Jameco Indians who first lived there. About two years later another section of middle Queens was bought from the Indians. At first the region was known as Whitepot, from the legend that the land had been bought with three white pots. Today it is called Forest Hills.

The Bronx was known to the Indians as Keskeskeck. In 1639 it was bought by the Dutch West India Company, but at first no one settled there. Then, as we have seen, a Danish immigrant, named Jonas Bronck, became the first white colonist when he purchased fifty acres between the Harlem and Aquahung Rivers. The latter stream became known as Bronck's River and now, of course, is the Bronx River.

Religious dissenters trickled into the Bronx from New England. In 1643 John Throgmorton settled on the skinny peninsula we call Throgs Neck. The next year Anne Hutchinson, exiled from Massachusetts, took up residence on the banks of the stream now known as the Hutchinson River. Her family was wiped out by an Indian massacre. In 1654 Thomas Pell bought a large tract of land near Pelham Bay Park.

The upper reach of the Bronx constituting Van Cortlandt Park was originally a hunting ground for Mohican Indians. In 1646 it was included in a patroonship granted by the company to Adriaen Cornelissen Van der Donck. He was New Netherland's first lawyer and historian and served as one of Stuyvesant's Nine Men. Because of his wealth and social position, he was popularly known as *jonkheer,* meaning his young lordship. In time the name of the area was corrupted to Yonkers.

The story of Staten Island, lying south of Manhattan, started in 1630, when Michael Paauw was granted a patroonship that included the isle. At least three attempts were made to colonize the island, but each time the settlements were wiped out by Indians. The Dutch bought Staten Island a total of five times. In 1661 nineteen Dutch and French settlers established the first permanent colony on the island near the present site of Fort Wadsworth. They called it Oude Dorp, or Old Town.

The city of New Amsterdam and the colony of New Netherland had one and the same government until 1653, when the city got its own separate government. This happened because of a chain of circumstances forged in the year 1649.

The Nine Men had been emboldened by Kuyter's and Melyn's victory over Peter Stuyvesant. Disgruntled by his treatment of them and disheartened because his reforms had failed, they decided to go over his head, bypass the company, and appeal directly to the Dutch government at The Hague. Despite the governor's angry protests, the Nine Men drew up and sent to the homeland the famous Petition and Remonstrance of New Netherland.

Both papers were written by Van der Donck and were signed in July, 1649. The petition was a short report on the condition of the colony, with suggested remedies. The remonstrance was a lengthy explanation of the detailed history of the facts on which the petitioners based their appeal for changes. It spelled out the autocratic behavior and cross-grained personality of both Stuyvesant and his predecessor, Kieft. It posed questions about the expenditure of public funds. It criticized the administration of justice. It asked for trading concessions. It said that more farmers were needed in the colony.

Most important, the Petition and Remonstrance asked for: (1) administration of the colony by the Dutch government instead of by the company; (2) municipal rule for New Amsterdam instead of arbitrary rule by the director general; and (3) establishment of a firm boundary between New Netherland and New England by treaty between the Dutch and English governments. What did the Nine Men get? Point 1 was rejected: The Dutch government declined to take over the administration of the colony because it could not withstand the pressures brought to bear on it by the company. Point 2 was granted: The government agreed to give New Amsterdam the kind of municipal government enjoyed by cities in Holland. Point 3 was approved in theory: Although the government itself made no effort to settle boundary disputes, it did not object to the establishment of a commission to consider the issues.

Company directors were outraged by the effrontery of the Nine Men in appealing to the government. They sneered at the petitioners, denied the need for reforms in the colony, and upheld Peter Stuyvesant in everything he had done. This was all the ammunition he needed. Seeking revenge on the upstart members of his advisory board, Stuyvesant began by insulting them. He forbade them to use their reserved pews in the Dutch Reformed Church and branded them publicly as promoters of "schisms, factions and intestine commotions." Whenever a board member died or resigned, Stuyvesant refused to let his position be filled and so almost extinguished the board. But before the Nine Men vanished, they again appealed to the States General.

This time the Dutch government cracked down on the company. Its directors realized now that they had better concede a few points or risk losing the colony. Therefore, in 1652 the firm ordered Stuyvesant to grant New Amsterdam a burgher system of government modeled after that of the free cities of Holland.

The crisp evening of February 2, 1653, the birth of a new city was proclaimed. The ceremonies began with a parade down Broadway to the church within the fort. Old Peg Leg marched at the head of the procession, resplendent in his regimental coat studded with brass buttons from chin to waist. His coat skirts were turned back and separated to display his sulfur-hued breeches. His right hand held a long gold-headed cane, and his left hand rested on the hilt of his sword.

The bell ringer carried rich pew cushions for the dignitaries to use in the church. These grave-faced gentlemen wore long-waisted coats with skirts reaching almost to the ankles, vests with large flaps, and multicolored breeches. Their coats and vests were trimmed with big silver buttons and decorated with lace. On nearby pews they placed their low-crowned beaver hats. When all were assembled and the coughs had been stifled, Stuyvesant rose to speak. With his proclamation that the city was being granted municipal government, the town elders nodded at one another and preened.

Then Stuyvesant announced that he would appoint one schout, or sheriff; two burgomasters, or city magistrates; and five schepens, or aldermen. Appoint? Faces fell. In Holland these officials were elected by the people themselves. Slowly the townspeople realized that they had little cause for rejoicing. The governor went on to state that even after he had appointed these officials, his authority would not be diminished one whit. Often he would preside at their meetings, and always he would counsel them about matters of importance. Before Stuyvesant finished speaking, the congregation understood that the officials would function in name only. The people had begged for a loaf and been thrown a few crumbs.

Four days later the newly appointed city fathers met for the first time. Eighteen days after this, City Tavern was officially proclaimed the first City Hall. Not until the spring of 1657, however, were burghers registered. Thus, for the first time in the city's history, citizenship became an accomplished, legal fact.

Although Stuyvesant felt that he had local matters firmly in hand, he worried about external affairs. New Netherland thrust like a wedge between New England, to the northeast, and the English colonies of Maryland and Virginia, to the southwest. This Dutch-held gap along the Atlantic seaboard made it difficult for the English government to enforce its commercial regulations in America. A few Englishmen from Maryland and Virginia filtered into Dutch territory, but it was mainly New Englanders who encroached on the land claimed by the Hollanders. English and Dutch traders vied for the fur trade. New Amsterdam's tariffs were a source of irritation. For the Dutch West India Company, Stuyvesant claimed all the coast between the Delaware River and Cape Cod. The Dutch and English quarreled over ownership of the Connecticut Valley.

Matters worsened. At last Stuyvesant offered to confer in Hartford, Connecticut, with commissioners of the United Colonies of New England, consisting of Massachusetts, Plymouth, Connecticut, and New Haven. Stuyvesant agreed to negotiate because he realized that the New Englanders outnumbered the New Netherlanders. Indeed he thought them fifty times more numerous, whereas the odds were actually sixteen to one. This margin still prevented Stuyvesant from engaging in power politics. Setting forth with attendants, he made the four-day trip from New Amsterdam to Hartford, where he was received courteously.

Stuyvesant proposed that negotiations be conducted in writing since he didn't speak English fluently and this procedure would ensure greater accuracy. His very first paper, though, raised a storm because it was datelined New Netherland. The New England delegates insisted that the name Connecticut be substituted. Peg Leg Peter apologized. He said that the paper had been drafted before he left New Amsterdam and then translated and copied by his English secretary en route to Hartford.

The week-long conference ended in a stalemate. Finally, all agreed to submit the issues to four arbitrators, two for the English and two for the Dutch. Stuyvesant, who seems to have relied on his English subjects living on Long Island, appointed two of them—Thomas Willett and George Baxter. The four arbitrators came to a decision that was accepted by both parties to the dispute—the Treaty of Hartford of 1650. Six years later the Dutch government ratified the agreement. The English government never did. Although the treaty did not become legally binding, it served awhile as a method for both sides to get along.

Long Island was divided between the Dutch and English, but not evenly. Stuyvesant sacrificed a great deal of real estate by allowing the English to win the larger eastern end of the island. When terms of the treaty were revealed to the Nine Men, they angrily declared he "had ceded away territory enough to found 50 colonies each four miles square." They kept harping on this subject; whereupon Stuyvesant threatened to dissolve the body, then and there. Actually, he had been powerless against the English. The treaty, however, didn't end all trouble with other colonies.

Rhode Island, which did not belong to the New England confederation, started a little war of its own against the Dutch. Its soldiers were led by Captain John Underhill, the very Englishman who years earlier had saved New Amsterdam during the Indian war. Subsequently he had bought property at the site of Locust Valley, Long Island. Annoyed by Dutch discrimination against English settlers and provoked by Stuyvesant's tyranny, Underhill had incited riots, for which he had twice been arrested by the Dutch. Seething with rage, he now set out with twenty men and took an unoccupied Dutch fort on the Connecticut River, thus ending Dutch sovereignty in New England.

Besides intercolonial quarrels, Stuyvesant had to contend with overseas affairs that impinged on New Netherland. Oliver Cromwell seized England, and in 1651 the first British Navigation Act was passed. This forbade the importation of goods into England except in British ships or those of the country producing the merchandise. It was intended to prevent rival sea powers—especially Holland—from carrying goods to the American colonies. British sea captains searched and seized Dutch merchant ships. As a result, in 1652 war broke out between England and Holland. The next year the United Colonies of New England girded for war on New Netherland, charging that the Dutch had conspired with the Indians against the Connecticut colonies.

Stuyvesant ordered his people to build a fortified wall in New Amsterdam along what is now Wall Street. This stretched 2,340 feet from the East River to the Hudson River. Along this line, stakes were hammered 3 feet into the ground, their exposed 9-foot lengths ending in sharp tips. Earth was packed along the inside of the wall for Dutch soldiers to stand on when they fired at an approaching enemy. A land gate was cut in the wall opposite the present Trinity Church, while a water gate toward the east gave access to the Brooklyn ferry. Cattle were driven out the land gate mornings and back in again at night.

But no assault came. This was the result of a quarrel that developed among the United Colonies of New England. Massachusetts, with a larger population than the other three members combined, was called on to contribute the most men and money. It refused, for it lay at a greater distance from the Dutch than its colleagues. Besides, it didn't really believe that the Dutch were inciting the Indians. Nevertheless, Oliver Cromwell dispatched a fleet from England to conquer what is now New York City. The expedition was supposed to be aided by the New Englanders. Before an attack could be mounted, however, peace between England and Holland was declared.

New Netherland enjoyed comparatively greater religious freedom than church-ruled New England. Stuyvesant, however, was a religious bigot. From the time the first Dutch minister arrived to the very end of the Dutch occupation, not a single religious group other than the Dutch Reformed Church was allowed to put up a house of worship. Even so, in 1655 a Dutch pastor complained: "We have here Papists, Mennonites and Lutherans among the Dutch. Also many Puritans or Independents, and many atheists and various other servants of Baal among the English under this government, who conceal themselves under the name of Christians."

The first Catholic priest visited Manhattan in 1643. A French Jesuit, named Father Isaac Jogues, he did missionary work among the Indians of Canada and upper New York State. The first Irish Catholic layman who settled here was Hugh O'Neal. He married a Dutch widow the very year that Father Jogues paid the city a short visit. Apparently the Jesuit heard O'Neal's confession. In 1646 Father Jogues was killed by Indians, and in 1930 he was canonized as a saint. It was, however, a long time before Catholics came to New York in large numbers.

The first Jew to settle here was Jacob Barsimon; he arrived from Holland on July 8, 1654. The next month twenty-seven Jews landed after a long and exhausting voyage from Brazil. They were the descendants of Jews expelled from Spain and Portugal in 1492 by King Ferdinand and Queen Isabella. The original refugees had found a haven in Holland and then, after the Dutch took part of Brazil, had gone there to live. But in 1654 Recife, the last Dutch stronghold in Brazil, was captured by the Portuguese. Faced with persecution from the Inquisition, the twenty-seven remaining Jews fled to New Amsterdam. They left Brazil in such haste that they didn't even collect debts due them, for on their arrival here the skipper of their ship auctioned off all their goods to pay for their passage.

Soon more Jews arrived from Curaçao. Annoyed by their presence, Stuyvesant wrote the Dutch West India Company to beg that "none of the Jewish nation be permitted to infest New Netherland." Company directors wrote him that the Jews had sustained a loss in the capture of Brazil, held shares in the company, and must therefore be allowed to settle in New Netherland, provided they took care of their own poor.

Stuyvesant fumed but was powerless because no Jew became a welfare case. At first the only trade open to the Jews was that of slaughtering. Despite this, they prospered and began to play an active part in civic affairs. Before the end of Stuyvesant's reign they were permitted to own property, engage in foreign and domestic trade on a wholesale basis, and enjoy burgher rights. They were barred from public office, however.

The first Rosh Hashanah service in North America was held on September 12, 1654, when a group of Jewish men met secretly in New York City, probably in an attic or in a room behind a shop. This was the beginning of Congregation Shearith Israel (the Spanish and Portuguese Synagogue), the oldest existing Jewish congregation in North America. New York Jews held their first public service in 1673 on Beaver Street, in a rented room. By 1695 the Jews had their first synagogue, a house on Mill Street (now South William Street).

In 1656 they acquired a plot for their first cemetery. No trace remains of this earliest Jewish burial ground in North America, but it may have been located a little north of Wall Street. In 1682 members of Congregation Shearith Israel established their second cemetery, a plot fifty-two feet long and fifty feet wide. Located south of Chatham Square, this burial ground is today a small triangle on St. James Place between James and Oliver streets.

All in all, but in spite of Peter Stuyvesant, the Jews were treated better in New Amsterdam than in most American colonies. The prevailing attitude toward the Quakers was different—different and worse. A group of Quakers expelled from Boston arrived here by ship in August, 1657. Two of the women began preaching in the streets; whereupon Stuyvesant had them locked up inside the fort prison. After an examination they were ordered out of the city and colony and were placed on a ship bound for Rhode Island.

Another Quaker, Robert Hodgson, made his way to Heemstede, or Hempstead, Long Island, where he intended to spread the word about the new Society of Friends. While strolling in an orchard, he was seized and led before a local magistrate, who took away his Bible and imprisoned him. For twenty-four hours he was tied in a painful position. The Hempstead magistrate also arrested two women who had sheltered Hodgson. One of them was nursing an infant. Word was sent to Stuyvesant that other Quakers had been captured. He ordered them brought to New Amsterdam.

Hodgson was lashed facedown in a cart. The women were roped to the cart's tail. In this fashion the three prisoners were conveyed over rough roads to the city and thrown into separate dungeons. After Hodgson had endured vermin and filth, and near starvation for several days, he was brought before Stuyvesant. The governor and council tried him, but the prisoner was not allowed to speak in his own defense. He was sentenced to be chained to a wheelbarrow and suffer hard labor for two years, unless he paid a $240 fine.

The destitute Quaker was unable to pay. Stubbornly he declared that he had done no wrong, had broken no law, was unused to manual labor, and so would do no work. After he had finished speaking, he was stripped to the waist and beaten with a tarred rope until he sagged to the ground. Strong men stood him up again. Once more he was beaten. Blow after stinging blow rained on his back. Then, his flesh waffled with welts, he was left, still chained to the wheelbarrow, to lie under an autumn sun until he fainted.

That night Hodgson was thrown back into his filthy dungeon. The second day he was flogged—and the third day. At last he was brought again before Stuyvesant, who commanded him to work or be lashed every day until he did. Boldly looking at his tormentor, Hodgson asked what law he had broken. The governor didn't bother to answer. The Quaker cried that he never would submit to Stuyvesant's will, so back to the dungeon he went, and for the next two or three days he was kept there without even bread or water. Still he refused to give in.

Now began new torture. Hodgson was dragged to a room, where his mutilated skin was bared once again. He was suspended from the ceiling by his wrists, with a heavy log tied to his feet. In this taut position he was lashed again and again and again. Two days later the torture was repeated. Sobbing, Hodgson begged to see a fellow Englishman, and at last a poor Englishwoman was allowed to visit him. She bathed his wounds and wept in pity. Later she told her husband that she didn't think the wretched fellow could live until morning. The husband went to the sheriff to offer him a fat ox to allow the prisoner to be removed to his own house until he recovered. This couldn't be done, the sheriff said.

By now, this torture having become common knowledge, people began muttering about their governor. Hodgson wasn't the only Quaker persecuted in the colony just then, although he suffered the most. Dutch ministers, unlike most burghers, sided with Stuyvesant and wrote the Dutch West India Company of their alarm at the spread of sectarianism in New Netherland.

Meanwhile, the governor's sister, Mrs. Verlett, caught the note of public discontent, and her gentle soul winced at what he had done. She marched into Peter's presence, tongue-lashed him for his cruelty, and denounced and upbraided him until at last Stuyvesant agreed to let the man go. Hodgson was freed, but he was banished from the colony.

Other Quakers met secretly at Flushing, Long Island, in the homes of Henry Townsend and John Bowne. Both men were arrested. Stuyvesant's action infuriated and saddened all the people of Flushing and nearby towns. After all, Flushing's charter of 1645 declared the settlers were "to have and enjoy liberty of conscience, according to the custom and manner of Holland, without molestation or disturbance." Obviously, the governor himself was the lawbreaker. On December 27, 1657, thirty-one Dutchmen and Englishmen drew up a protest addressed to Stuyvesant. Six of the thirty-one, being illiterate, merely made their mark on the document; they were courageous men, willing to face the fiery governor along with the others.

This Flushing Remonstrance has been called the first American Declaration of Independence. Among other things, it said:

> The law of love, peace and liberty in the states extending to Jews, Turks and Egyptians, as they are considered the sons of Adam, which is the glory of the outward states of Holland, so love, peace and liberty, extending to all in Christ Jesus, condemns hatred, war

and bondage. And because our Saviour saith it is impossible but that offenses will come, but woe unto him by whom they cometh, our desire is not to offend one of his little ones in whatsoever form, name or title. . . .

The Flushing sheriff traveled to New Amsterdam and handed the protest to Stuyvesant, who angrily banged his wooden leg and ordered the sheriff arrested. Then the governor cracked down on other Flushing officials. The town clerk was jailed for three weeks. Two justices of the peace were suspended from office. For a long time afterward no Long Island resident dared to shelter Quakers openly, but the sectarians continued to hold secret meetings in the Flushing woods. They managed to get news of their persecution to the Dutch West India Company in Holland, whose directors then ordered Stuyvesant to keep hands off the Quakers.

As we have seen, the Treaty of Hartford took away from Stuyvesant much of Connecticut, which he originally claimed for the company. Now, except for New Amsterdam, only the part of the Atlantic coastline between the Delaware and Hudson rivers came under his rule. Because the Delaware River emptied into the Atlantic to the south of the Hudson, the Dutch called the Delaware the South River and spoke of the Hudson as the North River. Even today the first leg of the Hudson just north of the Battery is sometimes called the North River.

Stuyvesant was irked by the existence, proximity, and rivalry of New Sweden. This colony on the Delaware River included parts of the present states of Delaware, New Jersey, and Pennsylvania. About half the colonists were Finns, since Finland was then part of Sweden. The population of New Sweden never rose to much more than about 300 inhabitants, but Stuyvesant would not leave them alone.

In 1651 he built Fort Casimir on the site of New Castle, Delaware. Three years later the Swedes captured it, thus gaining control of the entire Delaware Valley. In 1655 Stuyvesant led an expedition of hundreds of soldiers, on seven men-of-war, back to the Delaware River and recaptured Fort Casimir. He and his men also took Fort Christina, about thirty-five miles below the present site of Philadelphia. Then New Sweden disappeared from the map.

For ten years—from 1645 to 1655—the Dutch in and around Manhattan had not been troubled by Indians. Of course, a few minor incidents did occur, and the Dutch discriminated against the Indians by charging them double fare for the East River ferry ride, but nothing serious happened. Then, while Stuyvesant and most of the town's able-bodied men were subduing the Swedes on the Delaware River, open conflict broke out here.

A former sheriff, named Hendrick Van Dyck, had a farm on Broadway just south of the present Exchange Alley, or perhaps a block and a half below the site of Trinity Church. As twilight thickened one September day in 1655, he saw somebody moving stealthily among his heavy-laden peach trees. Tiptoeing closer, Van Dyck realized that an Indian woman was stealing his fruit. He pulled out a pistol and fired. The woman gently slumped to earth, and in that tragic moment Van Dyck triggered the historic Peach War.

When news of the murder reached the dead woman's relatives and friends and spread to neighboring tribes, the Indians suffered shock. Then they exploded with the cry "Death to the woman killer!" They were well aware that Stuyvesant had left the town almost defenseless by sailing away with most of his soldiers.

At daybreak on September 15 the prows of 64 canoes sliced through the morning mist along the high banks of the Hudson. A little below the stockade at Wall Street the craft glided to the shore. About 500 braves, armed with bows, arrows, and tomahawks and daubed with war paint, leaped out, made fast their canoes, and then raced into the city. Soon they were joined by others until 2,000 marauders fanned through the streets.

The Indians didn't instantly massacre the inhabitants. They began with psychological warfare by breaking into houses under the pretext that they were searching for their ancient enemies, the Iroquois. This transparent deceit heightened the menace. Alarmed Dutchmen struggled into pantaloons as their wives stared, wide-eyed with terror. Children screamed at the sight of dusky strangers in the kitchens. Council members assembled quickly and held a hurried conference. Realizing that the townspeople were outnumbered, these officials decided to put up a brave front. They strolled out into the open to the midst of the sullen intruders and asked to see their chiefs.

When the sachems advanced and identified themselves, the Dutch invited them to a parley inside the fort. There the white men tried to pacify the red men. At last the chiefs agreed to withdraw their warriors to Governors Island, but after filing out of the fort, the Indians did not leave as promised. Instead, all the rest of the day they loitered about the southern end of Manhattan, muttering menacingly.

At dusk they gathered and broke toward Broadway, screaming

and surging directly toward Van Dyck's home. He stood uncertainly at his garden gate. An arrow flashed through the evening sky and gashed into his side, wounding him gravely, but not mortally. A neighbor who tried to help had his scalp sliced with a war hatchet.

Frantically, the town elders tried once again to locate the chiefs to avert more bloodshed. Then the Indians slew a Dutchman. Now the colonists opened fire on the invaders, driving them back to the shore, back into their canoes. Even as they paddled out into the Hudson, the Indians twanged a volley of arrows into the counterattacking Dutchmen, killing one and wounding several others. Swift-stroking across the river, the Indians landed at Hoboken, set fire to every dwelling there, turned to Jersey City to reduce it to ashes, and then proceeded to Staten Island, where they wreaked havoc.

The Peach War lasted only three days, three terrifying days, but by the time it ended, the entire countryside had been put to the torch. About 100 white persons were killed, about 150 others were dragged into captivity, and 7 men and 1 woman were tortured to death. In addition, 28 plantations were destroyed, 500 head of cattle were slain or driven away, and huge quantities of grain were burned. All for a few peaches!

During the brief outbreak Mrs. Stuyvesant, her sons, and the rest of the family were guarded at the Stuyvesant farm by ten French mercenaries hired for the emergency. News of the attack was sped to the governor in Delaware, but he was unable to return until October 12.

Panic still prevailed when he arrived. Stuyvesant, who had always adopted a reasonable Indian policy, was careful to give the natives no cause to maraud again. His sturdy leadership, zeal, resourcefulness, and military know-how finally gave the people a sense of security. Soldiers were posted at outlying farms. Ship passengers ready to flee the colony were ordered ashore to join the troops "until it should please God to change the aspect of affairs." Funds were raised to strengthen the vulnerable city wall.

But now the Indians were ready to negotiate. Their fury was spent. They grumbled about the portions of food consumed by their prisoners. One Dutchman wanted to continue the war to get revenge, but the governor flatly disagreed. "The recent war," he rasped, "is to be attributed to the rashness of a few hotheaded individuals. It becomes us to reform ourselves, to abstain from all wrong, and to guard against a recurrence of the late unhappy affair by building blockhouses wherever they are needed, and not permitting any armed Indians to come into our settlements."

Stuyvesant's cool judgment prevailed. Still, he was able to negotiate the release of only forty-two white persons. Twenty-eight of them were ransomed by paying the Indians seventy-eight pounds of gunpowder and forty bars of lead. At last peace was concluded with the red men—or at least some of them. White prisoners held at Esopus were not released. This community, now known as Kingston, New York, perched on the west bank of the Hudson River eighty-seven miles north of New Amsterdam.

The Dutch West India Company suffered so many reverses in various parts of the world that it wound up a commercial failure. By 1661 New Amsterdam was bankrupt. That year, in a frantic effort to protect its investment, the company tried to lure discontented Englishmen to New Netherland from their native country. The Dutch government helped by seeding Great Britain with glowing descriptions of the Dutch colony "only six weeks' sail from Holland . . . land fertile . . . climate the best in the world."

This practice irritated English authorities. As we have seen, they objected to the very existence of New Netherland. It blocked their westward expansion, denied them the continuous belt of English colonies along the coast necessary for protection from the French, and interfered with enforcement of the Navigation Acts.

Because of bitter rivalry with Holland for control of the seas and business profits, the English Parliament, as has been noted, passed several acts of trade and navigation. But Dutch smugglers in the New World loosened England's grip on trading among the English colonies. Although the Treaty of Hartford had reduced the Dutch holdings, the British weren't satisfied. They encouraged the rebellion of restless English towns on Long Island. Peter Stuyvesant thrice convened delegates from towns adjacent to New Amsterdam but never could satisfy all their demands.

Charles II became the king of England for the second time in 1660. Two years later he granted a charter to the English colonists of Connecticut. Because this area included settlements which the Treaty of Hartford said belonged to New Netherland, tension mounted between Dutch and English colonists.

On March 22, 1664, Charles gave a present to his brother, James Stuart, the Duke of York, later to become King James II. Upon the duke Charles conferred all Long Island, its neighboring islands, and all the territory lying between the west side of the Connecticut River and the east side of Delaware Bay. This, of course, embraced the Dutch colony of New Netherland. By now the English had launched an undeclared war on the Hollanders, the Second Anglo-Dutch War.

Even British historians admit that the English acted like pirates. The king and duke knew that the war would be popular with the trading classes at home, for they intended to break Dutch control of slave-trading ports on the African coast and to seize land in the New World. The duke ordered Colonel Richard Nicolls to lead an expedition against the Dutch in America. This was kept a secret lest the Dutch government dispatch a fleet to protect Dutch interests. The English didn't issue a formal declaration of war until 1665. Meanwhile, the king lent his brother 4 men-of-war and 450 soldiers.

News of this small armada was brought to Peter Stuyvesant by an Englishman in New Netherland. He, in turn, had heard about it from a British merchant whose ships sailed from England to this city. Stuyvesant reacted quickly. He confined to port some Dutch ships ready to sail to Curaçao, sent agents to New Haven to buy provisions, stationed lookouts along the coast to watch for the British fleet, borrowed money, and ordered gunpowder rushed from Delaware to New Amsterdam.

Then word arrived from the Dutch West India Company that the English ships were not headed for New Amsterdam. Instead, according to this rumor, they were en route to Boston, where the king's men were to insist that Church of England rites be observed.

Everyone relaxed. Stuyvesant let the Dutch vessels sail for the Caribbean, and he departed for upstate New York to pacify Indians. So for the second time the governor was absent from New Amsterdam during an emergency. Fortunately, a messenger caught up with him to report that the English squadron was indeed bearing down on the city. Stuyvesant got back to town just three days before enemy masts loomed against the horizon.

The English ships anchored off Coney Island below the Narrows. Two days later Colonel Nicolls demanded the surrender of New Amsterdam. Stuyvesant's courage cannot be questioned, although his judgment, as in the 1644 attack on St. Martin Island, is open to debate. He resolved to fight.

This was a foolhardy decision. Stuyvesant admitted as much indirectly, for shortly before the enemy arrived, he told the Dutch

West India Company that the English in America outnumbered the Dutch "and are able to deprive us of the country when they please." In 1664 there were 50,000 English colonists in Maryland and Virginia, plus an equal number in New England. New Netherland's 3 cities and 30 villages had a total population of only about 10,000 persons. New Amsterdam itself boasted only 1,500 inhabitants, and Stuyvesant could muster no more than 200 militia and 160 regular soldiers.

Dutch colonists had been lax about throwing up their defenses, arguing that the company or the Dutch government should pay for all fortifications. Now, partly because of their own folly, they were helpless. The Wall Street palisade was falling apart. The city was open along the banks of both rivers. Food was scarce. Despite the gunpowder sent from Delaware, there still wasn't enough on hand. The fort, which didn't even contain a spring or well, couldn't withstand a siege. If an invader landed on either shore, he could stand on the hills of Broadway at pistol-shot range and look down into the fort's interior.

English negotiators rowed to a wharf under a white flag of truce. Stuyvesant received them with starchy courtesy, pointing out that England and Holland were not formally at war. The British then produced a letter from Nicolls stating his terms. These were liberal, considering that all the power was on his side. He promised to grant Dutch citizens freedom of conscience and religion. He declared that he would not interfere with their private property, inheritance rights, or customs. They would be permitted to trade directly with Holland. Public buildings and records would be respected. City officials could remain in office awhile; later, elections would be held. When the English diplomats had been rowed back to their men-of-war, the burgomasters urged Stuyvesant to accept these conditions "in the speediest, best and most reputable manner." He refused. They argued. In a fit of temper he tore Nicolls' letter to shreds. A crowd gathered. Some people cursed stiff-necked Peter, while others cursed the company. By this time they knew about Nicolls' letter, although they were unaware of its contents. "The letter!" they cried. "The letter!"

After Stuyvesant stamped out to take up a position on the fort, his secretary gathered the scraps of paper, pasted them together, and handed the mended document to the burgomasters. They quickly announced the terms, and almost everyone wanted to give up.

As the enemy fleet sailed into the Upper Bay and closed in on the

Battery, the governor stood on a rampart near a gunner who was holding a burning match near a cannon. Stuyvesant growled, "I must act in obedience to orders!" Near him stood a minister, who cried, "It's madness!" Laying a hand on Stuyvesant's shoulder, the pastor pleaded, "Do you not see that there is no help for us either to the north or to the south, to the east or to the west? What will our twenty guns do in the face of the sixty-two which are pointed toward us on yonder frigates? Pray, do not be the first to shed blood!"

At that moment a messenger brought Stuyvesant a document signed by ninety-three of the principal citizens—including one of his own sons. They begged him not to do anything that would result in the slaughter of the innocent and reduce the city to ruins. The gunner still held the match at the ready as the governor read the paper. His eyes were sad; his lips, white. At last he signaled to the gunner to put out his flame. Then, more to himself than anyone else, Peter Stuyvesant muttered, "I had rather be carried to my grave." Five minutes later a white flag waved above the fort.

Chapter 4

THE ENGLISH NAME IT NEW YORK

IT HAD been so easy. Without declaring war, without firing a shot, without spilling a drop of blood, the English took the forty-year-old Dutch city of New Amsterdam on August 29, 1664.

They renamed it New York in honor of the Duke of York, its new lord proprietor. York is a compound of two ancient words, which mean place at the water, a fit title for so great a seaport.

The day after the surrender the burgomasters and schepens transacted municipal business as though nothing had happened. The next Sunday the chaplain of the English troops conducted the first Church of England rites ever observed here. The transition from Dutch to British rule did not greatly disturb most citizens, for they felt nothing could be so oppressive as a soulless corporation and a high-handed governor. But Peter Stuyvesant took it hard. To Holland he sent an explanation of his own conduct, describing how helpless he had been at the critical moment. Then he retired to the shaded quietude of his country estate.

The surrender of the city was an event of deep significance for all America. As historian John Fiske said, "Few political changes have been greater in their consequences. By transferring from Dutch into English hands the strategic center of antagonism to New France, it brought about an approach toward unity of political development in the English colonies and made it possible for them to come together in a great federal union."

Except for one brief interruption, New York was to be ruled for many years by the last of England's royal Stuarts, James Stuart— first as the Duke of York and then as King James II. His authority over the new English colony was as absolute as that formerly enjoyed by the Dutch West India Company. His henchmen wielded all legis- lative, executive, and judicial power, subject only to approval by the king and Privy Council of England. James, who never visited his American empire, chose well when he selected Colonel Richard Nicolls as his first governor.

Nicolls was about forty years old when he succeeded Peter Stuy- vesant. Tall and erect, gray-eyed, genial and polite, and somewhat curly-haired, Nicolls was a bachelor. The son of a lawyer, university- trained Nicolls read Greek and Latin classics in the original and spoke Dutch and French as fluently as his native English. He utterly charmed the Dutch citizens, who signed a letter proclaiming Nicolls "a wise and intelligent governor, under whose wing we hope to bloom and grow like the cedar on Lebanon." He repaired Fort Amsterdam and renamed it Fort James. He offered to let any Dutch- man go back to Holland, hoping none would do so, and none did. Of course, he was careful to ship the Dutch soldiers back home.

This first English governor found himself at the head of a strange assortment of people. The Dutch made up three-quarters of the population, but the other quarter consisted of English, French, Swedes, Finns, Portuguese, and Negroes—most of the Negroes having been brought here from Brazil. From the time of the first English settlers there had been frequent marriages between the Dutch and the English. Educated citizens spoke both languages, but many busi- nessmen were unable to translate from one language to the other.

Because of the growing influx of Huguenots, some records were kept in French. All in all, the city was a veritable Babel.

Society was rigidly stratified. The immigrants brought along their Old World prejudices, which they handed down to their children. A line was clearly drawn between master and slave, master and indentured servant, aristocrat and tradesman, rich and poor. The common people felt they had small chance of rising in the social scale. Because of patroonships, the first wealthy class consisted of landowners. Only later did trade and shipping elevate to prominence men of humble origin.

The colonists owned several kinds of livestock—goats, hogs, oxen, sheep, cattle, and horses. Goats cost little, bred prolifically, and yielded milk and meat. Hogs overran the streets. Some farmers preferred English swine because they were hardy and could endure cold weather without shelter, but Holland hogs grew heavier and yielded more pork than the English kind. Oxen hauled wagons and pulled plows.

Dutchmen had brought their own stolid cattle to the New World. With the inauguration of livestock fairs in the city they gazed for the first time on the red English cattle shipped here by New Englanders. Local farmers soon learned that superior cattle could be bred by mating Holland bulls and English heifers. Milk was sold from house to house by countrymen bearing wooden yokes on their shoulders. From each end of the yokes dangled chains, attached to huge tin milk cans. Thus laden, the dairymen trudged about the city, crying, "Milk come!"

Because fences were scarce, most livestock grazed at large. This resulted in confusion and in conflicts about ownership until Nicolls ordered the branding of all cattle and horses. Roundups were held in Manhattan. To corner, halter, and lead wild bulls to market was a dangerous sport. The English imported bulldogs, which soon became popular among butchers. The bowlegged broad-jawed animals were trained to seize a bull by the nose and hold down its head until a rope could be slung about its neck.

When the English arrived, most of the horses in the colony were of Dutch strain. Heavy and awkward, they were good for farmwork but for little else. After the first English horses had been imported from New England and the mother country, Governor Nicolls introduced horse racing into America. Out on Long Island, near the town of Hempstead, he found a long narrow plain covered with fine grass and unmarred by sticks or stones. There Nicolls built a racetrack, called the Newmarket Course for the famous racetrack outside London. Then the governor scheduled a series of horse races, "not so much for the divertisement of youth as for encouraging the bettering of the breed of horses which, through neglect, have been impaired."

Apparently the first race was run in 1665, and others were run in the two following years. We know for certain that a contest was held in 1668 because Yale University owns a silver dish with this inscription: "1668: runn att Hampsted Plains, March 25."

Two months after the city had been captured, Nicolls called a meeting of leading citizens, including former Governor Stuyvesant. Nicolls said that he hoped they would take the customary oath of allegiance to British authority. This did not mean, he explained, that they would be renouncing allegiance to the Dutch government. Presumably, the oath would result in dual citizenship. Some Dutchmen protested. Then the English governor pointed out gently but firmly that all Dutch inhabitants must renew the titles to their lands in the name of the Duke of York. After more discussions and explanations, 250 residents of the city and the adjoining countryside swore fidelity to British overlordship. Even Stuyvesant took the oath.

The Dutch West India Company now ordered Peg Leg Peter back to Holland to explain his surrender to the English. Before sailing, he obtained from the burgomasters and schepens a certificate testifying to his good character. Upon his arrival in Holland he blamed the loss of the colony on company officials, who had left him without adequate means of defense, without a single warship, and with only a few barrels of gunpowder. Angrily, they countercharged that Stuyvesant was guilty of cowardice and treason.

While this dispute bubbled overseas, in New York, Stuyvesant's nephew, Nicholas Bayard, was appointed secretary of the council. Bayard was a mere youth in age and appearance but, thanks to his mother, as self-possessed as a mature man. Peter Stuyvesant's elder son, Balthazar, quit the colony to live in the West Indies, but his younger son, Nicholas William Stuyvesant, chose to remain.

At the time of the conquest Broadway was a street only from the Battery to Wall Street, continuing north as an Indian trail. Nearly a century passed before Broadway became a street reaching as far as the Commons, or City Hall Park. To the river along the west side of Manhattan the British gave the name of Hudson, for their countryman who first explored it. Staten Island became Richmond County in honor of the Duke of Richmond, the illegitimate son of King Charles II. Then, sailing up the Hudson in force for the first time, the British took Fort Orange and changed its name to Albany, for the Duke of York's Scotch title—the Duke of Albany.

Unable to quarter all his English soldiers within the fort, Nicolls sought to billet them in private homes, offering to pay householders for their food. However, some enlisted men and officers behaved so badly that they were turned out of respectable houses. Irate citizens finally agreed to pay an assessment for feeding and lodging the soldiers elsewhere, rather than shelter them in private homes. This change pleased the people, but not the soldiers themselves. In a letter to the Duke of York the governor complained that "not one soldier to this day since I brought them out of England has been in a pair of sheets, or upon any sort of bed but canvas and straw."

At first Nicolls let the conquered people retain their Dutch form of municipal government. When the burgomasters and schepens completed their terms of office on February 2, 1665, they named their successors, as before. This happened just twelve years to the day that Stuyvesant had granted them their limited powers. The new officials were promptly confirmed by Nicolls and announced by the usual ringing of a bell. Three of the eight men were Huguenots.

However, the Duke of York ordered Nicolls to alter the city government to conform to the customs of England. Accordingly, on June 12, 1665, he issued this proclamation: "I, Richard Nicolls, do ordain that all the inhabitants of New York, New Harlem and the Island of Manhattan are one body politic under the government of a Mayor, Aldermen, and Sheriff, and I do appoint for one whole year, commencing from the date hereof and ending the 12th day of June, 1666, Mr Thomas Willett to be Mayor. . . ."

Thus did Thomas Willett—by appointment, not election—become the first mayor of New York City. Born in England, he emigrated in 1629 to Plymouth, Massachusetts. Willett began trading operations between New England and New Amsterdam, profited mightily, bought real estate here, and became a permanent resident. Despite his Puritanical heritage and pinched features, he roistered with the easygoing Dutch. Nicolls selected Willett for office because of his popularity. However, the new mayor enjoyed more dignity than power, the governor retaining for himself and his council the right to impose taxes and make laws. Nicolls and the council also functioned as a court of assizes, the supreme tribunal of the province.

Besides changing New York City's form of government, Nicolls sought to bring into line the nearby towns of the colony. At Hempstead, Long Island, he convened a meeting of thirty-four deputies from seventeen communities on Long Island and in Westchester County. With the help of his secretary, Matthias Nicolls (no relation), the governor had been studying various laws of the New England colonies. Using these as guides, he had drawn up a code of laws to govern his own territory.

When he explained his conclusions, the delegates were shocked. Unlike the New England laws, the code did not grant self-government to the people or give them a voice in levying taxes. A ten-day debate ensued. Nicolls shrewdly accepted a few minor changes but insisted that he alone would appoint all civil officials. If the delegates wanted a larger share in government, they would have to appeal to King Charles. Because they were powerless at the moment, they adopted this civil and criminal code, known as the Duke's Laws.

One provision stipulated that death would be the penalty for denying the true God, for murder, treason, kidnapping, and striking one's parents, and for some other offenses. But—significantly—witchcraft was not listed under capital offenses because it was not recognized as a crime. However, when so-called witchcraft was alleged to result in murder, the charge became murder.

Nicolls' comparative enlightenment saved New York from the witchcraft delusions and persecutions that blotched the reputation of New England. The Dutch themselves cherished their long tradition of tolerance. Although some witchcraft trials had been held in the Netherlands, the last of record had taken place in 1610—long before the Dutch had settled New Amsterdam. Throughout the witch-hunting seventeenth century New York remained free of the madness except for two minor cases.

The first came to trial on October 2, 1665. Ralph Hall and his wife, Mary, were brought by the sheriff to the court of assizes in New York City. The Halls lived on an island, now known as City Island, in Long Island Sound, just off the eastern shore of the Bronx. The husband and wife were accused of murdering George Wood and his baby by the use of witchcraft. Both pleaded not guilty, and a jury decided: "We find that there are some suspicions by the evidence of what the woman is charged with, but nothing considerable of value to take away her life. But in reference to the man, we find nothing considerable to charge him with." The court ruled that Ralph Hall should be held responsible for his wife's appearance at the next session of court and every other session so long as the Halls remained within the province. Then they were released. On August 21, 1668, before Governor Nicolls left for England, he released the Halls from all "bonds of appearance or other obligations . . . there having been no direct proofs nor further prosecution of them or either of them since."

Two years later some Westchester residents demanded that a rich widow, named Katherine Harrison, be sent back to her hometown of Wethersfield, Connecticut. It was stated that "contrary to the consent and good liking of the town, she would settle amongst them, and she being reputed to be a person lying under the suspicion of witchcraft, hath given some cause of apprehension to the inhabitants there." Like the Halls, she was tried in New York and set free.

In 1665 the British declared war on the Dutch, thus launching the Second Anglo-Dutch War. France supported the Dutch in a desultory fashion. Plague and fire wracked London, adding to the general woes of Englishmen.

New Yorkers became innocent victims of this war, which was caused by rivalry in commerce and fishing. Neither King Charles II of England nor the Duke of York could render any real assistance to the newly taken province. The Dutch held the upper hand at sea, and vessels owned by New Yorkers were seized by Dutch privateers almost in sight of the harbor. Abundant nature provided many of the colonists' wants, but the shipping crisis prevented them from exchanging raw materials for finished goods from the Old World. They were unable to get badly needed Indian goods—blankets, woolens, guns, powder, and lead, which had always been traded to the Indians for furs.

Nicolls wrote the Duke of York to urge that British merchant ships be sent to New York, where commerce languished. Necessities of all kinds grew scarce. Unable to make the province turn a profit, the governor could raise money only by borrowing. He realized that New York, with its gigantic harbor, was fated to become the chief port of the American continent. But lacking a helping hand from across the sea, he could not transform this potential into reality. Forced to pay his British troops himself, Nicolls ran through his private fortune. Finally, he became so oppressed by money troubles that he wrote both the king and the duke begging to be relieved of his command.

The Stuarts were slow to reply. Before releasing this able man, they wanted to make sure that they wouldn't lose New York. On July 21, 1667, the Peace of Breda ended the Second Anglo-Dutch War, and news of the treaty reached here on the same ship bearing the recall of the weary governor. The settlement was generally favorable to the Dutch, but they made a historic error of judgment. They let the British keep the colony of New York, while they retained Surinam, also known as Dutch Guiana. The tiny enclave on the northeastern shore of South America counts for little today, compared with the power, wealth, and prestige of New York.

Nicolls' replacement was Colonel Francis Lovelace. Handsome and gracious and a polished man of the world, Lovelace was also narrow-minded and greedy. Perhaps his fanatical devotion to the Stuarts blinded them to his flaws. In their behalf he had endured imprisonment in the Tower of London under Cromwell. For this and services rendered, he was knighted.

When Lovelace landed in New York in the spring of 1668, he was nearly forty years old. Accompanying him were his two younger brothers, Dudley and Thomas, who hoped to line their pockets at the expense of the colonists. Nicolls broke in his successor, taking Lovelace on trips throughout the province to acquaint him with its problems. Lovelace was smart enough not to make any premature changes in the form of government that Nicolls had established. His regime, like that of his predecessor, was autocratic, but not oppressive.

Most New Yorkers were sorry to see Nicolls leave. Even those who had chafed under some of his orders had come to love the man. He had arrived as a conqueror, but he left as a friend. An impressive dinner was given for him in the square stone house owned by Mayor Cornelius Steenwyck on the corner of Whitehall and Bridge streets. The guests marveled at the mayor's marble tables, velvet chairs trimmed with silver lace, Russian leather chairs, French nutwood bookcases, alabaster statues, tall clock, muslin curtains in the parlor and flowered tabby curtains in the drawing room, and oil paintings by old Antwerp masters. A few days later, on August 28, 1668, Nicolls was led to his ship by the largest procession yet seen in Manhattan.

During Nicolls' four-year rule the population had remained about at a standstill. When Lovelace took over, the city contained about 1,500 inhabitants and 380 houses. The entire colony of New York held no more than 6,000 persons, compared with the 40,000 colonists in New England. However, New York City was not a crude frontier town. Indeed, Lovelace wrote the king: "I find some of these people have the breeding of courts, and I cannot conceive how such is acquired." No printing press existed here, the only one in America being located at Cambridge, Massachusetts. Yet three Dutch girls, using books imported from Europe, became fine Latin scholars.

With England and Holland at peace, New York began to prosper. Several Bostonians moved here and invested in real estate, one of them buying five houses on Broadway. All kinds of business increased. Nine or ten vessels could be seen in the harbor at the same time. Huge quantities of wheat were shipped to Boston. A clatter and bang rose from New York's reactivated shipyards. A rich fishing bank was discovered near Sandy Hook. Oil-yielding whales were taken off the eastern tip of Long Island and even in New York Harbor.

Clothmaking was widespread here as early as 1670. This we know from an eager-eyed Englishman, named Daniel Denton, who visited New York about then. After getting home, he wrote a book, called *A Brief Description of New York, Formerly Called New Netherland, With the Places Thereunto Adjoyning*. Published in London in 1670, it was the first printed description of the city in the English language.

Denton noted that the tobacco grown here was as good as that cultivated in Maryland. Smoking was as important to the Dutch as to the English. One day, Denton said, two New York Dutchmen raced each other on horseback, each rider clenching a short pipe between his teeth. One horse stumbled and pitched its rider onto the ground. The man wasn't hurt. The pipe still in his mouth, he pulled himself into a sitting position. He continued to puff furiously and enjoyably, paying no attention to the fact that his horse was running away.

During Governor Lovelace's administration much real estate changed hands. For the final time Staten Island was acquired from the Indians. On April 9, 1670, Lovelace bought it in the name of the Duke of York. Although land prices had risen, he got the island at bargain rates—some wampum, coats, kettles, gunpowder, lead, guns, axes, hoes, and knives. Surveyors sent from England laid out lots and declared the island the "richest land in America."

About the same time a man named Isaac Bedloe made improvements on a small island he had obtained by patent from Governor

Nicolls. Today this is called Liberty Island because the Statue of Liberty stands on it. The colonists then named it Great Oyster Island, to distinguish it from Oyster Island (now Ellis Island). But Governor Lovelace proclaimed that Bedloe's property should be known as Love Island, and he designated it as "a Priviledged place Where no warrant of Attachment or arreast shall be of force or be served unless it be by ye peace of Criminall Matters."

An island in the East River, just off mid-Manhattan, a place known now as Roosevelt Island, was bought by a British officer, Captain John Manning. Ferries began operating across the Harlem River to the north of Manhattan and across the Hudson River between New York and New Jersey. Some Barbados merchants, named Morris, bought the Bronck estate and gave this part of the Bronx its present name of Morrisania. University Heights in the west Bronx perches on the site of the old manor of Fordham, which Lovelace granted to a conniving Dutchman, named Jan Arcer. This real estate promoter was so clever at seizing land from the Indians that his neighbors dubbed him Koopall, or Buy-All.

In the early months of Lovelace's regime the city suffered a severe epidemic, the first of record but by no means the last. Its victims burned with fever and swelled into grotesque shapes. The governor set aside a day of prayer and atonement for the swearing, drunkenness, and impiety that he believed responsible for this disease.

No bluenose himself, Lovelace persuaded some Dutch, English, and French families to form a little club to promote sociability. The members were fluent in all three languages. They met in one another's homes from 6 to 9 P.M., twice a week in winter and weekly in summer. From silver tankards they drank punch made from Madeira wine, rum, and brandy—not diluted, as in England, but straight.

Lovelace continued Nicolls' policy of religious toleration. He helped the Dutch Reformed Church get a good minister from Holland and gave this divine a generous salary, a rent-free house, and free firewood. In 1671 the Lutherans established their first church here. The same year the Quakers, who had huddled under trees during Stuyvesant's regime, held their first meeting under the roof of an inn. In 1672 these Quakers were visited by the founder of their sect, the Englishman George Fox, then making a missionary trip to America.

The first commercial exchange was started by Lovelace when he ordered merchants and "other artificers" to meet every Friday between 11 A.M. and noon near the bridge over the canal. This was at Exchange Place and Broad Street.

Lovelace also began the first postal service in America. Because events in Europe influenced affairs in New York, the governor decided that news from abroad must be received as quickly as possible. Because Boston lies nearer to Europe than this city does, Lovelace laid out the first mail route between these two communities. For the first postman he chose a fat but hardy horseman, named John Archer. On January 22, 1673, Archer leaped onto his horse just outside Fort James at the tip of Manhattan. He rode north up Broadway to the present City Hall Park, angled northeast to the Bowery, and headed north to Harlem. The people there watched excitedly as Archer strode into a tavern for a draught of the famous Harlem beer. Then, flicking foam from his lips, Archer sprang back into the saddle and crossed the Bronx River on a bridge erected by Lovelace. Marking his trail-blazing route with slashes on tree trunks and using boats to cross other rivers and inlets, the courier wound his way through Connecticut, into Massachusetts, and on to Boston. Archer's ride was the origin of the famous Old Post Road, or Boston Post Road.

At first this service ran only once a month, and few letters were exchanged. Then, as New Yorkers became accustomed to it, they deposited ever more dispatches in a locked box in the colonial secretary's City Hall office. Whenever Archer returned from Boston, he headed for a coffeehouse. People flocked there to watch with delight as he dumped the contents of his mail pouch on a broad table.

The Dutch government had let Peter Stuyvesant leave Holland and return to New York. In February, 1672, the grizzled former governor died on his Bowery estate, now fronting the Boston Post Road. His body was interred in a vault in a chapel a few steps from his house. Almost immediately, family servants whispered that they saw his ghost prowling about the farm. Later, when streets were cut through this part of the city, neighbors vowed that a tap-tap-tapping, as if from his peg leg, emanated from his tomb.

One month after Stuyvesant's death the Third Anglo-Dutch War erupted in Europe. Like previous Continental wars, it affected New York City.

King Louis XIV of France wanted to extend his empire, destroy Dutch trade rivalry, and crush Holland for sheltering political writers who criticized him. To achieve all this, the French monarch sought help from his cousin, Charles II of England. By promising to give Charles more French mistresses, enough money to dispense with Parliaments, and 200,000 pounds a year as long as the war lasted, Louis secretly won the English king's consent to join his attack on the Dutch and all their possessions.

In March, 1672, British ships swooped down on Dutch vessels in the Mediterranean, and French soldiers invaded the Netherlands. In partial retaliation the Dutch outfitted an expedition in Holland to recapture New Netherland. This was done secretly. Commanders of the new Dutch fleet were given a code, the figure 163 standing for New York. Finally, 19 men-of-war, carrying full crews and 1,600 soldiers, left Holland for the New World.

Only now did the British publicly declare war on the Dutch. A copy of Charles' formal declaration was sent to New York, and Governor Lovelace had it read aloud in front of the fort and City Hall. In a covering message the king warned the governor to place the city in a posture of defense. Lovelace set men to work repairing the fort. He recalled British soldiers from Albany, Kingston, and Delaware. Even so, he was able to raise only 330 fighting men.

Several ships owned by New York merchants were captured in European waters. After that, all eastbound vessels sailed in convoys for mutual protection. Navigation was restricted on the Hudson River, and New York's commerce fell off so steeply that local merchants found themselves on the verge of bankruptcy.

Time passed. No menacing Dutch fleet appeared. Lovelace relaxed and failed to complete repairs on the fort. He took a short trip to the Bronx to settle a question about the new postal route. There, from a swift-riding messenger, he received word that a Dutch armada had been sighted off Sandy Hook. The governor hurried back to the city, but unable to confirm this report, he decided it was a false alarm. And since Indians threatened British towns elsewhere in the colony, Lovelace foolishly ordered many of his soldiers back to their outposts. This left only eighty warriors in Fort James. Then the governor left town again, this time for New England to straighten out still other postal problems. He placed the city in the hands of the sheriff, Captain John Manning.

A second dispatch rider caught up with Lovelace at Hartford and reported that a Dutch fleet had anchored in the Narrows just below New York City. This time the news was true.

Since Governor Lovelace could not get back in time to take charge, responsibility fell on Captain Manning. However, the fort wasn't finished, only a handful of soldiers was available, and the townspeople were divided among themselves. Englishmen burned with indignation at the thought that they might fall into the hands of the enemy, while Dutchmen welcomed what they regarded as a liberation force. Some local Dutchmen rowed out to the Dutch ships to reveal the fort's weaknesses; others spiked the guns set up in front of City Hall.

Under a flag of truce two Dutch admirals sent an officer to Captain Manning with the demand that he surrender. "We have come to take the place which is our own," they said, "and our own we will have." Manning tried to stall until Governor Lovelace could return to the city. But after an exchange of several notes the Dutch ships edged closer to Manhattan. This brought them within range of the fort. Now the admirals gave Manning only half an hour to make up his mind. There was a nervous upending of hourglasses in the fort and aboard the ships. The period of grace was extended. At last the impatient Dutch fired broadside into the fort. The defenders fired back, but to no avail. After perhaps 700 shots had been traded, several English soldiers being killed and wounded, 600 Dutch soldiers landed on the shore of the Hudson River just behind the site of the present Trinity Church and deployed south toward the fort.

New York City surrendered to the Dutch on August 9, 1673. Once again the tricolored flag of the Dutch republic waved over the fort.

In Holland, meantime, the startling successes of the French invaders led to a revolt among the Dutch people. Fortunately, they found a leader in young William, the third Prince of Orange, making him their stadholder (chief executive officer), their captain general, and their admiral for life. William's mother was the daughter of Charles I of England; thus, William was a nephew of the Duke of York, whose American colony had just been recaptured by the Dutch.

New York City was renamed New Orange in honor of William of Orange. Administration of the city and province was not returned to the heartless Dutch West India Company but was assumed by the Dutch government itself. A Dutch captain, named Anthony Colve, was made governor-general of the province, which once again became New Netherland.

When Lovelace got back to the city, he found that he not only had lost his title and power but was also in financial trouble. A speculator, Lovelace had bought much real estate in and around town without always paying cash. Now creditors fell on him, and he was arrested for debt. At first the Dutch authorities said that he could leave within six weeks after he had paid everything he owned. When he was unable to make restitution, though, they let him sail sooner. For losing the province with its three cities and thirty villages, Lovelace was severely reprimanded by Charles II and the Duke of York, and all his large British estates were confiscated.

John Lawrence was mayor of New York when the Dutch retook the city. Thomas Willett, the first mayor, had served two divided terms, the first in 1665 and the second in 1667. The Dutch seized all of Willett's New York property, so he moved to Rhode Island, where he helped found the town of Swansey. He died in 1674, and the remains of New York's first mayor lie today in Rhode Island soil.

The government and the people of Holland were eager to end the Third Anglo-Dutch War. At the very least they hoped to stop British attacks so that they could turn their full military might against the French invaders. Weary of the carnage in their homeland, they were willing to sacrifice their overseas colony of New Netherland. In December, 1673, the Dutch government informed the English king that it wanted to negotiate peace, offering him New Netherland as bait.

The Treaty of Westminster, signed in February, 1674, ended hostilities between England and Holland. Under its terms the Dutch agreed to restore New Netherland and the city of New Orange to the English.

First word of the treaty was brought here by two men from Connecticut, and as a reward for bearing bad news, they were cast into dungeons. New York Dutchmen gathered on street corners to denounce the States General and the Prince of Orange. One angry citizen shrilled that the Dutch would oppose submission to the English "so long as they could stand with one leg and fight with one hand."

Despite this uproar and despite his own dejection, Governor Colve received orders from the Dutch government to transfer the city to the proper English representatives. King Charles II gave the Duke of York a new patent to his former colony of New York. The duke appointed Major Edmund Andros his new governor. On November 1, Andros arrived here aboard a frigate. Governor Colve asked for a few days in which to complete plans for the transfer of power.

The last entry in the court records of New Orange, the last statement ever written by a Dutch official in this city, reads as follows:

"On the 10th November, Anno 1674, the Province of New Netherland is surrendered by Governor Colve to Governor Major Edmund Andros in behalf of His Majesty of Great Britain."

For fifteen months the city had been called New Orange. Now, for the final time, it was given the name New York City.

Chapter 5

THE LEISLER REBELLION

IN A CEREMONY held in front of City Hall the public executioner broke Captain John Manning's sword over his head for surrendering the city to the Dutch. Thus disgraced, the Englishman retired to his estate on what we now call Roosevelt Island.

The very year that the British recaptured the city, the Dutch West India Company was dissolved. Later it was revived under the same name, but it never again influenced New York.

During the next 109 years of their rule the British did little to promote education, never establishing free schools. The public school system inaugurated by the Dutch withered under the new regime. From time to time, however, various churches set up primary and secondary schools. On the other hand, slavery increased far more rapidly under the British than under the Dutch, and eventually this brought tragedy and disgrace to the city.

Many rich merchants lived here. As early as 1674, 94 burghers had estates valued at more than 1,000 guilders each. Twenty-two estates were worth between 5,000 and 10,000 guilders each. Hendrick Philipsen, the richest man in town, had assets of 80,000 guilders. In that era, planters worth 500 guilders were considered wealthy. About this time rich people began using silverware, although forks did not become common until after 1700.

Surrounded by abundant natural resources, New Yorkers were stupidly wasteful—chopping down trees, for example, with no thought of conservation. Windmills remained popular after the British took over. For a while the Boston Post Road was allowed to languish because fears of the Dutch had vanished and the French had not yet become a menace.

From the beginning of the city's history down to the present, men in the same line of work settled in the same part of town. Shoemakers, to name one group, congregated in Broad Street. Using the bark of trees for their tanning process, they converted animal skins into leather for shoes, boots, harnesses, men's breeches, and waistcoats and into the leather petticoats and jerkins worn by women. Their tanning pits emitted an acrid stench. At last the tanneries were declared a public nuisance and driven outside the town limits. Four shoemakers bought property just south of the present Manhattan end of the Brooklyn Bridge and set up shop there, only to be driven farther north about twenty years later.

The first Britain governor after the recapture of the city was Major Edmund Andros, not quite thirty-eight years of age. The life-span then was far shorter than it is now, and men rose to eminence at an early age. Another favorite of the royal Stuarts, Andros was a man of unblemished character, firm purpose, administrative ability, energy, and zeal. Like his predecessor Nicolls, he spoke French and Dutch as fluently as English. Andros belonged to the Church of England. The lieutenant governor, Anthony Brockholls, was a Roman Catholic.

Andros got off to a good start. Once again the Duke's Laws were proclaimed in effect. The new governor did not pack all public offices with Englishmen but parceled out these positions among English, Dutch, and French citizens. Unable to straighten out the colony's chaotic currency, Andros did succeed in nearly every other reform he instituted. He reorganized the militia, repaired the fort, strengthened the harbor defenses, increased trade, beautified the city, and pacified the Indians.

In 1676 the Great Dock was constructed along Water Street from Whitehall Slip to Coenties Slip. For the next seventy-four years it was the only dock in the city. Seven public wells, two in the middle of Broadway, were drilled, householders near each well being assessed one-half the cost of their maintenance. In 1677 Andros ordered work begun on the first insane asylum in the province of New York. In Dutch days the streets were never lighted at night. Andros decreed in 1679 that on moonless nights every seventh house must display a lantern containing a lighted candle. The expense of the streetlights was divided among the seven property owners adjacent to each lantern.

A city-appointed chimney sweep roamed the streets, crying aloud that his services were available to householders. For the first time the city began to support paupers, and the first welfare case was "Top Knot" Betty, who got three shillings a week. Peaches and apples grew in abundance, but the Dutch drank imported rum or brandy, which they called kill-devil. In 1679 a visiting missionary wrote with a sense of awe: "In passing through this island we sometimes encountered such a sweet smell in the air that we stood still." Corn was New York's principal crop for many years. Imported wheat, however, did so well in the local soil that raising wheat became even more profitable than growing corn or trading furs.

To make flour from wheat, the grain must be ground, sifted, and blended. At first the Dutch ground the wheat by hand; later, by windmills. Under the English, horse mills began to displace windmills. The Dutch had created a demand for flour, not only within the colony but also in the West Indies and elsewhere. Unfortunately, it was of an uneven quality and could not be produced in great quantities. Governor Andros now realized that not even the most honest and able miller, toiling in isolation, could produce standardized flour in sufficient bulk to meet the growing demand.

New York flour already was popular, but Andros decided to improve its manufacture and packaging by creating a monopoly. In 1678 he granted a few leading citizens the exclusive right to bolt all flour and bake all bread and hardtack. Bolting means sifting with a cloth screen or sieve. The milling process separates the flour portion of the wheat kernel from the germ, bran, and most of the harder parts of the endosperm.

This monopoly at the bottleneck of the Hudson valley wheatlands made New York City the granary of America. Cries of outrage arose from neighboring towns and people hurt by the monopoly, but it resulted in the city's first great business boom. In the long run the entire colony benefited, for as the improved flour created ever wider demand, there was a need for more farms to grow grain and more ships to transport the finished product overseas. In the city itself the manufacture of flour became the leading industry, with almost two-thirds of the citizens dependent on it in one way or another. New buildings were erected, land values increased, shipbuilding flourished, more beef cattle were slaughtered, and city revenues rose.

During Andros' regime and that of his successor a series of Bolting Laws was passed. Although some were repealed, amended, or ignored, they increased the city's wealth threefold over the sixteen years that the monopoly lasted. Throughout this period other colonies tried in vain to overcome New York's lead in the flour industry. However, they forged ahead in other ways.

Boston, founded in 1630, or 6 years after New York City, was growing fast. Philadelphia, laid out in 1682, was 58 years younger than New York. When Philadelphia was founded, New York City contained about 2,000 white persons, plus Negroes and slaves. Three years later Philadelphia held 2,500 inhabitants, while the whole province of Pennsylvania boasted more than 8,000 colonists. Thus, Pennsylvania grew as fast in three years as New York had grown in a half century. Pennsylvania's greater religious tolerance played a part in this growth.

New York had many religious sects, and not only did they quarrel with one another, but disputes also raged among members of the same sects. In 1678 the Reverend Charles Wolley arrived to become the chaplain at Fort James. The only English minister in the entire province, he kept a diary and noted with chagrin the religious acrimony prevailing here. Two other pastors had not spoken to each other for six years. One was German-born Bernhardus Frazius, a Lutheran. The other was Dutch-born Wilhelmus Van Nieuwenhuysen, a Calvinist.

One evening Wolley asked both men to his house without letting either know the other had been invited. "At their first interview,"

Wolley recorded, "they stood so appalled as if the ghosts of Luther and Calvin had suffered a transmigration." The English pastor quickly suggested that the opponents converse in Latin, and if either uttered one word in Dutch, he would be penalized a bottle of Madeira wine. Wolley hoped to dilute their hostility in alcohol and a neutral tongue. The dumbfounded Lutheran and Calvinist nodded agreement. Then Wolley uncorked a bottle of wine, started their tongues wagging, and discovered that the Calvinist had a taste for spirits. Before the evening ended, the erstwhile enemies were chattering in Latin so rapidly that Wolley could not keep up with them.

New Yorkers of all faiths were terrified in the fall of 1680 by the appearance of an enormous comet that streaked through the sky for more than five weeks. They fasted and humiliated themselves to appease what they considered to be the wrath of God.

Governor Andros became the target of criticism. He was accused of showing too much favor to Dutch shipping and of letting the people of Boston engage in the fur trade with Indians. When the Duke of York heard these rumors, he ordered Andros to London to justify his conduct. Andros sailed in 1681, fully expecting to return. After all, his bolting monopoly had increased New York's revenue. Even so, Andros hadn't made enough profits to satisfy the greedy duke, so he was relieved of his command in America. Then, to save face for both of them, the duke made Andros a gentleman of the king's chamber and gave him a lease to the island of Alderney.

About this time the duke was closeted in London with his friend William Penn. This wealthy Quaker was the son of Admiral William Penn, who had captured the island of Jamaica for England. After the admiral's death his son inherited a claim on the Crown for 16,000 pounds lent by his father to Charles II. In payment of the claim the king gave the younger William Penn a charter for Pennsylvania. An ardent believer in freedom of conscience, Penn wanted to create a haven for Quakers in America. Now, during their private interview, the duke lamented that he couldn't collect taxes or raise enough revenue in New York, that indeed he had half a mind to sell his colony to anyone offering a fair price for it.

"What?" cried Penn. "Sell New York? Don't think of such a thing! Just give it self-government, and there will be no more trouble."

The duke took Penn's advice. In 1683 he chose Colonel Thomas Dongan to succeed Andros as governor of New York. Dongan was an Irish Catholic of extremely liberal views. He was accompanied here by an English Jesuit, Father Thomas Harvey. Later they were joined by two other Jesuits, Father Henry Harrison and Father Charles Gage, as well as by two lay brothers. Mass was celebrated for the first time in New York City—inside Fort James—on October 30, 1683. Because Dongan was the first Catholic appointed to high office in New York, the people were prejudiced against him at the onset and were somewhat suspicious.

The duke had ordered Dongan to permit people of all faiths to worship in New York, provided they did not disturb the peace. This was not so benevolent as it seemed. Both as the Duke of York and later as King James II, James Stuart schemed to enhance the power of the Catholic faith, which he had embraced as a convert. A fanatic, he pretended to tolerate all faiths, hoping to revive Catholicism in Protestant England and establish it in New York. He gave Dongan this order only for tactical reasons.

Agreeing with William Penn that New Yorkers needed more self-government, the duke told Dongan to permit elections to be held. About this time some Long Island townspeople refused to keep paying taxes without representation. They complained about the greater freedom and prosperity of the colonies on either side of them. They wanted a government consisting of a governor, a council, and an assembly, the assembly members to be elected by freeholders of the colony.

On August 25, 1683, Dongan ordered the election of such an assembly. Two months later seventeen elected representatives sat down with the governor and ten councilors in Fort James. The first bill passed by the assembly vested supreme and permanent legislative power in the governor, a council, and the people. It guaranteed every freeholder and freeman the right to vote for representatives. It specified that no man should be tried for any offense except by a jury of twelve peers. It declared that no tax could be imposed except by direction of the assembly. It spelled out other liberties and privileges. However, Dongan's charter was more democratic in appearance than in reality. Furthermore, it wasn't actually a charter, but only a legislative act. Governor Dongan consented to it, but the measure had to be approved by the Duke of York. It was sent to London. Before the duke signed the document, he found himself the new king of England.

In 1683, after the English manner, the province of New York was divided into counties. Four lay within the present city of New York. They were the counties of New York (Manhattan), Kings (Brooklyn), Richmond (Staten Island), and Queens. The Bronx did not become a separate county until 1914. Most Americans think of a county as a geographical area larger than any municipality lying within it. However, New York City's counties are physically smaller than the municipality itself. At present the city's five *counties* are political subdivisions of the *state*. The same five counties also are known as *boroughs* when they are considered political subdivisions of the *city*.

The names given the counties were vivid reminders of the royal Stuarts: New York County was named for the Duke of York; Kings County, for his brother, King Charles II of England; Queens County, for Charles' wife, Catherine of Braganza; and Richmond County, for the Duke of Richmond, the king's illegitimate son by the Duchess of Portsmouth.

Also in 1683, the city of New York was divided into six wards: South, Dock, East, North, West, and the Out Ward (Harlem). The freemen annually elected an alderman for each ward.

Charles II died in 1685, and the Duke of York ascended the throne of England as King James II. Now the proprietary colony of New York became a royal colony. In a proprietary colony ultimate power is vested in one or more private individuals. In a royal colony the king is supreme. When King James examined the Dongan charter, he decided that it granted too many liberties, and he refused to sign it. As king, James concerned himself not only with the colony of New York but also with all the American colonies. Wishing to simplify administration and strengthen the line of defense against the French of Canada, he formed a Dominion of New England, which included all the colonies north and east of the Delaware River.

The Dominion of New England was established in 1686, and the colony of New York was annexed to it. James chose Edmund Andros as the dominion's governor-general, plucking him out of exile and knighting him. Sir Edmund selected Boston for his headquarters. The new lieutenant governor, Captain Francis Nicholson, was ordered to New York. The colony's erstwhile governor, Thomas Dongan, was told to resign.

In 1685 King Louis XIV of France had revoked the Edict of Nantes, thus denying Protestants the right to practice their religion in France. This sent a tidal wave of frightened Huguenots tumbling out of France to other parts of Europe and to the New World. Many refugees came to New York, bringing skills, such as silversmithing, which added to the city's cultural life. In 1688 the first Huguenot church was established in New York. The same year another group of exiles settled on Long Island Sound northeast of the city, founding the community of New Rochelle, named for their hometown in France, La Rochelle.

James of England promptly wrote Louis of France to congratulate him on his persecutions. James still connived to reestablish Catholicism in his native land. There had been no widespread conversions to the Church of Rome as he had hoped. His appointment of more Catholics to office, together with other measures, brought on the English Revolution of 1688, which in turn sparked a revolution in New York.

English Protestants finally grew so fearful of the king's swelling tyranny that they cast about for a leader to replace him. Their choice fell on William of Orange, the stadholder of Holland, who, besides being the king's nephew, had become his son-in-law by marrying his daughter Mary. William was a Calvinist and wholly free of religious prejudice. The Protestant party now secretly invited the Dutch Protestant to invade England and strike down the Catholic despot. William landed on British soil on November 5, 1688. James abdicated and fled to France. The conquering Dutchman and his English wife became King William III and Queen Mary II of England.

News of their accession was received in America with rejoicing. This seemed the moment for sundering the hated Dominion of New England. The various colonies disliked the dominion because it imposed a centralized rule and deprived them of their charters.

The people of Boston jailed Governor Andros and chose a council of safety "to preserve the government until directions arrive from England." This is known to history as New England's Glorious Revolution of 1689. The Dominion of New England split into about a dozen independent units. In New York the lieutenant governor, Nicholson, declined to proclaim William and Mary the new monarchs of England until he received official word from them. They were slow to act in this regard. Nicholson was less concerned with religion than he was with maintaining law and order.

New York Protestants, who loathed Popery, were afraid that James might hack or plot his way back to power. Revolts broke out in Queens, in Westchester County to the north, and in Suffolk County on Long Island. Nicholson was eyed suspiciously. A Protestant? Perhaps he was a secret tool of the Catholic James.

The day after Nicholson learned that Andros had been imprisoned in Boston, he heard that England and France had started fighting again. Actually, war was not declared until May 7, 1689. Thus began the second Hundred Years' War between France and England. In America it was called the French and Indian Wars. On this side of the Atlantic the conflict was a struggle between the French colonies and the English colonies. At issue was the question of which would rule the New World.

Nicholson repaired Fort James and ordered the militia to drill. Many English regulars, usually stationed in New York, had been sent to Maine, where French-supported Indians were attacking frontier settlements. This left only a few professional soldiers in the fort at the lower tip of Manhattan. Other than these regulars, there were only 6 militia companies in the city of 3,500 inhabitants. The militia was led by a colonel.

The senior captain, Jacob Leisler, now leaped into the center of the city's history. Born in Germany and the son of a minister, Leisler had emigrated to New York at the age of twenty. He married the widow of a rich Dutchman, accumulated a fortune of his own, became a leading citizen, and served as a deacon in the Dutch Reformed Church. Sharp in business dealings, he nevertheless bought the freedom of a poor Huguenot family about to be sold into servitude for nonpayment of their ship's passage to the city. Stocky, gusty, carelessly dressed, both profane and pious, Leisler was a coarse-grained fellow of mulish stubbornness.

He imported liquor, among other things. At just this time there arrived a cargo of wine consigned to him. Leisler refused to pay the duties because the collector, Matthew Plowman, was a Catholic and therefore unqualified to collect customs under the new Protestant monarchs. Other merchants, taking their cue from Leisler also balked.

Leisler despised and feared James II and Popery. Although the Protestants of New York did not know it, James afterward informed Pope Innocent XI that he had always intended to force Catholicism on the American colonies. Moreover, James' coreligionist, Louis XIV of France, ordered an expedition to attack and conquer New York City, as Cromwell once had intended to do. So there was some substance to anti-Catholic rumors in New York. Few Catholics lived anywhere in the city, but Staten Island was said to be swarming with them. Nicholson was supposed to have crossed the Upper Bay in a small boat to conspire with these Catholics. Former Governor Dongan, still in these parts, was preparing to destroy the city. James himself was about to land on a Jersey beach at the head of a French army.

These spreading rumors caused panic. Some people demanded that all local Catholics be disarmed. Nicholson's every act was distorted and misinterpreted. Seeking to blunt the terror of a French invasion, he suggested that each militia company take turns guarding the fort. One evening Captain Abraham De Peyster's company mounted guard. Lieutenant Henry Cuyler told one of his men to stand sentinel at the sally port, but a sergeant of the regulars protested that Nicholson had given no such orders. When Nicholson heard of the incident, he summoned the militia lieutenant into his presence.

"Who is the commander of this fort?" Nicholson demanded. "You or I?"

The lieutenant said that he had acted under Captain De Peyster's orders.

Nicholson barked, "I'd rather see the town on fire than be commanded by you!"

Before sunrise the next day, May 31, 1689, there buzzed from mouth to ear word that the lieutenant governor had threatened to burn New York to the ground. What's more, he planned to massacre all Dutch citizens who entered the fort the following Sunday to attend church. Leisler's company rushed to his house, led by a sword-brandishing sergeant, who cried, "We're sold! We're betrayed! We're going to be murdered!" He begged Leisler to lead them as they captured the fort. Leisler refused. Off raced the sergeant and the other soldiers. When they got to the fort, they were let inside by Lieutenant Cuyler. Left behind, Leisler brooded a few minutes, then hurried to the fort, and took command.

A little before dark he sent a group of his men to a house where Nicholson was dining. They demanded that the lieutenant governor surrender the keys to the fort. Indignantly, he refused. After they left, Nicholson sped to City Hall to confer with his council about this "confused business." An hour later another militia captain, named Charles Lodowick, marched his own company into the council chamber and demanded the keys. Realizing that the militia had turned against the government, Nicholson now handed them over.

Later that evening all the militia captains gathered in the fort to discuss what should be done. They were far from unanimous about a complete break with British authority as represented by Nicholson. Now appeared the schism which divided the populace into two factions for years to come. The patroons, rich fur traders, merchants, lawyers, aristocrats, and Crown officers opposed the clean break urged by Leisler, himself a wealthy merchant. His followers consisted of small shopkeepers, small farmers, sailors, poor traders, and artisans. It was rich against poor, aristocrats against democrats. Leisler orated about the treacherous designs of the deposed James, the insidious fanaticism of all Catholics—especially priests—and the dangers of an attack by the Catholic hordes of the French king. He denounced Nicholson as a traitor, warned that a massacre might occur the following Sunday, and roared his loyalty to the new Protestant monarchs.

After much hesitation the captains finally agreed to take turns governing the city until explicit orders arrived from England. Leisler, flushed with triumph, drafted a paper stating that New York was threatened by Nicholson and promising to hold the fort until the proper person arrived to take command. One after another, in the glow of shadow-splashing candles, the captains signed this document on the head of a drum. With this act all real power passed from the lieutenant governor and the council.

Down through the ages the greatest revolutionary leaders have been men who could articulate clearly what the masses felt and thought only dimly and dumbly. Leisler was such a man. At first, apparently, he was entirely sincere. William and Mary should have been proclaimed in New York more quickly than they were. They should have trumpeted their authority, made plain the chain of command, and issued royal statements to restore order. Instead, partly because of the slowness of transportation and communication, they allowed time for Leisler to step into the vacuum.

How Leisler seized control of the city, tried to extend his power to the rest of the colony, chafed for lack of royal recognition, and changed from a well-meaning liberator into a tyrant—this is a long story. In his growing megalomania, Leisler compared himself with Cromwell, denounced all who opposed him, and ordered dissidents dragged to jail. Still, not a drop of blood was shed, and Leisler never executed anyone.

For two years he ruled New York. Despite all his mistakes and excesses, he did convene the first congress of the American colonies.

At his invitation, representatives of the various provinces met in New York on May 1, 1690, to plan an attack on the French Canadians. Never before had the colonies voluntarily cooperated in a common cause. Their efforts came to nothing, and Leisler spent much of his fortune fruitlessly. However, the French became so embroiled in war with Iroquois Indians that they did not send a military expedition down the Hudson to take New York, as was their intention.

Leisler raged over the failure of his attack on Canada and sulked because William and Mary sent him no mark of their favor. His behavior became so erratic and his rule so tyrannical that petitions criticizing him were sent to the monarchs in London. Old women taunted him in the streets, and a few daring souls threw stones at him.

On September 2, 1689, the king and queen had named Colonel Henry Sloughter the new governor of New York, but he didn't arrive until the next year. By then Nicholson and Dongan and all priests had fled the colony in fear of their lives. The new governor sailed from England with a fleet of British ships, but they were separated in a raging storm. The first three vessels to reach New York were commanded by Richard Ingoldsby, the new lieutenant governor of the colony. He led a force of regular troops.

Ingoldsby ordered Leisler to admit his men into the fort. Leisler refused to recognize Ingoldsby's authority or to surrender the fort without a written order from King William or the new governor. Unfortunately, Ingoldsby carried no official documents of any sort. His papers were aboard the frigate *Archangel,* conveying Sloughter here, and this ship had grounded on a Bermuda island and was waiting for repairs.

Ingoldsby knew his rights, even though he lacked the papers to prove it. After waiting four days, he disembarked his soldiers and quartered them in City Hall. He demanded the release of those of Leisler's prisoners whom the king had appointed to the council. All this infuriated Leisler and convinced him that Ingoldsby and his men were Catholic conspirators trying to capture the fort for James II. There were demands and counterdemands. Six weeks passed. At last Ingoldsby and some anti-Leislerians began to collect militia to reinforce the regulars.

Leisler gave Ingoldsby two hours to disband his forces. When the lieutenant governor balked, Leisler ordered his troops to fire on the king's men. A few were killed and wounded. Even worse, from Leisler's viewpoint, some of his own followers threw down their arms and scattered to their homes.

Two days after this clash, which further divided the two New York factions, Sloughter's ship arrived belatedly at the Narrows. A rowboat was sent to the *Archangel* with news of the bloody crisis in the city. Governor Sloughter landed, marched to City Hall, and read aloud his commission. Then he ordered Ingoldsby to demand the instant surrender of the fort.

Leisler behaved like a madman. He bellowed that he would not give up the fort until he got a written order from the king addressed to him personally. As midnight neared, a second demand was made of Leisler. Now he sent his son-in-law, Jacob Milborne, to say that it was against his principles to surrender the fort at night. Sloughter, with a flick of his fingers, signaled his soldiers to seize Milborne and throw him into jail. So ended the night of tension.

The next morning Leisler sent Sloughter a conciliatory letter, disclaiming any wish to keep the fort for himself. But he added that there were certain points he wanted clarified. Ignoring the letter, the governor commanded Ingoldsby to order the fort's defenders to lay down their arms and march out. He promised freedom from prosecution for all but Leisler, Milborne, and their closest advisers. Leisler's troops obeyed. The demented dictator was left alone and helpless.

He and his staff were charged with treason. They also were accused of murder for firing on the king's men and thereby causing wanton destruction of life. After a week's trial Leisler, Milborne, and six others were found guilty and sentenced to death. However, the six subordinates were pardoned, leaving Leisler and Milborne to pay the supreme penalty. Although Sloughter considered them knaves unworthy to live, he hesitated about signing their death warrants because an appeal had been sent to the king by Leisler's adherents. The anti-Leislerians invited the new governor to a wedding feast and plied him with liquor until he put his shaky signature to the execution papers.

On a dark and rainy May morning Leisler and his son-in-law were led to gallows erected at what was to become the Manhattan end of the Brooklyn Bridge. A large crowd gathered despite the bad weather. To many of the frightened onlookers Leisler still was a hero, the man who had saved them from Popery and aristocratic rule. Other witnesses gloated at the spectacle of this tyrant about to meet the fate he deserved.

In his final moments Leisler behaved with dignity. Granted the chance to make a speech, he said in part, "So far from revenge do we depart this world that we require and make it our dying request to all our relations and friends, that they should in time to come be forgetful of any injury done to us. . . ."

The trapdoors were sprung. The two men fell, danced on the air a few moments, and then perished. Their enemies cried in exultation. Their friends groaned in sorrow, women fainting and men weeping. Then Leisler's faithful followers dashed to his broken body to snatch up souvenirs to keep the rest of their lives.

Chapter 6

PIRATES INFEST NEW YORK

JACOB LEISLER's death that rain-swept day of May 16, 1691, was not in vain. However much he may have overreached himself, he taught the poor and oppressed not to kneel before the rich and royal. He divided the electorate into two parties—popular and aristocratic. Agreeing on practically nothing, they split the city for years to come. But their everlasting quarrels prevented the British governors from gaining undisputed mastery of the colony.

Governor Henry Sloughter's first act after Leisler's arrest and before his execution was to issue writs for the election of a representative assembly. It met in a Pearl Street tavern on April 9, 1691. This date marks the beginning of continuous constitutional government in New

York. The party opposing Leisler won a majority of representatives, and the governor named as members of his council the most bitter enemies of Leisler.

Sloughter died so suddenly the following July that it was rumored he had been poisoned. Six doctors examined his body; this was the first autopsy ever held here. Finding a high alcoholic content in the corpse and learning that the governor suffered from delirium tremens before his death, they concluded that he had died after a drunken debauch.

The council chose Major Richard Ingoldsby to take charge of things until the arrival of the new governor, Benjamin Fletcher. Heavyset, florid, and greedy, Fletcher did not appear until August of the following year. Anti-Leislerians welcomed him with a great parade. From that year, 1692, dates New York's custom of honoring notables and celebrating important events with impressive parades.

After Fletcher had taken office, his handsome six-horse carriage was seen everywhere, carrying Mrs. Fletcher and her daughters, gowned in the latest European finery. The new governor was an opportunist, little concerned about the colonists. At the time the chief source of riches was land, and Fletcher gave property to his favorites. By bribing him, a wealthy man could get any real estate he wanted. Because only propertied men could vote, Fletcher not only swindled honest people out of their land but also reduced most of them to tenant farmers.

During his regime the city lost its bolting monopoly. In 1678, when the first Bolting Act was passed, the city owned only 3 ships, 7 sloops, and 8 small boats, while the city revenue came to only 2,000 pounds a year. In 1694, when the last act was repealed, the city boasted 60 ships, 62 sloops, and 40 boats. Then too, its annual revenue had risen to 5,000 pounds, and the number of houses had doubled.

As the result of pressure from other communities, the manufacture and packaging of flour and bread were thrown open to all competitors. Within two years bread became scarce in the city. Bakers couldn't buy flour cheaply enough to bake it for their customers at the former prices. An inventory revealed that only a week's supply of wheat, flour, and bread was on hand for the city's nearly 7,000 inhabitants.

Such was the genesis of three significant trends: (1) Strife between Leislerians and anti-Leislerians split the citizens into popular and aristocratic parties. (2) Fletcher's venality inaugurated a corrupt alliance between bad politics and big business. (3) The Bolting Acts and their repeal set city against country and country against city.

Most prominent families were related by marriage—sometimes doubly and trebly connected. Class distinctions were emphasized by clothing. A gentleman might bedeck himself in green silk breeches trimmed with silver and gold thread, a gold-embroidered blue coat, a lace shirt, scarlet and blue hose, a powdered and pompadoured wig, and a silver-hilted sword. Even upper-class schoolboys owned three pairs of gloves and wore gold or silver buttons and blue or red stockings. New York's gaudy fashions contrasted sharply with the drab garb of New England Puritans.

A Boston gentlewoman visiting New York at this time had a sharp eye for ladies' fashions. She considered the local Englishwomen more chic than their Dutch counterparts. The Dutch *vrouws* favored loose gowns with unlaced waists. Wealthy Dutch females prided themselves on their ornamental headdress, the jewels on their fingers, and their earrings.

New Yorkers loved fun. They whipped about the countryside in sleighs during the winter, enjoyed drinking in smoky taverns, almost entirely ignored the Sabbath, and consumed huge quantities of good food. A delicacy of the day was orange butter, made according to this recipe: "Take new cream two gallons, beat it up to a thicknesse, then add half a pint of orange-flower-water, and as much red wine, and so being become the thicknesse of butter it has both the colour and smell of butter." Drunkenness was common. At a City Hall dinner honoring Mayor Stephanus Van Cortlandt, he became so intoxicated and merry that he snatched off his hat and wig, skewered them on the tip of his sword, set fire to them, and waved them happily over the banquet table.

Despite the heavy drinking done by men, divorce was rare. A very few divorces did occur in the 1670's, but in the century preceding the Revolutionary War not a single divorce was granted in the colony of New York. In fact, there was no way of dissolving a marriage except by a special act of the legislature. Most weddings were performed by justices of the peace instead of by ministers.

In 1693 the Church of England became the colony's official religion. Two years later, though, a local Anglican chaplain complained that only 90 families adhered to the English Church. There were 20 Jewish families, 260 Huguenot families, 45 families of Dutch Lutherans, 1,754 families subscribing to the Dutch Reformed Church, and 1,365 families of English Dissenters. Dissenters meant all Protestant groups disputing the authority of the Anglican Church.

Only six Catholics lived here in 1696. For more than three-quarters of a century after the flight of Dongan, Nicholson, and the Jesuit fathers, the few remaining Catholics lacked a place of worship and lived in fear of persecution. The war between England's Protestant king and France's Catholic king so agitated New Yorkers that in 1691 they banned "Romish forms of worship" here. Even worse was to come.

Fearful that the French would descend from Canada and attack New York, the British in America, helped by the colonists, launched expeditions against New France in 1693, 1709, and 1711, only to fail each time. The British knew that many leading French explorers were Jesuit priests and believed that they tried to incite Indians against the English colonies.

Because of this, on August 9, 1700, the province of New York enacted a law that all Jesuits, priests, or any other ecclesiastics ordained by the Pope must leave before November 1, 1700. Any who remained after that date, taught Catholic doctrines, used Catholic rites, or granted absolution "shall be deemed and accounted an incendiary and disturber of the public peace and safety and an enemy to the true Christian religion and shall be adjudged to suffer perpetual imprisonment." Any Jesuit who escaped from prison and then was recaptured would be put to death. Any citizen who knowingly hid a priest could be fined 200 pounds.

This cruel law was really passed for political and military reasons. As one historian said, "In directing severe penalties against the priests, the legislators fancied they were warding off the blows of tomahawks."

Upstate New York from the Hudson westward to the Genesee River was the home of a powerful Indian confederation, known to the French as the Iroquois and to the English as the Five Nations. It consisted of Mohawk, Oneida, Onondaga, Cayuga, and Seneca tribes. In 1715 the Tuscarora tribe, fleeing northward from the Carolinas, was admitted to limited privileges within the confederation, which then became known as the Six Nations.

About 1700 the Five Nations stood at the peak of their power. They watched the growing Anglo-French rivalry for control of North America. New York was most directly affected because of its long border along the southern edge of New France. The Iroquois chiefs, skilled in diplomacy, realized that they held the balance of power and tried to play the British and French off against each other, winning first this concession and then that.

New York City took part in these abortive invasions of Canada. In 1693 the city sent 150 soldiers to Albany, and although the expedition failed, the men were received with honors when they returned. In 1709 supplies were gathered here; men, ships, horses, and wagons were requisitioned; and 20 carpenters built boats and canoes. Although this project was abandoned, New York had to issue paper money to pay the debts accumulated. Again in 1711, preparations for war whipped the city into a frenzy, markets being taken over for the construction of boats, but this invasion, too, came to nothing.

In 1693 the lower tip of Manhattan was named the Battery. A battery, of course, is an emplacement where artillery is mounted. To defend the city, Governor Fletcher constructed an emplacement on the rocks along the waterfront from what is now the foot of Greenwich Street to the corner of the present Whitehall and State streets. This southwestern tip of the island commanded the approach to the Hudson River. Ninety-two cannon were mounted in firing position. Fletcher also ordered the fort repaired once again. Decade after decade the fort needed attention because it was maintained by men ignorant of military engineering and because funds earmarked for the stronghold often were spent on other projects.

Turning from war to peace, Fletcher helped the first printer set up shop in New York. He had heard of a Quaker, named William Bradford, the official printer of Pennsylvania. Bradford got into trouble in Philadelphia because of a book he published. Tried and acquitted, he was so harassed by authorities that he decided to return to England. When Fletcher learned of this, he induced the New York council to pass a resolution offering forty pounds a year to a royal printer of the colony of New York. Bradford accepted the position.

He began operating New York's first printing press at 81 Pearl Street on April 10, 1693. Besides printing city laws, he published lawbooks and other volumes. One of his first was a fifty-one page booklet entitled *A Letter of Advice to a Young Gentleman Leaving the University, Concerning His Conversation and Behavior in the World.* This was an odd choice because New York contained no college, let alone a university.

In 1696 Governor Fletcher ordered Bradford to reprint an issue of the London *Gazette* that reported progress in England's war with France. The same year Parliament passed another Navigation Act. New Yorkers were now told to buy all their manufactured goods from England or through England. These items could be brought here only in English-built ships skippered by English captains and worked by crews three-quarters of whom must be English-born. New Yorkers were forbidden to engage in manufacturing. In addition, because English authorities wanted to protect farmers in the homeland, only a fraction of the crops harvested in New York would be purchased. Yet the colonists were not allowed direct trade with any other nation.

All this added up to a boycott penalizing and paralyzing the city's trade. But wealthy merchants found ways to evade the laws. They felt justified in cheating the king of revenue whenever they could turn a profit. As a result, smuggling became an accepted way of life. Another factor favored contraband trade. England was so busy warring on France that it could not patrol the seas in the New World.

This situation led to the birth of the privateer—the owner of a private vessel preying on naval and merchant ships of an enemy in time of war. Any government official could issue a letter of marque to a privateer. These letters authorized the privateers to capture enemy ships. The word "marque" comes from the French and Provençal *marca,* meaning seizure or reprisal.

Unhappily for the English king, privateers were often men of easy conscience; they did not discriminate among enemy ships, neutral ships, or even ships belonging to their own kind. They halted, boarded, and plundered any craft that might be laden with treasure. Thus, many privateers became out-and-out pirates.

King William's warships were so busy in French waters that the Indian Ocean was left virtually unguarded, and it was there that the richest prizes were taken. Ships owned by the English and Dutch East India companies plied between their homelands and India. Now, with increasing frequency, pirates fell on them, killing and plundering.

After a pirate had captured one or more ships and taken aboard all the treasure he could carry, he sailed for New York. Here he would pull out of his pocket a tattered letter of marque and swear that he had acted as a lawful privateer in seizing this Oriental loot from a French ship. New York merchants, eager to buy goods denied them by the English Navigation Acts, never asked questions about the origin of a cargo.

Thus did New York City become the world's principal market for the sale of pirates' wares. The freebooters knew that if they put into leading European ports, they themselves might be seized; their ships, impounded; their cargoes, confiscated. In New York, however, they were greeted warmly by colonists hungry for trade. For more than a decade the city's streets swarmed with swashbuckling pirates clad in blue coats trimmed with pearl buttons and gold lace, white knee breeches, and embroidered hose, with jeweled daggers flashing from their belts. They swilled liquor in taverns, spun lurid adventure stories, and tipped everyone from the potboy to the governor.

Governor Fletcher had found a new kind of graft. Although he was the king's man, he sold protection to the pirates. He controlled the harbor and cooperated with greedy merchants. Three thousand miles of water protected him from interference by home authorities busy prosecuting the war with France.

Local shops displayed Oriental rugs, carved teakwood tables, ivory fans, and vases of hammered silver and brass. New Yorkers became familiar with strange gold and silver coins—Arabian dinars, Hindustani mohurs, Greek byzants, French louis d'or, and Spanish doubloons. Excited by the influx of such wonderful wares and currency, local merchants sent their own ships to the island of Madagascar, where pirates had established their own colony.

Of course, voyaging between New York and Madagascar was risky business. Local ships might fall prey to other pirates or be captured by English or Dutch frigates as receivers of stolen goods. But the profits were too juicy to resist. A big cask of wine cost 19 pounds here, but Madagascar pirates were willing to pay 300 pounds. A gallon of rum worth only 2 shillings here brought 3 pounds there. In 7 years one New York merchant made $500,000 by trading with pirates. This Red Sea trade, as it was called, became the foundation of many a New York fortune lasting to the present day. Some of the city's current society leaders are descendants of black marketeers.

Many pirates and privateers who traded here were educated and well bred. Not only did they walk the streets safely, thanks to Governor Fletcher, but they also dined in wealthy homes and danced with eligible belles. In this category was the most notorious pirate of them all—Captain Kidd.

Born in Scotland about 1645 and thought to be the son of a Presbyterian minister, William Kidd went to sea, became an able mariner, sailed all over the world, and finally rose to the rank of captain. Eventually he owned several ships of his own. Not a breath of scandal tarnished his name when he came to New York to live, in 1691. Everyone knew that he was a privateer because he paid fees to the king through the governor. Nonetheless, he was a highly respected citizen. Kidd served with credit against the French in the West Indies, chased a hostile privateer off the New York coast, and received 150 pounds from the city council. He helped build the first Trinity Church and bought a large lot for himself on the north side of Wall Street.

The year of his arrival, Captain Kidd married the beautiful and twice-widowed Sarah Oort Cox. His wedding certificate styled him Gentleman. The newlyweds settled down in a handsome stone house one block east of Hanover Square, then a fashionable part of town. They owned 104 ounces of silverware, and Mrs. Kidd boasted the first big Turkish rug ever seen in New York. Their other household items included a dozen Turkey-work chairs, a dozen double-nailed leather chairs, two dozen single-nailed leather chairs, one oval table, three chests of drawers, four feather beds, three chafing dishes, four brass candlesticks, three barrels of cider, and a fine wine cellar.

The Leislerian party in the city accused Governor Fletcher of complicity with pirates and accepting bribes from them. He protested his innocence. Then various East Indian governments, irked by the piracy practiced at the expense of their subjects, threatened reprisals against the English East India Company. In turn, this firm complained to the British government. About the same time King William began to wonder why the prosperous colony of New York produced such scanty revenues.

After a discussion with Richard Coote, Earl of Bellomont, and with other Privy Council members, the king decided to act. He would replace Fletcher with Bellomont and send his new governor to New York with explicit orders to stamp out piracy. The king also planned to outfit a frigate and dispatch it to the Indian Ocean to protect legitimate English merchantmen and appease the angry Indians.

Visiting London just then were Captain Kidd and a respected New York merchant, named Robert Livingston. Bellomont told Livingston about the king's proposed expedition. The New Yorker then suggested to the nobleman that Captain Kidd, "a bold and honest man," should lead it. Bellomont reported this recommendation to the king. On October 10, 1695, an agreement was signed in London between Bellomont, on the one part, and Livingston and Kidd, on the other.

The king was to get 10 percent of all profits from Kidd's foray into the Indian Ocean, with the balance to be divided between Bellomont,

Livingston, and Kidd. Bellomont and a syndicate of rich men financed four-fifths of the venture, the rest being paid by the other two partners. Kidd was ordered to render a strict account of all his prizes. Livingston posted a bond guaranteeing that Kidd would live up to the contract. From the king Captain Kidd received a commission to arrest and bring to trial all pirates he captured, plus a letter of marque entitling him to seize French vessels.

Kidd then outfitted a 275-ton 36-gun frigate, the *Adventure Galley,* and hired enough crewmen to sail her from Plymouth to New York. Here he recruited a full complement of sailors, buttoned himself into the handsome uniform of a British naval officer, and bade farewell to his wife and small daughter. Escorted by merchants and public officials, Captain Kidd marched to Wall Street and the East River, where he boarded his cannon-bristling ship and set sail for the Indian Ocean.

Bellomont, the colony's new governor, didn't arrive here until 1698. Immediately the nobleman aligned himself with the Leislerians, the democrats. He began cracking down on pirates and on New York merchants working hand in hand with them. The more deeply Bellomont probed, the more convinced he became that many local aristocrats had accumulated their wealth dishonestly.

While this aristocrat battled aristocrats, New Yorkers learned of Captain Kidd's astonishing behavior. The pirate hunter had turned pirate. Finding no French ships in the Indian Ocean, he captured native trading vessels, pretending they held French passes and so were fair prizes. Furthermore, he attacked and plundered ships indiscriminately. Sailors landing on the quays of London and New York told blood-chilling stories about Captain Kidd's raising the dreaded black flag, burning ships, plundering the Madagascar coast, setting fire to homes, pillaging, and slaughtering. It was said that he tortured Moors and Christians, Englishmen and Americans, until they revealed the site of hidden treasures.

All this, of course, embarrassed King William and Governor Bellomont, who issued orders for Kidd's arrest. Kidd abandoned the *Adventure Galley* and sailed for America in one of his prizes, named the *Quedagh Merchant.* Upon landing in the West Indies, he deserted this ship as well, transferred his booty to a sloop, and proceeded to Gardiners Island at the eastern end of Long Island.

There have arisen many legends about what Kidd did next. Apparently he buried part of his treasure on the island, and from there he wrote to Bellomont, professing innocence. Kidd was arrested, sent to England, and tried for the murder of one of his sailors and also for piracy. Found guilty on all charges, he was hanged at Execution Dock in London on May 23, 1701. His wife and daughter continued to live in New York.

With the opening of the eighteenth century the province of New York, despite its prosperity, lagged behind Connecticut and Massachusetts. In wealth and population Connecticut was at least twice as great as New York. Massachusetts also grew faster and built more ships than New York and prided itself on Boston, undeniably the largest city on the American continent. Nevertheless, changes continued to take place here. New streets were laid out, and for the first time the city assumed responsibility for cleaning streets. The first bridge across the Harlem River linked Manhattan and the Bronx. The city's few paupers had to wear badges identifying them as indigents. Stinking tanning vats were driven even farther north. A second City Hall was built, and the first Trinity Church was erected.

Within the province of New York the Church of England was set up, at first in just the four counties of New York, Queens, Richmond, and Westchester. By royal charter the parish of Trinity Church was created, and New York property owners elected wardens and vestrymen to administer the parish's temporal affairs. They voted to tax all citizens, regardless of religion, to pay for an Anglican clergyman. Trinity's first rector was the Reverend William Vesey; a New York street is named for him.

Trinity is important in the city's history. The mother of other churches in the area, it became perhaps the wealthiest parish in the world because it was granted a large tract of valuable land. This property was the target of lawsuits, filed one after another for more than a century.

Now, however, a church building was needed. Because the Church of England was the established religion here, this structure was quasi-public. Everyone of means, including Jews, donated funds for its erection. The government also allowed Trinity to seize all unclaimed shipwrecks off the New York coast and permitted it to claim stranded whales for conversion into oil and whalebone.

This first Trinity Church went up on the west side of Broadway at the head of Wall Street, on the site now occupied by the third and present Trinity. It was first used for religious services on March 13,

1698. A squat barnlike structure, 148 feet long and 72 feet wide, the church faced the Hudson River rather than Broadway. It received a steeple many years later.

Time and weather had taken their toll of the building at 71-73 Pearl Street which, since 1653, had served as the first City Hall. The five-story structure became so dilapidated and dangerous that the council and courts moved into temporary quarters elsewhere. Obviously a new City Hall was needed. Nearly all of the north side of Wall Street was owned in alternate sections by Colonel Nicholas Bayard and Abraham De Peyster. To the city De Peyster gave a strip of his land as a site for a new public structure. The lot was on the northeast corner of Wall and Nassau streets, where the Subtreasury Building now stands. The cornerstone of the second City Hall was laid in 1699, and the building was completed the following year.

Wrangling continued between the common people and the aristocrats. Governor Bellomont, firmly behind the Leislerians, did all in his power to break up the huge estates of the landed aristocracy. This was fiercely resented by Colonel Bayard, who, besides being a property owner, had once served as mayor. Bayard allegedly tried to stir the local troops to rebellion, and he mailed stinging criticisms of the governor to the authorities in London. For this he was arrested, charged with high treason, found guilty, and condemned to death. Before he could be executed, however, Governor Bellomont died of natural causes. Bellomont was succeeded by Edward Hyde, Lord Cornbury, who set Bayard free.

Of all New York's governors, Cornbury was by far the most eccentric and perverted. One prominent citizen compared him to a maggot. Although Cornbury had a wife and seven children, he dressed in women's clothes, pranced on the ramparts, and minced through the streets until he was dragged out of sight by his own shamefaced soldiers. It is conceivable that the governor was a transvestite, a latent homosexual who satisfied his subconscious desires by masquerading as a female.

Cornbury's efforts to mask his homosexuality led him into fetishism —adoration of a localized part of the body. He fell madly in love with his wife's ear. Then he fell out of love with Lady Cornbury's ear and cast lascivious eyes elsewhere, neglecting his wife and withholding her pin money. As a result, she begged and stole, and she borrowed gowns and coats from other ladies, which she never returned. She had the only carriage in town, and when the rattle of wheels was heard, New York's society leaders peeped through curtains and cried, "There comes my lady!" Then they would hide their valuables. Whatever Lady Cornbury admired during a visit, she always sent for the following day. She also forced the daughters of best families to sew for her.

Besides the dissolute behavior of the governor and his wife, the townspeople had to endure a natural holocaust. In the summer of 1702 the first great epidemic struck the city: a scourge of yellow fever. Many terror-stricken citizens fled from Manhattan to Staten Island and New Jersey. Governor Cornbury removed his wife and children to Long Island. In a few weeks more than 500 New Yorkers died of yellow fever.

In 1707 New York was visited by an Irish preacher, the Reverend Francis Makemie, called the Father of American Presbyterianism. When he and a companion, named John Hampton, preached here, Governor Cornbury had them arrested. Although the charge against Hampton was not pressed, Makemie was accused of being "a Jack-of-all-trades, doctor, merchant, attorney, preacher, and—worst of all —a disturber of governments." At his trial he was defended by three able lawyers, one of whom argued defiantly: "We have no established church here. We have liberty of conscience by an act of assembly made in William and Mary's reign. This province is made up chiefly of dissenters and persons not of English birth." The court acquitted Makemie but required him to pay costs of eighty-three pounds. The case ended the prosecution of Protestant Dissenters, but for years to come Catholics and Jews still suffered inequities.

Cornbury's ineptitude, depravity, and grafting resulted in his dismissal. Then he was arrested for debt and thrown into prison here. Released after his father's death had enabled him to discharge his obligations, he left for England and died there. For a second time Lieutenant Governor Richard Ingoldsby served temporarily as the governor until a successor could be found. The choice fell on Robert Hunter, who arrived in 1710. A soldier, courtier, scholar, and wit, Hunter knew many of England's leading men of letters. Shortly after landing he wrote to Jonathan Swift, the satirist, that "this is the finest air to live upon in the universe."

Just before this the armies of Louis XIV of France had overrun the Rhineland in Germany, and many inhabitants, called Palatines, fled to England. Queen Anne paid the fare for 40 of the refugees, who continued to New York, landing on Governors Island in 1708.

When Governor Hunter arrived, he led a fleet bringing 3,000 more
of these displaced persons to the city. Thus began the first big wave
of German immigration. Most Palatines settled on the Hudson River
north of New York City, hoping to manufacture masts, tar, and other
naval stores for England's warships. They proved totally unfit for
this kind of work.

The number of Negro slaves had increased. There are no reliable
figures about the proportion of colored to white people in the city, but
it is known that all wealthy whites owned slaves, some as many as
fifty. Even people of moderate means had three to six household
slaves, whom they regarded as impersonally as they did chairs and
tables. In 1711 a slave market opened at the eastern end of Wall
Street.

The Negroes were treated so badly that they became sullen. Tension developed between them and their masters. A Negro woman
and an Indian man were burned at the stake in New York City for
murdering their master, mistress, and five children. Negroes were not
encouraged to embrace Christianity because most whites believed
they lacked souls. For two years one slave unavailingly begged his
master for permission to be baptized. Marriages between Negroes
were performed by mutual consent and did not receive the blessing
of the Church. After colored people died, they were buried in a
potter's field without religious rites. About the only white man who
showed concern for them was a Frenchman, Elias Neau. He opened
a school for Negroes.

About 1 A.M. on April 7, 1712, twenty-three Negroes gathered in
an orchard in Maiden Lane. They were armed with guns, hatchets,
and knives. By launching a dramatic revolt, they hoped to incite
other slaves and massacre all the white people in town. After a
whispered conference under the trees, two Negroes sneaked to the
nearby home of Peter Van Tilburgh. One of them was owned by
Van Tilburgh and nursed a grudge against him. Swiftly they set fire
to the main house and an outhouse and raced back to the orchard. As
the flames reached to the sky, all twenty-three conspirators marched
toward the fire, their weapons at the ready. The eerie light and
crackling flames soon aroused nearby householders, who jumped out
of bed and sped to the scene. They were jumped by the armed
Negroes, who killed nine of them and wounded five or six others.

Governor Hunter was awakened and told that the slaves had re-
volted. He ordered a cannon fired from the fort to alert the towns-

people and dispatched soldiers to the disturbed area. When the regulars appeared, the Negroes faded into the shadows, broke, and ran, slaying one or two other whites during their retreat. Some quaking rebels found refuge within deep woods; others, inside barns; and still others, in reed-thick marshlands. Hunter realized that they could not be spotted that night. He posted sentries at the Harlem River bridge, at the ferry slip to Brooklyn, and elsewhere so that the Negroes would be unable to slip off the island of Manhattan. After daybreak the regular soldiers, aided by the militia, beat bushes and swamps and searched barns until all the culprits were flushed from cover— All, that is, except six, who killed themselves rather than endure the terrible fate awaiting them.

The town churned with rage and fear. White people told one another that this never would have happened if Elias Neau hadn't opened a school for Negroes and stuffed their minds with inflammatory ideas. What need had Negroes of education? All they had to know was to do as they were told, work hard, and keep their places. The kindhearted Neau was abused so shrilly that for a while he hardly dared appear in public.

Then, as with one diseased mind, the white colonists settled down to the punishment of the colored revolutionaries. The seventeen surviving rebels, together with four more slaves who were implicated, were arrested, tried, and convicted. One was a pregnant woman, so her sentence was suspended. Another woman, however, was hanged. Some Negroes turned state's evidence by confessing that they had known about the plot. They were banished from the province after they had testified at the trials.

The others were tortured and killed. A slave, named Robin, who had stabbed his master in the back was suspended alive in chains without food or water until he expired after days of unspeakable anguish. A couple of Negroes, one of them owned by Nicholas Roosevelt, were burned alive over a slow fire. The acrid odor of singed flesh irritated the nostrils of spectators during the eight to ten hours the Negroes suffered. Another slave, who had wounded a constable, was stripped to the waist, tied to the end of a cart in front of City Hall, dragged through lower Manhattan, and lashed bloodily ten times at every street corner.

One prisoner was broken on the wheel. His eyeballs bulging in terror, he was bound, face up, on a large cartwheel set on a platform. Then the wheel was raised to an inclined position so that every onlooker could have a clear view. After that, the public executioner picked up a sledgehammer, raised it high above his head, and slammed it down on one bound arm. Slowly, deliberately, panistakingly, the hammer rose and fell, rose and fell, blow after thudding blow, smashing to pulp the arms and legs of the shrieking black man. Now the attack was directed to the trembling torso until one murderous whack over the heart killed the condemned. Twenty-one Negroes were executed.

Chapter 7

OF QUEESTING AND FRIBBLES

THE YEAR after New Yorkers killed the slaves, they began drinking tea. The new beverage slowly displaced hot chocolate as their favorite nonalcoholic drink. Beer remained popular, while Madeira held first place among wines, followed by canary, claret, Burgundy, port, brandy, and champagne.

People welcomed tea because the city's wells had become polluted. Some visitors got sick after drinking the local water. About the only available pure water came from a spring that fed the Collect. Mounted over the spring was a pump that made it easy for water vendors to fill casks, load them onto carts, and hawk the water about the streets.

Housewives eagerly bought it for brewing tea. The Tea Water Pump was the city's chief source of water until 1789.

One of the Collect's outlets flowed across Chatham Street, now called Park Row, and was spanned by a bridge. A favorite spot for lovers, it became known as the Kissing Bridge. Another attraction was a nearby racetrack. From time to time swains and their maidens, making this trip north of the city, could not get home by dark and spent the night in one of the nearby roadhouses. Because rooms were scarce and heating was scant, the stranded couples bundled. The Dutch called this queesting. The young man and his girl lay down together in bed, wearing all their clothes or most of them, with or without a board separating them. The custom was not supposed to be an invitation to romance, but love, which laughs at locksmiths, was not to be baffled by buttons.

Bundling was more common among the poor than among the rich. Stylish young ladies wore hoopskirts, which could not be tucked under covers. The women looked like handbells, their slim torsos bulging at the waistline into huge petticoats stiffened by whalebone. Fastened on this rigid framework was damask, brocade, silk, satin, or velvet.

New York's gay young blades were called fribbles, meaning frivolous. Even more colorfully clad than women, fribbles adorned themselves in purple coats lined with sky-blue silk, cinnamon-colored breeches, dove-colored hose decorated with golden clocks, and red-heeled shoes. Dainty ruffles of white Holland shirts peeped through the front of their gold-threaded red-satin waistcoats, and their wrists were frilled with still more ruffles. Their long-tailed coats and their vests shone with big silver buttons engraved with their initials.

No gentleman would appear in public without wearing a powdered and scented wig. The styles of wigs changed from decade to decade. In the second decade of the eighteenth century the Ramillies headpiece was the fashion. This wig was designed by an enterprising barber after the Battle of Ramillies, fought in 1706 in Belgium. It consisted of a bushy coiffure, liberally powdered, pulled together behind into a queue, and tied with a large ribbon. Despite this outward elegance, nobody bathed very often.

Slaves imitated their masters by wearing wigs and gay colors. One runaway slave boasted a blue-lined jacket made of kersey, a coarse and ribbed woolen cloth; a red-lined white vest sparkling with yellow buttons; light-colored breeches made of drugget, another variety of woolen material; and black stockings and square-toed shoes.

According to Governor Robert Hunter, few New Yorkers wore clothing of their own making, except for "planters and poorer sort of country people." Beaver hats were fashioned and exported, as was linseed oil. In an attempt to compete with the shipping industry of New England, shipbuilding was encouraged in New York. William Walton, rich from trading with the Spanish West Indies and South America, established a great shipyard on the East River at the foot of Catherine Street between what are now the Brooklyn and the Manhattan bridges. Meats and vegetables were bought at public markets, but most other wares were sold at auctions, called vendues. Merchants served free drinks to people attending auctions, and the higher the customers became, the higher the bidding went.

Twenty-five gallons of free wine were consumed by townspeople on the green before the fort when news arrived that the Treaty of Utrecht, signed on April 11, 1713, had ended war between England and France. Shouting and singing, the wine guzzlers cavorted around a huge bonfire, which cost the city more than twenty-five pounds. With peace, local prices dropped and trade revived.

More attention began to be paid to local improvements. Broadway's hills were leveled from Maiden Lane northward to present-day City Hall Park. Two rows of shade trees were planted along the flattened section, adding to those along the lower part of Broadway. As the foliage greened and thickened, young men and women arose at five o'clock in the morning to stroll the thoroughfare. A favorite evening pastime was a row on the Hudson River at the hour when the water deepened from blue to mauve, while the Jersey Palisades purpled into black.

In 1723 the city was visited by a promising youth, who almost settled here. His name was Benjamin Franklin. Born in Boston, he worked there as a printer's apprentice for his brother James. After quarreling with his brother, young Ben decided to leave. Later he wrote in his autobiography:

> I found myself in New York, near 300 miles from home, a boy of but 17, without the least recommendation to, or knowledge of, any person in the place and with very little money in my pocket. . . . I offer'd my services to the printer of the place, old Mr. William Bradford. . . . He could give me no employment, having little to do and help enough already; but says he, "My son at Philadelphia has lately lost his principal hand, Aquila Rose, by

death; if you go thither, I believe he may employ you." Philadelphia was a hundred miles further; I set out, however, in a boat for Amboy, leaving my chest and things to follow me round by sea.

Thus, by a hairsbreadth, New York lost Benjamin Franklin, printer, author, inventor, scientist, statesman, philanthropist, diplomat, signer of the Declaration of Independence, and America's first world citizen.

Bradford, who urged Franklin to go to Philadelphia, founded New York's first newspaper on November 1, 1725. Called the New York *Gazette,* it was published weekly in Bradford's shop at 1 Hanover Square. Since he was the royal printer, his newspaper became largely a governmental organ. The *Gazette* contained little more than outdated European news, local customhouse entries, and three or four advertisements, most of them about runaway slaves.

Two years after his newspaper started, Bradford issued the first historical work published in the colony of New York. Entitled *A History of the Five Indian Nations,* it was written by Cadwallader Colden. Born in Ireland, Colden was graduated from the University of Edinburgh, studied medicine in London, came to America, settled first at Philadelphia, and then moved to New York in 1718. Next to Benjamin Franklin, he may have been the colonies' most eminent scientist and philosopher of the time.

In 1727 Greenwich Village was a small thriving community just north of New York. It was connected to the city by a road nearly parallel with today's Greenwich Street. In New York itself, goldsmiths profited; the first Baptist church was erected on Golden Hill, the former name of John Street between William and Pearl streets; the Merchants' Coffee House was put up at Wall and Water streets; the first city library was founded; Cherry Street was laid out and named for the cherry orchard belonging to Richard Sackett; Frankfort Street honored Jacob Leisler's hometown in Germany; America's first smelting furnace was built here; the manufacture of lampblack was begun; smallpox killed about 500 people in just a few weeks; and the city got its first fire engines.

New York's 9,000 inhabitants lived in wooden houses, for the most part, in 1731. They were always afraid of fire. Two public officials, called viewers, regularly inspected chimneys and hearths to make sure that they remained clean. By law a three-fireplace homeowner had to keep two leather buckets handy at all times. Only one bucket was required for a house with fewer than three fireplaces. If the house was rented, the landlord had to pay for the buckets and paint his initials on their sides. Every brewer was ordered to keep six buckets, and every baker three buckets. Private citizens always had bags large enough to hold their valuables; in case of fire they threw the full bags out the windows into the street.

Despite these precautions, fires were commonplace. Finally, the city fathers sent to London for two fire engines. The New York City Fire Department was born on December 3, 1731, when the engines arrived and were unloaded at the Battery. Hundreds of curiosity seekers gazed in wonder at the strange contraptions as forty volunteers dragged them from the dock to City Hall. There the mayor, Robert Lurting, accepted the vehicles and christened them Fire Engine No. 1 and Fire Engine No. 2. Then they were lugged inside sheds behind City Hall. Both engines were thirteen feet long; each had a large tank, a set of piston rods, pipes, and a rear nozzle. Twenty men were needed to work one of them. No. 1 was activated by a huge treadle moving up and down like a seesaw, and No. 2 was operated by levers that turned like a windlass. Both engines were mounted on wooden block wheels, and neither had a steering wheel. To turn a corner, the fire engines had to be lifted off the road. They were gorgeous to behold, but at their first fire the house burned down.

The city's first theater opened on December 6, 1732. A fat Dutchman, named Rip Van Dam, owned a warehouse at Maiden Lane and Pearl Street, and this was converted into a playhouse. Holding about 300 bench-huddling spectators, the New Theatre was decorated with a sign urging the audience not to spit. The makeshift foyer held a stove that was a fire hazard, so playgoers brought along the foot warmers they used in church. At one end of the room stood a rude stage illuminated by candles. The only other light was provided by more candles stuck onto nails projecting from a barrel hoop hung from the ceiling.

The first known play presented in New York was a comedy, called *The Recruiting Officer*. Penned by an Irishman, George Farquhar, it was an amusing story based on his own experiences when he had been sent to a small English town to collect soldiers to serve in Queen Anne's War. During the play's New York run the action was interrupted from time to time by stagehands snuffing out smoking candles in the footlights. Nonetheless, the show was a success, and the English cast remained here two years with a repertoire staged under makeshift circumstances.

During this period theater owner Rip Van Dam was more concerned with reality than illusion. Born in Albany, he had moved to New York and become a rich merchant and shipowner. For many years he served as a city councilor. He fathered fifteen children and never learned to speak English fluently. Governor William Burnet had been succeeded by John Montgomerie, who died here on July 1, 1731, probably a victim of smallpox. Until Montgomerie's successor arrived, Van Dam served as governor of the province. Then, on August 1, 1732, the new governor took over. He was Colonel William Cosby, another needy, greedy retainer of the English court sent to New York to fatten both his ego and his purse at the expense of the colonists.

Cosby soon demanded that the assembly grant him a huge cash gift above and beyond his generous salary. Then, for himself, his sons, and his brother-in-law, he tried to seize choice parcels of land in the Mohawk Valley far north of the city. He gave one son a lucrative office in New Jersey, took bribes, sold governmental positions, destroyed legal deeds belonging to the city of Albany, and threatened to resurvey all land patents on Long Island. Three-quarters of the colonists hated him, but the governor only smiled and barked, "What do you suppose I care for the grumbling of rustics?"

Cosby then demanded half the salary Van Dam had received during the thirteen months he had run the province. Van Dam, his Dutch blood boiling, refused to knuckle under to the grasping governor. Van Dam was popular, his cause was just, and he was supported by everyone except the petted, privileged members of the court party.

Now Cosby was puzzled about how to prosecute Van Dam. He couldn't bring the matter before the supreme court because it concerned equity and the supreme court was exclusively a court of law. He couldn't proceed in chancery because, as governor, he was its chancellor ex officio and could not sit in his own case. He was afraid to bring suit at common law because he knew a jury would decide against him. Therefore, Cosby created a special court, consisting of supreme court justices who would sit as barons of the exchequer. Then he directed the attorney general to bring action before them in the king's name.

Lewis Morris was the chief justice of the supreme court, and its other members were James De Lancey and Frederick Philipse. Van Dam was represented by James Alexander and William Smith. They argued that the governor could not create an equity court. Morris agreed with them, but De Lancey and Philipse ruled for Cosby. Even so, the case was dropped, and Cosby never got any money from Van Dam.

Now the frustrated governor turned his full wrath against Chief Justice Morris, removing him from office and appointing De Lancey in his place. This further inflamed the people against Cosby. Morris became the leader of the party opposing the governor, and De Lancey took command of the governor's, or court, party. Despite the fact that most people sided with Van Dam and Morris, they found themselves almost powerless. The courts were controlled by Cosby, the legislature was forbidden to meet, and it was difficult to get permission to hold elections.

Furthermore, William Bradford's New York *Gazette* was controlled by the court party. Leaders of the people's party probably knew that the governor was writing lies about them to officials in London, but they could not combat his vile accusations. In horror, they realized that the governor was plotting to crush all vestiges of liberty in the colony. Friends of Van Dam and Morris, hoping to save themselves, decided to establish a newspaper of their own. They chose John Peter Zenger as editor.

Chapter 8

THE PETER ZENGER TRIAL

BORN IN GERMANY, Peter Zenger was a thirteen-year-old when he came to New York with his widowed mother, a brother, and a sister. They were among the Palatines brought here by Governor Hunter.

The next year Zenger was apprenticed to William Bradford, and he still worked for the old master printer in 1725, when Bradford began publishing New York's first newspaper. Zenger realized that his employer's periodical was filled with little except "dry, senseless and fulsome panegyrics," so he left Bradford to set up his own printing shop. Except for theological tracts, he wasn't given much to publish. To supplement his income, he played a church organ. Just as he was on the verge of bankruptcy, the leaders of the people's party offered to subsidize him.

On November 5, 1733, eight years after the appearance of the city's first newspaper, Zenger began publication of its second, the New York *Weekly Journal*. Like Bradford's *Gazette,* it consisted of a small folio sheet, but the paper was of poor quality, the type was inferior, the dates were often wrong, and the proofreading was sloppy. Still, the *Journal* was livelier than the *Gazette*. One of the *Journal*'s advertisements said: *"Whereas,* the wife of Peter Smith has left his bed and board, the public are cautioned against trusting her, as he will pay no debts of her contracting. N.B.—The best of Garden Seeds sold by the said Peter Smith at the Sign of the Golden Hammer."

Slowly the English language was replacing the Dutch tongue, but only a minority of New Yorkers could read and write. This didn't matter too much because those who could read passed along the news to the illiterate, and soon they had news aplenty. Zenger basked in his sudden fame, but his backers never let him forget that they had set him up in business to attack the Cosby administration.

Many of the *Journal*'s articles needling the governor and the court party were actually written by leaders of the people's party. Zenger, however, was legally responsible for all copy in his paper. James Alexander, who had served as Van Dam's attorney, apparently provided most of the satirical stories. The second issue of the *Journal* included an article on freedom of the press—at a time when such a concept was virtually unknown. Indeed, most editors in England spent almost as much time in jail as they did in their printing shops.

The *Journal*'s attack was a diversified one. It printed logical arguments to appeal to thoughtful men. It indulged in witticisms, satires, parodies, squibs, ballads, lampoons, and verbal caricatures. Issue after issue contained mock advertisements about strayed animals that New Yorkers recognized as lackeys of the governor. The sheriff was represented as "a monkey of the larger sort, about four feet high" which had "lately broke his chain and run into the country." The city recorder was described as "a large spaniel, of about five feet five inches high," that "has lately strayed from his kennel with his mouth full of fulsome panegyrics." The *Journal* even said flatly, "A governor turned rogue does a thousand things for which a small rogue would deserve a halter." Week after week after week the attack continued until Governor Cosby and his sycophants were nearly driven mad.

Finally, acting for the governor, Chief Justice De Lancey called the attention of the grand jury to two "scurrilous ballads" in Zenger's paper. The ballads were ordered burned by the hangman. Next, the Cosby-dominated council declared that four issues of the *Journal* contained "many things tending to sedition and faction, and to bring his Majesty's government into contempt, and to disturb the peace." These, too, were ordered burned by the hangman near the pillory on the east side of what is now City Hall Park.

Council members directed city magistrates and aldermen to attend this ceremony. They refused. Even the hangman balked. The sheriff, who had been ridiculed in the *Journal*, had to command one of his slaves to burn the papers. At this disgraceful rite, held on November 2, 1734, the only people present were some British soldiers and a few of the governor's toadies.

Cosby and the council now asked the assembly to help prosecute Zenger, but the stiff-necked assembly members tabled the request. Attorney General Richard Bradley then filed an information charging seditious libel, and on November 17 the printer was arrested, marched to City Hall, and locked in a cell on the third floor. For three days he was held incommunicado, and for one week his *Journal* was silenced. The townspeople, 10,000 strong, seethed with excitement and indignation. Plainly the arrogant governor intended to force them to bow down to his will.

Alexander and Smith, who had represented Van Dam, assumed the defense for Zenger and had him brought before Chief Justice De Lancey on a writ of habeas corpus. They also submitted an affidavit arguing that since Zenger was worth no more than 40 pounds, except for his clothes and tools, moderate bail should be set. Instead, the judge placed bail at 400 pounds for Zenger and at 200 pounds each for two bondsmen. The sum probably could have been raised by Zenger's wealthy backers, but they may have hoped to dramatize the case by allowing him to languish in jail.

Their strategy worked. Receiving permission to speak to his wife and assistants through a hole in his prison door, Zenger dictated articles for his revived paper. His lawyers argued in court that Chief Justice De Lancey was not qualified to preside over Zenger's forthcoming trial. They declared that the wording of De Lancey's commission proved it had been granted by the governor "during pleasure" instead of "during good behavior," the proper phrasing of King's Bench commissions. The frontal attack so infuriated the judge that he shouted at the audacious attorneys, "You have brought it to the point, gentlemen, that either we must go from the bench or you from the bar!" Then he disbarred both men. They protested unavailingly, and New Yorkers seethed.

Month after month passed, and still John Peter Zenger crouched by the hole in his iron door, dictating diatribes. These were read with relish by men frequenting the Black Horse Tavern on William Street. Glasses of ale and rum were drunk in honor of the stubborn prisoner.

Finally, on August 4, 1735, Zenger's trial began. It was a hot sultry day, and sweat poured down the faces of spectators jammed into the courtroom. Most business came to a halt in the city that opening day, for people sensed that at long last they were locked in open combat with their tyrannical British overlords.

After disbarring Alexander and Smith, Chief Justice De Lancey had appointed attorney John Chambers to represent Zenger. Chambers was an able lawyer, but he didn't care to become a martyr. In behalf of Zenger he entered a plea of not guilty. Attorney General Bradley opened for the Crown, accusing the printer of publishing newspaper items that were "false, scandalous and seditious." Chambers countered weakly.

At this point an impressive, handsome, bewigged man arose from his seat among the spectators and said to the chief justice, "May it please your honor, I am concerned in this cause on the part of Mr. Zenger, the defendant." He identified himself as Andrew Hamilton.

Andrew Hamilton? He was the most famous lawyer in all America! Born in Scotland, he had emigrated to this country, had settled in Philadelphia, and had become first attorney general of Pennsylvania and then speaker of that colony's assembly. Hamilton was as renowned for his polished manners as for his ice-cold logic. Now the governor's henchmen and benchmen realized they had a fight on their hands. Although the Philadelphia lawyer did not supplant Chambers as Zenger's attorney, he ran the show for the defense from that moment on. The only people not surprised by Hamilton's appearance were Zenger's backers, who had planned the maneuver and kept it a deep secret.

In a clear and silvery voice Hamilton made a few introductory remarks, ending with these words: "I do, for my client, confess that he both printed and published the two newspapers set forth in the in-

formation, and I hope in so doing he has committed no crime."
Thereupon Attorney General Bradley declared that the jury must decide in favor of the king.

"By no means!" cried Hamilton. "It is not the bare printing and publishing of a paper that will make it libel. The words themselves must be libelous—that is, false, scandalous and seditious—or else my client is not guilty."

In those days the common law held that the greater the truth, the greater the libel. Pointing this out, the attorney general argued that the truth of a libel was no defense and could not be admitted as evidence. He was backed up by the chief justice, who said to Hamilton, "The law is clear. You cannot justify a libel." Hamilton, however, insisted that he would prove the truth of the statements published by Zenger and declared that it was the right of the jury to decide the intent of publication. By this line of attack Hamilton showed that he intended to air the delinquencies of New York's royal administration. He went on:

> Years ago it was a crime to speak the truth, and in that terrible court of Star Chamber many brave men suffered for so doing. And yet, even in that court and those times, a great and good man durst say what I hope will not be taken amiss of me to say in this place, to wit: "The practice of informations for libel is a sword in the hands of a wicked king, and an arrogant coward, to cut down and destroy the innocent. . . ."

All that hot summer of 1735 the trial of John Peter Zenger raged in the packed and stifling City Hall courtroom, while Philadelphia watched and Boston watched and even London watched, and men everywhere oppressed by British tyranny harkened to a new hope and took heart. Minds were stirred as seldom before, while new horizons seemed to unfold with each utterance of the silver-tongued Andrew Hamilton. Once and for all, this trial destroyed the notion that government officials are immune from criticism. It created a climate of civil disobedience. It marked the beginning of a movement for independence.

At last, in a courtroom throbbing with silence, except for his pulse-quickening voice, the Philadelphia lawyer delivered his memorable summation, saying in part:

> The question before the court—and you, gentlemen of the jury —is not of small or private concern. It is not the cause of a poor

printer, nor of New York alone, which you are now trying. No! It may in its consequences affect every freeman that lives under British government on the main of America! It is the best cause. It is the cause of liberty! And I make no doubt but your upright conduct this day will not only entitle you to the love and esteem of your fellow citizens, but every man who prefers freedom to a life of slavery will bless and honor you, as men who have baffled the attempt of tyranny, and by an impartial and uncorrupt verdict have laid a noble foundation for securing to ourselves, our posterity, and our neighbors, that to which nature and the laws of our country have given us a right—the liberty both of exposing and opposing arbitrary power—in these parts of the world, at least—by speaking and writing *truth!*

The moment Hamilton finished speaking, spectators jumped to their feet. They cheered. They applauded. The chief justice bellowed and pounded for order. The jury retired and then returned after only a few minutes of deliberation. The foreman of the jury was asked to announce the verdict. In a firm voice he said, "Not guilty."

Never before in the history of the city had there been such shouting, thumping, stamping, whistling, clapping, and cheering in a courtroom. Strangers hugged one another, women wept, and one judge threatened to jail the leader of the demonstration; but nothing could quell this tribute to the champion of liberty, Andrew Hamilton. His face flushed with joy, he resisted attempts to raise him upon the shoulders of yelling men, who wanted to carry him from the courtroom in triumph. Zenger beamed and shook the many hands thrust toward him.

To the printer's surprise and disappointment he was marched back upstairs to his prison cell, where he had to spend one final night until money was collected to pay for his keep during his imprisonment. Thus, he missed the victory banquet for his defender held that evening in the Black Horse Tavern.

This was a public testimonial for Hamilton, paid for by the city corporation, with liquor flowing in abundance and everyone pressing close to the guest of honor. The new mayor, Paul Richard, gave the principal address and then presented Hamilton with a gold box that contained a scroll bestowing on him the freedom of the city. After the banquet Hamilton was escorted to a ball, attended by citizens fighting the administration of Governor Cosby. The next day, as Hamilton left for his home in Philadelphia, he was accompanied to his barge by a crowd waving banners and cheering. A cannon boomed a final salute.

Zenger's acquittal was the world's first great victory for freedom of the press. However, it was not an end, but a beginning. A half century passed before the British government enacted into law the precedent established in this case: the right of a jury in seditious libel to pass on the truth of the matter published. Not until 1805 did the New York State legislature uphold the principle of freedom of the press, and not until 1821 was this principle incorporated into the state's constitution.

Yet long after Zenger and Hamilton had died, the American statesman Gouverneur Morris declared, "The trial of Zenger was the germ of American freedom—the morning star of that liberty which subsequently revolutionized America."

The Zenger case also gave us a figure of speech that has lasted to the present day: "as sharp as a Philadelphia lawyer."

Chapter 9

THE CITY GOES MAD

MORTIFIED by Zenger's acquittal and weakened by tuberculosis, Governor William Cosby died in 1736. Publicly the people faked grief, but privately they drank toasts to the passing of the tyrant and turned lightheartedly to other interests.

Ladies larded their hair with orange butter, flocked to public balls, vied for the attention of the newly arrived dancing master, and took French and Spanish lessons. Elaborately gowned, they attended the city's first public musical concert, held on January 21, 1736, in the home of a vintner, named Robert Todd. It was staged for the benefit of Charles Theodore Pachelbel, a German musician who came here from Boston to play the harpsichord.

Underneath the culture and gaiety of society the poor suffered, and crime increased. Beggars were put to hard labor, and cruel punishments were inflicted on criminals. A garden was fenced in so that hogs could not eat the roots and herbs grown for the poor. Indigent sick were lucky to get one of the six beds in the house of correction erected on the site of the present City Hall.

In the spring of 1737, when word reached New York that smallpox and spotted fever were raging in South Carolina, the city fathers established the first local quarantine. They ordered a pilot boat to lay in wait near Sandy Hook, the thin peninsula curving from the Jersey shore toward the Lower Bay of New York. Local doctors transferred from this boat to incoming ships to examine passengers and cargo. If infection was found, the vessel had to anchor just off the island that now holds the Statue of Liberty. The quarantine was ineffectual; smallpox broke out near the Battery two years later.

Frightened residents fled to the healthier climate of Greenwich Village north of town. Lieutenant Governor George Clarke, who had assumed charge after the death of Governor Cosby, let the assembly meet in a small house on the Hudson River two miles upstream. The largest Greenwich Village estate was owned by Peter Warren, a dashing British naval captain in charge of the fleet stationed here. He bought 300 acres on the west side of the village near the Hudson, and later the city granted him more land for his military feats. On high ground near the present intersection of Charles and Bleecker streets, Warren erected a magnificent poplar-shaded mansion, whose broad veranda faced the Jersey highlands and the hills of Staten Island. Then he was elected a Member of Parliament for the English city of Westminster and left New York in 1747, never to return.

Ever since the slave insurrection of 1712 New York's white citizens feared the local Negroes. Treatment of slaves became harsher and more repressive. The whites called the Negroes the black seed of Cain. If three slaves were found chatting together on the street, they were caught, tied to whipping posts, and lashed forty times on their naked backs. The same number of lashes was given to Negroes who carried clubs while strolling without permission outside their masters' grounds. John Van Zandt horsewhipped his slave to death for having been picked up at night by city watchmen. The coroner's jury declared that "correction given by the master was not the cause of his death, but that it was by the Visitation of God."

In 1741 New York had 10,000 inhabitants, including 2,000 slaves.

Some of these were called Spanish Negroes because a British warship captured a Spanish vessel in West Indies waters, brought her to New York, and sold the Negro crew members as slaves. About the same time African tribesmen were thrust suddenly into eighteenth-century New York; their barbaric looks and uncouth behavior terrified white people. Other fears added to the growing public anxiety. With England and Spain at war, perhaps Spain would send a fleet to attack the city. And what were Spaniards? Catholics, of course.

The slaves, poor and underprivileged, were certainly petty thieves. In the spring of 1741 silverware, money, and linen were stolen from Robert Hogg's house at the corner of Broad and Mill (now South William) streets. Suspicion fell on one of his blacks, who had met other slaves in a tawdry tavern on the Hudson River at the present corner of Greenwich and Thames streets. The place was run by a shifty white man, named John Hughson, who was already considered a receiver of stolen goods. Now police searched his premises—in vain.

Working for Hughson was a white indentured servant, sixteen-year-old Mary Burton. She had been born in England, served a jail term there, and then been shipped to New York. After the police had left her master's place, she whispered to a neighbor that the items stolen from the Hogg home were hidden in Hughson's house, but— mercy!—he would kill her if he learned that she had told. The neighbor repeated this to the authorities. They arrested Mary Burton for alleged complicity in the theft, threw her into jail, and then promised her freedom if she turned informer.

Hating her master and basking in the attention paid to her by city officials, Mary began to talk. As a result of her "confession," the police arrested Mr. and Mrs. Hughson, together with a prostitute, called Peggy Carey. At their trial in City Hall, Mary Burton testified about a Negro, known as Caesar Varick. Slaves were called by their masters' surnames. Mary said that Caesar had left stolen goods and money with Peggy Carey. This was denied by Peggy. Mary also claimed that Caesar had given part of his loot to Hughson to hide. Hughson admitted that he had stashed away silver and linen. The police arrested Caesar and also nabbed another Negro, named Prince Amboyman. Although they denied taking part in any robbery, stolen goods were discovered under the kitchen floor of the house owned by Caesar's master.

This was where matters stood until 1 P.M. on March 18, 1741, when fire broke out on the roof of the governor's house inside the fort. The city's two fire engines responded, but a brisk southeasterly wind and the dryness of the cedar shingles thwarted the efforts of the firemen. In less than two hours the governor's house, the chapel, the secretary's office, the stables, and the barracks were ashes. Lieutenant Governor Clarke said that the blaze had been caused by careless workmen repairing a gutter.

A week later sparks flew from Captain Peter Warren's house in downtown Manhattan. A few days afterward still another fire started in the storehouse of John Van Zandt, the Dutchman who had whipped his slave to death. Despite suspicions, it was proved that a careless smoker had dropped pipe embers inside the place. Then another and another and another fire started, sometimes as many as four a day.

New Yorkers grew apprehensive. With the outbreak of still another blaze the police arrested a Spanish Negro, who lived next door to the destroyed house. Under questioning, he seemed evasive. Now white people began muttering. One after another, they cried, "The Spanish Negroes! The Spanish Negroes! Take up the Spanish Negroes!" The police jailed other Spanish Negroes, along with a slave, called Quack. Asked about the origin of the fires, he stammered incoherently. City magistrates became so alarmed that they met to ponder the possibility of arson, and even as they sat, still another fire trembled like a cockscomb along the roof of a second storehouse. Apprehension then churned into terror, and terror curdled into universal panic. Here, there, everywhere in town, Negroes—even some known to have helped quench the flames—were seized indiscriminately. So many were jailed that the magistrates couldn't possibly examine them all.

On April 11, 1741, the council met to discuss the worsening situation. City Recorder Daniel Horsemanden vowed that they "must necessarily conclude that the fires were occasioned and set on foot by some villainous confederacy of latent enemies amongst us." He urged the lieutenant governor to issue a proclamation offering an amnesty and a reward to anyone giving information about the alleged plot.

Clarke now offered 100 pounds to any white informer; 45 pounds to free Negroes, Indians, or mulattoes; and 20 pounds and freedom to slaves. He also promised an automatic pardon to informers.

The proclamation was read to Mary Burton, who began spouting sensational charges about Caesar Varick, Prince Amboyman, and Cuff Philipse. According to her, these slaves often met at Hughson's tavern to chatter about burning the fort, putting the torch to the entire city, and massacring all the white people. Mary also said that Mr. and Mrs. Hughson had promised to help. Then, after the slaves had taken over, they planned to establish a monarchy, with Hughson as king and Caesar as governor. Except for the Hughsons and Peggy Carey, according to Mary, no other white person had overheard the diabolical plot.

Her fantastic story was believed by the magistrates. They petted and praised Mary Burton, who became the town heroine. Then Peggy Carey was promised a pardon and reward if she would support Mary's allegations. Despite Peggy's low morals, she refused to slander innocent persons. But now the authorities applied pressure by convicting her of receiving and hiding stolen goods. The sentence? Death! Also condemned to die were Caesar and Prince and Sarah Hughson—John Hughson's mulatto daughter by one of his Negro slaves.

Peggy Carey gulped and begged to be examined a second time. Now she "confessed" to wildly outlandish matters. Last December, she stuttered, she had attended a Negro meeting in another evil tavern, run by John Romme, a white man. He had told the slaves that if they would set fire to the city, slay all the white people, and bring their plunder to him, he would help them escape to a land where they could live in freedom the rest of their lives. Peggy obviously was telling the authorities what she thought they wanted to hear. Although some found it difficult to swallow her words, they managed to do so and begged for more. After all, the public was clamoring for victims. Peggy now said that she remembered the names of seven of the conspirators. When they were led into her presence, she accused them to their faces. Meanwhile, John Romme heard of Peggy's lies and scampered out of town. His wife, however, was arrested.

Several fires broke out in Hackensack, New Jersey, across the Hudson River. Later two Negroes were convicted of arson and burned at the stake, although there wasn't a shred of evidence against them. In New York's jail the quaking Negroes now began accusing one another to save their hides. Sarah Hughson was granted a stay of execution. On May 11, 1741, Caesar and Prince were hanged on a small island in the Collect. They admitted being thieves, but to the end they denied plotting to burn down the town.

Next, the Hughsons and Peggy Carey were convicted of receiving stolen goods. Apparently realizing that she was already doomed, Peggy now declared that she had lied in accusing Mr. and Mrs.

Hughson of complicity, but when she spoke the truth, nobody listened. On the other hand, everybody wanted to believe Mary Burton's lies. Mary suddenly remembered seeing a slave give Hughson twelve pounds to buy guns. Also, her master had hidden these weapons under his attic floor. Police dashed there, ripped up the boards, and found nothing.

One Negro prisoner became clever at prying "confessions" from his cellmates, and circles of accusations spread like ripples on a slimy pond. Even ignorant slaves understood that to tell the truth meant to confess to a lie. On May 29 two Negroes, Quack and Cuffee, became the first persons convicted of the conspiracy itself—not just of thievery. When Quack spun an unlikely tale about setting fire to the governor's mansion, nobody cared to remember that the lieutenant governor had attributed the blaze to careless workmen. Not a single lawyer defended the accused. Instead, every attorney in town sided with the prosecution. Even James Alexander and William Smith, who had acted so nobly for Rip Van Dam and John Peter Zenger, now joined in demands that the Negroes be put to death.

Quack and Cuffee were ordered burned alive. Their execution was to take place just behind the present New York County Courthouse at the intersection of Baxter, Worth, and Park streets. In this grassy valley hundreds upon hundreds of spectators watched with excitement as the fagots were piled high. The condemned slaves were questioned by their masters for the last time. Eager to save themselves, Quack and Cuffee blabbed everything expected of them. Hoarsely they "confessed" that the plot had originated with John Hughson, that Mary Burton had indeed told the truth, and that she could name many more conspirators if she cared to do so.

The sheriff then halted the proceedings. He said that it was his duty to report the confessions to the lieutenant governor. Meantime, he would march the prisoners back to jail. The crowd roared in protest. Excited voices cried that they were not to be cheated of watching two damnable blacks burn to death. Listening to the hubbub and noting the menacing gestures of men closest to the stakes, the sheriff reversed himself. The trembling Negroes were tied, the fagots were lighted, and Quack and Cuffee perished in screaming agony.

Their dying "evidence" led to the trial of seven other Negroes, six of whom were executed on June 7. The seventh slave saved his life by implicating fourteen others. One of these, in turn, won an amnesty by betraying still more slaves. Further burnings and hangings followed. At last, on June 12, Mr. and Mrs. John Hughson and Peggy Carey became the first white people to die because of the alleged conspiracy.

Seven days later a deadline was set for pardons and rewards, the lieutenant governor ordering all conspirators to confess before July 1. Now the shower of accusations became a deluge. Terrified Negro prisoners had learned that it did no good to protest their innocence. In desperation they felt that they might save themselves by faking guilt, compromising others, and then bargaining for their own freedom. They talked. Oh, how they talked! As lies tumbled from their lips, it seemed as if a veritable convention of slaves had gathered in John Hughson's house.

Up to now Mary Burton had implicated no white man except Hughson, although Peggy Carey had accused John Romme. Suddenly Mary pretended to remember that John Ury, a white schoolmaster, was also involved. He was arrested on a charge of urging Quack to set fire to the governor's house and of being an undercover Catholic priest. The law of 1700 condemning to death any priest in the province was still in effect. However, Ury claimed to be a clergyman of the Church of England and said that he sometimes held Anglican services in his home.

Sarah Hughson, the illegitimate daughter of John Hughson, had been reprieved from time to time. Now she was told that Mary Burton had accused John Ury of being the chief conspirator. What did she know about it? At first she said that Ury merely had visited her father's place with another white man, who considered renting the Hughson house. More pressure was applied to Sarah. She realized that she would be executed, after all, unless she concocted a tale that satisfied authorities.

Sweat standing on her forehead, Sarah promised a complete confession if she were pardoned. A pardon was promised. Then she invented a voodoolike story. She swore that Ury had sneaked into her father's house one night and joined a group of Negroes assembled there. He had chalked a circle on the floor and stepped into the center of it while holding a crucifix. As the slaves had taken places around the rim of this circle, Ury had sworn them to secrecy about the plot, had baptized them, and had forgiven them their sins.

Sarah's "confession" was reported to Mary Burton, who agreed it was true. Mary then denounced a soldier, named William Kane. Fearing for his life, he testified that he had been sworn into the plot by

Hughson in Ury's presence and that Ury had tried to convert him to Catholicism. Then a confectioner, named Elias Desbrosses, came forward to charge that Ury had once asked if he stocked the type of wafer used in the Catholic ritual. After all, Ury could read Latin, and of course, all priests read Latin.

About this time Governor James Oglethorpe of Georgia wrote to New York warning that priests disguised as doctors and dancing masters were to be Trojan-horsed into the English colonies. At a signal these Papists would set fire to the principal cities to forestall an expedition the British planned to launch against Havana from America. This was during the Anglo-Spanish-English war. New Yorkers remembered that in 1740 the Spaniards had attacked Florida. They feared that New York City would be the next Spanish target, because it had always been one of the most desirable prizes when European powers were locked in combat.

Thefts, fires, fears, accusations, confessions, executions, and now this chilling word from Georgia's governor—all blended and fermented until the city bubbled with mass hysteria. Everyone went mad. Neighbor shrank from neighbor. Strangers walked warily. People hastened to accuse others of imaginary crimes lest they themselves be accused. Everything seemed to add up: The Papists wanted to dominate the New World. The Spaniards were monsters of cruelty and intrigue. Negro slaves sought revenge. The Negroes were willing tools of the Catholic Spaniards.

That summer of 1741 New York City was as demented as Salem, Massachusetts, during the witchcraft delusion of 1692 and as psychotic as England in 1678, when a rogue, named Titus Oates, ranted about a Catholic plot to kill the king. Except for the Draft Riots of 1863, this was the worst blot on the city's history. It was the ugliest orgy of Negro persecutions occurring anywhere in America during the colonial period. Between the eleventh of May and the twenty-ninth of August, 154 Negroes were jailed, 14 were burned alive, 18 were hanged, and 71 were banished to the West Indies. During the same period 24 white persons were imprisoned, and 4 of them were executed.

Ury, the last of the victims, was hanged on August 29, 1741. The reign of terror might have continued if Mary Burton, dizzy with success, had not begun to accuse responsible citizens. This gave pause to New Yorkers eager to shed the blood of black men. But blue bloods? That was different. Scores of families already had fled the city to escape reckless accusations. No one felt secure. Finally, the city fathers began to doubt Mary Burton, so they paid her blood money and escorted the lady out of town. That was the last ever heard of her.

The massacre ceased. Accusations fell off. Everyone breathed more easily. No doctor or dancing master was revealed as a Spanish agent or Papist incendiary. No Spanish fleet attacked the city. As people regained their sanity, they began to regard the episode as a nightmare. Time cooled their heads, warmed their hearts, and left them ashamed of themselves. Within ten years all Negroes who met property qualifications were allowed to vote.

Chapter 10

DUEL FOR EMPIRE

FRANCE now became more menacing than Spain. The French sent a fleet to the New World with orders to burn Boston, and although the attack failed, French soldiers raided upper New York State. As always, the French and the British vied for help from the Six Nations. New York's new governor, George Clinton, offered a bounty to every Indian bringing in an enemy scalp.

In 1746 hundreds of Oneida and Mohawk warriors, squaws, and papooses glided down the Hudson in canoes so that the sachems could confer with the governor. Beaching their craft on the western shore of Manhattan, they disembarked and set up camp at what is now the eastern end of the Holland Tunnel. Then the braves filed down Broadway, carrying poles hung with the scalps of dead Frenchmen. Upon reaching the fort, they powwowed with the white men, declared an end to their friendship with the British, and vowed that they would slay no more Frenchmen. New Yorkers watched silently and anxiously as the Indians left.

Philadelphia feared an invasion from Canada as much as New York did, and four Pennsylvanians came here to borrow cannon. One of the men was Benjamin Franklin, then clerk of the Pennsylvania assembly. After returning home, he wrote about the conference with Governor Clinton:

> He at first refused us peremptorily; but at dinner with his council, where there was great drinking of Madeira wine, as the custom of the place was, he softened by degrees and said he would lend us six. After a few more bumpers, he advanced to ten; and at length he very good-naturedly conceded eighteen. They were fine cannon, eighteen-pounders with their carriages, which we soon transported.

This wine-guzzling governor ruled the colony and city of New York from 1743 to 1753, or longer than anybody since Peter Stuyvesant. Then, wracked with rheumatism and richer by 80,000 pounds, Clinton wanted to go back to England. The people were equally eager to see him depart. On October 7, 1753, Clinton welcomed his successor, thirty-eight-year-old Sir Danvers Osborn, still mourning his wife's death a decade earlier. His brother-in-law, the Earl of Halifax, got him this job in the New World, hoping that a change of scenery would brighten his spirits.

Three days after Osborn arrived, he was sworn into office by Clinton. As the new and the retiring governors paraded from the fort to City Hall and back, spectators shouted oaths and shook their fists at the detested Clinton. At first he shrugged off their hostility but finally took refuge within the fort. The more sensitive Osborn, shaken by the demonstration, murmured to Clinton, "I expect like treatment to that which you have received before I leave this government."

The next evening, while dining with Lieutenant Governor James De Lancey, the new governor complained that he felt ill and told his host, "I believe I shall soon leave you the government, for I find myself unable to support the burden of it." A doctor was summoned, but Osborn ignored his advice, merely taking a bowl of broth. Dismissing his servant at twelve o'clock, he spent the rest of the night burning private papers and laying out a small sum of money owed to a friend.

Osborn was a guest in the home of Joseph Murray, the colony's leading lawyer, because the governor's mansion was being redecorated. Just as dawn pearled the horizon on October 12, the young governor slipped out of the Murray household and walked into the garden. It was bounded by a high wooden fence, topped with spikes. Osborn climbed onto a board a few feet off the ground, took a silk handkerchief from his pocket, fashioned it into a noose, cast the loop over a couple of spikes, thrust his head through the handkerchief, and stepped off the board.

About eight o'clock that morning people began shouting in the streets, "The governor has hanged himself!" In excitement and bewilderment officials gathered in the Murray home. Osborn's secretary revealed that he had made an attempt on his life once before in anguish over the death of his wife. Now it was ruled that Sir Danvers Osborn had committed suicide while insane. After a dispute about giving a suicide a religous burial, he was laid to rest with full religious rites.

The Reverend Henry Barclay, rector of Trinity Church, who officiated at the funeral, took part in a more pleasant activity the following year. This was the establishment of present-day Columbia University. In those days lotteries were the usual means of raising money for colleges. Back in 1746 New Yorkers had persuaded the assembly to hold a lottery for a local college, and 2,250 pounds had been realized. Five years later a second lottery had brought in 3,443 more pounds. The total sum was vested in a board of ten trustees appointed by the assembly. One trustee was a Presbyterian, two belonged to the Dutch Reformed Church, and the other seven were members of the Church of England and served as Trinity vestrymen. When the assembly gave them the right to consider offers from citizens or counties wanting the college, Trinity's vestrymen offered some Trinity land as a campus.

The lone Presbyterian trustee, William Livingston, protested. He wanted a state college supported by the legislature, not an institution dominated by the Church of England. The local Anglican party, headed by De Lancey, fought back. After a furious controversy the Anglicans won. The college charter declared that the college president "forever and for the time being" must belong to the Church of

England. Moreover, the college's morning and evening services had to be conducted in the liturgy of this Church.

The sixth college in the British colonies received its charter on October 31, 1754. It was named King's College in honor of King George II. Its first president was a Church of England minister, the Reverend Dr. Samuel Johnson, of Stratford, Connecticut, tutor of the De Lancey grandchildren. His 250-pound salary was so inadequate that the vestrymen also named him assistant pastor of Trinity. Before construction began on the college buildings, the first class met in the vestry room of Trinity Church's schoolhouse.

For ten shillings the parish gave the college some land on the west side of Broadway. Bounded by Church, Barclay, and Murray streets, the campus sloped down to the Hudson River. An English writer vowed that it "will be the most beautifully situated of any college, I believe, in the world." The cornerstone was laid on August 23, 1756, and during the celebration that followed, the first toast was drunk to George II. No one mentioned that the mere sight of a book threw him into a rage. Two years later eight students were graduated with bachelor of arts degrees.

Across the sea the heavy-jowled bug-eyed king died of a stroke in 1760. He was succeeded by his twenty-two-year-old grandson, George III, a mama's boy who couldn't read until he was ten and who suffered neurotic disturbances. Eventually he went insane. The new monarch's first ambition was to stunt the growing power of the English Cabinet and become a real king. As he left Westminster Abbey the day of his coronation, a large jewel fell from his crown—an omen remembered when Great Britain lost the American colonies.

George casually referred to these colonies as his farms and let them go to weed. Until then the thirteen colonies lacked a central issue to unite them. Profit-conscious New York merchants, proud Virginia planters, and sea-battling Massachusetts mariners had little in common. But George III, his ministers, and Parliament acted so stupidly and repressively that the colonists began drawing together and finally rebelled.

In the seventy-year duel for empire, England had fought successive wars with France, partly in America and partly in Europe. A treaty signed in 1763 gave England control of North America from the Atlantic to the Mississippi and from Spanish Florida to the Arctic Sea. The wars had saddled the English with an enormous public debt.

British officials felt that the colonies ought to shoulder part of this load because now that Canada had been wrested from the French, the American provinces were no longer threatened by an invasion from the north.

Still, a few thousand French Canadians smoldered on the far side of the St. Lawrence River, and several hundred thousand hostile Indians bore watching. To guard this new empire, 10,000 British troops were to be sent to America, and the king's men thought the colonists should share this military expense. First, however, the English decided to break up the smuggling that put American customhouses in debt year after year.

The Navigation Acts would be enforced strictly, the colonies would be taxed, more power would be given to the admiralty courts, and royal governors would be told to demand compliance with the new acts pouring out of England. All these measures provoked the colonists, but they did not act in unison until the Stamp Act was passed in 1765. News of this outrageous law reached New York on April 11, 1765, and touched a spark to a long train of powder.

Chapter 11

THE STAMP ACT REBELLION

ANGERED by the Stamp Act, malcontents took direct action on April 14, 1765. They spiked the guns in the fort, then headquarters for England's small standing army in America.

During the recent Seven Years' War all the colonists had prospered, for British soldiers had spent money freely and contractors had reaped huge profits. However, after most of the troops had been withdrawn and the war contracts had been lost, there began a postwar depression, which was intensified by Parliament's trade acts. Prices soared. Real estate values fell. Creditors squeezed debtors. One bankruptcy followed another until a New Yorker wrote: "It seems as if our American world must inevitably break."

The Stamp Act was to go into effect on November 1, 1765. Unlike the new trade laws, it was meant not to control commerce, but to collect revenue. Under its terms Parliament insisted that the colonists pay direct taxes. In the past, taxes had been levied indirectly by imposing requisitions on colonial assemblies, which then appropriated the needed funds. Money raised by the Stamp Act would be used not to reduce the British debt, but to pay part of the cost of maintaining the 10,000 soldiers to be sent to America. Since this army would cost 350,000 pounds a year and the Stamp Act would yield only 60,000 pounds annually, British officials didn't feel that they were being unreasonable. Besides, the law would operate almost automatically. All legal transactions and various licenses would require a stamp.

The colonists didn't want a standing army in America. They weren't greatly concerned by the cost of the tax. What bothered them was the principle: taxation without representation.

Tax stamps were already used in England, but the situation there was different because the British were represented in Parliament— after a fashion. Twenty-nine out of every thirty Englishmen could not vote, but as William Pitt said, everybody at least had the right to cheer at elections. The colonists lacked even this fun, so New York newspapers shrilled with alarm, as did other American periodicals.

But what happened if the colonists refused to buy stamps? Well, they couldn't get a marriage license, buy a newspaper, draw up a will, receive a college diploma, file a lawsuit, purchase an insurance policy, send a ship from the harbor, or drink in a tavern. Even dice and playing cards were to be taxed. A total of forty-three groups of business and social transactions would require stamps, costing from twopence to ten pounds.

And who would collect the tax? Stamp masters—Americans, to be sure, but deep-dyed loyalists, who knew the right people in London. Each would be paid 300 pounds a year. There was a rush of applicants, but those chosen soon found themselves the most hated men in America. For example, Zachariah Hood of Maryland had his store demolished, was burned in effigy, and received threats against his life. Quaking with fear, he flung himself upon a horse and galloped toward New York, riding so hard that his steed died on the way. After getting another mount and reaching the city, he hid in Flushing. There he was discovered, however, and forced to resign his royal commission.

A New York paper soon published this tentative cry for independence:

> If then the Interest of the Mother Country and her Colonies cannot be made to coincide (which I verily believe they may), if the same Constitution may not take Place in both (as it certainly ought to do), if the welfare of the Mother Country necessarily requires a Sacrifice of the most valuable natural Rights of the Colonies, their Right of making their own Laws and Disposing of their own Property by Representatives of their own choosing—if such really is the Case between Great Britain and her Colonies, then the Connection between them ought to cease.

The New York assembly was in recess when news of the Stamp Act arrived. The first formal defiance came from Virginia. In the house of burgesses, Patrick Henry bitterly denounced the bill and asked fellow members to pass seven resolutions, which he whipped out of his pocket. Although four were rejected, all seven were reprinted by colonial newspapers. Thus the Virginia Resolves, as they were called, fluttered up and down the coast, like burning leaves from a forest fire, and inflamed other hearts.

James Otis now proposed in the Massachusetts legislature that the thirteen colonies send delegates to New York to sit as a congress and discuss resistance to the Stamp Act. On October 7, 1765, twenty-seven men from nine colonies met in City Hall; Virginia, New Hampshire, North Carolina, and Georgia were not represented. This Stamp Act Congress brought together rich men in coats of mulberry velvet and poor men clad in plain broadcloth. Collectively they were the best brains on the continent.

With its 18,000 inhabitants, New York had grown larger than Boston but still lagged behind Philadelphia. Under a new city law, householders had been ordered to cover their roofs with slate or tile to reduce the danger of fire, but the law was largely ignored. Visitors walking along flat-stone sidewalks and crossing cobblestone pavements praised the clean streets. They saw diamond-studded women and gentlemen dipping snuff from handsome snuffboxes and learned that many literate citizens read Shakespeare, Swift, Pope, Addison, and Hume.

Autumn is New York's most delightful season, but the delegates had little time to enjoy it. After gathering in City Hall, they soon divided into two factions—radicals and conservatives—and for the next three weeks debated how to act toward the mother country. At last they drew up resolutions of colonial "rights and grievances" and petitioned the king and Parliament to repeal the Stamp Act. They declared that taxation without consent violated one of an Englishman's most precious rights, and they still considered themselves Englishmen.

On Ocober 22, while the congress conferred, the ship *Edward* arrived from England with the first stamps consigned to New York, packed inside ten boxes stowed in various parts of the vessel. Their arrival was announced at 10 P.M. by the thunder of cannon from a man-of-war in the harbor. The next morning the *Edward* docked at the Battery. Two thousand people flocked there to jeer, so nervous officials did nothing until the crowd had dispersed. Later that night seven boxes were unloaded—the fear of a rising wind cut the work short—and transported secretly to the fort.

The next day dawn broke on rude posters nailed here and there in town. These warned: "The first man that either distributes or makes use of stamp paper, let him take care of his house, person and effects." Signed *Vox Populi,* the posters added: "We dare." The threat frightened the elderly scientist Cadwallader Colden, the new and unpopular lieutenant governor. He postponed opening the boxes until the just-appointed governor, Sir Henry Moore, arrived. Apparently Major Thomas James, who commanded the fort, thought differently. He was quoted as saying he would "cram the stamps down the throats of the people" with the end of his sword. By then more munitions and men had been added to the fort. Clad in scarlet coats, white breeches, and cocked hats, infantrymen and artillerists stirred restlessly and wondered what would happen next.

On October 31—"the last day of liberty," the patriots called it— royal governors throughout America swore to enforce the Stamp Act. At 4 P.M. more than 200 New York merchants met in George Burns' tavern at Broadway and Thames Street and signed an agreement to boycott British goods until the act was repealed. This, the first of the historic nonimportation agreements, laid the foundation of American manufacturing. The New York *Gazette* declared in huge type: "IT IS BETTER TO WEAR A HOMESPUN COAT THAN LOSE OUR LIBERTY!" Crowds clattered over cobblestones, shouting threats and singing defiant ballads. They were led by direct actionists, calling themselves the Sons of Liberty. James McEvers, the city's stamp master, looked, listened, and resigned. Lieutenant Governor Colden hid inside the fort.

The next day the Stamp Act was supposed to go into effect. However, the stamps were not distributed. Many offices remained closed. Buildings were hung with black crepe. Even backgammon boards and diceboxes in the Merchants' Coffee House were shrouded in black. Flags dangled at half-mast. Muffled church bells tolled. Again a street crowd gathered to mutter and grimace. Now, for the first time in the city's history, there appeared a new phenomenon—the mob. City magistrates warned Colden that they feared an outbreak. Marines disembarked from warships, and soldiers dogtrotted from Turtle Bay on the East River, bringing the fort's strength up to 30 officers and 153 enlisted men. As the day wore on, city merchants, barbers, sailors, cartwrights, teamsters, blacksmiths, and tavernkeepers were augmented by farmers, who streamed in from the countryside. By 7 P.M. all came together on the Commons.

There the Sons of Liberty whipped them into a frenzy as darkness fell. Torches, lanterns, and candles were lighted, their smoke idling straight up into the windless sky. Working by the glow, the mob made an effigy of the gray-haired lieutenant governor holding a stamp in one hand and then hung the figure from a mock gallows. Next, an image of the Devil was constructed and thrust so close to the figure of Colden that Satan seemed to be whispering into his ear. Both effigies were hooted and jeered. Now they were put in a cart and trundled onto Broadway. Men shot pistols at them. The shouting, dancing, disorderly crowd churned down Broadway toward the fort. Colden's coach house lay just outside its walls. The mob broke in, hauled out the lieutenant governor's gilded coach, and transferred his effigy to its top amid wild cheers.

Colden, hearing these shouts from within the fort, sagged in terror. Before the mob arrived, soldiers had sallied forth and knocked down a wooden fence in front of the fort so that rampart-posted gunners could potshot attackers. Torchbearing screaming men now scrambled over the broken boards and surged toward the fort. From a rampart, Major James cried, "Here they come, by God!" Men hefted heavy timbers to batter at the fort's doors. Bricks and rocks were thrown at parapets and ramparts. Faces distorted in fury, the rabble dared the cannoneers to fire. Major James stepped forward for a better look. Seeing him above their heads, the crowd bellowed with renewed anger. Again they lunged forward. Royal gunners held matches near the touchholes of their cannon. A massacre seemed to be in the making.

But the soldiers held their fire. No cannon belched. No musket cracked. An impasse had been reached. When mob leaders realized that they couldn't break into the fort, they urged their followers to fall back. Slowly, sullenly, the mob withdrew. The watching gunners breathed more easily. In a last defiant gesture, however, the rabble collected pieces of the broken fence, piled them under Colden's coach, thrust torches into the kindling, and howled with glee as the carriage and its effigy burned to ashes.

Then, as the mob straggled back up Broadway, someone remembered that Major James had rented a house on the Hudson at the foot of Warren Street, just below King's College. Why not tear it apart? Excited men turned and ran downhill to the major's temporary home. Screaming with frenzy, they battered down doors, charged inside, smashed furniture, made bonfires of chairs, broke china, slashed open feather beds, tore up books, ripped plants out of the garden, and destroyed the summerhouse. The place was a shambles when they finally left at two o'clock in the morning.

Nothing less than surrender of the stamps would satisfy the mob. Colden, already hanged in effigy, now heard of threats to kill him in fact if he did not give up the stamps. Tacked to the door of the Merchants' Coffee House was a poster calling for a frontal attack on the fort on November 5. Although the new governor was expected to arrive soon, Colden couldn't afford to wait.

He communicated with General Thomas Gage, commander in chief of all British forces in North America. Gage, married to an American, warned Colden that if the fort opened fire, civil war would follow. Colden then decided not to distribute the stamps. Instead, he would turn them over to the mayor and aldermen and wait for the governor to take further action. So now, amid wild rejoicing, the city fathers marched to the fort, picked up seven boxes of stamps, and deposited them in City Hall.

The ship that brought Sir Henry Moore here on November 13 carried a second shipment of stamps. The only colonist ever to become governor of New York, Sir Henry had been born in Jamaica, serving there as lieutenant governor between 1755 and 1762. A sensible man, he decided on a policy of conciliation here. Contrary to Colden's advice, he opened the gates to the fort and invited the people inside to watch as he was sworn into office. They arrived in great numbers and behaved well as the king's commission was read aloud. Sir Henry later stripped the fort of much of its artillery and suspended his own power to execute the Stamp Act.

Meanwhile, news of the disorders in New York and in the other colonies finally reached London. George III was annoyed by the "abandoned licentiousness" of his overseas subjects. Reactionaries screamed for cannon and dragoons to teach the upstarts a lesson, but British moderates termed the riots only "important occurrences."

In New York, with tranquillity restored, people talked of nothing but the agreement to boycott British goods. Leading citizens formed a Society for Promoting Arts—that is, for encouraging domestic manufacture. The rich set the tone of resistance by wearing garments made of cloth produced locally, and even Governor Moore donned homespun. Farmers tripled their flax harvest, housewives sat long hours at spinning wheels, and mourners wore less black cloth to save material.

The boycott by New York and the other colonies soon began to hurt British commerce. London merchants formed a committee to lobby for repeal of the Stamp Act, and petitions poured into Parliament from English seaports and manufacturing towns. Early in 1766 the House of Commons opened debate on this vital issue. William Pitt, the aging orator, rose from a sickbed and hobbled on crutches into the House to declaim, "I rejoice that America has resisted!" He urged total repeal of the act because it "was founded on an erroneous principle."

At 3 A.M. on April 26, 1766, New Yorkers were startled from sleep by the bonging of every bell in the city. Bleary-eyed and disheveled, they shuffled out into the streets to learn that the Stamp Act had been repealed. Actually, the news was premature. When confirmation arrived on May 20, however, the city went mad with joy. Men drank toasts, congratulated one another, fired pistols and muskets, lighted firecrackers, broke windows, and even ripped knockers off doors in their delirium. However, the city fathers postponed the official celebration until June 4, to combine it with the birthday of George III, toward whom all now felt grateful.

On that date the populace met on the Commons to feast on two barbecued oxen and to drink twenty-five barrels of beer and a hogshead of rum. Cannon fired salvos, a military band played "God Save the King," and everyone cheered himself hoarse. Not long afterward New Yorkers decided to erect a statue to George III.

In their effusion of gratitude New Yorkers forgot about the Declaratory Act. Although the king and his ministers had repealed the Stamp Act to save British businessmen from ruin, they had no intention of surrendering the Crown's authority over the colonies. The very day of repeal Parliament passed the Declaratory Act, which affirmed that the king and Parliament "had, hath, and of right ought to have the full power and authority to make laws and statutes of sufficient force and validity to bind the colonies and people of America, subjects of the Crown of Britain, in all cases whatsoever."

There stood the handwriting on the wall—plain enough to be read by anyone who cared to look. Moreover, the Quartering Act of 1765 was still in effect. It required American legislatures to provide the king's troops with barracks or other shelters; straw for bedding; cooking utensils; firewood for cooking and heating; and rum, cider, or vinegar to ward off scurvy. All this, the colonists slowly realized, was also taxation without representation. The Quartering Act fell most heavily upon New York because it was the headquarters of the British army. The New York assembly refused to comply with every provision of the act but did set aside a building containing nothing but four bare walls. The redcoats took one look at their stark quarters and grumbled. The longer they camped there and the longer they went without supplies, the angrier they became.

On the night of July 21 four British officers got drunk in a Broadway tavern and then wandered out to break streetlamps near King's College. The barkeeper followed them to protest and was slashed by a sword. After two orderlies had joined the roistering officers, the half-dozen British regulars staggered down Broadway, shattering other lamps. They encountered four members of the night watch, and a fight followed. One or two policemen were wounded, and a couple of soldiers were knocked down. One officer was jailed in City Hall.

The other soldiers sped to General Gage's house at 9 Broadway, his sentries sounded an alarm, and soon a dozen more warriors ran out of the nearby fort, fixed their bayonets, and advanced upon City Hall. On the way they met other policemen, wounded some, proceeded to the jail, and freed the prisoner. The next day the officer was rearrested, and another brawler was seized. The two Englishmen were brought before the mayor and aldermen, who bound them over to the supreme court. In the end the defendants were fined twenty pounds for each broken lamp.

During the celebration of the Stamp Act's repeal, a pine tree, proclaimed a liberty pole, was planted on the northwestern corner of the Commons. Eager to exalt the king and to weaken Parliament, the Sons of Liberty decked the tree with a sign reading: "George III, Pitt and Liberty." From time to time patriots gathered there to pledge their fortunes and honor to freedom.

British soldiers watched these ceremonies with sour eyes. On the first anniversary of repeal the regulars could contain themselves no longer. They crept from their barracks one night and hacked down the tree. The next day the Sons of Liberty put up another pine—the trunk encircled with iron bands to thwart the blows of an ax. Soldiers now tried unsuccessfully to blow up the tree with gunpowder. When citizens gathered to guard their emblem, the redcoats fired across the street into the Broadway tavern where the Sons of Liberty held meetings. Nobody was hurt, but General Gage hurried to the scene and dispersed his men.

Under the cover of darkness on August 10 the soldiers managed to fell the liberty pole. Nearly 3,000 angry New Yorkers swarmed onto the Commons to demand an explanation. After a heated exchange of words the mob threw brickbats at the regulars. They counterattacked with fixed bayonets and wounded two or three citizens. When General Gage was notified, he dispatched his aide-de-camp to size up the situation, but the officer was attacked by the mob and retreated to save his life.

Two days later the Sons of Liberty erected a third liberty pole and swore that no British soldier would be allowed to patrol the streets. As tempers flared, the breach between the townspeople and military widened. When General Gage tried to review a regiment on the Commons, a crowd of people, shouting that the place belonged to them, sought to push through the bayonet-bristling regulars formed in the traditional British square.

George III denounced New York as "rebellious" and decided to punish it to terrorize other colonists. Governor Moore was told to sign no legislation passed by the assembly until it complied with every article of the Quartering Act. Under this pressure the assembly voted by a majority of one to provide for the troops.

Besides disciplining New York, the British government now turned legislative guns against all the colonies. Chancellor of the Exchequer Charles Townshend put through a series of laws taxing many colonial imports, such as glass, lead, paper, and tea. Revenue from the Townshend Acts was to pay the salaries of colonial governors and judges. This struck at the root of America's political liberty, for the colonies had won almost complete self-government by financial control of royal officers. Trials for evasion of the Townshend Acts, the colonists also learned, would be held in admiralty courts without juries.

This time Boston raised the first cry for a boycott. At first New York and Philadelphia did not cooperate. But after George III had sent more troops to Boston because of an "insurrection" there and after they had heard rumors that still more regulars were coming to America, New York merchants finally signed a second nonimportation agreement in 1769. Once again it was patriotic to buy American.

Although the situation hurt British mercantile interests, it also damaged local merchants, shopkeepers, and artisans. The English had banned the use of paper currency, and specie was scarce. Some people, who preferred profits to patriotism, began smuggling British goods into the city.

For example, there was Simon Cooley, who had emigrated from London and was a haberdasher, jeweler, and silversmith. When it was discovered that he had imported British wares, he said that they had arrived long before the boycott had begun. Cooley promised not to sell any more English items, but greed got the better of him. He not only displayed his merchandise but also sent to England for more. Local papers denounced him as an ingrate, liar, and knave. Fearing for his life, Cooley hired British soldiers to guard his shop. When General Gage heard of this private use of his regulars, he withdrew them. Then the defenseless Cooley learned a mob was heading for his store. Hastily closing it, he ran to the fort to hide. Bellicose citizens demanded that he explain himself on the Commons. At last Cooley walked with quaking knees to the public meeting place, begged for pardon, and solemnly vowed to observe the nonimportation agreement.

Whenever citizens and soldiers met, they acted like the fighting cocks then popular in New York. The tension finally erupted in the Battle of Golden Hill, fought on January 18, 1770—nearly two months before the Boston Massacre and more than five years before the Battle of Lexington. Really more of a donnybrook than a battle, it took place on a golden wheatfield topping a knoll on John Street between William and Pearl streets.

The night of January 13 a group of regimentals made another attempt on the liberty pole. When enraged citizens closed in on them, the soldiers charged and drove the crowd into the Sons of Liberty's tavern, piled inside after their quarry, broke down doors, smashed windows, and demolished furniture. Before anyone was hurt, an officer appeared and ordered his men back to their barracks.

The next morning 3,000 townspeople gathered around the still-standing liberty pole to declare that all armed soldiers found on the streets at night would be treated as "enemies to the peace of the city." The redcoats retaliated by posting signs saying that the Sons of Liberty could boast of nothing "but the flippancy of the tongue." Two maligned members, Isaac Sears and Walter Quackenbos, followed six or seven soldiers carrying these signs. Just as a redcoat began pasting one in place, Sears collared him and roared, "What business do you have putting up libels against the inhabitants of this city?" Quackenbos grabbed a second soldier with limp posters dangling over one arm. A third soldier reached for his sword. Sears wheeled and threw a ram's horn at him, scoring a direct hit on the head. Sears and Quackenbos frightened off the other soldiers and marched their prisoners to the home of Mayor Whitehead Hicks.

As a crowd gathered in front of his house, Hicks sent for an alderman to discuss the situation. The fleeing soldiers had sounded an alarm in the barracks, and now twenty regulars double-timed it toward the mayor's place. They were armed, and a couple of their leaders were drunk. When they heaved in sight, citizens grouped themselves protectingly before Hicks' home. The soldiers halted, whipped out swords, and fixed bayonets. A few unarmed people ran to nearby sleighs to break off rungs for use as clubs. Then, their breaths frosting the January air, the two hostile parties confronted each other.

The alderman arrived, conferred indoors, and stepped outside with the mayor, who ordered the soldiers back to their barracks. After muttering indecisively, the redcoats moved on. However, instead of heading for their quarters, they turned toward Golden Hill. They still held naked swords in their hands. Some citizens tagged along, begging them to sheathe the weapons. The soldiers swore and plodded ahead. When they reached the crest of the hill, they were joined by other British regulars, who had run to the scene. Now the reinforced body of soldiers turned to curse the people and denounce the city fathers.

One warrior seemed to be an officer in partial disguise, for he wore silk stockings and neat buckskin breeches. He signaled the attack: "Soldiers, draw your bayonets, and cut your way through them!" The regulars fell upon the nearest townspeople, crying, "Where are your Sons of Liberty now?" A cutlass gashed a Quaker's cheek. Wounds were inflicted upon a tea-water man and a fisherman. A sailor was slashed on the head. Another sailor was stabbed with a bayonet. Two soldiers even attacked a small boy. Another soldier lunged at a woman.

At last city magistrates and members of the watch arrived and dispersed the regulars. Sixty British redcoats took part in the Battle of Golden Hill. They did not escape unscathed, for many were badly beaten. One wounded citizen perished of his injuries, and he may have been the first American to die in the Great Revolution.

The next day other skirmishes threw the city into wild excitement as bells clanged and horsemen threw themselves on their mounts to spread the news to other parts of the country. New York was by no means the only American city where disorders occurred. The hatred of Bostonians for British troops quartered on them led to the famous Boston Massacre on March 5, 1770.

By then Chancellor of the Exchequer Charles Townshend was dead. His successor, Lord Frederick North, later the Prime Minister, regarded the Townshend duties as "preposterous." He felt that the British had stirred up American bees without getting any honey, since revenue from the Townshend Acts came to only about one-tenth the cost of collection. So the very day of the Boston Massacre, North submitted a bill calling for the withdrawal of all the Townshend duties except that on tea. He kept the tea tax as a symbol of Parliament's supremacy over the colonies. In America the British concession broke down the nonimportation agreement.

Back in 1766 the New York assembly had voted 1,000 pounds to pay for a statue of George III "to perpetuate to the latest posterity . . . its deep sense of the eminent and singular benefits received from him . . . but in particular in promoting repeal of the Stamp Act." This gilded lead equestrian sculpture arrived here on the *Britannia* on June 4, 1770. After having been mounted on a tall pedestal at Bowling Green, it was unveiled the following August 16 —only seven months after the king's men had attacked New Yorkers on Golden Hill.

Although the colonists resumed buying British goods, they still balked at tea because of the tax. The threepence a pound levy was not burdensome, but again a principle was at stake. Since tea could not be grown in the colonies, people substituted sassafras, balm, and sage or enjoyed the real thing smuggled here from Holland.

In 1773 the British East India Company, which imported tea from India, was almost bankrupt. Parliament granted the firm the right to ship surplus tea directly to America without paying English import duties. This gave the company a virtual monopoly in the colonies, and merchants here were threatened with ruin. *The Alarm,* a leaflet distributed in New York at the time, denounced both the East India company and British officials. New Yorkers burned an effigy of a certain William Kelley, then in London, because they believed that he had encouraged the shipment of tea to America. Temporarily calling themselves the Mohawks, the Sons of Liberty issued a broadside stating that Americans were "determined not to be enslaved by any power on earth." They added that any merchant allowing India tea to be stored in his warehouse could expect reprisals.

The tea-bearing ships soon began arriving. The first one reached Boston on November 27, 1773, and the following December 16, Bostonians disguised as Indians dumped 342 chests of tea into the harbor. Soon after, Paul Revere galloped into New York with news of the Boston Tea Party.

Finally, on April 22, 1774, the ship *London* arrived here with the first tea consigned to New York. She tied up at the wharf at 4 P.M., and immediately a group of citizens boarded her to question the captain, James Chambers. He denied that his cargo included tea. Skeptical leaders of the boarding party growled that they planned to open every crate aboard his vessel. Captain Chambers then admitted that eighteen boxes of tea were stored belowdecks. The news was passed along to Sons of Liberty ashore, and they began painting their bodies as Mohawk warriors in preparation for raiding the ship that night.

At 8 P.M. the crowd at the dock would not wait for the "Indians." In everyday clothes people surged up the gangplank, spilled onto the deck of the *London,* and climbed down into her hold. They found the teaboxes, hoisted them topside, ripped them open, and spilled the leaves into the Hudson.

When news of the tea raids reached George III, he vowed that he would give the Americans "a few bloody noses to remind them of their duty!" Because Boston had been the first city to defy British authority, it would be starved into submission. Parliament passed the Boston Port Act, closing the harbor to all shipping. Once again New England horsemen galloped down the coast, scattering skull-and-crossbones handbills as a warning to other cities. New Yorkers met on the Commons to denounce the new act and take up a collection for suffering Bostonians. Perhaps one speaker that day was a seventeen-year-old King's College student, named Alexander Hamilton, making his first public appearance. New York promised Boston a 10-year food supply, and soon a flock of about 125 sheep set out for that hungry city.

Now, as other reprisals from the British government fell thick and fast, Americans united in a firm stand against England. The First Continental Congress met in Philadelphia and drew up a declaration of rights and grievances. Lord North made an unsuccessful attempt at conciliation. British troops and colonial militiamen clashed at Lexington and Concord. A Virginia planter, named George Washington, was appointed commander in chief of the provincial forces. The Battle of Bunker Hill was fought. Two weeks later Washington reached Cambridge and took command of an army of New Englanders. The British army lifted its siege of Boston and withdrew. Then, on April 4, 1776, General George Washington left Boston for New York City.

Chapter 12

REVOLUTIONARY WAR

HE STOOD six feet three in his black boots with their pointed toes. Wide-shouldered, deep-chested, and big-bottomed, he held himself as erect as an Indian and walked majestically. His legs and arms were long. His shapely head seemed small in proportion to his height and weight. Set far apart in his long face and divided by a heavy nose were steely blue-gray eyes. Because his false teeth bothered him, he kept his lips pressed together. A cocked hat topped his powdered brown hair, and he was uniformed in a blue coat, golden epaulets, and buff-colored breeches.

Well groomed most of the time, George Washington was dust-flecked the afternoon of April 13, 1776, when he rode his horse into

New York City at the head of five regiments. These soldiers reinforced troops sent here earlier from Boston. No British forces were left in New York. Governor William Tryon and his redcoats had abandoned the fort and taken refuge on the *Duchess of Gordon,* which lay in the harbor. For a time this ship became the colony's floating capital.

During Washington's first days in New York he stayed in a private house on lower Broadway. When his wife joined him, they moved into a mansion abandoned by Abraham Mortier, former paymaster general of British military forces in America. This grand house lay in Lispenard's meadows at the present corner of Varick and Charlton streets. To help make her husband comfortable, Martha Washington bought a feather bed, bolsters, pillows, bed-curtains, crockery, glassware, and other household items.

In 1776 New York had a population of 20,000 and extended about a mile north of the Battery. The province ranked seventh in population among the thirteen colonies. However, because of the city's geographic position and fine harbor, Washington considered it of "infinite importance." As he wrote Congress, he had transferred his army here from Boston because he considered New York the key to the coming campaign. If the British seized the city, they could control the Hudson River, and then, as Washington put it, "stop the intercourse between the northern and southern colonies, upon which depends the safety of America."

This view was shared by General William Howe, the new commanding officer of the king's forces in North America. Except for dark eyes and more pointed features than Washington's, Howe looked surprisingly like the American. Howe's brother, thick-lipped swarthy Admiral Richard Howe, headed all naval operations in America and now was leading a British fleet in this direction. With superior land and sea forces the Howe brothers were exceedingly mobile and could control America's waterways. But where would they strike first?

When General Howe left Boston the month before, most colonists expected him to head straight for New York. Instead, he took loyal Bostonians to Halifax, picked up more troops, and then set sail again. Not long after Washington had reached New York, another British fleet, under Admiral Peter Parker, attacked Charleston, South Carolina, only to be driven off. Anxious New Yorkers expected any day now to see the masts of one or more English fleets standing off Sandy Hook.

The work of fortifying the city had begun before Washington arrived; now he redoubled the effort. Manhattan would be difficult to defend because it was surrounded by water and America had no real navy. Therefore, Washington threw up defenses to hamper the landing of an invasion force. An elaborate system of forts, redoubts, batteries, barricades, and trenches was constructed along Manhattan's shores and on Brooklyn Heights, commanding the Upper Bay.

Lacking cavalry, the American army was a badly balanced force of infantry and artillery. More than 200 cannons were trundled into position by sweating soldiers. The men panted as they stamped shovels into the earth. They swore as they swung picks at solid rock. Munition carts thudded over cobblestones. The old Battery fort was partly demolished, and a barricade arose 200 yards north on Broadway. Drums snarled, flags fluttered, and more and more volunteers tramped into the city until Washington had 20,000 men.

Many Tories, expecting persecution by patriots, had fled. Patriots, too, had left for fear of bombardment by British warships. Despite the reduced population, it was difficult to find quarters for all the soldiers. At first they lodged in barracks and private houses; later they all went into tents, except for one regiment that lacked canvas. This was truly becoming an American army, rather than a collection of Colonial militia.

For the first time masses of men from the thirteen colonies came together and noted in surprise how different they were. Lean frontiersmen, many more than six feet tall, wore leather leggings and moccasins, Indian style. Marylanders favored green hunting shirts. Pennsylvania regiments sported all colors of the rainbow. Pious Connecticut troops regarded New Yorkers as a wicked lot. Aristocratic Virginians were shocked to see New England officers and enlisted men fraternizing. Rhode Islanders stared at New Jersey riflemen clad in short red coats and striped trousers.

As usual, the army attracted prostitutes, gamblers, and saloonkeepers. North of the city, near the present Washington Square, there was a squatters' camp of huts and tents housing loose women and lusty men. Cynics dubbed it the Holy Ground. "The whores," a shocked New England colonel wrote his wife, "continue their employ which is become very lucrative. . . . I was never within the doors nor 'changed a word with any of them except in the execution of my duty as officer of the day in going the grand round with my guard of escort, have broke up the knots of men and women fighting, pulling caps, swearing, crying 'murder!' " Drunken soldiers actually had their heads and arms and legs cut off.

Some of the Tories left in town were stripped, tarred and feathered, and ridden through the streets on rails. This rough treatment resulted as much from fear as from resentment, and there really were grounds for such fear. From his floating refuge in the harbor Governor Tryon directed a conspiracy of British officials and hundreds of loyalists to end the war by murdering or capturing American leaders, by inciting American troops to mutiny, and by seizing or destroying local army supplies. Two of Washington's own bodyguards were bribed. A third, who pretended to accede, revealed the plot.

The Tory mayor, David Matthews, was arrested and charged with "dangerous designs and treasonable conspiracies against the rights and liberties" of Americans. One ringleader, a member of Washington's bodyguard, was Private Thomas Hickey, a deserter from the British army. He tried to poison the general by stirring Paris green in a dish of peas. Hickey was put on trial. Refusing to name any conspirators, he defended himself so weakly that he was sentenced to be hanged. Stripped of his uniform, the disgraced private was led to a field near Bowery Lane, where 20,000 persons watched him dangle at the end of a rope. This was the first military execution of the Revolution and the first in the history of the American army. Although no other defendant was convicted, Washington kept Mayor Matthews in jail, being convinced that he too was involved in the plot.

At daybreak on June 29 an American, named Daniel McCurtin, glanced out of his waterfront home and stiffened with shock. The harbor was a forest of British masts. General Howe had arrived from Halifax with more than 100 vessels. In the next few days more and more ships heaved into sight. Admiral Richard Howe brought an entire army from England in a second fleet. Then Admiral Peter Parker arrived from Charleston with his fleet. Ships of the line, frigates, transports, and other vessels—nearly 500 in all—rocked at anchor on the very threshold of New York. It was the greatest expeditionary force ever mounted by England.

Included in this army of 32,000 soldiers were 9,000 German mercenaries. In 1776 perhaps 1,000,000 men of fighting age lived in

Britain, but the American war was so unpopular there that the government couldn't recruit or impress enough fighting men at home. King George tried unsuccessfully to hire soldiers from Russia and Holland. At last he got mercenaries from petty German princes, among them the Landgrave of Hesse-Cassel. American patriots wrongly called all of them Hessians and regarded them with corrosive hatred.

During this awesome buildup of British strength in New York Bay the Second Continental Congress in Philadelphia adopted the Declaration of Independence. Washington ordered the document read aloud to all his soldiers on July 9, 1776. Here and there in New York regiments were drawn up on parade grounds, the men spick-and-span in their uniforms, bayonets fixed on heavy muskets. One hollow square was formed in front of the present City Hall, and Washington sat astride his horse within this square as an officer began reading aloud, "When in the course of human events—" That evening, as bells clanged and men cheered, a mob spilled down Broadway to Bowling Green and pulled to earth the statue of George III. Washington later reprimanded the few soldiers who took part in this affair, but he was glad that the statue's 2 tons of lead melted down into 42,088 bullets for his army.

Meantime, 10,000 British and German soldiers had landed on Staten Island, where they set up camp, tore down fences for firewood, swilled Jersey applejack, and roamed drunkenly through the thickets. A British officer wrote that "a girl cannot step into the bushes to pluck a rose without running the most immediate risk of being ravished."

Time passed, and still there was no British attack. Both General Howe and Admiral Howe genuinely liked Americans and, before leaving England, had been named by the king to act as peace commissioners. So, before both sides locked in combat, the Howe brothers put out peace feelers. Under a flag of truce a British officer landed in Manhattan with a letter for "Mr. Washington." This envoy was received by an American officer who said, "Sir, we have no person here in our army with that address." Of course, there was a *General* Washington. After the proper form of address had been resolved, Washington met with a British lieutenant colonel, who reported that the Howe brothers wanted to settle the unhappy differences with America. Suspicious of this olive branch and unsure of the Howes' authority, Washington refused to treat with the British high command.

Now the English attacked. At dawn on August 22, 1776, a vanguard of troops shoved off from Staten Island near the western end of what today is the Verrazano-Narrows Bridge. Under a bright sun and on calm water the redcoats ferried across the Narrows in 88 craft specially built for this amphibious operation. They were in a carefree mood. When their boats grounded on the flat beach of Gravesend Bay in Brooklyn, they jumped out, splashed ashore, ran to nearby apple trees, shinnied up, and threw apples at one another. No American force opposed this invasion. Back and forth across the mile-wide Narrows the landing craft plied, until by noon 15,000 British had been transferred to Long Island. Three days later they were reinforced by 5,000 Hessians.

Washington hadn't known whether the first enemy thrust would come at Manhattan or Brooklyn. He realized that to hold New York City, he must hold Brooklyn Heights, but this meant splitting his 19,000 effectives between the two places. Long before the British landed on Long Island, the Americans had thrown up forts and earthworks from Gowanus Bay on the south to Wallabout Bay (later the Brooklyn Navy Yard) on the north. These strongholds were protected on the eastern inland side by thickly wooded hills. Stretching southwest to northeast, the hills were almost impassable except where they were cut by four roads. The enemy now lay on the flatlands to the south.

On each of the two days after the British landing Washington left his New York headquarters and ferried across the East River to reconnoiter. Convinced that the big British push was being made against Brooklyn, he rushed over reinforcements until 7,000 Americans faced 20,000 Englishmen and Germans. Unfortunately, two-thirds of Washington's men on Long Island were militia. Some had been under arms less than two weeks, and none had ever faced an enemy in battle. Discipline was so lax that some wandered miles beyond their fixed posts.

Worst of all, Washington and his generals neglected one of the four passes cut through the hills. This was the Jamaica Pass, just west of the present intersection of Fulton Street and Broadway in Brooklyn. Only five young militia officers were left to guard it.

The Battle of Long Island was fought on August 27, 1776. That morning the sun rose "with a red and angry glare." Later the day turned clear, cool, and pleasant. About 8 A.M. Washington once more arrived from Manhattan, this time to lead his troops in action.

Despite his service in the Seven Years' War and at the siege of Boston, never before had he directed a stand-up battle. It also marked the first time that Americans and British clashed in formal battle array in the open field.

Superior in numbers, weapons, experience, discipline, and strategy, the British pushed north. Most of the important action took place within the 526 acres now constituting Prospect Park. Perhaps the most dramatic and gallant episode occurred near Third and Eighth streets just west of Brooklyn's Fifth Avenue. There a Maryland battalion tried to hold off the enemy long enough for retreating Americans to scamper into the forts. The price they paid was 684 casualties. Standing on a hilltop and watching this action through fieldglasses, Washington groaned, "Good God! What brave fellows I must this day lose!"

By early afternoon most Americans who had not been shot, bayoneted, captured, drowned, or driven panic-stricken from the field were cooped up within forts and redoubts on Brooklyn Heights. They were frightened. They were bloody and tired. They sweated out the danger of a British frontal attack. They nibbled biscuits "hard enough to break the teeth of a rat," as one private expressed it. But General Howe was not willing to risk a headlong charge on these strongholds. His caution won a battle and helped lose a war. With a little more daring Howe might have captured George Washington and the entire Long Island army and put an end to the revolution then and there.

Up at four o'clock the next morning, Washington saw that the British still lay on their arms and that the wind kept enemy warships from closing in to bombard his position. He ordered even more Americans across the East River to reinforce his beleaguered men. The afternoon came and went with still no British attack. Toward evening a cold rain began and developed into a downpour that made it impossible for the Americans to build cooking fires. Their ammunition became wet and useless. In some trenches men stood waist-deep in water. All that night the northeasterly wind blew.

The second day after the battle Washington was hard at work by 4:30 A.M., writing Congress about the "engagement between a detachment of our men and the enemy" on August 27. This chore done, he sent orders to Manhattan to gather all available boats and assemble them by dark on the west side of the East River. Next, he held a war council with his seven generals in the Brooklyn forts. Beset by a superior land force and in peril of being cut off from escape by the British fleet, the Americans agreed to evacuate.

Soon after dusk the first boats from Manhattan nosed into the Brooklyn shore at what today is the eastern end of the Brooklyn Bridge. The northeasterly wind still kept enemy warships from closing in for the kill. Now a fog fell like a white pillow on the area. Besides blurring vision, it muffled sound. Speaking in whispers, groping through blackness, and squashing along muddy paths, American soldiers filed down to the evacuation point. A few panicked and tried to rush the boats and crawl over comrades' heads to get a seat. But most of the shivering miserable men behaved well and stepped in orderly fashion into scows, barges, and rowboats; anything that floated had been brought to the scene. The craft were manned by seafaring New Englanders, who rowed with aching muscles from the east shore to the west and back again, all that fog-shrouded night. The last man to pick his way down slippery steps into a boat was George Washington.

By seven o'clock on the morning of August 30 the last of his 10,000 men were back on Manhattan. They brought all their food, equipment, and arms, leaving behind only a few heavy and rusted cannon. A British military critic later wrote that "this retreat should hold a high place among military transactions." Howe's victory at the Battle of Long Island was indecisive because he let the American army regroup. England had lost its golden opportunity.

On September 7, 1776, for the first time in history, a submarine made an underwater attack on a warship. A Yale graduate, named David Bushnell, designed this submarine and managed to present his idea to Washington, who gave the thirty-four-year-old inventor all the money and men he needed to construct his strange craft.

Bushnell's submarine was made of huge oak timbers, scooped out and fitted together in the shape of a clam. Because of its appearance it was called Bushnell's *Turtle*. The oak timbers were bound with iron bands, the seams were calked, and everything was tarred to make the vessel watertight. The *Turtle* was big enough for one man to stand inside. Seven hundred pounds of lead stored in the bottom kept it upright. Two foot-operated pumps enabled the operator to dive or ascend. The submarine's forward movement was provided by a hand crank that turned a two-bladed wooden screw propellor.

Bushnell and Washington planned to use the crude submarine to blow up one of the British warships anchored in New York Harbor. Sergeant Ezra Lee, of Lyme, Connecticut, was chosen to operate the *Turtle*. One night a whaleboat towed the submarine to the foot of Whitehall Street at the Battery. An egg-shaped magazine, containing 130 pounds of gunpowder, was attached by a screw to the back of the submarine. The Americans hoped that the magazine could be detached from the *Turtle* and fastened to the underside of a British man-of-war. A timing device would give Lee 30 minutes in which to escape.

Bushnell, Washington, and a group of American officers gathered at the Battery at midnight on September 7 to watch Lee depart on his historic mission. The night was so dark that the enemy on nearby Governors Island could not see what was going on. After the sergeant had submerged, he steered his craft by a compass set near decayed phosphorescent wood, called foxwood. This eerie glow was his only light. Busily working his controls, Lee glided through the black and silent water of the harbor out toward Admiral Howe's flagship, the sixty-four-gun *Eagle,* anchored off Staten Island.

As planned, the submarine came up under the keel of the *Eagle.* Protruding from the top of the submarine and operated from inside was a drill. Lee tried to force this screw into first one spot and then another on the *Eagle* but was thwarted by iron plates reinforcing her copper sheathing. He worked hard and long until dawn began creeping over the harbor. Lee realized that he had to make a getaway, but to his dismay he discovered that his compass wasn't working. Time after time he had to surface to get a visual fix on the Battery.

The *Turtle* was spotted by red-coated British soldiers and blue-clad Hessian mercenaries standing on the parapets of Governors Island. Puzzled by the craft's odd shape, some of them climbed into a barge and pushed off to investigate. Having failed to blow up the flagship, Lee now decided to try to destroy the barge. He disengaged the magazine holding the gunpowder. It floated free of the *Turtle.* The men in the barge hastily rowed back toward Governors Island.

The tide was flowing shoreward. The dangerous egg-shaped magazine swirled into the East River, where it exploded thunderously but did no harm. Water, wood, and iron flew high into the air. Lee painfully cranked his way back to the Battery, where Washington and the others were waiting for him. There the weary sergeant climbed out of the *Turtle* to receive congratulations for his daring. Although he had not managed to accomplish his mission, he had thrown a scare into the enemy. One British officer wrote that "the ingenuity of these people is singular in their secret modes of mischief."

In the Battle of Long Island the Americans had suffered some 1,500 casualties, while the British had lost only about 400 men. King George was so pleased that he conferred the Order of the Bath on General Howe. The Tories thought that the war was almost over. Howe felt that the Americans now might be willing to talk peace, and he arranged a conference with their representatives. Congress chose John Adams, Edward Rutledge, and Benjamin Franklin to learn the British intentions. On September 11 they met in a stone mansion in the southwestern corner of Staten Island, across from Perth Amboy, New Jersey.

With every courtesy, Howe received the American delegates in a large room, decorated with a moss carpet and green sprigs. Including dinner—consisting of excellent claret; cold ham, tongue, and mutton; and delicious bread—the meeting lasted three hours. Howe did most of the talking, saying that he had a brotherly feeling for Americans. Despite his every appeal, the committee reported to Congress that Howe seemed to have no authority except to grant pardons if America gave in. If it did so, there was no certainty that its grievances would be redressed. The war went on.

Now a scorched-earth policy was discussed by Congress, Washington, his generals, and other influential men. Should New York be burned to the ground? It was of no use to the Americans because the British controlled the city's waterways. Most inhabitants had fled, and two-thirds of all local property was owned by loyalists. By destroying the city, the Americans would deprive the British officers of a headquarters and the loyalists of housing. Washington couldn't make up his mind, but when Congress finally decided against razing New York, he concurred.

Washington now disposed his troops for the Battle of New York City. He left 5,000 men in the city itself near the Battery. He posted 5 brigades along the East River, chiefly near Kip's Bay, at East 34th Street and at Turtle Bay, at East 45th Street. Then he withdrew the bulk of his army to the high ground between 125th Street and the northern tip of Manhattan. For his new headquarters Washington chose the vacant house of Colonel Roger Morris, a Tory refugee in England. This house, later called the Jumel Mansion, still stands at Edgecombe Avenue and 160th Street. Washington now had his troops strung out the 13-mile length of Manhattan. The two ends were fairly strong, but the center consisted of green militia.

Howe struck at the center. Having kept his men idle since August 27, he launched an attack the hot Sunday of September 15. About 11 A.M. British warships, which had sailed up the East River, opened fire with 80 guns against American entrenchments near East Thirty-fourth Street. For 2 hours this heavy bombardment pinned the Americans in their lines. Then, as the last shell slammed to earth and the smoke drifted away, the first wave of British and Germans crossed the East River in 84 flatboats. The clustered redcoats looked to one observer like "a clover field in full bloom." The invaders jumped ashore at Kip's Bay. Washington's raw recruits, stunned by artillery fire and frightened by glinting sunlight on bayonets, broke and ran without firing a shot. The British captured 20 American officers and about 300 men.

Washington was three miles to the north when the bombardment began. He vaulted into the saddle and galloped to the scene of action. When he arrived at the present intersection of Lexington Avenue and Forty-second Street, he saw some of his men throwing away coats, hats, knapsacks, and even muskets in a wild scramble for safety. "Take to the cornfield!" Washington roared. "Take to the wall!" But most of the frenzied militia ignored him and kept running. Washington crimsoned with rage. Dashing his hat on the ground, he bellowed, "Are these the men with whom I am to defend America?" Still on horseback, he yanked his sword from its scabbard. The blade flashed as he laid its broad side on the shoulders of the men nearest him—privates, a colonel, and even a brigadier general.

Whack! *Damn ye!* Whack! Sixty to seventy Hessians trotted toward Washington, hoping to capture the American commander in chief. He was so blinded by rage that he took no notice of them. But his terrified foot soldiers bolted in every direction, leaving the general and his aides to face the attackers without a single musket. Fortunately, a young officer seized the bridle of Washington's horse and pulled him away. Sputtering and cursing, he was hustled north toward Harlem and safety.

The main body of British troops now pushed farther inland, spreading as far north as Murray Hill, rearing between Thirty-fourth and Forty-second streets, Third Avenue, and Broadway. There they were halted by General Howe. His objective for the day had been to capture Murray Hill. Now he wished to rest his men and wait for reinforcements. The British and German soldiers grounded their arms in meadows stretching south from the present Grand Central Station.

Murray Hill was named for Robert Murray, whose mansion stood at the corner of what is now Park Avenue and Thirty-seventh Street. According to legend, his wife beguiled General Howe and his staff into dallying in her home so that the Americans might escape. This isn't quite true. That sweltering day Mrs. Murray did send a servant to invite Howe to stop for refreshments, and he accepted her hospitality. Far from being a *femme fatale,* however, she was a middle-aged Quaker lady with twelve children. Besides, as we know, Howe had already decided to pause.

Meantime, American troops left in the toe of Manhattan learned that most roads leading north were held by the British. At first they thought that they would have to cut their way through the enemy to join Washington's force in Harlem. But Aaron Burr declared that he could lead them to safety without a fight and without detection. The Americans began sneaking up a road on the west side of Manhattan. About the same time a British column started pushing up the Boston Post Road on the east side of the island. Separating the two hostile columns by only about two miles were a tangle of swamps and trees and low hills, constituting the present Central Park. It was a silent and secret race along parallel roads, for neither force knew about the other. Burr won, bringing 5,000 American soldiers into Washington's camp.

The western end of the present West 125th Street was then a valley, called the Hollow Way. The American army lay on the hills to the north. Advance posts of the British lay on the hills to the south. Their front lines were less than two miles apart.

In the early morning on September 16, Washington sent out a reconnoitering party of 150 Connecticut rangers, led by Major Thomas Knowlton. The general stood on a hill at 126th Street to watch them as best he could. Near 112th Street and Riverside Drive, Knowlton's men ran into British pickets. They clashed. Then, with a skirl of bagpipes, kilted Black Watch warriors advanced to help the pickets. The outnumbered Americans soon broke off the engagement and retreated in orderly fashion two and one-half miles north.

Superior in force, the cocky British followed, descending into the Hollow Way. When the pursuers came within sight of the main American army, a British bugler blew a call—not the signal to attack, but the call of hunters who have killed a fox. At this insult Americans quivered with rage. Until then Washington had been undecided about what to do. Now he feinted at the advancing British as though to offer open battle, at the same time sending two columns of Americans by detours to fall on the enemy's rear.

The outraged Americans did more than feint. Pouring down from the hills, they counterattacked in force. The very militiamen who had fled from Kip's Bay the day before raced with ferocious yells toward the advancing scarlet lines. The affair developed into a general engagement, which raged for two hours. Then the redcoats faltered, stopped, broke, and retreated. Whooping with joy, the Americans pushed them back to a buckwheat field on the present site of Barnard College. Again the enemy fell back, this time to an orchard farther south. Twice more the British gave ground, retreating to what is now 103d Street. But Washington, realizing that he would be outnumbered in a major conflict, ordered his men to halt before British reserves could be thrown into action.

This Battle of Harlem Heights did not change the relative position of either army since no new ground was captured and held. Technically, though, it was an American victory. Various historians have reported different casualty figures, but all agree that American losses were far fewer than those of the British. Morally, too, it was a triumph for the Americans. They had proved that the British army was *not* invincible.

Four days later fire broke out in New York City. It started in a wooden tavern, called the Fighting Cocks, on a wharf near Whitehall Slip and was spread by a gale blowing from the south. The origin of the blaze remains a mystery, but the British and Tories called it a plot to destroy the city. Amid crackling flames and falling timbers, half-naked people staggered through the streets in terror. Ordinary people, aristocratic loyalists, and British soldiers and sailors tried in vain to fight the fire. Tories claimed that holes had been cut in fire buckets. People suspected of touching off the conflagration were spitted on bayonets, hanged, and even tossed alive into the flames. The city's most prominent landmark, Trinity Church, crashed in ruins. One-fourth of the city was left a smoking blackened wasteland. Thousands of homeless people were reduced to beggary. All this was a major disaster to the British high command, which had chosen the city as its headquarters. Washington, who had considered and then rejected the idea of putting the city to the torch, commented, "Providence, or some good honest fellow, has done more for us than we were disposed to do for ourselves."

The day after the fire a twenty-four-year-old American, with blue eyes, blond hair, and a fair complexion, was brought to General Howe's headquarters at East Fifty-first Street and First Avenue. He was not an arsonist, but a self-confessed spy. His name was Nathan Hale. Disguised as a teacher, he had penetrated enemy lines in and around the city to sketch fortifications and jot down other pertinent military facts. After his capture in Brooklyn he admitted to being a captain in Washington's army and a spy. Howe questioned the handsome youth and turned him over to the British provost marshal, and on September 22, 1776, Nathan Hale was hanged—perhaps at Third Avenue and 66th Street.

For several weeks the British let Washington occupy Harlem Heights. Rather than risk a bloody frontal attack, Howe finally decided to use his warships to land part of his army behind the Americans. The foggy night of October 12 a British force was put ashore on Throgs Neck, a slim peninsula jutting out from the Bronx into the East River. Washington had anticipated this move. His Pennsylvania riflemen, crouched behind a woodpile, threw back the enemy in confusion. Howe then made a second landing, three miles north in Westchester County. This jeopardized Washington's army, and he pulled back to White Plains, which was then isolated country. The Battle of White Plains, fought on October 28, resulted in the defeat of 1,400 Americans by 4,000 British.

Washington still had 2,500 men left to defend the last bit of Manhattan held by the Americans. This was Fort Washington, perched on a rocky cliff 230 feet above the Hudson, at what is now the eastern end of the George Washington Bridge. Fort Lee stood on the Jersey Palisades just across the river. In a direct line between the two forts the Americans had sunk ships and lowered chevaux-de-frise—heavy timbers studded with iron spikes. Congress had asked Washington to bottle up the Hudson to prevent the British from breaking through to the north. However, the sunken barriers proved ineffectual; enemy ships sailed over them without damage.

Since Fort Washington's main function had been to guard the eastern end of the water barrier, there was no point now in trying to defend it against Howe's gathering might. Major General Nathanael Greene commanded the fort. Unwisely, he elected to make a stand. His troops were jammed within a space barely large enough for

1,000 men. And since the fort lacked a well, water had to be scooped up in buckets from the Hudson far below.

At the head of 5,000 soldiers, Washington retreated across the Hudson, into New Jersey, and down to Hackensack to set up camp. On November 16 he was back at Fort Lee. From a distance of less than one mile he looked through field glasses across the river and saw his brave men being stabbed to death by Hessian bayonets. Helpless and forlorn, Washington sobbed at the grisly sight.

The fall of Fort Washington was one of the greatest American disasters of the war. Greene lost a staggering amount of precious armament and equipment, and hundreds of prisoners were marched down the length of Manhattan and herded into makeshift prisons in churches, sugarhouses, and ships. What's more, the overall battle for New York City, from Long Island to Fort Washington, cost the Americans hundreds of lives and more than 4,400 prisoners.

Now the entire city was held by the British, who continued to occupy it for the next 7 years. Only about 3,000 civilians were left when the king's troops took over, most people having fled. Now British and German soldiers swarmed in, along with Tories from the countryside and other colonies. They soon boosted the population to 33,000. One loyalist wrote that New York was "a most dirty, desolate and wretched place." It had been dug up by the Americans for defense, shelled by British warships, and charred by fire. Slowly the city became the capital of Tory America, as well as Britain's greatest military base. Business boomed.

There was a great housing shortage. A cluster of shanties and tents, known as Canvas Town, arose amid the blackened ruins of the city. On the front doors of houses left standing after the fire, officials painted *G. R.,* for George Rex, meaning that they were commandeered in the king's name. The families of British and German servicemen poured into town. Added to these was the usual horde of prostitutes. An Englishman visiting St. Paul's Chapel, which survived the fire, wrote: "This is a very neat church and some of the handsomest and best-dressed ladies I have ever seen in America. I believe most of them are whores." A trader, named Jackson, contracted to supply 3,500 women to entertain His Majesty's troops in America and brought to New York doxies from England, as well as Negroes from the West Indies.

Rentals rose. Prices soared 800 percent. Food and firewood became dear. Profiteering, black-marketeering, smuggling, and graft flourished. Everyone cheated everyone else. Some greedy men made quick fortunes. In fact, even Tories felt that the British might have won the war had it not been for the colossal graft of barracks masters, quartermasters, the commissary of artillery, the commissary of cattle, the commissary of forage, and the commissary of prisoners.

The countryside for a radius of thirty miles around the city became a no-man's-land, wherein irregulars from both armies raided and plundered and burned and killed. Because the slaughter of cattle was a common goal, the British marauders were called Cowboys, and the American guerrillas were known as Skinners.

Life's uncertainty bred a feverish gaiety. Manners and morals relaxed. British officers promenaded in glittering uniforms, drank heavily, fought duels, frequented taverns, celebrated the king's birthday, and promoted cricket matches, horse races, bullbaiting, boxing matches, and golf games. They escorted young ladies to dances, balls, teas, receptions, and dinners. On December 7, 1767, David Douglass had opened the city's first real playhouse, the John Street Theatre, halfway between Broadway and Nassau Street. During their occupation of New York the British took over the theater, founded the Garrison Dramatic Club, and presented amateur theatricals. The social whirl reached its peak with the visit of seventeen-year-old Prince William Henry, the third son of George III, who later became King William IV. In New York he was saved from drowning while ice skating and met twenty-three-year-old Post Captain Horatio Nelson, destined for immortality as the hero of Trafalgar.

But the plight of the common people worsened, especially after another fire had consumed 300 more houses. Rich Tories and British officers held charity drives to alleviate the suffering, but almost no one worried about American soldiers cooped up in prisons around town. Given wretched food or none at all, they were jammed elbow to elbow and received no medical care. The worst of the makeshift jails were the prison ships. About 11,000 Americans, or more than the total killed by British muskets throughout the entire war, perished on these fetid vessels.

The Englishman in charge of the prisoners, Provost Marshal William Cunningham, was sadistic and greedy. As he lay dying in 1791, he confessed, "I shudder at the murders I have been accessory to, both with and without orders from the government, especially while in New York, during which time there were more than two thousand prisoners starved in the different churches, by stopping their rations, which I sold."

New York was occupied longer and suffered more than any other great American city. Of the Revolution's 308 battles and engagements, 92 took place in various parts of New York State, while 216 occurred in and around the other colonies. The war ended with the surrender of Lord Charles Cornwallis at Yorktown, Virginia, on October 19, 1781.

Victorious American troops did not reoccupy New York City until November 25, 1783. For decades afterward this was celebrated as Evacuation Day. During the preceding weeks nearly 15,000 frightened Tories shipped out of here, and into the vacuum rushed Americans eager to buy loyalist property at bargain prices.

According to the timetable agreed to by British and American forces, the king's men were to quit the city beginning at noon, November 25. Most people awakened early that historic day and noted with delight that the weather broke clear, if cold. A Mrs. Day who ran a boardinghouse on Murray Street near the Hudson River flew an American flag over her place. When this was reported to Provost Marshal Cunningham, he sent word that she was to take it down. She refused. About 9 A.M., while Mrs. Day was sweeping in front of her door, Cunningham himself appeared in a scarlet coat and powdered wig. He commanded her to haul down the rebel flag. Again she refused. He seized the halyards to do the job himself; whereupon Mrs. Day took her broom and clobbered him until powder rose in a white mist from his wig and gore gushed from his nose. With his "front as red as his back," Cunningham retreated. This was the last conflict of the war.

An hour earlier, at 8 A.M., American light infantry reached McGowan's Pass in upper Central Park and closed in so near the British rear guard that officers on both sides could chat with one another. Then the British gave way, and the Americans followed as far as a barrier thrown across the Bowery, where they broke ranks and lounged about to wait. Shortly after the noon deadline the redcoats headed for the East River, stepped into rowboats, and were ferried out to the waiting British fleet. Now the Americans pushed all the way south and occupied the Battery fort.

Everybody was eager to see General George Washington, the man who had held the American army together by sheer willpower. He had been waiting in Harlem. Now, escorted by a body of Westchester Light Horse, he rode down to the Bull's Head Tavern on the Bowery between Bayard and Pump (now Canal) streets. There he was greeted by a whooping crowd of townspeople, some on horseback, some afoot. When he tugged his horse's reins to start the final leg of his triumphal entry, they trooped along behind him. The procession wound up at Cape's Tavern at Broadway and Thames Street, where a reception was held for the commander in chief.

A young woman who witnessed Evacuation Day wrote:

> The troops just leaving us were as if equipped for show, and with their scarlet uniforms and burnished arms, made a brilliant display. The troops that marched in, on the contrary, were ill-clad and weather-beaten, and made a forlorn appearance. But then they were *our* troops, and as I looked at them, and thought upon all they had done and suffered for us, my heart and my eyes were full, and I admired and gloried in them the more because they were weather-beaten and forlorn.

Now Washington was ready to say farewell to his officers before heading toward his Mount Vernon home. The chosen place was Fraunces Tavern at Pearl and Broad streets. The date was December 4, 1783, a lovely winter's day. By noon the general's officers packed the Long Room, named for the Indian term for a council lodge. A few minutes later Washington entered, looking tired. Everyone stood up to greet him. He acknowledged the tribute with a nod of his be-wigged head and moved over to a linen-draped table holding a buffet luncheon. Nobody ate much. The booted officers ached at the thought of parting with the man who not only had led them to victory but also had refused a crown. Swords clanking and spurs jangling, they drifted about aimlessly. Washington accepted a glass of wine; but his strong fingers shook, and his head hung low. The men filled their glasses and stared dully at the ruby-colored wine.

Finally, Washington began speaking: "With a heart full of love and gratitude I now take my leave of you. I most devoutly wish that your latter days may be as prosperous and happy as your former ones have been glorious and honorable." Washington raised his glass to his lips and drank the wine. The officers emptied their glasses.

As Washington put down his drink, his eyes filled with tears, and his iron will almost broke. In a choking voice he said, "I cannot—" He stopped and gulped, and his face was ashen. "I cannot come to each of you, but I shall feel obliged if each of you will . . . will come and take me by the hand."

There was a dead silence. All stood transfixed. Then a board creaked as 280-pound General Henry Knox, standing nearest Washington, swung his bulk toward his commander in chief. Knox's eyes brimmed with tears. He grasped Washington's hand. The two huge warriors stared deeply into each other's eyes and then, engulfed by memories of their years together, hugged each other. Washington kissed Knox on the cheek. Both wept. Neither said a word. Later, when Washington stepped aboard a barge at the Whitehall Slip, his jaw muscles throbbed convulsively.

Chapter 13

—————◄●►—————

THE DOCTORS' RIOT

AN EARTHQUAKE rocked New York in November, 1783, and jarred a man off his chair in lower Manhattan. A few months later John Jacob Astor strode onto the scene. This yellow-haired butcher boy from Germany took up where nature left off, for he shook the city and nation in his own titanic way. He became the so-called landlord of New York, manipulated the city government for his own purposes, and wound up the richest man in America.

Handsome and square-jawed and a smooth talker despite his broken English, Astor was twenty-one when he landed in the city that spring of 1784. Born eight miles from Heidelberg in a sleepy place, called Walldorg, or Village in the Woods, he was the fifth child of a German butcher. The family name was spelled variously as Ashdour, Aschtor, Ashdoor, and Ashdor. From his birthplace he emigrated to London to work for his brother George, who made musical instruments. He learned some English there, then continued to America with high hopes and seven flutes.

Another brother, named Heinrich, or Henry, already lived in New York. Henry had followed Hessian troops here to sell them provisions, and after the war ended, he changed from sutler to butcher. He was one of thousands of Germans who, genuinely liking the Americans they had been taught to hate, elected to remain in the New World after the Revolution. Henry wanted to hire his younger brother to stick pigs, but the lad had greater ambitions.

Jacob took a job as a helper to a German baker in Pearl Street, trotting up and down Broadway, sidestepping stray swine and balancing a tray of cakes on his hand. It was the fur trade, however, that really interested him. Soon Jacob went to work for a Quaker fur merchant, flogging moths out of stored pelts. Astor got in on the ground floor of a booming business, for the interruption of the fur trade during the war had boosted prices abroad. A beaverskin bought from an Indian in upper New York for $1 sold in London for $6.25.

The year of Astor's arrival this city became the state capital, the colony of New York having changed into the state of New York after a state constitution had been adopted in 1777. Except for five sessions, New York City served as the seat of state government until Albany became the capital in 1796. City affairs, formerly controlled by the British, now fell into the hands of the new state. George Clinton, New York's first American governor, appointed James Duane the city's first mayor after the Revolution. Duane was a rich man, whose house on Pine Street had been nearly destroyed during the British occupation. However, no damage was done to his country estate near the present Gramercy Park. The name of this park is said to be derived from Krom Moerasje, or Crooked Little Swamp, formed by Cedar Creek, which once flowed from Madison Square to the East River.

New York City also became the capital of the new nation when Congress convened here on January 11, 1785. For five years the city served as the seat of the federal government, such as it was. At first there was no constitution, there was no president, and Congress sat as a single chamber. The nation was like a crazy quilt of thirteen patches, each of these thirteen states loosely stitched together by the

Articles of Confederation. Jealous of one another and behaving like arrogant little republics, the states tugged in different directions and frayed the slight threads holding them in one piece. Until the federal government was reorganized under the Constitution in 1789, Congress rarely was attended by twenty-five members, although it was entitled to ninety-one representatives.

For some time after the Revolution, blackened bricks and jack-strawed timbers bore witness to the two fires that had ravaged New York while the British held it. Shipping having been throttled, wharves sagged and rotted. Dogs and pigs picked their way through badly paved, poorly lighted streets and fought over garbage, just as the town's 12,000 inhabitants quarreled among themselves. Lawsuits multiplied as people vied for property and trade. Vice flared in the tented area called Canvas Town. As many as 6 criminals were hanged at once from gallows inside a painted Chinese pagoda within City Hall Park.

However, the city's magnificent harbor, its fine business reputation, and its cosmopolitan atmosphere attracted people from the northern part of the state, from New Jersey, from New England, and even from Ireland. Two hundred foreigners were naturalized in New York the first year after the war. The Friendly Sons of St. Patrick was organized by Irish Catholics—and Presbyterians. Unlike the British, eighteenth-century Americans accepted Catholics at face value.

The first priest to officiate regularly in New York was a Jesuit, the Reverend Ferdinand Steenmayer. During the war he donned a disguise, called himself Mr. Farmer, and slipped into the city to minister secretly to Catholics in a house on Wall Street. When the British left, he appeared openly, gathered his scattered flock, and celebrated mass in a loft over a carpenter's shop on Barclay Street, then in the suburbs. In 1784 the state legislature repealed the law of 1700 banning "Papish priests and Jesuits," and the next year New York's first Catholic church was incorporated. On October 5, 1785, the cornerstone was laid for St. Peter's Church at Barclay and Church streets. By this time 2,000 Catholics lived here.

As Catholic prospects brightened, Trinity Corporation dimmed. The state legislature disestablished the Church of England and put all religious sects on an equal footing. The Revolution had all but extinguished Trinity Parish because most of its clergy and parishioners had been loyalists. A change of name and form seemed necessary, so Trinity became a Protestant Episcopal Church within the Anglican community, which included the Church of England. But Trinity still owned valuable Manhattan real estate and in time struggled back to power. However, it lost its influence over King's College, which re-opened as Columbia College.

Commerce was crippled now by many adverse factors. Trade between New York and the West Indies was cut off by English regulations. American goods could not enter British ports except in English ships. Britain dumped its manufactures here.

Casting about for new markets, New Yorkers sent a ship, called the *Empress of China,* to Canton and opened up trade with the Orient. Then too, Alexander Hamilton established the Bank of New York, the first bank in this city and the third in the nation. Its first home was the Walton Mansion, called the most beautiful house in America and located near what today is the western end of the Brooklyn Bridge. The Chamber of Commerce, born in 1768 and staunchly loyalist throughout the war, was reorganized as the Chamber of Commerce of the State of New York. A young Scotsman, named Duncan Phyfe, later to become America's best cabinetmaker, labored amid wood shavings as an apprentice to a local coachmaker.

Even as New Yorkers pulled themselves up by their bootstraps, they found time for fun. Incredible though it may seem, buffalo hunts were held in New York City with buffalo imported from Kentucky.

Visiting Europeans marveled at the speed of the city's postwar recovery. Most of the city still lay to the east of Broadway. Pearl Street (then Queens Street) had buildings from four to six stories high along its mile and one-half length. Most new houses were "framed buildings with brick or stone fronts and the sides filled in with brick." Luxuriously dressed damsels took the afternoon air in painted carriages, flocked to the theater, and doted on dances.

They were the daughters of the landed gentry who now controlled the city. For the time being, land remained the chief source of wealth. Then, in historic progression over the next many decades, economic power passed from landlords to shipping merchants to bankers to railway magnates to industrial trusts. In the era immediately after the Revolution rich property owners tried to prevent the laboring class from having any say in government. Not until 1804 was the city charter amended to allow all male New Yorkers paying twenty-five dollars' rent a year to vote for aldermen. Not until 1833 could these citizens vote for their own mayor.

The situation bred discontent. In 1785 journeymen shoemakers went on strike, and a General Society of Mechanics and Tradesmen was formed. Its members were butchers, hatters, potters, carpenters, masons, tallow chandlers, sailmakers, coachmakers, coopers, rope-makers, stonecutters, tailors, cutlers, tanners, bookbinders, saddlers, bakers, and ship carpenters.

Even though Philadelphia was still the largest city in the country, New York's population doubled between 1783 and 1786. However, in 1788, 1 out of every 7 men in the city was jailed for debt. The next year, at a dinner given by the mechanics' society, loud applause greeted this ominous toast: "A cobweb pair of breeches, a porcupine saddle, and a hard-trotting horse to all the enemies of freedom!" In 1790 only 1,303 of the 13,330 male residents of the city owned enough property to entitle them to vote for governor.

No formal political party existed, the people being loosely grouped into the rich and the poor. Each group had its own idea of what freedom meant. This class struggle colored the question of what kind of federal government Americans should have.

Congress—poorly attended, lacking money, without the means of raising revenue—degenerated into a debating society. A speaker in the Massachusetts house of delegates actually spoke of Congress as a foreign government. The new nation was coming apart at the seams. To avert this catastrophe, our forefathers drafted a federal Constitution, calling for a strong central government. It had to be ratified by nine of the thirteen states before it could become effective. Thorny questions were posed: How could the rights of man be reconciled with the protection of property? Did the Constitution assure government strong enough to save the Union without destroying the states?

The debate over ratification became so intense that two political factions arose. Adoption of the Constitution was urged by the Federalist party, representing the rich and wellborn. This party was led by George Washington, Alexander Hamilton, John Adams, and John Jay. The Anti-Federalist party, headed by Thomas Jefferson, drew its strength from the poor and humble. It insisted that all powers not specifically granted to the federal government by the Constitution should be reserved to the states.

Most citizens of New York City favored the Constitution. However, Governor Clinton, a majority of state legislators, and most up-staters preferred a confederation. The entire state bubbled with political fermentation. The campaign for ratification was fought largely in newspapers. On October 27, 1787, New York's *Independent*

Journal, or Weekly Advertiser published the first of a series of articles explaining and defending the Constitution. A total of eighty-five essays were printed, each signed Publius but actually written by three men—Hamilton, Jay, and James Madison. These *Federalist Papers* are considered the most important contribution to political thought ever made in America.

Before enough states had ratified the Constitution to make it the law of the land, the doctors' riot broke out here. In 1788 the town's only shelter for the ill was New York Hospital, a three-story structure atop a small hill west of Broadway between Duane and Reade streets. However, it was still not used as a hospital because British troops occupying it during the war had left the building in a sorry condition. Medical professors from nearby Columbia College had converted two of its rooms into a dissecting laboratory for their students. Human corpses were needed for this work. Although it was illegal to possess any part of a body, the students dug up corpses from city cemeteries —public and private alike. As more and more graves were violated, townspeople hired guards to protect their dead the first few nights after burial. Rumor distorted facts, excitement mounted, and every physician in town fell under suspicion.

Such was the mass mood one April morning in 1788, when some boys began playing in the rear of the nearly deserted hospital. Looking up, one lad saw a huge sausage dangling at a laboratory window. Looking more closely, he realized it was a human arm. With a scream like ripping silk, he fled. The other boys looked, screamed, and ran. Clattering through the streets, they told everyone they met about the fearsome thing they had seen. Soon startled men took up their cry. Individuals clustered into knots, the knots merged into a crowd, and the crowd churned into a mob that marched up the hill to the hospital. The rabble broke in and found that the boys had told the truth.

Enraged men now fell on doctors and students. They tore the laboratory apart. They smashed valuable medical equipment. Respectfully, they scooped up bits of human organs and arms and legs. Staff members were saved from death only by the timely arrival of Mayor Duane, Sheriff Robert Boyd, and other city fathers. For their own safety they were hustled off to jail in City Hall Park. Then city officials persuaded the mob to bury the specimens of human flesh and to disperse. No blood was shed.

The next morning, however, a muttering crowd again gathered

near the hospital. As more and more people arrived, the muttering rose to hoarse shouts. One man cried that the hospital should be searched a second time. Another suggested that other cadavers were being used in Columbia College. So the mob swarmed into the hospital. Next, the college was combed. Now someone shouted that corpses were being hidden by doctors in their own homes. Shrieking people fanned throughout the city and broke into private dwellings. Some rowdies passed the residence of Sir John Temple, the British consul general. Mistaking "Sir John" for "surgeon," they ransacked his home.

That afternoon the mob converged on the jail to chant threats against the physicians and medical students who had found asylum behind bars. Voices roared, "Bring out your doctors! Bring out your doctors!" Frenzied citizens tore down a fence surrounding the jail, smashed its windows, and battered its stout oak doors. They screamed that they would kill every doctor in town. Up scurried Mayor Duane and other officials to plead with the mob, only to be howled down. The mayor then called for the militia. A dozen helmeted musket-carrying militiamen arrived on the double, but the maddened throng drove them back down Broadway under a shower of stones and brickbats. The mayor sent for reinforcements. Eighteen more militiamen responded, faltered, and fell back.

Now the panic-stricken doctors and students at the jail windows hammered at hands trying to drag them to their death. All was turmoil, noise, madness. Alexander Hamilton tried to reason with the mob, but he may as well have debated with a hailstorm. The governor stumbled over his own sword and hurt himself. John Jay, the dignified Secretary of Foreign Affairs, was bashed on the head with a rock. Baron Friedrich Von Steuben, inspector general of the army under Washington, bellowed like a Prussian drillmaster, but without effect.

The mayor, shouting to make himself heard, ordered out a troop of regular soldiers, who marched toward the rioters. Reluctant to shed blood, Duane hesitated about commanding them to fire. More bricks and stones arched through the air. One laid open the baron's scalp. As he fell, he screamed, "Fire, Duane! Fire!" The mayor barked an order. Muskets belched. Bodies slumped to earth. Groans soured the afternoon. Five persons were killed, and about eight wounded. Before a second volley could be fired, the rest of the crowd scattered.

After quiet had been restored, the beleaguered doctors and students were slipped out of prison and sent to the country for a time. The next year the state legislature passed the first American law regulating the practice of anatomy. Doctors could experiment on the bodies of executed murderers, arsonists, and burglars, but the corpses of respectable citizens had to be left alone. In 1791 New York Hospital opened with eighteen patients; but for years thereafter the place was regarded as a chamber of horrors, and because many mistrusted physicians, people turned to quack remedies.

Meantime, the new federal Constitution was ratified by state after state—but not by New York. Tempers flared as Governor Clinton and his followers dragged their heels. Federalists and Anti-Federalists vilified one another in newspapers and pamphlets, on street corners, and in social gatherings. Local Federalists threatened to secede the city from the state unless New York's constitutional convention took positive action. When New Hampshire became the ninth state to ratify the Constitution on June 21, 1788, New York had either to unite with the majority or to withdraw from the Union.

On July 23 townspeople staged a great parade, honoring the adoption of the Constitution. The procession began at 8 A.M. and lasted until 5 P.M., despite showers. Then 5,000 celebrants sat down to an open-air banquet in the Bowery. Three days later New York became the eleventh state to ratify the Constitution.

State legislators, however, were so avid for power, that they couldn't agree on a method for choosing Presidential electors. As a result, New York did not vote in the election that made George Washington our first President.

In 1789, the year Washington was inaugurated, Jacob Astor made his first real estate investment in Manhattan. Now an independent fur dealer who sold musical instruments as a sideline, Astor bought property between the Bowery and Elizabeth Street for forty-seven pounds. Later he picked up two adjoining lots. Shortly before his death, many years afterward, Astor was to wail, "Could I begin again, knowing what I know now, I would buy every foot of land on the island of Manhattan."

Chapter 14

THE CAPITAL OF THE NATION

GEORGE WASHINGTON was notified on April 14, 1789, of his election as the first President of the United States. He had hoped to end his days at Mount Vernon, preferring the privacy of home to the pageantry of power, but his sense of duty compelled him to accept the office. He declined to accept the salary that went with it. Washington, one of the richest men of his time, was so land-poor that he had to borrow money to pay his travel expenses to New York for the inauguration. On April 16 he left his estate and headed north.

His trip turned into a triumphal procession. Alexandria, Georgetown, Baltimore, Philadelphia, and Trenton—all greeted him with high honors. And in a ceremony of exceeding splendor Washington was received in New York on April 23.

The nation's first Presidential mansion stood at 3 Cherry Street just east of the present City Hall; today the site is occupied by one of the granite supports of the Brooklyn Bridge. The house had been erected in 1770 by Walter Franklin, a merchant, for whom nearby Franklin Square was named. When Franklin died in 1780, the house passed to his son-in-law, Samuel Osgood of Massachusetts, whom Washington made our first Postmaster General. Osgood rented the house and its contents to the President-elect for 900 pounds a year.

New Yorkers called Osgood's house The Palace. Actually, it was a rather modest square brick building three stories high with a row of five windows across the front. Furthermore, it wasn't in Manhattan's fashionable residential area, then near Wall and Broad streets. Its ceilings were so low that a lady's headdress of ostrich feathers once touched the candles in a chandelier and burst into flame. One wall of the drawing room held a large portrait of Louis XVI in his state robes, a gift to Washington from the French king. The President-elect had eighteen servants, some clad in red and white livery. Although he had rejected a salary, he accepted $25,000 a year for expenses.

His inauguration was scheduled for Thursday, April 30, 1789. At dawn that great day the skies were overcast. Soon, though, the sun came out. The city's population of 30,000 was swollen by visitors from all parts of the Union. Private houses overflowed with guests, hotels were jammed, and strangers slept in tents hastily erected in fields and lots.

That morning all were jolted awake by gunfire heralding the occasion. Donning holiday attire, the people breakfasted on bacon, meat pastries, fish, cheese, and bread and jam, washing all this down with ale. Into town jogged mounted farmers, who nodded at grooms rubbing down horses and oiling harnesses. Packet boats brought multitudes down Long Island Sound and the Hudson River. The Brooklyn-Manhattan ferry was packed. Standing at the rails and gazing at the waterfront, passengers counted 100 ships rocking at anchor. Then, lifting their eyes, they stared at strange flags fluttering from the roofs of foreign legations.

Business was suspended for the day. By 8:30 A.M. the streets had begun to fill up, and men and boys climbed onto the roofs of buildings near City Hall. This two-story building, with its central cupola, slanting roofs and four thin chimneys, was now known as Federal Hall because Mayor Richard Varick had lent it to Congress.

At 9 A.M. church bells summoned people to pray for George Washington. Soon afterward John Adams rode into town. Two days previously the crusty Massachusetts lawyer had been sworn in as Vice-President. Adams felt peevish. There had been eleven candidates for Vice-President, and he hadn't received enough votes to satisfy him. About the same time James Madison, the frail Virginian who considered Adams vain and gauche, emerged from his lodgings at 19 Maiden Lane.

About 10:30 A.M. Senators and Representatives, still arguing about how to address the new Chief Executive, drifted into Federal Hall. By noon they had taken their seats, the Representatives on the first floor and the Senators on the second. John Adams annoyed some Senators with his fussy questions, such as: "Gentlemen, I wish for the direction of the Senate. The President will, I suppose, address the Congress. How shall I behave?" After a brief discussion a joint Congressional committee went to Washington's home to escort him to Federal Hall. The delegation, headed by Senator Ralph Izard of South Carolina, reached the mansion at 12:30 P.M.

The solemn-faced men found Washington clad in a brown suit of homespun broadcloth, presented to him by a Hartford mill. Washington usually wore imported silk, but that day he chose an American product to encourage domestic manufacturing. His somewhat drab appearance was relieved by white silk stockings, metal buttons embossed with eagles, cuff buttons studded with thirteen stars, and a sword encased in a white leather scabbard. Washington's powdered wig was caught behind in a silk bag.

Now he bowed to the committee members. Senator Izard announced that Congress was ready to receive him. Washington bowed again, took his cocked hat from an aide, and walked outdoors. A waiting crowd cheered as the tall, stately Virginian stepped into a cream-colored coach, decorated with cupids holding festoons of flowers in their pink hands. Hitched to the carriage were four superb horses, their prancing legs rippling in elongated shadows over cobblestones. A liveried postilion mounted the near horse, and two uniformed coachmen climbed into their rear seats.

The order of march had been carefully planned. Details were overseen by six mounted masters of ceremonies, led by Colonel Morgan Lewis. After surveying everything critically, Lewis flashed a signal, and the procession moved south to band music. During the half-mile ride to Federal Hall, Washington sat erect, his lips tight over his wooden teeth, his blue-gray eyes masking his emotions, now and then bowing stiffly to shouting spectators massed along the streets.

Arriving at the Capitol, Washington stepped from his coach and was ushered inside. Surrounded by dignitaries, he walked to the second floor and entered the Senate chamber, a room forty feet square and fifteen feet high. The arched blue ceiling glittered with a sun and thirteen stars. The chamber held several fireplaces and eight large windows, four of them opening on a southern balcony.

Senator Izard escorted Washington down the main aisle and formally introduced him to Vice-President Adams. Adams asked Washington to be seated. The President settled in a crimson damask-covered chair. Adams had prepared a little speech, but in this tense moment he couldn't remember what he wanted to say. After an awkward silence Adams presented Washington to the assemblage and said, "Sir, the Senate and the House of Representatives of the United States are ready to attend you to take the oath required by the Constitution, which will be administered by the chancellor of the state of New York."

Washington replied, in a low voice, "I am ready to proceed."

Everyone rose. The chief notables led Washington out of the Senate chamber onto the balcony fronting on Wall Street and facing south down Broad Street. Alexander Hamilton watched from a window of his home at 33 Wall Street. The moment Washington appeared on the balcony, a roar welled from the waiting multitude. He bowed three times, sat down in a chair, and, overcome with emotion, dropped his head into his hands. The crowd hushed. Chancellor Robert R. Livingston, a red-headed man wearing black robes, asked if he was ready to take the oath of office. Washington nodded.

But no Bible could be found in Federal Hall. Livingston, grand master of the New York Masons, hurriedly sent a messenger to a nearby Masonic lodge to fetch one. When the Bible arrived, it was put on a crimson cushion held by Samuel Otis, secretary of the Senate. Otis was so short that his head barely showed above the Bible. Washington stood up, his deep-set eyes scanning the packed streets and crowded roofs. Again the spectators cheered. Washington placed his big right hand on his chest in mute and humble acknowledgment. Then, gently, unwaveringly, his hand came down on the open Bible. Fixing his eyes on Chancellor Livingston, he repeated the words: "I do solemnly swear that I will faithfully execute the office of the President of the United States and will, to the best of my ability, preserve, protect, and defend the Constitution of the United States." Then he didn't wait for Otis to lift the Bible to his lips but leaned down and kissed it. As he straightened up, he murmured, "So help me, God!"

"It is done!" cried Livingston with tears in his eyes. "Long live George Washington, President of the United States!"

The crowd took up the chant: "Long live George Washington, President of the United States!" An American flag rippled up a flagpole on Federal Hall, church bells bonged, the Battery cannon roared, a fifteen-gun salute thundered from a Spanish warship in the harbor, and a wave of cheers crashed against the great man himself. Livingston was so choked with emotion that he could only wave his hat. Like him, some spectators, cheeks frozen with ecstasy, eyes misting, and throats hardening, merely flourished their hats over their heads. Others shouted themselves hoarse. Later several people said that they could die happy, having seen George Washington sworn in as President. Overpowered by the thunderous ovation, Washington's granite will almost cracked. He swallowed hard, stood briefly in trembling dignity, bowed solemnly, and then withdrew inside the Senate chamber.

After fumbling through his inaugural address, he was escorted to nearby St. Paul's Chapel to pray. By an irony of fate, at almost the same moment George III entered St. Paul's Church in London to offer thanks for the return of his sanity. During his recent period of mental confusion the king had muttered over and over again, "I shall never lay on my last pillow in peace and quiet as long as I remember my American colonies."

Because Washington found the Cherry Street house too small for his needs and too far out of town, he moved. For the second executive mansion he chose the finest private building in town, the four-story McComb House at 39 Broadway. On the sidewalk just outside this brick dwelling a fateful decision was made.

Congress was deadlocked on two issues: Should the federal government pay state debts incurred during the war, and where should the nation's permanent capital be located? As sectional rivalries thickened, these questions became intertwined. Northern states, with the largest debts, favored the assumption of state debts by the federal government. Southern states, most of them solvent, opposed the plan. Northern states wanted the capital in the North. Southern states wanted it in the South.

Secretary of the Treasury Alexander Hamilton, leader of the Federalists, advocated a strong central government. He felt that assumption of state debts would establish the nation's credit and force creditors to look to the federal government for payment, thus winning their support of the new nation at the expense of the states. If the federal government took over all debts, then it must get all revenues. Secretary of State Thomas Jefferson, leader of the Democratic-Republicans, felt that federal authority was already too great. As a Southerner, he wanted the nation's capital located farther south—say, on the banks of the Potomac River.

One day when Jefferson was about to enter Washington's house, he was stopped by Hamilton. Jefferson was so tall that he was known as Long Tom. Hamilton was so short that he was called the Little Lion. The oddly matched pair locked arms and walked back and forth for half an hour, discussing the issues. Hamilton, the New Yorker, warned Jefferson, the Virginian, that the nation might fall unless a compromise was reached. Jefferson agreed. They worked out a deal: Hamilton agreed to lobby for a Southern capital if Jefferson solicited Southern votes for assumption of state debts. The fate of the national capital was decided on a sidewalk of New York.

Philadelphia was chosen as a temporary capital until a new federal city could be built on the Potomac. On April 12, 1790, Congress met for the last time in New York, and on April 30 George Washington left the city, never to return.

Having consolidated all war debts, Congress now issued $80,000,-000 in government stocks. There was a scattered market for these securities, as well as for the shares of banks and insurance firms then being created. But trading was unorganized, being carried on in various coffeehouses, auction rooms, and offices. People were reluctant to invest unless they knew that they could sell their holdings whenever they chose. A group of merchants and auctioneers decided to do something about the situation. On May 17, 1792, twenty-four of them met under a buttonwood tree at 68 Wall Street and drew up an agreement that laid the foundation for the New York Stock Exchange. Antwerp had got its exchange in 1460; Paris, in 1726; and London, in 1773.

No longer the federal seat, New York still offered much to interest its citizens. Workmen leveled the ruins of the Battery fort erected in

1626. A second Trinity Church arose on the site of the first fire-stricken building. Governors Island was transformed from a brambled wilderness into a picnic resort. The city's first country club, the Belvedere, went up on a block now bounded by Montgomery, Clinton, Cherry, and Monroe streets.

Less than a month after Washington's inauguration, the New York branch of the St. Tammany Society had been reorganized as the Tammany Society or the Columbian Order. Named for a legendary Indian chief, called Tammany, and ostensibly created for fraternal purposes, it was in truth a counterbalance to the Society of the Cincinnati, founded six years earlier. The Cincinnati consisted of officers of the Continental army; membership was handed down to eldest male descendants. Tammany hoped to oppose this hereditary aristocratic society. At first Tammany took no prominent part in politics, but over the years it developed into the most powerful and ruthless political group in the nation.

Under Tammany auspices the city's first Columbus Day celebration was held on October 12, 1792. A gubernatorial campaign almost resulted in civil war in the city. Yellow fever struck repeatedly, hypnotism proved ineffectual against it, and some of the thousands of victims were buried in symbolic yellow sheets. A tornado slammed into town like a wet bullwhip. The first mental patient was admitted into New York Hospital. Bellevue Hospital for contagious diseases, later becoming perhaps the best-known hospital in the nation, was established on the East River three miles north of Wall Street. Enlightened people denounced slavery. Business boomed, and Broadway lots brought ever higher prices. In 1793 houses were numbered systematically for the first time.

In 1794, as thirty-one-year-old Jacob Astor slogged through upper New York and Canada buying furs, Cornelius Vanderbilt was born on Staten Island. His great-great-great-grandfather, a poor farmer named Jan Aertson, had left the village of Bilt, in Holland, to emigrate to the New World in 1640. The big bawling baby born on May 27, 1794, near the Kill Van Kull, on Staten Island, was christened Cornelius Van Derbilt. In time the last name evolved into Vanderbilt, and after Cornelius had become a shipping magnate, everyone called him Commodore. Only two years after his birth an event that partially shaped his life occurred here.

A Connecticult Yankee, named John Fitch, had built the first steamboat ever to carry a human being. On August 27, 1787, this craft plied up and down the Delaware River at three or four miles an hour, propelled by twelve big wooden paddles. The next year Fitch got a patent for the application of steam to navigation. By 1796 he was ready to try out his fifth boat in New York.

For his experiment Fitch chose the sixty-foot-deep Collect, or Fresh Water Pond. One summer day spectators gathered under the hickory and chestnut trees fringing the sheer cliffs of the Pond and watched as the tall, lanky Fitch made ready. Stepping into his eighteen-foot yawl, he jackknifed his long legs under him and tended his iron pot of a boiler, while a lad stood in the stern and steered with an oar. The parasol-twirling ladies and cane-swinging men were witnessing a historic event, for this marked the first time a steamboat was propelled by a screw propellor.

Although Fitch's experiment was a success, he could get no backers to finance him. His pioneering boat was abandoned on the shore of the Collect, where it decayed and was carried away, piece by piece, by poor children in need of fuel. Discouraged by lack of recognition, Fitch killed himself two years later.

People sought more lasting entertainment, but the John Street Theatre, the only one in town, had become old and shabby and altogether too small for the city's expanding population. On May 5, 1795, the cornerstone was laid for the Park Theatre, America's first outstanding playhouse. Located on Park Row north of Ann Street and east of City Hall Park, it was as elegant and beautiful as any London theater of the day, cost $130,000, and seated 1,200 spectators. Managers Lewis Hallam and John Hodgkinson opened it on January 29, 1798, with their production of Shakespeare's *As You Like It.* During the premiere, as was the custom, gentlemen sat with their hats on. In 1808 Stephen Price bought the majority interest in the management and inaugurated the policy of importing foreign players. His emphasis on using one celebrated actor in every play resulted in the birth of the star system and in the decline of stock companies.

The Park Theatre was designed by Joseph and Charles Mangin, refugee brothers from France's Reign of Terror. Another Frenchman then living in New York was Louis Philippe. Proficient in geography and mathematics, this genial and simple man taught school here to support himself while in exile. His lodgings were modest and small. Whenever he entertained, at least half his guests had to perch on his bed because there weren't enough chairs to go around. After returning to his homeland, Louis Philippe served as the Citizen King of France from 1830 to 1848.

New York's lack of good drinking water and the belief that brackish water spread yellow fever gave sly Aaron Burr a chance he sought. A lawyer, who shared with Alexander Hamilton the cream of the local law practice, Burr was politically ambitious. He wanted to found a bank as a stepping-stone to political power. However, the two city banks already in existence were controlled by Federalists, who tried to stop the state legislature from granting other bank charters.

In August, 1799, late in the legislature's session, Burr introduced a bill to create the Manhattan Company to supply the city with pure water. On the face of it, this was a worthy civic measure, so few lawmakers bothered to read the full text. Had they done so, they would have found a provision that "the surplus capital of the company may be employed in any way not inconsistent with the laws and Constitution of the United States or the State of New York." Actually, the bill created a bank, not a water supply company.

To maintain his charter, Burr had to go through the motions of improving the city's water. He sank a well near Broadway just north of the present Spring Street and laid a few miles of wooden pipes under the main streets. About the only use ever made of this well was to hide the body of a beautiful girl who had been murdered.

Gulielma Elmore Sands was a pert twenty-two-year-old, who lived in a rooming house on Greenwich Street not far from the Hudson River. On December 22, 1799, eight days after the death of George Washington, her disappearance set the stage for the city's first noted murder mystery. A few days later her remains were found in Burr's well.

Suspicion fell on her fiancé, a gay blade, named Levi Weeks. His rich uncle retained an able battery of lawyers, including Alexander Hamilton and Aaron Burr. The jurors pondered just four minutes and then declared Weeks not guilty. With this, the dead girl's landlady turned to Hamilton and cried, with venom unbecoming a Quaker, "If thee dies a natural death, then there is no justice in heaven!" Four years later Burr killed Hamilton in a duel.

Chapter 15

THE HAMILTON-BURR DUEL

AT THE OPENING of the nineteenth century Chicago didn't even exist. Boston, once America's largest city, had slipped to third place. New York was creeping up on Philadelphia, now the nation's most populous city. Nearly half a million settlers had pushed to the far side of the Allegheny Mountains, and Philadelphia remained the gateway to the West. A German visitor commented, "If Philadelphia should become extinct, everybody in New York would rejoice, and vice versa. New York is the vilest of cities, write the Philadelphia journalists. In New York they speak no better of Philadelphia."

New York was part rustic, part urban. Blackberries grew on Bleecker Street, and a glass chandelier dangled from the vaulted dome of the Park Theatre. At the foot of Greenwich Street fishermen hauled nets onto the beach, while gentlemen and ladies promenaded on fashionable Wall Street. The town had grown north of the Battery a distance of only about one mile, with gardens and vacant lots interspersed among the dwellings.

There remained the inefficient charm of the narrow and crooked streets which followed early footpaths, but Broadway was straight and lined with poplars. An English traveler, noting Broadway's maximum width of seventy feet, compared it favorably with Oxford Street in London. Between Murray and Canal streets the Broadway hills were graded, and the roadbed was lowered twenty-three feet at one site. In the main, Broadway rose gently northward, and pedestrians strolling south could still see the Upper Bay and even down to the Narrows. In the north, Broadway ended at what today is Astor Place, where it ran into a fence marking the southern boundary of a farm, owned by Captain Robert R. Randall, the rich son of a privateer.

The Bowery remained a dusty country road lined with quaint Dutch cottages, and boys stole peaches from the orchard left by Peter Stuyvesant. Another Kissing Bridge spanned a small creek at the present intersection of Fiftieth Street and Second Avenue. The Boston Post Road turned eastward below Madison Square and bent its crooked way to Harlem. It cost four cents to cross from Brooklyn to Manhattan on horse ferries, small craft moved by paddle wheels, which were turned by four horses trudging around a shaft on the boats. Inns were crowded, and as many as eight guests slept in a single room.

Everyone's ears were assaulted by a cacophony of cries from chimney sweeps, milkmen, bellmen, and bakers. Old Negro mammies peddled mint, strawberries, radishes, and steaming hot yams. Hotcorn Girls wandered barefoot and shawl-wrapped through the streets, with cedar baskets in the crooks of their arms, crying in singsong voices, "Hot corn! Hot corn! Here's your lily-white corn! All you that's got money—poor me that's got none! Come buy my lily-white corn and let me go home!"

On solemn and dreary Sundays heavy chains were strung across streets near churches to keep away noisy traffic. At dinner tables people were beginning to use forks with four tines, instead of the two-prong and three-prong kinds. Men who sympathized with the radicals of Paris struggled into the queer trousers that had become the badge of the democrat, pantaloons so long that they reached armpits. Fashions became ever more extravagant. Dandies brushed their hair from the back toward the front, looking as though they had walked backward into a hurricane.

New York State had developed into a grazing and dairy area, and cowboys rounded up cattle not far from the city. The Hessian fly, unwittingly brought in by mercenaries during the Revolution, blighted wheatfields and lowered the quality of New York's once-famous grain. Another unwanted import, the house rat, was multiplying annoyingly. A good dwelling rented for $350 a year. In the next 19 years John Jacob Astor was to invest an average of $35,000 a year in Manhattan real estate. Lotteries flourished, and business was good. Seamen groused because they were paid only $10 a month. Their anger might have sharpened had they known that the beautiful and talented actress Mrs. Robert Merry earned more than $100 a week performing at the Park Theatre.

One theater devotee, who stared at the statue of Shakespeare in the lobby, was Washington Irving, a seventeen-year-old with an oval face, chestnut hair, and blue-gray eyes. Born at 131 William Street, named for George Washington, and coiner of the phrase "the almighty dollar," Irving became the first American author of international renown. He hadn't yet heard of a six-year-old named Cornelius Van Derbilt, who was making poor marks in a school on Staten Island. Jacob Astor, now thirty-seven years old and worth $250,000, strode arrogantly into the Tontine Coffee House, where lesser men hastened to invite him to share a chunk of raw codfish and a glass of spirits. And an impressionable nine-year-old named Peter Cooper —later an inventor, manufacturer, philanthropist, and perhaps the best-loved man in New York—witnessed something in City Hall Park that he never forgot. Cooper later wrote:

> There I stood by and saw two men whipped at the whipping post, one a white man and the other a black man. The white man's back resembled, from his shoulders to his hips, just one bloody blister. The screams of that man will always remain in my memory. The scream of that man was perfectly frightful. He would scream, get a little lower down, and it seemed as if it was beyond his endurance.

Until the election of 1800 the first two Presidents of the United States, George Washington and John Adams, belonged to the Federalist party. Now Thomas Jefferson was the candidate of the Democratic-Republican party. Aaron Burr, a member of Jefferson's party, whipped the Tammany Society into a formidable political machine for the first time. Jefferson's supporters agreed with Tammany to let Burr become Jefferson's running mate. Thirty-nine young members of Tammany collectively bought a house and lot so that they could meet the property qualification to vote, but a court ruled their scheme illegal.

State legislatures named Presidential electors. New York was the pivotal state in the election. John Adams, running for reelection as a Federalist, got only sixty-five votes. Jefferson and Burr tied with seventy-three votes each. This threw the election into the House of Representatives. After much balloting Jefferson won. He became President, and Burr, the New Yorker, became Vice-President.

Jefferson believed that Burr had tried to win the Presidency for himself despite the arrangement with Tammany. The new President regarded Burr as "a crooked gun, or other perverted machine, whose aim or shot you could never be sure of." Alexander Hamilton found out differently. Not long after the inauguration Jefferson was visited in Washington by Matthew L. Davis, a Tammany sachem and a Burr henchman. Davis told the lanky Virginian to his face that he held the Presidency only because of Tammany's help. Jefferson listened intently. When Davis finished, the President flicked out a hand and caught a fly. Then, with the air of a professor, he asked the Tammany leader to note the remarkable disproportion between one part of the insect and its entire body. Getting the point, Davis returned to New York in a sour mood because he considered Jefferson an ingrate.

Burr agreed with Davis, but it was Alexander Hamilton, not Jefferson, whom Burr regarded as his chief rival. Fate had entwined the lives of Hamilton and Burr. Hamilton was the illegitimate son of a hot-blooded West Indian beauty and a handsome ne'er-do-well. Burr was wellborn, a grandson of the cool New England theologian Jonathan Edwards. Burr was one year older than Hamilton. In some ways the two men were much alike. Both had been officers during the Revolutionary War and had served on Washington's staff. Both had founded a bank and a newspaper. Both practiced law in New York and owned town houses and country estates just outside the city. They met socially, and Hamilton even lent money to Burr; but Hamilton considered Burr a dangerous politician. Hamilton had used his influence with Washington to prevent Burr's appointment as brigadier general. And, as Burr well knew, when the election had been thrown into the House of Representatives, Hamilton had lobbied against him and caused him to lose the Presidency. Burr bided his time, letting thoughts of Hamilton marinate in the brine of his resentment.

In 1802 the idea of building a bridge across the East River was proposed to the state legislature, only to meet with ridicule. This project was not realized until the opening of the Brooklyn Bridge eighty-one years later. With the growth of population, City Hall on Wall Street became inadequate, so in 1802 a prize was offered for the best design for a new building. The $350 prize was won by John McComb, Jr., a Scotsman, and Joseph Mangin, a Frenchman. It was Mangin who, with his brother, had designed the Park Theatre.

The site chosen for the new City Hall was the northern side of the little plain known in turn as the Commons, as the Fields, and, after its enclosure within a fence in 1785, as the Park. Not until 1871 was it legally established as City Hall Park, which it is today. It was a beautiful area shadow-dappled by elms, poplars, willows, and catalpas. In 1803 Mayor Edward Livingston laid the cornerstone for this third and present City Hall, the celebration continuing all that day of September 20 and far into the night.

The building's exterior, a gracious blend of French Renaissance and American Colonial design, was essentially Mangin's inspiration. McComb oversaw the interior details and the magnificent marble stairway. The copper roof was imported from England. City Hall was faced in white Massachusetts marble, varying in thickness from five to eighteen inches. Delivery of the stone posed many problems. McComb bribed political hacks who maintained roads, and he tested the bridges over which the marble had to pass.

The eastern, southern, and western sides of City Hall were covered with the white marble, but the city fathers decided to save $15,000 by using brownstone on the northern rear side. After all, the city lay south of the new building, and its back "would be out of sight to all the world." Obviously, nobody ever would build farther north.

The new edifice was not used until July 4, 1811, and wasn't fully completed until 1812. Having spent half a million dollars on it, New Yorkers hoped that their City Hall would become the most handsome structure in the world, and it indeed became the finest public building in America. At the time the Capitol at Washington, D.C., was still under construction.

Then there rose in New York another building less noble in design and purpose than City Hall. A fat butcher built an open-air bull-

baiting arena, seating 2,000 persons. A bull was led into this amphi-
theater and tied to an iron ring sunk into the ground. The rope was
long enough for the animal to run around in wide circles. Then bulldogs were set on the captive bull. Spectators bet on how many dogs
would be killed by the bull or how long the pack would need to tear
the beast to pieces. Sometimes a buffalo was substituted for the bull.

In 1804 a secession plot touched off a train of events that ended with
the most famous duel in the annals of the nation. Diehard New England Federalists were disgusted with President Jefferson. They connived to withdraw from the Union and set up a Northern Confederacy,
consisting of New England and New York. Federalist leader Alexander Hamilton was offered a role in the scheme. Even though his
party had differences with that of Jefferson, Hamilton never forgot
how once, on the sidewalk outside Washington's New York residence,
Jefferson had helped him maintain the Union. Now he turned thumbs-
down on the plot.

Then the plotters approached smart, ambitious, and bitter Aaron
Burr. Burr belonged to Jefferson's party and Jefferson had edged
him out of the Presidency. He got no federal patronage from Jefferson
or state patronage from Governor George Clinton. Burr was Vice-
President of the United States, true, but this did not satisfy him.
Aware of his discontent, the New England schemers made him a
proposal. If he ran for governor of New York, they would influence
their New York friends to vote for him. After his election he could
resign as Vice-President, lead New York State out of the Union, and
join it to the new confederacy. Then, as his reward, he would become
president of the new nation.

Too crafty to commit himself forthrightly to such an intrigue, Burr
did promise that if he were elected governor, he would guarantee an
administration "satisfactory to the Federalists." Political wheels began to turn. New York's leading Federalists met in an Albany tavern
to decide whether to nominate Burr, the Democratic-Republican, for
governor. Influenced by their New England friends, many were well
disposed toward him. But up rose Hamilton, Burr's nemesis, to read
a paper criticizing Burr. Hamilton convinced Federalist leaders that
Burr's nomination might lead to "dismemberment of the union."
Judge Morgan Lewis was chosen in preference to Burr. Every word
spoken by Hamilton was overheard by Burr's spies, hidden in an adjoining room of the tavern.

Denied the nomination by the Federalists, Burr also was rejected by the Democratic-Republicans. He ran as an independent candidate for governor and opened campaign headquarters on John Street. His followers, called Burrites, included most members of Tammany. Hamilton then threw all his political weight against Burr, split the Federalists, and caused Burr's defeat. Morgan Lewis became the new governor.

This was the last straw, Burr decided. Every time he tried to advance his career, he was blocked by Hamilton. So the Vice-President of the United States cold-bloodedly provoked the former Secretary of the Treasury into a duel. One June day, about two months after the election, into Hamilton's law office, at 58 Wall Street, strode William P. Van Ness, a young lawyer who was a personal friend and political associate of Burr's. Van Ness handed Hamilton a note from Burr, asking Hamilton to explain remarks that he had allegedly made about Burr. Two days later Hamilton replied in a way that Burr considered evasive. More notes passed back and forth. On June 27 Burr formally challenged Hamilton to a duel. Even though he opposed dueling, Hamilton accepted. The two antagonists were to meet on the field of honor at 7 A.M. on July 11, 1804.

Burr prepared by practicing with a pistol at his country estate. Hamilton, however, went about his business as usual, seeing clients and appearing in court. He did straighten out his affairs so that his wife and seven children would suffer less in the event of his death. Resolved not to fire at Burr, Hamilton wrote: "My religious and moral principles are strongly opposed to the practice of duelling, and it would ever give me pain to be obliged to shed the blood of a fellow-creature in a private combat forbidden by the laws."

Several people knew of the impending duel, but nobody tried to stop it. On July 4, one week in advance, Hamilton and Burr met at the annual banquet of the Society of the Cincinnati, which Hamilton had headed since Washington's death. The former army officers drank heartily, and Hamilton seemed as vivacious as usual. His friends asked him to sing his favorite ballad, called "The Drum." After a moment's hesitation Hamilton raised his voice in a solo. Burr seemed more silent than usual that day. As Hamilton began singing, Burr, elbows on a table, turned toward him, staring into the face of his opponent.

For their duel they chose a secluded spot at Weehawken, New Jersey, across the Hudson River due west of Manhattan's present Forty-second Street. About twenty feet above the water a little ledge was niched into a cliff. Six feet wide and thirty-six feet long, this grassy area was screened by cedars from boatmen below or pedestrians above. No footpath led to the spot. One got there only by boat and then by scrambling up rocks.

That historic morning Burr arrived before Hamilton, as prearranged. Burr was accompanied by his second, Van Ness, and by another friend, Matthew L. Davis, who had watched in disgust when Jefferson had lectured him about a fly. Davis stayed in the boat that brought them to the spot. Burr and Van Ness picked their way up to the ledge, doffed their coats, and began clearing away bushes and limbs of trees so that a big enough opening could be made. They were still engaged in this work when, a few moments before seven o'clock, Hamilton arrived in another boat with his second, Judge Nathaniel Pendleton; Dr. David Hosack; and a boatman. The physician and boatman remained below as Hamilton and the judge climbed to the dueling ground. Burr pulled on his coat and bowed to Hamilton, who returned the courtesy. The seconds exchanged greetings.

Then Van Ness and Pendleton drew lots to determine which should decide where the combatants must stand. Pendleton won. Again they drew lots to decide which should give the word to fire. Again Pendleton won. The two seconds carefully stepped off twelve paces. Pendleton placed Hamilton at one end. Van Ness stationed Burr at the other. A case holding a brace of dueling pistols was opened. The weapons were loaded under the gaze of the rivals. Pendleton gave one to Hamilton, and Van Ness handed the other to Burr. Then Van Ness stepped back out of the line of fire.

Pendleton solemnly explained to the two principals the rules already agreed on. When he cried, "Pre*sent!*" they were to raise their pistols and fire at will. Now Pendleton stepped back. Both combatants wore hats, although it was a bright warm summer morning. The dipping of breeze-stirred leaves spilled shadows into the hollows of their tight cheeks. All was silence except for the drone of a flower-flirting bee nearby and the soft *slap-chunk* of little waves on the rocks below.

"Gentlemen, preee-ee-*sent!*"

At Pendleton's command Burr raised his right arm, slowly and deliberately, took aim, and fired. A slug slammed into the right side of Hamilton's belly a little above the hip. His muscles contracted, pulling him up onto his toes. He spun to the left—oddly enough—and fell on his face. As he fell, his fingers tightened in a spasm, squeezing off a shot from his pistol, the bullet ripping through the limb of a cedar tree above and to the left of Burr. After a moment of brittle silence Burr advanced toward Hamilton with regret showing on his face, but after one look he turned away silently.

Pendleton shouted for Dr. Hosack. The physician scrambled up the rocks. Van Ness quickly opened an umbrella and held it in front of Burr's face so that Hosack would not be able to testify that he had seen the Vice-President. Then Burr and his second descended the cliff and boarded their boat. The doctor found Hamilton half sitting on the earth and half supported in Pendleton's arms. Hamilton looked up, recognized Hosack, murmured, "This is a mortal wound, doctor," and fainted. The doctor ripped open his coat and tore away his shirt. Placing his fingers on Hamilton's wrist, he could feel no pulse. He laid his hand over Hamilton's heart but could detect no movement. Hosack and Pendleton picked up the bleeding man and carried him laboriously down the rocks to the boat, where the boatman helped ease him into the craft.

They shoved off from the Jersey shore, heading for the Manhattan waterfront estate of Hamilton's friend Samuel Bayard. The doctor rubbed Hamilton's lips, temples, neck, and wrists with spirits of hartshorn, or ammonia. When they had rowed about fifty yards, Hamilton began to breathe perceptibly. He sighed. His deep-set eyes fluttered open, and he stared about vacantly. Between long breaths he murmured, "Pendleton knows that I did not intend to fire at him."

Brought back to Manhattan, Hamilton lingered in great agony. As he lay on his deathbed that night, Tammany members celebrated at Martling's Long Room, toasting the victorious Aaron Burr, who had shut himself up in the library of his country place. But after Hamilton had died at half past two the following afternoon, the men of Tammany found it expedient to take part in the public mourning. The funeral was one of the most impressive in the city's history. Alexander Hamilton's death drove his twenty-year-old daughter insane, converted Aaron Burr into a social leper, and resulted in widespread revulsion against dueling. Hamilton was buried in Trinity Churchyard.

When Washington Irving was a boy, he had gone to a school at 37 Partition (now Fulton) Street run by an old soldier, named Benjamin Romaine. This was a private institution, as were all other New York schools. They were maintained by churches. No education was given to the children of unaffiliated parents. Obviously, something had to be done, or many of the new generation would grow up in ignorance. On April 9, 1805, the state legislature passed an act incorporating a free school society.

Public School No. 1 opened on Chatham Street on April 28, 1807. Before the end of the year 150 pupils were enrolled. The educational system first used here was devised by an Englishman, named Joseph Lancaster. The schoolmaster taught pupils, who in turn taught children in lower grades. This meant that fewer schoolmasters were needed, an economy appreciated by the rich. After all, a part of the excise duties was now being used to support the schools.

Besides education, the city fathers were concerned about the growth of population. In 1807 the state legislature named a three-man commission to plot Manhattan's undeveloped land. Because the chief engineer was John Randall, Jr., this first real city plan was called the Randall Plan. From today's East Houston Street northward to 155th Street Randall laid out a gridiron or rectangular system of north-south avenues crossed at right angles by east-west streets.

The Randall Plan made no allowance for the shape of the land, preferring to iron out Manhattan's hills by force instead of by blending man's needs with nature's gifts. It was too late to do anything about Greenwich Village's streets, which cut diagonally southwest to northeast. However, there was serious talk about abolishing Broadway altogether, for people believed that the city's business life would center on the Boston Post Road. Almost no space was allotted for public parks, an oversight that later cost the city millions of dollars.

Undeveloped land was divided into lots 100 feet in depth. As often happens during a land boom, householders put exorbitant values on houses in the path of a proposed street. When the city wouldn't pay their prices, they set dogs on public surveyors. One new avenue was laid out on a line that cut in half the kitchen of a vegetable woman; she and her neighbors bombarded surveyors with cabbages and artichokes.

Citizens laughed at the commissioners for laying out the city as far north as the wilderness of 155th Street. The officials replied:

> It may be a subject of merriment that the commissioners have provided space for a greater population than is collected at any spot this side of China. . . . It is not improbable that considerable numbers may be collected at Harlem before the high hills to the

south of it shall be built upon as a city, and it is improbable that *for centuries to come* [italics added] the grounds north of Harlem Flat will be covered with homes. . . .

As a matter of fact, just before World War II a total of 3,871 persons lived in a single Harlem block. If all Americans had lived together that closely, the nation's whole population would have fitted into one-half the area of New York City.

In 1807 New York was nicknamed Gotham. It seems that three young men—Washington Irving, his brother William, and James Kirke Paulding—wrote essays poking fun at the foibles of their fellow townsmen. This wasn't difficult because manners were ridiculously formal. For example, one gentleman always spoke of *Mr.* Julius Caesar and *Mr.* Homer. This jumble of essays was called *Salmagundi,* meaning a hash made of minced veal, pickled herrings, anchovies, and onions served with lemon juice and oil. After they had appeared in newspapers, the *Salmagundi* squibs were published in a yellow-backed pamphlet small enough to be carried in a lady's purse. Eight hundred copies were sold the first day of publication, and this started the Knickerbocker school of literature.

New Yorkers chuckled, even though the essays mocked them. The authors dubbed the city Gotham because of something that had happened in the English village of Gotham in the thirteenth century. King John planned to visit Gotham and buy a castle there. The villagers, realizing that they would have to maintain this estate, decided to act like idiots and scare away the king. John was amazed to see them trying to rake the moon's reflection out of a pond, joining hands around a thornbush to keep a cuckoo from flying away, and doing other foolish things. Wanting no part of such madmen, the king decided not to settle in Gotham. The villagers later chortled that "more fools pass through Gotham than remain in it."

The year of *Salmagundi* also produced the first New York guidebook. Written by Dr. Samuel Latham Mitchill, its pomposity amused and irritated Washington Irving. He was surprised to learn how few New Yorkers realized that the city once had been called New Amsterdam. Irving, who was making no progress as a lawyer, consulted local libraries and in twenty-two months wrote *A History of New York From the Beginning of the World to the End of the Dutch Dynasty.* Because he pretended that it had been written by an antiquarian named Diedrich Knickerbocker, his work became known as

Knickerbocker's History of New York, and it also gave the city its symbol—Father Knickerbocker. The word means baker of marbles.

As New York became a literary center, the age of steam navigation began. For twenty years inventors had experimented with a variety of steamboats, and Robert Fulton, son of an Irish immigrant, learned from all of them. Unlike the luckless Fitch, Fulton got financial backing from wealthy Robert R. Livingston, who had become minister to France after he had sworn in Washington as President. Fulton and Livingston met in Paris. The inventor ordered an engine built in England, and when he got back to New York, he found it lying on a wharf near the Battery. He had it hauled to Charles Brown's shipyard on the East River, and there he oversaw the construction of his steamboat.

The *Clermont* was 150 feet long and 13 feet wide. To play it safe, Fulton equipped her with a mast and sail, although she had a huge paddle wheel on each side. After she had been finished, the *Clermont* was towed to the foot of Amos (now West Tenth) Street on the west side of Manhattan.

One August morning in 1807 Fulton prepared to cast off for the most memorable steamship trip in history. The forty-two-year-old inventor was a reserved man with a solemn face; he was tall and slender, with large dark eyes, a high forehead, and curly brown hair. A crowd of skeptics gathered on the banks of the Hudson. Uneasy passengers aboard the ship shifted their weight from one foot to another. At last the paddle wheels stirred the water into white foam, and the ship began to move. Then she stopped. From the shore arose murmurs of "I told you so!" Fulton asked the spectators and passengers to be patient for half an hour.

After he had adjusted the balky engine, he again gave the signal to cast off. Now the paddle wheels not only turned but also kept moving and, since they were uncovered, threw up torrents of water, drenching the passengers. The *Clermont* was fueled by pine knots that cast sparks and ashes out of the skinny smokestack. Warding off this fiery deluge, the passengers looked as fearful as though they were crossing the river Styx. As the hissing thumping black monster crept up the Hudson, crews of passing river sloops fell to their knees to pray, cows along the shore stuck their tails into the air and bucketed into woods, and a farmer ran home to tell his wife that he had seen "the devil on his way to Albany in a sawmill."

The first stop for fuel was at Clermont, Livingston's estate 110 miles above New York; later the ship was named for this place. She made the 150-mile trip to Albany at an average of 5 miles an hour, thus completing the first real voyage ever made by a steam vessel anywhere in the world. Fulton and Livingston won a monopoly of steamboat travel in New York waters, but soon other men built and operated steamships elsewhere.

When Fulton had been in Paris, he had presented his idea for a steamboat to Napoleon. The emperor had been so impressed that he had ordered his marine minister to discuss the matter with Fulton, but nothing had been done for three years. By then it was too late. After Fulton's success on the Hudson, Napoleon sighed: "I should have been master of the world, but those idiots of savants made fun of his invention!"

Napoleon's ambition kept Europe in bloody turmoil the first decade of the nineteenth century. England and its allies—but especially England—kept him from achieving his desires. Eager to make any sacrifice for "six hours' control of that wet ditch"—the English Channel—Napoleon sold Louisiana to the United States for money to invade England. The invasion never came off, but the headlong clash between France and Great Britain was felt in America.

Neither European power paid much attention to the rights of neutrals, and the United States was by far the most important neutral. As France and England produced war matériel and fed huge armies, the demand for American produce soared, and the United States merchant marine multiplied. Each nation tried to keep American goods away from the other. Both were high-handed in halting American ships to search them. And the British impressed American seamen. As tensions mounted, it became apparent that something had to give.

Chapter 16

JOHN JACOB ASTOR
FOOLS THE PRESIDENT

TOWARD five o'clock on the afternoon of April 25, 1806, an American coastal sloop, called the *Richard*, was approaching New York after a trip from Brandywine Creek in Pennsylvania. She reached a point two miles from Sandy Hook and a quarter mile off the Jersey shore. Suddenly three cannon shots were fired at her. They came from the *Leander*, one of three British warships that had been lying off New York, stopping coasters, searching merchantmen, seizing ships, and capturing American sailors. The first shot splashed into the water forty yards off the *Richard*'s bow. The second arched directly over her. The third ripped off the head of John Pierce, the *Richard*'s helmsman.

When New Yorkers heard that the British had killed an American within sight of shore, they flared with anger. The previous day the *Leander*'s purser had come to town and bought food for his ship. Now that Pierce was dead, the outraged citizens seized two provision-laden boats at the wharf. Three other food-carrying craft had started down the bay, but swift American vessels overhauled them at Sandy Hook and brought them back to the city. All of the *Leander*'s captured supplies were loaded into ten carts and dragged by a noisy crowd to almhouses, where the food was given to the poor.

The body of the murdered sailor was exposed to view on Burling Slip, then in the Tontine Coffee House, and finally in City Hall. Thousands seeing it muttered threat's against England. The council denounced Pierce's death and the unprovoked attack by a British warship, voted a public funeral, asked ships in the harbor to half-mast their flags, and requested church sextons to toll the bells.

Although the beheading of the American seaman aroused less excitement outside New York, President Jefferson ordered the *Leander* to leave local waters. This did not end the friction. First the British and then the French, by a series of unilateral orders and decrees, cracked down on American commerce so harshly that the entire nation suffered. Still, both combatants sought American goods. During the first decade of the century American tonnage more than doubled, and American manufacturing boomed. The construction of the new ships increased the demand for sailors, whose wages rose from eight to twenty-four dollars a month. Because this was more than British seamen were paid, they deserted from every privateer and frigate entering American ports. In New York most English vessels left the harbor shorthanded.

This provoked British authorities into ever more brazen violations of the rights of American ships and sailors. Tars were dragged aboard English ships while clutching American citizenship papers. Moreover, despite Jefferson's order to the *Leander*, fleets of British frigates prowled the waters off New York, ambushed French privateers, and searched American ships for contraband goods and sailors.

Although most British and Americans abhorred the thought of open conflict, the two nations began drifting into a second war. Congress passed four major acts restricting shipping in the hope of avoiding a clash, but to no avail. The second of these measures was the famous Embargo Act. It outlawed all international trade to and from American ports. Jefferson felt that it would teach England and

France to honor neutral commerce. The ban later was extended to America's inland waters and land-borne commerce to halt the sky-rocketing trade with British Canada. Actually, the embargo hurt America more than it hurt any European power.

Congress passed the Embargo Act on December 22, 1807, and Jefferson signed it. A few minutes later express riders galloped out of Washington with instructions to port collectors at New York, Baltimore, and Philadelphia. One weary horseman clattered into New York at 5 A.M. and awakened the local port collector. The sleepy official was told to forbid the departure of any ship for any foreign port. Coming wide-awake, he rustled a printer out of bed, and by 7 A.M. handbills announcing the new law were being distributed in the streets of Manhattan.

It was like poking a stick into a beehive. People poured out of houses to fill the streets with humming confusion. Merchants, ship-owners, sailors, and other citizens thronged to the wharves. Those with vested interests wanted to put to sea before the new law could be enforced. By 8 A.M. a little fleet of half-laden half-manned ships had spread their sails and were beating down toward the Narrows. None had clearances. Apparently most got away, for the port collector didn't send his boats after them until ten o'clock.

Fearful that the embargo would ruin them, Americans mournfully dubbed it O Grab Me—"Embargo" spelled backward. Before long, shipping came to a halt as the federal government enforced the ban along the Atlantic seaboard. Business in New York almost ground to a halt. Unemployment rose. Some citizens even began to starve. Sailors, beached through no fault of their own, became angry. On January 9, 1808, they led a mob through the streets, some demonstrators carrying signs demanding work and bread. The seamen also petitioned the mayor "to provide some means for our subsistence."

A soup kitchen was set up, and work relief projects were instituted. Some of the unemployed got jobs building City Hall. Others were assigned to the Brooklyn Navy Yard, which the federal government had bought in 1801 from a shipbuilder, named John Jackson. Marshes were drained, and hills leveled. Earth from the cuts was dumped into the Collect, for this once-pure pond, thoughtlessly used as a garbage dump, had become so putrid that it needed to be filled in.

Jacob Astor didn't worry about relief projects. He was too busy scheming how to cheat the federal government and his competitors. Finally, he perfected his plan.

One day a Chinese presented himself to Dr. Samuel L. Mitchill, author of the city's first guidebook. Mitchill was also a professor of natural history, a United States Senator from New York, and a friend of President Jefferson's. Despite his eminence, he was considered deficient in common sense. The Chinese introduced himself as a merchant, named Punqua Wingchong. He said that he had been in New York for nine months attending to business. Now he wanted to go home to China because of pressing family matters, such as the rites connected with his grandfather's death. The American embargo made this impossible.

Mitchill sympathized with the plight of the honorable gentleman. On July 12, 1808, the doctor wrote a letter to President Jefferson introducing the bearer. Punqua Wingchong was now in Washington, said Mitchill, "to solicit the means of departure, in some way or other, to China; but he feels at the same time a strong desire to see the Chief Executive officer of the United States." By this time Jefferson had left Washington to visit his home at Monticello. The Chinese wrote the President there and enclosed Mitchill's letter. Jefferson was touched by the story. Besides, he thought that it might be wise for the administration to extend a courtesy that would be appreciated in the Celestial Court.

The President wrote to Secretary of the Treasury Albert Gallatin, recommending that Wingchong's request for a ship be granted. He enclosed a blank passport and urged the Secretary to "direct all the necessary details." Gallatin went to work. On what ship did the Chinese—now referred to as a mandarin—propose to sail to China? On the *Beaver*. And what did the honorable Chinese wish to take aboard ship? Well, besides his personal effects, his attendants, and their luggage, about $40,000 worth of merchandise, including furs. Gallatin knew that the *Beaver* was owned by Jacob Astor. In fact, Gallatin and Astor were close friends. Always the scrupulous public servant, Gallatin never mixed business with pleasure. Once Astor's name had crept into the affair, he had misgivings. Still, the President had asked him to do all he could, so on August 3 Gallatin forwarded the passport to New York's port collector and explained why the President was willing to make an exception to the embargo.

Then Punqua Wingchong, sleek in a silk coat gay with peacock buttons, shuffled up the gangway onto the 427-ton *Beaver* to take a cup of tea with her skipper. On August 13 the shipping column of the New York *Commercial Advertiser* printed this one-line announcement: "Yesterday the ship *Beaver*, Captain Galloway, sailed for China."

It was like splashing cold water onto a hot stove. People sizzled with indignation. Business-starved merchants and shippers, forbidden to dispatch theirs ships to foreign shores, denounced the affair as a hoax. One of them wrote Jefferson: "The great Chinese personage was no mandarin, not even a Hong Kong merchant, but a common Chinese dock loafer, smuggled out from China, who had departed from that country contrary to its laws, and would be saved from death on his return only by his obscure condition."

The President, embarrassed at becoming Astor's dupe, ignored the letter. Gallatin was upset because tongues were already wagging about his friendship with Astor. The Secretary wrote the President: "Had I any discretion as to the application itself, I would have hesitated; for I apprehend that there is some speculation at bottom; and every deviation from the general rule is considered favourtism [*sic*] and excites dissatisfaction."

But by now there was nothing anyone could do, for the fast-flying *Beaver* was far beyond the reach of any American patrol boat. On June 1, 1809, she returned to New York with a full cargo of chinaware, spices, silks, and tea. Because of the embargo, grocers clamored for tea, the Souchong brand fetching the price once asked for imperial gunpowder tea. Since the *Beaver* was the first ship from China in more than a year, Astor made a profit of $200,000 on her merchandise. This was his biggest single coup to date. He had gulled the President of the United States; hoodwinked his friend, the Secretary of the Treasury; outmaneuvered the New York port collector; and beaten New York businessmen who stuck to the law. Yes, Astor was proud of himself. He took part of the money and bought a huge farm stretching from Broadway to the Hudson River in what is now mid-Manhattan.

The same year, 1809, in New York, 1,300 men were jailed for no crime except that of having been ruined by the embargo Astor defied. The city looked like a wasteland. Waterfront streets were almost deserted. Grass grew on wharves. Ships were dismantled, their decks stripped and hatches battened down. Coffeehouses were nearly empty. Other buildings were shut or advertised for sale. The next year 1,050 New Yorkers were thrown into debtors' prison for debts of less than $25.

On March 1, 1809, in a face-saving gesture, Jefferson signed the

Nonintercourse Act, repealing the embargo and reopening trade with all nations except France and Great Britain. Three days later he was succeeded in the Presidency by his friend James Madison. Like his predecessor, Madison exhausted every effort to preserve peace, but in vain.

Jacob Astor had much to lose if war broke out. Among other things he owned a lucrative fur post, called Astoria, at the mouth of the Columbia River northwest of the present city of Portland, Oregon. One day in 1812 Astor got into a coach in New York and started for Washington to plead with Madison to maintain neutrality, but halfway there he heard that the President had signed a resolution declaring that the United States was at war with England. Astor turned around and headed home. He lost Astoria, worth $800,000. Astor could afford it. A few years later he was dealing in narcotics, writing a Constantinople merchant to "please send returns in Opium" for a consignment of 1,500 red-fox furs.

New Yorkers were divided on the issue of war. Despite the indignities suffered at the hands of England, many yearned for peace. The *Commercial Advertiser* printed this headline: "MOST AWFUL CALAMITY." A strong minority of merchant princes not only opposed the war but also openly proclaimed admiration for the enemy. Although they had lost ships to the British, they more than compensated for these losses by marine insurance and inflated profits from the goods they managed to bring to port. But while they sat safely at home and counted their gains, their hired seamen had jeopardized their freedom on the high seas. Sailors, eager to get even with the British for seizing 6,000 shipmates, roared with joy when war began.

At a mass meeting in City Hall Park it was resolved "to lay aside all animosity and private bickering, and aid the authorities in constructing fortifications." Senator Samuel L. Mitchill, for all his bumbling, got generous federal defense appropriations for New York. When the war started, the city contained four arsenals and two forts. One fort, known at first as the Southwest Battery, had been completed in 1807. Standing on a cluster of rocks a short distance from the southern tip of Manhattan, it had walls 8 feet thick, massive bolt-studded doors, and gun embrasures. The other fort, Castle Williams, located on Governors Island, had been finished in 1811. Called the Cheesebox because of its circular shape, it was 200 feet in diameter, with red sandstone walls 40 feet high and 8 feet thick.

These strongholds held artillery practice. Training their guns on an old hulk of a ship anchored in the Upper Bay about 1,000 yards distant, they blasted away for 2 hours. The Southwest Battery missed only 3 of the 40 rounds it fired, while Castle Williams scored all but 3 of the 30 shots it discharged.

This markmanship was comforting, but what was to prevent the British from slipping in via Long Island Sound and dropping down the East River or from launching a land attack from the north? Two more forts were erected at Hell Gate. A line of other forts, block-houses, and entrenchments was constructed across upper Manhattan, and still more forts were built in the offshore waters. Shipyards hummed, and within four months after the declaration of war twenty-six privateers were outfitted here.

Matthew L. Davis of Tammany Hall was now the army's commisary general. He called for bids to provision the New York forts. Boatmen vied for the contract in the hope of escaping military service, submitting outrageously low bids. Not so twenty-year-old Cornelius Van Derbilt, who had become the most ambitious boatman in the city. "Corneel," as he spelled his name, entered the highest bid of all —and got the contract. When Davis was questioned about letting the contract to the highest bidder, he growled about boatmen trying to escape duty by submitting absurd bids.

The tireless Van Derbilt profited greatly during the War of 1812. By day he ferried passengers back and forth between Manhattan and Staten Island. By night he supplied the forts with provisions.

Governor Daniel D. Tompkins, who also held the rank of major general, had called up the militia to protect the city. Among those summoned was twenty-two-year-old Peter Cooper, a frail and lanky lad, who was sent to Brooklyn to drill. This was a tedious chore. Besides, it took him away from his business when the country was short of clothing, and Cooper had just invented a machine for shearing cloth. At last he found a substitute, whom he paid to take his place in the ranks.

In addition to the militia, several volunteer companies were formed in the city. For the most part they consisted of the town's young elite. Perhaps the most elegant outfit was the light infantry known as the Iron Grays. These well-bred men elected their own captain, six-foot-two-inch Samuel Swartout. One junior officer was thirty-one-year-old Washington Irving, the personable literary chap, who was five feet six inches tall.

One evening Irving headed for Albany aboard a Hudson River

steamboat, which stopped at Poughkeepsie to pick up passengers. From these newcomers Irving learned that the British army had captured Washington, D.C., and burned several public buildings, including the White House. A man, lolling in the dark on a settee, overheard this news and blurted, "Well, I wonder what Jimmie Madison will say now?" Flushing with rage, Irving swung at the man, but his glancing blow did little damage. "Sir!" Irving stormed. "Do you seize on such a disaster only for a sneer? Let me tell you, it is not now a question about Jimmie Madison or Johnny Armstrong. The pride and honor of this nation are wounded. The country is insulted and disgraced by this barbarous success, and every loyal citizen should feel the ignominy and be eager to avenge it!" When the boat docked at Albany, Irving bounded ashore and offered Governor Tompkins his services. The governor made the author his aide-de-camp with the rank of colonel.

Irving's anger may have been due to guilt, for despite membership in the Iron Grays, he was lukewarm about the war until he heard that the nation's capital had been burned. Just as this news jolted him into action, so did it jar other indifferent New Yorkers. Now they feared that their own city might be attacked. Panic set in. Newspapers once critical of the administration now shrilled defiance of the British. Tammany members, Freemasons, and other volunteers helped complete Fort Greene on Brooklyn Heights. Even a seventy-two-year-old woman pushed a wheelbarrow.

The city was not attacked. The British failed in their attempt to invade New York State via Lake Champlain. On land the War of 1812 was fought along the Canadian frontier, around the Great Lakes, and at Washington and New Orleans. Much action took place on water, and Americans scored notable victories. During the war 120 privateers sailed from New York Harbor and captured 275 enemy ships.

Great Britain and the United States signed a treaty in Ghent, Belgium, on December 24, 1814. This guaranteed America's independence but didn't even mention the issues for which the war had been fought—impressment of sailors, the right to search ships, and the status of neutral trade. All three had become academic because of Napoleon's downfall. In those days ocean trips took so long that word of the signing didn't reach New York until February 11, 1815. In the blue smudge of twilight a pilot hopped out of a boat at a wharf and ran uphill through foot-deep snow toward the New York *Gazeteer*.

He reached the office just as it was about to close. When he caught his breath, he whispered hoarsely, "Peace! Peace! An English sloop of war is below with news of a treaty of peace!"

People whooped and dashed out into the snow and shot off fireworks and drank rum and danced in glee. They continued to celebrate for several days, staging a succession of dinners and balls and illuminations, building fancy Temples of Concord and Bowers of Peace. Soon the price of sugar fell from $26 per hundredweight to $12.50, and tea dropped from $2.25 to $1 a pound. Jacob Astor, grown soft and flabby, let the little people enjoy their little delights. By cleverly arranging to get news of the peace treaty ahead of everybody else, he had unloaded his wares at wartime prices. He had also made $500,000 lending money to the federal government at steep interest rates. Next to Stephen Girard, the Philadelphia merchant and financier, Astor was the richest man in America.

Now Broadway had been built north a distance of 2 miles, now the city boasted 100,000 inhabitants, and now New York had become the largest city in the United States.

Chapter 17

SAWING OFF MANHATTAN ISLAND

Two SAILORS scampered up the rigging of a ship idled by embargoes and war. When they got to the top, they unlashed an empty tar barrel capping the mast for protection from the elements. As they lifted it off, one seaman cried, "Have a care below! Off comes Madison's nightcap!" Then the sailors heaved the barrel down onto the wharf, where a waiting crowd made a bonfire of it.

The mast-capping barrels were called Madison's nightcaps because many people blamed President Madison for the trade-crippling war. Now that the conflict was over, now that American ships might again plow the seas, the uncapping ceremony was repeated day after day. It symbolized the good times everyone felt were at hand. New Yorkers drank toasts to Peace and Plenty and to Peace, Commerce, and Prosperity. Jacob Astor soon had three fleets scouring the seas. Washington Irving didn't tarry to watch the beginning of the boom but sailed in 1815 for Europe, where he remained the next seventeen years. He was surprised to feel a lump in his throat as he left his hometown.

The city's first St. Patrick's Cathedral was dedicated on May 6, 1815, on Mulberry Street just north of Prince Street, an area then so wild that foxes were caught in the churchyard. Despite some bigotry, life was becoming easier for Irish Catholics. It was decided in court that priests did not have to reveal secrets of the confessional. Pope Pius VII had created the diocese of New York, consisting of the state of New York and the eastern part of New Jersey. St. Peter's Church was unable to accommodate the city's growing Catholic population, so this second Catholic edifice was erected. Not merely a church but a cathedral, it was named for St. Patrick, the patron saint of Ireland.

Another current attraction was the busy waterfront. Thousands of spectators watched the work of calkers, riggers, and sailmakers, who earned four dollars for a ten-hour day. Shipyards rang with hammerblows and cries as keel after new keel was laid. Vessels couldn't be built fast enough to meet the demand. As soon as they were finished, crews were hired, manifests were drawn up, and shipping clerks bustled about self-importantly.

During the war, when foreign trade had come to a standstill, domestic manufacturing had expanded, and Americans had been proud to wear homespuns. Now they hungered for the superior products of Great Britain, which led the United States in the Industrial Revolution. They yearned for Yorkshire cloth, Scotch muslins, silks, bedcovers, and toothbrushes—everything they could buy.

Because war-impoverished Europe was unable to absorb the huge inventories piled up in British warehouses, English manufacturers dumped their goods in America. They didn't even wait for orders. To these shores they dispatched not just a few ships but great fleets. Never before had such heaps of merchandise been sent abroad. In one three-day period sixty-five cargo-laden vessels tied up in New York. In a single week auction sales of British wares exceeded $460,000. During April, May, and June, 1815, the duties paid at the New York customhouse came to $3,900,000. The city swarmed with buyers eager to pay any price asked of them.

Most imports were sold by auctioneers, many of whom became rich overnight. Although auctions had been common before the war, they had been used chiefly to dispose of damaged goods. Now British manufacturers sent their best goods to New York agents, who turned them over to auctioneers. Consumers got better bargains this way than by buying from local merchants. The governor and state council of appointments granted licenses to only a few auctioneers; in 1816 there were just twenty-nine of them in New York.

One auctioneer got rich so fast that he retired at the age of forty. This was Philip Hone, who served one term as mayor, took part in civic affairs, was a Whig leader, hobnobbed with celebrities, and set the style in fashion—but is best remembered for his 2,000,000-word diary. Hone was tall and fastidious, an arrestingly handsome man, with blue eyes and a clean-cut face.

At first the British were willing to sell here at a loss. Apparently they hoped to stifle the American manufacturing that had sprung up during the war. Then too, beef, tallow, butter, hams, and potatoes from Galway and Newry undersold local produce. When American buyers ran out of money, the auctioneers gave them credit. Thus, many consumers went into debt. While flooding American markets with British manufactures and produce, England closed its ports to American ships. So British manufacturers and shipowners and American auctioneers flourished as American manufacturers and wholesale merchants and importers withered. By the autumn of 1815 the American wool and cotton industry was prostrated, and eventually three-quarters of American factory owners failed.

Among those forced to the wall was Peter Cooper, who lost out as a manufacturer of shearing machines. Resignedly turning first to cabinetmaking and then to the grocery business, he vowed that he would always oppose free trade. Congress passed the nation's first protective tariff in 1816, but by then most of the damage had been done. Moreover, the British destroyed this tariff wall by faking sales and invoices.

The depression gripping New York was aggravated by immigration. From the beginning of the American Revolution to the end of the Napoleonic wars only a trickle of Europeans had left home. When the continent settled into temporary peace, though, foreigners began to arrive in the United States by the thousands, and New York was the favorite port of entry. Between 1820 and 1920 about 70 percent of all aliens entered America through the port of New York, many of them settling in the city. The population grew fast, but poverty and crime grew faster.

One-seventh of New York's population soon lived on charity, and the debtors' prison overflowed. This gloomy jail had a cellar honeycombed with dungeons for solitary confinement. The first floor was occupied by the families of the jailer and the keepers. It also had a bar, where prisoners lucky enough to own a few coins bought liquor at outrageous prices. The second floor was filled with relatively well-to-do debtors, who called themselves the Middle Hall Society. Most debtors, however, were confined on the third floor, which lacked light at night and sometimes fire in winter. Since neither the city nor the state gave them so much as a crust of bread, they depended on private charity for their food.

Poor people outside debtors' prison tried to escape their misery by frequenting the city's 1,900 licensed grogshops and the 600 other establishments where rum was sold without a license. Dead cats and dogs polluted the air, dust and ashes were thrown into the streets, and except for the most popular thoroughfares the streets were cleaned only once a month.

The sorry state of affairs caused conscientious New Yorkers to take stock of themselves. Not so Jacob Astor, who was scooping up Manhattan real estate at bargain prices, or Cornelius Van Derbilt, who was prospering as a steamboat captain. High-minded citizens studying the situation leaned more to a moral than to an economic interpretation. They decided that the whole problem was due to drunkenness, together with ill-advised and ill-regulated charity.

In his *History of the Great American Fortunes,* Gustavus Myers said: "A study of the names of the men . . . who comprised the New York Society for the Prevention of Pauperism, 1818-1823, shows that nearly all of them were shippers or merchants who participated in the current commercial frauds. Yet this was the class that sat in judgment upon the poverty of the people and the acts of poor criminals and which dictated laws to legislatures and to Congress."

One man who owed a debt of only fifty dollars was kept in debtors' prison and fed by a humane society for three years before death ended his misery. Another spent six years in that fetid jail. At last the state legislature forbade the imprisonment of debtors for sums of less than twenty-five dollars. Justice of another kind was meted out to a certain Lawrence Peinovie, who got two years in jail for biting off his wife's nose. "This," cried the mayor, "is the first offense of its kind to blur the escutcheon of the republic!"

Yellow fever added to the city's woes. The first new case broke out on June 17, 1822, in Rector Street just below Trinity Church. In those days no one knew that this acute infectious disease is transmitted by a certain kind of female mosquito. However, all soon recognized its symptoms—flushed face, dull pain, a red and pointed tongue, yellowing of the whites of the eyes and the skin of the body, nausea, black vomit, delirium, convulsions, coma, and then death on about the eighth day.

By the middle of July the epidemic was spreading with fearful rapidity. The city fathers ordered quicklime and coal dust spread in the gutters and set fires to "purify" the air. They fenced off every block in which new cases appeared. Nothing did any good. By August all business had been suspended, and the only sounds in the city were the footsteps of doctors and the rumbling of hearses.

On the day that 140 persons died, a ship anchored at Governors Island. Among its passengers was Charles Mathews, the great English mimic. When he heard the size of the death toll, he refused to land. Word of his anxiety was sped to Stephen Price and Edmund Simpson, co-managers of the Park Theatre, who had brought Mathews here. Simpson and a physician boarded the vessel to try to persuade the entertainer to come ashore. The forty-six-year-old actor was tall and thin; his face was disfigured, and one leg was shorter than the other as the result of his having been thrown out of a gig in England. All his life he was neurotically melancholy, but this did not lessen his talent as a comedian. Now he limped about deck, muttering that he could feel the pestilence in the air, crying that every cloud carried death, and moaning that each wave in the harbor was charged with poison.

The producer and the doctor suggested that Mathews might feel safe if he landed in New Jersey instead of in New York. He agreed. Mathews was escorted to a cottage on the road to Hackensack. He paced the floor in terror all that first night. After staying in his bedroom a few days, however, he couldn't stand further confinement. Strolling out into the chicken yard, he practiced his mimicry before an audience of hens and roosters.

Mathews was not the only one terrified by the yellow fever. Residents of lower Manhattan fled by the thousands to upper Broadway and to Greenwich Village. The ferry that normally ran between Brooklyn and Manhattan now bypassed the tip of the island and berthed at the Village, which had exploded into a boomtown. At first some people had to sleep in fields. Then wooden buildings rose almost overnight. Business was conducted in temporary booths, and prices soared.

Living on John Street in lower Manhattan at the time was an old Negro woman, named Chloe, who sold flowers and cleaned the offices of lawyers along the street. The attorneys were fond of her, and with sick people dropping like flies on the cobblestones, they urged Chloe to join them in their flight to Greenwich Village. She refused to budge. Shrugging, the lawyers left without her.

For a while there was serious talk of abandoning lower Manhattan entirely and creating a new city in Greenwich Village. What we now know as Bank Street got its name because banking offices, removed from Wall Street, were opened there. One Saturday morning a minister saw corn growing along Hammond (now West Eleventh) Street, but on the following Monday the same site held a house accommodating 300 boarders. A group of Scottish weavers settled in what is today West Seventeenth Street, then a country lane; built a row of modest dwellings; and resumed their handweaving. They called their new street Paisley Place in memory of their hometown of Paisley, Scotland.

By the end of October the weather had turned cold, and frost diamonded the earth for the first time that season. This dispelled fears. The first part of November New Yorkers flocked back to the city they had considered abandoning forever. Bank Street retained its name, although the countinghouses returned to Wall Street. As the makeshift buildings in Greenwich Village were vacated, laborers moved in, seeking low rents.

When the lawyers got back to their John Street offices, there was Chloe, still alive, still smiling, her small quarters filled with dogs and cats, goats, and birds. These were pets left behind by attorneys and householders in their frantic flight out of town. Having cared for them throughout the plague, Chloe now returned them to their owners. Everyone was so touched by her courage and compassion that an important artist was commissioned to paint a portrait of her surrounded by the pets whose lives she had saved.

Soon after the end of the epidemic New Yorkers were taken in by an amusing hoax. A market had been built behind what became

Police Headquarters, located at 240 Centre Street between Grand and Broome streets. It was called the Centre Market. Butchers, farmers, fishermen, and others gathered there daily to sell their wares and to gossip. A certain teller of tall tales usually was surrounded by a crowd who enjoyed his yarns. He was John De Voe, a retired butcher commonly called Uncle John. One of his cronies was a retired carpenter, known to the idlers as Lozier, although this was not his real name.

One afternoon Lozier walked up to a group around Uncle John and asked what they were talking about. "Well," said Uncle John with a straight face, "we have had a long conversation about New York Island, and we've come to the conclusion that it's getting too heavy at the Battery end. Too many buildings there. Fact is, the situation is becoming dangerous. So-o-o, our intention is to have it sawed off at Kingsbridge and turn that end down where the Battery is now located. But the question is, How shall it be done, since Long Island appears in the way? Some think it can be done without moving Long Island at all—that the bay and harbor are large enough for the island of New York to turn around in. Others say, though, that Long Island must be detached and floated to sea far enough, then anchored until this grand turn is made, and then brought back to its former place."

A gleam flickered in Lozier's eyes, for he always enjoyed a practical joke. Deadpan, he asked questions about the technical problems involved and made a few suggestions. That day, the next day, and almost every day for the next two or three months, Lozier and Uncle John solemnly explored the subject of sawing off Manhattan. In addition to their regular audience, they attracted strangers taken in by the hoax.

Lozier slowly emerged as the genius who would mastermind this great engineering feat. He declared that the project needed hundreds of workmen, and of course barracks must be built for them at the northern tip of Manhattan, where the sawing would be done. They would have to build 24 sweeps, each 250 feet long. When finished, these would be placed on opposite sides of the northern and southern tips of Manhattan to sweep the island around after it had been sawed off. Naturally, the ironwork on the sweeps would have to be constructed with care. This was a challenge to a blacksmith whose shop was near the market; he begged to be allowed to take charge of this part of the plan.

Although the blacksmith's wife scoffed, every few days he con-ferred with Lozier about the dimensions and specifications of this or that portion of the huge sweeps. Word spread about this exciting job, and soon other men presented themselves to Lozier, asking to be en-rolled. Graciously accepting each volunteer and never betraying him-self with a smile, Lozier said that he especially needed pitmen. He had enough sawyers to work on the ground, but he wanted deep-chested fellows to labor in the earth, as well as under the surface of the Harlem River itself. Of many applicants he anxiously asked whether they were long-winded. Yes, indeed, they assured him.

The dupes who had dedicated themselves to this historic feat brought in others who wished to share the glory. They urged Lozier to name the day that operations would begin. The jokester, over-whelmed by the mass response to his prank, hedged. They insisted. At last he set a date on which they would gather and trek to the north-ern tip of Manhattan to set up camp. One work force was to gather at the Bowery and Spring Street. The other would meet at the junc-tion of Broadway and the Bowery, now called Union Square. All were told to bring along wagons, tools, food, and their wives, who would cook and wash for them once they arrived at Kingsbridge.

Came the great day. Vast numbers of people appeared at the designated spots with all the equipment ordered by Lozier. But where was Lozier himself—the leader, the visionary, the great engineer? He was nowhere to be seen. Hour after hour wore on, and still Lozier failed to arrive. Gradually, painfully, everybody realized that he had been duped. Not wishing to admit this, however, most people pre-tended that they had known from the start that it was a hoax and had just gone along for the fun of it. Trying to erase their own images as fools, they ridiculed the men who stormed about, muttering threats against Lozier. Then the disenchanted went home, and within a few days hardly anyone would admit that he had wanted to help saw off Manhattan.

But Lozier feared that the dupes might want to saw him off. He holed up in his home and remained there for the next several weeks. Since his victims knew him only as Lozier, they could not find him. When he finally emerged, he wore a disguise and used his real name. Manhattan remained intact.

Considering the relative sophistication of New Yorkers, the story would sound incredible were it not for a mood then in the air. Most minds were open to the impossible. Everyone knew that the greatest engineering feat in the history of America was nearing completion. This was the construction of the Erie Canal.

The story of New York City cannot be told without reciting the epic of the Erie Canal. This artificial waterway in upper New York State augmented the city's leadership, converted it into a metropolis, assured its position as the nation's most influential port, confirmed it as the gateway for European immigration, transmuted it into the country's commercial and financial center, and touched it with greatness. In the words of Lewis Mumford, New York City became "the mouth of the continent, thanks to the Erie Canal." It was the longest canal in the world, built in the shortest time, with the least experience, for the least money, and to the greatest public benefit. It revolutionized the American capitalistic system by proving that large sums of money could be raised for public works through the sale of state bonds. It opened up the Middle West. It set off a craze for canal building. It became the nation's golden cord.

The Appalachian Mountain Range paralleling the Atlantic seaboard stood like the Great Wall of China between the coast and the interior. Although it had been penetrated, transportation and communication between these two areas were still difficult. At the end of the War of 1812 the hinterland of America consisted for the most part of a vast unpeopled bowl, whose natural resources lay untapped. Rivers provided the easiest method of travel. However, the St. Lawrence River did not give access to the Great Lakes. The Mohawk River in upper New York connected with the Hudson River at Rome, New York, but from Rome one had to travel overland to reach the West.

Roads were little more than ruts through forests, muddy in wet weather and dusty during droughts. Wagon wheels thudded into boulders and tree stumps. Drivers were happy to travel twenty miles a day. Between 1800 and 1830 chartered companies built turnpikes and charged tolls for their use, but overland travel remained slow, rough, and dangerous. Besides, the tolls were so high that farmers and merchants could not afford to move their products over the pikes. To avoid these fees, some wagoners resorted to shunpikes, or detours around tollgates. As a result, the turnpikes failed.

To transport wheat from Buffalo to New York cost three times its market value; corn, six times its value; oats, twelve times. It cost $100 a ton to move wheat from Buffalo to Albany and $120 a ton for the entire distance from Buffalo to New York. Transportation from the Great Lakes to Montreal cost only a third as much as the long overland carries to New York. So the commerce of the interior followed the natural waterways to the markets—down the St. Lawrence to Montreal, down the Delaware to Philadelphia, and down the Mississippi to New Orleans.

After the initial hardships of homesteading, settlers wanted necessities and luxuries made in Europe and on the eastern seaboard. These items were too bulky to be transported profitably by land. Farmers were able to pay for machine-made wares only if they could get their produce to the more populous Atlantic coast and sell it at a fair price. Moreover, unless this commerce were deflected down the Hudson River, New York City would lose its commercial leadership.

Even before America won its independence, there was talk of connecting the Atlantic and the Great Lakes via the Hudson River and the Mohawk Valley. In 1773 an Irish-American, named Christopher Colles, lectured in New York about the possibilities of such a canal. In 1786 a man asked the Chamber of Commerce of the State of New York for financial aid in building a canal, but although the chamber thought well of his scheme, it turned him down for lack of funds.

The problem seemed insuperable. The Mohawk Valley was a wilderness for the most part, while the Montezuma Swamp, near Syracuse, was a treacherous marshland. President Jefferson said that "talk of making a canal three hundred and fifty miles through a wilderness is little short of madness." President Madison thought that the canal would cost more than the entire resources of the nation. Scoffers spoke of it as "a big ditch," in which "would be buried the treasure of the state, to be watered by the tears of posterity." State legislators at Albany feared that it would boost taxes so high that angry voters would refuse to reelect them. New York City's representatives at the state capital shunned what they considered upstate improvements.

Perhaps the only man who never lost faith in the canal was De Witt Clinton; certainly he deserves the most credit for it. Of Dutch and Irish descent, Clinton was born at New Windsor, near Newburgh, New York, on March 2, 1769. He belonged to an aristocratic family; his father was General James Clinton, and his uncle, George Clinton, became the first governor of New York State and twice was Vice-President of the United States. A precocious lad, De Witt studied in an academy at Kingston and then enrolled at the age of fifteen as a junior in Columbia College, the first student to be admitted to the college under its new name. At seventeen he was graduated at the head of his class and delivered a commencement address in Latin.

Admitted to the bar two years later, De Witt Clinton never practiced much law. Instead, he became private secretary to his uncle, Governor Clinton, who also named him secretary of several boards. Thus, at an early age he gained much political experience and influence. He rose to fame because of his vigorous mind, forceful character, and awesome dignity. Although he seldom won love, he forever excited admiration; even his enemies respected his towering intellect.

A heavy man, more than six feet tall, De Witt Clinton moved with massive deliberation. He had a well-shaped head, a broad forehead, a Grecian nose, curly chestnut hair, clear hazel eyes, and a complexion as fair as a woman's. Once, after a political defeat, he shut himself up on his Long Island farm and drank for days on end. Then, snapping out of alcoholic self-pity, he again charged into public affairs. Clinton was that wondrous blend of a visionary-realist who aims high, but not too high, and accomplishes almost everything he sets out to do.

Speaking from the steps of City Hall one day, he predicted that within a century the city would be built up solidly from the Battery to the northern tip of Manhattan. The crowd hissed him. Even a gentle Quaker turned to a man beside him and said, "Don't thee think friend Clinton has a bee in his bonnet?" He did indeed have a bee in his bonnet—the idea of linking the Atlantic with the Great Lakes. Nothing could discourage him, not even the Tammany newspaper that printed this doggerel: "Oh, a ditch he would dig from the lakes to the sea,/The Eighth of the world's matchless Wonders to be,/Good land! how absurd! But why should you grin?/It will do to bury its mad author in."

In 1810 the state legislature had appointed a commission to explore a route for a canal across upper New York State, and Clinton became one of its seven members. No armchair theorist, he journeyed through the Mohawk Valley, jotting down his keen observations in a notebook. Clinton and his fellow commissioners reported to the legislature that it would be feasible to dig a canal for about $5,000,000.

In 1811 the commissioners asked other states for financial aid, but Ohio was the only one to respond. The next year the commissioners tried for a federal subsidy but were turned down. They then recommended that New York State proceed alone and got a go-ahead signal from the legislature. But the War of 1812 delayed the project.

When peace came, all the friends of the canal had given up in despair—all but De Witt Clinton. Along the proposed route, landowners, blind to their own interests, asked fantastic prices for their properties. State and local politicians refused to vote the necessary appropriations. It seemed foolish to try to dig a canal more than 350 miles long through a wilderness. All the nation's existing canals totaled only 100 miles; the longest one was not quite 28 miles in length. When the Albany legislators killed the canal project, Clinton appealed directly to the people.

In the fall of 1815 he convened a great meeting of New York merchants in the City Hotel and read aloud his long memorial on the subject. This appealed to the self-interest of the merchants, whose business would boom once the canal was built. They ordered thousands of copies of his memorial printed and distributed throughout the state. Other merchants, shopkeepers, and manufacturers around the state held mass meetings. Finally, more than 100,000 New Yorkers signed a petition demanding that the legislature take positive action.

In April 1816—the month Brooklyn was incorporated as a village —the legislature named five new commissioners and gave them $20,000. The new board members elected Clinton president and went to work so energetically that by fall the canal route had been explored and surveyed and maps and profiles had been drawn.

Now a great deal of money was needed. Disappointingly, President Madison vetoed a federal bill that would have given New York State $1,500,000 for the canal. In 1817 the state legislature authorized the canal commissioners to do everything necessary to raise all the money they sought. The canal was to be built between Albany and Buffalo.

In addition to pursuing his pet project, De Witt Clinton served ten one-year terms as mayor of New York City and was elected to three three-year terms as governor. On the Fourth of July, 1817, only three days after his reelection as governor, Clinton turned the first shovelful of earth.

Construction of the canal was a formidable task. Eighty-three locks had to compensate for the difference of 650 feet in elevation between Buffalo, the high western end, and Albany, the low eastern end. Some lock machinery had to be imported from Europe. Transportation of materials was slow and difficult. Underbrush had to be cut away, trees felled, and stumps extracted from the soil.

The Erie Canal has been called America's first school of engineering, for when it was started, the nation had no professional engineers. The work was directed by brilliant amateurs, many of them lawyers, who learned as they went along. One man surveying the route hadn't even seen a transit before. These dedicated dabblers came up with new inventions—a machine to pull trees out of the ground, a grubbing machine that could remove forty stumps a day, a two-bladed plow to cut roots, and a new cement that quickly hardened under water.

This first massive public works project coincided with the first tidal wave of immigration from Ireland, and the hardy sons of Erin supplied most of the muscle power. Mainly small farmers, their uncouth appearance provoked barbed comments from New Yorkers. Local rowdies engaged in Paddy-making. They would fashion a dummy from rags, smear its painted mouth with molasses, string potatoes or codfish around its neck, stick a whiskey bottle in one pocket, and then erect this travesty in a public place on the eve of St. Patrick's Day.

The self-proclaimed upper classes should have been grateful to these bogtrotters, for Irish sweat put money in their pockets. The immigrants worked under appalling conditions, digging from one red-painted stick to another through thick woods, rocky barrens, and miasmic swamps. They floundered through mud and tried to fight off swarms of mosquitoes. One summer, in the Montezuma Swamp near Syracuse, 1,000 laborers were struck down by malaria, ague, and typhus; many of them died.

The Erie Canal was made 363 miles long, 4 feet deep, 28 feet wide at the bottom, and 40 feet wide at the surface. Instead of the estimated $5,000,000, it cost nearly $8,000,000.

At ten o'clock on Wednesday morning, October 26, 1825, the canal was declared officially open as the first boat moved from Lake Erie into the man-made waterway. De Witt Clinton headed the distinguished passengers aboard the elegant packet, the *Seneca Chief*. The news was announced by a battery of cannon stretching 500 miles from Buffalo to Albany and then to New York City. At Buffalo the sound of the first cannon was the signal to fire the second one, and so on down the line; the message rode the airwaves from Buffalo to New York City in 81 minutes. Later, when the *Seneca Chief* and her flotilla escort reached this city, Governor Clinton upended a green keg ringed with gilded hoops and poured Lake Erie water into the

Atlantic off Sandy Hook, saying, "May the God of the heavens and the earth smile most propitiously on this work, accomplished by the wisdom, public spirit and energy of the people of the state of New York, and may He render it subservient to the best interests of the human race. . . ."

What did the Erie Canal do for New York City? A German duke, who visited the city in 1825, said that it seemed to be attracting "nearly the whole commerce of the country." This was only a slight exaggeration, for Manhattan merchants captured control of well over half of the nation's imports and more than one-third of its exports. They served as middlemen for America's farmers and England's manufacturers.

New York City set the pace for this nation's first great business boom. In the early months of 1825 at least 500 new merchants set up shop here. That first year 12 new banks and 13 new marine insurance firms were established. The city's banking capital rose from $3,400,000 in 1800 to $25,100,000 in 1825. The new canal made it possible to ship bulk goods more quickly and cheaply between the east coast and the interior. Previously, it had taken 3 weeks and cost $120 to move 1 ton of freight from New York to Buffalo; now it took only 8 days and cost just $6. Raw products from rural areas arrived here via the canal to be turned into factory-made goods.

The city's population exploded. Real estate values skyrocketed. In anticipation of this growth, 3,000 new houses were built in 1824, but there still weren't enough dwellings to go around the following year. Shops and stores doubled their rents. With old structures being torn down, new ones rising, and the streets almost impassable, all was hubbub.

From 1825 to 1850 Greenwich Village's population quadrupled. Farther uptown, Franklin Delano Roosevelt's great-grandfather, James Roosevelt, profited by selling his farm between 110th and 125th streets just east of what is now 5th Avenue. Two houses with marble fronts, probably the first in the nation, were erected at 663 and 665 Broadway. For the first time gas streetlights appeared in the city south of 14th Street.

The year the canal opened, 11 percent of the city's inhabitants consisted of aliens, and each day more poured in from abroad. Merchants began displacing the landed gentry as the city's social leaders, and both groups worried about the changing complexion of society. With the removal of property qualifications the suffrage was extended, all white males now being allowed to vote. This was not to the liking of the old guard. The Federalists' chancellor, James Kent, warned: "The growth of the city of New York is enough to startle and awaken those who are pursuing the *ignis fatuus* (foolish fire) of universal suffrage. . . . It is rapidly swelling into the unwieldy population, and with the burdensome pauperism of an European metropolis. . . ."

In 1825 a seven-story tenement was erected at 65 Mott Street, the Society for the Reformation of Youthful Delinquents opened the House of Refuge, and the first organized gang appeared.

Chapter 18

THE GANGS OF NEW YORK

NEW YORK CITY was "the tongue that is lapping up the cream of commerce and finance of a continent," as Dr. Oliver Wendell Holmes expressed it, but this meant nothing to Rosanna Peers. She sold rotten vegetables.

Produce was scarce and costly that booming year of 1826. Early vegetables had not yet reached here from the South, and nobody ate tomatoes because they were considered poisonous. Rosanna Peers displayed brown-streaked cabbages and tattered lettuce outside her ramshackle shop on the northern side of what is now Foley Square, but they were a cover-up. Her real business was conducted in a dingy back room, where she sold rotgut rum for less than it cost in saloons.

Lacking a liquor license, she had taken her blind piggy to market.

It was in Rosanna Peers' back room that the city's first organized gang came into existence. Called the Forty Thieves, it was led by Edward Coleman. All day long and half the night he sprawled in Rosanna's hideaway, dispatching henchmen to the nearby slum area to slug, steal, rob, and kill. Rosanna's place also bred the city's second gang, the Kerryonians, whose members had been born in County Kerry, Ireland. Less ferocious than the Forty Thieves, the Kerryonians seldom ventured far from Rosanna's and did little fighting, devoting themselves mainly to hating the British.

For the next century the gangs of New York terrorized the city, waged hundreds of street battles, and won the community the reputation of the most wicked city in the world. Except for a few freed slaves hanging about their fringes, the first gangs consisted almost entirely of Irishmen. The Irish, arriving in droves, lacked money and education and skills. They were met with contempt by native New Yorkers and welcomed only in the city's worst slum—the Five Points district.

A squalid area lying northeast of the present New York County Courthouse, Five Points was formed by the intersection of five streets —Anthony, Orange, Cross, Little Water, and Mulberry. Today Anthony is Worth Street, Orange is Baxter Street, Cross is Park Street. Vanished altogether is Little Water Street. Only Mulberry Street has kept its original name. The Five Points opened onto a small triangular park with the cynical name of Paradise Square. Today this is the southwestern corner of Columbus Park.

Such was the core of what became the largest Irish community outside Dublin. The first ten or fifteen years of its existence the Five Points was fairly decent. The city had no day police, but by night a sole watchman was able to keep peace in the Five Points. He was paid $1.87½ cents a night and wore a fireman's leather helmet from which the frontpiece had been removed. Because of this, New York's cops once were called Leatherheads.

About 1820 the Five Points began to deteriorate. It stood on the site of the old Collect, or Fresh Water Pond, and the landfill hadn't been packed solidly enough. Buildings slowly sank into the moist soil, their doors springing on hinges and their façades cracking into wooden grins. Respectable families fled from the decay to better parts of the city, and the Irish moved in. Clannish by nature and shunned by native New Yorkers, the Irish clustered by the thousands in the wretched rookeries, with their dank cellars and fetid garrets. Lacking other means of earning a living, the Irish carved out criminal careers.

The predominant landmark in the Five Points was the Old Brewery. It stood just behind what today is the New York County Courthouse. Erected in 1792 on the shore of the Collect and known at first as Coulter's Brewery, it produced beer that became famous in all the eastern states. Time, weather, and neglect reduced its five stories to ruins. In the words of Herbert Asbury, "It came to resemble nothing so much as a giant toad with dirty, leprous warts, squatting happily in the filth and squalor of the Points." Converted into a multiple dwelling in 1837 but still called the Old Brewery, the monstrosity became the most infamous tenement in the city's history.

The murders, prostitution, perversion, drunkenness, brutality, thievery, and idleness in the Old Brewery and the Five Points were considered by native New Yorkers to be the natural condition of Irishmen. Philip Hone sniffingly noted in his diary that "they increase our taxes, eat our bread and encumber our streets, and not one in twenty is competent to keep himself." Genteel citizens shrank with horror from an evil they refused to analyze. It took a British historian, James Bryce, to say of the Irish: "There is a disposition in the United States to use the immigrants, and especially the Irish, much as a cat is used in the kitchen to account for broken plates and foods which disappears [sic]. . . . New York was not an Eden before the Irish came."

In 1826 John Jacob Astor, himself an immigrant, was paid $27,000 in rentals, but there is no evidence that he concerned himself about the plight of the poor Irish. Any son of Erin lucky enough to find a job was paid only 75 cents to $1.25 a day. Even so, this was better than life in the old country, where a laborer's wages ranged from 8 to 16 cents a day. Although rent and food were higher here, whiskey was cheaper—28 cents a gallon.

Unlike the Germans, who later arrived in family units, most Irish came as individuals. Thus, they lacked the tempering influence of family life. Besides, far from the public opinion of their native villages, uprooted Irishmen felt free of most moral restraints. Naturally, many decent and honest Irish settled here and later swelled the ranks of the city's police—"New York's Finest." In 1826 the city held nearly 30,000 Catholics, most of them Irish immigrants. The three Catholic churches were run by only six priests, who couldn't begin to cope with their countrymen, although one brave old priest broke up a Five Points riot by wading into the melee with a stole about his neck and a missal in his hand.

In the Five Points the root problems were ignorance, poverty, unemployment, ostracism, and political corruption. Churches and welfare agencies bewailed these conditions, but nothing was done to help the Irish until the late 1830's. Then it was too late, and by the 1840's the area had become the most vile slum on earth.

Gang leaders bore unmistakable Irish names—Farrell, Corcoran, Connolly, Ryan, Hurley, Doyle, and Hines. The gangs themselves were called the Patsy Conroys, O'Connell Guards, Bowery B'hoys, Chichesters, Roach Guards, Plug Uglies, Shirt Tails, Dead Rabbits, Atlantic Guards, Daybreak Boys, Buckoos, Hookers, Swamp Angels, and Slaughter Housers.

New York's first gangs did not consist of teen-agers but of grown men. There were more and larger gangs than at present. Gangs of hundreds of men were commonplace; one numbered 1,200 members. Small gangs grouped together into constellations of gangs, led by a supreme chieftain commanding absolute loyalty. Undeniably the gangsters were brave, but their courage was due to ignorance, insensitivity, and booze. Every battle was a fight to the finish—no quarter asked and none given. Gang leader "Dandy Johnny" Dolan stuck blades in the soles of his boots to enhance the gore when he trampled an enemy. Dolan also invented copper wedges, which he wore on his thumbs to make it easier to gouge out eyes.

Thriving on excitement, gangsters often were cruel just for the sadistic fun of it. One strolled up to an old man sipping beer and hacked open his scalp with a huge bludgeon. Asked why, the ruffian replied, "Well, I had forty-nine nicks in me stick, an' I wanted to make it an even fifty." Another plug-ugly seized a stranger and cracked his spine in three places just to win a two-dollar bet.

Themselves the victims of unhealthy slums, gang members averaged only 5 feet 3 inches in height and weighed between 120 and 135 pounds. But their bloody exploits created a legend, a bigger-than-life folk hero, like Paul Bunyan of the American Northwest and John Henry of the Mississippi River. This mythical figure, allegedly 8 feet tall, was called Mose, and a play entitled *Mose, the Bowery B'hoy* was first performed in 1849 at the old Olympic Theatre.

Among lowlifes the proper etiquette was to distinguish between American sons of bitches and Irish sons of bitches. To the non-Irish nearly every Irishman was known as "a damned Paddy." This hostility between native New Yorkers and Irish Catholic immigrants degenerated into the dangerous, superpatriotic, spread-eagle Know-Nothing movement. It was true that many liquor-loving Irishmen became drunk and disorderly, but native-born cops were quick to arrest them when they would have helped home an equally drunk and disorderly native American. For this reason the era's crime statistics may be distorted.

The contempt felt by most native New Yorkers for the Irish was not shared by Tammany Hall. In the beginning, what Irish Catholics sought from politics was not power but protection. Tammany, now an arm of the Democratic party organized in 1828, was eager to provide protection—at a price. Tammany helped Irishmen get their naturalization papers before the end of the waiting period. Whenever a gang leader got into trouble, a Tammany lawyer appeared for him in court, and a Tammany bondsman put up his bail. Tammany pulled strings to obtain licenses for the many Irishmen seeking to open saloons. If cops cracked down on Irish-owned bars and brothels, Tammany bribed key officials and arranged immunity from further raids. All Tammany asked in return was that the Irish prove their gratitude by voting Democratic regularly and even repeatedly. As a result of this interest in their welfare, the Irish gave Tammany fierce loyalty.

Because unskilled Irish competed for jobs with free Negroes, the sons of Erin had no love for colored men. Themselves persecuted, the Irish helped persecute Negroes and denounced the growing movement to abolish slavery. Effective in 1808, Congress forbade the importation of slaves into the United States. The ban was flouted by New York shipowners and others. In 1817 the American Colonization Society was formed to oust troublesome Negroes by settling them in Liberia, but the plan wasn't much of a success. Only 6,000 colored people were sent to Africa—a drop in the bucket, considering that in 1820 the South contained nearly 1,500,000 slaves, to say nothing of the free Negroes scattered throughout the North.

A state law, passed in 1817, abolished slavery in New York State as of July 4, 1827. The following autumn Judge William Jay alluded to this emanciption in his charge to a Westchester County grand jury:

> I cannot forbear to congratulate you on that event, so auspicious to the character and happiness of the community. . . . Within a few months more than ten thousand of our fellow-citizens have

been restored to those rights which our fathers in the Declaration of Independence pronounced to be inalienable, and to have been granted to all men by their Creator. As yet we have no reason to suppose that crimes have multiplied or the public peace disturbed by the emancipation of our slaves, nor can we fear that He who commanded us to do justice and love mercy will permit us to suffer by obeying His injunctions.

Philip Hone, the diarist and onetime mayor, was less optimistic. To his diary he confided: "The terrible abolition question is fated, I fear, to destroy the union of our states, and to endanger the peace and happiness of our western world."

New York's freed Negroes had no easy time of it. Most were manual laborers. Some managed small stores, fruitshops, oyster stands, and barbershops. All were excluded from the white man's churches and theaters. The nation's first Negro newspaper, *Freedom's Journal,* was established here in 1827 by Samuel E. Cornish and John Brown Russwurm, but it expired after three years. Small white boys solemnly told one another that if you kicked a Negro's shins, his nose would bleed.

Also in 1827, the New York *Journal of Commerce* was founded, in part as an abolitionist newspaper. It was created by Arthur Tappan, who, with his younger brother, Lewis, gained notoriety as one of the city's leading abolitionists. Both had been born in Northampton, Massachusetts, of solid Puritan stock and with starched Puritanical consciences. The Tappan brothers got their start in business by selling dry goods in Boston; but in 1814 Arthur moved to New York, and in 1827 he was followed by Lewis. They made a fortune with their dry-goods importing house, located on Hanover Square.

Sympathetic though they were to oppressed Negroes, the Tappan brothers acted like martinets toward their white employees. Any worker who smoked, played cards, or attended the theater was fired out of hand. Both Arthur and Lewis refused to keep chairs in their offices, for they felt that business would be conducted more briskly if visitors had no place to sit down. Yet Arthur was so ardent an abolitionist that he sank $30,000 into the *Journal of Commerce.* Later he sold the paper, which soon veered to the side of those favoring slavery.

It was remarkable that two wealthy merchants, such as the Tappan brothers should urge an end to slavery, for most businessmen considered the idea both foolish and dangerous. They were concerned more with profits than with principles. One New York businessman frankly said to an abolitionist minister:

> We are not such fools as not to know that slavery is a great evil, a great wrong. But it was consented to by the founders of our republic. . . . A great portion of the property of the Southerners is invested under its sanction, and the business of the North, as well as the South, has become adjusted to it. There are millions upon millions of dollars due from Southerners to the merchants and mechanics of this city alone, the payment of which would be jeopardized by any rupture between the North and the South. We cannot afford, sir, to let you and your associates succeed in your endeavor to overthrow slavery. It is not a matter of principle with us. It is a matter of business necessity. . . . We mean, sir, to put you abolitionists down—by fair means if we can, by foul means if we must!

This plain-speaking man was addressing an unusual pastor, since at first most ministers were hostile to abolitionism. After all, churches were built, pews rented, and ministerial salaries paid by the city's rich businessmen. The preachers, more concerned with buttering their bread than with trying on wings for size, hid behind tortured readings of the Scriptures. One New York cleric intoned from his pulpit that "slavery is a divine institution"; whereupon an abolitionist cried from his pew, "So is hell!"

Most newspapers also sided with the proslavery businessmen to safeguard advertising revenue. With Irish immigrants, wealthy merchants, preachers, and the press opposed to freeing the slaves, abolitionism was left in the hands of idealists and crackpots. They propagandized to arouse white men's consciences. Some hewed to just one line—liberation of slaves. Others—and they cracked the solidarity of the crusade—also clamored for different humanitarian causes, such as the rights of workers, the reformation of jails, the renunciation of debtors' prisons, more hospitals and orphanages, temperance, and equal rights for women.

Abolitionism's cradle was New England, and its creed was enunciated by two New England sons, William Lloyd Garrison and Wendell Phillips. Until they began ranting about the injustice of slavery, advocates of Negro freedom had behaved quietly and decorously—so much so, in fact, that the evils of slavery were all but smothered under a conspiracy of silence.

In 1831, the year Horace Greeley arrived in New York, this conspiracy was broken in Boston, broken violently by the appearance of Garrison's new periodical, the *Liberator*. In his first editorial Garrison roared:

> Let Southern oppressors tremble—let their secret abettors tremble —let their Northern apologists tremble—let all the enemies of the persecuted blacks tremble. . . . I *will be* as harsh as truth, and as uncompromising as justice. On this subject I do not wish to think, or speak, or write, with moderation. Tell a man whose house is on fire to give a moderate alarm. . . . I am in earnest—I will not equivocate—I will not excuse—I will not retreat a single inch— AND I WILL BE HEARD.

Arthur Tappan's *Journal of Commerce* never had raised its voice this way. Garrison's *Liberator* fulminated for the next thirty-five years without interruption, and the name Garrison became a red flag to white Southerners and to many of their Northern business associates. Tappan once bailed Garrison out of a Baltimore jail. Georgia's state senate offered a $5,000 reward for the apprehension and conviction of Garrison in a Georgia court. A South Carolina editor wrote to the editor of the New York *Evening Star* that abolitionism could be "silenced in but one way—*Terror—Death.*"

In 1832 there were seven morning and four evening newpapers in this city. Most vehemently opposed abolitionism. That year a twelfth paper, the New York *Sun,* was established by Benjamin H. Day. All the other papers sold for six cents a copy, but the *Sun* was priced at a penny. It was edited and printed at 222 William Street by Day, who vacillated on the issue of slavery versus freedom. He had a reporter and editor, named George W. Wisner, who was a passionate advocate of liberty for all Negroes. Day once grumbled, "Whenever Wisner got a chance, he was always sticking in his damned little abolitionist articles."

On December 4, 1833, the American Antislavery Society was organized in Philadelphia, elected Arthur Tappan its first president, and voted to set up permanent headquarters in New York. Tappan promptly founded its official organ, the *Emancipator,* and chose for its editor a Congregational minister from Massachusetts, Joshua Leavitt. Every month Leavitt sent copies of the *Emancipator* to members of Congress, and every month twenty to thirty copies were returned with insults scribbled in the margins. One Southern lawmaker wrote: "You damned infernal psalm-singing, negro-stealing son-of-a-bitch,

if you ever show your damned hypocritical face in the dist. of Columbia, I will make my negroes cowhide you to death!"

The governor of Alabama complained to the governor of New York
about the *Emancipator*. Tappan was marked for assassination. Vigilante groups were formed throughout the South. The New Orleans
Vigilante Committee offered $20,000 for the capture of New York's
Arthur Tappan. At Charleston, South Carolina, Tappan was hanged
in effigy. A storekeeper in Norfolk, Virginia, took up a subscription
for the delivery of Tappan's dripping head to him.

Even in New York abolitionists were attacked, and their homes
were stoned. Mrs. Lydia Maria Child, an abolitionist writer, said after
one New York antislavery meeting, "I have not ventured into the city
nor does one of us dare to go to church today . . . so great is the
excitement here. 'Tis like the times of the French Revolution when no
one dared trust his neighbors."

On the evening of July 9, 1834, some Negroes met in the Chatham
Street Chapel to hear a sermon by a Negro minister. In the audience
sat the white abolitionist Lewis Tappan, a jaunty figure despite his
Puritanical heritage. The meeting had just begun when members of
the New York Sacred Music Society broke in to proclaim that they
had rented the place for the evening. The Negroes, who had paid for
use of the chapel, refused to leave. There was an exchange of words,
then blows.

White men beat Negroes with lead-loaded canes, seriously injuring
two or three of them. The fight attracted a crowd, and a riot was in
the making when the police arrived and drove both whites and blacks
from the chapel. The fracas continued on the street. Tappan walked
away toward his home on Rose Street, just behind the present Municipal Building. Recognized as a damned abolitionist, he was followed
by a yelling mob that pelted his residence with stones after he had run
inside.

The next evening another proslavery crowd, still spoiling for a fight,
gathered in front of the chapel. Its doors were locked, but the agitators broke in and held an impromptu meeting. A rabble-rouser,
named W. W. Wilder, lashed passions with a speech denouncing
abolitionists, and as the meeting closed, there came cries of "To the
Bowery Theatre!"

Opened in 1826, the Bowery Theatre was the nation's first gaslighted playhouse and it seated 3,000 persons. It stood at the present
50 Bowery on the southeastern corner of the approach to the present

Manhattan Bridge. Burned down and rebuilt many times, it remained one of America's foremost theaters for nearly a century. That night of July 10, 1834, a benefit performance was being given for an English actor, George Percy Farren, whose cross-grained comments about Americans had irked New Yorkers.

The crowd at the chapel somehow got the idea that the Englishman's alleged anti-Americanism meant that he was an abolitionist. Leaving the chapel, rowdies headed for the theater, picking up reinforcements along the way, their menacing roars being heard in the showplace before their arrival. The theater doors were slammed shut, but when the mob got there, it burst through them, interrupting a performance by the American tragedian Edwin Forrest. From the stage he tried to pacify the intruders but was howled down. Before the Englishman could be found and maimed, the police appeared and herded everyone out of the theater.

Now agitators howled, "To Arthur Tappan's house!" Taking up the cry, the mob raced back down the Bowery, changed its collective mind, and turned instead toward the home of Lewis Tappan. He and his family escaped just before the throng surged into sight. The rioters took Tappan's place apart, stick by stick, saving only a painting of George Washington. Then they rampaged through town, torturing Negroes, raping prostitutes, and gouging out an Englishman's eyes and tearing off his ears.

This human violence followed on the heels of a natural catastrophe, for just two years earlier the city had been plagued by Asiatic cholera. For centuries the deadly disease had ravaged the Far East, but it did not spread to the Western Hemisphere until the nineteenth century. In 1831 cholera reached England, leaping from there to Ireland. The early part of June, 1832, an Irish immigrant ship brought the infection to Quebec, and on June 27 the first cases appeared in New York City.

A Mrs. Fitzgerald and her two children were found dead in their apartment at 75 Cherry Street. The police took one look and called a doctor. The deceased bore the unmistakable marks of Asiatic cholera: bodies shrunken from loss of fluid, skin dry and wrinkled, tongues white and dry, eyeballs shrunken, faces pinched, and cheeks hollow.

When the city fathers understood the situation, they ordered the streets cleaned as never before. This did no good. A coroner's jury sat in the case of a cholera victim found dead on a Harlem road, and of the twenty witnesses and jurors who appeared, nine soon died of cholera themselves. Terrified townspeople clustered in churches to pray for deliverance. Board of health figures were appalling: On Saturday, July 14, there were 115 new cases and 66 deaths; Sunday, 133 new cases, 74 deaths; and Monday, 163 new cases, 94 deaths. Doctors treated patients with dry friction, dry heat, opium, and brandy—without much effect. Every picture of a cholera patient of the period shows a brandy glass at his head.

Aside from going to church, most people stayed home. One lawyer took up the study of Greek to while away the clientless hours. Then panic set in. First to flee were the rich, who departed in such haste that they left their fine houses in shambles. They headed toward New Jersey, Westchester County, Far Rockaway, the eastern tip of Long Island, and Connecticut. Cornelius Vanderbilt now ran a fleet of steamships on Long Island Sound, and he and other steamboatmen profited from the panic. They sent overcrowded vessels to Connecticut ports, where alarmed citizens brandished pitchforks and guns and refused to let the ships dock. Driven from the harbors, the craft nosed along the Connecticut coast until they found deserted beaches where New Yorkers could land.

The next few weeks even the city's poor ran for their lives, fathers carrying tots in their arms, women clutching bags of food, and boys leading horse-drawn carts piled with pitiful belongings. Roads became traffic nightmares of plunging horses and cursing men and frightened refugees. That horror-haunted summer of 1832 nearly half the population of a quarter million left the city. But the poorest of the poor, the Irish of the Five Points, lacked the means to get out of town. The Five Points lay in the city's Sixth Ward, an area northeast of City Hall, and one-third of all cholera cases occurred in this ward. Business was paralyzed. Streets were empty. A butcher riding a cart from Houston Street down Broadway to Fulton Street in broad daylight saw no one en route except two watchmen.

In proportion to population, this was the worst epidemic in the city's history. Nearly 4,000 persons died of cholera between June 27 and October 19, 1832.

Plague was followed by fire. About 9 P.M. on December 16, 1835, a watchman was passing the corner of Merchant (now Beaver) Street and Pearl Street when he smelled smoke. In those days Beaver Street was narrow and crooked and filled with tall stores recently put up by dry goods merchants and hardware dealers. The watchman sounded the alarm for the city's worst fire in that era of disasters.

Fifty-five-year-old Philip Hone, the retired auctioneer and diarist, was writing in the library of his $25,000 house at 235 Broadway. Just a few blocks away at that very moment the city's other great diarist, fifteen-year-old George Templeton Strong, lolled in his bedroom of his father's three-story brick house at 108 Greenwich Street near Rector Street. A slender, fair-haired, precocious lad, G. T. Strong was a sophomore at Columbia College. Both he and Hone noted in their diaries that they first heard the fire alarm at about 9 P.M. Strong said that the temperature stood exactly at zero.

A northwester of nearly gale force scudded over icy streets and lashed snow into frozen surf. The moment Hone heard the news, he bundled up and struggled through the storm to see what was going on. Strong's father had a law office on Wall Street, but at first the elder Strong didn't think it necessary to plunge into the howling wind to look after his place. Soon, though, a man rushed into the Strong household and awakened the attorney, and the two then dashed into the night.

The fire started on the first floor of a five-story warehouse at 25 Merchant Street, at the corner of Pearl Street. This ground floor was rented by Comstock & Andrews, fancy dry goods jobbers. Apparently the blaze was caused by an overheated pipe. The watchman who discovered the fire was joined by fellow patrolmen, and they forced open the front door. The interior, filled with bolts of cloth and clothing, was such an inferno that the men backed away and tried to latch the door in place. At that moment flames licked through the roof. Wind-borne embers dashed against stores on the other side of Pearl Street, and within fifteen minutes the dumbfounded watchmen counted fifty other buildings ablaze.

Cholera had decimated the strength of the city's volunteer firemen. What's more, the previous night the fire fighters had battled a big conflagration at Burling Slip on the East River, and when the new alarm sounded, they were so exhausted that they responded slowly. Half an hour passed before they put the first water on the flames. Everything was pitted against them. Shorthanded and already worn out, they manned antiquated equipment. The city's water supply was scanty. Cisterns, wells, and most fire hydrants were frozen. Firemen had to beat their hoses to keep water from congealing in them. This worked for a while, but no sooner would water spray from a nozzle than it turned to ice in the air and fell as hail. Unremitting pressure of the ferocious wind lowered the water level of the East River just enough so that firemen on the docks above couldn't reach it with suction hoses. So the frustrated, exhausted, shivering firemen could do little more than watch as a large section of town went up in flames.

That bitter night the air was so clear that the fire's reflection was seen as far away as Philadelphia to the southwest and New Haven to the northeast. The blaze raged 16 hours before it was brought under control, and 3 days passed before the last spark was extinguished. When all was over and citizens took stock of the disaster, they found that 17 blocks of lower Manhattan, consisting of 52 acres, had been gutted. Exactly 693 buildings—about 500 of them stores—were destroyed. Only 1 structure was left standing in the afflicted area. Not a single life was lost, but property damage came to more than $20,-000,000.

The city's fire insurance firms, unable to pay policies in full, were ruined. Many banks closed. As a result, businessmen were unable to get money to rebuild their shops and factories. Thus, the great fire of 1835 was one of the causes of the panic of 1837.

Since the year 1762 the nation had experienced ten major depressions; two were especially severe. The panic of 1784-88 lasted forty-four months, while the panic of 1815-21 stretched out for seventy-one months. The depression beginning in 1837 was fated to endure for seventy-two months. In fact, it remained the worst panic in the nation's history until the Great Depression, which started in 1929.

The fire, however, was only one of many factors triggering the panic of 1837. States had piled up huge debts to build canals and railroads. People had speculated recklessly in buying land in the West—and even on Long Island. To check the speculation, President Andrew Jackson ordered all payments for public land to be made in gold or silver; this cramped banking operations. Banks overextended themselves. Interest rates were too high. Imports exceeded exports. Bad weather ruined crops. British bankers called in their loans. Stock prices fell. Real estate collapsed.

"This is the most gloomy period which New York has ever known," Hone scribbled in his diary. "The number of failures is so great daily that I do not keep a record of them, even in my mind. . . . All is still as death; no business is transacted." Depositors began a run on the city's banks, which held more than $5,500,000 of their securities. Hone "witnessed the madness of the people—women nearly pressed to death, and the stoutest men could hardly sustain themselves; but they held on as with a death's grasp upon the evidence of their claims, and, exhausted as they were with the pressure, they had strength enough to cry, 'Pay! Pay!' " The banks hired plug-uglies and ordered them to fire on the crowds if the situation got out of hand.

All coins vanished. Firms paid their workers in shinplasters. A real shinplaster was a paper plaster saturated with tar and vinegar and applied to a sore shin. During the American Revolution the word took on the meaning of fractional currency. Now the paper currency called shinplasters assumed every form and denomination, from the alleged value of five cents to five dollars. Badly printed, it was easy to counterfeit; in fact, counterfeiting became a flourishing business. Although workers didn't know if shinplasters had any value, they were compelled to accept them or starve.

Wages were cut. Jobs grew scarce. With the cessation of all ship-building for two years, shipyard employees were left idle. Building construction came to a halt, throwing 6,000 more laborers out of work. Soon every third workingman was unemployed. Job-seeking Negroes vied with the Irish, native Americans competed with the foreign-born, skilled craftsmen wrangled with the unskilled—and the puny labor movement collapsed. About 10,000 citizens lived in absolute poverty. The almshouse commissioners said that seven-tenths of all relief applicants were Irish women whose husbands were out of town. But—added the native-born anti-foreigner officials—the husbands were "very particular to be here to vote at the spring election."

This "year of national ruin," Horace Greeley was publishing a weekly, called the *New Yorker,* from an office at 18 Ann Street. Troubled by the misery he saw at every hand, Greeley wrote: "Mechanics, artisans, laborers, you cannot with safety give heed to those who prophesy smooth things. . . . We say to the unemployed, you who are able to leave the cities should do so without delay. . . . Fly —scatter through the land—go to the Great West." In issue after issue he repeated this advice until he became known as "Go West" Greeley.

He also claimed that local rents were higher in New York than in any other great city of the world. Agreeing, the City health inspector, Gerret Forbes, said, "We have serious cause to regret that there are in our city so many mercenary landlords who only contrive in what space they can to stow the greatest number of human beings in the smallest space." John Jacob Astor, the so-called landlord of New York, didn't suffer lack of space himself; his thirteen-acre Hell Gate estate on the East River gave him plenty of elbowroom.

Seventy-four years old when the panic began, his once ruddy skin sagging in gray pouches, Astor no longer needed his China trade or fur profits to earn money to buy ever more Manhattan real estate. Income from rent alone more than covered the price of his new land. While hungry men scrabbled for jobs that paid off in dubious shinplasters, Astor lent a friend $250,000. The old man also bought mortgages from people who couldn't keep up payments on their property and then promptly foreclosed, thus accumulating more land at ridiculously low prices. He made millions out of the panic.

Washington Irving, now back from Europe, was glad to take money from Astor to write an authorized history of *Astoria,* the old fellow's ill-fated trading post on the Pacific Coast. Despite the fame Irving enjoyed, he wrote: "My own means . . . are hampered and locked up so as to produce me no income." It was during the panic of 1837 that Irving coined his famous phrase, writing of *"the almighty dollar.* that great object of universal devotion throughout our land."

Cornelius Vanderbilt now owned the greatest fleet of steamers on Long Island Sound, and in 1837 the press began calling him Commodore. Arthur and Lewis Tappan failed in business. Philip Hone lost two-thirds of his fortune, but in the depth of the depression he wrote: "We had a handsome supper, with oceans of champagne." Meantime, a pale, sharp-faced painter, named Samuel F. B. Morse, who hadn't yet won fame with his telegraph, went twenty-four hours without food.

Speculation in flour boosted the price from $6 to $15 a barrel, and it was rumored that a few big flour and grain merchants were buying all the flour in town. On February 10, 1837, newspapers and placards announced that a protest meeting would be held in City Hall Park, at 4 P.M. on February 13, to denounce the high price of bread, meat, fuel, and rent.

Although it turned out to be a cold bleak afternoon, there gathered 6,000 persons, most of them Irish immigrants and nearly all of them in faded working clothes. Speaker after speaker reviled the rich, especially landlords and those who hoarded flour. One agitator cried, "Fellow citizens, Eli Hart and Company now have fifty-three thousand barrels of flour in their store! Let's go and offer them eight dollars a barrel for it, and if they do not accept—" A man who stood

near the speaker, noticing the presence of Mayor Cornelius W. Lawrence, Eli Hart, and a knot of policemen, whispered into his ear. The
orator then ended, in a softer voice, "If they will not accept it—we
will depart in peace."

But the crowd understood the speaker's meaning. With a roar,
people rushed down Broadway. Hart's big brick building stood on
Washington Street between Dey and Cortlandt streets. The worried
merchant gathered some cops and trotted toward his place; but at Dey
Street they were surrounded, and clubs were snatched out of the hands
of policemen. Hart's clerks tried to bar the store's three iron doors
and its windows, only to be assaulted before the place was secured.

Surging inside and swarming upstairs, the rioters rolled flour barrels to the windows and pushed them out. Dashed onto the icy pavement, the casks burst open, spilling flour everywhere. Then the mob
ripped open burlap bags holding wheat and spilled their contents on
the street; a fog of powder thickened the air. The mayor got to the
scene, mounted a flight of steps opposite the store, and tried to reason
with the vandals. Nobody listened. Angry people pelted him with
bricks and stones and hunks of ice until he retreated. The rioters tore
one of the store's iron doors from its hinges and used this as a battering ram to beat open the other two doors. Three streams of maniacal
people poured into the place to hasten the plunder.

The violence reached its peak at twilight. With Washington Street
knee-deep in flour and wheat, scores of tattered women waded in to
scoop the precious grain into boxes, pails, sacks, baskets, and aprons.
They worked fast and panted, and their breath bloomed like white
flowers before their pinched faces. They were helped by small boys,
one of whom was sentenced to hard labor in Sing Sing Prison. Finally,
as the edge of night crept over the city, two companies of national
guardsmen trotted up. The sight of their loaded rifles dispersed the
rioters.

The police arrested several vandals and began marching them toward the jail in City Hall Park. Other rioters jumped the cops and
rescued some of their friends. In the brief fight the police chief had
his coat torn off his back. Forty persons were convicted and sent to
Sing Sing, built in 1825. Two other stores near the Hart establishment
were attacked, and a total of 1,000 bushels of wheat and 600 barrels
of flour were destroyed. The next day the price of flour rose again.

The financial panic that began in 1837 ended in 1843. By this time
the city had a fabulous new water supply, and Irish Catholics had

reached a turning point in their political fortunes. The Democratic administration gave some Irishmen petty jobs, such as marshals, street inspectors, health wardens, lamplighters, fire wardens, dockmasters, weighers, clerks, and inspectors of pawnshops, junkshops, and meat markets. The lucky ones joined the white-collar class. Philip Hone wrote bitterly that Bishop John Hughes deserved "a cardinal's hat at least for what he has done in placing Irish Catholics upon the necks of native New Yorkers."

Chapter 19

DOWN WITH FOREIGNERS!

In his essay on fate, Ralph Waldo Emerson said, "The German and Irish millions, like the Negro, have a great deal of guano in their destiny. They are ferried over the Atlantic, and carted over America, to ditch and drudge, to make corn cheap, and then to lie down prematurely to make a spot of green grass on the prairie."

In the first half of the nineteenth century New Yorkers could not imagine how these foreigners could ever fertilize their culture and bring it to blossom. Aliens were no-good, whiskey-swilling trouble-makers. Far from greening the prairie, they soiled this city, huddling in stinking slums near aristocratic noses. It never occurred to society leaders that John Jacob Astor and other rich landlords helped create these slums. In the fall of 1835, on Broadway between Barclay and Vesey streets, Astor began building a magnificent hostelry, which dwarfed the largest hotels in London and Paris. At the same time a cramped, dark, airless, unsanitary tenement rose on Cherry Street.

Most foreigners were Irish, and the Irish were Catholic, and by 1835 abuse of Catholics had developed into mass hysteria. Butcher boys, born in New York and proud of it, beat up the Irish, who lamented that the Declaration of Independence had been changed to read "Life, Liberty and the pursuit of Irishmen." Bullies snarled that aliens not only deprived them of jobs but also accepted less money and thus kept down wages. This wasn't necessarily true. Irish stevedores struck for more pay, only to have their leaders jailed for rioting. If the Irish took less than the prevailing wage, they were scabs; if they demanded higher pay, they were termed agitators.

A scandalous book, entitled *Six Months in a Convent,* was published in Boston, and New Yorkers complained when the supply of copies failed to keep up with the local demand. Samuel F. B. Morse—remembered today for the telegraph and Morse code—was a New Yorker who brought out his own book, called *Foreign Conspiracy Against the Liberties of the United States.* He accused the Jesuits of plotting to win control of America.

The Native American Democratic Association was formed in 1835 by nativists who swore that "we as Americans will never consent to allow the government established by our Revolutionary forefathers to pass into the hands of foreigners. . . ." The association denounced office holding by aliens, opposed immigration, and attacked the Catholic Church. Irish-wooing Tammany then held a meeting at which the virtues of foreigners were proclaimed. Why, they had hearts of gold—these Irish peasants with their soft hats over one eye, their tailcoats, tight corduroy breeches, ribbed woolen stockings, thick shoes, and blackthorn shillelaghs.

In 1836 the Irish organized the Ancient Order of Hibernians. G. T. Strong, who experimented with chloroform and hashish, remarked, sniffingly, that "it's as natural for a Hibernian to tipple as for a pig to grunt." A famous comedian, named Tom Flynn, drank heavily for years and then took the pledge. He announced that he would deliver a temperance lecture in the Chatham Theatre, which he and Charlie Thorn managed. Tom was a turncoat to tipplers, but a hero to temperance ladies, so the night of his lecture the place was packed.

The stage was set with flats for a scene in *The Drunkard's Home*, and the only props were a table holding a water pitcher and a glass.

The audience applauded as Tom Flynn strode to the center of the stage, filled his glass from the pitcher, and began talking. How old Tom could talk! Mingling humor and pathos, he described the drunkard's downfall, moving the people first to laughter and then to sobs. For two hours, wetting his throat from time to time, Tom mesmerized everyone with his eloquence about the demon rum. Toward the end he soared to a Mount Everest of oratory as all held their breaths, and then—and then old Tom faltered, swayed, and fell to the stage. Friends swarmed over the footlights, picked up his limp body, and carried it to a nearby hotel. Those left behind exchanged pitying words about his sudden illness. In the group were militant temperance workers. One of them idly examined the water pitcher and glass Tom had used. He sipped from the glass. The colorless liquid burned like fire. Then horrified drys understood that the source of Tom Flynn's inspiration had been Old Swan—his favorite gin.

It was all very well for temperance people to urge New Yorkers to drink only water, but what kind of water did they have? A book, published in 1837, said, "There is not perhaps in the Union a city more destitute of the blessing of good water than New York." Seepage from boneyards and privies polluted the local water supply. A contemporary noted, "A person coming into the city from the pure air of the country, is compelled to hold his breath, or make use of some perfume to break off the disagreeable smell arising from the streets."

A Manhattan Company official admitted to Peter Cooper, now an assistant alderman, that the water tasted brackish in summer because when the company's wells dried up, the firm pumped river water into its pipes. Alderman Samuel Stevens urged the city council to ask the state legislature to repeal the privileges of the Manhattan Company.

Townspeople had five sources of water supply: the Manhattan Company's private wells; public pumps located in almost every block; the famous Tea Water Pump; Knapp's Spring, which supplied the upper part of town; and water carted in casks from the countryside, a source only the rich could afford. As far back as the days of the Revolution there had been talk of constructing a good water supply system, and dozens of committees had looked into the matter; but nothing was done. All plans were sabotaged by public apathy, differences of opinion about the schemes, and a power struggle between the city and private companies. City engineers now decided that the best source of supply was the Croton River, which rose in the southern part of Dutchess County, New York, and flowed through Putnam County.

New Yorkers voted for the Croton project in April, 1835. Brewers favored it because they needed better water to compete with Philadelphia beer. Many taxpayers feared the expense, but others were even more afraid of the recurrent fires that raked the city. New York now set to work to become the first big city in history to provide itself with an ample supply of pure water—far better than Rome in its days of glory.

Construction of the Croton system posed engineering problems second only perhaps to the Erie Canal. A dam had to be built at the Croton River 40 miles north of what today is Bryant Park. The parksite had been a potter's field, and 100,000 corpses were dug up and removed to a new burial ground on Wards Island. On the area now occupied by the New York Public Library there rose a reservoir capable of holding 20,000,000 gallons of water, its walls resembling an Egyptian temple.

The Croton Dam created a lake 5 miles long. This flooded Westchester field, and farmers, losing court battles, went after surveyors with shotguns. A masonry conduit was laid from Croton to New York. It was elliptical in shape, 8½ feet high and 7½ feet wide. Also constructed were 16 tunnels, one of them 1,263 feet long. In Westchester County alone the aqueduct spanned numerous brooks and 25 larger streams. High Bridge, a granite structure rising 114 feet above tidewater, bore the aqueduct across the Harlem River near what is now Yankee Stadium.

On June 28, 1842, G. T. Strong, then a young lawyer, wrote in his diary: "Croton Water is slowly flowing toward the city, which at last will stand a chance of being cleaned—if water *can* clean it." By July 4 the water was creeping up inside the new reservoir. On August 1 Strong scribbled: "There's nothing new in town, except the Croton Water, which is all full of tadpoles and animalculae, and which moreover flows through an aqueduct which I hear was used as a necessity by all the Hibernian vagbonds who worked upon it. I shall drink no Croton for some time to come. Jehiel Post has drunk some of it and is in dreadful apprehensions of breeding bullfrogs inwardly."

On October 14, 1842, New York celebrated the completion of the Croton system. That year New Yorkers used an average of only twenty-two gallons of water a day, but within a decade consumption soared to ninety. Now the city had pure drinking water. It had copious water for fighting fires. Fire insurance rates fell. Real estate increased in value. Health and sanitation improved—at least among the well-to-do.

The city's population nearly quadrupled between 1825 and 1855. Most immigrants settled in lower Manhattan, the former residents selling out and moving away. The built-up section of Broadway grew northward at the rate of about one mile each decade. By 1840, when Manhattan's population stood at 312,710, it had reached Fourteenth Street. Two years later a city inspector deplored the sorry condition of tenements and alleged that housing problems were caused in the main by the influx of foreigners. About 1,000 men, women, and children lived in filth and vice in the Old Brewery, which averaged a murder a night for almost 15 years. Most of these tenants were Irish.

Persecution had caused the Irish to become ever more clannish. Bishop John Hughes scorned priests who mingled with non-Catholics, calling them "Protestant priests." In 1837 a nativist, named Aaron Clark, became the city's first Whig mayor after conducting an anti-Irish, anti-Catholic campaign. One street orator had ranted, "What mean the systematic efforts of these foreigners to keep themselves distinct from the American people? . . . What motivates them to vote? What appeals stir them? Not American but foreign interests, the interests of Ireland. . . . The foreign politician, distinguished in a cassock, is behind the curtain and moves the wires. He it is who governs them. . . ."

In a city election two years later native New Yorkers were startled to read this handbill: "IRISHMEN, to your posts, or you will lose America. By perseverance, you may become its rulers; by negligence, you will become its slaves. Your own country was lost by submitting to ambitious men. This beautiful country you gain by being firm and united. Vote the ticket, ALEXANDER STEWART, Alderman, EDWARD FLANAGAN, for Assistant—both true Irishmen." An apologist for the Irishman, George Potter, author of *To the Golden Door,* believed that this poster was a savage propaganda hoax played on the Irish by fanatical patriots, and this seems likely. Up-and-coming Irish politicians were too canny to antagonize the majority of voters.

Tension between nativists and Irish Catholics exploded in the great school controversy. Beginning in 1801, New York State gave money to various churches for the education of poor children. De Witt

Clinton advocated public instead of religious education. In 1805 he
organized a public school system for New York City. Called the Free
School Society, it was created "to provide a free school for the education of poor children in the city who do not belong to, or are not
provided for by an religious denomination."

The Protestant-dominated society was a private corporation; voters
had no say in its management. In 1812 the state organized its own
public school system and let voters elect representatives to local
school districts. State funds continued to be given to New York City's
Free School Society, which passed them along to both Protestant and
Catholic churches. In 1823 it was discovered that Baptist schools
padded their enrollment books and forced teachers to kick back part
of their salaries. Two years later the state stopped giving money to
any Church schools. State education funds now were handed to
New York City's common council, which turned them over to the
Free School Society. In 1826 this group was renamed the Public
School Society.

In 1839 the society ran 86 local schools, with nearly 12,000 pupils.
The same year there were 7 Catholic schools in the city, attended by
about 5,000 pupils. Almost half the city's children went to no school
at all. Most Catholics kept their children out of the quasipublic
schools because these used Protestant Bibles and textbooks bristling
with anti-Catholic propaganda.

This situation caught the attention of William H. Seward, the upstate Whig who began his second term as governor in 1840. In a
message to the legislature he urged the establishment of schools in
which foreigners' children "may be instructed by teachers speaking
the same language with themselves and professing the same faith."
Historian Allan Nevins has written: "This was a dangerous piece of
folly. It would have undermined the ideal of non-sectarian education,
and the equally important ideal of public education in the English
tongue alone."

But Catholics gleefully seized on Governor Seward's remark. Into
action wheeled craggy-faced beak-nosed John Hughes, born in County
Tyrone, Ireland, and in 1837 named coadjutor bishop of New York.
On September 21, 1840, Bishop Hughes asked the city council for
a fair share of state funds for parish schools. The council voted down
his petition as unconstitutional.

The bishop then drafted a second petition, attacking what he called
the "falsehoods" of Protestant teachings in pseudopublic schools that

were "poisoning" the minds of Catholic children. Catholics were tax-payers, too, he pointed out. The bishop even offered to place parochial schools under supervision of the Public School Society in return for public aid. He announced his willingness to debate the issue in public. Uneasy council members reopened the matter.

A protest against the bishop's second petition was made by pastors of the Methodist Episcopal Church, which held the balance of power in the society. They said that the Catholics' real purpose was to use public funds to teach Catholicism not only to their own children but to Protestant children as well. They added, "If Roman Catholic claims are admitted, all the other Christian denominations will urge similar claims."

A two-day hearing began on October 29, 1840. Facing a hostile audience, Bishop Hughes appeared as the sole Catholic spokesman. Brilliantly and passionately, he orated more than three hours. He objected to the Public School Society on the ground that it violated the American principle of freedom of speech. He denied the charge that he wanted to preach Catholicism in public schools. He protested the use of textbooks calling Catholics "Papists." He bet Methodists $1,000 that they couldn't prove their charge that the Catholic Bible sanctioned the slaughter of non-Catholics. Newspapers primly reminded the bishop that there was a law against betting. The next day Protestant leaders rebutted him in speeches wildly applauded by spectators.

The city council postponed action on the bishop's second petition. Not a single daily paper supported him. Angry Catholics worked off their frustations by breaking up meetings of the Public School Society and by indulging in other provocative acts. Newspapers denounced this rowdyism. A city council committee conceded that Catholic complaints were "not wholly unfounded" and offered to compromise by expunging from textbooks all comments offensive to Catholics. Nonetheless, the city council rejected the bishop's second petition by a vote of fifteen to one in January, 1841.

Twice defeated by the city fathers, Bishop Hughes now turned to the state legislature. In February, 1841, he asked the state to change the law denying state funds to Church schools. He also called for the abolition of the Public School Society. State legislators, afraid of losing either Catholic or Protestant votes, adjourned without acting on the bishop's third petition.

Thrice thwarted, Bishop Hughes planned a new strategy. Unable to change the state law, maybe he could change the lawmakers. A statewide election was coming up. Two state senators and thirteen state assemblymen were to be elected from New York City. Four days before the fall election of 1841 the bishop convened a great meeting of Catholics in Carroll Hall. Since Whigs and Democrats opposed any change in the school system, he said, there was only one thing left for Catholics to do—pick their own candidates for state offices. For the first and only time in American history there was formed a Catholic political party, with its own slate of candidates openly pledged to support the position of the Roman Catholic Church.

Not a single Carroll Hall candidate was elected. However, the Catholic ticket split the Democratic vote so badly that Whig candidates squeaked to victory. Tammany leaders took fright. They realized that in the future they could whip the Whigs only with the help of Irish Catholics, who had won the balance of political power in the city. For some time Tammany had been helping Irish Catholics in various ways but had been keeping them out of office. Now Tammany began handing out political plums to them.

State Secretary John C. Spencer urged that control of New York City's school system be given to officials elected by the people. A bill embodying his ideas was introduced into the state legislature. Peter Cooper was one of many lobbyists sent from New York City to Albany to agitate against the bill. Despite their opposition, the measure was passed. Under its provisions, state funds were denied to *any* school in which *any* religious doctrine was taught. This disappointed Catholics and Protestants alike.

The compromise law was signed by Governor Seward on April 11, 1842. That night New York City gangsters beat up Irishmen, stoned the bishop's home on Mulberry Street, and broke windows in old St. Patrick's Cathedral. Other Catholic churches were saved from destruction only by prompt action by the militia.

Before long, however, New Yorkers began to prefer the new schools to the old ones. In 1853 the Public School Society disbanded and gave its property to the new board of education. Bishop Hughes now decided that the city's Catholics should create and maintain a complete educational system of their own. He told them, "Go build your own schools. Raise arguments in the shape of the best educated and most moral citizens of the republic, and the day will come when you will enforce recognition."

Chapter 20

THE ASTOR PLACE RIOT

RECOGNITION of another kind was accorded the Irish by Charles Dickens after a visit to one of their slums. The great English novelist wrote:

> Let us go again, and plunge into the Five Points. This is the place; these narrow ways diverging to the right and left, reeking everywhere with dirt and filth. . . . Debauchery has made the very houses prematurely old. See how the rotten beams are tumbling down, and how the patched and broken windows seem to scowl dimly, like eyes that have been hurt in drunken frays. Many of these pigs live here. Do they ever wonder why their masters walk upright instead of going on all-fours, and why they talk instead of grunting? . . .

When Dickens wrote these words in 1842, the times were awry. The rich got richer, and the poor got angrier. Immigrants knew that they were being put upon. Greedy property owners discovered that more money could be made from tenements than from respectable property. Transients paying weekly rates were jammed into decaying buildings, into flimsy barracks built in backyards, and into cellars converted into apartments. Well-to-do-tenants could demand and get repairs; the poor were unable to force landlords to do anything to improve their hovels.

In 1843 the city's two prisons held twice as many Irishmen as native New Yorkers. One rabid nativist shouted, "If I had the power, I would erect a gallows at every landing place in the city of New York and suspend every cursed Irishman as soon as he steps on our shores!" An investigating committee accused relief agencies of failing to learn the "wants, capacities, and susceptibilities" of the poor. As a result, the town's many private welfare agencies banded together as the Association for Improving the Condition of the Poor of New York City.

Ironically, in 1844 New York was known as the most prosperous and worst governed city in the world. In the election that year James Harper, a partner of the publishing firm of Harper & Brothers, ran for mayor as a reform candidate. He was a curious blend of arch reactionary, tinsel patriot, and businesslike administrator. During the campaign his adherents paraded the streets with banners that screamed: "No Popery!" Harper was elected.

New Yorkers now heard a rumor that some Irish in Philadelphia had trampled the American flag; tempers ran high here. Mayor Harper declared that no violence would be tolerated in New York, but the *American Republican* shrilled: "Blood will have blood! It cannot sink into earth and be forgotten." As tension mounted, Bishop Hughes posted thousands of Irishmen around Catholic churches and schools and warned that if a single church were burned, all of New York would be converted into "a second Moscow." Despite the bishop's intemperate remark and because of the mayor's sensible attitude, the city averted a bloodbath.

However, nativists organized more and more supersecret superpatriotic societies. In 1844 the Native Sons of America and the American Brotherhood were formed. In 1845 the Native American Party was created by foreigner-fearing fanatics, who called for a twenty-one-year period to precede naturalization. Although their program was aimed primarily at *Irish* Catholics, it frightened *German* Catholics. The Germans met in the Broadway Tabernacle at Broadway and Anthony (now Worth) Street and formally announced their "secession" from Rome.

New York City held 10,000 Jews in 1846, but because they kept to themselves and remained quiet, there was no overt anti-Semitism. That year 1 of every 7 citizens was a pauper. Irish and Negro women vied for jobs as servants, although the work paid only $6 a month, plus room and board. Astonishingly, the city's poverty-stricken Irish community collected more than $800,000 for victims of the famine that had broken out in Ireland.

The war with Mexico, which began in 1846, had little impact on New York City, but many Irishmen were glad to enlist in the army just for the food and shelter it provided. Now they jeered that if the nativists wanted to fight so much, why didn't they join the colors?

In 1847 Philip Hone wrote in his diary: "Our good city of New York has already arrived at the state of society to be found in the large cities of Europe; overburdened with population, and where the two extremes of costly luxury in living, expensive establishments, and improvident waste are presented in daily and hourly contrast with squalid misery and hopeless destitution."

Hone knew about luxury because he dined with aging John Jacob Astor. One night the diarist visited Astor's mansion at 37 Lafayette Place (now Lafayette Street) and then scribbled: "His life has been spent amassing money, and he loves it as much as ever. He sat at the dinner table with his head down upon his breast, saying very little, and in a voice almost unintelligible; the saliva dripped from his mouth, and a servant behind him to guide the victuals which he was eating, and to watch him as an infant is watched."

In 1848 Astor was eighty-four years old, and the fat of his body drooped like tallow drippings on a guttering candle. The last few weeks of his life the only nourishment he could take was milk from a woman's breast. For exercise his servants gently tossed him up and down in a blanket. One of Astor's rent collectors was present one day as this went on, and from the blanket Astor asked in a feeble voice if a certain woman had paid her rent. The agent said that she was a widow who had fallen on hard times. No, she hadn't paid yet, but maybe Astor could give her more time? "No! No!" Astor wheezed. "I tell you she can pay it, and she *will* pay it. You don't go the right way to work with her." Upon leaving his employer, the agent mentioned the matter to one of Astor's sons, who counted out the proper sum and told the agent to give it to the old man with the message that the widow had paid up. When Astor got his hands on this money, he snuffled, "There! I told you she would pay it if you went the right way to work with her!"

John Jacob Astor died on March 29, 1848, and was buried by six clergymen. Most of his $20,000,000 went to his second son, impassive heavyset William Backhouse Astor, then fifty-five years old. The eldest son, John Jacob Astor, Jr., had been a mental incompetent from early childhood. James Gordon Bennett of the *Herald,* who had called Astor a "money-making machine," now declared that half his fortune rightly belonged to the people of New York City. Their industry and intelligence, Bennett reasoned, had increased the value of Astor's huge holdings.

When Astor died, the city was a vastly different place from that which he had found when he arrived in 1784. Manhattan was built up solidly almost to Thirty-fourth Street, and already a row of houses stood on Forty-second Street. Philip Hone, who lived at 714 Broadway just below Waverly Place, exaggerated when he wailed, "The city of New York is so overgrown that we in the upper regions do not know much more about what is passing in the lower, nor the things which are to be seen there, than the inhabitants of Mexico or Grand Cairo." Hone noted that "Overturn, overturn, overturn! is the maxim of New York."

Broadway, between the Battery and Chambers Street, was being paved with granite blocks. Fifth Avenue, above Eighteenth Street, was a bumpy, unpaved road. The village of Yorkville held about 100 houses. G. T. Strong marveled in his journal: "How this city marches northward!"

The advance was helped by better transportation. The city's first public conveyances were stagecoaches holding four to six passengers. They were supplanted by larger horse-drawn omnibuses. Paris had its first omnibus in 1823; London, in 1829; New York, in 1830. Horse-drawn streetcars began running here in 1832. Three years later the "hurry-scurry of the Broadway and Wall Street" with their "driving, jostling, and elbowing" irked a British visitor, who went on to say, "Add to this the crashing noises of rapid omnibuses, flying in all directions, and carts (for even they are driven as fast as coaches are with us), and we have a jumble of sights and sounds easy to understand but hard to describe. The most crowded parts of London can scarce be compared with it." Bus rides were costly. In 1837 the city fixed fares at thirty-seven and one-half cents for less than one mile and at fifty cents for one to two miles.

New York *state's* first railroad, the Mohawk and Hudson, was chartered in 1826 and began operating in 1831 between Albany and Schenectady. The *city's* first railroad, the New York and Harlem, was chartered on December 22, 1831. It was promoted by Thomas Emmet, elder brother of Robert Emmet, the Irish martyr, but its first president was Allan Campbell. Its railroad cars were pulled first by mules, then by horses, and then by locomotives.

The pine-burning engines, running through the center of town, belched sparks and smoke and clanged bells and soon provoked public indignation. In 1839 a locomotive boiler exploded at Fourteenth Street, killing the engineer and injuring twenty passengers. As a result of this and other accidents, mobs tore up tracks on the Bowery. The city fathers then banned engines from the populous parts of town; horses pulled the railway cars from a terminal at Center and Chambers streets to the open countryside, where locomotives hooked onto them. Cornelius Vanderbilt invested in the line, and by October, 1839, double tracks had been laid from City Hall to Harlem. At a banquet celebrating this event, Philip Hone proposed this toast: "The locomotive—the only good *motive* for riding a man on a *rail*."

Just as the New York and Harlem contributed to the northward expansion on Manhattan, so did the Long Island Rail Road (L.I.R.R.) enable New Yorkers to live in the country and commute to the city. The L.I.R.R. began operations on April 18, 1836. Long Island farmers regarded its trains as natural enemies. Bonging bells, hooting whistles, and clattering wheels frightened cows out of giving milk. Cinders and soot blackened the washing hung out by farmers' wives. Ministers denounced the railroad for running trains on the Sabbath. Suffolk County farmers tore up tracks, burned down stations, and caused train wrecks by pulling spikes out of the roadbed.

In addition to railways, revolutionary changes in merchant shipping helped the city grow and prosper. After 1838 steamships, called packets, plied between New York and foreign ports, their success resulting from the regularity of their schedules. By 1840 New York was second only to London among ports of the world. It owned more than one-fifth of all registered American tonnage. It boasted sixty-three wharves on the East River and fifty on the Hudson. Then, beginning in 1843, came the clipper ships—long, narrow vessels with lofty sails, the most beautiful craft ever to sail any seas, faster than steam-driven packets. They were called clippers because they clipped time off speed records.

John Jacob Astor did not live long enough to see the Astor Place riot, which took place one block north of his home. He and other rich men had donated money for the erection of the Astor Place Opera House or Theatre—the terms were used interchangeably. It rose on a site bounded on the south by Astor Place, on the west by Broadway, on the north by Eighth Street, and on the east by what is now Fourth Avenue. Seating 1,800 persons, the building had classical lines and tall colonnades that gave it the look of a Greek temple. The opera house restricted admittance to those wearing kid gloves, so working-men dubbed it the kid-glove opera house. Verdi's opera *Ernani* was presented on the opening night, November 22, 1847.

The trouble began when co-managers William Niblo and James H. Hackett announced that the noted British tragedian William Macready, would appear in a four-week "farewell" engagement beginning on May 7, 1849. There was bad blood between Macready and America's greatest actor, Edwin Forrest.

Macready had passed the peak of his fame. Worried at the age of fifty-six about his being "far advanced in life," he suffered from mental depression and a dwindling fortune. Both talented and tem-perimental, the British star was gaunt and angular, with an odd nose, square jaws, a skinny neck, and grizzled hair. He called himself an aristocrat, sneered at American life, and blinked in surprise when his superior airs offended people. New York's social leaders preferred him to Edwin Forrest because of the American's lowly birth and im-passioned style of acting.

In 1849 Philadelphia-born Forrest was at the height of his popularity, the unchallenged star of the American stage and the first American tragedian to equal any British thespian. But the forty-three-year-old Forrest wanted more; he sought acclaim as the *world's great-est* tragedian. Unschooled, a coarse fellow with a ferocious temper, rugged and muscular, dark-haired and dark-eyed, Forrest radiated animal magnetism. A dabbler in politics, he was the hero of the com-mon man, although he was almost a millionaire.

While touring Great Britain, he dined with Macready, who said kind things in his diary about Forrest. However, when the American played Hamlet in London, he was hissed by the audience and reviled by the

British press. Forrest suspected that Macready was behind these insults. Forrest later went to Edinburgh to see Macready in *Hamlet* and hissed him. The outcry in British newspapers was echoed in New York newspapers, and by the time Macready arrived here, the actors' quarrel had attracted widespread attention.

Their feud was augmented by social unrest. In 1848 a wave of revolutions convulsed Europe. American workers despised all kings and aristocrats. New York festered with a hatred of foreigners. Macready was a foreigner, an aristocrat, and the pet of local society. He had been booked into the Astor Place Opera House, the very symbol of privilege. All these factors gave nativists a chance to propagandize their doctrine of "America for Americans." Two spread-eagle patriots began plotting.

One was Isaiah Rynders, a knife fighter, a gambler, and an English-hating Tammany politician. He owned the notorious Empire Club at 25 Park Row and half a dozen Paradise Square dives, bossed the Sixth Ward, and controlled all the vicious Five Points gangs. During a previous Macready engagement in New York, Rynders had interrupted the Englishman's curtain speech by leaping to his feet and shouting abuse.

The other plotter was E. Z. C. Judson, frontiersman, political propagandist, and writer, better known under his pen name of Ned Buntline, which he used to write hundreds of dime novels. In 1848 Judson became publisher of a weekly, called *Ned Buntline's Own*. The next year he headed a nativist group, the American Committee, and ached to start a fight between native-born Americans and aliens, between workers and aristocrats. The Macready-Forrest feud was the very opportunity he sought, and he turned a theatrical dispute into a sham patriotic crusade.

Although Forrest took no active role in the plot to humiliate his rival, he did nothing to stop it. The city seethed with excitement despite the *Herald*'s remark that it was silly for the public to get worked up about the relative merits of two "impertinent" actors. Other newspapers played up the issue. When Macready opened in the opera house on the evening of May 7, 1849, he was showered with rotten eggs, old shoes, and the like.

Chagrined and angered, the British star wanted to end his New York engagement then and there. In a petition signed by forty-seven distinguished New Yorkers, among them Washington Irving and Herman Melville, he was implored to continue. Macready gave in reluctantly. He agreed to appear again as Macbeth on the night of May 10. The same evening Forrest was to open in the Broadway Theatre a mile south of the opera house. The play was *The Gladiator*, and Forrest was to play the part of Spartacus, which gave him a chance to lead a stage assault on an oligarchy.

Newspapers heaped more fuel on the flames by printing articles headlined "Forrest and Macready." The *Evening Post* insisted that "the fullest and most effectual arrangements must be made for the preservation of order." It was rumored that the British crew of a Cunard liner docked here intended to rally to the defense of their countryman. The morning of May 10 New Yorkers found that the American Committee had plastered the city with posters bellowing: "Workingmen, shall Americans or English rule this city? The crew of the English steamer has threatened all Americans who shall dare to express their opinion this night at the English Aristocratic Opera House! We advocate no violence, but a free expression of opinion to all public men!"

The posters frightened Caleb S. Woodhull, who had been sworn in as Whig mayor only two days before. He called an 11 A.M. meeting in City Hall. Into his office filed the police chief, sheriff, recorder, and Niblo and Hackett, co-managers of the opera house. Also present was Major General Charles W. Sanford, commander of the national guard's Seventh Regiment. At the very moment they discussed ways to preserve peace, Bowery B'hoys raced through the streets, scattering notices that called on everyone to show up for the evening's fun.

At 4 P.M. Police Chief G. W. Matsell and his top officers arrived at the theater to make the arrangements decided on in the mayor's office. When Macready appeared at 5:40 P.M., Astor Place was filling with people. A force of 325 policemen reached the opera house shortly before 6 P.M. Matsell posted 200 of them in various parts of the building, ordered 50 to cover the rear along Eighth Street, and deployed the other 75 along Astor Place. The sky was overcast, and the temperature stood in the low fifties.

About this time General Sanford was assembling his 8 companies of guardsmen, numbering fewer than 300 men. Some mustered at the Washington Parade Ground (now Washington Square). Others formed farther downtown in the artillery drill room of the Centre Market, where they were issued 1,500 rounds of ball cartridges. A troop of light artillery was given two 6-pound cannon, plus a supply of grape and canister shot. At the arsenal there gathered 2 troops of cavalry—haphazardly uniformed milkmen and carmen astride their own horses.

When the theater's doors opened at 7 P.M., the sale of tickets exceeded the building's capacity of 1,800. Macready's friends outnumbered the Forrest fans 9 to 1. By 7:15 P.M. Astor Place from Broadway to the Bowery was a field of human flesh. At that moment Recorder Frederick Tallmadge arrived, as did word from General Sanford that his forces were ready. At 7:40 P.M., 10 minutes late, the curtain rose on *Macbeth.* Despite the rowdies in the audience, the first two scenes were played without incident.

Then, in the third scene, Macready strode onto the stage dressed as Macbeth and spoke his first line: "So foul and fair a day I have not seen." Rynders led his gangsters in a storm of hisses and groans. Macready's friends jumped to their feet to cheer and applaud and wave hats and handkerchiefs, but although they outnumbered the ruffians, they didn't make half the noise. For fifteen minutes both groups clapped and whistled and roared, all action on the stage coming to a halt. The police inside the theater stood with tensed muscles but did nothing, for they had been ordered by Chief Matsell to make no move unless he signaled them. Matsell sat in a loge where he easily could be seen. At last the play resumed; but the hubbub continued, and not a word of dialogue could be heard.

As the second act began, the crowd outside the opera house attacked the building. Nearby pavement had been broken up to lay sewer pipes, so the mob was well supplied with rocks. Although the theater windows had been barricaded with boards, they shattered under the impact of heavy stones. Windowpanes were reduced to slivers. The screaming, snarling, cursing mob heaved thousands of rocks and stones and bricks at the theater. Every nearby streetlamp was broken. Water hydrants were opened, flooding the pavement.

The police counterattacked with clubs. A cop thrust a hose through a window and sprayed the rioters with water, but this didn't faze them. At 8 P.M. the police captain of the Eighth Ward told the chief that his men could not retain their positions, let alone restore order. Policemen outside the theater were greatly outnumbered, the mob ranging somewhere between 10,000 and 24,000 persons. These troublemakers were carpenters, gunsmiths, organ builders, machinists, hucksters, printers, porters, sailmakers, clerks, marble cutters, plumbers, shoemakers, paper folders, and butchers—the working class. Most were young men; some were only fifteen years old. A few wore firemen's uniforms, carried ladders, and yelled, "Burn the damned den of aristocracy!"

At 9 P.M. the first militiamen arrived, and Mayor Woodhull squeezed into the theater to confer with the police chief, sheriff, and recorder. Now the mob was trying to batter down the doors. Between acts Macready found a pool of water on his dressing room floor; rocks had smashed overhead pipes. But the British star insisted on finishing the play, although he raced through acts IV and V.

A militia officer, with blood streaming down his face, begged the mayor for permission to fire on the mob. Woodhull gasped, "Not yet!" The officer shouted that his men would be stoned to death. The mayor, a politician to the bitter end, vanished and left the big decision to others. Not until the end of the play, not until Macready was back in his dressing room, and not until forty-five minutes after the military had arrived, was the order to fire given.

Swaggering back and forth in front of the crowd was Ned Buntline, clad in a monkeyjacket and cap, swinging a sword and bellowing, "Workingmen! Shall Americans or English rule? Shall the sons whose fathers drove the baseborn miscreants from these shores give up liberty?" The soldiers were frightened but shrank with horror at the thought of firing on fellow citizens. In the mayor's absence Sheriff J. J. V. Westervelt finally told the militia's commanding officer to let his men fire—over the heads of the rioters.

The soldiers raised their muskets and volleyed into the air. Mob members thought that blank cartridges were being fired and continued to advance, still throwing bricks and stones. Chief Matsell, now outside the theater, was hit on the chest by a twenty-pound rock. One ruffian tore open his grimy shirt, exposing red flannel underwear, and roared, "Fire into this! Take the life of a freeborn American for a bloody British actor! Do it! Ay, you darn't!" But the militia did dare. Now the soldiers were ordered to fire point-blank at the oncoming mob. Again and again and again they raked New Yorkers.

A boy was shot in the feet. One bullet bored through a man's head and scattered his brains on the pavement. A spectator—a tall and handsome Wall Street broker—was drilled through the head as he stood in Astor Place. A gangster was hit in the left eye. A Negro woman was shot through the cheek as she lay abed in a nearby house. Two men were felled when they stepped off a horsecar on the Bowery 150 yards from the theater. An Irish woman, walking with her husband two blocks from the scene, was wounded in one leg, which had to be amputated.

It was the worst theater riot in the history of the world. That night 22 persons were killed, and 9 others died of injuries within 5 days. A total of 150 persons were wounded. More spectators than participants were killed and injured. Many policemen and soldiers were wounded, but none perished. Macready, who escaped unhurt, was spirited out of town and up to New Rochelle.

That bloody evening eighty-six rioters were arrested and held prisoner awhile in the opera house. Among them was Ned Buntline. As he was being dragged under the stage, he broke away from his captors and tried to set fire to the building. Isaiah Rynders was not taken into custody. Ten of the eighty-six prisoners were found guilty of inciting riot and got prison terms, varying from one month to one year. Buntline received the maximum the law allowed—a year in jail and a $250 fine. He served time on Blackwells Island, and the day of his release he was met by rowdy friends and a band playing "Hail to the Chief." A coroner's jury held that "the circumstances existing at the time justified the authorities in giving the order to fire upon the mob."

Peaceful citizens were dismayed. The New York correspondent of the Philadelphia *Ledger* wrote: "There is a bitterness and a rancor remaining behind, which I fear will manifest themselves on future occasions. It leaves behind a feeling to which this community has hitherto been a stranger . . . a feeling that there is now in our country, in New York City, what every good patriot hitherto has considered it his duty to deny—a *high* and a *low* class."

Chapter 21

SLAVERY AND ABOLITIONISM

WILLIAM LLOYD GARRISON dressed carefully for the occasion. He knew that he and his fellow abolitionists faced a rough time when they opened the annual meeting of the American Antislavery Society in the Broadway Tabernacle that May 7, 1850.

With the *Herald* sputtering about "the annual congress of fanatics," Garrison didn't want to look odd to New Yorkers. Instead of wearing his queer turndown collar, he put on a fashionable stand-up one. The Bostonian and editor of the *Liberator* was of middling height, bald, and rather deaf. From behind silver-rimmed spectacles his big hazel eyes shone with a saintly expression.

Another scheduled speaker was Frederick Douglass, born in Mary-

266

land of a black slave mother and a white father. He was an eloquent orator with bushy hair and a tawny leonine face. In 1838 Dougl?ss had run away from his Baltimore master and come to New York. On Broadway he met another escaped slave, who warned him to shun other Negroes because some, for a meager reward, tipped off slave-hunters. White riffraff considered Douglass' presence at the Taber-nacle to be an affront. Their cutthroat leader, Isaiah Rynders, re-garded slavery as a divine institution. Before the meeting began, Rynders posted his tough Bowery B'hoys here and there in the audi-torium.

Garrison opened the session by reading from the Bible and then launched into his speech. Rynders jumped up and heckled him. An abolitionist choir started to sing, but Rynders and his hooting gang-sters brought the meeting to a halt. The same thing happened again that evening and the following day. Because Parke Godwin, an editor of the *Evening Post,* denounced the demonstrations, Rynders' mob decided to kill him. The editor was warned just in time.

In 1850 all Americans mulled the question of the extension of slavery west of the Mississippi River. Southern states, with more than 3,000,000 slaves, favored its extension. Northern states, con-taining only 262 Negro slaves, opposed it. New York City became a link in the system of routes and hideouts called the Underground Railroad, but the city's merchants sympathized with Southern plant-ers, whose debts they held.

Congress was deadlocked because neither its pro- nor its anti-slavery members held a working majority; both sides now agreed to the Compromise of 1850. This let California into the Union as a free state; set up the territories of Utah and New Mexico but left the slavery issue to be decided by their inhabitants; and amended the Fugitive Slave Act of 1793. Now anyone refusing to help a federal agent capture an escaped slave was guilty of treason. James Hamlet, a runaway slave who had worked in New York three years, was arrested and dragged back to Baltimore. John Jay, namesake and grandson of the first Chief Justice of the U.S. Supreme Court, headed the New York Young Men's Antislavery Society and acted as attorney for escaped slaves picked up in this city.

With the issues of slavery and nativism sundering the city and na-tion, New York writer Herman Melville unconsciously struck an ironic note in his 1850 novel *White-Jacket.* "We Americans," he said, "are the peculiar, chosen people—the Israel of our times; we bear the ark of the liberties of the world." Perhaps he was unaware that only one-third of the soldiers in the American army were native-born. In New York City the Irish accounted for 69 percent of all pauperism and 55 percent of all arrests. Homegrown Protestants were irked in 1850 when Pope Pius IX elevated the diocese of New York to an archdiocese and raised Bishop Hughes to archbishop.

Hughes preached an inflammatory sermon, called "The Decline of Protestantism." He vowed that the "true" church would "convert all pagan nations, and all Protestant nations, even England. . . . Everybody should know that we have for our mission to convert the world—including the inhabitants of the United States—the people of the cities and the people of the country, the officers of the Navy and the Marines, commanders of the Army, the Legislature, the Senate, the Cabinet, the President and all."

Perhaps the archbishop spoke recklessly because of the growing strength of Irish Catholics, who had organized military companies. In 1852 they staged the city's first St. Patrick's Day parade. One New Yorker, staring at the long line of marchers, cried, "Why, sure these can't be all Irish! There aren't so many in this city at least!"

Although the Irish were not particularly kind to Negroes, their sentimentality was tapped by *Uncle Tom's Cabin,* which was taking the country by storm. This was one of the most influential novels ever published. It was written by Mrs. Harriet Beecher Stowe, a sister of the Reverend Henry Ward Beecher, pastor of the Plymouth (Congregational) Church of Brooklyn. Visiting him, she said, "I have begun a story, trying to set forth the sufferings and wrongs of the slaves." Rather diffidently, he urged her to finish it. Beecher was an opportunist who courted popularity; he was slow in taking the anti-slavery stand for which he is now remembered.

In 1852 a dramatized version of *Uncle Tom's Cabin,* staged in Purdy's National Theatre on the Bowery, was sensationally successful. For the first time "respectable colored people" were admitted to the theater through a special entrance and seated in a parquet set off from the rest of the house. During its first New York season the play was seen and applauded by Bowery toughs who had broken up abolition-ist meetings.

Henry Ward Beecher was eager to ride on his sister's bandwagon. His Brooklyn church, on Orange Street between Henry and Hicks streets, had become one of the most influential in America. Beecher sent to Virginia for a beautiful mulatto girl about twenty years old and then let it be known she was fated "to be sold by her own (white) father . . . for what purpose you can imagine when you see her." This titillation drew such a crowd that traffic jammed around the church, and thousands had to be turned away.

Those lucky enough to get inside lapsed into silence as the rosy-cheeked Beecher mounted the platform with the mulatto girl. She was dressed from head to toe in virginal white. The preacher told her to loosen her hair, and gasps arose from churchgoers as glistening long tresses cascaded down her back. Then, sensually calling attention to the girl's beauty, Beecher auctioned her off. Men wept, women became hysterical, and money and jewelry were heaped into collection baskets. Having reaped headlines, Beecher later set the girl free.

This sensation was soon followed by another and longer lasting one. Some New York businessmen, eager to boost trade, decided to present the first world's fair ever held in America. They formed a corporation and sold $750,000 worth of stock in the venture, called the Exhibition of the Industry of All Nations. Many nations contributed to the 6,000 items of art and industry finally collected in the Crystal Palace.

This huge building, inspired by the London Crystal Palace, took shape in what is now Bryant Park, just west of the reservoir and fronting on Sixth Avenue. It was shaped like a Greek cross, with four wings of equal length at right angles. Except for the floors, it was made of iron and glass and considered fireproof. A translucent dome, Moorish in design and bubblelike in delicacy, soared over the center of the handsome structure.

The fair was opened in July, 1853, by President Franklin Pierce. It was a long hot summer, with the New York temperature reaching 100 degrees in the shade and 230 local residents dying of heat in one day. At first attendance was scant. When September's cooler days came, so did the crowds. People marveled at the biggest and best collection of sculpture and paintings ever assembled in America; at the model elevated railway carrying passengers around inside the House of Glass; at the nuggets and bars and chunks of gold newly found in California; and at armor from the Tower of London, Sèvres china, Gobelin tapestries, and Marochetti's statue of George Washington.

The fair did not make money. As early as October stockholders who had bought shares at $175 found them worth only $55. In 1854 the fair association went into bankruptcy. Some believed that P. T. Barnum, who had brought the Swedish singer Jenny Lind here, might be able to save the venture. He was made president. When he discovered that Crystal Palace creditors expected him personally to pay all its debts, he resigned.

In a final effort to save investments and reap a profit, the fair was reopened in 1854 as a permanent exhibit. Four years earlier the world's first elevator, built by Henry Waterman in his Duane Street shop, had been installed in a flour mill at 203 Cherry Street. The invention of the elevator made possible a side attraction to the fair —Latting Tower. Created by Warren Latting, erected just north of the Crystal Palace, made of timber braced with iron, and rising 350 feet into the air, this 8-sided landmark suggested a lesser Eiffel Tower. Its steam elevator lifted passengers aloft, where they could gaze out over the city and countryside. But this $100,000 project also failed because the nearby reservoir with its tall walls provided a more spacious vantage point where people could walk and gawk without cost. The Latting Tower burned down in 1856.

A little more than two years later, on October 5, 1858, G. T. Strong wrote in his diary: "Recent rains had laid the dust, and the air was cool. There was an alarm of fire as we emerged from the tunnel at Thirty-First Street, and a majestic column of smoke was marching southeastwardly across the blue sky, and men said the Crystal Palace was on fire. . . ." Arsonists apparently ignited paper in the building's lumber room. More than 2,000 spectators were inside, and the doors were closed; but all managed to escape, one man being rescued seconds before the dome collapsed. Within fifteen minutes the entire structure with all its precious exhibits was a molten mass of ruins. Total damage ran to $2,000,000.

But another civic wonder began to restore New Yorkers' pride. This was Central Park.

The Randall Plan of 1807-11 had failed to provide the city with enough parks. In 1844 William Cullen Bryant, the poet-editor of the New York *Evening Post,* declared that New Yorkers should have some place where they could find solitude. In an editorial he called for the establishment of a park between Sixty-eighth and Seventy-seventh streets from Third Avenue to the East River. He kept up the campaign, but nothing was done. Battery Park, once the world's best seaside resort, had decayed into a foul wasteland. In 1850 London's 1,442 acres of parks gave 500 acres of breathing space to every 100,000 inhabitants. New York's fewer than 100 acres of parks afforded only 16 acres to every 100,000 inhabitants.

The disparity between London and New York was pointed out by Andrew J. Downing, a prominent American landscape gardener and editor of a horticultural journal. In 1851 Mayor Ambrose C. Kingsland told the city council that there was "no park on the island deserving the name." The same year the state legislature gave the city permission to buy Jones' Wood, which stretched from the East River to the present Park Avenue between Sixty-sixth and Seventy-fifth streets. Downing spurned this area as too small "for a city that will soon contain three quarters of a million people." His opinion and the fact that Jones' Wood was difficult to reach caused the project to be abandoned.

The city council named a three-man committee to inspect other sites. In 1852 it recommended the area now known as Central Park because it was more central to the city than Jones' Wood. Despite its better location and greater area, it hardly seemed suitable. Barren, treeless, pierced by outcroppings of rocks, and studded with quarries, the site was used as a shantytown for 5,000 squatters. They lived in huts and ate garbage and kept 100,000 animals and fowls. Horses, cows, pigs, goats, chickens, geese, dogs, and cats trampled the scant vegetation, tore roots out of the ground, and left it naked. Water was plentiful, streams veining the earth in all directions and natural springs bubbling up between rocks. Most of the creeks, however, ended in swamps that polluted the air. Most of the squatters were Irish and German. When they learned that their reeking enclave was about to be taken over by the city, they swore to fight off any invasion.

There was other opposition to the park. The city was built up only to about Thirty-fourth Street. Horsecar lines had reached Forty-second Street, but above that lay a wilderness. Some people thought that it was silly to convert this into a park. Fortunately, the city fathers realized that even this empty space would be lost unless they acted quickly. They appointed park commissioners, who armed themselves with guns against the squatters and with deodorizers against the stench and then tramped over 760 acres lying north of what today is Fifty-ninth Street. They decided to lay out a park running north and south 2½ miles and reaching east and west ½ mile. More than 7,000 lots lay within this area. Some were owned by the city; some, by the state; some, by private citizens. It became necessary to buy 376 acres. These were purchased in 1856 at an average price of $7,500 per acre.

A nationwide contest was held to select the best plan for landscaping the terrain. Of the thirty-three ideas submitted, the best was prepared by Frederick Law Olmsted and Calvert Vaux. They split the $2,000 prize money, and Olmsted was named architect in chief, while Vaux became his assistant. From 1857 to 1870 Andrew H. Green was executive officer and president of the Central Park commission.

Work on the park began in the depression year of 1857 and provided jobs for 4,000 men. Most were Irish, since 87 percent of all foreign-born laborers in the city had come from Ireland. Olmsted, who had seen famous gardens in France and Italy, did not try to shape the rough terrain of Central Park into a formal pattern. He worked with nature, instead of against it. Vaux contributed the idea of sinking the east-west transverse roads below ground level to hide crosstown traffic from strollers in the park.

Another city landmark was taking shape about this time. In 1850 Archbishop Hughes had announced his intention of building a second St. Patrick's Cathedral. He asked 150 rich Catholics to give $1,000 each to pay for the initial cost. Within a few weeks 103 men donated the requested sum, while 2 non-Catholics made voluntary contributions.

Hughes planned to build on a block bounded by the present Fifth and Madison Avenues and Fiftieth and Fifty-first streets, a knoll sloping northward toward Central Park and southward toward Forty-second Street. The site was another wilderness, and many people ridiculed the archbishop's plan. The land had been owned by Catholics since 1828. It had been bought at a foreclosure sale by trustees of the old St. Patrick's Cathedral and St. Peter's Church for use as a cemetery. However, the land proved too rocky to serve this purpose.

Hughes chose as architect thirty-two-year-old James Renwick, Jr., an Episcopalian. The son of a Columbia College professor and himself a Columbia graduate at nineteen, young Renwick was a civil engineer, not a professional architect. As assistant engineer of the Croton water system, he had supervised construction of the reservoir in Bryant Park. Renwick taught himself architecture and studied European cathedrals.

The archbishop wanted the decorated Gothic style of the thirteenth century, like that in the cathedrals of Cologne and Rheims. Decorated Gothic is free of both the heaviness of the earlier period and the over-ornamentation of the later. Renwick changed his plans many times, but they had been completed by 1853.

Nearly 200,000 Catholics lived in New York, with its 5,980 taverns and 2,000 beer parlors. The *Tribune* estimated that one-half to three-quarters of all groggeries were owned by Catholics and added, "Catholics sell much more than their proportion of the liquor drunk in this country." Partly because of this bad publicity, the archbishop inserted in the cathedral's building contract a clause forbidding workmen to drink on the job.

On August 15, 1858, before an audience of 100,000, Archbishop Hughes laid the cornerstone of the new St. Patrick's Cathedral. Work began the next day. Laborers dug through the soil to bedrock. The cathedral's foundation stones were huge blocks of blue gneiss granite quarried in Maine. The walls were to be made of marble from Pleasantville, New York, and Lee, Massachusetts.

New York's fast-changing face caused *Harper's Magazine* in 1856 to make a complaint that sounds familiar even now:

> The other day they were tearing down the Irving House. It is too old; it has been built at least ten years. . . . New York is notoriously the largest and least loved of any of our great cities. Why should it be loved as a city? It is never the same city for a dozen years altogether. A man born in New York forty years ago finds nothing, absolutely nothing, of the New York he knew. If he chances to stumble upon a few old houses not yet leveled, he is fortunate. But the landmarks, the objects which marked the city to him, as a city, are gone.

Peter Cooper did not hold with such old-fogy notions. He favored progress—the more the better. By this time his glue factories and ironworks had made him $2,000,000, but his attitude toward wealth differed from that of his rich contemporaries. Cooper wrote: "I cannot shut my eyes to the fact that the production of wealth is not the work of any one man and the acquisition of great fortunes is not possible without the cooperation of multitudes of men." Having been denied a technical education, and being interested in the welfare of the working class, Cooper announced in 1852 that he planned to build his own college.

Five years later he incorporated the Cooper Union for the Advancement of Science and Art. It had two main objectives: (1) free education for all without regard to race, creed, color, sex, or economic status; and (2) the furthering of adult education. In 1859 the state legislature authorized Cooper's college to grant degrees and certificates in all its courses.

For many years Cooper had been buying lots in the vicinity of what became Cooper Union. Today the site is bounded on the north by East Ninth Street, on the west by Fourth Avenue, on the east by Third Avenue, and on the south by Astor Place. It stood just east of the Astor Place Opera House, which in 1854 became the Clinton Hall Library.

Cooper erected a seven-story brownstone building as massive as it was plain. To support the floors, he used wrought-iron beams arranged in grids, and by replacing heavy stone arches with thin piers, he increased the usable space. Cooper Union's Great Hall was located in the basement. Cooper put it there for safety, reasoning that if fire and panic broke out, fewer people would be hurt scampering upstairs than stampeding downstairs. He installed a gigantic fan that circulated air through small vents under the seats. The ventilating system continued to work well for the next hundred years.

When the Great Hall opened in 1858, the New York *Times,* which had begun publication on September 18, 1851, said that it was "not equalled by any room of a similar nature in any city of the United States." Down through the decades the vast auditorium, seating 2,000 persons, was the scene of meetings which led to formation of such organizations as American Red Cross, the Volunteers of America, and the National Association for the Advancement of Colored People.

Cooper spent $630,000 to build his college, which opened on November 2, 1859, in the year that Washington Irving died. Although he gave it to the city's workers forever, Cooper failed to set up an endowment fund for its operation, counting on rents and outside help to keep the place going. The first two floors were set aside for shops; but their rental was inadequate, and the public was slow to contribute money to the college.

It was the nation's first free private college and the first to provide adult education. Cooper never ran the institution with an iron hand, for he believed in striking sparks by rubbing one mind against another. As a result, the phrase "a Cooper Union audience" became proverbial to describe intellectuals. Cooper himself often met with students in nearby McSorley's Ale House, which had opened in 1854 at 15 East Seventh Street. For his famous white-haired customer McSorley kept a special chair with an inflated rubber cushion and a pewter mug with Cooper's name engraved on it. Cooper Union men (women were excluded from McSorley's) enjoyed hoisting a drink with the old boy.

In some ways Peter Cooper was as naïve as Little Red Riding Hood. A loyal Tammany member, he was slow to realize that the Democrats were plunging the city ever deeper into corruption. A man of goodwill, he found it difficult to penetrate the disguise of a wolf named Fernando Wood.

Chapter 22

---◄●►---

THE POLICE RIOT

FERNANDO WOOD was born in Philadelphia in 1812 and moved to New York City with his parents as a lad of nine. At the age of twenty he opened a "Wine and Segar Shop" at 322 Pearl Street but failed because he spent too much time dabbling in politics.

After he had managed a tobacco factory in Virginia, where he picked up Southern sentiments, Wood came back to New York and established a grocery-groggery one block from the waterfront. He made a fortune selling bad liquor to drunken sailors and struck up friendships with underworld characters. He invested this money in five sailing ships, one becoming the first to reach San Francisco after the discovery of gold in California. Wood next made a killing in Manhattan real estate. All this time he and his brother, Benjamin, ran local lotteries as licensed gamblers under a Louisiana charter. By 1849, when Wood was thirty-seven, he had become so rich that he retired from business to devote himself entirely to his greatest love—politics.

Known to all as "Fernandy," Wood pretended to be just one of the boys. Twinkly were his blue eyes, and soft was his voice. A slender graceful man standing five feet eleven inches, his head crowned with a shock of dark-brown hair, Fernando Wood was as handsome as a Greek god. In the election of 1854 bullyboy Isaiah Rynders was for him. The underworld was for him. Saloonkeepers were for him. Tarts were for him. Abortionists were for him. And enough decent, but hoodwinked, people were for Wood to elect him mayor, although he bought votes.

Taking office on January 1, 1855, he declared in his inaugural message that he was "a man of honor, a friend of labor and industry, and a protector of the poor." An intelligent man with a real knowledge of government, "Fernandy" Wood instituted some reforms during his first two-year term of office. However, after his reelection in 1856 he dropped his mask. His true nature was revealed in his mishandling of the police riot.

In 1844 Mayor Harper had tried to put the cops into uniform, but they had balked. As freeborn Americans, they argued, they would not wear "livery" and look like servants. By 1853 they had given in and donned a uniform, consisting of a blue coat with brass buttons, a blue cap, and gray trousers. This was the first completely uniformed, tax-supported, full-time police force in the city's history, but citizens complained that their police were "the worst in the world." Among other things, Police Chief George W. Matsell took bribes from the city's leading female abortionist. Corruption became so flagrant that the state stepped in and took over the police.

In 1857 the legislature created a new police district from the counties of New York, Kings, Richmond, and Westchester. In those days Westchester included what is now the Bronx. The governor appointed five police commissioners to run the new state police district—with the mayors of New York and Brooklyn serving as ex officio members. Frederick Tallmadge was named police superintendent. The new state force was called the Metropolitan Police; the old city one, the Municipal Police.

The state now ordered the city to disband its force. Mayor Wood refused, declaring that the act creating the Metropolitan Police was unconstitutional. He urged the Municipal Police to stand by him. Its 1,100 members voted, and 800 of them—all Democrats—affirmed their loyalty to the mayor. The other 300 resigned to serve as a cadre for the new Metropolitan Police force, which opened headquarters in White Street and recruited new men to fill its ranks. The state went through the motions of trying the 800 cops who stood by Wood. The city did the same with the 300 who deserted him.

New York now had two police departments, each of equal strength and each regarding the other as an outlaw force. Five Points criminals danced in the streets to celebrate the vacuum of law enforcement. Decent people walked warily and knew that sooner or later the two hostile groups would clash, leaving them utterly without protection. This fateful day fell on June 16, 1857.

The street commissioner had died. His deputy claimed the right to succeed him. However, the deputy wasn't rich enough to bribe Wood, and the mayor rejected him. The Republican governor then appointed a Republican, Daniel D. Conover, to the post. Meantime, after a Democrat, named Charles Devlin, had paid $50,000 to Democratic Mayor Wood, he too was named street commissioner.

With the governor's commission in his pocket and accompanied by a dozen friends, Conover walked to City Hall to take over the office. Wood's police threw them out. Conover and his friends fought back but were overwhelmed. Conover then marched to a Republican judge and swore out two warrants for the arrest of the mayor. One charged Wood with assault, the other with inciting to riot. The captain of the Metropolitan Police, George W. Walling—one of the 300 men who had deserted the mayor—was ordered to serve one warrant upon Wood. By now the mayor had posted 500 of his Municipal Police outside City Hall, keeping a reserve force inside.

Despite this imposing array and despite the mob that gathered in front of City Hall to sympathize with the mayor, Captain Walling walked alone up the front steps. He was permitted to enter the mayor's office, where Wood sat behind a desk, one hand clutching his ornate staff of office. The captain said that he had come to arrest the mayor. Wood refused to recognize the warrant's legality or the captain's power. The captain smiled, walked around one end of the desk, and grabbed the mayor by the arm. Twenty Municipal Police swarmed into the room, seized the captain, dragged him through the corridors of City Hall, and threw him out into the park. The obstinate captain tried again and again to get back into City Hall but was blocked each time. He was still arguing with a captain of the Municipal Police when fifty Metropolitan Police arrived on the double to rescue him and serve the second warrant on the mayor.

The mob—described by G. T. Strong as "a miscellaneous assortment of suckers, soaplocks, Irishmen, and plug-uglies"—hissed and booed the Metropolitan Police. The state cops wore plug hats and frock coats, and their new badges glistened in the sun. But they were outnumbered by the mayor's "Municipals" in their blue coats, armed with revolvers, slingshots and locust clubs.

The "Mets" advanced toward the main entrance of City Hall. The Municipals fell on them. There, on the steps of the official seat of government of the largest city in the United States, two rival police forces clashed in combat. Clubs whirred through the air. Skulls cracked. Fists thudded into faces. Bloodied men, knocked off their feet, rolled helplessly down the steps. Disabled Mets were beaten and kicked by the crowd as they lay on the ground. A few hardy Mets bulled their way into City Hall. The Municipals battered them outdoors again. Some bruised and bloody Mets fled, leaving companions writhing on the earth under a hail of blows from cursing gangsters. When the fracas was all over, most of the Mets had been injured, twelve of them seriously, and one remained a cripple the rest of his life.

Mayor Wood and his cohorts now gathered in his office to celebrate their victory. Meantime, Captain Walling had prevailed on the city recorder to order Sheriff J. J. V. Westervelt to arrest the mayor. The sheriff consulted his attorney, who said that it was his duty to take the mayor into custody. Walling, Westervelt, and the lawyer strode to City Hall and pushed their way through the threatening mob. The sheriff walked with dignity, face grim, head crowned with plug hat, and sword clanking at his heels, holding aloft his own staff of office. Under orders from Wood the Municipals fell back and let the three men enter the mayor's office. The trio told him to submit to arrest. Wood shouted, "I will never let you arrest me!"

Just then the beating of drums was heard through the windows of City Hall. The national guard's Seventh Regiment, flags flying, was marching down Broadway toward the waterfront to board a ship for Boston to help celebrate the anniversary of the Battle of Bunker Hill.

Met officers ran to the soldiers and cried for the attention of their commanding officer, Major General Charles W. Sanford. He halted his men. The Mets excitedly asked him to come to their aid. This, after all, was what the militia was supposed to do when the city's peace and dignity were threatened.

General Sanford marched his men into City Hall Park and surrounded the building. Now some Metropolitan Police commissioners appeared. Standing in the sun, the general, sheriff, and commissioners conferred. Then the general barked an order. Soldiers clicked bayonets onto muskets. They fell into place behind their general as he strode fierce-faced up the steps into City Hall. Entering the mayor's office, the general announced that he represented the state's military power, that he was going to take the mayor into custody, and—glaring menacingly about him—that he would brook no interference. The mayor submitted.

However, Wood was released on bond and never stood trial. Civil courts held that the governor had no right to appoint a city street commissioner and that Mayor Wood's appointee was entitled to the office.

But which of the two rival police forces was legitimate? While the issue was argued in courts, members of both departments strode New York's sidewalks, more concerned with their private feud than with the public weal. Local criminals ran wild, robbing, murdering, and looting. During the summer of 1857 respectable people were held up at gunpoint in broad daylight on Broadway and other thoroughfares. A Met would arrest a robber. A Municipal would attack the Met, while the holdup man ran away to sin some more. Then the Met and the Municipal would fight it out between themselves.

Into this power vacuum rushed gang members, who staged the biggest gang fight in the city's history on July 4 and 5. The Dead Rabbits and the Bowery B'hoys, deadly antagonists, tried to settle their ancient grudges. Barricades were thrown across streets. Between 800 and 1,000 toughs battled so ferociously that 2 regiments of militia were required to put down the disturbance. When it was all over, 10 men were dead, and more than 100 wounded.

The state supreme court upheld the law creating the state police force; in early autumn the court of appeals confirmed the finding; a few weeks later Mayor Wood disbanded his city police force. This threw 1,100 men out of work and contributed to the depression of 1857. The Mets hurt in the brawl at City Hall sued the mayor and received judgments of $250 each. However, Wood never paid, and the city finally settled the claims.

Germany's revolution of 1848-49 precipitated a wave of emigration that rose higher every year. Between 1852 and 1854 more than half a million Germans came to America, and although many moved West, enough remained in New York to constitute the city's largest foreign-born group next to the Irish. Most Germans were better educated and more highly skilled than Irishmen; many had a background of labor organization and played an important role in the city's trade union movement. The city's first German language newspaper, the *Staats-Zeitung,* established in 1834 as a weekly, became a daily in 1850. Germans helped organize the Communist Club of New York in 1857. This was six years after Karl Marx had begun writing weekly letters for the New York *Tribune* about European politics, economics, and war. Although some German laborers donated money to build a Catholic church on Third Street, many of their fellow immigrants were anti-Catholic. This angered fanatical nativists, who denounced the Germans as atheists, anarchists, and Reds.

Along the Bowery, between Houston Street on the south and Twelfth Street on the north, the Germans created their own *Kleindeutschland,* or Little Germany. Here they established a *Volkstheater,* a lending library, singing societies, gymnastic clubs, and beer gardens. Caring little for hard liquor and unable to afford wine, they quaffed vast quantities of beer, there being 1 beer garden for every 200 Germans. They strode the streets of Little Germany clad in leather shorts, called lederhosen, kept to themselves, and were conspicuously different from the Irish because they spoke a foreign tongue.

Hatred of all foreigners rose as tens of thousands of Europeans landed on America's shores. Supersecret societies multiplied under such names as the Supreme Order of the Star-Spangled Banner and the Wide-Awakes. New York City teemed with sixty of these dark-lantern lynch-minded groups. Horace Greeley lumped all together under the term "Know-Nothings," because whenever a man was asked if he belonged to such a society, he would say that he knew nothing about it. There were secret grips and secret signs, and meetings were called by cutting colored paper into distinctive shapes and scattering them on sidewalks. This mumbo jumbo attracted members hoping to escape their drab lives by identifying themselves with something that must be very powerful because it was mysterious. For the frustrated and ignorant, the confused and bitter, the Know-Nothings also acted as a bridge between the decline of the Whig party and the rise of the Republicans.

Abraham Lincoln said, "When the Know-Nothings get control the Declaration of Independence will read, 'all men are created equal except Negroes and foreigners and Catholics.'" By 1853 New York had the world's largest anti-Catholic library. Irish domination of politics evoked the saying "Erin e Pluribus, Unum go Bragh." There was a revival of Paddy-making—the creation and humiliation of scarecrow figures supposed to resemble Irishmen. Itinerant anti-Catholic preachers roamed streets and parks, protected by Protestant bullies, shrilling a gospel of hatred for all foreigners. An agitator, named John S. Orr, wore a white gown, blew a horn, and called himself the Angel Gabriel. Linking Popery and slavery as "twin sisters," he cursed the Irish and cried that even though the Negro had a black skin, the Irishman was black inside. Archbishop Hughes appealed to Catholics to stay away from such street meetings, but hot-tempered sons of Erin clenched their fists and sailed into their tormentors.

One Know-Nothing leader was Bill Poole, a butcher, bartender, and street brawler, who specialized in gouging out eyes. He met his match in cocky little Patrick "Paudeen" McLaughlin, and when their free-for-all was over, Bill Poole died. With his last breath he gasped, "I die an American!" Because of this precious remark, as George Potter has said, "nativists translated this gutter gladiator into a hero-martyr." In 1858 the Association for Improving the Condition of the Poor lamented, "Our city, operating like a sieve, lets through the enterprising and industrious, while it retains the indolent, the aged, and infirm, who can earn this subsistence nowhere."

Among the infirm were patients in the state quarantine hospital at Tompkinsville, in the northeastern corner of Staten Island. Neighbors feared infection and felt that the pesthouse kept down property values. For ten years they petitioned the legislature to remove the building, but nothing was done. When yellow fever reappeared in 1858, the Castleton board of health said, "The board recommends the citizens of the county to protect themselves by abating the abominable nuisance without delay." Copies of this inflammatory suggestion were posted throughout the island. Now people took matters into their own hands. They struck on the night of September 1, while the Metropolitan Police commissioners and other civic leaders were gathered in Manhattan to celebrate the completion of the first Atlantic cable.

The Staten Island plot was hatched by 30 men of wealth and social prominence. That warm evening they met for a final briefing under a tree on Fort Hill, a stronghold erected by Hessians during the Revolution. Some of the conspirators wore masks. Each was given a handful of straw, a bottle of camphene, and a box of matches. Then they began marching, shadows amid shadows, toward the quarantine station. Other men fell into line until a mob, 1,000 strong, descended on the dreaded sanctuary.

Surrounding its many buildings was a brick wall too high for easy scaling, so the attackers used wooden beams as battering rams, pounding at the wall until they had smashed holes big enough to admit them all. Quarantine officials had armed stevedores with muskets, but the rioters grabbed the weapons from their hands. Now, whooping and screaming and fanning out across the grounds, the invaders set fire to a dozen structures. Smallpox patients were saved from fiery death only by heroic nurses. The main hospital building somehow survived the attack.

The next night the mob returned and succeeded in putting the torch to the main building. Its flames illuminated much of the island and the Upper Bay. Delirious patients, some near death, were carried out and laid on the grass, where they remained the rest of that night and most of the following day. A regiment of militia and a boatload of marines arrived after the riot was over.

G. T. Strong wrote in his diary:

> This is the worst villainy that has been perpetrated in my day. . . .
> This riot, robbery and arson, and murder, this outrageous assault
> on men and women struggling against smallpox and yellow fever,
> was in fact a mere operation in real estate, a movement which
> Staten Islanders consider justifiable for the sake of ten per cent increase
> in the market value of building sites and village lots.

Damages to state property came to $133,822. Arrests were made, the matter was aired in courts, but no one was convicted. The state closed the ruined quarantine station and converted a ship into a floating hospital for contagious diseases. Staten Island then became a popular summer resort.

One month after the quarantine riot City Hall was sold.

A Wall Street broker, Robert W. Lowber, had added to his riches by selling land to the city at exorbitant prices, sharing his graft with Mayor Wood and the city council. These officials agreed that the city would pay Lowber $196,000 for a certain parcel of land worth $60,000. But before Lowber got his money, Fernando Wood lost his bid for reelection, and a paint manufacturer, named Daniel F. Tiemann, became mayor. The new Republican mayor was politically inept, but as honest as Wood was larcenous.

Tiemann's reform administration refused to pay Lowber the sum promised him by Wood. The Wall Street broker sued and won. He demanded his $196,000 with interest, damages, and legal fees, bringing the total to $228,000. The city comptroller said that the city couldn't pay this amount because it had no funds "applicable" for such a transaction. Lowber turned the matter over to the sheriff, who was compelled to obey the court's decision. It now became his duty to seize city property that could be sold at auction to realize the amount of the judgment. One day in October, 1858, the sheriff announced that he was going to auction off City Hall and all its contents—including the mayor's chair.

Through the city raced a rumor that Fernando Wood would appear at the sale, buy City Hall, and then make the grand gesture of allowing city officials to use the building. Bullets of sweat creased the worried face of Mayor Tiemann. What a disgrace to let that scoundrel Wood pull such a coup! Tiemann was rich, but Wood was richer. As it turned out, Wood did not show up the day they sold City Hall. Mayor Tiemann bid on it through a clerk, relaxing only after the place was knocked down to him for the nominal sum of $50,000. Thus, for a short time City Hall was owned by one man. The city later bought it back from Tiemann at the price he had paid for it. The Wall Street broker was reimbursed, and there the matter ended.

Chapter 23

ABRAHAM LINCOLN ARRIVES

FERNANDO WOOD was elected mayor for the third time in 1859. Openly hostile toward Negroes, he denounced them as inferior creatures and declared that "the profits, luxuries, the necessities—nay, even the physical existence depend upon the products only to be obtained by continuance of slave labor and the prosperity of the slave master!"

The issue of slavery in all its ramifications—moral, religious, economic, political, and sociological—towered above other issues, such as fear of foreigners, anti-Catholicism, women's rights, and temperance. Since 1808 the importation of slaves into the United States from Africa or the West Indies had been prohibited by federal law.

285

At first Congress did little to enforce the law. After 1820, however, when slave running was made a capital crime, an agency was set up to suppress this trade. Even so, not a single person was executed under the act until the outbreak of the Civil War. With an increase in the price of slaves in the 1850's, New York experienced a boom in slave trading. Horace Greeley called the city "the nest of slave pirates."

Between 1852 and 1862 a total of 26 schooners and brigs belonging to the port of New York were charged by the federal government with engaging in the slave trade. Men who smuggled in slaves were called blackbirders, while the Negroes themselves were referred to as black ivory. The favorite New York rendezvous of the blackbirders was Sweet's Restaurant, at Fulton and South streets, where many a nefarious deal was plotted. One successful slave-trading ship was a beautiful 95-foot yacht, the *Wanderer*, which sailed under colors of the New York Yacht Club. Her skipper and part owner was W. C. Corrie, who fronted for a syndicate of Southerners but was elected to the local club because of the quality of his craft. The *Wanderer* picked up more than 400 Congo Negroes and landed them on one of the Sea Islands of Georgia. When this act of piracy was disclosed, Corrie was merely expelled from the New York Yacht Club.

The Reverend Henry Ward Beecher, who turned to every breeze, said, "My earnest desire is that slavery may be destroyed by the manifest power of Christianity. If it were given me to choose whether it should be destroyed in fifty years by selfish commercial influences, or, standing for seventy-five years, be then the spirit and trophy of God, I had rather let it linger twenty-five years more, that God may be honored, and not mammon, in the destruction of it." This pious remark vexed Horace Greeley, who suggested in the *Tribune* that he would "wish to take the sense of *those in bondage* before agreeing to the twenty-five years' postponement for the glory of Christianity." Frederick Douglass, the former slave, growled, "With a good cowhide, I could take all of that out of Mr. Beecher in five minutes!"

From the time the first horse-drawn streetcars began running in New York, Negroes had been barred from riding them. In 1855 a court affirmed their right to ride in all public conveyances, but transit companies paid no attention to the ruling. One Sunday a Negro minister, the Reverend James C. W. Pennington, urged his parishioners to stand up for their rights. He boarded a Sixth Avenue car and, in a display of passive resistance, refused to get off at the request of the conductor. He was forcibly ejected.

The financial panic that wracked the city and the nation in 1857 provoked Southern resentment of Northern control of the cotton trade. Until the outbreak of the Civil War—when the South owed $200,000,000 to the North—the money manipulators of New York dominated every phase of this business, from plantation to market.

The New York *Evening Post* declared that "the city of New York belongs almost as much to the South as to the North." James D. B. De Bow, a New Orleans magazine editor, proclaimed New York "almost as dependent upon Southern slavery as Charleston itself." When the London *Times* asked De Bow what he thought New York would be like without slavery, he replied, "The ships would rot at her docks; grass would grow in Wall Street and Broadway, and the glory of New York, like that of Babylon and Rome, would be numbered with the things of the past."

This was what Northern businessmen feared. As trade with the West declined during the panic, these hardheaded traders reassured Southerners of their continuing friendship. It disturbed them when eighteen firms and individuals in Columbus, Georgia, pledged themselves not to trade with any New York firm hostile to the South. Deeper grew the cleavage between Northerners and Southerners, and louder their voices.

In Illinois a senatorial candidate, named Abraham Lincoln, said, "A house divided against itself cannot stand. I believe this government cannot endure permanently half slave and half free." The New York *Tribune* sent a correspondent to cover the Lincoln-Douglas debates, and Lincoln kept a special pigeonhole in the desk of his Springfield office for letters from Horace Greeley. When members of the American Antislavery Society met again in New York in 1859, James Gordon Bennett's *Herald* sneered: "They are down upon everybody and everything except their own little set of crazy demagogues and fanatics." Henry J. Raymond's *Times* explained attendance at abolitionist sessions this way: "People go to hear them just as they would go to a bull-baiting or rat-killing match, if these were respectable."

The afternoon of Saturday, February 25, 1860, an odd and ugly man stepped ashore from a ferry at Cortlandt Street. His furrowed face and weatherworn look and his ungainly clothes and loose-jointed gait seemed to mark him as a Westerner. Topping his six-foot four-inch height was a tall beaver hat that made him appear even taller. Wisps of black hair stuck out from the rim of this hat. His ill-fitting suit hung in wrinkles on his badly proportioned figure, with its scraggy neck, narrow chest, and long arms. In one big bony hand he carried an old-fashioned carpetbag. Set deeply within the gaunt clean-shaven face, the gray eyes of Abraham Lincoln gazed for the first time on New York.

No one was at the dock to meet him. A New York lecture agent had invited Lincoln to the city in behalf of the young men of Henry Ward Beecher's church. However, because of a conflict in dates, his engagement was now sponsored by the Young Men's Republican Union of New York City. This group hoped to prevent the nomination of Senator William Henry Seward as Presidential candidate of the new Republican party. Aware that Seward was the front-runner, Lincoln was gratified to read a friendly story about himself in Greeley's *Tribune*. Still alone, he checked into the Astor House, where gentlemen were requested to park their pistols in the cloakroom.

The next morning Lincoln crossed over to Brooklyn to hear a sermon by Beecher, whom he considered "the greatest orator since St. Paul." Sunday afternoon an Illinois Congressman took Lincoln slumming through the notorious Five Points—always a must for out-of-town visitors.

A cold rain was falling on Monday when some young Republicans called for Lincoln at the Astor House. When he said that he wanted to buy a new hat, they drove him to Knox's Great Hat and Cap Establishment at Broadway and Fulton Street. Because Knox made a hobby of collecting politicians' hats, he gave Lincoln a new silk topper in exchange for his beaver hat. Back on the street, noticing that the rain was turning into a wet snow, Lincoln may have wondered if bad weather would reduce attendance at Cooper Union that evening. He stared at Broadway horsecars, their sides gay with pictures painted by well-known artists, and then drew up in front of 643 Broadway, where Mathew B. Brady ran a photo studio. In the reception room Lincoln met George Bancroft, the eminent American historian. Then Brady ushered Lincoln into an inner room and posed him standing erect, his left hand resting on a book on a small table. Lincoln looked directly into the lens of the camera, his gaze soft and gentle, his lips somewhat melancholy. The photographic session over, Lincoln was driven to his hotel to dress for the evening.

Thickening snow gummed the streets as Lincoln struggled into the new suit he had brought along for this, his first appearance before an Eastern audience. It was a black broadcloth frock coat, much too small and badly wrinkled from confinement in his carpetbag. His low collar exposed his thin neck, and the right side of the collar wouldn't stay down. Onto his big feet he pulled new boots so tight that he limped all evening. As Lincoln later confessed, he was ashamed of his appearance.

Despite the traffic-snarling snowstorm, 1,500 persons paid 25 cents each to hear this strange man from the West. Although Lincoln had lost the senatorial race to Stephen A. Douglas, he had written to a disheartened friend: "Quit that. You will soon feel better. Another 'blow-up' is coming; and we shall have fun again." Already there was talk of Abraham Lincoln as a dark horse candidate for the Presidency.

Gathered in Cooper Union that night, as Greeley said, was the "intellect and moral culture" of the city of New York. Ticket holders strolled into the Great Hall and sat down in revolving chairs upholstered in red leather. About 8 P.M. Lincoln was led past the thick white pillars, under the glass chandeliers with their hissing gas jets, and onto the stage, where he sat down. One man staring at the seated Lincoln felt that there was something strange about his posture, and soon he understood what it was: Although Lincoln's long legs were crossed, both feet were flat on the floor of the platform. Then bearded William Cullen Bryant arose and introduced Abraham Lincoln of Illinois. Applause sounded like rain on a tin roof.

Unkinking his lanky frame, Lincoln stood up, tucked his left hand under a coat lapel, smiled wanly, and waited until the noise subsided. At last he began in a falsetto voice: "Mr. *Cheer*man—" There were titters from the audience. Lincoln gulped, his Adam's apple riding up and down. Again he began in his Kentucky drawl, his voice still cracked with stage fright, speaking too softly to be heard in the back of the room. People yelled, "Louder!" Steeling himself, Lincoln went on to plod more deeply into his well-researched and well-reasoned speech, gaining confidence, his voice deepening in pitch and growing in volume. As he forgot his audience and concentrated on his message, Lincoln seemed transformed. His fixed gaze became hypnotic, and for the next hour and a half he held the breathless attention of the sophisticated New Yorkers. He said:

> Even though much provoked, let us do nothing through passion and ill temper. Even though the southern people will not so much

as listen to us, let us calmly consider their demands, and yield to them if, in our deliberate view of our duty, we possibly can. . . . Wrong as we think slavery is, we can yet afford to let it alone where it is, because that much is due to the necessity arising from its actual presence in the nation; but can we, while our votes will prevent it, allow it to be spread into the national territories, and to overrun us here in these free states? . . . Neither let us be slandered from our duty by false accusations against us, nor frightened from it by menaces of destruction to the government, nor of dungeons to ourselves. Let us have the faith that right makes might, and in that faith let us to the end dare to do our duty as we understand it.

Lincoln's New York speech that evening of February 27, 1860, was received by his audience with prolonged cheers. The next morning four New York newspapers ran the full text. It was also published in pamphlets and distributed by the tens of thousands across the land, together with reproductions of Brady's photograph depicting a statesmanlike Lincoln. Republicans were so impressed that Seward lost much of his early support, and three months later Lincoln won the Republican Presidential nomination. Lincoln always remembered New York with special fondness, saying, "Brady and the Cooper Institute made me President."

As election day neared, Southerners spoke ever more menacingly about seceding from the Union. The New York *Evening Post* met this talk with what it called "the following choice lines of Mother Goose. 'Says Aaron to Moses, let us cut off our noses; Says Moses to Aaron, it's the fashion to wear'em.' " Then, in a serious vein, the *Post* declared, "If a State secedes, it is revolution, and the seceders are traitors."

Lincoln's election as President on November 6 was the signal for overt action by South Carolina, the proudest and most aristocratic of all Southern states. Its legislature called a state convention, whose delegates at 1:15 P.M. on December 20, 1860, declared that "the union now subsisting between South Carolina and the other States, under the name of 'The United States of America,' is hereby dissolved."

In the White House, President James Buchanan dolorously told John Cochrane of New York he believed that he was the last President of the United States. The New York *Herald* jibed that just as Lincoln had once split rails, so was he now splitting the Union. Alexander T. Stewart, a New York department store magnate, wrote that "the refusal at Washington to concede costs us millions daily." New York bankers and merchants—anxious about the $150,000,000 or so they had advanced to Southerners in long-term crop loans—told Congress that the federal government would be left penniless if it did not allow South Carolina to go its own way.

Southern agents shipped increasing quantities of muskets from New York to states south of the Mason and Dixon line. The New York *Journal of Commerce* said ominously, "There are a million and a half mouths to be fed daily in this city and its dependencies; and they will not consent to be starved by any man's policies. They will sooner set up for themselves against the whole world." Mayor Fernando Wood agreed. On January 7, 1861, in the most extraordinary message ever received by the city council, the mayor *recommended that New York secede from the Union and become a free city.*

He believed that dissolution of the Federal Union was inevitable. He felt that the city should not jeopardize its profitable trade with the South by taking an anti-Southern stand. He hoped to free the city from domination by the state legislature. He schemed to capture the rich customs duties now pouring into the city and being absorbed by the federal government. "If the confederacy is broken up," Wood argued, "the government is dissolved, and it behooves every distinct community, as well as every individual, to take care of themselves."

The mayor's proposal did not win favor even among members of his own Democratic party. Greeley blasted him: "Fernando Wood evidently wants to be a traitor; it is lack of courage only that makes him content with being a blackguard." The *Evening Post* scoffed that it never suspected Wood of being a fool, regardless of whatever else he might be, and archly asked if the seceding city should take along Long Island Sound, the New York Central Railroad, and the Erie Canal. When Lincoln heard the news in Springfield, he grinned and told a New Yorker, "I reckon it will be some time before the Front Door sets up housekeeping on its own account." In the nation's capital Secretary of the Treasury John A. Dix, a New York Democrat, issued this order: "If anyone attempts to haul down the American flag, shoot him on sight."

No flag came down, but none went up over City Hall on the day Lincoln was inaugurated as President of the United States. Flouting city tradition, Mayor Wood refused to let the Stars and Stripes wave above the seat of government of the nation's most powerful city.

On April 12, 1861, the first shot of the Civil War was fired by a Southerner at Fort Sumter, in Charleston, South Carolina. Poet-editor Walt Whitman wrote:

> News of the attack on fort Sumter and *the flag* at Charleston Harbor, S.C., was receiv'd in New York city late at night and was immediately sent out in extras of the newspapers. I had been to the opera in Fourteenth street that night, and after the performance was walking down Broadway toward twelve o'clock, on my way to Brooklyn, when I heard in the distance the loud cries of the news-boys, who came presently tearing and yelling up the street, rushing from side to side even more furiously than usual. I bought an extra and cross'd to the Metropolitan hotel where the great lamps were still brightly blazing, and, with a crowd of others, who gather'd impromptu, read the news, which was evidently authentic. For the benefit of some who had no papers, one of us read the telegram aloud, while all listen'd silently and attentively. No remark was made by any of the crowd, which had increas'd to thirty or forty, but all stood a minute or two, I remember, before they dispers'd. I can almost see them there now, under the lamps at midnight again.

From the Reverend Henry Ward Beecher, a rosy-cheeked follower of the Prince of Peace, came this shrill cry: "Give me war redder than blood and fiercer than fire!"

Chapter 24

THE DRAFT RIOTS

A FORMER New York policeman, named Peter Hart, helped save the American flag at Fort Sumter in that first battle of the Civil War. In the early morning of April 12, 1861, Southerners opened fire on the federal-held stronghold in Charleston Harbor and kept up the bombardment for thirty-four hours. The second afternoon, a few minutes before one o'clock, an enemy ball shot off the tip of the fort's flagpole. Down fluttered Old Glory. Peter Hart, then a sergeant in the United States army, dashed out onto the littered parapet, carrying a long pole. A captain and two lieutenants ran to his aid. Amid a tempest of shot and shell the four soldiers fastened the pole to a gun carriage and raised the colors once more.

In New York during the opening days of the war a famous widow sat in her home making American flags. Her husband had been Captain James Lawrence, the naval officer who had won immortality during the War of 1812 by shouting, "Don't give up the ship!" He had died of his wounds and lay buried in Trinity Churchyard.

As newspapers issued one extra after another, Mrs. Lawrence showed her little granddaughter how to scrape lint with a carving knife. A visitor, a flip young man known as "Poke" Wright, dropped by. He made an insulting remark about the American flag. The old woman looked up in astonishment and then cried, "No one can speak with disrespect in *my* house of the banner under which my husband fought and died!" Pulling her frail body out of a chair, she charged the rascal with her knife, driving him out onto the street. Her shrill anger attracted pedestrians, who grabbed Wright, forced him to his knees, and made him cheer the flag.

This symbolized the changed attitude of most New Yorkers upon the fall of Fort Sumter. A merchant wrote: "There is but one feeling here now, and that is to sustain our flag and the government at all costs." A Charleston man who ordered flour from another New York merchant got this reply: "Eat your *cotton,* God damn ye!" The Planters Hotel at Albany and Greenwich streets, long popular with Southerners, quickly closed. Tammany Hall had opposed war with the South, but now, sniffing public opinion, it issued a loyalty proclamation and sent a regiment to the front.

Mayor Fernando Wood issued his own bland proclamation, urging everybody to obey the laws of the land. Remembering that only four months earlier the mayor had suggested that the city secede from the Union, G. T. Strong wrote in his diary: "The cunning scoundrel sees which way the cat is jumping and puts himself right on the record in a vague general way, giving the least possible offense to his allies of the Southern democracy." A mob chased *Herald* publisher James Gordon Bennett up the street and insisted that an American flag be displayed from his building; Bennett had to send out an office boy to find one. The supply of bunting ran short as nearly every private and public building flew Old Glory.

The previous year work had ceased on the new St. Patrick's Cathedral for lack of money. Now a halt was called to the landscaping of Central Park, and Frederick Law Olmsted went to Washington as general secretary of the Sanitary Commission. The city took on a military appearance, as camps were set up in City Hall Park, at the

Battery, on Staten Island, on Rikers Island, and at Atlantic and Flatbush avenues in Brooklyn. Cannon ringed the new Croton Fountain in City Hall Park. Private houses and public buildings were taken over by the army for offices and recruiting stations. The Brooklyn Navy Yard hired more men.

President Lincoln called for 75,000 three-month volunteers on April 15, and within 10 days 8,000 well-equipped men from this city left for the front. For days afterward the slap and scuffle of marching feet resounded in streets as volunteers from upper New York State and from New England flowed through the city en route to threatened Washington. The local Irish, Germans, Poles, Italians, and Scots organized their own regiments. Firemen banded together into regiments of Zouaves. In their drill and dress they imitated Algerian light infantry of this name. Their gaudy uniforms consisted of baggy trousers, gaiters, open jackets, and turbans or fezzes. Oddly clad, too, were members of the Seventy-ninth New York Highlanders. On ceremonial occasions the officers wore kilts, while the men donned pantaloons of the Cameron tartan in honor of their colonel, James Cameron.

A physics professor left Columbia College to join the new Confederate army. A few Columbia students enlisted and fought, but they did not enroll en masse, as did Harvard boys, and war fever never gripped Columbia, as it did, say, the University of Wisconsin.

Free Negroes tried to enlist, but they were rejected at first. New York was still a segregated city. In 1860 voters had defeated a bill giving Negroes the right to vote without meeting property qualifications. Black men persisted in their clamor to bear arms against the South. Visiting here was a South Carolina white woman, who cried, "Just think how infamous it is that our *gentlemen* should have to go out and fight niggers, and that every nigger they shoot is a thousand dollars out of their own pockets!" The first local company of colored soldiers was mustered on February 9, 1864. All told, 200,000 American Negroes served in the Union army.

The New York Sabbath Committee declared it would be unholy of soldiers to fight on Sunday. The Reverend Stephen H. Tyng, of St. George's Episcopal Church on Broadway, said that it was a historic fact that "the party who attacks in war on Sunday has invariably been defeated." General Robert E. Lee, who had spent five years in New York strengthening local forts, took command of all Southern forces. Tiffany's began making swords, medals, corps badges, and other military insignia. Brooks Brothers turned out uniforms for generals

Grant, Sherman, Sheridan, and Hooker and for thousands of their men.

The largest mass meeting in the city's history was held in Union Square to pledge loyalty to the Union cause. Crowd estimates vary from 100,000 to 250,000 persons. Whatever the exact number, the multitude was so vast that speeches were made from 5 different stands erected in the square. Fernando Wood presided because he was mayor, but scowling men muttered that they might run him out of office unless he took a strong pro-Union stand. This warning was echoed by a boy perched in a tree: "Now, Fernandy, mind what you say! You've got to stick to it this time!" People laughed, and Wood spoke as ordered. The rabid patriotism of New Yorkers galled Southerners, who felt betrayed by the one group of Northerners they had considered their friends. The Richmond *Dispatch* editorialized: "New York will be remembered with special hatred by the South for all time."

The Rebels, with superior leadership, won the first two engagements of the war. After the First Battle of Bull Run, demoralization spread throughout the North, and Greeley wanted an armistice. In the *Tribune* he wrote: "The gloom in this city is funereal—for our dead at Bull Run were many, and they lie unburied yet. On every brow sits sullen, scorching, black despair." Spirits drooped even lower after the Battle of Ball's Bluff. Then came incredible news of how some New York units had conducted themselves on the field.

At Bull Run the First New York Fire Zouaves distinguished themselves. However, another group of Zouaves panicked their first time under fire. Basically brave men, they were such individualists that they defied discipline. Then too, the Seventy-ninth New York Highlanders, who had volunteered for three *years* of service, mutinied when three-*month* volunteers left the front.

Early victory faded from sight, and defeatism corroded the North. A Confederate major from Mississippi rashly made his way to New York, swaggered from one Broadway saloon to another, and boasted how he had chewed up Union soldiers at Bull Run. He was clapped into prison, but people shuddered at his words. August Belmont, a Rothschild agent in New York, wrote that thousands of people were sorry they had voted for Abraham Lincoln. Bennett of the *Herald* roared, "The business community demands that the war shall be *short;* and the more vigorously it is prosecuted, the more speedily it will be closed. Business men can stand a temporary reverse. They can easily make arrangements for six months or a year. But they cannot endure a long, uncertain and tedious contest."

Greeley, who blew hot and cold about the Lincoln administration, first used the word "Copperhead" in the *Tribune* on July 20, 1861. Copperheads were Northern Democrats who opposed the war policies of the Republican President and favored a negotiated peace. New York became the nest of these snake-named conspirators. According to *A Short History of New York State:* "The peace faction was particularly strong in New York City, which from the elections of 1860 to Appomattox provided more moral support to the Confederacy and more opposition to the war than any other important section of the North."

The first two war years the Union's fighting men consisted of four grades of troops—regular army, state militia, three-*month* volunteers, and three-*year* volunteers. Most were volunteers, since this was a people's war fought by amateurs, rather than by professional soldiers. In April, 1862, the Confederacy began drafting men, and the following July New York State passed a weak draft law. Lincoln's first call for 75,000 three-month volunteers proved inadequate, so he asked again and again for various quotas to serve various periods of time. Not enough men stepped forward to replace battle losses and the thinning of ranks because of illness. On March 3, 1863, the first federal American draft went into effect. All able-bodied Northern white males between the ages of twenty and forty-five became liable for military service.

The draft was "profoundly repugnant to the American mind," according to the New York *World,* controlled by Fernando Wood and August Belmont. Wood's brother, Benjamin, headed the *Daily News,* which said, "The people are notified that one out of about two and a half of our citizens are to be brought into Messrs. Lincoln & Company's charnelhouse. God forbid!" The proslavery *Journal of Commerce* snarled that the war itself had become the work of "evil-minded men to accomplish their aims."

Even though his own state had already passed a draft act, Democratic Governor Horatio Seymour challenged the federal government's right to conscript citizens. By protesting the quota assigned to New York State, he postponed the first local draft lottery. On July 4, in New York City, the governor made one of the most inflammatory speeches ever uttered by a public official. Seymour shouted, "Remember this! Remember this! The bloody, treasonable and revolutionary doctrine of public necessity can be proclaimed by a mob as well as by a government!"

His words fell like sparks on a city rotten with crime and ripe for revolt. In 1862 nearly one-tenth of the population had been arrested on one charge or another, and between 70,000 and 80,000 criminals infested the town. Wages were low, and prices high; coal, for example, cost more than $10 a ton. A draftee could buy exemption from service by paying the federal government $300, but few unskilled workers had this much money. They muttered that it was a rich man's war, but a poor man's fight. It was known that John Jacob Astor, grandson and namesake of the late multimillionaire, was a colonel on General McClellan's staff and lived by himself at headquarters in a rented house with a valet, chef, and steward.

In New York City a recent strike had been broken by importing freed slaves willing to scab. This further incensed poor whites against Negroes. More than half the city's dwellers were foreign-born, most were Democrats, and 203,740 were Irish. Tammany Hall, dependent on the Irish vote, was eager to undermine the national war effort. The *Daily News* charged that the federal draft was a deliberate attempt to reduce the number of Democratic voters in the city.

The draft was scheduled to begin here on Saturday, July 11, 1863. The city was divided into districts, each having an enrollment office. There the names of eligible men would be drawn from revolving lottery wheels. City officials were not asked to take part in the draft; the War Department had appointed Robert Nugent chief provost marshal to oversee everything. Nugent, a colonel of the Sixty-ninth Regiment, an Irishman, and a Democrat, was named in the hope of assuring the city's Irish that the draft would be conducted fairly.

As the deadline approached, New York City was almost stripped of troops. Confederate General Lee had invaded Maryland and filled Pennsylvania with wild alarm. President Lincoln had asked the governor of New York to send 20,000 men for 30 days to resist the invaders, and 19 regiments of the state national guard had been rushed to the front. Only about 1,900 military men remained here. Of these, 1,000 belonged to various militia and volunteer companies still being organized; 700 were soldiers, sailors, and marines garrisoning the city's forts and manning the warships anchored here; and 200 were members of the Invalid Corps, or crippled and wounded soldiers protecting arsenals, armories, and munitions plants. A few of these invalids were detached from duty to protect draft offices. There was 1 constable for each of the city's 22 wards. The police force totaled only 2,297 men.

The infamous Draft Riots of July, 1863, were so well led that they constituted an organized insurrection, rather than a spontaneous mob uprising. Definite strategy may be seen in the efforts to cut off approaches to the city, to sever communications, to capture forts, to seize armories and munitions works with all their weapons and ammunition, and to plunder banks and federal treasury vaults. In fact, the mobs have been called "the left wing of Lee's army." G. T. Strong spoke of the "scoundrels who are privily engineering the outburst" as "agents of Jefferson Davis," the president of the Confederacy—but he stretched a point.

Some contemporary New Yorkers regarded the riots as a Catholic plot, since Protestant property was burned and looted, while no Catholic property was even threatened. This seems unlikely, for on several occasions lone Catholic priests turned back murderous mobs. It is true, however, that most rioters were Irish Catholics. Between 50,000 and 70,000 of them took part in the orgy, and some individual mobs numbered as many as 10,000 frenzied men and women.

On Saturday morning, July 11, Governor Seymour was vacationing at Long Branch, New Jersey, a two-hour carriage drive from New York City. He sent the state adjutant general from Long Branch to Washington to ask federal officials to postpone the draft. Lincoln's twenty-year-old son, Robert Todd Lincoln, on holiday from Harvard, was stopping in the Fifth Avenue Hotel, at Fifth Avenue and Twenty-third Street. Sir Winston Churchill's paternal grandfather, Leonard Walter Jerome, sometime adviser to Cornelius Vanderbilt and a big stockholder in the New York *Times,* puttered about his mansion, at Madison Avenue and Twenty-sixth Street.

Early that morning the police heard that the arsenal at Seventh Avenue and Thirty-fifth Street was to be raided by Knights of the Golden Circle, a secret society of Northerners siding with the South. The police superintendent, John A. Kennedy, sent a sergeant and fifteen patrolmen to the building, where they broke up a gathering crowd and then marched inside.

News of the Union victory at Gettysburg now reached the city, and optimists assured one another that the rebellion had been put down. Who wanted to be drafted when the whole shooting bang was about over? A sullen crowd collected in front of the Ninth District's enrollment office on the northeastern corner of Third Avenue and Forty-sixth Street, where the city's first draft lottery was to be held. Names and addresses of eligible men were written on white slips of paper. The papers were folded and dumped inside a wooden revolving drum. It was hand-cranked until the papers were thoroughly scrambled. This process was repeated again and again until 1,236 names had been picked. Then it was announced that the draft would be resumed the following Monday.

Saturday's evening papers published the results of this first local draft. As *Leslie's Illustrated* said:

> It came like a thunderclap on the people, and as men read their names in the fatal list the feeling of indignation and resistance soon found vent in words, and a spirit of resistance spread fast and far. The number of poor men exceeded, as a matter of course, that of the rich, their number to draw being so much greater, but this was viewed as a proof of the dishonesty in the whole proceeding.

That night Southern sympathizers visited saloons in the Five Points and along the waterfront, fanning the first flames of resentment.

On Sunday morning, in hundreds of homes, the meaning of the draft sank deeper into the minds of conscripted men, their wives, and their sweethearts. The city's seventeen detectives spread through streets to look and listen. Stormy-faced citizens gathered at corners to growl that some rich men had already paid their $300 and been excused from military duty. Messages flew back and forth among gang chieftains. Hoodlums collected bricks, clubs, stones, and other weapons and hid them. Superintendent Kennedy kept a guard at the arsenal and made full use of his detectives, but otherwise his Sunday assignments were routine. That evening several fires broke out in lower Manhattan, and firemen noted that the watching crowds were larger and more boisterous than usual.

Monday morning dawned hot and clear. About 6 A.M. men and women slunk out of Lower East Side slums, filtered to the West Side, and paused to regroup. They were joined by others until the crowd became enormous. Now it split into two detachments, which tumbled north up Eighth and Ninth avenues. Groups of men spun off from these main bodies and darted into side streets, yelling for workers to lay down their tools and join the fun. By the time respectable people sat down to breakfast, the mob had turned east and reached its rendezvous. This was a vacant lot just east of Fifth Avenue near

Fifty-ninth Street. Agitators climbed onto boulders and bellowed about the injustice of the draft.

At eight o'clock, augmented by newcomers, the human tide began moving again, this time southward, clattering in two thick columns down Fifth and Sixth avenues, cursing, singing, brandishing weapons, and screaming defiance of the federal government. At Forty-seventh Street the columns merged and wheeled east in one vast multitude, filling the street from curb to curb, requiring twenty-five minutes to pass a given spot. At Third Avenue the rabble turned south and tramped down the broad thoroughfare to the draft office at Forty-sixth Street, where another crowd was already assembled.

Although Police Superintendent Kennedy knew that trouble was brewing, he was not yet aware of how deadly it would become. He had sent a captain and 60 cops to reinforce the squad of patrolmen on duty at the uptown draft office. He also dispatched a captain, 4 sergeants, and 69 cops to another threatened draft office on Broadway at Twenty-ninth Street. That Monday morning, July 13, Kennedy had a total of only 800 policemen available for duty as the riots began.

Federal officials in the city began to stir uneasily. Major General John Ellis Wool was in charge of the Department of the East, with headquarters in New York City. The seventy-four-year-old general was muddleheaded and indecisive. Now he detached fifty members of the Invalid Corps from guard duty elsewhere and sent them limping toward Third Avenue horsecars to ride to the Forty-sixth Street draft office. By this time rioters were chopping down telegraph poles around the menaced building.

Ruffians along Second and Third Avenues halted the horsecars, and by 8:30 A.M. no more of these vehicles were moving on the avenues. G. T. Strong had heard the roars of the mob and boarded a Third Avenue car to go see what was happening. At Thirteenth Street he found the track blocked by a line of motionless cars stretching way up the avenue, so he got off and began walking. Above Twentieth Street all shops were closed.

At 9 A.M. so many alarming reports reached Police Headquarters, at 300 Mulberry Street, that Superintendent Kennedy sent this message over the police telegraph system: "To all stations in New York and Brooklyn: Call in your reserves and hold them at the station house subject to further orders." A millionaire merchant, named

George Opdyke, was now mayor of New York City. From his City Hall office Mayor Opdyke sent a request to Major General Charles W. Sanford to call out all the militia units left in town. As a result, the first military unit mustered on Monday—apart from the Invalid Corps already under arms—was the Tenth Regiment of the national guard. It assembled in the arsenal at Elm and Worth streets. The mayor also telegraphed an appeal to Governor Seymour to hasten to the city from his Jersey retreat.

Up at the Third Avenue draft office, for the next hour and a half, the police had little trouble coping with the mob surrounding the place. The lottery wheel stood on the ground floor, while the upper three stories were occupied by poor families. The Invalid Corps had not yet arrived. The cops, clubs drawn and faces tense, stood with their backs against the building as the draft lottery resumed. To complete the Ninth District's quota, 264 more names had to be picked. The mob extended half a dozen blocks north and south of Forty-sixth Street, pushing and yelling and hooting. A few reckless carriage drivers tried to whip their horses through the throng. Plug-uglies caught the bridles of horses, unhitched animals from their shafts, and forced drivers and passengers to get out. Bobbing up and down in the melee were placards reading: "No DRAFT!" The mob surged closer to the cops ringing the draft office. Its vanguard consisted of members of a street-brawling outfit, volunteer firemen in Engine Company 33, popularly known as the Black Joke. The Black Jokers jeered the cops and shouted so uproariously that those inside draft headquarters could barely hear themselves.

At 10:30 A.M. someone in the mob shot a pistol into the air. Then a volley of bricks and stones shattered windows of the draft office. The Black Jokers lunged toward the door. The police fought bravely but were overwhelmed. A police captain ordered his men to retreat inside the building. They backed through the door but were unable to slam it shut, so fast did the howling firemen pour in after them. Draft officials scampered out rear windows. In the halls the cops fought a hopeless rearguard action. Then they dived out windows into the alley and ran toward Second Avenue. Thousands of rioters surged inside. They broke the lottery wheel. They set fire to the building. The flames spread to an adjoining building. Loyal firemen raced up; but the mob kept them from dousing the blaze, and they had to stand by helplessly and watch the destruction of the entire block from Forty-sixth to Forty-seventh Street.

Moments later those on the southern fringe of the mob saw the Invalid Corps unit closing in. These veterans of battlefield horrors, their flesh and bones mending from wounds, had been delayed when the horsecars had stopped running. Now they walked and limped straight toward the mob, which wheeled and charged at them. The clash came at Third Avenue and Forty-second Street. The veterans were vastly outnumbered. Gangsters stoned them, killing one soldier and injuring half a dozen more.

The commanding officer ordered his front rank to fire blanks. The volley pricked the mob into greater fury and left half the troops defenseless. Snarling Irish plug-uglies lunged at the soldiers. The second rank of the Invalids fired real bullets, slaying and wounding six men and one woman. For a second the mob paused. Then, with ferocious roars, the ruffians fell en masse on the veterans, who did not have time to reload. Muskets were jerked from their trembling hands. Many were clubbed with the butts of their own weapons and shot point-blank in the belly. One veteran ran toward the East River and clawed his way to the top of a cliff. He was followed, caught, and hurled to death on the rocky beach below. Then his lifeless body was pounded to pulp by boulders so big that it took two strong men to lift and throw them. All told, a score of veterans were killed. Those able to run took to their heels. They abandoned wounded comrades, who were mutilated as they lay on the ground.

Meantime, Police Superintendent Kennedy had left his headquarters to make a tour of inspection. That hot summer day he wore civilian clothing and carried a bamboo cane. By carriage he drove to Forty-sixth Street and Lexington Avenue, where he heard the hoarse shouts of the mob and saw smoke charcoaling the sky. Kennedy got out and began walking east on Forty-sixth Street. He had gone only half a block when he was recognized. Gangsters rushed him, and one man in an old army uniform knocked him down. Kennedy jumped up and slashed the bully across the face with his cane. Kennedy was beaten to the ground again. He was kicked and stamped on. Once more he leaped up. A hail of blows hammered him to the edge of a hole dug in the street, and he was knocked into it. Up he bobbed. He fled across a vacant lot toward Forty-seventh Street, where another gang met him. He was slugged and slashed as he tried to escape to Lexington Avenue. There a thug pounded him into a deep mudhole. Kennedy pulled himself out and, muddy and bloody, staggered on until he collapsed in the arms of an influential citizen, named John Eagan.

This good Samaritan convinced Kennedy's attackers that the police superintendent was dead. He was indeed unconscious. Kennedy later was placed in a wagon, covered with gunnysacks, and driven to Police Headquarters. There a surgeon found seventy-two bruises and more than a score of cuts on his body.

In the nation's capital President Lincoln was getting telegraphic news of the riot from Sidney H. Gray, managing editor of the New York *Tribune*. At 11:45 A.M. the federal government ordered the city draft offices closed. This did not end the violence. The criminals, the poor, and the disloyal were out to seize control of the town, and they did. By tearing up tracks, they isolated the city from direct approach by train. They cut wires that cobwebbed the police telegraph system, but repairmen soon spliced lines and restored communications.

With Superintendent Kennedy unconscious, police command devolved upon police commissioners John C. Bergen and Thomas C. Acton. Bergen took charge in Brooklyn and on Staten Island. Acton, a prominent Republican and a founder of the Union League Club, assumed command in Manhattan. Intelligent and energetic, Acton received and answered more than 4,000 telegrams between Monday morning and Friday afternoon. All this time he neither slept nor changed clothes.

Monday noon a mob clattered toward the home of Mayor Opdyke, at 79 Fifth Avenue, near Fifteenth Street. Although the mayor had neglected to provide a guard for his residence, fifty neighbors now armed themselves and took up defensive positions. Supreme Court Justice George G. Barnard climbed onto the stoop of an adjoining house and spoke to the mob. Everybody knew that Barnard had been elevated to the court by William Marcy Tweed, and the fat Boss was everybody's friend. So the judge talked the crowd out of attacking the mayor's home.

Mayor Opdyke was in his City Hall office, where he now called for a special session of the city council. Because only half a dozen aldermen appeared, no quorum could be obtained. The mayor then issued a proclamation ordering the rioters to disperse. The Irish, who regarded the mayor as a Black Republican, reacted violently. A mob began to howl under City Hall windows. Since the mayor was in danger, Tweed and other Democrats persuaded him to seek safer quarters in the St. Nicholas Hotel, at Broadway and Spring Street.

Monday afternoon the city was mob-ruled. As Carl Sandburg has written: "Never before in an American metropolis had the police, merchants, bankers, and forces of law and order had their power wrenched loose by mobs so skillfully led." Now brutal Irishmen began attacking Negroes, whom they blamed for the war.

The Colored Orphan Asylum, on the west side of Fifth Avenue, occupied the entire block between Forty-third and Forty-fourth streets. It looked a little like the White House in Washington. Here were sheltered more than 200 Negro children under the age of twelve, together with 50 matrons and attendants. Soon after the abortive attack on the mayor's home, a mob of 3,000 persons gathered in front of the asylum and began shouting threats. The asylum superintendent, William E. Davis, barricaded the doors. Rowdies roared that they damned well would break in. The children's eyes widened in terror. Davis and other staff members herded them out the back and into a nearby police station. Later, under military escort, the children were taken to Blackwells Island. Moments after the asylum was evacuated, rioters stormed its front doors, broke them down, tumbled inside, smashed furniture, carried out toys and bedding, and then set fire to the place. While the vandalism was at its height, one little Negro girl, overlooked in the hasty departure, was found trembling under a bed. She was pulled out and beaten to death.

The middle of Monday afternoon the rioting spread to the downtown section of the city. Most stores had closed, but saloons stayed open to stoke people's fury with raw liquor. Jewelry shops were looted. Hardware stores were raided for guns and pistols and ammunition. Fires were set here, there, everywhere. Negroes were chased and cornered and strung up and tortured. Irish biddies knifed the flesh of hanged Negroes, poured oil into the wounds, set fire to the oil, danced under the human torches, and sang obscene songs.

(Despite the unspeakable cruelty of some of New York's low-class Irish, many of the city's Irishmen served with distinction in the Union army. At least 8 all-Irish regiments were formed here. Thousands of Patricks and Clanceys and Emmets donned the honorable blue uniform, a total of 150,000 Irishmen from all parts of the North swelling the ranks. Generals Meade, Rosecrans, Sheridan, Meagher, Sickles, Ord, and Gillmore were Catholic. At Fredericksburg, Virginia, an Irish brigade marched into battle flying Ireland's green flag with its golden harp. Later a color sergeant was found with the flag wrapped about his body, a bullet having pierced the flag and his heart. An Irish washerwoman followed some of her countrymen into combat during the Second Battle of Bull Run and stood tall and unafraid as she cheered them on.)

But here in New York, as drunken Irishmen lurched through the streets, decent people locked themselves in their homes. Peter Goelet owned a big house at Broadway and Nineteenth Street. With him lived his twenty-five-year-old nephew, Elbridge Gerry. The old man raised peacocks and pheasants and let them strut about the lawn. In normal times pedestrians stopped to peer at them between iron railings. On this day of peril young Gerry felt that the gorgeous plumage of the birds might attract the attention of rioters. He ordered the coachman to pull out all their colorful tail feathers. Divested of this weight, the peacocks and pheasants, looking like drunken acrobats, lost their balance and toppled over onto their beaks. Elbridge Gerry later became vice-president of the American Society for the Prevention of Cruelty to Animals.

One mob looted and burned a block of fine houses on Lexington Avenue near Forty-sixth Street. Another set fire to the draft office on Broadway near Twenty-ninth Street. Then this downtown mob, led by a giant carrying an American flag, a bobbing, throbbing, chanting mass of men and women, 10,000 strong and armed with guns, pistols, clubs, swords, and crowbars, clattered down Broadway, setting the torch to houses as they went and heading for Police Headquarters. Under the hot sun the rioters cast snake-weaving shadows. At the central office, as Police Headquarters was then called, 200 policemen had gathered, but 50 were too weak from wounds to be efficient. Commissioner Acton wired precinct houses to rush reinforcements at once. The besieged Eighteenth Precinct Station, on Twenty-second Street near Third Avenue, replied, "One of our officers, just in, says that not one of us can get to the central office, in uniform, alive. They will try in citizens' dress." Detectives who had mingled with the advancing mob now raced into headquarters, panting that if the rioters overran the central office, their next target would be the Wall Street area. There they planned to loot banks and plunder the Subtreasury Building. The alert was relayed to the Brooklyn Navy Yard, and two armed ships glided into position, one in the East River and the other in the Hudson, ready to rake the toe of Manhattan with their guns.

Sweeping sweat from his forehead, Acton decided to head off the mob before it neared the central office. Combat command was given to Inspector Daniel C. Carpenter, the senior uniformed officer in the department. Lining up 125 cops in front of headquarters, he said grimly, "We are going to put down a mob, and we will take no prisoners." Then he marched his men out of Mulberry Street west toward Broadway and turned north onto this wide thoroughfare. From the north as far as the eye could see, a lavalike hubble-bubble of people seethed and seeped down Broadway. The police trudged north. The mob inched south.

They met at Broadway and Amity (now West Third) Street, one block south of Washington Square and near the sumptuous hotel called the La Farge House. Scores of rioters swarmed into the hotel and beat up Negro bellboys and waiters. Out on the street, when the police heaved in sight, the mob halted. Then a huge club-waving bully sprang at Inspector Carpenter, marching several feet in front of his men. Carpenter ducked a blow that might have cracked his skull and killed the man with his nightstick. Patrolman Doyle slew a man carrying a "NO DRAFT!" sign. Patrolman Thompson captured the American flag from the giant. The mob let go with a storm of bricks and stones and opened up with firearms. Several cops slumped to the pavement. The rest closed ranks and charged, their clubs rising and falling, tattooing skulls on all sides. It was hand-to-hand combat, no quarter given, with the thud of nightsticks and the crunch of breaking bones, the howls of fury and shrieks of pain, sweaty bodies thudding against one another, blood and sweat dripping down weary arms and legs. For fifteen minutes all was confusion. Then the rioters broke and ran. The dead and dying and disabled littered the street and sidewalk. Gone was the threat to Police Headquarters.

The battle did not quell the riots. It was an island of success in a sea of defeats. In first one section of the city and then another, brutish mobs killed and tortured and looted and burned, and by 4 P.M. on that Monday of infamy every good citizen who was able to do so had left New York. Trains had stopped running at noon, after tracks had been spiked in the upper reaches of the city, so panic-stricken people jammed ships and boats and vehicles of every sort to get away. By evening it was impossible to hire a rig of any kind. Quaking Negroes fled afoot, skulking up alleys and bypaths, dodging hot-eyed pursuers, and racing and stumbling to the safety of woods and fields.

Monday evening some influential citizens called on Mayor Opdyke and General Wool in the St. Nicholas Hotel and urged that martial law be declared. The mayor said that this was the general's responsibility. The general said that it was the mayor's responsibility. Then the mayor was asked to issue a proclamation urging peaceful citizens to enroll in a volunteer force to defend life and property. With a shiver the mayor replied, "Why, that is *civil war* at once!" It was already civil war, whether the mayor admitted it or not. The general's chief of staff told the delegation that everything was under control, but it was not. The visitors left in disgust and went to the Union League Club, where they argued about what should be done. Some felt that the city was doomed. At last they wired President Lincoln to beg for troops. And despite the mayor's reluctance, some good people reported at Police Headquarters, where they were sworn in for emergency service and given clubs and badges.

The same evening a mob came together in City Hall Park and glared menacingly at the Tribune Building across the street in Printing House Square. Some began chanting, "We'll hang old Greeley to a sour-apple tree!" Others took up the cry "Down with the *Tribune*! Down with the old white coat that thinks a nigger as good as an Irishman!" (The eccentric Greeley was known for the white coat he wore.) Inside the Tribune Building the managing editor, Sidney Gray, shouted to his boss, "We ought to arm ourselves! This isn't a riot! It's a revolution!" Baby-faced Greeley sauntered over to a window, peered out nearsightedly, and said, "It's just what I expected. I have no doubt they'll hang me, but I want no arms brought into the building."

Defensive measures already had been taken at the nearby New York Times Building, the handsomest newspaper building of its day. Its editor, thickset Henry J. Raymond, had received two machine guns from the army. These were set up in northern windows overlooking the probable line of attack. Raymond manned one gun. The other was taken over by Sir Winston Churchill's grandfather, who had hastened downtown to help defend the property in which he held an interest.

In City Hall Park, thicker grew the mob, and more clamorous grew its thousand-voiced fury. After working themselves to fever pitch, the rioters now charged across Park Row, into Printing House Square, and up to the doors of the Tribune Building. Bricks arched across the darkening sky. Windows tinkled to extinction. Timbers thudded at the front doors, which splintered and gave, admitting bellowing hordes thirsty for the blood of Greeley. But before the first wave of attackers could surge up to the city room, 200 police erupted onto the scene, whanging nightsticks upon heads, brandishing cocked revolvers, and bucking and cursing and bulling their way through the mob until they broke its will to fight, turned it back, and saved the *Tribune* and Horace Greeley.

Mayor Opdyke finally acted. He wired the War Department in Washington, requesting that New York regiments at Gettysburg be returned to the city as fast as possible. He asked the governors of New Jersey, Connecticut, Rhode Island, and Massachusetts to hold troops in readiness. By 11 P.M. on Monday, in the city, 2 companies of soldiers intended for the battlefront had been sent instead to Police Headquarters. By midnight 2,000 regulars and militiamen had been made available for service. About this time the postmaster's house on West Eighty-sixth Street was burned down. Shortly before midnight a heavy rainstorm broke the heat, but at 12:15 A.M., rain or no rain, barbarians danced a death dance under the body of a Negro who had been hanged on Clarkson Street near Hudson Street. All that night the bullyboys of the Bowery and the Five Points drank and caroused and laughed like hyenas.

On Tuesday morning, before dawn, another Negro was assaulted at Washington and Leroy streets, knocked to the ground, and held there by a dozen bullies, while the leader of the mob dropped a twenty-pound rock on his head again and again and again. By 6 A.M. other mobs were roaring through the streets, chasing black men and setting fire to houses. Bells clanged as firemen raced here and there, trying to cope with the blazes. No store or shop or bank or factory opened its doors. No streetcar moved. No omnibus ran. Red-eyed householders, bestirring themselves behind shuttered windows, gulped coffee and wondered what the day would bring.

In New Jersey a leisurely breakfast was taken by New York Governor Horatio Seymour, who had not hastened to New York as requested. In New York City, at 197 Henry Street, Boss Tweed heaved his whalelike bulk out of bed in his red brick house and dressed carefully, for he hoped to play an important role in the day's events. At 6 A.M., 200 weary cops mustered at the central office and then marched up to the Union Steam Works factory, on Second Avenue just below Twenty-third Street, where heavy fighting had taken place on Monday afternoon. This was a munitions plant partly owned by the mayor; it held more than 4,000 finished carbines and muskets, plus ammunition. Before the sun bulged over the horizon, gang members began building street barricades. The longest one stretched a mile along Ninth Avenue, from Twenty-fourth to Forty-first Street.

The morning *Times,* loyal to the federal administration, printed a bold editorial, headlined "CRUSH THE MOB." This editorial said in part: "No man, whatever his calling or condition in life, can afford to live in a city where the law is powerless. This mob must be crushed at once. Every day's, every hour's delay, is big with evil: Let every citizen come promptly forward and give his personal aid to do good and indispensable work." On the other hand, Copperhead newspapers, such as the *World, Journal of Commerce, Express, Daily News, Day Book,* and *Mercury,* blandly referred to the rioters and murderers as "the people."

Before noon on that Tuesday, July 14, Governor Seymour finally arrived by ferry after a two-hour drive from Long Branch, New Jersey. Boss Tweed rode beside the governor in the first of two carriages that wheeled up Broadway to Mayor Opdyke's temporary office in the St. Nicholas Hotel. The governor, seeing the smoke hanging over the city and feeling the tension, went gray with fear. At the hotel Seymour conferred with the mayor, Sheriff James Lynch, and other city officials. They heard discouraging reports from commanding officers of each of the twenty-six police precinct houses. Even as they discussed the situation, fire was set to the Eighteenth Precinct Station, on East Twenty-second Street near Second Avenue, by Irishmen who had poured out of nearby tenements. The arsonists gloated over the damage done to "them bloody police."

State and city officials now crossed over to City Hall so that the governor could speak to the throng assembled there. Mayor Opdyke, trembling and white-faced, stood on one side of the governor. Boss Tweed, a smile parting his dark whiskers, took up a position on the other side. Horace Greeley left the Tribune Building and at great personal peril pushed his way to the steps of City Hall to hear the governor. Horatio Seymour was an elegant lithe man, standing six feet tall. His long lean face was clean-shaven; but a muffler of whiskers padded his throat, and ringlets of hair circled his bald pate. Graceful and cultured, the New York governor now faced a critical moment in his Copperhead career. He said:

> I come not only for the purpose of maintaining law, but also from a kind regard for the interests and welfare of those who, under the influence of excitement and a feeling of supposed wrong, were in danger not only of inflicting serious blows to the good order of society, but to their own interests. I beg of you to listen to me as your friend, for I am your friend and the friend of your families.

Friend? In the crowd before City Hall were some who had killed Negroes and invalid soldiers and cops, who had burned houses, who had looted stores, and who had run drunkenly amuck through the city. Also present were some good people, who bridled at the word "friend." Then the governor urged listeners to break up and retire peacefully to their own homes. He declared that the city could furnish its quota of soldiers with volunteers alone. He said, "I have received a dispatch that the draft is suspended. There is no doubt the conscription is postponed. I learn this from a number of sources. If I get any information of a change of policy at Washington, I will let you know."

Despite the governor's appeal, violence flared that Tuesday afternoon the length and breadth of Manhattan. A mob destroyed the bridge over the Harlem River. Also demolished was the Washington Hotel, at Broadway and Chambers Street. Rioters made ashes of the Weehawken ferryhouse, at West Forty-second Street and the Hudson River, when a saloonkeeper refused to give them all his liquor. Homes near Fifth Avenue and Forty-seventh Street were looted. Irishmen even strung up an Irish Catholic, named H. F. O'Brien, because he was colonel of the Eleventh Regiment.

In the White House in Washington, Abraham Lincoln read telegrams about the horrors being committed in New York. Along with feeling sorry for all innocents, he worried about his son. That Tuesday afternoon he wired the Fifth Avenue Hotel to ask Robert, "Why do I hear no more of you?" About the same time, in New York, a corrupt Tweed henchman, City Court Judge John H. McCunn, declared the federal Draft Act unconstitutional. An hour later Governor Seymour proclaimed the city in a state of insurrection. He also promised to maintain the right of every citizen to appeal to the courts when drafted, adding that "the decisions of the courts must be respected by rulers and people alike." This was politics; the governor knew that no mere city judge had the right to pass judgment on federal legislation.

Tuesday evening City Hall Park bristled with howitzers. The new citizen police force, grown 1,000 strong, was releasing cops and local soldiers for combat missions in the city. The New York *Times'* defenses had been augmented by 150 volunteers and 30 regular soldiers sent over from Governors Island. At 8 P.M. G. T. Strong tarried awhile in the Union League Club and heard rumors that the clubhouse was to be attacked that night. Half an hour later a wire was sent from the Fourth Precinct House, at 9 Oak Street, to Police Headquarters, reporting that a mob threatened to burn down the Brooks Brothers clothing store on the Lower East Side, at Catherine and Cherry streets.

A few police, disguised as civilians, were already on the scene. They were able to check the raid for a few moments, after which they were overwhelmed and beaten off. The rioters smashed into the store, lighted gas jets, broke windows, and began plundering the place. Up trotted police reinforcements. Thugs were struggling into new suits and stuffing their pockets with haberdashery. The police chased them from floor to floor. Some toughs slid down a rope dangling through a trapdoor into the basement. Waiting there were cops, who clubbed them senseless as fast as they descended. The next day a search of nearby slums turned up $100,000 worth of clothing. One dive yielded fifty new suits, while another held a gunnysack stuffed with ties and socks.

Late that Tuesday night every whorehouse in the city was attacked by mobs, who abused the harlots. At midnight Mayor Opdyke got a telegram from Secretary of War Edwin M. Stanton, announcing that five regiments, detached from the Union army, were being rushed to the city. All that night fire bells bonged as firemen raced from one burning building to another.

Wednesday opened with a downpour of rain, and by 10 A.M. the city was steaming like a Turkish bath. Wednesday, July 15, became the hottest day of 1863. Morning papers published a statement by Police Commissioner Acton that the backbone of the riot had been broken and that police were in control of the city, but G. T. Strong felt that "rabbledom is not yet dethroned." Fighting resumed before dawn. For the first time violence broke out in Brooklyn; a mob set fire to grain elevators and displayed this banner: "NO $300 AR-RANGEMENTS WITH US." In Manhattan the first big clash of the day took place on the site of the present Pennsylvania Railroad Station at Thirty-second Street and Eighth Avenue, where three Negroes were lynched. A gang of bestial women milled about the dangling bodies of the black men, gashing their flesh with knives, while more than 5,000 men cheered them on. Militiamen advanced, and the mob gave ground. One New Yorker believed that the mobs everywhere in the city were better armed and organized than they had been on Monday.

By this time word of the city's agony had reached the Confederate capital of Richmond, Virginia, and a clerk in the Rebel war department wrote in his diary: "We have *awful* good news from New York.

An *insurrection,* the loss of many lives, extensive pillaging and burning, with a suspension of the conscription."

Early Wednesday morning a mob tried to wreck an ironclad ship, the *Dunderberg,* under construction in a shipyard, but were frustrated by a company of regular soldiers. On Staten Island fifty men attacked Negro houses in Stapleton, burning one to the ground, sacking others, and beating a lame Negro unable to follow his friends into the woods. In Manhattan other rioters captured two howitzers by clubbing artillerymen, but the guns were of no value to the thugs because they lacked the proper ammunition. Aldermen met in City Hall, denounced the draft, and appropriated $2,500,000 to pay the $300 needed by poor men seeking to escape conscription.

Beginning at 6 P.M. on Wednesday, the largest battle thus far took place at Nineteenth Street and First Avenue. There rowdies clashed in 20 minutes of desperate fighting with 3 companies of regular soldiers, utterly routing them. Sixteen wounded soldiers were beaten to death by the mob. Gunfire sounded elsewhere in Manhattan, and smoke from burning homes coiled into the sky. Wary householders filled bathtubs, pots, kettles, and pails with water.

About 10 P.M. on Wednesday the Seventy-fourth Regiment of the national guard reached the city. Half an hour later a Buffalo regiment arrived. At 4 A.M. on Thursday the Seventh Regiment of the national guard landed at Canal Street and soon after daybreak marched in battle array through the Lower East Side. All told, 10,000 veterans of the Battle of Gettysburg poured into the city. Manhattan was divided into four military districts. Soldiers relieved police who had been fighting almost without pause since Monday. Nearly every policeman had been wounded, and the few who escaped injury were so bone-tired that they could hardly lift their arms.

Thursday morning, in a proclamation published in the newspapers, the mayor urged all citizens to open their stores and factories and go back to work. Most streetcar and omnibus lines resumed operations. However, a gunboat still stood guard at the foot of Wall Street.

Thursday afternoon, as the incipient revolution flickered and faded, the city was plastered with signs bearing an announcement from Archbishop Hughes. He said, "To the men of New York, who are now called in many of the papers rioters: Men! I am not able, owing to the rheumatism in my limbs, to visit you; but that is not a reason why you should not pay me a visit in your whole strength. Come, then, tomorrow at two o'clock, to my residence, northwest corner of Madison Avenue and Thirty-sixth Street. I shall have a speech prepared for you." The archbishop had moved uptown from Mulberry Street.

Thursday evening the last sharp clash took place near Gramercy Park, where regular solders roughed up rioters who were looting fine homes. Soldiers from West Point reinforced the regulars already thrown into the city. As the thud and cadence of ever more marching men sounded in streets, rowdies sullenly retired to their dirty dens. By midnight on Thursday peace had been restored, but bitterness lingered. G. T. Strong wrote: "Never knew exasperation so intense, unqualified, and general as that which prevails against these rioters and the politic knaves who are supposed to have set them going, Governor Seymour not excepted. Men who voted for him mention the fact with contrition and self-abasement, and the Democratic party is at discount with all the people I meet."

Friday morning the New York *Times* snapped: "The *Express* is a very curious journal. It 'begs' and 'implores' us to 'hush up' the statement that the President has not ordered the draft suspended. . . . We prefer, for our own part, to tell the truth and shame the *Express*. The draft itself ought *not* and must not be abandoned." Lincoln had overridden lesser federal officials who had called off the draft. The thirteen regiments of regulars now on duty in the city remained until the draft was resumed on August 19. Then it went off peaceably.

At 11 A.M. on Friday 4,000 persons gathered in front of the home of Archbishop Hughes. He had spent eight months in Europe as Lincoln's personal representative, successfully setting forth the Union's cause in France, Italy and Ireland. Now sixty-six years old and a sick man only six months from death, the archbishop tottered out onto a balcony and sat down in a chair. He wore a purple robe and other insignia of his high ecclesiastical office. He told the throng:

> I have been hurt by the reports that you are rioters. You cannot imagine that I could hear those things without being pained grievously. Is there not some way by which you can stop these proceedings and support the laws, of which none have been enacted against you as Irishmen and Catholics? . . . Would it not be better for you to retire quietly—not to give up your principles or convictions, but to keep out of the crowd where immortal souls are launched into eternity, and, at all events, get into no trouble till you are at home? . . . When these so-called riots are over, and the blame is justly laid on Irish Catholics, I wish you to tell me in what country I could claim to be born—

Came a clamor of voices: "Ireland!" The archbishop went on:

> Yes, but what shall I say if these stories be true? Ireland—that never committed a single act of cruelty until she was oppressed! Ireland—that has been the mother of heroes and poets, but never the mother of cowards! I thank you for your kindness, and I hope nothing will occur till you return home, and if, by chance, as you go thither, you should meet a police officer or a military man, why, just—look at him.

Archbishop Hughes had not spoken until five days after the riots had begun. According to Joel T. Headley, a historian and former secretary of state for New York: "The address was well enough, but it came too late to be of any service. It might have saved lives and much destruction had it been delivered two days before, but now it was like the bombardment of a fortress after it had surrendered—a mere waste of ammunition. The fight was over, and to use his own not very refined illustration, he 'spak' too late."

The Draft Riots of July, 1863, stand as the most brutal, tragic, and shameful episode in the entire history of New York City. Politicians encouraged mob violence. Law and order broke down. Mobs seized control of America's largest city. Innocents were tortured and slaughtered. The Union army was weakened.

No one will ever know exactly how many people were killed. The New York *Post* said that the bodies of rioters were boated across the East River and buried secretly at night. Governor Seymour, who tried to minimize the tragedy, told state legislators that "more than a thousand" civilians, policemen, and soldiers had been slain. Police Superintendent Kennedy, after recovering from his injuries, told G. T. Strong that 1,155 persons had been killed—not counting those smuggled to their graves. Social historian Herbert Asbury wrote that "conservative estimates placed the total at two thousand killed and about eight thousand wounded, a vast majority of whom were rioters." Four days of rioting in New York City produced casualties numbering almost half the total of Americans killed in the American Revolution, just about as many as perished in the War of 1812, and more than all the battle deaths in the Mexican War.

More than 100 buildings were burned down, and about 200 others were damaged and looted. The property loss has been estimated variously at from $1,500,000 to $5,000,000. Business suffered in another way, too, for of the thousands who fled the city, many did not return for several months.

The federal government investigated but took no other action. The identity of the men who planned and led the riots was never disclosed. Of the 50,000 to 70,000 men and women who had taken an active part in the insurrection, only 19 were tried and convicted. None was a ringleader. The 19 men got an average of 5 years each in jail. Governor Seymour, on the other hand, tried but failed to remove police commissioners Acton and Bergen, who had done all in their power to quell the uprising.

Carl Sandburg wrote: "So delicate and combustible was the subject that neither party cared to go into details about those New York riots, the Democrats because their record was so lawless and shameful, the Republicans because they were still conducting the draft over the country." Perhaps the most trenchant judgment was made by George Templeton Strong: "This is a nice town to call itself a centre of civilization!"

Chapter 25

CONFEDERATES TRY
TO BURN DOWN NEW YORK

THE IMPACT of the Civil War on the city was varied and colorful. When hostilities began, New York was suffering from a recession. Scores of firms went bankrupt, and thousands of men were thrown out of work. Employers took advantage of the labor surplus to cut wages from an average of $1.25 to 85 cents a day. Women were paid only $1 to $3 a week. At the same time Arnold Constable & Company sold lace at $1,000 a yard, lace parasols at $500 each, and shawls at $1,500.

By the fall of 1861 the recession had ended, and the city was prospering as never before. But it was a selective prosperity. Wages lagged behind price rises. Workers, plunged into even greater poverty, organized unions and walked off jobs. Newspaper publishers broke a strike by the printers' union. Streetcar drivers lost their bid for an 11-hour working day. For a second time war increased Cornelius Vanderbilt's fortune; he chartered his fleet of ships to the federal government. Cotton, once the chief export from New York, fell off to a trickle. On the other hand, torrents of wheat left Manhattan docks for England. Officers of a Russian fleet anchored here donated $4,760 to buy fuel for the poor. But William B. Astor raised his rents 30 percent.

Corruption fell like a leper's shadow on the city, as well as on the rest of the country. Lincoln sighed that "few things are so troublesome to the government as the fierceness with which profits in trading are sought." The New York *Tribune* advocated the gallows for New York profiteers who sold the army rotten blankets and "rusty and putrid pork." Mayor Opdyke made a fortune as a secret partner in a munitions firm. Edwin D. Morgan, governor of New York State when war broke out, was a brother-in-law of Secretary of the Navy Gideon Welles, of Connecticut. Welles gave Morgan permission to buy ships for the navy at a 2.5 percent commission, and within a few months Morgan had profited by $90,000. The House Select Committee on Government Contracts said, "Worse than traitors in arms are the men pretending loyalty to the flag, who feast and fatten on the misfortune of the nation, while patriot blood is crimsoning the plains of the South, and bodies of their countrymen are mouldering in the dust."

The city's social fabric was torn by the excitement of the times, the grief of separation and death, easy money, and increased tension between rich and poor. Morals degenerated. Broadway teemed with women of easy virtue. Saloons were crowded. Luxury shops and restaurants catered to the new rich. Men wore diamond buttons on their waistcoats, and women powdered their hair with gold and silver dust. The *Herald* estimated that an average of $30,000 was spent in the city each night just for entertainment—or a third more than in Paris. After attending *The Follies of a Night* to raise money for army relief, G. T. Strong mourned in his diary that "the spectacle of lavish luxury tonight was a little suggestive of fiddling while Rome is in full blaze at its corners."

Far from this revelry and graft, Billy Yank fought on and on until, by the autumn of 1864, the South was losing the war and knew it. Union forces controlled the Mississippi, General Lee had failed in his second attempt to invade the North, General William T. Sherman's army had captured Atlanta, and the South's resources were about exhausted. In a spirit of desperation and vengeance the Confederates tried to burn down New York City.

This plot had the approval of Judah P. Benjamin, successively the Confederacy's attorney general, secretary of war, and secretary of state. Already he had underground agents in Canada just across the border from New York State. They raided Union territory, tried to free Rebel prisoners, and encouraged rebellion in the North by Southern sympathizers. The Canadian-based Rebel who masterminded the scheme to incinerate New York City was Jacob Thompson, former U.S. Senator from Mississippi and onetime Secretary of the Interior in President Buchanan's Cabinet.

Benjamin gave $300,000 to Thompson, who slipped part of the sum to members of the Sons of Liberty, a secret society of treasonable Northerners and an offshoot of the Knights of the Golden Circle. Thompson heard that in New York City alone 20,000 persons were ripe for revolt against the Lincoln administration. He decided to strike on November 8, election day. Abraham Lincoln, the Republican President, would be running against former General George B. McClellan, the Democratic candidate. More New Yorkers were against Lincoln than for him.

With the development of the plot against New York, messages were carried between the Confederate capital, at Richmond, Virginia, and the Rebel base of operations at St. Catharines, a Canadian town northwest of Niagara Falls. Thompson was unaware that his principal courier was a double spy whose loyalty lay with the North. All the dispatches he carried were copied and sent to Washington so that even Lincoln knew of the conspiracy against New York. On November 2 Secretary of State William H. Seward sent a telegram to Charles Godfrey Gunther, an independent Democrat who had been elected mayor of New York on December 1, 1863. Seward warned him to beware of a scheme to burn New York on or about November 8. The mayor reported this to Police Superintendent Kennedy and to General John A. Dix, who commanded the Department of the East, with headquarters in New York City. Although both men were skeptical, they alerted their subordinates.

The day before the election General Benjamin F. Butler arrived here at the head of 7,000 to 10,000 troops. Washington officials remembered all too well the disgraceful Draft Riots. Aware of the anti-

Lincoln feeling in New York, they anticipated election disorders. Meantime, a hitch developed in Thompson's plans, causing him to postpone his undercover strike against the city. Election day came and went without much trouble. Lincoln was reelected, but in New York City he lost to McClellan—78,746 to 36,673.

Thompson now picked eight daring young men for the fire raid on New York. Their leader was Lieutenant Colonel Robert Martin of the Confederacy's Tenth Kentucky Cavalry. He was tall and slender, his swarthy hawklike face bearing the stamp of resolution. Disguised as civilians and using fictitious names, the eight Rebel soldiers slipped into New York from Canada. Upon reaching this city, they made contact with local plotters, using their homes and stores as meeting places.

Federal Secret Service agents, alerted by the Union's double spy, trailed the arsonists to the city and kept them under observation. However, the Rebels acted so innocently that the federal men became convinced that they were on the wrong trail. The eight young men heard a sermon by the Reverend Henry Ward Beecher, attended a lecture given by humorist Artemus Ward, enjoyed the theater, and in general conducted themselves blamelessly. The Union agents on their trail must have been rather stupid; otherwise, they would have traced the Rebels to suspicious meetings.

As days passed with no action taken, the local co-conspirators began to get nervous. At last they tried to persuade the Confederate spies not to burn down the city. But on November 15 General Sherman destroyed Atlanta's military resources and began his spectacular march to the sea. When Confederate Colonel Martin and his seven picked men read New York newspaper articles praising Sherman's gutting of Atlanta and heard rejoicing on the sidewalks of New York, they bitterly resolved to go ahead with their plan despite the mounting reluctance of their local hosts.

Second in command to Martin was Confederate Lieutenant John Headley of Kentucky. Headley later wrote an account of this episode, and because of this we can follow him step by step that fateful day of Friday, November 25, 1864.

A New York chemist who sympathized with the South made a self-igniting fire bomb, which the Rebel agents called Greek fire. Consisting of turpentine, phosphorus, and rosin, the liquid was supposed to burst into flame when exposed to air. It was poured into bottles, and each bottle was wrapped in paper. At 6 P.M. that Friday the eight men met in a secret cottage and were given ten bottles apiece. They stuffed them into their coat pockets.

Two days earlier the conspirators had registered at various hotels throughout the city. Each man had signed in at several different hotels. For example, Headley had taken rooms in the Astor House, the City Hotel, the Everett House, and the United States Hotel. The Rebels planned to set as many fires as possible at about the same time, making conditions as difficult as possible for the city's volunteer firemen.

At 7:20 o'clock that Friday evening Headley walked into the lobby of the Astor, where he was registered as W. L. Haines of Ohio. From the desk clerk he got the key to Room 204 and sauntered to his quarters. Once inside the room he lighted the gas jet against the autumn twilight. Then he pulled the blankets and sheets off his bed and loosely draped them on the headboard. Next, he piled the chairs, bureau drawers, and wooden washstand on top of the bed. Around these he stuffed newspapers. Suddenly he reflected that he did not know how quickly his fire bomb would work or if it would make any noise. To be on the safe side, he unlocked his door and put the key on the outside so that he could make a fast getaway. Out of one coat pocket he drew a bottle, carefully uncorked it, and then spilled the fluid on the rubbish. With a soft *whoosh!* the liquid fluttered into flame, and the entire bed was ablaze before Headley could get out of the room.

He locked the door, strolled down the hall, descended the stairs to the lobby, left his key with the desk clerk, and sauntered out onto Broadway. Then he walked to the City Hotel, where he was registered under another alias, and repeated the performance. Having left the City Hotel, he headed toward the Everett House, glancing toward the Astor as he strode along. A bright glare lighted up the room he had occupied there, but as yet no alarm had been given. Next, Headley set fire to his Everett House room. He had just started for the United States Hotel when fire bells began clanging throughout the city. That evening G. T. Strong was attending a meeting of the Sanitary Commission, and although he heard the Calvary Church bell toll mournfully, he didn't know at first what this signified.

Headley now touched off a fourth fire in his room at the United States Hotel. All had gone according to plan, he felt, but as he left his key with the desk clerk, he thought that the man glanced at him curiously. In that moment Headley remembered something. Each time he had registered at a hotel he had carried a black canvas bag, because it would have looked suspicious to seek lodgings without luggage. But each of his four bags was empty. Had this been discovered by the clerk at the United States Hotel? Well, it was too late to worry now.

As Headley strolled back onto Broadway, it sounded to him as though a hundred bells were ringing, and he saw great crowds gathering in the street. By the City Hall clock he noted that the time was 9:15. Eager to learn how his first blaze was doing, he walked back toward the Astor. No panic was to be seen there, but to Headley's surprise, a horde of shrieking people poured from Barnum's museum across the street. The plot had not included firing the museum.

Headley couldn't tarry because his job was still not done. He walked south on Broadway and turned west toward the Hudson River waterfront. Tied up there were ships and barges of every kind. Having used four bottles of Greek fire in his four hotels, Headley had six left. Skulking from one dark corner to another, he pulled these bottles out of his pockets, one by one, and threw them here and there among the vessels. All touched off fires. One struck a barge loaded with bales of hay, making an especially spectacular blaze.

Leaving that part of the riverfront in flames, Headley now dodged back to Broadway and again walked to City Hall. Crowds clustered about the flame-scalloped hotels and Barnum's museum. Having threaded his way through the unsuspecting multitude, the Confederate spy boarded a horsecar heading north. At the corner of the Bowery and Prince Street he swung off the vehicle to see what had happened at the Metropolitan Hotel. It was burning. Headley had walked only half a block when he recognized a man in front of him as Robert Kennedy, one of his associates. Just for the fun of it, Headley closed in behind Kennedy and slapped him on the shoulder. In a flash, Kennedy squatted, went for his gun, and whirled around. Headley laughed just in time, and Kennedy recognized him. Kennedy took his hand from his pistol and chortled that he ought to shoot Headley for giving him such a scare. Then, standing there on the Bowery, the Rebels exchanged stories of their adventures.

Kennedy said that after he had set fire to the hotels assigned him, he had gone to Barnum's museum to see what happened. A few minutes after he arrived at the showplace, fire bells began clanging throughout the city. Kennedy started down a stairway, intending to leave the museum. The thought occurred to him that "it might be fun" to start a panic there. He had one fire bomb left. He cracked it on the edge of a step as one cracks an egg. Instantly it flared up. Kennedy ran out of the burning building and mingled with throngs near the Astor House and the City Hotel. He overheard people muttering that the Rebels were trying to burn down the city.

The six other Confederate agents had also proceeded with their nefarious work. One, named Ashbrook, had been assigned to destroy the Winter Garden theater. That evening Edwin Booth was playing the role of Julius Caesar to raise money for a statue of Shakespeare. The theater adjoined the La Farge House. After Ashbrook set fire to the hotel, he tossed a bottle of Greek fire into the theater. The audience screamed in terror, but some coolheaded men took charge of the situation and averted a tragedy.

Headley and Kennedy returned to Broadway to gaze on their handiwork. As Headley later wrote, "there was the wildest excitement imaginable." The two spies felt their skins tighten as New Yorkers shouted that they would hang the guilty Rebels or burn them at the stake. The agents also suffered pangs of disappointment when they discovered that every blaze had been quickly brought under control, except the fire at the St. Nicholas Hotel, which was badly damaged. Hotel employees had been efficient in dousing the flames, and volunteer firemen had performed heroically. Headley concluded that the New York chemist had purposely made a weak mixture of Greek fire after the Confederates had refused to abandon their plot.

Instead of scurrying out of the city, the eight Rebel agents stayed the night. Headley parted from Kennedy and found Colonel Martin. About two o'clock in the morning Headley and Martin booked new quarters, where they slumbered until ten o'clock Saturday morning.

Then they went for breakfast to a Broadway restaurant near Twelfth Street. The place was filled with excited people, reading the morning papers to find out what had happened the night before. Headley and Martin offhandedly ordered food and then bought copies of the papers. Front pages were devoted to news of the fire raid. The *Herald* said that the city "has undoubtedly had a most wonderful escape." It was pointed out that although the enemy combustible had blazed up when exposed to air, the flames had failed to take hold on the surfaces of the targets. Headlines told of the "DISCOVERY OF A VAST REBEL CONSPIRACY." Suspicious black bags had been found in various hotels. Several people already had been arrested. Newspapers printed all the fake names used by the Confederate agents when they had checked into their hotels. Authorities were said to have full knowledge of the plot. They predicted that all the villains would be caught, for every avenue of escape was being guarded. All told, nineteen hotels, two theaters, Barnum's museum, several vessels, and some stores, factories, and lumberyards had been set on fire.

Headley stiffened a little in his restaurant chair when he read that the clerk at the United States Hotel had given police a description of his looks, manners, and habits and had said that the suspicious-looking man had left a black bag that was entirely empty. Ah, so the clerk *had* noticed! Headley's flicker of anxiety had been justified, after all.

Scanning the papers and noting how specific was the information possessed by officials, Headley and Martin realized that they had been under observation part of the time. Police had arrested a Mr. McDonald, who ran a store where they had sometimes met before registering in the hotels. Had McDonald confessed? Headley and Martin finished breakfast and sauntered out of the restaurant. Because hotelkeepers were offering a $20,000 reward for apprehension of the criminals, New Yorkers by the thousands would be on the lookout for them.

That evening all eight Rebel agents boarded a northbound train and slipped out of town without detection. Eventually they reached Toronto and safety. From his Canadian sanctuary, Jacob Thompson had to report to Confederate Secretary of State Benjamin that his picked men had failed to burn down New York. Robert Kennedy, the man Headley had bumped into on the Bowery, tried to work his way south through Detroit but was captured. The Union's double spy had done his work well, and federal authorities did indeed know the identities of the arsonists. Kennedy was brought to New York, tried before a military commission, and hanged at Fort LaFayette.

The South was in desperate straits. With the opening of 1865 only two Confederate armies were left in the field. Below the Mason and Dixon line, transportation had broken down, ports were blockaded or captured, Union troops held croplands, hunger spread, the Rebel army's morale was shattered, and civilians demonstrated against the Confederate government. After Atlanta there was nothing left to oppose Sherman, whose men fanned north through South Carolina, inflicting even more damage than they had in Georgia. No single Southern defeat was due to lack of arms, but the will to win had drained from Rebel hearts. Lee evacuated Richmond, and when the news reached New York, diarist G. T. Strong wrote: "Never before did I hear cheering that came straight from the heart. . . . I walked about on the outskirts of the crowd, shaking hands with everybody, congratulating and being congratulated by scores of men I hardly even knew by sight. Men embraced and hugged each other, *kissed* each other, retreated into doorways to dry their tears and came out again to flourish their hats and hurrah."

This was on April 3. Three days later, just as twilight softened the city, a young Confederate officer pulled himself out of the Lower Bay, climbed up a seawall, stepped over a fence, and stood on the Battery. Water dripped from his gray tunic with its yellow collar and cuffs; water sloshed from his faded yellow-striped blue trousers. He was Captain William R. Webb of the Second North Carolina Cavalry. Webb was one of 1,500 Rebel prisoners held in Castle Williams on Governors Island. He had escaped, slid into the water, and swum 3,200 feet to the southern tip of Manhattan. A civilian, seeing the dripping man, asked how he had happened to fall into the bay. "I swam across," Webb replied. "I escaped from the prison stockade over there." He pointed. "I am Captain Webb of the Confederate army." The civilian laughed and went about his business. So did other New Yorkers who saw the strange figure, although Webb always identified himself. For three days the Rebel captain wandered about the city. No one bothered to report him to the authorities. Who cared? The war was won.

At 3:45 in the afternoon of Palm Sunday, April 9, 1865, General Robert E. Lee of the Confederacy surrendered to General Ulysses S. Grant of the Union in the courthouse of Appomattox Village, 95 miles west of Richmond, Virginia. In the evening of Good Friday, April 14, John Wilkes Booth shot Abraham Lincoln as the President sat in Ford's Theatre, in Washington, D.C. Lincoln died at 7:22 the following morning. When the news reached New York City, men and women sobbed. Strangely, during the week after Lincoln's death the number of arrests in New York for drunkenness and disorder was lower than in any week for many years. On April 24, Lincoln's body lay in state in City Hall on the way to its final resting place in Springfield, Illinois. Even the poorest of New York's poor spent 25 cents for a tiny flag with a scrap of crepe attached.

With the war won and Lincoln dead, the city took stock of itself.

It had supplied the Union army with 15,000 soldiers and contributed $400,000,000 to the war effort. The North came out of the conflict richer than it had entered it, and business in New York had been greatly stimulated. However, the population had dropped from 813,669 to fewer than 727,000.

Now, front and center, there strolled a fat man who licked his chops. They called him Boss Tweed.

Chapter 26

THE TWEED SCANDALS

WILLIAM MARCY TWEED was a huge man. He stood 5 feet 11 inches tall, and his weight varied from 280 to 320 pounds. Like some other fat men, he was light on his feet, and the ladies said that he waltzed divinely. His head was big and rather pointed. He had coarse features, a prominent nose, a ruddy complexion, a brown beard, and bright blue eyes, which twinkled when he was amused. When angered, he could stare down almost anyone—even a rowdy who held a gun against his potbelly.

Tweed laughed easily. A man of enormous appetite, he consumed gargantuan meals. Endowed with almost limitless energy, he worked most of the time. He was fond of power and money and canaries and flowers and women. Happily married and proud of his wife, Tweed also was devoted to his eight children. Nonetheless, he had two mistresses. One was a tiny blonde who didn't reach to his shoulder. Tweed lavished $1,800,000 on his kept women, but this meant nothing to a politician who cheated the city out of $5,500,000 in a single morning. Fond of massive jewelry, he wore a huge diamond in the front of his shirt.

Tweed was rough in manners and humor, spouting profanity in basso profundo. His speech was so thick that it was sometimes difficult to understand him. He drank heavily until a doctor said that he was endangering his health. Tweed never smoked and often moralized about the evils of nicotine. Although he quit school at the age of fourteen, Tweed bent college graduates to his iron will. He liked to breed dogs and confusion. He was the first city politician in the United States to be called the Boss. He enslaved New York City and the state of New York, and he planned to put America into one of his huge pockets.

Tweed became the third largest property owner in the city, lived in baronial splendor in a Fifth Avenue mansion, and kept a country house, whose mahogany stables were trimmed in silver. Devoid of religious faith, he believed in just two things—himself and power. He owned a yacht and some people's souls. He radiated animal magnetism, was a genius at making friends, and remained loyal to them regardless of what they did. He thoroughly understood the mass mind. Tweed looked a little like Falstaff and acted a lot like Captain Kidd, and if he had not been such a monster, he might have been a great man. The complete cynic, he said:

> The fact is that New York politics were always dishonest—long before my time. There never was a time when you couldn't buy the board of aldermen. A politician coming forward takes things as they are. This population is too hopelessly split up into races and factions to govern it under universal suffrage, except by the bribery of patronage or corruption. . . . I don't think there is ever a fair or honest election in the city of New York.

Unhappily, there was some truth in this. It was by studying the methods of Fernando Wood that Tweed learned to make citizens of aliens so they could vote for him and his henchmen. As historian James Bryce once wrote: "Plunder of the city treasury, especially in the form of jobbing contracts, was no new thing in New York, but it had never before reached such colossal dimensions."

There was nothing in Tweed's heritage or the circumstances of his birth that gave a clue to his future. One of his ancestors emigrated here from Scotland, which has a river called Tweed. Three generations of Tweeds had lived in New York City before he was born on April 3, 1823, at 24 Cherry Street. His father, Richard Tweed, made chairs. William was the youngest in a family of three boys and two girls.

Bill Tweed ran with the Cherry Hill gang and soon took command of it. The boys liked to steal pigs' tails from butchershops and roast them over fires in hidden places. Bill, who was large for his age, could cut off a pig's tail with one slash of a knife. He worked in his father's chair factory, became a salesman for a saddle and harness shop, learned bookkeeping, juggled figures for a tobacco firm, did some selling for a brush concern, wound up a junior partner, saved money, and went into the chair business with his father and a brother.

The young men of his day joined volunteer fire companies because firemen wore gaudy uniforms, dashed about the city, and played a big role in politics. Tweed helped organize Americus Fire Engine Company No. 6, known as the Big Six. Its symbol was a tiger—a fact which was to plague Tweed in years to come. Totally without racial or religious prejudice, Tweed befriended Irishmen, Germans, anyone and everyone. In 1850 he made his first bid for public office. He ran for assistant alderman—but lost. Instead of sulking, he did all he could to dilute the strength of the Know-Nothing movement, thus winning more friends among immigrants.

The next year Tweed aimed higher and was elected an alderman. At the time the city council consisted of twenty aldermen and twenty assistant aldermen, nearly all of them so venal that they were openly called the Forty Thieves. Neither position paid a salary, but council members were powerful because they appointed police in their respective wards, granted licenses to saloons, and awarded franchises. It was a grafter's dreamboat, and away Tweed sailed. For example, only a few weeks after he had become an alderman, Tweed acted for the city in buying land for a new potter's field. Available were 69 acres on Wards Island worth only about $30,000. Tweed paid $103,450 of the city's money for the property and then split the difference among his cronies and himself.

Before the end of his two-year term as alderman, Tweed was elected to Congress. A poor public speaker, ignorant of national interests, and bored with Washington, he swilled liquor and chased women instead of attending to business. Coming back to his hometown, he again ran for alderman, but being out of touch with local politics, he was beaten by a Know-Nothing candidate. The defeat endeared him all the more to his foreign-born friends. In 1855 Tweed was elected to the city board of education, whose grafting members sold textbooks and peddled appointments to teachers. To cite just one instance, a crippled young schoolmarm had to slip $75 to the board for her job, which paid only $300 a year. With Tweed's election to the county board of supervisors in 1857, he really was off and running.

Legally, the city was the creature of the state. Actually, the city enjoyed more independence than the state had intended. This was partly because state, county, and city governments overlapped and clashed and wallowed in such chaos that local politicians seized control. In 1857 the Republican-dominated state legislature tried to break the Democrats' grip on the city's political machinery. It took local finances out of the hands of the city council and gave them to a reorganized and strengthened county board of supervisors. Under this new setup six Republicans and six Democrats had to be elected to the board. Upstate Republicans felt that the presence of half a dozen Republicans on the board would guarantee good government. It didn't.

Besides controlling the city's purse strings, the county board of supervisors had charge of public improvements and the appointment of election inspectors. The latter power was of vital significance. Inspectors were influential because on election day they watched the polls, and if they could be corrupted, elections could be thrown. Tweed, who always recognized the weak links in a chain, took instant action. The day the inspectors were to be named, one of the six Republican board members did not attend the meeting of the supervisors. Tweed had paid him $2,500 to stay away. Republicans, after all, could be as venal as Democrats. From that day, Tweed dominated the board of supervisors. Now it consisted of six Democrats against five Republicans, and soon other Republican members sold out to Tweed. Firmly in charge of the financial arm of government, Tweed used this power to extend his authority over other branches of the city administration.

Such was the origin of the first Tweed Ring. A writer of the era defined a Tweed Ring as "a hard band in which there is gold all round and without end." Every contractor, artisan, and merchant wanting to do business with the city had to pay Tweed and his henchmen 15 percent of their total bill before the board of supervisors would grant them a contract. Years later, when confessing his crimes, Tweed said, "Pretty nearly every person who had business with the board of supervisors, or furnished the county with supplies, had a friend on the board of supervisors, and generally with some one member of the Ring. And through that one member they were talked to, and the result was that their bills were sent in and passed, and the percentages were paid on the bills. . . ."

When an overt fix was considered by the board, Tweed induced the two or three Republicans who declined to vote with him to refrain from voting at all. Then, if an indignant citizen howled about the haul, Tweed could cluck, "But, sir, there was only one vote cast against the measure!" Tweed served on the board thirteen years and was elected president four times. Whether president or not, he called the shots at board meetings, shifting from menacing bluster to silky smiles and noisily moving to suspend the rules or to adjourn, as the tactics of the day dictated.

While gathering the board into his smothering bear hug, Tweed also captured Tammany Hall. At first he was influential only in his own Seventh Ward. But his magnetism, quick-wittedness, and energy won the loyalty of some men ruling other wards. This made him a leader. Then he brought the other leaders under his power. This made him the boss.

Tammany Hall was a general term for two intertwining but separate entities maintained by the Democratic party in New York City. One body was the Tammany Society. This was a *social* organization, which consisted of clubs scattered throughout the city and catered to the needs of citizens at the grass-roots level. The other body was the New York County Democratic committee. This was a *political* organization, which exercised the real power. In theory, its governing body was a central committee, but this had so many members that it was cumbersome. In practice, the affairs of the central committee were directed by a small executive committee. Prominent in the executive committee were leaders of the Tammany Society, and this is how the two entities blended. Tweed took over Tammany Hall by being elected grand sachem of the Tammany Society and by gaining control of a majority of the executive committee of the New York County Democratic committee. Now he rode herd on the city's Democratic party and its primaries and its patronage.

Because New York was predominantly Democratic, whoever controlled the Democratic party controlled the city. In 1868 there was only one Republican ward among the twenty-two wards of the city; therefore, whoever won the Democratic nomination for a given office was sure to be elected. And Boss Tweed dictated nominations. Then, come election day, Tweed's ward leaders hired bullies to intimidate Republican voters, drifters and crooks were bribed to vote several times each, Tweed judges naturalized thousands of aliens with the understanding they would vote Democratic, and Tweed's candidates won. Most of the voters were Irish or German and blindly followed Tweed because he had led the local fight against the Know-Nothings.

The power pattern would not have been effective if decent people had fought it from the start. But, apathetic about politics and zealous about making money, they abdicated their civic responsibilities. The Civil War had stimulated Northern industry. Manufacturing became more important than merchandising. As a result, merchant capitalism gave way to industrial capitalism. The war ushered in a wave of prosperity, and New Yorkers forgot public spirit in greed for profits. They speculated wildly in stocks, hoping to become rich overnight. In 1866 a New York weekly, called the *Round Table,* said, "A strange craziness is abroad in the land. Some mysterious spirit of evil has led our people into the blindest, wildest infatuation . . . wild and foolish speculation. . . . At least half the people are living beyond their means."

According to a member of the Union League: "This decline in the public tone was not confined to the vulgar and ignorant. It affected all ranks and professions, perhaps most marked where it would naturally be least looked for and most abhorrent—in the clerical calling. . . ." Soon Henry Ward Beecher, perhaps the best-known minister in the land, was to be accused of adultery, and although the jury failed to reach an agreement, many people felt that he had been guilty of impropriety. The Union League member continued: "No doubt it (the decline in the public tone) affected injuriously many of the leaders of all parties and every school of politics; the senate, the bench, the bar, and the pulpit, as well as the ranks of trade and the directors of the banks, insurance companies, savings institutions, and even the boards of education."

G. T. Strong sadly noted in his diary: "The city government is rotten to the core."

Political corruption works two ways: Someone gives, and someone takes. Money-minded men were willing to pay bribes to power-minded

Boss Tweed. People were so busy piling up wealth that they didn't understand what was happening to the city until it was too late. For his part, Tweed gave generously to the poor, who jolly well knew that he was stealing from the rich but considered him a sort of Robin Hood. They thanked the Boss by maintaining him in power. As James Bryce observed: "The government of the rich by the manipulation of the votes of the poor is a new phenomenon in the world." Just before Christmas one year, so the story goes, Police Justice Edward J. Shandley asked Boss Tweed for a donation for relief of the poor in the Seventh Ward. Tweed promptly wrote out a check for $5,000. When Shandley cried jestingly, "Oh, Boss, put another naught to it!" Tweed grinned, picked up his pen again, said, "Well, here goes!" and raised the $5,000 check to $50,000.

By January 1, 1869, Boss Tweed was lording it over both the city and the state. On that date his henchman, John T. Hoffman, was sworn in as governor. After he had been admitted to the bar at the age of twenty-one, Hoffman had worked his way up through New York City's Democratic ranks. Elected city recorder in 1860, he had been the youngest man ever to hold this position. Although he had not been completely enslaved by Tweed and opposed him on one notable occasion, Hoffman had become mayor of New York City on January 1, 1866, with Tweed's help. Frauds and thefts had flourished during his two-year term in this office, but Hoffman's name could not be connected with them. In 1868 Tweed had seen to it that Hoffman had been elected governor. Hoffman was tall, slender, and stately and had black eyes. A *Sun* reporter said that his black mustache made him look like "a Spanish grandee or a first-class German metaphysician."

The same January 1, 1869, Abraham Oakey Hall took office as mayor of New York City. After he had been graduated from New York University, he had entered Harvard Law School but left it to go to New Orleans with his family. There he had become a newspaper reporter. He had abandoned this career, entered a New Orleans law office, and then come back to settle in New York City. In 1854 he had shown up in Albany as lobbyist for the Republican party. Hall detested Abraham Lincoln, and after the rail-splitter became President, Hall turned Democrat. Wholly an opportunist and once a fervent Know-Nothing, he switched sides again and became an apologist for the Catholic Church. He wooed local Germans and Irish so cloyingly that he became known as Von O'Hall. His more popular nickname, though, was Elegant Oakey, for he dressed like a dandy. Hall's debonair appearance amused Tweed. However, the Boss had a sober appreciation of this brilliant eccentric who knew the law so well. Tweed made him mayor. Hoffman was legal and legislative adviser to the Tweed Ring. A small man with a heavy dark mustache and a scrubby black beard, he wore pince-nez on a black string.

Peter Barr Sweeny was city chamberlain. Next to Tweed, Sweeny was the most important member of the Tweed Ring. He was known as Brains or Bismarck. Sweeny had been born on Park Row, where his father had kept a saloon. He had been graduated from Columbia College, become an astute lawyer, been elected to the state senate, lobbied there for stagecoach companies, and been chosen district attorney here; but he had broken down during the trial of his first case and resigned in humiliation. A quiet reserved man, he was most effective in private offices and in political caucuses held behind closed doors. Well read, Sweeny knew about the fortunes amassed in the rebuilding of Paris under the direction of Baron Haussmann and understood how public improvements may be used for private profit. Despite his erudition and subdued nature, Sweeny became involved with a woman who worked in a Turkish bath and was said to have had a child by her. He was the Tweed Ring's silent adviser, and his principal job was to control the judiciary. Sweeny was of medium height and slight of build, with a low forehead, deep-set eyes, and black bristly hair and mustache.

Richard B. Connolly was city comptroller. He acted as financial adviser to the Tweed Ring. Born in Ireland, he had come to America as a young man, worked in Philadelphia as an auctioneer's clerk, and then moved to New York City. Here he had been appointed to the customhouse, switched to the job of discount clerk in the Bank of North America, and gained local political experience in Tweed's Seventh Ward. Connolly had served two terms as county clerk, twice been elected to the state senate, become general manager of the Central National bank, and had risen in Tammany Hall. A Uriah Heep in mannerisms, cringing in the presence of Boss Tweed, and tyrannical to his own underlings, Richard Connolly merited the nickname of Slippery Dick. His broad face was clean-shaven, and he brushed his hair forward from his ears.

Three judges rounded out the inner circle of the Tweed Ring:

George G. Barnard was presiding justice of the state supreme court. For a while he posed as a reformer, but soon everyone understood that he was Tweed's vassal. Barnard was handsome of face and figure, overbearing, and insolent.

Albert Cardozo was a justice of the state supreme court. The only Jewish member of the Tweed Ring and of Portuguese extraction, Cardozo was learned and industrious but was such a scoundrel that he sold justice as a fishwife sells flounders. His son, Benjamin Nathan Cardozo, later redeemed the family name by serving honorably and wisely as an Associate Justice of the United States Supreme Court.

John H. McCunn was a judge of the superior court. He had tried to nullify the federal Draft Act during the Draft Riots, and this had brought him to Tweed's attention. When Tweed barked, McCunn jumped through hoops.

Tweed himself was the Boss, the leader of Tammany Hall, the president of the county board of supervisors, the street commissioner, and a state senator. Through Hoffman, Hall, Sweeny, Connolly, Barnard, Cardozo, McCunn, and the 12,000 other persons who received patronage from him, he controlled the entire machinery of the city and state governments—executive, legislative, and judicial—with the sole exception of the court of appeals. He named the men he wanted elected to office—and they were elected. He spelled out the laws he wanted enacted—and they were enacted. Should an innocent dare to bring charges against Tweed or any of his underlings, the Boss lifted a finger, and one of his judges ruled in his favor. He controlled the city police, mostly Irish and Democrats, even paying the police commissioner out of his own pocket. He bought the silence of most newspapers by subsidizing them with unnecessary city advertising and by bribing editors and reporters. He emasculated the New York County Republican committee by buying off its members. He smothered reform movements in money. And by 1869 he was stealing more than $1,000,000 a month from the city treasury.

This still wasn't enough to satisfy him. Bloated with success and brazenly confident, Boss Tweed sometimes shut his bright-blue eyes and dreamed of taking over the United States of America. How? He planned to make John T. Hoffman the nation's President, raise A. Oakey Hall to the governorship of New York State, and himself become a U.S. Senator in order to work his black magic in the upper chamber of the Congress. Connolly would stay home and watch the store as city comptroller. Before he could launch this grandiose scheme, there was one thing Tweed had to do.

He wanted a new city charter. Powerful though he was, he had to tack indirectly toward his goals under the current charter. By streamlining legal technicalities, he would be able to work smoother and faster. For one thing, Tweed hated to ask the state legislature to pass city tax bills. He practically owned the legislature, true, but this cost him a lot of money in bribes. The state's lawmakers were paid only $300 a year, so they were always eager to milk money from anyone wanting legislation They would introduce a bill striking at a large corporation—including a city, such as New York—and then wait to be paid to withdraw the obnoxious measure. No railroad ever got a favor without bribes. Bills were attacked and defended in terms of who paid how much to whom. These freebooters worked generally as individuals until Tweed became a state senator. Then he whipped them into a disciplined band, which rode roughshod over the few honest legislators. Handing out greenbacks like cabbage leaves, Boss Tweed was the man to whom every grasping lawmaker looked before voting on any bill.

Tweed paid about $1,000,000 in bribes to get his new city charter passed at Albany, but pass it did. On the afternoon of April 5, 1870, only two of the thirty-two members of the state senate voted against it. Governor Hoffman immediately signed the bill and then handed the pen to a beaming Tweed. That night the Boss held court, dispensing free champagne to all comers. He had explained to the businessmen of New York City that he sought municipal autonomy for their hometown. Peter Cooper and others, who should have known better, believed him. When Tweed returned from the state capital, he was greeted here like a conquering hero.

What did this Tweed charter do? Seemingly it gave control of the city back to the city at the expense of the state, which pleased the advocates of home rule. It increased the power of the mayor by granting him the right to appoint department heads and all other important city officers without anyone's approval. Before this, the governor had made many of these appointments. What's more, the mayor could now appoint his favorites for terms of four to eight years, thus assuring continuity of power regardless of reformers. Under the charter it was impossible to discharge department heads for incompetency or dishonesty, except by unanimous consent of the six judges of the court of common pleas. To Tweed, who had bribed a Republican to stay away from a meeting of the board of supervisors, this provision meant nothing; in a crisis one of the six judges would fail to appear. The charter weakened the city council by forbidding it to regulate the affairs of any city department. It wrested control of Central Park from the original commissioners. It ended state supervision of city police.

Worst of all, perhaps, the charter created a board of audit to consist of the mayor (Hall), the comptroller (Connolly), and the commissioner of public works (Tweed, whom Mayor Hall quickly appointed to this new post). According to M. R. Werner in his book *Tammany Hall:* "The Tweed charter was *carte blanche* for members of the Ring to enter the city treasury with shovels and load their wagons with gold." Later, when Tweed was confessing, he explained how this three-man board of audit had enriched the ring: "—The understanding was that the parties to whom we advanced money, and whom we had confidence in, should, through our influence, advance bills for work purporting to be done for the county or the city—more particularly for the county—and they should receive only fifty percent of the amount of their bills."

In addition to graft and corruption, New Yorkers were plagued with a transportation problem. After the Civil War, traffic became a headache. A state senate committee said that "the transit of freight and passenger trains by ordinary locomotives on the surface of the street is an evil which has already endured too long. . . ." The New York *Herald* grumbled that "modern martyrdom may be succinctly defined as riding in a New York omnibus."

Between 1831 and 1858, 8 city railroads had been incorporated. In 1860, 6 of them remained in operation. Additionally, 16 omnibus companies controlled 544 licensed stages over fixed routes to all parts of the city below Fiftieth Street, as well as to neighboring villages. By 1864 there were only 12 such lines and 61,000,000 passengers a year. By 1865 the traffic snarl had become so great that it was almost impossible to get around town. By 1866 a pedestrian bridge had been built across Broadway at Fulton Street. In 1867 the *Evening Post* complained that workers had to spend more than four hours a day getting to and from their jobs. Mark Twain shook his head over the "torrent of traffic" and accused city officials of winking at the overloading of streetcars. Boss Tweed had both the streetcar and the stage companies in his pocket. All public vehicles were filthy and smelly, lighted at night by one faint kerosene lamp and warmed in winter only by straw strewed on the floor.

Most stores and offices still lay within the downtown area, and employees had to live fairly close to their places of business in order to get to work. Lacking good transportation, they couldn't spread out. Because Manhattan was long and narrow and because it lacked bridges to Brooklyn and New Jersey, the population could expand in only one direction—north.

The world's first underground railroad system opened in London in 1863. Then a Michigan railroad man, Hugh B. Willson, raised $5,000,000 to dig a subway in New York under Broadway. Cornelius Vanderbilt, who was slowly acquiring control of the New York Central, snorted that he'd be "underground a damned sight sooner than this thing!" Boss Tweed was against Willson's subway, too, because it would compete with transit lines he already controlled. Tweed gave the word to Reuben E. Fenton, Hoffman's predecessor as governor, and Fenton promptly vetoed a bill calling for construction of Willson's underground railroad. Thus did Tweed delay New York's subway system by nearly half a century. The New York *Times* criticized Fenton, saying: "There is not enough room on the surface of the city to accommodate the traffic which its business requires."

Now the only solution to the traffic problem was to build above the ground—in the air. In 1867 the state legislature authorized construction of an experimental line of elevated railway track stretching the half mile between the Battery and Dey Street along Greenwich Street. It had been suggested by a bearded inventor, named Charles T. Harvey. Tweed laughed, people jeered, and almost nobody thought that the train in the sky would work. On July 1, 1868, a crowd gathered to watch as the frock-coated stovepipe-hatted Harvey took his seat in a dinky car looking a little like a primitive automobile, except for the fact that it perched thirty feet above Greenwich Street. This was not a self-propelled locomotive. Its boiler turned a wheel that wound in a cable and moved the car. To everyone's astonishment, the vehicle picked up speed of five miles an hour and hit a peak of ten. The trial run of the world's first elevated had proved a success.

Tweed glowered. Harvey nonetheless got enough financial credit to extend his Ninth Avenue elevated line north toward the Hudson River railroad terminal, at Thirtieth Street near the Hudson River. In 1869 Vanderbilt merged the Hudson line with his New York Central and also broke ground for the first Grand Central terminal, on Forty-second Street at Fourth Avenue. Tweed felt that if Harvey's elevated ever reached the new depot, it was sure to succeed, so he took action. As a state senator, he pushed through the legislature a bill branding the elevated as a public nuisance and permitting him, as city commissioner of public works, to tear it down within ninety days. However, for the first and only time during the 1870 session of the legislature, the lawmakers crossed Tweed by voting down his bill. Tweed, who had set back New York's subways, was not permitted to delay its elevateds.

Meanwhile, a strange subway was secretly being bored through the ground under Manhattan. The man behind this mystery was a genius, named Alfred Ely Beach. An inventor, he had designed a typewriter, which he jokingly called a literary piano. A publisher, he was co-owner of the New York *Sun* and had founded a score of other periodicals. For a while he had an office overlooking City Hall and a home at 9 West Twentieth Street, and traffic was so dense that it took him almost an hour to get from one place to the other.

In 1866 Beach began experimenting with pneumatic power, making models of mail tubes. The next year, during the American Institute Fair held in the Fourteenth Street armory, he built a plywood tube six feet in diameter and a block long on the armory floor. Inside this tube was a ten-passenger car. Using a big fan, Beach blew the car from Fourteenth Street to Fifteenth Street and then sucked it back. Hundreds of people enjoyed this ride, and Beach now knew that he could propel a train through a pneumatic tube.

The inventor was aware that Tweed had killed Willson's hope of building a subway, and he knew about the graft involved in obtaining transit franchises. He decided not to seek a franchise from corrupt city officials, telling his brother, "I won't pay political blackmail. I say let's build the subway furtively." He asked the state legislature for a charter to dig what he characterized as a pneumatic mail tube system under Broadway. In 1868 the bill crossed the desk of State Senator Tweed, who failed to understand its implications. Beach got his charter. Soon he had a gang of laborers burrowing a tunnel 21 feet under Broadway just west of City Hall. This hole in the ground was only 312 feet long, running a single block from Murray Street on the south to Warren Street on the north. The project went on in complete secrecy, the workmen dumping bags of earth into wagons whose wheels were muffled to avoid all noise. The digging was finished in only 58 nights. Then the men bricked in the tunnel, which had an outside diameter of 9 feet and an inside diameter of 8 feet.

On February 26, 1870, New Yorkers awakened to find that they had a one-block subway. The *Herald* blared: "FASHIONABLE RE-

CEPTION HELD IN THE BOWELS OF THE EARTH!" Tweed was furious. City and state officials, aware of his anger, stayed away from the new marvel, but the people flocked to see it. They were overwhelmed by the subway's waiting room, which was nearly half as long as the tunnel itself. All was elegance, the walls frescoed, paintings hung here and there, a grand piano standing in stately splendor, a fountain bubbling, and a tank glistening with goldfish—all lighted by zircon lights. Beach purposely had made the waiting room impressive in the hope of winning popular support for the battle he anticipated with Boss Tweed.

New Yorkers were delighted with their pneumatic subway, but Beach still had to ask the state legislators for a new charter. After all, he had built a transit line instead of a pneumatic postal system. What's more, he wanted to extend his subway the length of Broadway. Now the state governor was John T. Hoffman, whose political future lay with Boss Tweed. The lawmakers passed Beach's transit bill, but the governor vetoed it. In an editorial the *Tribune* stormed, "Of course it was to be expected that, as long as Tammany had no hand in the scheme and saw no chance of converting it into a swindle, its influence would be used against it."

This was in 1871. The next year the people threw Hoffman out of office, and in 1873 a third Beach bill came before the legislature. It won the approval of both the lawmakers and the new governor, John A. Dix. By this time, however, the city was writhing in the grip of a depression, and Beach could not get enough capital to extend or even maintain his subway. Late in 1873 Governor Dix withdrew Beach's charter with "the greatest reluctance." Not until the beginning of the twentieth century was New York to get a permanent subway.

In 1871 self-propelled steam locomotives replaced the cable-winding engines on the Ninth Avenue elevated, whose tracks now pushed north of Thirtieth Street. Vanderbilt's Hudson River railroad thrust even farther north, making it possible for Yonkers to become a separate city in 1872. The same year Vanderbilt wangled through the legislature a bill forcing New York City to pay $4,000,000 to improve the roadway of his New York Central tracks on Park Avenue. On February 1, 1872, the New York Council of Political Reform declared publicly that for a long time the city had been swindled out of at least $1,000,000 a year in the development of surface railroads.

Expansion of elevated railways marked the first real advance in the city's rapid transit. English visitors liked New York's elevated better than their own London subway. A German geographer, who saw New York in 1873, said that its transportation facilities were better than those of any European city. Improved transit caused a real estate boom that made ever more money for Tweed and his henchmen. On the inside of everything, they bought property where improvements were to be made and then sold this land to the city at fantastic sums. The strip that became Riverside Drive should have cost only $1,400,000, but the Tweed Ring had run the cost up to $6,000,000 by the time the purchase was made in 1872.

Three years later the state legislature passed the Husted Act, empowering New York's mayor to appoint the city's first rapid transit commission. Its members chose elevated railways as the best medium for moving New Yorkers around the city speedily. They also selected Second, Third, Sixth, and Ninth Avenues as routes for these railways. Rail by rail, pillar by pillar, the elevateds took shape overhead; the tracks were thirty feet high in most places and even higher in others. On narrow streets the aerial railroads were built right over sidewalks and almost flush with the sides of buildings.

The Third and Sixth Avenue elevateds were the first to begin operations in 1878. Each train consisted of four cars, painted light green, their interior upholstery finished in dark brown. Trains ran from 5:30 A.M. until midnight. The fare was ten cents a ride except during rush hours, when it cost five cents. Conductors collected tickets threaded with silk as a protection against counterfeiting. The engines started with a jerk that jolted the spines of passengers. The clatter and rumble of the sky trains frightened horses on the streets, while the soot, cinders, and burning coals they dropped infuriated pedestrians and housewives. People living on the second and third floors of tenements, on a level with the passing cars, lacked privacy unless they pulled down their shades. Oil squirted into their parlors when their windows were open. Property values declined all along the elevated lines. Despite these drawbacks, New York now had a transit system of which it could be proud—for a time.

The same could not be said of the interstate Erie Railroad, whose tracks were reaching the Midwest. Its flaking rails sank into rotten ties and undulated beneath the wheels of passing trains. Nonetheless, since it offered the possibility of plunder, a group of rapacious tycoons fought one another for possession of this down-at-the-heels line. Because their fiscal war was waged in New York courts and the Stock Exchange, this railroad was called the Scarlet Woman of Wall Street.

Cornelius Vanderbilt, rapidly developing into the nation's top railway magnate, wanted this Scarlet Woman. Boss Tweed, who had served as a representative of the Vanderbilt interests in Albany, favored Vanderbilt at first. Judge Barnard therefore issued the injunctions Vanderbilt demanded in the Erie war. Vanderbilt's chief antagonist was shy, swarthy, wispy Jay Gould, a financial wizard who liked to raise orchids. Gould nervously twisted his feet as he talked, and Mrs. Abram S. Hewitt shuddered and said that he had the eyes of a snake. Gould bribed Tweed to come over to his side by offering him more money than the $19,000 Vanderbilt handed the Tweed Ring. Gould gave the Boss a block of Erie stock, had Tweed and Sweeny elected to the Erie's board of directors, and paid Tweed $1,500,000 for "legal" services and expenses—Judge Barnard having proclaimed Tweed an attorney-at-law. The judge then handed out the injunctions sought by Gould and denied those Vanderbilt wanted. Gould won the Erie war, and Tweed happily helped him defraud the railway's investors.

Using the money milked from the Erie, Gould then schemed to corner the market in gold. In the 1860's the United States was not on the gold standard. Monetary values were expressed in terms of paper money. Gold was scarce, and the scarcity resulted in high interest rates. By 1869 the federal treasury held in reserve $95,000,000 in gold, but only $15,000,000 worth of the precious metal circulated throughout the country. Gould planned to rake in this $15,000,000 and then set his own price on gold. He felt that he could make a fast killing and reap enormous profits before gold could be imported from Europe—provided one thing: provided the federal treasury did not sell any of its $95,000,000 in gold. Vital to his plot was knowledge of what the government might do once he made his move.

As his chief ally Gould picked James Fisk, Jr., a shameless financial buccaneer, who was short and round and merry. "I was born to be bad," Fisk said of himself. His mustache was "the color of a Jersey cow" and as long and pointed as the spikes of a catfish. Fond of champagne and chorus girls, Fisk was as charming as he was ruthless. He helped the shy Gould by playing host to the important people they set out to capture.

Ulysses S. Grant was President of the United States at the time, so Gould and Fisk cultivated Abel Rathbone Corbin, who had married Grant's sister. Into their scheme they drew Daniel Butterfield, whom Grant had named as head of the New York subtreasury without really studying his qualifications. Gould and Fisk were unable to involve Grant's private secretary, Horace Potter, but they did entertain the President himself. Fisk called himself an admiral because he owned a fleet of steamships plying the waters off Long Island, and he and Gould took Grant sailing. They tried to worm out of him some hint about the treasury's gold policy. They implied that if the United States kept gold at a high price, this would help sell American grain in Europe, thus aiding the American farmer. Grant kept mum. The plotters decided to go ahead anyway. Corbin wrote an article entitled "Grant's Financial Policy," and Gould managed to get all but the last paragraph printed in the New York *Times* as an editorial.

Since the nation was on a paper standard, gold was bought and sold as a speculative commodity. The trading took place in the Gold Exchange, established in 1864 on the corner of Broad Street and Exchange Place. Everyone called it the Gold Room. In the center of the room stood a fountain containing a bronze statue of Cupid, a dolphin in its arms. A tiny stream of water spouted from Cupid's head to a basin below. A mechanical indicator inside the room and another on an outdoor wall over the sidewalk told the current price of gold. Such was the setting of the most frenetic day thus far in the history of Wall Street.

On September 2, 1869, Gould bought $3,000,000 worth of gold through more than 40 brokers. The price rose 5 points in two days. Because Gould told Fisk that President Grant had forbidden Secretary of the Treasury George S. Boutwell to sell any of the government's gold reserve, Fisk also began buying. As the price of gold soared, other traders became suspicious, and newspapers urged the government to break up the gold conspiracy. Secretary Boutwell hurried from Washington to New York, looked into the situation, but decided to do nothing until instructions arrived from Grant. It was difficult to reach the President, who was visiting a small Pennsylvania town. When at last he heard the news, he became disturbed. Grant got back to Washington on September 22, and that day gold closed at 140½ points. The next day, when it reached 144, the panic began. Throughout the nation, manufacturers and other businessmen, thinking that gold might hit a peak of 200, ordered their agents to buy at any price.

Then came Friday, September 24, 1869—infamous Black Friday.

Brokers in the Gold Room and crowds on the sidewalk outside watched apprehensively as the price of gold went up, up, up. This meant ruin for hundreds of thousands of Americans, because bankers' paper was unsalable except at a high premium, while merchants' paper could hardly be sold at any price. Gold transactions that day amounted to more than $400,000,000. As telegraph lines *dit-dah-ditted* the news across the country, business from Boston to San Francisco ground to a halt. Speculators, merchants, and workers realized that their futures depended on what was happening in New York's Gold Room.

In Washington the President and Secretary Boutwell were kept informed of minute-by-minute developments. When the price reached 160 at about 11:30 A.M., one man fainted in the Gold Room, and many wept openly. Secretary Boutwell nervously suggested to President Grant that they sell $3,000,000 of the nation's gold reserve. Grant mentioned $5,000,000, but Boutwell wired the subtreasury in New York to sell $4,000,000. Butterfield, the man in charge of the subtreasury, may have tipped off Jay Gould about the selling order, for now Gould switched tactics and began unloading. Jim Fisk, unaware that Gould was doublecrossing him, urged his broker, Albert Speyer, to buy more and more and more. A few minutes before noon, when gold reached its high of 162½, everyone learned that the New York subtreasury intended to sell $4,000,000 worth of gold the next day.

Fortunes were lost. Wall Street brokerage houses failed. Railway stocks shrank. The nation's business was paralyzed. An observer in the Gold Room wrote that "the spectacle was one such as Dante might have seen in the inferno." Half a dozen men went temporarily mad. A broker, named Solomon Mahler, slunk home and killed himself. A little man with glassy eyes staggered about the floor, croaking, "I'm Albert Speyer! Some people have threatened to shoot me. Well, shoot! Shoot!" Men cursed and screamed and laughed maniacally and dashed from one trading post to another. Their nerves were tighter than the gut of an Indian's bow. Half-moons of sweat stained the armpits of their jackets. From time to time they wobbled to the fountain to dash cool water on their burning faces.

The frenzy inside the Gold Room reached the people on the sidewalk outside, fermenting the crowd into a mob that howled for the hides of Jay Gould and Jim Fisk. A national guard regiment was ordered to stand by to "quell the riot in Wall Street." But Boss Tweed, forever loyal to fellow scoundrels, gave the plotters police protection. Gould, who had failed to corner all the gold in circulation but who nonetheless made a profit of $11,000,000, said smoothly, "I regret very much this depression in financial circles, but I predicted it long ago. I was in no way instrumental in producing the panic." Fisk, who had lost money but soon found a way to repudiate his contracts, spoke with his usual impudence: "A fellow can't have a little innocent fun without everybody raising a halloo and going wild."

Greedy to the last, neither cared about the suffering they had inflicted on numberless innocents. Tweed didn't care, either.

Monarch of all he surveyed, affecting the grand manner in public, and arrogant to friend and foe alike, Tweed had become giddy with success. A once great city had degenerated into Tweedsville. While the Boss ate oysters at Delmonico's, rode behind sleek trotting horses, cruised aboard his yacht, and beamed on champagne-swilling cronies, New York fell into ruins.

It was filthier than Naples. Dirty streets and defective sewer pipes resulted in abnormally high death rates. Tweed's stables were superior to any tenement in town. Public buildings sagged into dilapidation for want of proper maintenance. Produce was unloaded on rotting wharves. Every day was Mardi Gras for thieves and harlots. The annual tax levy rose from an average of $4.33 per person in 1860 to $25.11 in 1870. Between 1869 and 1870 the city debt soared from $36,000,000, to $97,000,000, and the town teetered on the edge of bankruptcy. G. T. Strong lamented in his diary: "To be a citizen of New York is a disgrace."

Tweed became arrogant because he became careless, and he became careless because it had been so easy to plunder the city. For example, in a couple of hours one morning Tweed and his henchmen stole more than $5,500,000. Here's how it happened: Under the new Tweed charter the new board of audit consisted of Tweed, Hall, and Connolly. At one of the board's first meetings, on May 5, 1870, the trio authorized the payment of an additional $6,300,000 for the new courthouse they were building. Nearly 90 percent of this sum was padding, and they pocketed the extra $5,500,000. The same day six Negroes were arrested for playing penny poker in the basement of 208 West Thirtieth Street.

When the sands of time begin to run out for any man, it is difficult to detect the first grain, but for Tweed it may have begun to trickle into infinity on December 24, 1869. On that date *Harper's Weekly* published a cartoon showing members of the ring breaking into a big box marked "Taxpayers' and Tenants' Hard Cash." Fletcher Harper owned this courageous magazine, and George William Curtis was its editor. The cartoon came from the pen of German-born Thomas Nast, who wore his hair crew cut in the fashion of Prussian officers. A fierce handlebar mustache and pointed beard emphasized the virility of this clear-eyed man. A gifted cartoonist and caricaturist, Nast created the symbolic Republican elephant and Democratic donkey, and soon he was to paint some stripes on Tammany.

In the spring of 1870 Comptroller Connolly complained that he wasn't getting a big enough cut of the loot. He told Tweed that other members of the ring would be unable to swindle the city at all without him. Tweed asked what he had in mind. Connolly said he wanted 20 percent instead of just 10. Tweed decided that this could be managed by doublecrossing Mayor Hall and City Chamberlain Sweeny. From that time on, Hall and Sweeny got what they thought was 20 percent of the take, although it was really only 10 percent.

Toward the end of the summer of 1870 James Taylor died. He had been Tweed's partner in the New York Printing Company, which, not surprisingly, did far more business than other printing firms. Taylor also had been one of the three directors of the New York *Times*. While Taylor was alive, the *Times* did not attack Tweed, but now that he was dead, the influential morning paper fell under the control of George Jones, who detested the Boss. Although no one confused George Jones with St. George, he began hunting the dragon.

On September 20, 1870, the *Times* published its first attack—not as a news article on page one, but as an editorial inside the paper. It was written by the *Times*' managing editor, Louis J. Jennings, who wielded his pen like a broadsword. Born in England, Jennings had worked on newspapers in London and India, and years after the Tweed exposé he returned to Great Britain and wound up as a Member of Parliament. Now, day after day, Jennings lambasted Tweed, making such charges as: "No Caliph, Khan or Caesar has risen to power or opulence more rapidly than Tweed I. Ten years ago this monarch was pursuing the humble occupation of a chairmaker in an obscure street in this city. He now rules the State as Napoleon ruled France, or as the Medici ruled Florence. . . ." Jennings dealt mainly in invective because the *Times* lacked enough hard facts to make the kill.

In January, 1871, Jimmy Watson died as the result of a sleighing accident. His official title was county auditor, but his unofficial job was bookkeeper and paymaster for the Tweed Ring. The *Times* could howl its head off about the way the city was run, but proof of corruption could only be obtained by access to the ring's books, and no one but Connolly and Watson ever saw these doctored documents. So far the *Times* didn't know that Watson had issued a $66,000 voucher to an imaginary man with the outlandish name of Philippo Donnoruma or that the fellow who had cashed it had signed it with the anglicized name of Philip Dummy. If you're going to bilk the public, you may as well have some fun while doing it. Although Watson's salary was only $1,500 a year, he had become a millionaire and lived in a mansion at 42d Street and Madison Avenue. The sleighing accident happened on January 24 at the corner of 8th Avenue and 130th Street. Newspaper readers tilted their eyebrows and pulled down the corners of their mouths when they read that Watson's mare, killed in the collision, was worth $10,000. For the week that Watson lingered on his deathbed, Tweed kept some of his plug-uglies handy to thwart a last-minute confession.

In the spring of 1871 James O'Brien decided that he, too, wanted a bigger slice of the melon. Tweed had made O'Brien county sheriff. This office paid no salary; but the sheriff was entitled to keep all the fees he collected, and they were enormous. O'Brien panted for power, as well as plunder. He dreamed of displacing Tweed as grand sachem of Tammany and Hall as mayor of New York. O'Brien helped organize a maverick group within Tammany, known as the Young Democracy, only to have Tweed beat its ears off. But when O'Brien finished his profitable term as sheriff, he brazenly submitted a bill for $350,000 in "extras" he claimed the county owed him. Tweed, the granddaddy of grifters, wasn't going to let an upstart get away with a haul like that. He bellowed like a wounded rhinoceros and stamped his foot, and that was that. Or so Tweed thought. O'Brien withdrew his claim and returned to the fold of tweedledum democracy. Secretly, though, O'Brien decided to try to get the goods on the Boss and blackmail him.

After Watson's death a nonentity, named Stephen C. Lyons, was made county auditor, but he soon faded from sight. Matthew J. O'Rourke, former military editor of a newspaper, became the new auditor. Connolly's faith in O'Rourke was misplaced, for he began copying incriminating terms from the secret books of the ring. About the same time O'Brien asked Connolly to find a job for his friend

William Copeland. Connolly thought O'Brien had made his peace with the Boss; after all, the former sheriff was trustee of a group collecting funds to raise a statue of Tweed. So Connolly obliged O'Brien by putting Copeland to work on some books in his office. A spy for O'Brien, Copeland also started copying fraudulent accounts. No one knows if O'Rourke and Copeland were aware that each was playing the same dangerous game.

Copeland fed facts and figures to O'Brien. O'Brien then told the Boss he would publish this proof unless he got the $350,000 he wanted. Tweed apparently considered this a bluff. But soon thereafter O'Brien called at the office of the *Sun* with evidence of the ring's corruption under one arm. No one there would touch this dynamite. O'Brien then trudged to the *Times,* which kept calling for an examination of the city's financial records. If all was well, the paper argued, why object to publication of the figures? The *Evening Post,* which sided with Tweed, protested righteously that Connolly could not open these books because only city aldermen had this power.

One steaming hot night in the first week of July, 1871, the balding O'Brien opened the door of Jennings' office at the *Times.* The former sheriff mopped his brow and said vaguely, "Hot night." The managing editor replied in a flat voice, "Yes. Hot." O'Brien fingered a big paper envelope he carried and said, "You and Tom Nast have had a tough fight." Jennings nodded and said, "Still have." O'Brien remarked, "I said—*had.*" He laid the envelope on Jennings' desk and added, "Here's the proof to back up all that the *Times* has charged. They're copied right out of the city ledgers." Jennings' muscles tightened, but he did not move until O'Brien left his office. Then he pounced on the envelope.

A couple of days later O'Rourke also came to the *Times* with his copies of the ring's books. His data included some information missing from the O'Brien collection. Now the *Times* had the hard facts and figures with which to expose the most astonishing story of graft in the history of New York.

On July 8, 1871, the newspaper began publishing the inside story of the Tweed Ring. At first Tweed shrugged this off as a partisan attack by a Republican journal, but the *Times* kept it up day after day, revealing one secret after another. In its July 22 issue it printed this front-page headline: "THE SECRET ACCOUNTS . . . PROOFS OF UNDOUBTED FRAUDS BROUGHT TO LIGHT . . . WAR-

RANTS SIGNED BY HALL AND CONNOLLY UNDER FALSE PRETENSES."

This and subsequent revelations told of fraud so cunning and monumental that it was appalling. Contractors and merchants overcharged the city at the behest of the ring and then kicked back the excess to ring members. Some bills were absolutely false in both amounts and prices. The city was charged for work never done. Streetlamps were often painted on rainy days so that the paint would run off immediately, thus creating extra work and giving more pay to Tweed's followers. The city paid money to imaginary persons, imaginary firms, and imaginary charitable institutions. In six weeks alone the Boss added 1,300 names to the city payroll, which ultimately rose from 12,000 to nearly 15,000 persons. Some did no work whatsoever. William "Pudding" Long, who walked Tweed's dogs, was paid $100 a month as an interpreter, although he couldn't read or write *any* language.

The permit bureau spent $2,842 to collect $6 worth of permits. Andrew J. Garvey, the ring's plasterer, got $133,187 for two days' work. George S. Miller, its carpenter, was paid $360,747 for one month's work. At $14 per ream of paper, plus other marked-up items, the city's stationery bill for one year came to $1,000,000. The city paid $170,729 for 35 to 40 chairs and 3 or 4 tables. At $5 per chair this sum would have entitled the city to 34,145 chairs, and if they had been placed side by side in a straight line, they would have reached the 4½ miles from City Hall to the arsenal in Central Park opposite East Sixty-fourth Street.

The prime catch-all for this graft was the new County Courthouse, located behind City Hall, on the corner of Chambers and Centre streets, just west of the present Municipal Building. It gained renown as the House That Tweed Built. In 1858 a bill authorizing its construction and providing $250,000 for this purpose had been passed. Work began in 1862, but before it was finished, it needed many repairs. By 1867 some of its rooms had been put to use, but the structure wasn't completed until 1872. Its total cost came to more than $12,-000,000. At the most, the building and all its equipment couldn't have cost more than $3,000,000, but of course, Tweed and his fellow rogues pocketed the other $9,000,000. The *North American Review* estimated that the three-story courthouse cost New York taxpayers more than four times the cost of the Houses of Parliament.

The *Nation,* a weekly magazine founded in New York in 1865, now joined the *Times* in attacking the Tweed Ring. Back in 1868 the *Nation* had daringly used the phrase "the notorious Supervisor Tweed," but it had not crusaded so vigorously as either the *Times* or *Harper's Weekly.* The *Nation's* editor was liberal Irish-born Edwin Lawrence Godkin, a Utilitarian philosopher.

Thomas Nast's cartoons in *Harper's* also became more frequent and savage now, and his drawings made Tweed look like a bloated vulture. On November 11, 1871, Nast created the emblem of the predatory Tammany tiger, inspired by the tiger painted on the fire engine belonging to the Big Six, Tweed's onetime volunteer fire company. The cartoons frightened Tweed, who rumbled, "Let's stop them damned pictures! I don't care much what the papers write about me— my constituents can't read. But—dammit!—they can see pictures!" (Indeed, nearly half the people of New York were foreign-born, and most of Tweed's supporters were illiterate.)

The Boss, who really did care what was written about him, now counterattacked. He growled that if he were twenty-five years younger, he would kill *Times* owner George Jones with his bare hands, and he mumbled something about having Thomas Nast horsewhipped. Ring members pointed out that the *Times'* managing editor, Jennings, was an Englishman and married to an actress. They spread rumors that Jennings had been discharged from the London *Times* for printing lies. The New York *Sun,* still aligned with Tweed, archly commented that "the decline of the *New York Times* in everything that entitles a paper to respect and confidence has been rapid and complete. . . ."

Charles Nordhoff was fired as managing editor of the *Evening Post* for criticizing Tweed; then the *Post* stoutly defended the Boss. Mayor Hall forbade all city employees to eat in the basement of the nearby Times Building. The mayor also upheld Tweed in Hall's own newspaper, the *Leader.* Ring members then tried, but failed, to prove that the real estate title to the Times Building was defective. Tweed thought of trying to buy the *Times* itself, but George Jones snorted that he wouldn't sell under any circumstances. Next, the ring caused a bill to be passed in the state legislature, and Tweed's vassal, Governor Hoffman, signed it. This weasel-worded law gave the appellate division of the state supreme court the power to hold any critic of Tweed or his ring in contempt of court and send him to jail. Two of the three appellate judges, Barnard and Cardozo, were owned by Tweed.

His whisper squads now spread the lie that Nast had left Germany to escape military service, although Nast had been a child of six when he had landed in New York. The cartoonist received threatening letters; one enclosed a drawing of him with a thread tied around his neck like a noose. *Harper's Weekly* was owned by Harper & Brothers, and now the Boss banned all their books from public schools. Fletcher Harper refused to be frightened into silence. A Tweed emissary offered Nast a $50,000 bribe to drop his attacks on the ring and leave for Europe. Nast refused. "Slippery Dick" Connolly offered George Jones of the *Times* the fantastic sum of $5,000,000 to forget the whole thing. Jones not only brushed this aside but dared the ring to sue the *Times* for libel.

Tweed, usually a master of mob psychology, now made a damaging mistake. For the first and only time during a newspaper interview he lost his temper when reporters badgered him about the disclosures in the *Times*. "Well," he snarled, "what are you going to do about it?" He failed to anticipate an utterance of a character in a book, by Alfred Henry Lewis, entitled *The Boss:* "Th' public is a sheep, while ye do no more than just rob them. But if ye insult it, it's a wolf!"

The righteous and outraged wolves held a historic mass meeting in Cooper Union on the sweltering evening of September 4, 1871. So hot and sticky was the Great Hall that aging Peter Cooper, G. T. Strong, and other dignitaries adjourned to a nearby committee room. This was the meeting that brought to the surface an undercover adversary of Boss Tweed—the masterful and emotionless politician Samuel J. Tilden. Slight of figure and racked by illness, Tilden had a big nose and small eyes. His droopy left eyelid lent him a baleful look. Snake-cold, withdrawn, and ignorant of human nature, a man who thought five times before doing anything, Tilden had become a millionaire as a corporation lawyer, and he had risen to power in the Democratic party. When the Tammany tiger first began stalking the city, Tilden belonged to the organization and must have known much of what was going on. He held his tongue, however, for he hoped to become President of the United States, and it would have been unwise to cross Tweed prematurely. Now that Tweed seemed to be on the run, Tilden closed in for the kill, thinking that this would further his political future.

William F. Havemeyer, a sugar merchant and former mayor of New York, chaired the Cooper Union meeting. Many of the city's leading business and professional men were there, the *Times'* exposé having convinced them of Tweed's venality. When attorney Joseph H. Choate mentioned Tweed's name, there arose cries of "Pitch into the Boss! Give it to him! He deserves it!" Two days before, the *Nation* had hinted that Tweed should be lynched; the usually responsible magazine declared that such violence would no more constitute a real lynching than had the execution of Robespierre, the French revolutionary who had loosed the Reign of Terror on Paris. On this tense torrid evening Judge James Emmott shouted, "Now, what are you going to do with these men?" People screamed, "Hang them!" Serious consideration was given to forming a vigilance committee like that which Californians had organized in the days of the gold rush. Wiser heads prevailed, however. A respectable Committee of Seventy was set up under Tilden's leadership. Resolutions were passed, and a program was presented for prosecuting the Tweed Ring. One of the seventy committee members was John Foley, chosen for his Irish name since most of Tweed's followers were Irish.

Two days after the mass meeting Foley brought a taxpayer's suit asking for an injunction to restrain the mayor, comptroller, and others from (1) paying any city money to anyone and (2) issuing any more bonds. When the case was given to Judge Barnard, who liked to whittle, some people felt that it was like presenting a matchstick to an ax killer. Foley's suit would end up on the floor among other wood shavings from the judge's pocketknife. Everyone understood the significance of the suit, for it marked the very first time that Tweed's total power had been challenged in a court of law. To the stunned surprise of all—especially Tweed—Judge Barnard granted the injunction. Samuel J. Tilden apparently promised to make Barnard governor of New York State if he doublecrossed Tweed, and this is just what the judge did. Barnard's betrayal nearly drove Tweed insane. He even considered suicide.

Then Comptroller Connolly, quaking with fear, visited Tilden, babbled about some of the frauds, and threw himself on the mercy of the reformers. On the night of September 11, 1871, someone broke into Connolly's office and stole 3,500 incriminating vouchers, which were burned in the City Hall furnace. This may have been done at the suggestion of Mayor Hall, who now called on Connolly to resign. Tilden advised Connolly to appoint Andrew H. Green, one of the Committee of Seventy, deputy comptroller with the full powers of comptroller. After Green had taken office on September 18, it was reported that Mayor Hall had gone mad and was tearing out his hair.

Duplicates of the burned vouchers, or most of them, rested in a bank used by ring members, and now the duplicates fell into the hands of the Tilden forces. Here was more proof of corruption.

Charles O'Conor was named the state's special attorney general to prosecute Tweed. A week later Tilden swore out a complaining affidavit. A grand jury indicted the Boss on 120 counts, boiling down to the charge that the board of audit had passed fake claims and that much of the plunder had been paid to Tweed. About 1:30 P.M. on December 16, 1871, Sheriff Matthew Brennan, one of Tweed's creatures, had to arrest the Boss in his own private office in the department of public works at 237 Broadway. Jay Gould of the Erie Railroad and other friends instantly put up bail for Tweed. The Boss soon resigned as commissioner of public works, as a director of the Erie, and as grand sachem of Tammany. However, he clung to his office of state senator.

Tweed's trial did not begin for more than a year, his lawyers winning one postponement after another on the grounds that they needed time for preparation. He was represented by seven eminent attorneys, including Elihu Root, who later became United States Secretary of State under President Theodore Roosevelt. Mayor A. Oakey Hall stubbornly finished his term in City Hall but was succeeded on January 1, 1873, by William F. Havemeyer, mayor for the third and last time.

At last, on January 7, 1873, Tweed was brought into the court of oyer and terminer. Tilden, who hoped to be elected governor despite his alleged promise to Judge Barnard, testified against Tweed. So did Andrew J. Garvey, whom the *Times* called the "Prince of Plasterers." Garvey squirmed in the witness chair and during a recess was approached by Tweed, who growled into his ear. Later, when Garvey was asked what the Boss said to him, the plasterer replied piously, "His language was blaphemous." Despite the judge's instructions, which almost demanded a verdict of guilty, the trial ended in a hung jury. Nine jurors held out for acquittal, while three wanted to find Tweed guilty. Most were men of low character, intelligence, and education, and one had lobbied for Tweed in Albany. Almost everyone believed that Tweed's lawyers had packed the hung jury.

Tweed's second trial began on November 5, 1873. This time the prosecutors went to great pains to keep Tweed henchmen off the jury. Nine days were spent in picking the jurors, but the trial itself lasted only four days. The same facts were presented more briefly. This time

Garvey was not called, and Tweed exercised his legal right not to take the witness stand. This second jury found the Boss guilty of 102 offenses. Three days later he was brought back to court for sentencing. Judge Noah Davis said in part:

> Holding high public office, honored and respected by large classes of the community in which you lived, and, I have no doubt, beloved by your associates, you with all these trusts devolved upon you, with all the opportunity you had, by the faithful discharge of your duty, saw fit to pervert the powers with which you were clothed in a manner more infamous, more outrageous, than any instance of like character which the history of the civilized world contains!

Tweed's lips quivered as the judge then sentenced him to 12 years in prison and fined him $12,750. The date was November 19, 1873.

But the court of appeals soon reduced Tweed's sentence to a mere year in jail and a token fine of $250. When Tweed was registered at the Tombs, the warden asked his occupation. Chins held high, Tweed replied, "Statesman." Religion? "I have none." In the Tombs the Boss enjoyed relative luxury, for he occupied a room, not a cell. Cracked windows were replaced with new glass panes, the floor was covered with a dark-green rug, five chairs were provided for visitors, and the famous prisoner could ease his bulk into either a leather lounge or a rocking chair.

Tweed later was removed to the county's grim penitentiary on Blackwells Island. While he sat it out there, Samuel J. Tilden was elected governor for having helped put the Boss behind bars, and a new law enabled the state to sue for money stolen from the public treasury.

Tweed served the full year. The day of his release he was rearrested because a $6,000,000 civil suit had been filed against him. Bail was set at the unheard-of sum of $3,000,000. Unable to provide this security, Tweed was taken to the Ludlow Street Jail for debtors. This county jail, located in the rear of the Essex Market, extended from Ludlow to Essex Street. As a member of the county board of supervisors, Tweed had overseen construction of the brick prison, in which he now became an unwilling guest. Each of its eighty-seven cells was ten feet square, but the Boss occupied the warden's quarters, consisting of two rooms. There Tweed took up residence on January 15, 1875.

How much did the Tweed Ring steal? The exact amount will never be known because the reformers couldn't find every document revealing the true figures. But apparently Tweed and his henchmen filched about $30,000,000 in cash. Considering the bribes paid to the ring by rich men for cutting their taxes, the plunder from the rigged sale of franchises, the issuance of bonds at extravagant interest rates, plus the sale of other privileges, taxpayers probably lost a total of $200,000,000.

What happened to Tweed's cronies? None suffered so much as the Boss himself. Cunningly having assigned their spoils to their wives, brothers, and close friends, most of them fled to Canada, England, and Europe. Mayor Hall was tried, but when a juror died, the trial had to be called off; at his second trial he was acquitted. Judge Barnard was impeached. Judge Cardozo resigned under pressure. Judge Mc-Cunn was deposed and died of heartbreak three days later. The new city fathers, realizing that the loot was beyond the law's reach, promised immunity to Connolly, Sweeny, Garvey, and others if they would give back part of the swag. How much did the city recover? After all expenses had been deducted, a mere $876,241 of the $30,000,000 to $200,000,000 that had been stolen.

Tweed's Fifth Avenue mansion and other properties were attached to repay a portion of his thievery. On October 8, 1875, the state supreme court denied his appeal from the huge civil suit pending against him. The Boss worried about his fate if he lost this new case. Meantime, his status as a prisoner was more like the life of Riley than that of Jean Valjean. Almost every afternoon he strolled out of the Ludlow Street Jail, flanked by two guards, stepped into a carriage, drove to the sparsely settled northern section of the city, took a pleasant walk, and then stopped to dine with his wife en route back to jail.

Late in the afternoon of December 4, 1875, Tweed got out of the carriage in front of the brownstone house his family now occupied at 647 Madison Avenue, between Fifty-ninth and Sixtieth streets. On that day's outing he was accompanied by William M. Tweed, Jr.; Warden Dunham; and a deputy keeper, named Edward Hagan. As Tweed walked up the stoop, he looked for and found a secret mark on one of the steps. Once inside the four men sat down in the parlor, where they were joined by Tweed's son-in-law. Darkness fell, and the gas lamps were lighted. About 6:15 P.M. the Boss said that he would like to go upstairs to see his wife. He left. Five minutes later the warden turned to young Tweed and said they'd better leave. Tweed's son climbed the stairs. A moment later he clattered back down, shouting that he couldn't find his father. Tweed's overcoat still hung on a rack in the hall, but he had escaped. While the warden and deputy keeper nervously searched the house, young Tweed tugged at his hair and screamed that his father had ruined the family.

Tweed had paid $60,000 for help in making his getaway. He may have had the assistance of a smuggler, named Lawrence, with whom he had struck up a friendship in the Ludlow Street Jail. The faint mark on the stoop had told Tweed that this was the chosen day. Instead of going upstairs in his home, Tweed had walked out the back door and cut through his backyard to Fourth (now Park) Avenue. The split second he reached the avenue, a wagon drew up close, and a man's hand reached out and groped toward him. Another confederate, posing as a pedestrian, muttered, "All right—get in!" Tweed crawled into the wagon, and once inside he was covered up. The vehicle jogged across town to a Hudson River pier, where the Boss was transferred to a rowboat. Under the cover of December darkness he was rowed to the New Jersey shore.

After landing, he was whisked to an old farmhouse in a lonely wooded area back of the Palisades, and there he hid for three months. He shaved off his whiskers, clipped his hair, donned a wig, and wore gold-rimmed spectacles. So far as any rambler could tell, he was an infirm gentleman, named John Secor, who needed rest and fresh air. Following his ninety-day confinement in New Jersey, Tweed was smuggled to a shad fisherman's hut on Staten Island.

From there a small schooner took him to Florida, and for a while he hid out in the Everglades. Next, he rode a fishing smack to Santiago, Cuba. He left Santiago in a bark, named the *Carmen,* and on September 6, 1876, landed at Vigo, Spain. By this time he had been traced to Cuba, where it was learned that he had departed for Spain. Secretary of State Hamilton Fish asked Spanish authorities to arrest Tweed. Although Spain and the United States had no mutual extradition treaty, the Spaniards voluntarily obliged. They sent to London for a photograph of Tweed, but none being available, they used a Nast caricature of the Boss.

Tweed was arrested, and the U.S. cruiser *Franklin* sped from the Mediterranean to Spain to bring him back to America. When the ship steamed into New York Harbor, the broken Boss was transferred to a tug that put him ashore at Pier 46, where a curious crowd had gathered. Tweed was now gaunt and poor. Picking his way down a plank from tug to pier, he lost his balance, fell forward, and tumbled into a heap of coal.

Back in the Ludlow Street Jail, Tweed learned that his fair-weather friends had escaped prosecution by turning state's evidence and returning part of their loot. He raged. For the first time he offered to confess everything and did so—fruitlessly. He later said that he had been promised his freedom if he would testify, but the promise was not kept. Cared for in jail by a faithful Negro servant, recognizing passersby, and reciting their personal histories, Tweed finally caught a cold that developed into bronchial pneumonia. He began to die on the morning of April 12, 1878. That noon the clock on the nearby Essex Market started to bong the hour, and just as its last stroke reverberated throughout the jail, William Marcy Tweed died.

Chapter 27

THOMAS EDISON LIGHTS THE CITY

PROGRESS was the magic word in the latter nineteenth century. In New York, as elsewhere in America, the prevailing mood was an optimistic faith that everything was fated to get bigger and better, that people would become richer and happier. Science was a ringmaster taming wild nature, a horn of plenty pouring out so many inventions that progress seemed inevitable.

In this spirit, and while Boss Tweed still languished in jail, some notable New Yorkers gathered on the evening of May 11, 1877, in the Hotel St. Denis, at Broadway and Eleventh Street. They came to watch Professor Alexander Graham Bell, of Boston, demonstrate a strange new device, called the speaking telephone. He proved that he could speak to an assistant two miles away in Brooklyn. Bell's success that night marked the beginning of New York's place in telephone history.

Six days later the first interstate telephone conversation was held between a man in New Brunswick, New Jersey, and Professor Bell in Chickering Hall, at Fifth Avenue and Eighteenth Street. Soon the renowned vaudeville team of Edward "Ned" Harrigan and Tony Hart presented a sketch, called *The Telephone,* on the stage of the Theatre Comique, at Broadway near Spring Street.

The Telephone Company of New York was incorporated in August, 1877, but it failed. In the autumn of 1878 the Bell Telephone Company of New York was organized. The next March it opened New York's first commercial telephone exchange at 82 Nassau Street, and the following autumn the city got a telephone directory, a small card bearing 252 names. The first telephone operators were boys, but soon they were replaced by bustle-wearing girls. Instead of starting a telephone conversation by saying, "Hello," subscribers shouted, "Ahoy!"

The New York Stock Exchange got its first telephone in 1879. Five years later the first regular long-distance service in history went into operation between New York and Boston; in 1885, between New York and Philadelphia; and in 1892, between New York and Chicago. Telephone concerts became the rage, piano solos played in Philadelphia and elsewhere being heard in New York.

Rich people enjoyed the convenience of telephones, but almost everyone complained about the telephone wires cobwebbing the sky. Telegraph wires had been bad enough. In the bitter winter of 1874-75 ice had felled telegraph poles and wires all over the city, and mounted fireman, called Cowboys, patrolled the slick streets, warning pedestrians against the danger of live wires. In 1878 a British visitor wrote: "In the old or lower part of the city . . . against the sky, you look upon a perfect maze of telephone and telegraph wires crossing and recrossing each other from the tops of houses. The sky, indeed, is blackened with them, and it is as though you were looking through the meshes of a net."

That year, 1878, William C. Whitney, the city's corporation counsel, said that communication firms needed no special authority to bury their wires and cables under the streets, but the companies were slow to spend money for such a changeover. In 1881 the first underground telephone cables were laid in Attleboro, Massachusetts, and the next year Boston followed suit. In 1884 the New York state legislature ordered "all telegraph, telephone and electric light wires and cables" removed from the surface of New York's streets before November 1, 1885.

The law had little effect. Telephone poles rose to 50 feet, then to 60, 70, and 80. In 1887, 90-foot telephone poles were installed along West Street, bordering the Hudson River in lower Manhattan. Each was bisected by 30 double crossarms, looking like ladders mounting toward heaven, and each was strung with 300 separate telephone wires. They remained until after the blizzard of 1888.

New York responded to the nineteenth century's avid interest in natural science by founding the American Museum of Natural History. J. Pierpont Morgan was one of seventeen rich men who asked the state legislature for a museum charter. It was granted in 1869. The museum founders soon raised $52,000, with which they bought, among other things, a famous collection of stuffed mammals and birds owned by Prince Maximilian of Germany. This and other early collections were housed at first in the arsenal in Central Park. About eighteen acres of land were acquired along Central Park West between Seventy-seventh and Eighty-first Streets, and in 1874 President Grant laid the cornerstone of the museum's first building.

At the site an underground stream—one of many that lace Manhattan—cost the contractor a fortune because he had to divert it and sink foundation walls strong enough to resist the water pressure. This first building, of Victorian Gothic style and later known as the south-central wing, was opened on December 22, 1877, by President Rutherford B. Hayes. By then Morgan had been elected the museum's treasurer, a title he held for fifteen years. Far from being just an exhibit of old bones and stuffed birds, the museum developed into a dynamic research laboratory, a school for advanced study, a publishing house for scientific manuscripts, the sponsor of exploring parties sent out all over the world, and probably the finest institution of its kind anywhere on earth.

It was a great day for New York's Catholics when St. Patrick's Cathedral was dedicated on May 25, 1879. Except during the Civil War, when construction stopped, passersby for more than twenty years had gawked at laborers hard at work on the Gothic Revival masterpiece. Now that all the scaffolding had been removed and the grounds tidied up, New York newspapers hailed it as the noblest temple ever raised to the memory of St. Patrick.

Archbishop John Hughes had been succeeded by Brooklyn-born Archbishop John McCloskey, who in 1875 became America's first Roman Catholic cardinal. On the day of dedication a host of Catholic dignitaries, headed by six archbishops and thirty-five bishops, watched solemnly as John Cardinal McCloskey walked around the outside of the Cathedral to bless it. The granite exterior resembled the Cologne Cathedral, and the interior suggested the Cathedral of Amiens—a forest of white marble piers, kaleidoscopic stained-glass windows, dominated by an impressive rose window twenty-six feet in diameter. St. Patrick's ranked eleventh in size among the great cathedrals and churches of the world.

The year 1879 also marked the first use of the name Madison Square Garden. Several years earlier the New York and Harlem Railroad had abandoned its depot on the block bounded by Madison and Fourth avenues from Twenty-sixth to Twenty-seventh Street. P. T. Barnum and another showman, named W. C. Coup, leased the property and erected a one-story building with a square four-story tower. They called it the Great Roman Hippodrome. While overseeing the construction job, Coup had a nervous breakdown. He sold his interest to Barnum, who put on entertainment combining the features of a circus, menagerie, and museum. Barnum then sold the place to Patrick S. Gilmore, official bandmaster of the Union army during the Civil War. The best-known bandleader of his day, Gilmore changed the name to Gilmore's Concert Garden. Finally, in 1879, the name was again altered to Madison Square Garden. It was the first of four separate buildings to bear the name, two of them on the original site.

Bullfights were held in New York City in 1880. A promoter, called Angel Fernandez, built a bullring at the corner of 6th (now Lenox) Avenue and 116th Street in Harlem. Downtown New Yorkers got there by taking either the Sixth Avenue or the Third Avenue elevated. That summer billboards announced that "a first-class company of Spanish bull-fighters under the direction of the famous Spanish Espada, Angel Valdemoro," would be brought to the city for this gala occasion. Puzzled New Yorkers had to be told that *espada* means swordsman.

The bulls were shipped from Texas. The general admission was $1.50, the arena doors opened at 3 P.M., and the fights began at 5 P.M. Among the 3,000 to 4,000 persons attending the first of the 3-day fights were parents who dragged along children. Admission for tots under eight was half price. Most youngsters enjoy horror scenes, but these must have been disappointed, for no gore flowed. The rosettes were glued onto the bulls instead of being stuck into them. Rubber caps were placed on the bulls' horns, and the matadors were not allowed to kill the beasts.

More refined diversion than bullfighting was offered New Yorkers in 1880 with the opening of the Metropolitan Museum of Art. At a dinner held in Paris about a dozen years earlier, John Hay had suggested that New York City establish a museum not for art's sake, but for the sake of humanity. Hay was a man of cultivated tastes who had served as private secretary to President Lincoln, and when he made this suggestion, he was first secretary of the American legation in the French capital. His idea fired the interest of the Union League Club, and the chairman of its art committee called a meeting to discuss it. Committee members felt ashamed that New York had no art gallery to compare with those already established in several smaller American cities. Poet-editor William Cullen Bryant was named chairman of a committee of fifty to launch a campaign to raise $250,000 for a public art museum. Another patron was J. Pierpont Morgan, who now controlled the Vanderbilt properties.

The museum's first full-time director was Italian-born, American-naturalized Luigi Palma di Cesnola. While serving as American consul to the island of Cyprus from 1865 to 1877, he had excavated Greek and Roman ruins and put together the Cesnola Collection of Cypriote Antiquities, the largest of its kind in the world. His stone sculptures, bronzes, pottery, and the like were bought by the new museum.

Its trustees had acquired property in Central Park along the west side of Fifth Avenue from Eightieth to Eighty-fifth Street. This had been a disgraceful area; nearby Seneca Village, the largest and foulest squatter camp in the park, had stunk up the neighborhood. Now there rose the first permanent wing of the Metropolitan Museum of Art. Until the building was completed, the museum occupied two temporary homes. The first was at 681 Fifth Avenue, in a place once known as Allen Dodworth's Dancing Academy. The large skylighted dance hall was converted into a picture gallery whose walls were hung with 175 paintings, mostly of Dutch and Flemish masters, brought from Europe. When the growing collection began to overflow the renovated dance hall, the museum moved into its second temporary home, a mansion on the south side of Fourteenth Street just west of Sixth Avenue.

In 1880, when the city's shopping center reached Fourteenth Street, the museum was able to move into its permanent home. The first wing, set well back from Fifth Avenue, was a red brick structure designed in the Tuscan Gothic style. As New York City dedicated one new institution after another, American Presidents were kept busy shuttling back and forth between the national capital and New York. On March 30, 1880, President Hayes formally opened the Metropolitan Museum of Art. It became one of the greatest museums of art on earth.

In the early part of the 1880's New York streets flickered under the glow of gaslights more picturesque than efficient. At twilight it was pleasant to watch lamplighters making their rounds, using a long stick to poke open one side of each square gas lamp, turn on the jet, and set it aflame. But the lights were dim, costly, and troublesome.

A scientist, named Charles Francis Brush, had invented an electric arc light, and by 1879 his creation was illuminating Cleveland's Public Square. In December of that year the first Brush arc lights were installed in New York on Broadway from Fourteenth to Twenty-sixth Street. By July, 1880, Brush had erected one 6,000-candlepower lamp atop a 160-foot pole in Madison Square and another in Union Square. They could be seen from the Orange Mountains of New Jersey 16 miles away, but their dazzling brilliance was unbearable at close range. Women complained that the lamps made their faces look ghostly white.

At this time Thomas Alva Edison was "fired with the idea of an incandescent lamp as opposed to the arc lamp," as he expressed it. Born in Ohio of a Dutch father and Scottish mother, young Edison had only three months of formal schooling. He was tutored by his mother and at the age of twelve read *The Decline and Fall of the Roman Empire*. He went to work as a tramp telegraph operator but vowed that he would become an inventor. In late May or early June, 1869, he arrived in New York for the first time, nearly penniless and deep in debt. The only friend he had here was not at home, so the boyish-looking twenty-two-year-old trudged the streets the whole night through.

The next few days he lived on 5-cent meals of apple dumplings and coffee. That infamous Black Friday when Gould and Fisk tried to corner the gold market, Edison stood on a telegraph booth to watch in wide-eyed wonder as men went mad and fortunes were lost. Amid the frenzy a telegraph operator held out his hand and cried, "Shake, Edison! We're okay. We haven't a cent." Edison later said, "I felt happy because we were poor." By the time of his death his many inventions had spawned business interests worth more than $25,000,000,000; the New York *Times* declared that this gave Edison's brain the highest cash value in history.

The quality, utility, and volume of his brainchildren quickly brought financial independence. By 1876 Edison had taken out 122 patents. By 1878 he had a home and laboratory at Menlo Park, 7 miles northeast of New Brunswick, New Jersey. He searched 13 long months for an incandescent lamp to replace the arc lamp. At last he discovered carbonized cotton filaments and produced a light bulb that burned 40 hours.

The first public demonstration of Edison's new electric lamp was held at Menlo Park on December 31, 1879. Two days later the "Wizard of Menlo Park" held a special preview for New York City aldermen. He had strung his lamps along wires so that he could light or extinguish any bulb without affecting the others. Although the aldermen were impressed, they did not care to spend city money to subsidize Edison's plan to light the sidewalks of New York. After all, the Brush Electric Illuminating Company of New York was already doing that job.

Edison appealed to private investors, and soon the Edison Electric Illuminating Company was incorporated with a capitalization of $1,000,000 to light stores and homes. Officials of the various gas companies, aware of Edison's great reputation, watched his every move with glum eyes, hoping that he would fail. The creation of a central power station and commercial lighting system was the biggest project Edison had ever undertaken. All the equipment had to be "home-devised and home-made," as Edison put it.

J. Pierpont Morgan, the financier, always welcomed new ideas. In January, 1881, he went to New Jersey to find out for himself if Edison's lights could be used to illuminate private homes. (Back in

1859 a professor, named Moses Gerrish Farmer, had lighted his own parlor in Salem, Massachusetts, with lamps powered by a galvanic battery in the cellar.) Edison convinced Morgan that an electric lighting system could be installed in a house. The banker promised that when he moved to 219 Madison Avenue, he would buy an Edison system. Before Morgan changed residences, however, James Hood Wright had installed a generating plant in his home in the Fort Washington section of Manhattan.

In the autumn of 1882 Morgan moved his family to Madison Avenue and Thirty-sixth Street, and soon thereafter the renovated house was wired for electricity. Morgan's son-in-law, Herbert L. Satterlee, said in his biography of the banker:

> This apparatus was one of the very first ever made. . . . A cellar was dug underneath the stable . . . in the rear of the house, and there the little steam engine and boiler for operating the generator were set up. A brick passage was built just below the surface of the yard, and through this the wires were carried. The gas fixtures in the house were wired, so that there was one electric light bulb substituted for a burner in each fixture. Of course there were frequent short circuits and many breakdowns on the part of the generating plant. Even at the best, it was a source of a good deal of trouble to the family and neighbors. The generator had to be run by an expert engineer who came on duty at three P.M. and got up steam, so that at any time after four o'clock on a winter's afternoon the lights could be turned on. This man went off duty at 11 P.M. It was natural that the family should often forget to watch the clock, and while visitors were still in the house, or possibly a game of cards was going on, the lights would die down and go out. If they wanted to give a party, a special arrangement had to be made to keep the engineer on duty after hours. The neighbors complained of the noise of the dynamo, and Mrs. James M. Brown next door said that its vibrations made her house shake. . . .

Edison, too busy to give the Morgan house personal attention, promised his stockholders that his commercial generating station would begin operations almost any day. To impress the men who counted most, he chose to light offices in the financial and communications center of the city. This was an area bounded by Spruce Street on the north, Nassau Street on the west, Wall Street on the south, and Pearl Street on the east. Realtors, aware of the capital Edison had raised, charged him $75,000 for two old four-story buildings at 257 Pearl Street.

He commissioned engineer Charles T. Porter to build six 240-horsepower engines capable of running at a maximum of 700 revolutions per minute. Edison himself went to work on the first of six 110-volt dynamos—"built them by guesswork," he later admitted. Sensitive to the public anger at overhead wires, Edison elected to run his electric wires under the streets, and in the summer of 1881 gangs of laborers began digging. Electricity was such a strange new phenomenon that most people believed it was a liquid that might flow into their basements. To educate his own workers, Edison opened a night school for them at 65 Fifth Avenue. While his underground tubes were being laid, Edison was summoned to the office of the city commissioner of public works, who snapped, "You are putting down these tubes. You need five inspectors to look after this work. Their salary is five dollars a day. Good morning!"

Edison was constantly on the go, supervising each detail of his monumental project, watching as each connection was made, and trusting no one to do things right. At night he stretched out on piles of pipes in the growing power station and fell asleep instantly. By October 1, 1882, he had strung wires into the homes of 59 customers, and although the power had not yet been turned on, there was a great demand for securities in his company. Issued with a par value of $100 per share, this stock advanced rapidly—sometimes as much as $100 *an hour*. It rose to $500 a share, then $3,000, then $5000, then $8,000. Gashouse workers grumbled that soon they would lose their jobs. But by the time Edison inaugurated his commercial lighting system, he had only 85 homes fully wired with a total load of 400 bulbs.

Having postponed the premiere many times and fearful that it might be a fiasco, Edison shunned any fanfare that great day. He stayed up all the previous night to rehearse his men in their new jobs after the first switch had been thrown. Despite his precautions, reporters for the metropolitan papers and for some scientific journals were on hand. Monday, September 4, 1882, they gathered in the dynamo room at 257 Pearl Street, along with some directors of the Edison company.

All eyes were on Thomas Alva Edison. The thirty-five-year-old inventor was of less than average height and was already beginning to flesh out. A handsome man, he had gray eyes, a sturdy chin, a large and sensitive mouth, a prominent nose, and large ears. Locks of hair hung in careless disarray over his domed forehead. When he concentrated on a theoretical problem, his eyes were those of a dreamer;

in an emergency they were the eyes of a man of action; in moments of relaxation they were as boyishly mischievous as those of Tom Sawyer. Tom Edison spat on the floor. He swore manfully. He said "git" for "get." He pronounced "does" as "doos." But on this day of days in his life he did not wear his usual baggy pants and rumpled jacket. Instead, he had struggled into a Prince Albert coat, a white cravat, a starched shirtfront, and a white derby hat.

At 3 P.M., with summer sunlight smiling on downtown Manhattan, Edison signaled his chief electrician, John W. Lieb, to pull the master switch and thus light offices and homes with his electricity. The effect was anticlimactic, like striking matches in the glare of a bonfire. Not until the descent of velvet dusk could the radiance of this man-made illumination be appreciated.

The New York Times Building, at 41 Park Row, had been wired. The next day a *Times* article said:

> To each of the gas fixtures in the establishment a bronze arm was attached, and the electric lamps were suspended from the ends of these arms. . . . The light was more brilliant than gas, and a hundred times steadier. To turn on the light nothing is required but to turn on the thumbscrew. . . . As soon as it is dark enough to need artificial light, you turn the thumbscrew and the light is there, with no nauseous smell, no flicker and no glare.

Only one dynamo went into operation that first day, but Edison declared that it would run forever, provided there was no earthquake. It did function eight years with only one minor stoppage. But other small troubles occurred that first day—such as the blowing out of underground safety catch boxes—and Edison raced from the plant first to one spot and then to another to make repairs. Soon his collar had been torn off, and his white derby hat was stained with grease.

A few days later a policeman rushed into the central station to report trouble at Ann and Nassau streets. Edison and a helper trotted to this corner and found a junction box leaking onto the moist street. Later Edison said:

> When I arrived I saw a ragman with a dilapidated old horse come along the street, and a boy told him to go over to the other side of the road—which was the place where the current leaked. The moment the horse struck the electrified soil he stood straight up in the air, and then reared again. The crowd yelled, the policeman yelled, and the horse started to run away. . . . We got a gang of men, cut the current off . . . and fixed the leak.

Aware of J. Pierpont Morgan's influence, Edison personally over-saw the installation of lights in the white marble Drexel Building, at Wall and Broad streets, where Morgan had his private office. On that notable day of September 4, 1882, Edison scurried down to the build-ing to turn on the lights himself.

The first few months after the Edison system went into operation, no customer received a bill. Fourteen months later there were 508 subscribers and 12,732 bulbs, but each bulb cost $1. Trouble of one kind or another was forever developing. If it wasn't a leak from an underground junction box, it was a fire in a house or shop wired for electricity. New Yorkers were pleased with Edison's invention and agreed that it was superior to either gas or arc lights, but in the fol-lowing decade they were slow to adopt it.

Chapter 28

BUILDING BROOKLYN BRIDGE

THE BROOKLYN BRIDGE was opened on May 24, 1883. During the previous two and a half centuries of New York's history no bridge had spanned the East River to connect Manhattan Island with Long Island.

John Augustus Roebling, the man destined to succeed in this undertaking, was born in the German state of Thuringia in 1806. Brilliant, imaginative, and ambitious, Roebling studied at the Royal Polytechnic Institute in Berlin, then the world's best engineering school. Roebling was twenty-five years old when he came here in 1831. He was a many-sided genius, like Leonardo da Vinci, Benjamin Franklin, and Goethe. He was a master of mathematics, a scholar who put together a magnificent private library, a philosophy student who wrote a 2,000-page book on the universe, a musician who played the piano and flute, a linguist who spoke German and English and French, an engineer, a technologist, and an inventor. Despite all his many abilities, Roebling had just one ambition—to become a builder of great bridges. He was a man in a hurry. Forever fighting the clock, Roebling refused to see anyone five minutes late for an appointment. Still, his compassionate nature attracted both men and women.

Peter Cooper came to know this young man, instantly recognized his genius, and encouraged him. Cooper had a son-in-law, named Abram S. Hewitt, who was later elected mayor of New York. On June 19, 1857, Roebling wrote Hewitt a letter in which he proposed to build a bridge across the East River. During the 1840's the idea of such a bridge had been raised, because in winter months the ferry trip between New York and Brooklyn was slow and uncomfortable and dangerous. Most New Yorkers regarded the project with indifference because they lived where others wished to come, but many Brooklynites who worked in Manhattan had to use the ferry twice daily. Roebling was the first *engineer* to suggest that a bridge was feasible. Hewitt had his letter published in the New York *Journal of Commerce.*

By this time Roebling had fabricated the first wire rope in America, established a wire factory in Trenton, New Jersey, built several suspension bridges, and won a good reputation. However, publication of his letter aroused little interest because of New Yorkers' smugness and because of the outbreak of the Civil War. After the war Roebling submitted to a group of Brooklyn civic leaders a set of plans calling for construction of a bridge twice as long as any in existence and capable of bearing a load of 18,700 tons. He estimated that it would cost $4,000,000.

Except for a few enlightened New Yorkers, such as Hewitt, enthusiasm for the Brooklyn Bridge came not from the people of Manhattan, not from public officials, but from a small group of Brooklyn's private citizens. One prominent New Yorker said, "Our city is not a jealous city, but then to ask it to build a bridge in order to send its trade to a neighboring city is asking a good deal even from the best of natures." Another New Yorker warned that a bridge would "drain the resources of the city of New York in order to fertilize the sandy wastes of Long Island." The Union Ferry Company, which was transporting thousands of commuters a year between Brooklyn and New York, certainly did not favor the bridge.

The winter of 1866 proved decisive. So bitterly cold was the weather and so choked with ice was the East River that ferry traffic became annoyingly slow. Brooklyn's daily commuters figured that it took them longer to get to Manhattan than it took railway passengers to make the 150-mile trip from Albany to Manhattan.

On the frigid evening of December 21 a Brooklyn businessman, named Alexander McCue, was surprised to see William C. Kingsley drive up to his home in a carriage. Kingsley was a prominent contractor and a Brooklyn civic leader. He already had convinced McCue that a bridge could and should be built. Now Kingsley asked his friend, "Will you drive with me to Mr. Murphy's this evening? I want to get him to consent to prepare a bill for the bridge."

Henry C. Murphy had been editor of the Brooklyn *Eagle*, had risen to power as the Democratic leader of Brooklyn, had served a term as mayor, and was now a state senator. That winter evening he was resting on his estate in what today is Owls Head Park in western Brooklyn near Colonial Road and Wakeman Place. After hearing Kingsley's invitation, McCue had looked out a window of his home and shivered. However, McCue was impressed with Kingsley's electric personality and hoped that he would win over Murphy. Climbing into Kingsley's carriage and pulling buffalo robes over their laps, the two men braved the night to drive to the Murphy estate.

The senator was astounded to see them emerge from the winter wasteland but hurried them inside so that they could get warm in front of a roaring fire. After they exchanged pleasantries, Kingsley explained their mission. He declared that a bridge was badly needed. Senator Murphy raised objections. Kingsley met all of them. Kingsley went on talking, knitting a logical argument that fascinated Murphy. At last, raising a hand in a gesture of surrender, the senator said that he agreed. It was late in the morning when Kingsley and McCue left Murphy's home, but they had his promise to draft an enabling bill.

Senator Murphy's measure was passed by the state legislature on April 16, 1867. It granted a charter to a company of private citizens to build a toll bridge across the East River between Brooklyn and Manhattan. Kingsley was so optimistic that even before the bill passed, he signed contracts worth thousands of dollars for construction materials. Thirty-nine investors—most of them from Brooklyn, a few of them from New York—met on May 13, 1867, to organize the

New York Bridge Company. Three days later Murphy was elected its president, and three committees were appointed. John A. Roebling was made chief engineer at $8,000 a year. He predicted that this "will not only be the greatest bridge in existence, but it will be the greatest engineering work of this continent and of the age."

Although the company was privately owned, the state permitted New York and Brooklyn to buy part of its stock. At a meeting of New York's city council it was proposed that the city buy $1,500,000 worth of bridge securities. The aldermen, with their usual avarice, forbade the city comptroller to make this purchase unless and until some money changed hands. Bridge company officials, bending to political reality, gave Boss Tweed $65,000 to pass along to the boys in City Hall. For this service Tweed got 560 shares of stock, with a par value of $40,000, for himself.

By the end of 1868 Brooklyn had subscribed $3,000,000 worth of securities and New York half as much, the total capital issue being $5,000,000. The biggest single subscriber was William C. Kingsley. Despite the fact that money now was available, many people doubted the wisdom of the whole project. They were staggered by the length of the span Roebling proposed. Owners of the East River ferries fought the bridge. Editor Horace Greeley and Brooklyn Mayor Martin Kalbfleisch expressed their nervousness. That Roebling! Now he wanted to use steel wire in the bridge instead of iron wire. Why, this never had been done in the history of the world! To allay fears, Roebling invited a board of prominent engineers to review his construction plans, and in May, 1869, they unanimously agreed that for strength and durability Roebling's bridge was more than adequate.

Congress passed a bill authorizing construction of the bridge, and President Grant signed it. The Secretary of War ordered three military engineers to ascertain if shipping along the East River would be impeded by the proposed bridge. They recommended raising the span from 130 to 135 feet above the river at mean high water, and Roebling agreed. The height became standard for future bridges over navigable waters in America. When the War Department approved the project on June 21, 1869, the last legal hurdle had been cleared.

Laborers went into action on January 2, 1870, by starting to clear the site in Brooklyn where the bridge's granite and limestone tower would be erected. It took a total of thirteen years and five months to build the Brooklyn Bridge. On December 30, 1873, Alfred E. Smith was born in a four-story tenement at 174 South Street in Manhattan just below the growing structure. "The bridge and I grew up together," he said in later years. "I spent a lot of time superintending the job. I have never lost the memory of the admiration and envy I felt for the men swarming up, stringing the cables, putting in the roadways, as the bridge took shape." As many as 600 workmen were employed on it at the same time, and more than 20 lives were lost before the project was finished. Al Smith added, "I often heard my mother say . . . that if the people of New York had had any idea of the number of human lives sacrificed in the sinking of the caissons for the towers of the Brooklyn bridge, in all probability they would have halted its progress."

The Brooklyn Bridge was one of the first bridges to use pneumatic caissons for working under water. Sandhogs labored in yellow pine chambers 9½ feet high and about 50 feet square. Lighting was a problem: Calcium lights were expensive, oil lamps were smoky, gas lamps raised the temperature, and even candles were costly. At last 14 calcium lights and 60 gas burners were installed at a cost of $5,000. From time to time fires started, pneumatic chambers blew out, and sandhogs developed the bends.

On July 6, 1869, John Roebling stood on a Brooklyn wharf surveying the locations of the main piers, when his right foot was crushed between an oncoming ferry and the ferry slip. He was rushed to his son's home in Brooklyn Heights, where his toes were amputated without anesthesia. Lockjaw set in, and the great bridge designer died on July 22 at the age of sixty-three.

His thirty-two-year-old son, Washington A. Roebling, had worked with his father a full year before this fatal accident. Himself a graduate engineer, Washington Roebling inherited his father's engineering skill, Germanic thoroughness, courage, and analytical powers, if not all his creative brilliance. One month after his father's death, Washington Roebling was made chief engineer of the project. It now became his passion to complete his father's dream, but in the spring of 1872 the son was carried out of a caisson suffering from the bends. Only thirty-five years old, his days of physical exertion were over, for he was left partially paralyzed and doomed to a lifetime of suffering. Even the mere sound of a human voice was unbearable to him.

The onetime aide had to find his own aide. Fortunately, his wife filled the bill. Emily Warren Roebling was a remarkable woman. Under her husband's guidance she studied engineering, mastered higher mathematics, served as an extension of his brain, and functioned as field marshal on the construction site. In their Brooklyn Heights home Washington Roebling crouched in a wheelchair at the window, field glasses at hand, to watch from an agonizing distance as the work went on, day by day, month by month, year by year.

At times construction stopped for lack of funds. Then, in 1875, the state legislature took over the project and converted it into a public trust. Thus, two-thirds of the bridge was paid for and owned by the city of Brooklyn, while one-third was paid for and owned by New York City. At long last the formal opening was scheduled for May 24, 1883.

The dedication of the Brooklyn Bridge was an event of national importance. Nearly every state sent representatives, and railroads ran excursion trains from neighboring cities so that thousands of non-New Yorkers might attend. Business was suspended for the day, and schools were closed. Flags fluttered from windows and ships, grandstands were erected on buildings near both ends of the bridge, and tens of thousands of Sunday-clad people thronged toward the grand new structure.

Glorious spring weather crowned the celebration. The sun warmed people perching on fire escapes, glinted from the buttons of marines, and burnished the gray and white uniforms of the "Dandy" Seventh Regiment. Women shielded their coiffures with gay parasols, but the sunlight spun in golden whorls on the tops of men's silk hats whenever they turned their heads. Chester A. Arthur, once collector of the port of New York but now President of the United States, had arrived from Washington with his Cabinet members to take part in the opening of the bridge. The President was suffering from stomach cramps that day, and his muttonchop whiskers quivered a little with pain; but he rallied when he neared the Manhattan approach to the bridge and saw the stupendous crowd. He was accompanied by Grover Cleveland, now the governor of New York, a massive man with a walrus mustache and heavy jowls. With Arthur and Cleveland was New York's bearded and handsome mayor, Franklin Edson. The three dignitaries and other officials walked to the middle of the bridge as cannon roared, sirens shrieked, horns blatted, and a million people cheered. At the center of the bridge they were met by the mayor of Brooklyn, thirty-two-year-old Seth Low, the youngest mayor in Brooklyn's history. Low accepted the bridge in behalf of his community, while Edson accepted it in the name of New York.

Washington Roebling was unable to be there because of his crippled condition. Tended by his misty-eyed wife, he sat at a window of their Brooklyn Heights home to watch the event through field glasses held in trembling hands. He choked with pride in his accomplishment, and he ached with pain because his father had not lived to share the moment of exultation. Across the sun-flecked river and to the lonely window came the crash of bands and the cries of people. That evening the President of the United States, the governor of New York, and the mayors of New York and Brooklyn, together with other notables, marched to the residence of Washington Roebling to take his hand, bow low, and pay homage to the engineer who had sacrificed his health to build the Brooklyn Bridge.

With the possible exception of the Suez Canal, opened in 1869, the Brooklyn Bridge was the greatest engineering feat in the world since completion of the Erie Canal. It was the first bridge to connect New York and Brooklyn, the first to use steel cables, and the greatest structure to date made of steel, and it had the longest span of any bridge on earth. It inspired more paintings and etchings, novels and short stories, plays and poems, photographs and conversations than any other suspension bridge in the world. Above all, the Brooklyn Bridge made inevitable the consolidation of New York and Brooklyn, thus adding stature to the giant metropolis.

Decoration Day fell six days after the gala opening, and holiday-happy people promenaded across this Eighth Wonder of the World. J. Pierpont Morgan's yacht was being brought out of winter drydock, and ten-year-old Al Smith was playing with boyfriends under the Manhattan end of the bridge. About 4 P.M. Smith and his pals were dumbfounded when the air began raining coats and hats and parasols and pocketbooks. Craning their necks to look up, they saw a line of struggling people, heard chilling screams, and sensed that panic had broken out.

Newspapers had printed scare stories about the danger of soldiers marching in step across the new bridge; it was believed that their rhythmic tread would set up vibrations capable of destroying the bridge. Someone may have remembered these warnings that Decoration Day as regiments of the national guard marched onto the span, for suddenly there was a shriek of fear. This triggered a stampede among the promenaders. Mad confusion ensued. People tried to run to the shore. They struggled to push past one another. They fought. They clawed. They climbed on top of each other. They throbbed with terror—without knowing why. Bridgeworkers tore out railings on both sides of the bridge to relieve the pressure, but it was fifteen minutes before the panic was quelled. Twelve persons were trampled to death or pushed off the bridge. In addition to the dozen fatalities, thirty-five people were injured.

After the shock of the disaster had worn off, the bridge became a place of pleasure and recreation. Al Smith doted on singing "Danny by My Side," whose opening line is "The Brooklyn Bridge on Sunday is known as lovers' lane."

Chapter 29

METROPOLITAN OPERA HOUSE OPENS

THE METROPOLITAN OPERA HOUSE was built because of a tiff between titans.

With the growth of capitalism and the expansion of trade after the Civil War a new breed of millionaires was born. The old family-proud aristocrats of New York watched uneasily as the new plutocrats jockeyed for an inside track on the social scene. Bitterness deepened when the new millionaires refused to stay in their places and eat the dust of the old millionaires.

The socially correct place to be seen was in a loge of the ancient Academy of Music on the northeast corner of Fourteenth Street and Irving Place. Since its opening in 1854 the Academy had been the

377

operatic and cultural center of New York. Snobs felt that they had to attend the Academy, not necessarily to enjoy the music, but to be seen by people who counted. Unfortunately, the shabby old opera house held only eighteen loges, or boxes, and for years these had been sold out by the season to wealthy patrons of time-honored lineage. As a result, the new millionaires had to sit in orchestra seats on the main floor. At performance after performance the old millionaires sneered down on the new breed. The plutocrats tried sneering up at the aristocrats, but sneers, like waterfalls, seem to flow better downhill. The situation finally became unbearable to the lowly seated men, who were now gathering the financial power of the city and nation into their hands.

William Henry Vanderbilt, who liked to boast that he was the richest man in the world, offered $30,000 for one box for the 1880-81 opera season. The Academy's governors haughtily rejected his bid. Vanderbilt refused to put up with this final insult. If he couldn't get what he wanted in the old Academy of Music, he and his friends would build their own opera house. What's more, they planned to make it the most magnificent in the entire world. When news of the decision reached August Belmont, the greatest power at the Academy, he tried to snuff out the cultural revolution by offering to add twenty-six boxes to the Academy for use by the new millionaires, but by then it was too late.

On April 8, 1880, the Metropolitan Opera-house Company, Ltd., was incorporated by Vanderbilt, Jay Gould, the broker Henry Clews, and others. Twenty days later they organized formally and elected J. N. A. Griswold president. The next month they spent $600,000 to buy property bounded by Broadway and Seventh Avenue from Thirty-ninth to Fortieth Street. Let the Academy of Music stay on the fringe of the shopping district, which had reached Fourteenth Street. Vanderbilt and his associates proposed to erect their new opera house within easier reach of upper Fifth Avenue, already blossoming into the city's fashionable residential area.

They chose J. Cleveland Cady as their architect and gave him $430,000 to spend. Although Cady was one of the most prominent architects of the day, he had never designed a theater of any sort; in fact, he is reported to have boasted that he "had never entered a playhouse." Down to the year 1966 New York opera-goers suffered from his lack of experience, for only half the stage could be seen from certain seats in the "Met." Cady, however, was not at all confused about which goose was laying this golden egg. More than anything, the new plutocrats wanted loges from which they could be seen clearly from all sides. Cady gave them more boxes, bigger boxes, and more prominent boxes than those installed in any opera house in history. He also understood that the Met's interior had to be decorated more ostentatiously than even the most luxurious opera houses of Europe. He spent money so freely that patrons had to organize something called the Metropolitan Improvement Company to underwrite completion of the building.

The Met's stage was made bigger than the stages of the opera houses of Paris and St. Petersburg. Its seating capacity of nearly 3,500 almost equaled the capacity of the largest opera house in the world, Milan's La Scala, which could accommodate 3,600. For all its interior opulence the Met's exterior was as bleak as a warehouse. Finished in Italian Renaissance style, its façade consisted of plain yellow bricks. Colonel James H. Mapleson, impresario of the Academy, sneeringly called the Met that "new yellow brewery on Broadway." Even disinterested persons were struck by the ugliness of the seven-story building, whose Broadway side included rent-producing stores.

Both the Metropolitan Opera House and the Academy of Music scheduled the opening of their 1883-84 season for the evening of October 22. Manager Henry E. Abbey of the Met presented Gounod's *Faust,* starring Christine Nilsson in the role of Marguerite. Colonel Mapleson of the Academy featured Bellini's *La Sonnambula,* with diva Etelka Gerster in the starring role. A certain Mrs. Paran Stevens, torn between curiosity and tradition, compromised by spending half the evening at the Met and the other half at the Academy.

At 3 P.M. on the day the Met was due to open, its several floor levels were still littered with plaster shavings, powdered whitewash, raw lumber, messy paintpots, and a carpet of dirt. Could it really open on schedule? "It will be ready by eight o'clock," proclaimed impresario Abbey. Inside the building 700 cleaning women bustled about, while on the outside gangs of husky men tore down the last of the scaffoldings. By 7:30 P.M. 10,000 curiosity seekers were thronging nearby streets. About half an hour later carriages were snarled in a traffic jam extending three blocks in every direction from the Met. Silk-hatted gentlemen and bejeweled ladies stepped out of their stalled vehicles to push and shove their way through crowds to the doors of the new house.

After pressing inside, they were shown to their seats by ushers clad in bottle-green uniforms studded with gold buttons. The Goulds and Morgans and Schurzes—representing the new plutocracy—were gratified to note the presence of the Astors and Belmonts and Goelets —representing the old aristocracy. As for the Vanderbilts, members of this family occupied no fewer than five loges. William Henry Vanderbilt himself, savoring to the utmost this moment of triumph, had as honored guest in his box none other than Sir John Duke Coleridge, the Lord Chief Justice of England.

The resplendent evening marked a transition in the history of New York, as power passed from the old order to the new. Before this, no such audience had ever gathered in one spot in America. The Met was crowded with men whose total wealth was estimated at more than $500,000,000. The Met won the battle hands down; Colonel Mapleson soon thereafter closed the Academy of Music with the melancholy words "I cannot fight Wall Street."

It was an era of velvet and vice, of magnificence and misery. Henry George, the economist and reformer, who had moved to New York three years earlier, wrote in the year the Met opened: "Civilization, as it progresses, *requires* a higher conscience, a keener sense of justice, a warmer brotherhood, a wider, loftier, truer public spirit. Failing these, civilization must pass into destruction." George pointed out that shirtmakers were paid only thirty-five cents for every dozen shirts they produced. "The main source of the difficulties that menace us," he went on to say, "is the growing inequality in the distribution of wealth." Then he painted a verbal picture of life outside the Metropolitan Opera House:

> Take in imagination such a bird's-eye view of the city of New York as might be had from a balloon. The houses are climbing heavenward—ten, twelve, even fifteen stories, tier on tier of people living, one family above another, without sufficient water, without sufficient light or air, without playground or breathing space. So close is the building that the streets look like narrow rifts in the brick and mortar, and from street to street the solid blocks stretch until they almost meet; in the newer districts only a space of twenty feet, a mere crack in the masonry through which at high noon a sunbeam can scarcely struggle down, being left to separate the backs of the tenements fronting on one street from the backs of those fronting on another street. . . .

Not only were the rich getting richer and the poor getting poorer, as Henry George pointed out, but there was also a dizzying increase in the *tempo* of this widening split. Economically and socially, America was disintegrating, and nowhere in the nation could this be noted more vividly than in New York. Oppression by the rich evoked rebellion by the poor. Sobersided Grover Cleveland said:

> Communism is a hateful thing and a menace to peace and organized government, but the communism of combined wealth and capital, the outgrowth of overweening cupidity and selfishness, which insidiously undermines the justice and integrity of free institutions, is not less dangerous than the communism of oppressed poverty and toil, which, exasperated by injustice and discontent, attacks with wild disorder the citadel of rule. . . .

The year 1886 was blotched by depression, mass unemployment, strikes, and lockouts. Among other labor disorders, New York's streetcar employees struck for shorter hours. While city aldermen took bribes in exchange for franchises paying enormous profits to rapid transit owners, the workers themselves were paid a pittance for slaving up to 16 hours a day. Most aldermen were indicted for bribery, New Yorkers turned in anger on their public servants, and labor leaders decided to channel the mood to their own ends. The Central Labor Union (C.L.U.), organized in 1882, now banded together 207 separate unions, representing 50,000 workers in New York, Brooklyn, and Jersey City. Then, deciding to plunge into politics, the C.L.U. pledged support to Henry George in the forthcoming mayoralty race. The Democrats nominated Abram S. Hewitt. The Republicans picked Theodore Roosevelt.

"Thus began the most stirring campaign in the city's history," according to historian Allan Nevins, "for never before or since have men of such ability contended for the prize." Labor leader Samuel Gompers, who supported Henry George, said in his autobiography that "the campaign was notable in that it united people of unusual abilities from all walks of life." With labor trying to seize control of America's largest city and with amateurs warring on the nation's most powerful political machine—Tammany—the eyes of all Americans turned toward the New York battleground.

Henry George was already famous. His classic, *Progress and Poverty,* had been translated into German, French, Dutch, Swedish, Danish, Spanish, Russian, Magyar, Hebrew, and Chinese and had sold millions of copies. In this book George argued that rent is robbery; that wealth is the product of labor applied to natural resources; that interest is the part of the result of labor that is paid to capital;

and that capital is the fruit of labor, not its master. His theories influenced tax legislation around the world and colored the thinking of
people as different as Leo Tolstoy and Sun Yat-sen. In the fall of
1886 Henry George was forty-seven years old. Short, quivering with
nervous energy, his reddish hair fringing the bald spot on his head
and his strong jaw encased in a sandy beard, George was sometimes
called the little red rooster.

Abram Hewitt felt ancient and weary that election season. He was
sixty-four years old and had a white beard. The eminent son-in-law
of Peter Cooper and himself a millionaire and philanthropist, Hewitt
had served for many years in Congress and did not care to return to
Washington. Ironically, six years earlier he had employed Henry
George as a ghostwriter. Now he scorned his former hired hand, declaring that only Abram Hewitt could save New York from socialism,
communism, anarchism, nihilism, and revolution.

Theodore Roosevelt was a mere twenty-eight years of age and only
six years out of Harvard. However, he had written three books and
served three years in the New York state legislature. An aristocrat,
Roosevelt was regarded as a maverick by his peers, who considered a
political career beneath the dignity of a gentleman. But the thin-
waisted scion, even then sporting the mustache that later delighted
caricaturists, threw himself into the campaign with cyclonic fervor.

When 34,000 laborers signed pledges to work and vote for Henry
George; when the United Labor party was organized in behalf of
George; when a priest, named Edward McGlynn, declared George to
be inspired "by the same love of justice as was taught by Christ";
when the brilliant agnostic, attorney, and orator Robert Ingersoll
called on fellow Republicans "to show that their sympathies are not
given to bankers, corporations and millionaires," Tammany became
frightened.

Richard Croker, the new boss of Tammany, sent an emissary to
George, offering a deal: If George would stay out of the mayoralty
race, Tammany would guarantee his election to Congress. George rejected the offer and then charged that Hewitt was a captive of
Tammany. Hewitt, in turn, charged that George was a captive of
radicals. The campaign developed into a duel between George and
Hewitt, with Roosevelt largely ignored. Young Teddy tried to attract attention by shouting about "the countless evils and abuses already existing," but some Republicans joined Ingersoll in crossing
party lines and voting for George.

Hewitt won the election, and Roosevelt came in a poor third. Second-place Henry George complained that he had been cheated out of the mayor's office by Tammany trickery. Certainly there were illegal registrations, bribery, and manipulation of the ballot count, but historians disagree on whether this fraud was sufficiently widespread to throw the election to Hewitt. In any event, he gave the city an able administration.

Chapter 30

CREATION OF THE STATUE OF LIBERTY

THE STATUE OF LIBERTY was the brainchild of a Frenchman, named Édouard René de Laboulaye. He once wrote that "the folly of love and the madness of ambition are sometimes curable, but no one was ever cured of a mania for liberty." A popular author, liberal politician, student of the American Constitution, and hero worshiper of George Washington, De Laboulaye rivaled the dead Lafayette in his extravagant admiration of everything American. He venerated the American Revolution more than the French Revolution because he was deeply religious and the revolution in his fatherland had taken on antireligious overtones.

A Parisian, he owned a country house in Glatigny, near Versailles,

384

and in the summer of 1865 he invited a number of French intellectuals to visit him there. Among these writers, artists, and politicians was a thirty-one-year-old sculptor, Frédéric Auguste Bartholdi, busily working on a bust of his host. That pleasant afternoon the conversation turned to the subject of gratitude among men of different nations; whereupon someone recited the heroic deeds of Frenchmen in America during the American Revolution.

"There," said De Laboulaye, "you have the basis of the American feeling for the French—an indestructible basis. The feeling honors the Americans as well as us, and if a monument should rise in the United States as a memorial to their independence, I should think it only natural if it were built by united effort—a common work of both our nations." As chairman of the French Antislavery Society, he thought partly of American abolitionists, whom he admired. As a historian, he looked forward to 1876, when America would celebrate the hundredth anniversary of her independence.

The idea of a monument was novel, but nothing was done immediately to translate it into reality. Bartholdi never forgot it, though, and six years later he again visited De Laboulaye. They discussed the coming centennial of American independence. Bartholdi said, "I think it would be well to offer the Americans a statue—a statue of liberty." He toyed with the thought of leaving for the United States to suggest the idea to Americans and to ask them to share the cost. De Laboulaye cried, "Go to America! Go see the country, and bring us back your impressions. If you find a happy idea—one that will rouse public enthusiasm—we may take up a subscription in France."

In 1871 the French sculptor sailed for America. As his ship steamed into New York Harbor, he dashed off a watercolor of the statue he hoped to see erected at this gateway to the nation. Everything about New York looked so big that he decided only a big statue would do. Visiting Egypt as a youth of twenty, Bartholdi had been deeply impressed by the size of the Pyramids and the Sphinx. Now, as the Statue of Liberty took shape in his mind, he wrote: "The details of the lines ought not to arrest the eye . . . the surfaces should be broad and simple, defined by a bold and clear design, accentuated in the important places . . . it should have a summarized character, such as one would give to a rapid sketch."

Armed with letters of introduction to influential Americans, Bartholdi spent nearly half a year traveling around the country. He received encouragement from notables like Henry Wadsworth Longfellow. After the sculptor returned to France, his proposal was approved, and in 1875 the Franco-American Union was formed with Professor de Laboulaye, now a member of the Chamber of Deputies, as its head.

Since the statue was to be a gift to the American people from the French people—not from French officialdom—no funds were solicited from the French government. Over the next seven years money was raised by a variety of devices—lotteries, theatrical benefits, and the like. French composer Charles Gounod wrote a song for the campaign, and the composition was presented at a benefit performance in the Paris opera house. France was poor. Some Frenchmen could give no more than a sou—worth half a cent—but at last the equivalent of $250,000 was raised. This sum came from thousands of individuals, from 181 cities including Paris, and from 10 municipal chambers of commerce. Now that the French had done their part, to the Americans was left the task of underwriting the cost of the pedestal on which the statue would stand.

Bartholdi took no payment for his many years of work on the statue. The money collected in France was spent for materials and the wages of workmen helping the sculptor. Bartholdi did, however, obtain a patent on his figure; in 1876 he registered two small bronze models at the U.S. Patent Office. Besides the glory of the project, which obsessed him, he hoped to earn an income from the sale of souvenirs fashioned after the statue. In 1874 Bartholdi made his first design of Miss Liberty, using his handsome mother as a model.

Construction began in Paris in the foundry yard of Gaget, Gauthier & Cie., on high ground three-fifths of a mile to the northeast of the Arch of Triumph. Because a project of such magnitude demanded more than artistic genius, Bartholdi hired artisans, engineers, carpenters, plasterers, and contractors to help him. He also prevailed on Alexandre Gustave Eiffel, the famous French engineer who later built the Eiffel Tower, to design an iron framework for the statue.

In 1877 the growing figure was visited by former President Grant in the course of a trip around the world. Aging French novelist Victor Hugo tottered into the foundry yard to have a look. The statue's thumbnail was a foot long, a child could stand up inside the thumb, and because bigness excites attention, more than 300,000 persons viewed the figure while it was under construction.

Bartholdi promoted it with all the skill of P. T. Barnum. In 1876 he shipped the torchbearing right arm to Philadelphia for display at that city's Centennial Exposition. De Laboulaye's hope of completing the memorial in time for the hundredth anniversary of American freedom could not be realized, but 9,000,000 visitors to Philadelphia saw part of it. In 1877 the right arm was sent from Philadelphia to New York, where it was exhibited in Madison Square Park. Here it remained until 1884, when it was returned to Paris to be fitted to the rest of the figure.

Bartholdi's first sketch had shown the Statue of Liberty rising from Governors Island in the Upper Bay of New York, but he later decided that nearby Bedloe's Island would display it to better advantage. On February 9, 1877, President Grant had urged Congress to accede to the wish of "many distinguished citizens of New York" by approving the use of Bedloe's Island as a site for the monument. Thirteen days later Congress granted this wish.

Americans now had to build and pay for the foundation and pedestal on which the statue would perch. At first an appeal for funds met with apathy and ridicule. The New York *Times* whimsically suggested that the statue be placed at the Battery to make it easier for people to scrawl their names on it. John D. G. Shea, who later became the first president of the Catholic Historical Society of the United States, wrote an article criticizing "Our Great Goddess and Her Coming Idol."

America's nine-year financial drive began in 1876, when the Union League Club appointed a fund-raising committee. This was two years after Bartholdi had begun working on the figure in Paris. Because money only dribbled in, on January 2, 1877, a group of civic leaders met in the Century Club and organized the American Committee of the Statue of Liberty. The original committee consisted of 114 members, but it was later enlarged to more than 400. They prevailed on President Grant to ask Congress to pass a joint resolution acknowledging the forthcoming gift from France and announcing that the pedestal would be built by private subscription. Although the Senate and House passed the resolution and although committee members now had this enormous prestige behind them, few contributions were made. Wealthy patrons of the arts were unsure about the artistic merit of the statue. Poor people felt that the rich could better afford to finance the pedestal than they could.

On May 25, 1883, Édouard René de Laboulaye died in Paris without knowing whether his brainchild actually would arise in the New

World. Four days later on Bedloe's Island a trumpetblast signaled the evacuation of the island's marine hospital so that digging could begin. Charles Pomeroy Stone was chosen as engineer in charge of preparing the site. A Union general during the Civil War, he had later gone abroad and become commander in chief of the Egyptian army.

Meantime, plain-faced Emma Lazarus had become interested in the continuing appeals for funds. She was born in New York in 1849, was the daughter of wealthy parents of Portuguese-Jewish descent, and had her first book published when she was only eighteen. As her contribution to the Statue of Liberty, she wrote a sonnet that was read publicly for the first time on the evening of December 3, 1883. This was opening night of the Bartholdi Statue Pedestal Art Loan Exhibition, held in the National Academy of Design, and there author F. Hopkinson Smith recited the now-famous line: "Give me your tired, your poor, Your huddled masses yearning to breathe free. . . ."

On January 4, 1884, the pedestal stood fifteen feet high, about one-sixth its intended height of eighty-nine feet. There work stopped because the $125,000 raised by the committee was exhausted. A new American President, Chester A. Arthur, urged Congress to appropriate enough money to complete the pedestal, but a bill to this effect was killed in committee. The New York state legislature passed a measure giving New York City permission to contribute $50,000, but Governor Grover Cleveland vetoed it on "constitutional grounds." Such was the state of affairs when Joseph Pulitzer entered the picture.

Of Magyar-Jewish ancestry, born in Hungary in 1847, and emigrating to America in 1864, Pulitzer became first the most famous reporter in St. Louis and then owner of the fabulously successful St. Louis *Post-Dispatch*. This failed to satisfy the tall and reedy journalist with the tangled black hair and reddish beard, who stared at the world with dimming brown eyes behind almond-shaped spectacles. He propelled himself into New York journalism on May 10, 1883, by purchasing the New York *World* from Jay Gould. On March 13, 1885, Pulitzer's *World* declared, "Money must be raised to complete the pedestal for the Bartholdi statue. It would be an irrevocable disgrace to New York City and the American Republic to have France send us this splendid gift without our having provided even so much as a landing place for it."

Bartholdi himself had not been idle. Whenever New Yorkers dragged their feet, the wily French sculptor pretended to offer his statue first to Philadelphia and then to Boston. When the word got around, bids for the statue came from other cities—Chicago, Cleveland, St. Louis, Minneapolis, and Baltimore. Now Pulitzer goaded New Yorkers into taking positive action. To finish the concrete pedestal with its granite facing, $100,000 more was needed. The *World* started its patriotic drive by contributing $1,000 and offering to print the names of every donor regardless of the amount given.

Day after day, week after week, the *World* kept up a drumfire of publicity, printing front-page editorials and displaying a semipermanent cartoon of Uncle Sam standing hat in hand. It published this note: "I am a little girl nine years old and I will send you a pair of my pet game bantams if you will sell them and give the money to the Statue." A man wrote: "Since leaving off smoking cigarettes I have gained twenty-five pounds, so I cheerfully inclose a penny for each pound." A total of 121,000 Americans, most of them New Yorkers, sent money to the *World;* 80 percent of this was in sums of less than $1. By August 11, 1885, Pulitzer's campaign had raised $101,091. A check for $100,000 was sent to the statue committee, while the balance was spent on a silver gift for Bartholdi.

In the Paris foundry yard the Goddess of Liberty was disassembled, and its hundreds of parts were packed into 220 crates. At Rouen they were loaded aboard the French ship *Isère,* which weathered a stormy ocean crossing and arrived off Sandy Hook on June 17, 1885. General Stone and New York aldermen boarded a tug to go down to meet the ship. After boarding her, they were ushered into the captain's cabin, where General Stone was handed legal documents conveying the statue from France to the United States.

With completion of the pedestal, workmen began putting Miss Liberty together again. Some iron beams and copper plates were mislabeled. Time and again one or another section of the statue was hoisted into the air, only to be lowered when it could not be fitted into a particular niche. Although this was dangerous work, not a single laborer was injured or killed.

At last the 225-ton statue, an impressive 305 feet 1 inch from the base of its pedestal to the tip of its torch, rose to its full height and gazed seaward in warm welcome to the world. Will Durant, the historian, called it the most famous statue in the world.

The Statue of Liberty was dedicated on Thursday, October 28, 1886. To New York for the occasion came the great of America and a few leading Frenchmen. The sum of $9,000 was set aside to entertain the official French delegation, headed by Bartholdi and Count Ferdinand Marie de Lesseps. The eighty-year-old De Lesseps was a French engineer and diplomat representing the Franco-American Union. He had designed the Suez Canal, which had opened in 1869, and as recently as 1881 he had begun to dig the Panama Canal, which the French never completed.

For a week the weather had been vile, and on the day of dedication it failed to clear up. A Cuban correspondent for an Argentinian newspaper described it this way: "The day was bleak, the sky leaden, the ground muddy, the drizzle stubborn. But human joy has rarely been so bright." President Grover Cleveland arrived from Washington and was received in the elegant town house at Fifth Avenue and Fifty-seventh Street owned by his Secretary of the Navy, William C. Whitney. The thickset walrus-mustached President met handsome bearded Bartholdi and De Lesseps of the silver upturned mustache. Whitney beamed on this tableau through his pince-nez. Because a parade was scheduled to start from Madison Square at 11:30 A.M., the celebrities forsook lunch to emerge from the Whitney mansion and climb into waiting carriages.

By this time a river of humanity had poured across the Brooklyn Bridge and flowed in fleshy whorls and eddies in and about City Hall Park. Now and then the people glanced up at wet flags dangling limply from nearby buildings. Raindrops diamonded the hats of marching soldiers; water gurgled into the brass instruments of oompahing musicians; the cheeks of proudly strutting Negroes were silver-veined with unheeded trickles of water. The squash of shoes on pavements provided a counterpoint to the martial music as the parade slithered from Madison Square down to the Battery.

President Cleveland reviewed the marchers. Then, accompanied by members of his Cabinet, the governors of many states, French dignitaries, and other notables, he was driven to the Hudson River at West Thirty-third Street to board the U.S.S. *Despatch*. Full-rigged ships of the U.S. navy thundered a 21-gun salute to the President. Fog hugged the river's surface and obscured the upper part of the statue. An armada of nearly 300 yachts, French warships, excursion steamers, and tugs groped their way toward Bedloe's Island. Thousands of spectators at the Battery peered through the mist at the distant statue. An estimated 1,000,000 persons, ashore and afloat, took part in this gala event.

The 2,500 elite guests of the day disembarked on the island and took seats on a temporary platform at the base of the pedestal. Whenever they lifted their chins to look up, raindrops trickled down their throats. In the murky height above them a French flag, stained by the rain, clung to the contours of Miss Liberty's face. The fifty-two-year-old Bartholdi and 3 helpers panted up the 167 steps from the ground to the top of the pedestal, walked inside the giantess, trudged the 168 steps from Miss Liberty's feet to her head, and climbed the 54 rungs of a ladder leading into the torch.

Down on the soggy earth a teen-age boy quivered with excitement. As the son of the contractor who had built the pedestal, he had been granted the honor of signaling to Bartholdi when to unveil the face of the statue. Most eyes were on President Cleveland, whose huge fingers were locked across his great belly.

The ceremony began. The Reverend Dr. Richard S. Storrs of Brooklyn read the invocation, but boat whistles erased many of his words. Then Count De Lesseps, his majestic mustache defying the elements, read in French some prepared remarks from large loose sheets of paper, italicizing his meaning with quick Gallic gestures. His voice was inaudible to the waiting Bartholdi, high above his head.

William Maxwell Evarts stood up. Born in Boston, now United States Senator from New York and chairman of the Statue of Liberty committee, Evarts was an orator whose talent was better suited to an indoor hall than to a rain-swept island. When the Senator paused a moment to rest his voice, the contractor's son thought that he had finished speaking. The boy waved his arm at Bartholdi. The sculptor and his helpers tugged at ropes, the French flag slithered off the face of Miss Liberty, and people and ships exploded in a bedlam of cheers and whistles. Evarts looked up in surprise. He gasped. He resumed speaking, but the pandemonium was so loud that he could not be heard. The tumult was augmented by a broadside fired from the flagship of the American naval squadron and a band's brassy rendition of "My Country 'Tis of Thee." Evart's lips still moved in pantomime. President Cleveland, courteous as ever, made a pretense of listening to him.

At last Evarts finished. The President got up and said a few words about accepting the statue from the French in behalf of the American people. He was followed by Chauncey M. Depew, another renowned orator. Depew had a hulking nose, thin lips, and long sideburns, and he wore a gates-ajar collar and lapelled waistcoat. His rhetorical flourishes wearied the audience, which had been sitting in the chill and rain since 3:15 P.M. Finally the benediction was pronounced by Henry C. Potter, bishop of the Protestant Episcopal diocese of New York, who removed his soaked mortarboard and let the raindrops fall on his eyelids.

It was done. The world's best-known statue had been dedicated, and from this day forward it stood at New York's doorway, a permanent reminder of an elusive ideal. Spiritually it belonged to all mankind—not just to New Yorkers, not just to Americans. It developed into a shrine, where all might worship. Perhaps an attendant said it best when he murmured, "Whoever visits the Statue of Liberty feels that he has come home."

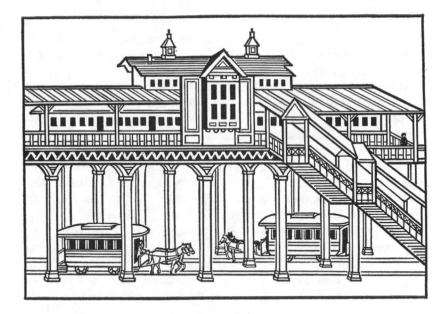

Chapter 31

THE BLIZZARD OF 1888

THE AIR was soft. Birds twittered in trees. Farmers worked their fields. It had been the mildest winter in seventeen years, and now it seemed about over. This Saturday, March 10, 1888, wedges of geese honked through the heavens toward Canada, red-breasted robins skittered across greening lawns, bushes budded in Central Park, and Walt Whitman sent the New York *Herald* a poem about the first flower of spring.

The weatherman decided to make one last check before calling it a day. He was Elias B. Dunn, jokingly called Farmer Dunn because the nation's forecasting service recently had been transferred to the Department of Agriculture. Dunn and 3 assistants staffed the local

393

Weather Bureau atop the 5-story Equitable Building, at 120 Broadway. Rising from the roof to a height of 150 feet above the street was a pole topped by a wind gauge.

Dunn phoned coast guard headquarters at Peck Slip on the Lower East Side. Stationed up and down the Atlantic seaboard were weather observers, who dispatched reports to the coast guard by telegraph or carrier pigeons. That day they had nothing unusual to announce. Dunn next opened a telegraph line to Washington. The news was much the same. On the basis of these reports Dunn drew up his Sunday forecast for New York and vicinity: "Cloudy followed by light rain and clearing." Then he took a hydraulic elevator down to the lobby of the Equitable Building and left for his home in Brooklyn.

Sunday, March 11, was a relatively warm day. At noon the temperature rose to a high of forty degrees. Still, it was a gloomy day, for the sun never came out. Telling one another that winter was over at last, New Yorkers opened windows to air their rooms and went to church as usual. In the afternoon, as predicted, rain began falling— warm and gentle raindrops that peppered the dry pavements. Then, to everyone's surprise, the light rain thickened and quickened and developed into a downpour, which exploded into a cloudburst.

Gutters choked on muddy waters. The temperature sank. People began to grow uneasy. The drumming downpour flooded basements, slowed horse-drawn streetcars, and delayed the city's four elevated lines. Although New Yorkers had no way of knowing it at the time, around Washington and Baltimore the rain turned to sleet, and ice congealed on telegraph and telephone wires. Two separate storms were zeroing in on the eastern seaboard—one moving down from the north in a southeasterly direction, the other blasting up from the south in a north-northeasterly line.

Sunday was "Farmer" Dunn's day off; but as he watched from a window of his home, he began to worry, so he bundled up and left for his office. Ice slashed through the sky on a rising wind. Streets and sidewalks glinted with slick layers of ice. Before Dunn arrived at the Equitable Building at 5 P.M., his assistants put out Monday's forecast: "Fair and warmer." Hastily shucking off his coat, Dunn tried telegraphing Washington weather headquarters. No response. He worked the telephone. No answer. However, he was able to raise coast guardsmen at Peck Slip. They said that they hadn't heard from any of their weather spotters in hours. At 6:50 P.M., with the temperature down to 36 degrees and still sinking, Dunn issued a revised forecast, predicting a cold wave. At 10 o'clock that Sunday night Alfred E. Smith's mother told her fourteen-year-old boy to shutter the family candy store in the basement of their new home, at 12 Dover Street, on the Lower East Side.

On Monday morning, March 12, about ten minutes after midnight, the sleet and ice changed into dry snow, which whisked through the city in blinding clouds. At dawn seventeen-year-old Bernard M. Baruch arose in his home at 49 East Sixtieth Street, tugged heavy clothing onto his six-foot frame, and trudged through growing snowdrifts thirty-nine blocks to the College of the City of New York, at Lexington Avenue and Twenty-third Street. Baruch was surprised to find few fellow students in his classroom. Meantime, down on the Lower East Side, Al Smith hopped out of bed and bounded to a window with the rapture of a boy seeing the first big snowfall of his life. Already the Smith candy store in the basement was buried under snow and could not be reached from inside the building. Al Smith didn't give a hoot about the storm itself; he fretted about his Scotch terrier bitch and her four puppies shivering in a back room down there.

By five o'clock that Monday morning all railway service in and out of the city had come to a halt. Not a single ship entered or left the greatest port in the world. The mercury dropped lower and lower. The wind rose higher and higher. When gusts roared to seventy-five miles an hour, the snowstorm became a hurricane, descending on the city like a raid of white-sheeted Klansmen. In some narrow streets the wind blew straight up toward the sky. From the edge of every tall building a flapping, weaving, lashing banner of snow rippled through the turbulent air.

J. Pierpont Morgan, the fifty-year-old financier, marched manfully out of his home at 219 Madison Avenue, climbed into his cab, and rode downtown to his office in the Drexel Building. About the same time Roscoe Conkling left his home on Twenty-ninth Street for his Wall Street law office. The former Congressman and U.S. Senator was still handsome and athletic, despite his fifty-eight years. That very day the New York *Herald* published a story from Buffalo reporting a Conkling for President boom, but few subscribers received copies of the paper.

About 7 A.M., with the thermometer sinking to 21 degrees and the hurricane worsening, many city dwellers plunged outdoors in a holiday mood. They enjoyed bucking the elements as their primitive ancestors had done. Class distinctions disappeared. In the face of a common hazard people were uncommonly helpful to one another.

Of course, the storm imposed special responsibilities on men like Henry D. Purroy, the fire commissioner. At 7:45 A.M., using the only city telegraph line still working, he sent this message: "I am snowed in at Fordham. No trains running. Impossible to reach city. Spare no expense to keep the department working." His dispatch reached Firemen's Hall, a three-story building at 127 Mercer Street, and was read with a frown by Fire Chief Charles O. Shay.

Julian Ralph of the New York *Sun*, perhaps the greatest reporter of his day, described the blizzard this way:

> The wind howled, whistled, banged, roared and moaned as it rushed along. It fell upon the house sides in fearful gusts, it strained great plate glass windows, rocked the frame houses, pressed against the doors so that it was almost too dangerous to open them. It was a visible, substantial wind, so freighted was it with snow. It came in whirls, it descended in layers, it shot along in great blocks, it rose and fell and corkscrewed and zigzagged and played merry havoc with everything it could swing or batter or bang or carry away. At half past ten o'clock, not a dozen stores on Fulton Street had opened for business. Men were making wild efforts to clean the walks, only to see each shovelful of snow blown back upon them and piled against the doors again.

There was something almost supernatural about the storm. A *Herald* reporter wrote:

> A horror of darkness deepened on the crowded city and the terror-stricken population cowered at the awful sounds which came from the throat of the whirlwind. . . . The heavens darkened and a great roaring sound came from the thundering clouds. It seemed as if a million devils were loose in the air. . . . Sign boards were stripped from the fronts of stores and hurled through the storm clouds. Hats were picked up and carried out of sight. As the afternoon wore away, men and women were blown flat on the ground or picked up into the air and thrown against buildings. Hundreds of pedestrians were cut and bruised. Many were run over. The very mail wagons had to be abandoned. They were left in all sections of the city.

Sixty-six-year-old Mayor Abram S. Hewitt did not stir out of his 4-story house at 9 Lexington Avenue, and a good thing this was, for many people who suffered exposure that day took to their beds and never rose again. Only 23 of the 600 members of the New York Stock

Exchange were on the trading floor when the opening gong rang. About 1,200 people worked for the American Bank Note Company, but only 40 of them showed up. Department stores had advertised spring sales for this very day, and although some stores did open, they were staffed by mere skeleton crews. One hardy housewife trudged 6 blocks to B. Altman & Company to buy a single spool of thread, but that was the only Altman transaction of the day. Macy's spring sale was a failure.

The previous Friday a man, named Edward Meisinger, had bought 3,000 unclaimed snow shovels at the bargain price of $1,200 for the downtown department store of E. Ridley & Company. Because the weather had been soft and sunny at the time, a *Herald* reporter had dubbed the hardware buyer "Snow Shovel Ed." Now the snowshoe was on the other foot. The Ridley firm quickly sold its shovels at $1 apiece for a fast profit of $1,800. By this time men were tramping down Broadway on snowshoes, while on Fifth Avenue other sturdy souls ventured forth on skis. Rubber boots worth $3 sold for $10 a pair.

Monday's total snowfall was only eighteen inches, but the wind drove it into drifts thirty feet high in places. A man standing at a Broadway and Ann Street window watched in disbelief as a snowbank grew before his eyes until it covered the fence around St. Paul's Chapel. On Second Avenue another man awakened late with a hangover. His first-story window was completely covered with snow. Aware that his eyes were open, but seeing only a white blankness, the man went mad.

Walls of snow blocked all the streets west of Seventh Avenue. Traffic halted. Horse-drawn streetcars bogged down, and although first four horses, then six horses, and finally eight horses were hitched to one car, the cars couldn't be budged. Steam trains were immobilized in the suburbs, some plowing to a stop in a deep railroad cut at Spuyten Duyvil just north of the city limits. A New York Central locomotive tried to butt through snow packed in the Fourth Avenue tunnel, only to topple off its rails. Some idiot asked Chauncey M. Depew, president of the New York Central, if the line could maintain its train service. Depew snorted, "Trains! Why, we don't even know whether we've got a railroad left!"

Vehicular traffic on the Brooklyn Bridge was halted, and police warned pedestrians not to walk across in the shrieking storm. Now Brooklyn was entirely cut off from Manhattan. After various adventures, ferryboats gave up trying to reach Manhattan; thus, Staten Island and New Jersey also became inaccessible. A few brave and greedy cabdrivers still slogged through the streets. Some poured whiskey into their horses to keep them from freezing to death, and the price of a cab ride rose to thirty dollars, then forty dollars, and ultimately to more than fifty dollars.

When elevated railroads had first been proposed, their advocates said that bad weather couldn't possible affect their operation. Now, however, all the steam trains on the four lines snorted to a halt, stranding 15,000 passengers high above the streets. On the Sixth Avenue line a backlog of trains stretched from Fourth to Twenty-eighth Street. At first commuters sat and shivered in the unheated wooden coaches. The slamming wind teetered the cars on their rails, frightening passengers into believing that the trains would be dumped onto the streets below. Some panic-stricken people left the coaches and climbed down onto the narrow paths by the side of the track, but this exposed them to the full force of the hurricane.

The fire department tried to send hook-and-ladder companies to the rescue; few could force their way through the snowpacked streets. Men and boys propped ladders against elevated structures and brought victims down to safety at prices ranging from 5 cents to $1. A Negro, whose fee was 25 cents, collected more than $100 in an hour or so. One stalled train couldn't be reached by ladders. Its 30 passengers sat it out for 15 hours; but by lowering a cord to a saloon directly below them, they were able to hoist up buckets of booze, so they survived cheerfully and bibulously. At Third Avenue and Seventy-sixth Street an elevated train chugging through the murk crashed into the rear of a stalled train; 14 passengers were hurt, and the engineer of the moving train later died of head injuries.

The snow still buzzed like angry white bees, and the wind thudded into buildings like a berserk ram. Windows shattered. Glass slashed through the air. Bricks were torn loose from chimneys. Cornices toppled from buildings. So many pedestrians were felled by flying debris that an eyewitness swore the streets looked like snowy battlefields. Men, women, and children were treated at hospitals for gashed cheeks, broken limbs, and frostbitten fingers and toes. Drunks toppled into snowbanks and froze to death. In City Hall Park four girls trying to wade through the snow fainted from exhaustion. They were rescued by a burly cop, who dragged them by their wrists, two at a time, out of the park and into the safety of the Astor House.

Before noon that Monday every hotel room was packed. At the Astor House one bank rented a single room for ten of its clerks. Another bank crammed thirteen employees into a single hotel room; still another, a total of fifteen. Besides sleeping on beds and cots, in closets and bathtubs, men sprawled on billiard tables and floors. State armories were thrown open, and within these shelters men and women, complete strangers to one another, huddled together in sleep. Police stations held open house, and many a respectable citizen snored in a cell for the first time in his life.

Saloons, bars, grogshops, gin mills, and billiard parlors stayed open all night, offering hospitality to anyone lucky enough to make his way to them. Unable to get home, marooned in odd places, with time weighing heavily on their hands, and exhilarated by this white crisis, New Yorkers indulged in a mass binge. Steve Brodie, something of a celebrity because he claimed to have jumped from the Brooklyn Bridge two years before, now owned a bar at 114 Bowery. Over the door he nailed this sign: "A free drink of whiskey to anyone that needs it and has not got the money to pay for it. Come in if you need it. Steve Brodie."

The wind's eerie wail frightened dogs and birds. A man standing at a window of the Fifth Avenue Hotel, at Fifth Avenue and Twenty-third Street, saw "a veritable rain of sparrows falling dead from the eaves of nearby buildings." Luckier sparrows flitted through the briefly opened doors of hotels; although it was against the law to feed them, people did. Five hundred warmth-seeking birds dashed themselves to death against the façade of the Old London Building, at Broadway and Waverly Place.

Monday afternoon, about 1:30, Roscoe Conkling decided to leave his Wall Street office since no client had showed up. He planned to head for the New York Club. Conkling later said:

> There wasn't a cab or carriage of any kind to be had. Once during the day I had declined an offer to ride uptown in a carriage because the man wanted fifty dollars, and I started up Broadway on my own pins. It was dark and it was useless to try to pick out a path, so I went magnificently along, shouldering through drifts and headed for the north. I was pretty well exhausted when I got to Union Square and, wiping the snow from my eyes, I tried to make out the triangle there. It was impossible. When I reached the New York Club at (Fifth Avenue and) Twenty-fifth Street, I was covered all over with ice and packed snow, and they would scarcely

believe that I had walked from Wall Street. It took three hours to
make the journey.

Conkling did not mention that when he arrived at the club's thresh-
hold, he crashed full length like a timber felled by a lumberjack. As
a result of this harrowing experience, Conkling developed pneumonia
and mastoiditis and died the following April.

Monday noon Macy's had dismissed all its employees, but when
the salesgirls got to the doors and saw the storm's fury, they were
afraid to venture out. Executives then announced that they could
spend the night in the store if they wished. Sighing with relief, the
girls turned back inside, took off their coats, and made themselves as
comfortable as possible. Food was brought in from nearby restaurants,
cots were set up in the furniture department, and all settled down for
the night.

Into the dingy New York *World,* at 32 Park Row, walked a bearded
man with snowshoes strapped to his back. Introducing himself as
Richard Farrelly, he told the editors that besides having newpaper
experience, he knew a great deal about cold weather because he had
spent much time in the frozen north. He proposed that they hire him
to cover the storm, and they did. Now a temporary *World* reporter,
Farrelly laced on his snowshoes, buttoned his coat across his chest,
and butted out into the tempest. He couldn't be seen for very long by
editors at windows of the *World*'s city room. Farrelly clumped across
City Hall Park, checked into the Astor House, and was lucky enough
to get a room to himself. Ordering up some whiskey, he sat out the
storm in comfort and euphoria. Every now and then he would bundle
up, lunge back outdoors, plod over to the *World* office, and dramatically stagger inside, his coat snow-spangled and his breath coming
hard. Flicking snowflakes from his beard, he would sit down and write
thrilling stories about his adventures in the blighted city. His hoax
wasn't discovered until long afterward. Even though he was a charla-
tan, he was so talented that later he became managing editor of the
World.

Shortly after noon that Monday, J. Pierpont Morgan closed his
Wall Street office to head for home. Unlike Conkling, he had kept his
cab waiting. He climbed inside, and the driver whipped up the horse;
but they were just barely able to inch through mounting snowdrifts,
past stalled streetcars and beer wagons and hacks and butchers'
trucks, piled with carcasses from slaughterhouses. Morgan and his
driver often had to stop at a cross street to wait until an especially

vicious blast of wind died down. They got as far as Fifth Avenue and Thirty-sixth Street; beyond that they couldn't go. Morgan left his cab and struggled on foot toward home. Although this was only a block away, the heavyset Morgan was exhausted when he arrived. He crawled up the front steps and managed to ring the doorbell before collapsing. A servant pushed open the door and dragged him inside.

At 2:45 P.M. on Monday, March 12, 1888, the wind hit a peak of 84 miles an hour. The temperature was 10 degrees above zero.

New York was isolated from the world except for one transatlantic cable. Fortunately, a cable company had buried the wire connecting its office with the end of the submarine cable. Oliver McKee, Boston correspondent for the New York *World,* got in touch with his office by cabling from Boston to London, with London relaying his message to New York.

Monday night was the wildest the city had experienced. Two-thirds of the electric light poles in Manhattan had been blown down, and in Brooklyn all of them were felled. Streetlamps still burning gas were of no help since the frost had shut off the gas supply. With hardly a soul to be seen on the streets, New York looked like a ghost town. Indoors, however, a Mardi Gras spirit ruled. Champagne parties were held in fashionable hotels, while in the Tenderloin section of town, raw liquor was gulped in great quantities.

General William Tecumseh Sherman had taken refuge in the Fifth Avenue Hotel. Two years earlier Sherman had moved to New York and into a house at 75 West Seventy-first Street. Sixty-eight years old, his grizzled beard close-cropped, and deep lines plowing his forehead, Sherman was one of the town's celebrities. Everyone called him Uncle Billy. The old warrior was something of a man about town, and he attended all opening nights. Now, an unwilling guest in the Fifth Avenue Hotel, Sherman wondered what lay ahead for him that tempestuous night. Understandably, the hotel manager told his assistants to shift other guests from one room to another so that Uncle Billy could occupy a room by himself. Most of the night Sherman sat up to stare out at the blizzard. War is not the only hell.

Tenement dwellers were less fortunate. At 10 P.M., with the temperature down to 6 degrees above zero, gas jets were turned off, leaving them to grope about in darkness. When they ran out of coal and their stoves went cold, they huddled together for warmth. In Hell's Kitchen a flower-selling giantess, called Big Six, went berserk, attacked a cop, and banged about a total of six policemen before she could be subdued. As they threw her into a cell, she snarled, "You bastards! Don't you know how to treat a lady?"

Five new plays were scheduled to open on Monday evening, but none did. Only four theaters held their usual shows. Henry Irving and Ellen Terry, the stars of *Faust,* dined leisurely in the Hoffman House, a famous hotel on Broadway between Twenty-fourth and Twenty-fifth streets. The Hoffman House bar was the most famous in town because of Bouguereau's scandalous painting of a nude nymph surrounded by leering satyrs. Irving and Miss Terry thought that their performance at the Star Theatre had been canceled. Surprisingly, every seat in the playhouse was filled that evening, and at curtaintime a breathless messenger rushed into the Hoffman House to tell the stars that they were expected. The news was overheard by a dozen men dining in the hotel; whereupon they gallantly took turns carrying Miss Terry on their shoulders through a dozen snow-clogged streets to the theater, at Broadway and Thirteenth Street.

Another group of hardy playgoers packed Augustin Daly's theater on Broadway between Twenty-eighth and Twenty-ninth streets to watch Ada Rehan star in *A Midsummer Night's Dream*—an ironic choice on the night of the Great Blizzard. In Niblo's Garden, at Broadway and Prince Street, only five persons appeared, but actor-manager Daniel E. Bandmann presented *Dr. Jekyll and Mr. Hyde* anyway. Tony Pastor's Music Hall was located at Fourteenth Street and Third Avenue, near Tammany Hall. Exactly four customers arrived and bought twenty-five-cent gallery seats. Pastor invited them to occupy orchestra seats and sent word to Tammany politicians to come and see his show for nothing. Seventy Democrats accepted. At the end of the performance Pastor broke out a case of champagne, put out a spread of sandwiches, and held a midnight party for the customers, Democrats, and theater help.

The circus known as the Greatest Show on Earth was scheduled to launch its 1888 season that Monday night in the renovated Madison Square Garden. The *Evening Post's* critic, Charles Pike Sawyer, tramped through the storm to the Garden. Snowdrifts more than 5 feet high blocked most entrances, but workmen had kept one doorway clear. Sawyer sighed with relief when he found himself inside the huge gaslighted hippodrome. He and other newspapermen crowded around seventy-seven-year-old P. T. Barnum to urge him to cancel the performance since fewer than 200 spectators had appeared. However, in the best the-show-must-go-on tradition the white-haired Barnum lifted his hand in a grandiose gesture at 8 P.M., the band crashed a brassy counterpoint to the howl of the wind outside, and the circus began. In another *beau geste* the old impresario sent champagne to the ringside seats occupied by reporters and critics. They drank, grew merry, and finally climbed into the ring to make happy idiots of themselves, while the professional clowns took seats and cheered them on.

About 1 A.M. on Tuesday, March 13, a fight broke out in the main bar of the Hoffman House. The temperature had sunk to 3 degrees above zero. Some actors had gathered to soak up brandy and companionship and make a stand against the storm. Among those present was the noted Irish comedian Nat C. Goodwin, whose liquid blue eyes, Apollo-like face, and personal magnetism charmed one and all; a famous English leading man, Robert Hilliard, a strapping six-footer; and the renowned tragedian, Maurice Barrymore, of the slender nose and flaring nostrils, eyes burning in his lean face. The handsome and witty Barrymore had just moved to New York and occupied a brownstone house at Broadway and West Forty-seventh Street. Safe in bed that bitter night were his wife and three children—Lionel, ten; Ethel, nine; and John, six.

There in the Hoffman House, his face flushed with brandy, Barrymore sprang onto a table and, as gaslights flickered on his monocle, began reciting Mark Antony's funeral oration from Shakespeare's *Julius Caesar:* "Friends, Romans, countrymen, lend me your ears!" Few did lend him their ears, even though this was a free performance by one of the world's leading actors. A well-dress stockbroker, named Howard Burros, who had been chatting with a friend, turned toward the drunken declaiming actor and tried to silence him. Barrymore broke off his monologue, pointed dramatically at Burros, and snarled, "You, sir-r-rr, are an ignorant clod!" Burros snapped an insult at Barrymore. Barrymore's friends replied in kind, and the evening ended in a free-for-all. Barrymore had been lightweight boxing champion of England during his student days at Oxford; but he disdained to mix in the brawl, kept his perch on the table, and ignored the shattering of glasses and the smashing of furniture, his eyes flaming and his magnificent voice booming another famous line: "A horse! A horse! My kingdom for a horse!"

At 6 A.M. on Tuesday the temperature stood at 1 degree below zero, the snow stopped falling for a few hours, and the wind eased up. The worst of the Blizzard of '88 was over.

More than twice as much snow fell during the storm as had fallen all winter long. The 20.9-inch deposit set no local record, for more recent storms have left even more snow upon New York's streets. What distinguished the Blizzard of '88 above all others was the deadly combination of an erroneous weather forecast, an unprepared city, a heavy snowfall, a ferocious wind, and a bone-chilling cold. The exact number of deaths caused by the storm is unknown. Property damage was estimated at between $20,000,000 and $25,000,000. The *Dictionary of American History* calls it "the most famous blizzard in American history."

Chapter 32

NEW YORK'S FIRST SKYSCRAPER

ANOTHER STORM that struck New York in 1889 is of historical interest because it dashed itself against the city's first real skyscraper.

Until the 1870's none of New York's buildings was taller than five stories. Even so, it was difficult to rent the topmost floors because few people cared to trudge up many flights of stairs. Higher structures were erected as elevators improved. Elevators changed in size, shape, and operating principle. There were screw, hydraulic, steam, and finally electric elevators. As they became faster and safer, they won wider acceptance.

With the advent of the 1870's the city's five-story buildings were topped by others eight and ten stories high. Old-timers complained that they threatened "to shut out the sky," but enterprising men went on building them. In 1882 Cyrus W. Field put up the twelve-story Washington Building at 1 Broadway. This has been wrongly called the world's first skyscraper, but it was made of masonry, and true skyscrapers consist of steel skeletons.

These earliest tall buildings of solid masonry needed very thick walls to support the weight of each floor. As a consequence, the lower stories had such thick walls that they wasted a great deal of rentable floor space. A solid masonry structure was limited in height by the total weight it could support. With the development of elevators came the need for a new kind of construction that would allow the use of thinner walls all the way up the building.

The prototype of all skyscrapers was erected in Chicago, a city that was young and bold and short on precedent. After the disastrous Chicago fire of 1871 a flurry of new construction began on the shore of Lake Michigan. In 1884 an architect, named William Le Baron Jenney, built the Home Insurance Building in Chicago. It was only ten stories tall, and the Washington Building in New York soared to twelve stories. However, the Home Insurance Building was the world's first real skyscraper because it was the first to use steel skeleton construction instead of solid masonry. Its steel frame supported the weight of the thinner walls, as well as the weight of each floor

The success of the Chicago landmark proved that there was no reasonable limit to the height of buildings. Besides steel construction and elevators, however, a third element was required to erect skyscrapers. This was a tough thick bed of rock on which to build. Parts of Manhattan's stony subsoil were perfect for shouldering the enormous weight of high buildings.

In the spring of 1887 a young New York silk merchant, named John L. Stearns, bought a lot at 50 Broadway on the east side of the street just south of Exchange Place. Its Broadway frontage was so narrow that a building only twenty-one and one-half feet wide could be erected there. Stearns wanted to put up a building that would earn him money from office rentals. If he built the conventional stone masonry structure, its walls would be so thick that he would not have enough rentable space to turn a profit. The more he pondered the problem, the more he felt that he had a white elephant on his hands. Stearns turned for help to a young New York architect, named Bradford Lee Gilbert.

For more than six months Gilbert meditated. Then one day he

realized that the solution was to erect a building like a steel bridge stood up on one end. First, he would raise a steel skeleton framework six stories high. On top of this he would place a seven-story super-structure. The walls would be only twelve inches thick and bear no weight at all. The weight of the walls and floors would be transmitted to the steel columns and then down to the cement footings of the foundation. The thin walls would provide more floor space and thus command more rentals than the usual masonry structure.

New York's ancient and rigid building laws, geared to solid masonry structures, dictated the exact thickness of walls in office buildings. Gilbert and Stearns agonized through long negotiations with various city officials before they were granted a construction permit by the buildings department. When newspapers heard about the plan for the radical new building, they dubbed it the Idiotic Building. New Yorkers were positive that Stearns' building would be blown over in the first strong windstorm. An engineer even wrote an alarming letter to Stearns, who handed it to his architect. By now Stearns himself feared that his new building would topple and that he would be sued for unprecedented damages. Gilbert, whose faith in himself never wavered, said to Stearns, "I will make my offices in the upper two floors of the Broadway end. If the building falls, I will fall with it."

The statement satisfied Stearns, and work began on New York's first true skyscraper. The building was so slim that it began to look like a gigantic exclamation mark. Stearns named it the Tower Build-ing because it towered into the sky. Except for the roof, the thirteen-story structure was finished when a hurricane hit the city one Sunday morning in 1889. With gusts of wind reaching a velocity of eighty miles an hour, Gilbert and Stearns rushed from their homes to the Tower Building to share in the crucial test it was undergoing.

By the time they arrived at 50 Broadway, a crowd had gathered— at a safe distance—to watch the fate of the building. The spectators babbled to one another that it was damned well going to blow down. Janitors and watchmen scurried out of buildings across the street, jabbering that they didn't want to be crushed to death when it fell.

Gilbert grabbed a plumb line and began climbing a ladder left in place by workmen when they had quit work the evening before. Stearns followed at his heels. From the crowd arose screams: "You fools! You'll be killed!" The architect and businessman could barely hear them above the shriek of the hurricane. Stearns' courage gave out when they reached the tenth floor. There he sprawled full length on a scaffold and held on for dear life. Gilbert, who felt that the risk of his reputation was worth the risk of his life, continued to climb the ladder, rung by painful rung, his knuckles whitening with strain and gusts of wind battering him unmercifully. When he reached the thirteenth and top floor, he crawled on hands and knees along a scaffold. At a corner of the building he tugged the plumb line from a pocket, got a firm grip on one end of the cord, and dropped its leaden weight down toward the Broadway sidewalk. He later reported, "There was not the slightest vibration. The building stood as steady as a rock in the sea."

In that moment of triumph Gilbert rashly jumped to his feet on the scaffold. His hat had been tightly crushed on his head. Now he snatched it off and waved it exultantly. The wind knocked him down. It scudded him toward one end of the scaffold. He gulped. He prayed. Wildly he grabbed about him. Just as he was about to be swept off the end of the board and down to certain death, he caught a rope lashing about in the wind from an upright beam of the tower. His grip held. The rope held. He steadied himself, eased down onto his knees, and carefully picked his way back to the ladder. Climbing down the ladder, he was joined by Stearns at the tenth floor, and the two men then made their way slowly back to street level.

Spectators cheered the heroes of the hour and gave way to let them pass. Locking arms, their chins upthrust, the architect and the businessman marched up Broadway, dumbfounding Trinity Church members just leaving the morning service, by singing in unison: "Praise God from whom all blessings flow. . . ."

New York's first skyscraper had passed its first test. The thin walls Gilbert designed gave Stearns $10,000 a year in extra rental. New York was to become *the* city of skyscrapers, a man-made Rocky Mountain range wondrous to behold. The end result was the world's greatest concentration of the tallest possible buildings on the smallest possible site. One year after this memorable Sunday, with the opening of the sixteen-story Pulitzer Building near the Manhattan end of the Brooklyn Bridge, a guest stepped off the elevator at the top floor and asked in a loud voice, "Is God in?"

New York needed a large hall for orchestral and choral music. The Metropolitan Opera House was inadequate for concert music because an orchestra's best effects were lost in the vast recesses of its stage. Chickering Hall and Steinway Hall were suitable only for recitals. Theaters lacked the proper atmosphere for serious music. The Oratorio Society, founded by Leopold Damrosch in 1873, gave concerts in the showrooms of a piano store.

Damrosch also established the New York Symphony, and before he died in 1885, he passed along to his son Walter his vision of a huge music hall in New York. After his father's death Walter Damrosch became director of both the New York Symphony and the Oratorio Society. Serving on the society's board was Andrew Carnegie, the industrialist and philanthropist. Young Damrosch told Carnegie that a chorus as large as that of the Oratorio Society had to have a much larger place in which to perform. Carnegie preferred pipe organs and bagpipes to symphony orchestras and choral groups, but his wife, twenty-four years his junior, urged him to give the city a great concert hall.

Carnegie acquiesced, partly because he foresaw the use of such a hall as a lecture platform and partly because he hoped that such a building could pay its own way. He told Damrosch that he was willing to spend $2,000,000 to construct the building, but that other New Yorkers would have to maintain and expand the institution. In the spring of 1889 Carnegie organized the Music Hall Company, and that summer excavation began for the main building.

The chosen site was the southeastern corner of Seventh Avenue and Fifty-seventh Street, then considered far uptown. Saloons abounded in the neighborhood, and Carnegie, who never drank liquor, was annoyed when he heard that at the end of a working day his laborers headed for a bar run by a brewery on Fifty-sixth Street. He cut off this source of supply by buying the property and closing the tavern.

The Music Hall, as Carnegie Hall was first called, was designed by William B. Tuthill. Besides being an accomplished architect, Tuthill had an excellent tenor voice, played the cello, was secretary of the Oratorio Society, and knew all of New York's serious musicians. In those days acoustical engineering was in its infancy, but Tuthill methodically studied the acoustics of all the important European concert halls. When the cornerstone was laid on May 13, 1890, Carnegie said of the structure, "It is built to stand for ages, and during these ages it is probable that this hall will intertwine itself with the history of our country."

It was erected piecemeal over the next seven years—not just one building, but three buildings cunningly connected to look like one. Down to the present, strangers are confused by the fact that the eighth floor of one unit runs into the tenth floor of another. Tuthill designed the exterior of the main building in modified Italian Renaissance Eclectic, which one writer described as a "fat, brown-and-buff Romanesque pile." Its foyer was well marbled, and the auditorium was rich in red plush and gilt trimmings. Two tiers of boxes were constructed around 3 sides of the auditorium, which seats 2,760 persons.

To open the Oratorio Society's new home, Walter Damrosch planned a five-day six-concert music festival, and he persuaded Peter Ilich Tchaikovsky to conduct some of his own works. When the Russian landed here late in the afternoon of April 26, 1891, he was the first truly great composer to visit America. Tchaikovsky was not a conductor by profession. A morbid neurotic, he sometimes felt as if his head were falling off as he stood on the podium, and at a previous concert he had clutched his head with one hand during the entire performance.

Tchaikovsky had a ruddy complexion, a bitter and full-lipped mouth, piercing blue eyes, gray hair, and a gray beard, and he dressed meticulously. As members of the welcoming committee helped him pass through customs, he glanced about apprehensively. He suffered from what he called heart cramps, and he had endured nervous breakdowns, tried unsuccessfully to cure his homosexuality by marrying, and made a stab at suicide. He felt homesick now and grieved over the recent death of his sister. Upon reaching the Hotel Normandie at Broadway and Thirty-eighth Street, he sat down in his suite and wept.

The formal opening of Carnegie Hall was held on the evening of May 5, 1891. Seated in Box 33 was Andrew Carnegie, a tiny man with white beard and hair, his hard mouth hidden by his mustache and his bright eyes widely separated by a thick nose. He was applauded by the chorus, about 400 strong, massed on the stage behind the orchestra. Exactly at 8 P.M. Walter Damrosch lifted his baton, and the chorus began singing a popular hymn, "Old Hundred." Later that evening Tchaikovsky conducted the *Marche Solennelle,* one of his minor works, but this time he did not feel it necessary to keep his head from toppling off. His beat was firm, forcible, and a little harsh.

Tchaikovsky considered Carnegie Hall "magnificent." He was paid $2,500 for this and other appearances during the music festival, and before leaving here, he was entertained by Carnegie. The Russian composer liked the Scottish-born steel magnate, partly because Carnegie expressed admiration for Moscow, which he had visited two years before. Tchaikovsky was also impressed by Carnegie's simplicity and his talent as a mimic. The musician wrote in his diary: "He grasped my hands, declaring that I am the uncrowned but true king of music; embraced me (without kissing—here men never kiss), expressed my greatness by standing on tiptoe and raising his hands up high, and finally threw the entire company into raptures by showing how I conduct. He did it so seriously, so well, so similarly, that I myself was delighted."

Carnegie Hall did not pay its way, as Carnegie had hoped. Although it was well attended, its operating costs exceeded its income, so with many complaints Carnegie underwrote its annual deficits for many years. However, it was an artistic success. Few auditoriums have such excellent acoustics as Carnegie Hall, which became America's most important concert hall.

The world's largest cathedral began to take shape in Manhattan about this time. Called the Cathedral of St. John the Divine, it was the Mother Church of the Episcopal diocese of New York.

Back in 1828 the need for such a cathedral had been mentioned by John Henry Hobart, the third Episcopal bishop of New York. In 1872 the idea was revived by Horatio Potter, the sixth Episcopal bishop, who urged Episcopalians to erect the largest church in America. G. T. Strong discussed the plan with John Jacob Astor, grandson and namesake of the original John Jacob Astor. The grandson told Strong he would donate $100,000 toward the project, causing the diarist to write: "Often as I have thought of it, I never regarded the realization of such a conception as within the bounds of possibility till my casual talk with John J. Astor at the door of 68 Wall Street this morning. Why not try to make the dream a reality?" That was on May 27, 1872. The next year Bishop Potter obtained a state charter incorporating the Cathedral of St. John the Divine.

He was succeeded as bishop by his nephew, Henry Codman Potter, who had pronounced the benediction at the dedication of the Statue of Liberty. The new bishop appealed for funds, not merely from Episcopalians but from Christians of every creed. John D. Rockefeller, a Baptist, later contributed $500,000.

On October 31, 1891, the Episcopalians paid $850,000 for 11½ acres of land then occupied by an orphan asylum on the Morningside

Heights plateau, 3 blocks east of the Hudson River. The site was bounded on the west by Amsterdam Avenue, on the north by West 113th Street, on the east by Morningside Drive, and on the south by West 110th Street. Part of the Battle of Harlem Heights had been fought here. Architects throughout the world were invited to submit plans for the cathedral. The winners were two Americans, George Lewis Heins and Christopher Grant La Farge. They chose the Romanesque Eclectic style, deriving part of their inspiration from the Cathedral of Gerona in Spain, which La Farge had visited in his youth. The cornerstone was laid on St. John's Day, December 27, 1892.

Built in the shape of a cross, the cathedral was so oriented that a priest standing at the high altar faced the east. Its nave, 601 feet long, became the longest in the world. Its foundation, 72 feet below the surface at certain spots, rested on solid rock. Except for steel in the roof over the nave, the building was made entirely of stone. Its core was Maine granite. Its outer walls were Mohegan granite from Peekskill, New York. Its inner surfaces were Bedford (Indiana) limestone and Wisconsin dolomite. Its flying buttresses were placed inside, rather than outside, the structure.

Flanking the nave were columns so lofty that they added grandeur to the magnificent cathedral. The work of hoisting them into place was directed by Carrie A. Howland, wife of one of the contractors. A shipload of tall pine trees had to be brought here all the way from Oregon around Cape Horn in order to make a derrick tall and strong enough to lift the granite pillars. The trees were landed at a Hudson River dock, as were the columns. To move the columns from the waterfront to the cathedral site required the construction of a truck reputed to be then the largest in the world.

Set in the western and front façade of the cathedral was a great rose window, forty feet in diameter. Under this stained-glass marvel stood ponderous bronze doors, eighteen feet high, weighing twelve tons, and richly ornamented on the outside with bas-relief panels illustrating biblical scenes.

The first service in the unfinished cathedral was held on January 8, 1899. After the death of Heins, architect La Farge carried on alone until 1911. At that time only the choir, the apse, and a rough masonry shell at the crossing had been completed. Certain cathedral officials, who preferred the more traditional Gothic architecture, declared the original contract at an end and turned the commission over to Ralph

Adams Cram and Frank E. Ferguson. This was a disheartening blow to La Farge and largely cut short his creative career. Cram and Ferguson designed the rest of the building in French Gothic Eclectic.

Although more than $20,000,000 has been spent on the cathedral, it is only about two-thirds finished today. Still lacking are two western towers, not yet carried to their full height of 207 feet, and a central spire, designed to rise more than 400 feet.

St. Peter's in Rome is a church, not a cathedral; its 41,900,000 cubic feet make it the largest church in the world. St. John's in New York is a cathedral because it contains the bishop's throne; its 16,822,000 cubic feet make it the largest cathedral in the world. The Cathedral of St. John the Divine can seat 10,000 people and hold thousands of standees. A scientist has predicted that this massive pile of stone upon stone will endure for at least 5,000 years.

The first Waldorf-Astoria Hotel resulted from a feud and then a truce between two branches of the Astor family. In the 1880's the empress of American society was Carolina Webster Schermerhorn Astor, known to the elite as *the* Mrs. Astor. She had married William Astor, the second son of William Backhouse Astor, and at their wedding reception Ulysses S. Grant had become a little drunk. *The* Mrs. Astor lacked beauty and brains, wore a black wig because her hair was falling out, but rose to undisputed leadership in society because she had $50,000,000 and the personality of a Prussian drill sergeant.

On the southwestern corner of Fifth Avenue and Thirty-fourth Street she built a 4-story mansion costing $1,500,000 and spent $750,000 to furnish it. Her husband disliked social life, so she chose Ward McAllister as her chamberlain, secretary, and social arbiter. The third Monday of every January she gave a ball regarded as the crowning event of the social season. At first she limited her guests to 400. McAllister told a reporter, "There are only about four hundred people in fashionable New York society. If you go outside the number you strike people who are either not at ease in a ballroom or else make other people not at ease. See the point?" The phrase "The Four Hundred" came to mean society's elite.

Mrs. Astor received her guests while standing in front of a full-length life-size oil portrait of herself. She wore as many jewels as possible, among them a triple necklace of diamonds and a famous diamond stomacher said to have belonged to Marie Antoinette. Every pair of canvasback ducks consumed by her guests cost the equivalent of a worker's weekly wages, and her annual ball was paid for by rentals from miles of tenements.

Her nephew was William Waldorf Astor, a great-grandson of the original John Jacob Astor. He was tall and stooped, parted his hair in the middle, and was as eccentric as he was irascible. It galled him when voters twice refused to elect him to Congress. Equally irritating was his aunt's social glory, which he wanted for his wife, Mary Dahlgren Paul Astor. Despite the fact that his fortune was twice as large as his aunt's, he was unable to wrest the social leadership from her. Declaring that "America is not a fit place for a gentleman to live," he planned to move to England. First, however, he would try to humble his aunt.

He lived on the northwestern corner of Fifth Avenue and Thirty-third Street in a house inherited from his father, John Jacob Astor III. Only a garden separated his place from his aunt's. He planned to raze his house and on its site erect a hotel so tall that its shadow would fall on his aunt's residence and dwarf its grandeur. Furthermore, he would call it the Waldorf so that everyone who voted against him would have to pronounce this part of his name. He chose Henry J. Hardenbergh to design his hotel and George C. Boldt to run it.

No expense was spared to make the Waldorf the most sumptuous hotel in America. The building alone cost nearly $4,000,000, while furnishings came to $600,000. Construction never was hurried, every detail being planned and built with meticulous care. When completed, it stood 13 stories high and had 530 rooms and 350 private baths. On the rainy night of March 14, 1893, the new Waldorf was officially opened. This was a depression year, and one Sunday the hotel had only 40 guests and 970 employees available to wait on them. Quickly recovering, however, the Waldorf won widespread fame.

Less than a year later *the* Mrs. Astor capitulated. Unwilling to live within a shadow created by her nephew and seeking to remove herself from what she considered sordid commercialism, she engaged Richard Morris Hunt to design a new palace for her farther north on Fifth Avenue.

Her son, John Jacob Astor IV, was angered by his cousin's victory and envious of his new hostelry. He decided to tear down his mother's abandoned mansion and there erect a hotel even taller than the Waldorf. But money was thicker than bad blood. Boldt, who had leased the Waldorf, suggested that the two hotels be operated as one so that both cousins would make greater profits. Cautiously agreeing, they stipulated that every opening between the two structures be constructed in such a way that they could be bricked up and sealed off, should the occasion arise.

John Jacob Astor IV, sixteen years younger than his cousin, had a lean face, a sharp nose, long sideburns, and a pointed upturned mustache. He decided to name his hotel the Astoria for the trading post his great-grandfather had planted in Oregon at the mouth of the Columbia River. In the spring of 1895 he began to demolish his mother's mansion, and by the following summer the Astoria was well along in its construction. The Waldorf had no bar; patrons would drink vintage wine at their tables. The Astoria featured a huge four-sided bar that became famous. It also boasted an enormous carriage entrance and the first roof garden of any New York hotel.

The 17-story Astoria opened on November 1, 1897, and by a coincidence this, too, turned out to be a stormy evening. President William McKinley was unable to attend, but sent Vice-President Garret A. Hobart. The combined hotel, called the Waldorf-Astoria, cost $13,000,000. With its 1,000 rooms and 765 private baths, it was the world's costliest, largest, and most magnificent hotel. Hardenbergh, who designed both parts, immediately became the foremost hotel architect of his time. The German Renaissance edifice abounded in roofed galleries, balconies, gables, and clusters of chimneys. The Empire dining room was modeled after the grand salon in King Ludwig's palace at Munich.

"Meet me at the Waldorf" became a byword among New York's elite during the Gay Nineties and long afterward. The hyphenated hotel continued to function at that location until 1929, when it was torn down to make way for the Empire State Building.

Chapter 33

ELLIS ISLAND OPENS

In the nineteenth century New York grew faster than any other big city in the world because immigrants washed upon its shores in ever-increasing numbers. Now, however, there came a change in the ethnic nature of the influx. Before 1883 about 85 percent of the immigrants were from northern and western Europe. After that, a flood of foreigners began arriving from central and southern Europe.

In the 1880's more than twice as many aliens landed as had arrived in any two previous consecutive decades. In 1861 only 91,918 reached America, but 669,431 were admitted in 1881. Most of the aliens came through New York. They were fleeing from exploitation and from political and religious persecution.

In 1880 New York City had 80,000 Jews, most of them of German extraction. Then, in 1881, Czar Alexander III began persecuting Russian Jews by forbidding them to acquire land, establishing Jewish quotas in schools and universities, and instituting cruel pogroms. Terror-stricken Jews poured out of the Russian empire, their exodus becoming the greatest since the departure of the Jews from Egypt.

Between 1881 and 1910 a total of 1,562,000 Jews came to America. A majority remained in New York, and a majority of this majority settled in the Lower East Side, converting it into the world's largest Jewish community. By 1910 there were 1,252,000 Jews living there. Irishmen and Germans hastily left for other parts of the city, leaving New York's oldest dwellings to the newcomers. Walt Whitman did not share in the general scorn for the Russian Jews. In a letter written to his Russian translator in 1881, Whitman remarked on the amazing similarity between Russians and Americans.

It was not anti-Semitic Christians who first slandered Jews with the derogatory term "kikes." New York's long-established German Jews, noting that the names of many Russian Jews ended with *ki*, began calling them kikis, which gradually changed to kikes. Hoping to escape this embarrassing distinction and obtain credit from German businessmen, some Russians took German names. Efforts were made to exclude Jews from good jobs and neighborhoods, from clubs and schools. Many Lower East Side Jews became peddlers because little capital was needed to get into this line of work. Pushcarts were thickest on Hester Street, the chief market center on the Lower East Side. Jews were so fond of the theater they said their diet was "bread smeared with theater." The first Yiddish play in America was staged in New York in 1882. Second Ave. became the Jewish Rialto.

As a result of centuries of political oppression, most Jews were liberals, and many were Socialists. They spent so much time quarreling about different radical doctrines that the Irish easily maintained control of Tammany Hall. However, the Irish were slow to move out of the ranks of unskilled labor, whereas the Jews were quick to become first small merchants and then professional men.

Tammany Hall was reluctant to take Jews into its inner circle, but it did help the masses of Jewish immigrants. Seeking to maintain its reputation as the friend of the poor, Tammany gave the underprivileged of all faiths coal in winter, ice in summer, food on holidays, and favors the year around. In return, Tammany expected the votes of those whom it helped. Local Republicans tended to ignore the foreign-born and the poor.

Unlike the prodigal Irish, the Jews saved their money. According to an immigrant guidebook of that era, a Jew who earned fifty cents a day spent only ten cents for coffee and bagels and saved the other forty cents. But it wasn't long before Jews wanted to live as well as the older New Yorkers in better parts of the city. Jews could not be kept out of schools, so intense was their passion for education. Teachers and public officials alike were astonished by the intellectual zest of Jewish children. Police Commissioner William McAdoo cried, "Think of it! Herbert Spencer preferred to a fairy story by girls and boys!"

Like other immigrant groups, Jews made a rich contribution to the political and artistic life of New York and the nation. The year 1891 marked the arrival of Morris and Rose Gershovitz, born in St. Petersburg, Russia. Morris soon shortened his name to Gershvin. He is remembered today only because of his son, George Gershwin, the composer and pianist. In 1893 a frail Russian rabbi, Moses Baline, settled on the Lower East Side with his wife, Leah, and their children. One of their sons was four-year-old Isador Baline, commonly known as Izzy. The Izzy Baline of that day became Irving Berlin, another renowned composer. The Lower East Side also produced sculptors Jo Davidson and Jacob Epstein.

William Sulzer was a Christian and a Democratic politician who went out of his way to help the Jews. After serving nine terms in Congress, he became governor of New York State. Undeniably beloved by Jews, Sulzer is said to have shouted during a political campaign, "Every night a hundred million Jews in Russia kneel to pray for William Sulzer!" A heckler called out: "Jews don't *kneel* when they pray!" According to the story, Sulzer fixed his heckler with penetrating eyes and retorted, "They do when they pray for William Sulzer!"

Italian immigration into New York and the rest of America has been called modern history's greatest and most sustained movement of population from a single country. The first Italian to settle here was a Venetian craftsman, named Peter Caesar Alberti, who took up residence in Brooklyn in 1635. Twenty years later an Italian, named Mathys Capito, became a clerk in the New York municipal bookkeeping office. Many Italians fought for this country during the American Revolution. In 1806 Lorenzo Da Ponte, the author of many

Mozart librettos, emigrated to New York. Staten Island became a refuge for politicians exiled from Italy. Foremost among these, perhaps, was Giuseppe Garibaldi. After living from 1850 to 1854 on Staten Island, where he worked as a candlemaker, he went back to his native land to try to unify it.

In 1880 more than 12,000 native Italians lived in New York. Most congregated in Mulberry Bend, located on Mulberry Street between Bayard and Park streets, two blocks west of the Bowery. This slum area became known as Little Italy. A majority of the early Italian immigrants had been born in northern Italy. Beginning in the 1880's, however, the bulk of Italian immigrants arrived from southern Italy and from Sicily. Unskilled and illiterate peasants for the most part, they were regarded with disdain by northern Italians. Among the Sicilian newcomers were members of the dreaded Mafia, which had a long history of preying on helpless and ignorant peasants. They began terrorizing New York's transplanted Italians.

No ethnic or religious group, however, has held a monopoly on vice in New York. The city has known Irish gangsters, Jewish gangsters, Chinese gangsters, and Italian gangsters.

In 1880 Achille Luigi Carlo LaGuardia brought his bride to New York. They were the parents of Fiorello H. LaGuardia, who was born on December 11, 1882, in a tenement at 7 Varick Street in the Italian section of Greenwich Village. Fiorello LaGuardia became the first Italian-American to overthrow Irish-dominated Tammany Hall, and he finished his spectacular career as the greatest mayor in the history of New York City. At the time of his birth Greenwich Village was occupied mainly by the Irish and Negroes. As more Italians moved into the Village, the Negroes began to move out, gathering in an area just west of Columbus Circle in mid-Manhattan and on the Upper East Side. The year of LaGuardia's birth, Eamon De Valera was born here. De Valera, who became president of the Republic of Ireland, was the son of a Spanish father and an Irish mother. He was delivered on October 14, 1882, in the Nursery and Child's Hospital, at Lexington Avenue and East Fifty-first Street. The year 1882 also marked the birth of Franklin Delano Roosevelt at Hyde Park, New York.

Southern Italians were clannish. Despite the fact that they had shown enough spirit to emigrate to the New World, their outlook on life continued to be that of villagers. Intensely suspicious, they regarded everyone outside their own family as *forestieri,* or strangers.

Differences in customs and dialects, together with centuries-old prejudices, separated Abruzzese, Calabrians, Genoese, Neapolitans, Pied-
montese, Sicilians, Turinese, and miscellaneous others. Members of
each group huddled near one another in their new homes here.

Most Italian men arrived without their women, for they had no
intention of staying. They hoped to make a fortune and then to return to their native villages. As a result of this wish to go home, their
fear of strangers, their lack of skills, and their illiteracy, Italians were
slow in becoming Americanized.

Jews were also somewhat clannish and didn't want their children
to marry outside the group, but they considered their offspring to be
the equal of anyone else. The Italians lacked this confidence and pride
in their children. Stunted in outlook, many Italians fell victim to the
very kind of exploitation which had caused them to leave their homeland. Just as some vicious Irishmen had preyed on later-arriving
Irishmen, so did Italians fall into the hands of their own greedy people. A stereotype of the day was the padrone, an Italian straw boss
who took charge of fellow immigrants when they arrived, found them
jobs and apartments, acted as their brokers, and profited handsomely
from each transaction. Many padroni wound up as wealthy men, but
the masses of Italians went on working as common laborers.

Because Irish workmen predominated in the building trades, Italians at first found it difficult to break into this field. The backward-
ness of Italian immigrants enabled employers to play them off against
other workers by using them as strikebreakers. As a result, they were
sneered at as dagos. The word "dago," a corruption of the Spanish
proper name Diego, is the equivalent of Jack or Jim. Another derogatory nickname applied to Italians was guinea. Originally this word
was confined to Portuguese exploring for gold along the part of
western Africa then known as Guinea. Because southern Italians,
like the Portuguese, tended to be dark-skinned, the insulting term
"guinea" was applied to them.

The first Chinese known to have visited New York was Punqua
Wingchong, who figured in John Jacob Astor's hoax against the
Jefferson administration. He arrived in 1807 and left in 1808. Historians differ about the first Chinese who lived here. Some say that
it was Quimbo Appo, who landed in San Francisco in 1844 and
arrived in New York a few years later. Others declare that it was
Ah Ken, a Cantonese merchant who appeared in 1858, opened a
cigar store on Park Row, and made his home on Mott Street. An-

other contender was a Chinese sailor, called Lou Hoy Sing, who settled in New York in 1862 and married an Irish colleen, who bore him two sons. Wah Kee appeared in 1868 and established a fruitshop, at 13 Pell Street, which served as a blind for the gambling den and opium dive he ran secretly above this shop. In 1872 there were 12 Chinese in the Mott Street district, and in 1880 they numbered 700. From then on they arrived in New York by droves, although more settled in California than on the eastern seaboard.

New York became a haven for almost all nationalities—Hungarians, Bulgarians, Czechs, Poles, Bohemians, Rumanians, Latvians, Estonians. Lithuanians, Greeks, Turks, Austrians, Arabs, Lebanese, Spaniards, Albanians, Syrians, and others. The so-called melting pot never really dissolved their different identities. The process of assimilation resulted in something like vegetable soup. Although the ingredients retained their separate forms and flavor, they went well together. This was the way that liberals viewed immigration. Conservatives felt differently. As the tide of aliens rose, conservatives grew apprehensive and ultimately took alarm. Something of the spirit of the Know-Nothing era developed as Anglo-Saxons excitedly told one another that this immigration threatened the identity and character of the nation. Pride in ancestry dies hard. On December 23, 1894, the Society of Mayflower Descendants was organized in New York by descendants of the Pilgrims "to preserve their memory, their records, their history, and all facts relating to them, their ancestors, and their posterity."

On the other hand, Abram S. Hewitt, onetime mayor of New York, declared that every immigrant worker meant a $5,000 increase in the nation's wealth. Aleš Hrdlička, an American anthropologist born in Bohemia, once said, "So far as science is able to see, there has not been . . . a trace of any bad effect of these mixtures on the American people. Much rather otherwise. Probably a good part, perhaps a very important part . . . of the power and strength of the American people is the result of these very mixtures." Italian-born Edward Corsi, who became an important American political figure, remarked, "Roughly one-half the total population of the United States traces its beginning to Ellis Island."

Between 1855 and 1892 nearly 7,700,000 aliens entered this country through New York State's big immigration station at Castle Garden near the Battery and through the state's subsidiary depot on Wards Island in the East River. Conditions at Castle Garden became so bad that when Grover Cleveland was sworn in as governor in 1883, he devoted part of his first message to the problem. A state investigation resulted in better conditions there. With the increase in immigration, facilities at Castle Garden and on Wards Island became so inadequate that both were closed. In 1890 immigration control was transferred from the state to the federal government, and Ellis Island was chosen as the new immigration station.

On January 1, 1892, the first foreigners arrived at Ellis Island in the Upper Bay of New York Harbor. The island served as the main gateway to America until 1954. After numbing days and nights sardined in steerage, fretted by seasickness and homesickness and fear and a sense of rootlessness, many aliens arrived in a state of physical and emotional exhaustion. Their spirits did not revive until some—the lucky ones—walked into the main reception hall and up to the famous "kissing post," where they were reunited with relatives and friends who had preceded them to the New World. These scenes were very touching and very American because America is a nation of immigrants and New York City is the most cosmopolitan city in all of cosmopolitan America. Dutch blood flowed in the veins of patrician Franklin Delano Roosevelt, who once began a speech to the Daughters of the American Revolution with the words: "Fellow immigrants—"

Chapter 34

THE REVEREND PARKHURST
SAMPLES VICE

THE REPORTER wondered what he was doing in church. W. E. Carson of the *World* had been urged to attend the Madison Square Presbyterian Church on Sunday morning, February 14, 1892. Half-suspecting that the tip might be a hoax, but hesitant to overlook a good story, Carson strolled into the Gothic brownstone church at Madison Avenue and Twenty-fourth Street. Sitting down in a pew, he peered past green granite columns and soon spotted a frail and aging man, who held his silk hat between his bony knees. The reporter recognized him as Thomas C. Platt, Republican boss of New York State, who recently had declared war on Richard Croker, leader of Tammany Hall and thus boss of New York City.

Now the minister stepped into the pulpit. He was the Reverend Charles H. Parkhurst, a fifty-year-old man with a slender figure, a long and narrow face, nearsighted eyes peering intensely through rimless glasses, a chin cloaked in a Vandyke, and curly hair worn long at the sides and the back of his head. Dr. Parkhurst looked like the scholar he was. A graduate of Amherst College, he had also studied in Germany, and he knew Greek, Latin, and Sanskrit. That Sunday morning he wore a black clerical robe with a white starched bib at his throat.

He had spoken no longer than a minute when a gasp rose from the congregation, and the *World* reporter reached for a pencil inside his pocket. New York City, the pastor declared, was thoroughly rotten. He laid the blame squarely on Mayor Hugh J. Grant, District Attorney De Lancy Nicoll, and the police commissioners. "Every step that we take looking to the moral betterment of this city," Dr. Parkhurst charged, "has to be taken directly in the teeth of the damnable pack of administrative bloodhounds that are fattening themselves on the ethical flesh and blood of our citizenship. . . ."

The Presbyterians sat in a state of shock. The reporter scribbled notes as fast as he could. Republican Boss Platt narrowed his eyes as he schemed how to use this sermon for his own political ends. But no man present that day could foresee the full consequences of the remarkable sermon.

It shook the town because the *World* played up Carson's story. Mayor Grant angrily called on the minister to prove his allegations. Tammany politicians denounced Dr. Parkhurst as "un-Christian" and "vulgar." Charles A. Dana, editor of the *Sun,* urged that the minister be driven from his pulpit. Other pastors felt that if Dr. Parkhurst wished to denounce evil, he should have stuck to Sodom and Gomorrah. And District Attorney Nicoll ordered him to appear before a grand jury.

Nine days after his sermon the preacher was haled before the jury and asked for legal evidence of his charges. He had none. His attack had been based on newspaper articles never denied by public officials. Nearly everyone realized that vice was rampant in the city, but Dr. Parkhurst had not documented the case. The grand jury, which was partial to Tammany, rebuked him and called his charges sweeping and groundless. The jury sent its report to the court of general sessions, whose presiding judge agreed. Dr. Parkhurst was depressed. "I had waked up a whole jungle of teeth-gnashing brutes," he later said, "and it was a question of whether the hunter was going to bag the game or the game make prey of the hunter."

After moping a few days, Dr. Parkhurst sought the advice of commission merchant David J. Whitney, a founder of the Society for the Prevention of Crime. This was a private organization of clergymen, merchants, and lawyers. Parkhurst had been its president for the past year. Humiliated by the grand jury, he wanted to pick up where he had left off but didn't know how to proceed. Whitney urged him to make a personal tour of the underworld to collect evidence at firsthand. The merchant also put the minister in touch with a private detective, named Charles W. Gardner, who agreed to act as guide. This young man wasn't an altogether savory character, but Parkhurst didn't know it at the time. Gardner flaunted a huge mustache, which curled at the ends, and wore the hard hat popular with most private eyes of that era.

The detective and the pastor met in Parkhurst's home at 133 East Thirty-fifth Street. For six dollars a night, plus expenses, the detective agreed to show the cleric the seamy side of New York life. He also promised to hire other private detectives to collect further data on their own. As the two men conversed, young John Langdon Erving entered the room. One of Parkhurst's parishioners, Erving was tall and blond, a society dandy, and the scion of a rich family. It was decided that Erving would accompany his pastor and the detective on their outings. The three men agreed to meet on Saturday evening, March 5, in Gardner's apartment at 207 West Eighteenth Street. Naturally, they would need disguises. Gardner later wrote a book, called *The Doctor and the Devil, or Midnight Adventures of Dr. Parkhurst,* in which he told how he changed the pastor's appearance.

Their first night out on the town the three men stopped at Tom Summers' Saloon, at 33 Cherry Street, where they drank whiskey that tasted like embalming fluid and watched little girls buy booze at ten cents a pint to take home to their fathers. When the detective praised the pastor's ability to hold his liquor, Parkhurst closed his eyes and smiled. Next, they headed for a whorehouse at 342 Water Street, where painted women stood in the doorway soliciting trade. Two harlots grabbed Parkhurst, dragged him inside, and sat him down on a chair. He chatted easily with them, fended off their advances, and got away. The next stop was another red-light house, where a young prostitute asked Parkhurst to dance. To save the minister embarrassment, Erving danced with her, while Parkhurst sat and watched. Two old hags drifted up to him, begged him to buy them drinks, and he did. This so won the heart of a 200-pound crone that she leered at Parkhurst, asked him to call her Baby, and invited him upstairs. Again he managed to escape.

The night of March 9 the minister, detective, and socialite resumed their explorations. At Water Street and Catherine Slip they ducked into the bar of the East River Hotel, where they found two uniformed policemen enjoying drinks on the house. Parkhurst told Gardner to jot down their badge numbers. Then, acting like a roisterer, the minister ordered drinks for everyone in the bar. It cost Parkhurst only eighty cents to provide each of the sixteen customers with a whiskey. Next the trio visited a five-cent lodginghouse for men at 233 Park Row. Although this was a legal establishment, Parkhurst wanted to see it because Gardner had said that in places like this Tammany recruited voters to cast ballots frequently and fraudulently. In a room thirty feet wide and eighty feet long, dozens of foul-smelling bums slept on bare canvas cots; their stench drove Parkhurst out into the street.

On their next nocturnal trip the explorers headed for the Bowery and visited several brassy cabarets, known as concert gardens. Then they saw "tight houses," where all women wore tights. Brothels were classified by the nationalities of their inmates, so on Forsyth Street the three men visited a "German house." The madam said that the five scantily clad girls in the parlor were her daughters. Pushing on, the men got within a stone's throw of Police Headquarters, at 300 Mulberry Street, when they were accosted by fifty tarts. One woman enticed them to a house on Elizabeth Street, which she described as "a boarding house for the most respectable policemen in the city." By the time they left this place, Parkhurst had become ill from mixing his drinks, so the detective led him into a Third Avenue saloon for a glass of soda. As luck would have it, there sat a drunk who had gone to Amherst with the minister. When he greeted Parkhurst by name, the bartender looked up in surprise and fright, ordered the trio out of the place, and threw their money after them. Feeling better physically, Parkhurst demanded that Gardner "show me something worse."

In Chinatown, northeast of what is now Foley Square, they watched a game of fan-tan and then padded into the murky room of a nearby building, where they found a Chinese man, his Caucasian wife, and their eight-year-old son smoking opium. Next came a visit to the Negro district around Sullivan and West Houston Streets, called Coontown. Then Frenchtown on the southern fringe of Washington Square in Greenwich Village. Entire blocks consisted of houses of prostitution—of all kinds. Worst of all, to the sensitive Parkhurst, was a four-story brick house on West Third Street, called the Golden Rule Pleasure Club. There they were greeted by "Scotch Ann," who bade them enter the basement. This was partitioned into small dens, each containing a table and a couple of chairs.

As Gardner described it: "In each room sat a youth, whose face was painted, eyebrows blackened, and whose airs were those of a young girl. Each person talked in a high falsetto voice, and called the others by women's names." Puzzled, the minister turned to the detective and whispered a question. Gardner explained. For the first and only time Parkhurst was frightened. Running outdoors, he panted in horror, "Why, I wouldn't stay in that house for all the money in the world!"

The evening of March 11, the last time he ventured into New York's underworld, Parkhurst went with Gardner and Erving to a posh bawdyhouse at 31-33 East Twenty-seventh Street, just three blocks from Parkhurst's own church. They were welcomed by the madam, Mrs. Hattie Adams, who called eight young women into the parlor. Having recovered from his revulsion of the previous night, the minister hoped to see the very worst. Gardner paid five of the girls three dollars apiece to put on a dance. A broken-down musician, called the Professor, sat at a piano in the parlor, but the girls refused to perform until he was blindfolded. This done, they shucked off the Mother Hubbard gowns they wore, leaving themselves completely naked, and romped around the room while the Professor banged out a lively jig. They frolicked through a cancan, they danced with Erving, and finally they played leapfrog, with Gardner acting as the frog. Throughout this revelry the minister sat in a corner sipping beer and watching with a blank face. Hattie became suspicious of him, but Gardner assured her that he was a "gay boy from the West." The madam decided that maybe he was a pickpocket on vacation and tried pulling his whiskers, only to be rebuffed so sternly that she let it go at that.

Anti-Parkhurst newspapers later claimed that *he* had played the role of frog for the leapfrogging naked whores, but this was not the case. So celebrated did this episode become that delighted habitués of the Tenderloin district sang, "Dr. Parkhurst on the floor/Playing leapfrog with a whore/Ta-ra-ra-ra-boom-de-ay/Ta-ra-ra-boom-de-ay!"

From Hattie Adams' place the three men went to another brothel, on West Fourth Street, run by Marie Andrea. There they witnessed a "French circus." Gardner later said that this sickened him, but the minister "sat in a corner with his feet curled under his chair and blandly smiled." The detective also reported that "after their performance, the girls bowed like ballet dancers." After the three men got out of the place, Gardner asked Parkhurst what he thought of the spectacle they had just seen. "Think of it?" the minister cried. "It was the most brutal, the most horrible exhibition that I ever saw in my life!"

Never again did Parkhurst enter a brothel, den, dive, saloon, or any other place of low repute. He now had all the evidence he sought. In addition to his eyewitness tours, 4 other detectives hired by Gardner had visited 254 saloons. All told, the Reverend Dr. Parkhurst spent about $500 in this campaign.

He let it be known that on Sunday, March 13, he would deliver another sermon about corruption in the city. An hour before he began to speak, his house of worship was jammed, some people even sitting on the steps leading to the pulpit. On the lectern the minister placed a Bible, a hymnbook, and a stack of documents prepared with the help of Gardner and Erving. Launching into his indictment, Parkhurst said that at first he had not considered it part of his ministerial duties "to go into the slums and help catch the rascals, especially as the police are paid nearly five million dollars a year for doing it themselves." However, when he had realized that no one else would expose this vice, he had gone "down into the disgusting depths of this Tammany-debauched town."

Parkhurst picked up the documents from the lectern. These were sworn affidavits of what he had seen, affidavits from the detectives hired by Gardner, and a list of thirty houses of prostitution within the Nineteenth Precinct, where his church was located. "For four weeks," he cried, "you have been wincing under the sting of a general indictment and have been calling for particulars! This morning I have given you particulars—two hundred and eighty-four of them. Now, what are you going to do with them?"

His second sermon shocked the city even more than his first. Many citizens were horrified at the conditions he described. Others felt that the minister had been guilty of impropriety in crawling through the sewers of the underworld. He was accused of seeking personal publicity. Politicians pretended to worry that his findings might affect decent people. Some men of social and financial standing feared that reform would hurt business. The *Sun* declared that Dr. Parkhurst's usefulness as a minister had come to an end since he had instigated and paid for obscene performances. And Anthony Comstock felt jealous. Comstock headed the Society for the Suppression of Vice, which competed with Parkhurst's Society for the Prevention of Crime.

Parkhurst and his organization demanded that District Attorney Nicoll and the courts close the places he had visited. No action was taken. Since most police justices were creatures of Tammany Hall, they declined to issue warrants for the arrests Parkhurst wanted. Crime Society agents testified about disorderly housekeepers near the Essex Market court; but when they left the courtroom, they were attacked by a mob, and the police refused to protect them.

The next grand jury that convened was headed by an upright businessman, named Henry M. Taber. Under his influence the jurors summoned Parkhurst, gave him a friendly hearing, welcomed his affidavits, handed down indictments against two whorehouse madams, and questioned the city's four police commissioners, as well as a few police inspectors and captains. Nearly 90 percent of all police appointments, transfers, and promotions had been recommended by leaders of Tammany Hall; this explains why the men appearing before the jury showed very poor memories.

The grand jury declared: "(The police) are either incompetent to do what is frequently done by private individuals with imperfect facilities for such work, or else there exist reasons and motives for such inaction which are illegal and corrupt. The general efficiency of the Department is so great that it is our belief that the latter suggestion is the explanation of the peculiar inactivity."

Parkhurst hammered away, in sermon after sermon, about the unholy alliance between Tammany and the underworld. He received a flood of solid tips in letters from people afraid to sign their names. At last the Chamber of Commerce began to worry about the city's reputation; early in 1894 it asked the state legislature to investigate the city's police department. The legislature was controlled by Republican Boss Platt, who welcomed this opportunity to embarrass Democratic Boss Croker and the city's Democratic machine.

Clarence Lexow, a Republican state senator, was named chairman of a committee to conduct the probe. Committee members began by coming to New York and visiting Dr. Parkhurst, the acknowledged leader of the anti-vice forces. Now worldly enough to recognize the partisan composition and purposes of the legislative committee, he declined to give his full cooperation. Because he had been the first to raise his voice in public, committee members had to placate him. They let him name their counsel, John W. Goff, a brilliant lawyer, who at this time was above political influence.

Thus, in 1894, began the famous Lexow investigation of crime and corruption in America's greatest city. It became a national sensation. Never before had New York police been exposed so thoroughly. The committee's findings ran to nearly 6,000 pages in 5 thick books. The *World* gave massive publicity to this probe, which deeply impressed twelve-year-old Fiorello LaGuardia. When LaGuardia was three years of age, his family moved to the West, and his father was now an army bandmaster near Prescott in Arizona Territory. Whenever young LaGuardia rode into Prescott, he bought copies of the New York *World* at a drugstore. Much later he wrote:

> When I got home with the *Sunday World,* I would carefully read every word of the *World's* fight against the corrupt Tammany machine in New York. That was the period of the lurid disclosures made by the Lexow investigation of corruption in the Police Department that extended throughout the political structure of the city. The papers then were filled with stories of startling crookedness on the part of the police and the politicians in New York. Unlike boys who grew up in the city and who heard from childhood about such things as graft and corruption, the amazing disclosures hit me like a shock. I could not understand how the people of the greatest city in the country could put up with the vice and crime that existed there. A resentment against Tammany was created in me at that time which I admit is to this day almost an obsession. . . .*

The Lexow committee consisted of 7 members—5 of them Republicans; 1 an independent Democrat; and 1 a Tammany Democrat. They held their first meeting on March 9, 1894, in a third-floor room of the Tweed-built County Courthouse at 52 Chambers Street. The city had a population of not quite 2,000,000. The 4,000-man police force was run by a 4-man board of police commissioners. When it

* From *The Making of an Insurgent, An Autobiography: 1882-1919* by Fiorello H. LaGuardia. Copyright, 1948, by J. B. Lippincott Company. Published by J. B. Lippincott Company.

became apparent that the committee's counsel meant business, whorehouse keepers left town in droves, many heading for Chicago. A covert offer of $300,000 was made to counsel Goff to drop the probe, but he spurned this bribe. In 74 sessions the Lexow committee heard 678 witnesses and took 10,576 pages of testimony before its final meeting on December 29, 1894. Of these pages, 9,500 were about corruption in the police department.

In the middle of January, 1895, the Lexow committee issued a report. Although all worldly New Yorkers were generally aware of the situation, the report spelled it out in detail. Police bribery was so common that when a vaudeville actor wanted to impersonate a cop, he simply held one hand behind his back with the palm upturned. The report showed that woven into a web of corruption were policemen, judges, prostitutes, dope addicts, saloonkeepers, abortionists, robbers, gamblers, swindlers, bawdyhouse proprietors, politicians—and businessmen. In fact, M. R. Werner wrote that "the outstanding development of the Croker period in Tammany Hall was the beginning of an alliance between Tammany Hall and large corporate enterprise." Boss Croker became so frightened that he temporarily resigned his Tammany leadership and left for Europe, announcing that he needed a complete rest because he was ill.

Corruption began at the bottom, worked its way to the top, and then descended to the bottom again. Any ambitious young man who wanted to become a policeman had to pay a $300 bribe just to be appointed to the force. Police Commissioner James J. Martin admitted under questioning that 85 percent of his appointments to the police ranks were made on the recommendations of Tammany leaders and that in 5 years he had promoted only 2 men on merit alone. It cost a patrolman $2,500 to be promoted to sergeant. A captaincy was worth $10,000 to $15,000 in bribe money, although a captain's official salary was only $2,750 a year. To be elevated from captain to inspector cost from $12,000 to $20,000. The Lexow committee said that this promotion racket alone came to about $7,000,000 a year— a modest estimate, in its opinion.

Any policeman who paid for promotion expected to get his money back. A case in point was Alexander Williams, known as Clubber Williams because he said that there was more law at the end of a police club than in any courtroom. He was a sadistic brute who enjoyed beating up people. As a police captain, he was transferred from a not too lucrative downtown precinct to the Nineteenth Precinct, which embraced an area roughly bounded by Fourteenth to Forty-second streets and Fifth and Seventh avenues, now the city's garment district. This section was so wide-open and vicious and depraved that some people called it Satan's Circus. But Clubber Williams gave it another nickname. Upon taking over his new post, he drawled, "I've had nothing but chuck steaks for a long time, and now I'm going to get me a little of the tenderloin." The area became the Tenderloin.

Imposing tribute on every kind of illegal activity, Williams grew wealthy on graft and ultimately was promoted to police inspector. Ordered to appear before the Lexow committee, he admitted that he had been charged with clubbing more people than any other man on the force, that he had several big bank accounts, and that besides his home in the city, he owned a mansion in Connecticut and kept a yacht.

Saloons were supposed to close at 1 A.M. on weekdays and to remain closed all day Sunday. However, thousands of saloonkeepers paid the police $20 a month to stay open after the deadline and all day Sunday. Uniformed cops openly accepted free drinks in these places. The many houses of prostitution in the city paid from $35 to $50 a month to the police for protection. Madams also bought tickets to Tammany parties and picnics. Charles Priem, who ran a brothel at 28 Bayard Street, told the committee that in 6 years he had given the police $4,300 in regular payments, an "initiation fee" of $500 every time a new captain took over the precinct, and an annual Christmas gift of $100 to whichever man happened to be captain at the holiday season. One madam said that she had paid the police $150 a month for 10 years.

Besides this direct graft, the police had a hand in subsidiary graft connected with prostitution—the sale to whorehouses of beer, liquor, cigars, cigarettes, food, medical service, and so forth. Some high police officials and Tammany politicians had direct financial interests in bawdyhouses, and the cop on the beat was told to protect the establishments especially favored by city officials, judges, and millionaires.

Steamship owners paid police to guard their vessels from the time they arrived in port until they were unloaded. Pushcart peddlers paid cops three dollars a week to stand in the streets beside their carts. Sailmakers on South Street paid police for permission to hang out canvas banners proclaiming their trade. Bootblacks had to give a free shine to any cop demanding service. Whenever Charles Delmonico of the famous Delmonico's Restaurant staged a banquet, he asked his precinct house to assign a cop to duty at his entrance, and he paid the policemen five dollars an evening. Arthur Brisbane, then writing for the New York *World*, commented, "Another batch of the city's businessmen proved that they were just about as worthy of freedom as a Kaffir at the Cape."

George Appo, the son of a white mother and a Chinese father, told the Lexow committee that the city had 10,000 opium dens. One was located on West Forty-Second Street near Seventh Avenue. High police officials divided New York into districts so that they could be sure of getting their take from the city's 1,000 policy slip establishments; each paid from $15 to $35 a month to operate. Bailing out prostitutes was a valuable Tammany concession, and the police often shared in the proceeds of robberies committed by whores.

Perhaps the most damning evidence turned up by the Lexow committee was the fact that police did not consider themselves servants of the people, but their masters. Insolent, arrogant, and vicious, they produced a reign of terror as cruel as that of Cossacks during Old World pogroms. A man who had been robbed was beaten up by the policemen to whom he turned for help. A clergyman was thrown out of a precinct house where he had protested about streetwalkers. Some cops threatened to arrest any woman they found alone on the streets at night unless she gave them money. One patrolman clubbed sixteen people, including a fifteen-year-old girl, whom he bashed in the mouth with his fist while she was strolling on Broadway with her father. The Lexow committee said:

> The poor, ignorant foreigner residing on the great east side of the city has been especially subjected to a brutal and infamous rule by the police, in conjunction with the administration of the local inferior courts, so that it is beyond a doubt that innocent people who have refused to yield to criminal extortion, have been clubbed and harassed and confined in jail, and the extremes of oppression have been applied to them in the separation of parent and child, the blasting of reputation and consignment of innocent persons to a convict's cell. . . .

As the probe continued, the police department was deluged with cops applying for retirement. Croker wasn't the only one who pleaded illness; a long line of politicians and high police officials also took to "sickbeds." After Police Commissioner John McClave had been asked why his appointments and promotions had been followed by big deposits in his bank account, his spirits wilted, he resigned, and his lawyer thought that he might go insane. For the first time in the history of New York a police captain was sent to jail; he admitted accepting a basketful of peaches and another of pears from a commission merchant during a jury trial. And Police Superintendent Thomas F. Byrnes, seated in the witness chair, needed nearly 4 hours to account for the $350,000 he had amassed in real estate and securities.

As a result of the Lexow investigation, about seventy indictments were lodged against police officers, among them two former commissioners, three inspectors, one former inspector, twenty captains, and two former captains. Some were convicted, but higher courts reversed many of these verdicts. Several men were restored to duty on the force. Although this disappointed reformers, they hailed the Reverend Dr. Charles Parkhurst for starting the exposé. It was suggested that an arch be erected in his honor in Madison Square Park, that his birthday be made a national holiday, and that New York be renamed Parkhurst.

Following the Parkhurst investigation and Lexow hearings, Tammany was defeated in the election of 1894. William L. Strong—a Republican, a dry goods merchant, and a banker—was elected mayor with a mandate to reform the police department. He began by making a clean sweep of the board of police commissioners.

The new mayor remembered the name of Theodore Roosevelt, who, as a member of the state legislature in 1884, had conducted an earlier investigation of New York's police practices. By this time the thirty-six-year-old Roosevelt was working in Washington, D.C., as a member of the Civil Service Commission. Mayor Strong now offered to make him president of a new city police board here. Roosevelt accepted for three reasons: He found his civil service work rather routine, he wanted to return to his native state and enhance his image as a Republican reformer, and he was intrigued by the thought of ruling the police force in the nation's largest city.

The three other police commissioners chosen by the mayor were Colonel Frederick D. Grant, son of former President Ulysses S. Grant, a Republican, kindhearted, but a bit weak; Andrew D. Parker, an anti-Tammany Democrat, strong-willed and handsome, a former assistant district attorney, and a brilliant lawyer; and Major Avery D.

Andrews, a Democrat and a West Point graduate who had recently left the army to practice law. Thus, the bipartisan board consisted of two Republicans and two Democrats.

Among the police reporters curious about these new appointees were brash young Lincoln Steffens of the *Evening Post* and his sensitive friend, Jacob A. Riis of the *Evening Sun*. Riis was a Danish immigrant, who had investigated slum conditions and then written a book called *How the Other Half Lives*. Roosevelt was so impressed by Riis' book that he had made a point of becoming friendly with the reporter-author. Riis said of Roosevelt, "I loved him from the day I first saw him."

On May 6, 1895, when they were to take office, Roosevelt actually ran down Mulberry Street to Police Headquarters, while his three fellow appointees walked sedately behind him. Roosevelt yelled, "Hello, Jake!" to Riis and then bounded up the stairs, waving to all the reporters to follow him. In a second-floor office the retiring commissioners were waiting to be replaced. Roosevelt seized Riis, who introduced him to Steffens, and Roosevelt fired questions at the two reporters: "Where are our offices? Where is the boardroom? What do we do first?" The reporters led him to the boardroom, where the outgoing and incoming commissioners faced one another uneasily. The new commissioners were sworn in, Roosevelt shook hands vigorously all around, the old commissioners departed, and Roosevelt called a meeting of the new board.

As was prearranged, Roosevelt was elected president. Although the title gave him no more legal authority than that of his fellow commissioners, Roosevelt assumed from the start that he was superior to them. In his zest to begin the job of cleaning out the stables, he gave an impression of arrogance, which split the board from the outset. Grant and Andrews knew nothing about police work. Although Parker was somewhat familiar with conditions, he resented Roosevelt's domineering attitude. Roosevelt's own study of the city police department as an assemblyman had equipped him in part for his new post, but he wisely chose to pick the brains of two men closer to the situation—Riis and Steffens. They became his kitchen cabinet, which further alienated his colleagues. Parker snarled, "He thinks he's the whole board!"

Under orders from the mayor to clean up the police department, Roosevelt began by demanding that every patrolman in the city must enforce the law. When some failed to do so, he fired them. Although Roosevelt had been born in New York City, at 28 East Twentieth Street, he had ranched in the West and associated with cowboys. Whenever he wanted to summon Riis or Steffens, he would bang open the window of his second-floor office, lean out and give his famous cowboy yell *"Hi, yi, yi!"* Because of his fondness for cowboys, Roosevelt actually made a few of them mounted policemen.

Equally fond of what he called "the Maccabee or fighting Jewish type," Roosevelt urged strong young Jews to become cops. With an ironic chuckle, he once assigned forty Jewish policemen the job of protecting an anti-Semitic agitator.

For the first time in the department's history, Roosevelt named a woman as his secretary. The press hailed this appointment as "another illustration of the onward march of women."

Young Roosevelt's unorthodoxy extended even to his wearing apparel. He often wore a pink shirt, and instead of a vest he wrapped around his waist a black silk sash, whose tasseled ends dangled to his knees. His colorful attire and behavior delighted reporters. Brisbane wrote in the *World:* "We have a real police commissioner. His teeth are big and white, his eyes are small and piercing, his voice is rasping. He makes our policemen feel as the little froggies did when the stork came to rule them. His heart is full of reform and a policeman in a full uniform, with helmet, revolver and nightclub, is no more to him than a plain, every day human being."

Roosevelt's swollen ambition led Riis and Steffens to believe he was aiming for the White House. One day they bluntly asked him if he was working to become President of the United States. Roosevelt leaped up behind his desk, ran around it with clenched fists and bared teeth, and almost attacked Riis. "Don't you dare ask me that!" he roared. "Don't you put such ideas into my head! No friend of mine would ever say a thing like that, you—you—" Riis, who adored Roosevelt, was shocked, and his face showed it. Regaining control, Roosevelt lowered his voice and said to the two astonished reporters, "I must be wanting to be President. Every young man does. But I won't let myself think of it. I must not because, if I do, I will begin to work for it, I'll be careful, calculating, cautious in word and act, and so—I'll beat myself. See?" The three men remained friends.

Eager to observe everything himself, Roosevelt asked Riis to lead him on nighttime expeditions throughout the city. They would meet at 2 A.M. on the steps of the Union League Club and prowl about, hunting for delinquent cops. They saw policemen chatting in saloons, found one asleep in a butter tub on a sidewalk, and discovered others far distant from their assigned posts. One night Roosevelt surprised a beer-quaffing cop outside a saloon on West Forty-second Street, chased him fifty yards, collared the culprit, and brought him up on departmental charges the next day.

No policeman knew at what hour of the day or night Roosevelt's spectacles and teeth might come gleaming around a corner. As word of his nocturnal adventures spread from the police force to the citizens themselves, he was nicknamed Haroun al Roosevelt. A mischievous reporter disguised himself in a broad-brimmed hat and skulked throughout town, scaring people by chattering his teeth at them in the Roosevelt manner. Peddlers sold whistles shaped like "Teddy's teeth." Able to laugh at himself, Roosevelt said, when shown one of these novelties, that they were "very pretty." Then he added, "All short-sighted men have some facial characteristics of which they are unconscious. I cannot be blamed for having good teeth, or this characteristic of a shortsighted man."

Unwisely, Roosevelt kept saying "I" and "my policy," disregarding the feelings and advice of his three colleagues. Relations among the four men deteriorated so badly that Roosevelt found himself fighting, not only corruption, but attacks within the police board itself. In bitter exchanges the commissioners called one another names, such as faker and crook. Despite the schism, Roosevelt instituted so many reforms that he became a national figure. Newspapers across the country wrote laudatory articles about him. Even the London *Times* gave considerable space to the doings on Mulberry Street.

Roosevelt formed a police bicycle squad. He gave the police a telephonic communications system. He ordered training for police recruits before they were assigned to duty. He insisted that all policemen be polite to the public. He based promotions on merit. He fired "Clubber" Williams. Aware of the way the wind was blowing, Police Superintendent Thomas F. Byrnes, who had confessed to the Lexow committee that he was worth $350,000, voluntarily resigned.

In spite of these achievements, Roosevelt became as unpopular with the public, as with old-line cops on the force. He made the mistake of demanding the enforcement of all laws—good or bad. When he ordered the arrest of every saloonkeeper who sold liquor on

Sunday, an uproar followed. Workmen, who liked to slip into bars by rear doors for a friendly glass on Sunday, were outraged. The newspapers turned on Roosevelt. So did Mayor Strong.

Other blue laws also gave Roosevelt trouble. Among these were ordinances prohibiting soda fountains, florists, delicatessen owners, bootblacks, and ice dealers from peddling their wares on Sunday. Roosevelt vacillated between enforcing the ancient statutes and insisting that he was not interested in them. He did let the police close soda parlors. He gave the lie to a story that orders had gone out against flower selling, but the New York *Times* reported the arrest of a peddler who had sold five cents' worth of violets to a detective. Arrests of the petty offenders probably were the work of Tammany politicians, eager to get even with Roosevelt.

Citizens complained, policemen grumbled, the police board quarrels became ever more acrimonious, and Teddy Roosevelt soon found himself perhaps the most unpopular man in town. His life was threatened. He was shadowed day and night. An attempt was even made to catch him in a compromising situation.

Circus impresario P. T. Barnum had left a fortune of $4,100,000 and exactly $444,444.40 of this went to his nephew, Herbert Barnum Seeley. This blithe young man, who flitted about the fringes of New York society, decided to give a bachelor party for his brother, Clinton Burton Seeley, who was engaged to a society belle. Herbert invited 22 dashing young blades, some of them married men, to gather at 9 P.M. on December 19, 1896, in a private ballroom of Louis Sherry's fashionable restaurant, on Fifth Avenue at Thirty-seventh Street. That night, after the shades were drawn, champagne corks popped, and the revelry began. Three scantily clad girls undulated through sensuous dances. One already was notorious. Serious scholars of the belly dance can't agree whether she was an Algerian, named Ashea Wabe, or an Egyptian, named Fahreda Mahzar, but at the Columbian Exposition in Chicago she had performed the hootchy-kootchy under the pseudonym Little Egypt. At the Seeley party this little lady wore diamonds on her garters, and the men watching her soon wore diamonds in their eyes. Then, just as the party was getting interesting, in burst a police captain and 6 detectives.

Curiously, no arrests were made. In his autobiography Jacob Riis suggested an explanation for this omission. He said that Roosevelt's enemies within the police department raided the Seeley party in the belief that they would catch him there. The plot failed because Roosevelt did not attend the affair.

The young president of the police board finally wearied of his thankless job. He negotiated for an appointment as Assistant Secretary of the Navy and in April, 1897, resigned his New York post to return to the nation's capital. Although Roosevelt failed to rid the city of all corruption during his two years in office, he greatly improved the police department.

Chapter 35

HEARST WAGES WAR

WILLIAM RANDOLPH HEARST galloped onto the New York scene in 1895 like a one-man cavalry charge. For the next several decades his influence was felt not only in this city but also throughout the entire world.

He was born in San Francisco, the only child of a doting mother and of George Hearst, a multimillionaire mineowner, rancher, and Democratic Senator from California. Young Hearst studied at Harvard until he was expelled for sending every faculty member a chamberpot with his picture pasted on the bottom. After working briefly for the New York *World,* Hearst talked his father into buying the San Francisco *Examiner* for him in 1887.

Senator Hearst died in 1891 and left his widow $17,000,000. When Mrs. Hearst learned that her beloved son wanted to invade New York's world of journalism, she sold her seven-sixteenths interest in the Anaconda Copper Mining Company to the Rothschilds of London for $7,500,000 and gave the sum to him. For the bargain price of $180,000, Hearst bought the *Morning Journal* on October 7, 1895. The *Journal* occupied part of the *Tribune's* shabby little building at Park Row and Spruce Street. Hearst soon outfitted a magnificent office for himself on the second floor.

Only thirty-two years old when he took up residence in New York, Hearst was slender and stood six feet two inches tall. He had a long face, icy-blue eyes pinched together above a pointed nose, and blond hair. He behaved in a lordly, yet courteous, manner, spoke in a high-pitched voice, shook hands limply, and teetered back and forth on his heels while talking. He never smoked or drank or told dirty stories or swore in public. In private, though, he sometimes flew into tantrums. A megalomaniac, Hearst craved to become President of the United States.

Now that he owned the *Journal* and had more than $7,000,000 left to operate and promote it, Hearst began a vicious circulation war with Pulitzer's *World,* the leading newspaper in New York. Because the *World* always championed the underdog, Hearst decided to scrape up his own issues. He soon learned that Cuban patriots sought to free Cuba from Spanish tyranny. For more than a quarter century New York had been a haven for Cuban exiles plotting the downfall of the Spanish government on their island home. By 1898 the center of revolutionary intrigue in New York was 66 Broadway in the office of Horatio Rubens, a New York lawyer who sympathized with the Cubans. To this junta headquarters Hearst sent *Journal* reporters, and before long the *Journal* office itself was being frequented by swarthy exiles. Their tales about Spanish atrocities were only partly true, but Hearst believed them. In the fight for Cuban independence he thought that he had found the issue which would enable him to win his battle with the *World.*

With an audacity seldom matched in American history, Hearst assumed the role of spokesman for the United States. In a letter to a Cuban who called himself the president of the republic of Cuba, Hearst began by saying, "Sir: Will you kindly state through the *New York Journal,* acting for the people of the United States, the position of the Cuban Government on the offer of autonomy for the island by the Government of Spain? . . ." Even before William McKinley was inaugurated President of the United States on March 5, 1897, Hearst demanded that McKinley openly declare himself in favor of the independence of Cuba. When McKinley failed to do so at once, Hearst charged that he was "listening with eager ear to the threats of the big Business Interests. . . ." It was true that Wall Street did not want war with Spain because of American investments in Cuba. It was equally true that McKinley was influenced by business leaders, but the President hesitated because of his humanitarian impulses.

In one of Hearst's earliest signed editorials in the *Journal* he had announced that newspapers had the power to declare war. Seeking fame and eager to eclipse the *World,* Hearst now tried to plunge the United States into open conflict with Spain. Pulitzer hung back at first, but when he saw the *Journal* increase its circulation by whipping up a war spirit, he succumbed. Pulitzer actually said, "I rather like the idea of war—not a big one—but one that will arouse interest and give me a chance to gauge the reflex in our circulation figures."

With both papers trying to outdo one another as warmongers, their circulation figures shot to record-breaking heights. They published one extra after another, and when the Spanish-American War actually broke out, the *Journal* sometimes printed as many as forty editions a day. The *Journal* faked stories and photographs and sketches. Hearst sent illustrator Frederic Remington to Cuba to report the atrocities allegedly occurring there. Remington soon cabled Hearst: "Everything quiet. No trouble here. There will be no war. I wish to return . . . Remington." Hearst sent to Havana this memorable answer: "Please remain. You furnish the pictures and I will furnish the war . . . Hearst." As the *Journal* and the *World* piled one sensation on another, Edwin L. Godkin, editor of the New York *Evening Post,* declared:

> Nothing so disgraceful as the behavior of these two newspapers has ever been known in the history of journalism. Gross misrepresentations of facts, deliberate invention of tales calculated to excite the public, and wanton recklessness in the construction of headlines which outdid even these inventions, have combined to make the issues of the most widely circulated newspapers firebrands scattered broadcast throughout the community.

Under pressure of the *Journal* and *World* and the war hawks in Congress, President McKinley slowly began to abandon his position of neutrality. The Prime Minister of Spain said in bewilderment to an

American correspondent, "The newspapers of your country seem to be more powerful than the government."

On the recommendation of America's consul general in Cuba the 24-gun battleship *Maine* sailed into Havana harbor as a "friendly act of courte.y" to Spain. After she anchored there on January 25, 1898, the *Journal* boasted in a headline: "OUR FLAG IN HAVANA AT LAST." At 9:40 on the sultry night of February 15 the *Maine* blew up, killing 260 of her complement of 350 officers and men. Among the dead were 22 American Negroes, whom the Spaniards called Smoked Yankees. To this very day no one knows the cause of the explosion, but Hearst, Pulitzer, and other American jingoists seized on the tragedy as a reason for going to war. "Remember the *Maine*" became the slogan of the hour, and anyone voicing doubt that the Spaniards had blown up the battleship was branded a traitor.

President McKinley still hoped to preserve peace. For his fair-mindedness he was denounced by Assistant Secretary of the Navy Theodore Roosevelt as having "no more backbone than a chocolate éclair." Roosevelt was a leading warmonger. At a private Gridiron dinner in Washington, McKinley's closest adviser, Mark Hanna, spoke out against war. Roosevelt retorted, "We will have this war for the freedom of Cuba, Senator Hanna, in spite of the timidity of commercial interests." In the absence of his superior, the Secretary of the Navy, Roosevelt deployed warships so that they could take up what he considered the best offensive posture. In regard to the naval strength of the United States and Spain the ratio was about three to two in favor of the United States.

Aware that they would lose any war with America, Spanish officials conceded point after point, trying in almost every way to avoid open conflict. On February 18 the Spanish cruiser *Vizcaya* paid a courtesy call to the port of New York. When her commander learned of the loss of the *Maine,* he expressed regrets, half-masted his colors in mourning, and declined to take part in the scheduled ceremonies of welcome. Despite this, the *World* shrilled that the *Vizcaya* had treacherous intentions, saying, "While lying off the Battery, her shells will explode on the Harlem River and in the suburbs of Brooklyn." But the Spanish cruiser left New York without even firing a pistol shot.

Spain now asked for the recall of the American consul general in Cuba, Congress appropriated $50,000,000 for defense, the War Department began to mobilize the army, Pope Leo XIII appealed for peace, and the United States cabled an ultimatum to Spain. In the Knickerbocker Theatre at Broadway and Thirty-eighth Street audiences went wild with patriotism as the song "Unchain the Dogs of War" was introduced into the musical comedy *The Bride Elect*. Hearst sent *Journal* reporters throughout the New York area to interview mothers of sailors who had died in the *Maine*. Every day Hearst worked busily in his office in the Tribune Building. Pulitzer seldom visited the golden-domed World Building, directing his editorial staff from one or another of his five mansions or from aboard his yacht. Both the *Journal* and the *World* raised their price from one to two cents. The *Journal* introduced its readers to a new card game, called Game of War With Spain.

Because the American navy did not own a single troopship, the government began buying yachts, coastal steamers, seagoing tugs, and other vessels to transport troops to Cuba, to patrol the American coast, and to blockade our harbors. When J. Pierpont Morgan was told that the government wanted his yacht, the *Corsair,* he twisted and turned in every way to keep his beloved vessel, but without avail. The *Corsair* was taken to the Brooklyn Navy Yard, where her beautiful mahogany was ripped out. Hearst freely offered the government his yacht, the *Buccaneer*. John Jacob Astor placed his yacht, the *Nourmahal,* at the disposal of the United States, equipped an artillery battery, and later served as its lieutenant colonel. Jay Gould's daughter, Helen M. Gould, gave the navy $100,000.

On April 23 President McKinley called for 125,000 volunteers. Theodore Roosevelt resigned as Assistant Secretary of the Navy to organize the First Volunteer Cavalry Regiment. He wrote his family that he had plans for a "jim-dandy regiment" in case of war and that "it would be awful to miss the fun." He bought a uniform from Brooks Brothers in New York, sewed extra sets of pince-nez inside it, and rushed to San Antonio, Texas, where the regiment was being organized. The elite corps, which took the name of the Rough Riders, consisted of 1,000 cowboys, Indians, Ivy League athletes, and 4 New York policemen. Totally without military experience, Roosevelt accepted a commission as lieutenant colonel under the commanding officer, Colonel Leonard Wood, an army surgeon, who had fought Indians in the West. Unlike army regulars, who wore blue woolen shirts, the Rough Riders wore thin khaki uniforms.

On April 25 Congress declared that a state of war between the United States and Spain had existed since April 21. For the next two days the *Journal's* front pages asked, "HOW DO YOU LIKE THE JOURNAL'S WAR?" Someone apparently persuaded Hearst to remove the gauche boast, but in conversations with staff members he continued to refer to the conflict as "our war."

By this time New York had become the first motion-picture capital in history. When war was declared, two pioneer film makers saw an opportunity. J. Stuart Blackton and Albert E. Smith rushed to their movie studio on the roof of the Morse Building, at 140 Nassau Street, and made a short film, called *Tearing Down the Spanish Flag*. In the movie's climactic moment, Blackton's hand reached out from one side of the screen to pull down the Spanish colors. Shown in vaudeville houses throughout New York, the patriotic film became a smashing success.

Cables were cut between New York and Havana. The entrance to New York harbor was mined and patrolled. George B. McClellan, Jr., then a Democratic Congressman from New York, and later mayor of this city, declared in his posthumous memoirs, "The Spanish-American War was one of the most unnecessary that has ever been fought. Its alleged purpose, the freeing of Cuba, could have been attained without firing a shot, spending a dollar or wasting a man. . . ." * Nevertheless, McClellan warned the House of Representatives that "our seacoast was entirely undefended, that we had neither great guns nor ammunition, and that any of the first-class navies could lie outside New York and destroy the city without the guns of the city's alleged defenses being able to reach them."

Spanish Rear Admiral Pascual Cervera sailed with a formidable Spanish fleet from the Cape Verde Islands and steered west. Americans learned that he had left but did not know his destination. A rumor spread: He was going to descend on the Atlantic seaboard. Panic ensued. New York hastily reinforced its defenses. Rich New Yorkers raced out of town to inland points that seemed safer. The owners of Long Island summer hotels begged the government for protection. But instead of attacking New York or any other Atlantic port, the Spanish admiral turned up in the harbor of Santiago de Cuba on the southern shore of Cuba.

The war spirit affected gambling in New York. Whenever a phone

* From *The Gentleman and the Tiger, The Autobiography of George B. McClellan, Jr.,* edited by Harold C. Syrett. Copyright © 1956 by The New York Historical Society; copyright © 1956 by Harold C. Syrett. Published by J. B. Lippincott Company.

rang in a bookie joint, the man who answered would not say, "Hello," but "Havana." The correct response, indicating that the caller was to be trusted, was the muttered phrase "Remember the *Maine*." In 1897 a songwriter, named Charles K. Harris, had dashed off a sentimental ballad entitled "Break the News to Mother." This concerned the death of a fireman. After war broke out, Harris rewrote his lyrics, changing the fireman to a soldier. "Break the News to Mother" became a smash hit.

National guard units gathered in New York City armories the day after war was declared. Three days later the first company of volunteers set up camp on the Hempstead plains of Long Island twenty-two miles east of the city. The camp was called Camp Black for New York Governor Frank S. Black, whose term had ended in 1896. The Brooklyn *Eagle* erected a tent and displayed a banner inviting Brooklyn soldiers and their visitors to take their ease within the canvas shelter. Not to be outdone, the New York *Journal* proclaimed: "The bulletin service of the *Journal* is now perfected to such an extent that the news is posted on all the *Journal* boards in and out of the city at the same time it appears on the board at the main office." Camp Black had been thrown together so hastily that it was a squalid and uncomfortable post. With the usual cynicism of soldiers, New York boys decorated their tents with names such as The Suicide Club, Waldorf-Astoria, and Metropolitan Museum of Art.

On June 13 Roosevelt and his Rough Riders sailed out of Tampa. The main body of American troops left Key West between June 12 and 14. Beginning June 20, this land force of 17,000 regulars and volunteers landed at Daiquiri, 14 miles east-southeast of Santiago de Cuba. When war was declared, Cuba contained 155,302 Spanish regular troops and 41,518 Cuban irregulars. Cuban insurgents actively in the field against Spain numbered no more than 15,000. The day after American troops landed at Daiquiri, they began moving toward Santiago.

The most important land combat of the Spanish-American War consisted of 2 battles fought on July 1, 1898, near Santiago. At the village of El Caney, 4 miles northeast of the city, 7,000 United States troops took a strong post garrisoned by about 600 of the enemy. South of El Caney lay a series of ridges, known collectively as San Juan. The highest of these, San Juan Hill, was captured that July 1 by American forces.

The Battle of San Juan Hill was fought mainly by United States regulars. The Seventy-first New York was the only militia regiment present. Badly officered, sweating in wool shirts, and the black powder of their rifles emitting a telltale target every time they fired, members of the Seventy-first broke and then panicked. Their disgrace was witnessed by a *World* correspondent, Stephen Crane. His dispatch, published in Pulitzer's paper, angered Hearst, who called it a slander on the heroism of New Yorkers. Many men of the Seventy-first, that fateful day, recouped their morale and joined the regulars as individuals, but the black mark they had earned was not soon forgiven by the public.

A better performance was turned in by Negro soldiers from New York. Members of the Ninth and Tenth cavalries, composed entirely of Negroes, fought beside the Rough Riders and won their admiration. Roosevelt later wrote: "As I heard one of the Rough Riders say after the charge at San Juan: 'Well, the Ninth and Tenth men are all right. They can drink out of our canteens.'" Because of the valor of these Negroes, an area in New York City was dubbed San Juan Hill. This was located at the northern end of Hell's Kitchen, west of Columbus Circle, along West Sixty-first, Sixty-second, and Sixty-third streets.

Like Roosevelt, Hearst saw action in the war. After he gave his yacht to the navy, he bought another one, named the *Sylvia*. Wearing a yachting cap and sporting a pistol, Hearst led his own fleet of twenty cutters to Cuba. On July 3 Admiral Cervera's fleet tried to break out of Santiago Harbor. At that very moment Hearst's private fleet was circling the American fleet within range of American guns, compelling the American navy to hold its fire. After the Hearst navy had pulled out of range, the U.S. navy was able to bombard the fleeing Spanish ships.

Hearst was in Cuba a total of seventeen days. There he met a Cuban, named Honoré Laine, who had served him as a correspondent. This rebel told Hearst that forty Spanish prisoners taken at El Caney by the Americans had been turned over to his Cuban band. Hearst asked what the rebels had done with their Spanish captives. Laine replied casually, "We cut off their heads, of course." Since this was a war of his own making and since Laine was on his side, Hearst excused the barbarity, writing in a dispatch to the *Journal*: "The Cuban is tender and gentle. One seldom finds a man of more generous and gracious impulses than this Laine. His hour has come and he is lost in the almost savage enjoyment of it."

Santiago surrendered on July 17, and nine days later the Spanish government asked for peace terms. On August 4 the War Department authorized the removal of American troops from Cuba. Now arose a great controversy. More American soldiers had fallen victim to yellow fever, malaria, and typhoid than had died in battle. New York City objected to the landing of the army in its harbor because of the danger of these infectious diseases. At the time no one knew that malaria was caused by mosquito bite.

Finally, it was decided that the returning troops would be landed at Montauk Point on the eastern tip of Long Island, 127 miles from New York. In haste and confusion on those early days of August an army reception center was thrown together and named Camp Wyckoff, in honor of a colonel of the regulars killed at San Juan Hill. Hospital sites were staked out. Wells were drilled. Wires were strung along the ground. A strike by Brooklyn carpenters increased the problem of creating the camp from scratch. With no warehouses ready, army supplies could not be unloaded, so Long Island Rail Road freight cars were backed up from Montauk Point the 21 miles to Amagansett.

The omnipresent *Journal* put up three tents at Montauk. Soon the paper printed headlines about starving men, dying heroes, and food rotting on transports. One *Journal* banner shouted about "MURDER THAT IS BEING DONE AT MONTAUK." Red Cross workers hastened to the camp. Ladies' aid societies went into action. Society women sent their private chefs to the site. Soon the bivouacked soldiers feasted on pheasant and squab, champagne and brandy. Under the blistering sun and starry sky they lived in luxury. At last both the good and the bad came to an end. All the volunteers were discharged. The regulars were transferred to various army posts.

This shifted part of the load to New York City. Unconscious soldiers were taken off Long Island trains and driven to Bellevue Hospital. Other sick soldiers were found in the streets in a state of collapse. Doctors and nurses worked around the clock. Ultimately, all the city's hospitals became so jammed with bedridden soldiers that some had to be transferred to Newport and Boston.

A public outcry arose about the government beef served American soldiers during the war. Many men denounced it as "embalmed beef," and Roosevelt himself considered it "horrible stuff." Newspapers demanded that a special tribunal be established to decide the issue. After a three-month hearing a military court of inquiry ruled that there was no valid reason to believe that the beef was unfit to eat. The verdict failed to convince Fiorello LaGuardia, whose father had become ill after eating some of the meat.

The circulation war between the *Journal* and the *World* ended in a draw. Although Hearst had been unable to kill off the *World*, he succeeded in establishing his *Journal* as a force to be reckoned with in New York. His extensive coverage of the war cost him most of the $7,00,000 he got from his mother. Cable dispatches between Cuba and New York were priced as high as $2.12 a word. Both papers had published so many extras that newsdealers returned thousands of unsold copies at an enormous loss to both Hearst and Pulitzer. Each newspaper claimed a total circulation of 1,250,000, but cable bills, the rental of fleets of tugs, and the like had wiped out their profits. Both publishers were lucky that the war didn't last longer. Their rivalry resulted in a new phrase, "yellow journalism." This took its name from a comic strip in the *World* entitled "Hogan's Alley." Drawn by R. F. Outcault, its bad boy hero was called the Yellow Kid.

The Spanish-American War had been unnecessary, brief, inexpensive, patriotic, and relatively bloodless. The United States won hands down. This was a turning point in American history. The Spanish empire was virtually dissolved, and for the first time the United States gained an empire of its own. By acquiring the Philippines, Guam, and Puerto Rico under the peace treaty, the United States emerged as a world power. The center of gravity in this greatly expanded nation was New York City, which now expanded in its own way.

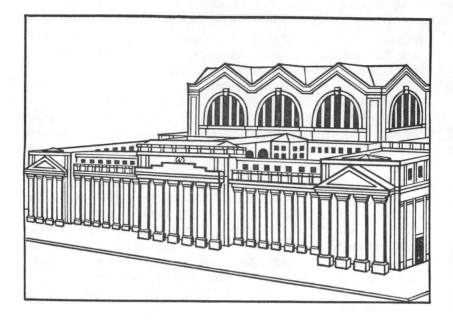

Chapter 36

CREATION OF GREATER NEW YORK

ANDREW HASWELL GREEN, who won a medal calling him "the father of Greater New York," was born in Massachusetts. He was the city's nineteenth-century Robert Moses. Historian Allan Nevins said of Green: "No citizen ever did more to improve and adorn the municipality."

Green was educated in an academy in his hometown of Worcester, groomed himself for West Point, gave up the idea of entering the army, became a clerk in a New York store, studied law, and entered into legal partnership with Samuel J. Tilden. Then he developed into a civic leader of vast ability and unspotted integrity. His activities

450

were so various and his influence so great that it is difficult to understand how one man could accomplish so much.

As city comptroller, he reestablished the city's credit following the Tweed scandals. He planned the American Museum of Natural History. He founded the New York Zoological Society. He established the American Scenic and Historic Preservation Society. He devised the plan to consolidate the Astor, Lenox, and Tilden Foundations as the New York Public Library. He was president of the Central Park commission, and a bench placed in the park honored him as "directing genius of Central Park in its formative period."

A man with a clear mind and forceful personality, Green had a strong nose, sunken eyes and a gray beard. For thirty years he was obsessed with the idea of creating an "imperial city," a proposal his enemies called Green's hobby.

Ever since 1686, when the Dongan charter was granted, New York City had consisted of just the island of Manhattan. However, consolidation of areas north, east, and south of Manhattan was predicted in 1857 by Henry C. Murphy, the former Brooklyn mayor who had sparked construction of the Brooklyn Bridge. Murphy said, "It requires no spirit of prophecy to foretell the union of New York and Brooklyn at no distant day. The (East) river which divides them will soon cease to be a line of separation, and, bestrode by the colossus of commerce, will prove a link which will bind them together."

It was in 1868 that Andrew H. Green first dreamed of integrating the areas around New York City into one great metropolis. He argued that the lines of unity had been laid down by nature when it "grouped together in a close indissoluble relation, at the mouth of a great river, our three islands, Manhattan, Long and Staten, making them buttresses and breakwaters of a capacious harbor."

The improvement of transit facilities gave impetus to his scheme, and a small step toward consolidation was taken in 1874. Three townships in what is now the western Bronx were taken from Westchester County and annexed to New York City. With that one stroke the city nearly doubled its area, jumped the Harlem River for the first time, and pushed north as far as Yonkers. Now the city, from the Battery to Yonkers, was sixteen miles long. In 1895 three other townships—or parts of townships—in the western Bronx were added to the city. These two annexations transferred a total of thirty-nine square miles from Westchester County to New York City.

The part of the city known today as Queens and Staten Island consisted of scattered villages. The situation in Brooklyn was very different. Incorporated as a village in 1816 and as a city in 1834, Brooklyn absorbed the communities of Greenpoint, Williamsburg, and Bushwick in 1855. It took over New Lots in 1866. It added Flatbush, New Utrecht, and Gravesend in 1894. Flatlands, the last township still outside the corporate limits, became part of Brooklyn in 1896. All these gains made Brooklyn the third or fourth largest city in the United States.

Acting on a petition by Andrew H. Green, the state legislature and the governor on May 8, 1890, jointly created "a commission to inquire into the expediency of consolidating the various municipalities of the State of New York occupying the several islands in the harbor of New York." Green was appointed chairman. He had won a skirmish; but many battles lay ahead, and ultimate victory was far from certain.

Many groups opposed consolidation. The people of Brooklyn preferred their slower pace of life to the frenetic tempo of Manhattan. New York businessmen thought that the addition of undeveloped areas might increase their tax burdens. Upstate Republicans were afraid that a metropolis might dominate the state. Because Brooklyn, Queens, and Staten Island were normally Republican, Tammany fretted lest their inclusion weaken its power.

Green and his colleagues advanced counterarguments. They pointed out that political separation had become a costly and cumbersome anachronism. Brooklyn's government duplicated that of New York. Staten Island and Queens residents suffered from restrictions imposed by small governmental units. Citizens of outlying areas would benefit from consolidation because of lower taxes, lower interest rates on mortgages, more public works, better business opportunities, and increased employment.

For all his logic, Green was able to accomplish little until his cause was taken up by Thomas C. Platt, the Republican boss of the state. Platt's motives remain a mystery. He may have felt that by uniting the Republican strongholds of Brooklyn, Queens, and Staten Island, he could bring the enlarged city under permanent Republican control.

In the prolonged drive to create Greater New York the pro and con forces were motivated by a variety of factors—political, economic, social, sectional, and selfish. Finally, an act of the state legislature, signed into law on May 4, 1897, called for consolidation on January 1, 1898.

This gave the city a new charter. (A charter is to a city what a constitution is to a state.) The city's counties and boroughs were declared to have common boundaries. A county is a political subdivision of a *state*. In New York City a borough is a political subdivision of the *city*. Manhattan became the county and borough of New York; Brooklyn became the county and borough of Kings; the villages lying north of Brooklyn became the county and borough of Queens; the villages of Staten Island became the county and borough of Richmond. Although the Bronx became a city borough in 1898, it did not become a county—the last county created by the state—until 1914.

Each borough could elect its own president. These borough presidents acted as local mayors responsible for some local improvements and administration. Legislative power for the entire city was vested in the sixty-member board of aldermen and the twenty-nine-member city council. Executive power was centralized in the mayor, whose term of office was increased from two to four years. Now came the question, Who would be the first mayor of Greater New York?

Boss Platt picked attorney Benjamin Tracy as the Republican candidate. Tracy, however, was unacceptable to a Republican party faction, which nominated Seth Low, former mayor of Brooklyn. Thus, the anti-Tammany forces were split in the expanded city's first election. Tammany Boss Richard Croker chose an obscure judge, named Robert A. Van Wyck, as the Democratic candidate. Van Wyck was elected the first mayor of Greater New York, and Tammany again vaulted into the saddle.

New York, Chicago, and Philadelphia had striven to win the title of the largest American city. With consolidation, New York City easily won. The new charter trebled the city's area and nearly doubled its population. It increased New York's total population by nearly 126 percent over the figure of the previous decade. New York now had 3,393,252 inhabitants to Chicago's 1,698,575. The city's extreme north-south length was 36 miles. Its maximum east-west breadth was 16½ miles. It contained a total of 320 square miles. The geographical center of the city now lay in northern Brooklyn

200 feet west of Reid Avenue between Van Buren Street and Greene Avenue. Among all the cities of the world New York was second in size only to London.

With the approach of January 1, 1898, the New York *Tribune* exulted: "The sun will rise this morning upon the greatest experiment in municipal government that the world has ever known—the enlarged city." Of course, some mourned the passing of Little Old New York. Among these was outgoing Mayor William L. Strong, who suggested holding a "funeral service." Indeed it began to appear that city officials planned nothing except a stuffy speech or two to celebrate the founding of Greater New York.

Into the vacuum rushed William Randolph Hearst. A city booster when it suited his purposes and addicted to fireworks, Hearst proposed that the *Journal* organize a fete and pay all the costs. Although no city father openly admitted it, Hearst's offer was accepted. *Journal* staff members collected $500 from Tammany Boss Croker, J. Pierpont Morgan, and others, together with smaller sums from average citizens. Hearst himself donated thousands of dollars to bring the total to more than $7,000. Singing societies, military units, bands, civic organizations, marching societies, and bicycle clubs were recruited. Carloads of fireworks were purchased. The *Journal* offered 10 silver loving cups as prizes for the best costume, the best float, and the best of everything among several participating groups. The leader of the Seventh Regiment band set to music an "Ode to Greater New York," which began: "Hail, thee, city born today,/Commercial monarch by the sea,/Whose throne is by Hudson's way,/'Mid thousands' homesteads join'd to thee."

Brooklyn's twenty-eighth and last mayor, Frederick W. Wurster, sat in Brooklyn's City Hall, soon to become Borough Hall, to perform his last official act. He turned over to Greater New York nearly $10,000,000 in Brooklyn funds. With consolidation the annual budget of the expanded city now exceeded $90,000,000. As Wurster sighed and signed, the weather worsened outside his windows. That evening of December 31, 1897, rain began falling. Gradually it turned into wet snow, but this did not dampen the spirits of citizens who gathered at Union Square to march to City Hall for the climactic moment of midnight. Men tippled freely, but the police were indulgent with drunkards on this great occasion. After the procession had got under way and while a horse-drawn float was mushing past the Broadway Central Hotel, at 665 Broadway, exploding fireworks frightened the horses. They bolted into a band, smashed several instruments, and injured 15 persons. Despite the accident, the celebrants danced through the dank streets to City Hall Park, which glowed in the garish glare of 500 magnesium lights.

As midnight approached, the crowd of 100,000 umbrella-huddling people broke into "Auld Lang Syne." Exactly at the stroke of 12 their voices hushed, and all waited breathlessly. Mayor James Phelan of San Francisco, sitting in that West Coast city, pressed a button that flicked an electric impulse 3,250 miles to New York City, and sent the new blue and white flag of Greater New York swishing up the staff on the cupola of City Hall. The waiting crowd roared. Near the post office at the southern end of City Hall Park a battery of field guns thundered a 100-gun salute, and skyrockets slashed into the murky heavens. Even the New York *Tribune,* hardly a Hearst admirer, admitted that this was the "biggest, noisiest and most hilarious New Year's Eve celebration that Manhattan Island has ever known." At long last, on January 1, 1898, at the mouth of the Hudson River, there was created the "imperial city" of which Andrew H. Green had dreamed.

Chapter 37

OPENING OF THE TWENTIETH CENTURY

J. PIERPONT MORGAN dealt himself another hand of solitaire and listened for the twentieth century. It was the night of December 31, 1899, and Morgan sat in the library of his Madison Avenue mansion. Logs crackled in the fireplace. To the left of the hearth stood a bookcase holding two metal statues of knights in armor, a clock perched between them. From time to time Morgan may have lifted his dark-hazel eyes to glance at the clock.

The hulking six-foot financier sat at his desk in his usual flat-footed position, toes turned out. With strong and well-formed fingers, he laid out the cards, playing almost automatically, as he did when he had something on his mind. A long cigar protruded from the paper cigar holder clenched in his teeth under his mustache.

456

Although it was almost midnight in Morgan's mahogany study, it was the high noon of capitalism in America, and no American stood out so starkly as he. Morgan was centralizing the control of industry and credit. He was the capitalist's capitalist. President William McKinley of the large head and barrel torso sat in the White House; but businessmen guided the nation's destiny, and Morgan guided the businessmen. Indifferent to social reform and defiant of public opinion, Morgan felt that he owed the public nothing.

The clock began tolling the hour of midnight. Morgan may have raised his massive head at the first bong. So the twentieth century had arrived? Very well. Within a little more than a year Morgan was to create the first billion-dollar corporation in history, the United States Steel Corporation. Bong!

At the turn of the century eighteen-year-old Fiorello LaGuardia was earning $100 a year as a clerk in the American consulate in Budapest, Hungary. James J. "Jimmy" Walker was a skinny nineteen-year-old attending LaSalle Academy, a business school on Second Avenue, and working as a part-time referee at prizefights in Brotty's Bar on Hudson Street. Alfred E. Smith was a slim twenty-six-year-old who worked for the city's commissioner of jurors, checking applications for exemptions from jury duty. Franklin D. Roosevelt was an eighteen-year-old standing an inch more than 6 feet but weighing only 146 pounds; he sang in Harvard's Freshman Glee Club. Robert Moses was an eleven-year-old boy, who had moved with his family from New Haven to New York in 1897; he felt that New York was too big, too crowded, too noisy, and too confused. Theodore Roosevelt, now forty-two, was governor of New York State, partly because he had become a hero of the Spanish-American War. William Randolph Hearst, at the age of thirty-seven, was cruising up the Nile in search of Egyptian art treasures.

The city, state, and nation this year of 1900 enjoyed prosperity. Never had such good times been seen from coast to coast. A New York minister exulted: "Laws are becoming more just, rulers more humane. Music is becoming sweeter and books wiser. Homes are happier and the individual heart becoming at once more just and more gentle." Except for the Boer War in South Africa, the Boxer Rebellion in China, and unrest in the Philippines, peace reigned throughout most of the world.

Sixty percent of all Americans lived in small towns or on farms. New York City itself had more than 2,000 farms, occupying nearly a quarter of its land. But the city was in the middle of a building boom. Land and buildings on Manhattan alone were valued at $3,600,000,000, having risen $2,600,000,000 since the year 1865. The city's 40,000 manufacturing establishments accounted for more than 60 percent of the manufacturing of the entire state. Hundreds of firms escaped taxes by incorporating themselves in other states, paid almost nothing for fire and police protection, yet asked the city for help whenever their underpaid workers struck. The shopping center had reached Twenty-third Street and was gliding north toward Thirty-fourth Street.

Wages were low. City employees put in a 10-hour day, with half an hour for lunch, but many had to work even longer. At 4 A.M. the streets were filled with people heading for their jobs, and any worker who reported late was sure to be penalized. To work from 5 A.M. to 9 P.M. was customary. Twelve-year-old boys and girls were allowed to earn wages if they went to school 80 days a year. Because of undernourishment, some children were slow to learn their lessons. Hundreds of youngsters lived on canal boats along the waterfront, seldom attended school, constantly played hide-and-seek with truant officers. There were hundreds, if not thousands, of homeless children in the city.

Nearly 7 percent of the population was illiterate, and 173,000 residents could not speak English. Of the city's inhabitants, 37 percent were foreign-born. About 25 percent of these immigrants came from Germany; 22 percent, from Ireland; 12 percent, from Russia; 11 percent, from Italy; 6 percent, from Austria; and 5 percent, from England. The remainder had arrived here from all other parts of the world. Although most Irishmen were still members of the working class, no longer were they caricatured on the stage as living in shanties and dressing in rags. The city's 700,000 Jews lived mainly on the Lower East Side. The 145,000 local Italians staged their first Columbus Day parade in 1900. Between 50,000 and 60,000 Negroes were residents of New York. The main Negro center was near West Fifty-third Street in Manhattan, although a large Negro community was also developing in Brooklyn.

New York was the last American city of any size to establish public high schools. The De Witt Clinton, Wadleigh, and Peter Cooper high schools were opened in 1897, and in 1900 one De Witt Clinton student was an energetic Irish boy, named Grover Whalen.

Only 13,700 of the 500,000 pupils enrolled in the elementary schools were graduated from the eighth grade.

Although Berlin had outstripped New York as the city of tenements, more than 1,500,000 New Yorkers lived in slums in 1900. Many European visitors, after one horrified look, concluded that the slum dwellers lived in misery worse than that in Berlin, London, or Paris. The section of Manhattan bounded by the East River, East Fourteenth Street, Third Avenue, the Bowery, and Catherine Street was probably the most densely populated area in the world. New York's poor lived under worse conditions and paid more rent than the inhabitants of any other big city on earth.

The average New Yorker was shorter and younger than his counterpart today. The mortality rate for children was more than five times higher then than now. Life expectancy at birth was much lower. Hospital conditions were horrible by modern standards. The city's water was first chlorinated in 1910, and milk was pasteurized for the first time in 1912.

Like artichokes, women were covered by layer after layer of clothing—chemise, drawers, corset, corset cover, and one or more petticoats. Skirts were so long that they merely showed the tip of the shoe. Ladies exposed much of their bosoms for a formal evening on the town, but during the day they wore shirtwaists with high collars. It was considered fashionable for well-dressed women to walk in such a forward-sloping position that they seemed to be falling forward. Gentlemen wore blue serge suits most of the time, and only dudes put on garters. Men's shoes had tips as sharp as toothpicks. In hot weather, men might remove their jackets in their offices, but never, *never* were they allowed to take off their vests. To appear hatless, whatever the season of the year, was unthinkable. Men wore derby hats in winter and hard straw hats in summer. Policemen wore long blue overcoats with two rows of nine brass buttons, a hard gray helmet, a leather scabbard holding a nightstick garnished with a fancy blue tassel, and a service revolver. Most cops were Irish, and almost all sported mustaches. Until 1902 they spent eighteen hours a day on patrol duty and then six hours more on reserve in the station house. They got one night off every twenty days —sometimes.

With Tammany in control again, the city was a free and easy place. On March 9, 1900, the New York *Times* said a Tammany "commission," consisting of a city official, two state senators, and the dictator of a poolroom syndicate, was raking in $3,095,000 a month in graft from gambling alone. New York had 25,000 prostitutes, and their come-on was: "It costs a dollar, and I've got the room."

Washington and Buffalo were better paved than Manhattan. Vehicular traffic here consisted mainly of hansom cabs, victorias shaped like gravy boats, and closed carriages, called broughams. At busy intersections trolley tracks crisscrossed one another in bewildering patterns. Because of the building boom and the quickening thrust of population toward the north, streets were ripped up much of the time. Manhole explosions were commonplace, and horses and drivers often were hurt by manhole covers hurtling into the air. This was the gaslight era, which reached its peak in 1914.

The social center of the city had advanced from Thirty-fourth Street and Fifth Avenue to Forty-ninth Street and Fifth Avenue. Never before had so much private wealth been concentrated in a single street as was on Fifth Avenue. In some of its mansions hostesses could serve dinner for 100 or more guests on a few hours' notice. India was famished, so it became fashionable to send shiploads of food from New York to the stricken country.

In the winter of 1900 Bernarr MacFadden opened a restaurant, at 487 Pearl Street, where most items sold for one cent. In addition to this penny restaurant, New York had a cafeteria in the basement of the New York Life Building, on Broadway four blocks north of City Hall. At most restaurants a regular dinner cost fifteen cents. Foreign-born laborers bought six rolls for a nickel and munched them on their way to work. In the evening, by paying a nickel for a stein of beer in a saloon, they were entitled to free bread, pickled herring, salami, or hard-boiled eggs. Butter cost nineteen to twenty cents a pound, and oleomargine was available. Macaroni factories were operating in the city. Chop suey had been invented here in 1896, but the dish, unknown in China at the time, was slow to win popularity. Ice cream sundaes, only three years old in 1900, came into favor more quickly than chop suey.

Shortly before the turn of the century New Yorkers became used to seeing automobiles. In 1890 the city granted the first charter to experiment with horseless trucks. By 1895 there were 300 motor vehicles operating in America. The nation's first automobile accident occurred in New York City on May 30, 1896, when Henry Wells of Springfield, Massachusetts, driving his Duryea motor wagon, collided with a bicycle rider, named Evylyn Thomas. She was taken to Manhattan Hospital with a broken leg. In 1897 electric taxicabs were introduced into the city by the Electric Vehicle Company, whose office and garage were located at 1684 Broadway. At the start of the automobile age no one could tell whether electric batteries or internal-combustion gasoline engines would prove superior. By 1898 there were more than 100 electric taxicabs on the streets of New York. Tires cost $40 apiece. In 1899 cars were banned from Central Park, and those chugging around the rest of the city had to observe a 9-mile-an-hour speed limit and carry a gong.

Jacob German was arrested in 1899 for driving on Lexington Avenue at the "breakneck speed" of twelve miles an hour. The same year America's first auto fatality occurred when a sixty-eight-year-old real estate broker, named Henry H. Bliss, was knocked down as he stepped off a southbound streetcar at Central Park West and Seventy-fourth Street. Bliss was taken to Roosevelt Hospital, where he died. Automobiles were regarded as a curiosity at first, but when the number of accidents rose, New Yorkers became critical of them. On December 27, 1900, the *Tribune* said editorially:

> A young woman was knocked down and fatally injured by an automobile vehicle while crossing Broadway on Christmas afternoon. She was a trained nurse, and therefore presumably intelligent, prudent, and active. The vehicle was moving rapidly, just how rapidly is not reported. The engineer in charge of it saw the young woman crossing the street and rang the gong in warning. Apparently, however, he did not abate speed of the machine nor attempt to steer it out of the way. He considered his responsibility fully discharged by the ringing of the gong.

Until 1900 almost all cars were custom-made and regarded as playthings of the rich. In that year the entire United States contained only 13,824 automobiles. Probably half the men and women of America had never seen a car. The nation's first automobile show was held in the old Madison Square Garden in 1900, 51 exhibitors displaying their latest models. Many were electric vehicles. Most were steered by rods, rather than by steering wheels. The show featured starting and stopping contests. Some cars were driven up a wooden ramp within the Garden to demonstrate how they could climb hills.

Some New Yorkers complained about the growing traffic problem. One of the best reporters in American history, Ray Stannard Baker, made this monumentally wrong prediction: "It is hardly possible to conceive the appearance of a crowded wholesale street in the day of the automobile vehicle. In the first place, it will be almost as quiet as a country lane—all the crash of horses' hoofs and the rumble of steel tires will be gone. And since vehicles will be fewer and shorter than the present truck and span, streets will appear less crowded."

In 1901 New York State ordered motorists to buy license plates at $1 apiece. The same year the Automobile Club of America, which had a clubhouse at Fifth Avenue and Fifty-eighth Street, sponsored a 464-mile endurance race between New York City and Buffalo. A French car won with an average speed of 15 miles an hour. On November 16, 1901, for the first time in American history, an auto exceeded the speed of a mile a minute in a race held by the Long Island Automobile Club on Brooklyn's Ocean Parkway. Within minutes, however, the speed record was broken.

The city's first traffic regulations for automobiles went into effect in 1903. Because the traffic situation worsened, the next year the state passed a law holding cars to a maximum speed of ten miles an hour in congested areas of the city. In 1905 the Fifth Avenue Coach Company introduced a twenty-four-passenger double-decked bus imported from France. The following year an automobile row began to develop along Broadway in the upper Fifties. In 1906 Woodrow Wilson, the president of Princeton University, said that "nothing has spread socialistic feelings in this country more than the use of the automobile" which represented "to the countryman . . . a picture of arrogance of wealth, with all its independence and carelessness." The Fifth Avenue line was so pleased with its French buses that it bought more of them and on July 30, 1907, removed the last of its horse stages from Fifth Avenue. Taximeter cabs made their first appearance in New York on October 1, 1907.

According to a traffic study made here in 1907, horse-drawn vehicles moved at an average speed of 11.5 miles an hour. (In 1966, during the daytime, automobiles crawled through Manhattan's central business district at an average speed of 8½ miles an hour.) The nation's first electric traffic signals were installed in Cleveland in 1914. New York City didn't get its first traffic towers until 1922, and by then the city was well along its way toward the automobile congestion that remains one of its most pressing problems.

London opened the world's first subway system in 1863. Ten

years later Abram S. Hewitt made a speech in Cooper Union calling for city ownership of all New York's rapid transit lines. A bill to this effect was soon introduced into the state legislature, but it was voted down. In 1877 cars hanging from an overhead rail were tried out in Brooklyn, only to prove unsuccessful. Elevated trains began crossing the Brooklyn Bridge in 1883. Three years later elevated roads carried 1,000,000 passengers a day and could hold no more. *Rapid* transit? It was a joke. Newspapers crusaded against indecent and inhuman congestion. Every seat was taken, and standees held onto leather straps and swayed and swore in the aisles. Pointing out that passenger traffic once again had outstripped all means of conveyance, the *World* asked, "Who will be the Moses to lead us through this wilderness of uncertainty?" Abram Hewitt seemed to be the man. He became mayor of New York in 1887. Appealing to the state legislature to study the problem further, Hewitt said, "The existing railroads have practically reached the limit of their capacity. Besides, though operated with great care and ability, they are not in reality satisfactory to any class of the community."

Cable cars, a form of transit inaugurated in San Francisco in 1873, had begun running in New York by 1885. The first local cable car rattled along 125th Street. It was drawn by a moving cable housed in a slot below street level; contact was established by a gripman standing in the front vestibule of the car. But soon the *Tribune* was crying that "the cable car is a Juggernaut, a murderer on wheels, a maimer of men and a destroyer of women and children."

Mayor Hewitt addressed the railway committee of the state senate and assembly on March 29, 1888. He urged that New York City be given the legal right to build its own subway system. His ideas were written into a bill introduced into the legislature, but the measure wasn't even reported out of committee. Neither Democratic nor Republican political bosses wanted a transit system rivaling the horsecars and elevateds in which they held a vested interest.

The mayor, the Chamber of Commerce, and others continued to agitate for a subway, and in 1891 the state passed a rapid transit act. This called for the creation of a board consisting of the mayor, city comptroller, and the city commissioner of public works. They could hold public hearings, listen to proposals, and then draft a plan for construction of a subway system. On October 21, 1891, city aldermen approved plans for an underground railway. Despite this, several powerful persons balked. Jay Gould, who partially controlled the elevated lines, was against it. Russell Sage, one of Gould's business associates, said contemptuously: "New York people will never go into a hole in the ground to ride. . . . Preposterous!" Chauncey M. Depew, president of the New York Central, warned that if New Yorkers used subways, they would develop claustrophobia. The Metropolitan Street Railway Company, undisputed master of surface transportation in Manhattan and the Bronx, fought its potential rival.

The city announced that it would accept bids for construction of the subway, but nothing happened; contractors were afraid to enter bids and begin construction because subway opponents might interrupt the work with lawsuits. In 1894 the state legislature created another rapid transit board, and in an election a majority of New Yorkers declared that they favored municipal ownership of subways. Over the next several decades the city built the subway system; then private companies took them over, but eventually the city got them back again.

In 1897 Boston became the first American city to inaugurate an underground railroad. The next year, while plans were being drafted for New York's subway, *Harper's Weekly* reported that the number of people commuting daily to Manhattan was greater than the total population of Cincinnati. About 100,000 commuters arrived by bridge and ferry from Brooklyn, another 100,000 or more came by ferry from New Jersey, and more than 118,000 arrived daily at the overcrowded Grand Central Station from Westchester County and from Connecticut. By 1900 New Yorkers were riding the city's streetcars—a billion times a year—or trying to. The same year an underground railway opened in Paris.

In New York a contractor, named John B. McDonald, wrote optimistically that "surface travel will be an oddity twenty years from now." McDonald wanted to build the subway. He had gained experience constructing tunnels in Baltimore for the Baltimore and Ohio Railroad. In February, 1900, he signed the first New York subway contract. For $35,000,000 McDonald agreed to build, equip, and operate the road for 50 years. He was a member of Tammany Hall and a close friend of Andrew Freedman, one of Boss Croker's financial partners. Since New Yorkers had voted for a subway system, Croker and his colleagues decided to profit from the inevitable by helping McDonald get the contract; they hoped that this would result in fat subcontracts for themselves. They also schemed to put thousands of Tammany voters on the payroll as day laborers.

But for all of McDonald's ability and political connections he didn't have enough money to swing this deal. To his aid came August Belmont II, who had succeeded his father as head of the banking firm of August Belmont & Company, and had retained close business relations with the Rothschild family. Belmont became president of the Rapid Transit Subway Construction Company, and Rothschild money poured into the project. On March 24, 1900, ground was broken for the subway in front of City Hall.

Twelve thousand laborers began tunneling through the earth. Most were Italian, Polish, and Irish, but among these brawny workers was a frail poet, named Edwin Arlington Robinson. Maine-born Robinson spent two years at Harvard and moved to New York in 1899. Slender and erect, with good breeding visible in every line of his scholar's face and his small mouth solemn and set, he peered through prim spectacles with burning brown eyes. So neurotically sensitive that he called himself "a man without a skin," Robinson smiled a twisted Yankee smile and admitted that "the world frightens me." When he arrived here, the only money he had earned up to then from poetry had been seven dollars for a sonnet praising Edgar Allan Poe. Threadbare and desperate, the shy New Englander took a job underground at twenty cents an hour for a ten-hour working day. Later his poems won him three Pulitzer prizes.

Robinson checked the loads of stones removed from the growing tunnels. By 1900 Governors Island had dwindled from 170 acres during the Dutch era to a mere 70 acres because of erosion by waves. Soil and stones dug from the ground were carted and barged to the island to enlarge it. Commuters saw this tangible evidence of a new kind of transportation and gave silent thanks. The subway's popularity was reflected in an advertisement declaring that Abbey's Effervescent Salt was "The Rapid Transit to Health."

In 1901, while the subway was still under construction, horses were taken off streetcars, which converted to electricity. This was a mere stopgap measure, and soon the electric streetcar became a menace. So fast and confusing were Brooklyn's trolley cars that harried Brooklynites dubbed themselves the Trolley Dodgers. A local baseball team, known successively as the Superbas, Kings, and Bridegrooms, ultimately became the Brooklyn Dodgers.

The first leg of the city's first subway went into operation for the first time on Thursday, October 27, 1904. The weather was crisp. The official ceremony began at 1 P.M. in the aldermanic chamber of City Hall. The city's new mayor was George B. McClellan, Jr., whose father had been one of Lincoln's generals and his Democratic rival for the Presidency. Thirty-nine-year-old McClellan was a scholar and author with a handsome, narrow, clean-shaven face. That great day a wearisome series of speeches was made. After the benediction had been pronounced, August Belmont gave the mayor a mahogany case containing a silver throttle. Taking out the throttle and waving it aloft, McClellan cried, "I now, as mayor, in the name of the people, declare the subway open." Then, donning a shiny silk topper and a chesterfield coat, McClelland led the procession out of City Hall.

Followed by other city fathers, Belmont, McDonald, and more than 200 whiskered and mustached Wall Street financiers, the mayor walked into a subway kiosk and down into the City Hall station. This was the southern terminus of the line. Standing in the station was the first train, 5 wooden cars sheathed in copper, their tops painted a flaming red. Each car seated 56 passengers. The front car, named the Belmont, had no doors on its sides. The celebrities had to board it via a door at the end. The mayor entered the motorman's closet and fitted the silver throttle into place. Photographers snapped pictures of him standing rigid and frozen-faced. McClellan had never operated any kind of train.

At 2:35 P.M. a cannon boomed in City Hall Park, whistles blew, bells rang, and the celebrity-packed train began to move. It headed north under Broadway, continued up 4th Avenue to Grand Central Station, turned west to Times Square, and then followed upper Broadway toward 145th Street. With McClellan still at the throttle, the train hit a top speed of about 45 miles an hour. The distance of 9.1 miles between City Hall and 145th Street was traveled in 26 minutes —exactly on schedule.

At seven o'clock that evening any and all New Yorkers were allowed to make this exciting trip. Tickets cost five cents each. A *World* reporter wrote: "Men fought, kicked and pummeled one another in their mad desire to reach the subway ticket office or to ride on the trains. Women were dragged out, either screaming in hysterics or in a swooning condition; gray-haired men pleaded for mercy, boys were knocked down and only escaped by a miracle from being trampled under foot. . . ."

Times Square became so congested with people that it looked like New Year's Eve. At the 145th Street subway station policemen struggled to control the throngs. During the confusion a passenger had his $500 diamond stickpin stolen; it was the city's first subway crime. The first day a total of 111,000 people rode the new rails. Friday it was 319,000; Saturday, 350,000.

Because this single line of the Interborough Rapid Transit Company was far from sufficient to solve the commutation problem, in the next few years ever more subway tracks pronged through the bowels of New York. In time the city's subway system developed into the most heavily traveled passenger railroad in the world.

Chapter 38

THE *GENERAL SLOCUM* DISASTER

A FEW MINUTES after nine o'clock on the morning of Wednesday, June 15, 1904, an excursion boat, named the *General Slocum,* left her pier at the foot of East Third Street and headed north up the East River. Although a light breeze blew from the south, the day was sunny, hot, and humid. The steamboat was a white three-decked side-wheeler with twin stacks that belched smoke as she gathered speed.

Aboard were about 1,400 passengers, mostly women and children. German-born or of German descent, they lived in Little Germany, on Manhattan's Lower East Side. They were parishioners of St. Mark's Lutheran Church, located at 328 East Sixth Street, and this was their annual Sunday-school outing. Flaxen-haired boys and girls carried fat picnic baskets which they planned to unpack at Locust Grove, on Long Island Sound. German men had gone to work as usual that day, happy that their wives and children could enjoy a day in the country. While the steamboat captain, William H. Van Schaick, stood his post on the bridge, a band aboard the ship played a Lutheran hymn, "A Mighty Fortress Is Our God."

As the vessel drew even with East 125th Street a fire was discovered in a cabin on the main deck, and the children's happy chatter thinned out. Since the passengers were women and children and since land was within easy reach on both port and starboard, the skipper should have beached his craft as quickly as possible and hurried his passengers ashore. Instead, he ordered an increase in speed. He planned to proceed under forced draft to North Brother Island, just off the southern shore of the Bronx, and disembark his passengers there. The engines pounded. The paddle wheels churned. The ship vibrated. The increased speed stirred up a breeze that spread the flames. The crackling fire rippled the length of the ship. Children screamed. Mothers grabbed tots to their breasts. Boys and girls climbed onto deck chairs and waved frantically toward the shore. Now the encroaching flames set their clothing afire. Terrified women tried to herd the children to the stern, but the panic-stricken screeching youngsters could not be managed. A girl in a blue dress leaped over the side, hit the hood of a paddle wheel, slipped off, and fell under the threshing wooden blade. Her screams ended in watery gurgles. Sixteen-year-old Albert F. Frese, who sorted mail in the Funk & Wagnalls publishing house, jumped from the stern, feet first, ankles together, arms rigid against his side. He swam to safety and lived to become treasurer of the firm.

By this time people on Manhattan's eastern shore were running along the riverbank, trying to keep up with the floating inferno. Others sped toward the waterfront in carts and wagons. Some threw barrels into the river for use as makeshift life preservers. Spectators shouted to the steamboat captain to head into shore. He ignored them. The doomed ship kept pounding upriver, while onlookers wept in frustration. Small boats took up the chase but were unable to catch the speeding *General Slocum*.

Docked at 134th Street was a barge owned by the Moran Towing Company. The barge captain sprang ashore and telephoned his boss, Eugene F. Moran, in downtown Manhattan. He shouted that the

General Slocum was on fire. Then he cried to Moran, "Get a tug!" Moran checked his operations sheet but found that he had none anywhere near the burning vessel.

About this time a wall telephone rang in the city room of the *World* on Park Row. A man, who failed to identify himself, said that he was standing in his office at 137th Street and could see a ship in flames heading north. The *World* rewrite man who took the call shouted to the city editor. The editor told a reporter to telephone Moran. The reporter asked Moran if he could provide a tug to rush *World* staff members to the scene. Moran said that they could get there faster by taking an elevated train at Park Row and getting off at the Port Morris station. Because of the anonymous caller and Moran's commonsense suggestion, *World* reporters beat their competitors to the scene of the tragedy.

By now the *General Slocum* was beached on North Brother Island. She listed. Smoke and flames enveloped her. Floating in the water and scattered along the shore were bodies blackened and bloody, torn and seared. Veteran reporters looked and wept. Then they scattered in search of phones. They delivered such sickening descriptions that rewrite men who took their stories dashed to the men's room and vomited.

Police estimated that 1,031 persons died in the fire, and a convulsive shudder ran through the city. German fathers came home to learn that their families had been wiped out. Some men died of grief. Some killed themselves. Others went mad. For three days hearses crunched through the streets of Little Germany, carrying bits and pieces of bodies to graves in the Lutheran cemetery in Middle Village, Queens. Not long afterward most German families moved away from that part of the Lower East Side because of memories too painful to bear.

There was, of course, an inquest. This proved that the *General Slocum* had not been carefully inspected, that her life preservers had been rotten, and that her crew had been virtually without emergency training. Although the steamboat company wriggled out of legal responsibility for the disaster, in 1906 Captain Van Schaick was sentenced to ten years at hard labor in Sing Sing for criminal negligence.

On May 30, 1905, a memorial fountain to the victims of the *General Slocum* tragedy was unveiled near the northwestern corner of Tompkins Square. A white shaft eight feet tall, it depicted a boy and girl gazing into space and bore this legend: "They were earth's purest children, loving and fair."

The New York *Times* was developing into a great newspaper under the guidance of its new owner, Adolph S. Ochs. Born in Cincinnati in 1858, he bought the Chattanooga *Times* in 1878 and made a success of it. Ochs invaded New York's fourth estate in 1896 by purchasing the faltering *Times*. In that year it had a paid circulation of only 9,000 copies. Ochs printed accurate news devoid of editorial bias, his policy paid off, and by 1900 the New York *Times* was showing a big profit.

Ochs was an ambitious man. He looked like George Washington and was delighted when strangers noticed this. Something of a dandy, Ochs was rich enough in 1900 to order tailor-made clothes from Rock's Fifth Avenue shop. In a letter to his mother he gloated: "Not bad for a country greenie from Tennessee, eh?" The *Times* was housed in a thirteen-story building at 41 Park Row, and Ochs' corner office measured only eight by ten feet. Gazing out on the statue of Benjamin Franklin in Printing House Square, Ochs dreamed of erecting the finest newspaper plant in the world—something to "wake up the natives."

In 1902 he bought a triangular lot at Broadway and Forty-second Street in an area called Long Acre Square. A center for the manufacture and repair of carriages and harnesses, it took its name from a section of London devoted to this same business. When Ochs made his purchase, the plot was occupied by the nine-story Pabst Building, which was now torn down. Construction of the Times Building posed vexing problems because the plot was so narrow, because of its triangular shape, and because a subway station was being built under it. Overcoming these engineering handicaps, architect Cyrus L. W. Eidlitz erected a beautiful twenty-five-story structure of Italian Renaissance design, suggesting Giotto's Campanile in Florence. When completed, the Times Tower became the city's second tallest skyscraper, topped only by the thirty-two story Park Row Building downtown.

It was dedicated at 3 P.M. on the bitterly cold day of January 18, 1904. Spectators jammed into the square were delighted by the building's terra-cotta and cream-colored brick and by its graceful lines. Ochs' eleven-year-old daughter, Iphigene, was handed a silver trowel for her part in the ceremonies. Her coat whipped by a crisp wind and warm in the heavy black tights her mother had made her wear, Iphigene advanced toward the great cornerstone as it settled into place. She wore gloves, and there is nothing in the world so dignified as a little girl wearing gloves. She smoothed the mortar with her trowel, struck the cornerstone three times, and then began her speech. To her horror, she flubbed one word. She was supposed to say, "I declare this stone to be laid plumb, level and square." Instead, she piped, in a childish voice, "I declare this stone to be laid *plump—*"

Although Ochs was rather vain, he never let his opinions interfere with his judgment as a newspaperman. The story about the dedication of the tower did not appear on page one of the *Times* the following day, but on page nine alongside social news.

City aldermen gave Times Square its new name in 1904, and the building opened for business in 1905. The New York *Times* then had a weekday circulation of 116,629 and a Sunday circulation of 54,795. It went on to become one of the three or four greatest newspapers in the world.

In 1908 the *Times* instituted its annual custom of saluting the New Year by lowering an electrically lighted ball six feet in diameter, down the tower's seventy-foot flagpole. When the ball touched the base at midnight, its lights went out and proclaimed the advent of another year.

So quickly did the *Times* grow in prestige and circulation that in 1913 it moved into the first part of still another plant at 229 West Forty-third Street, half a block west of the tower. As stores and theaters continued to advance northward up Manhattan, Times Square came to be known as the Crossroads of the World. Today the Times Square district consists of about thirty-four square blocks, three-quarters of a mile long by one-third of a mile wide. The area is the heart of New York's theatrical district.

Immigration reached a peak in 1907, a year of financial panic for New York and the rest of the nation. In those 12 months a total of 1,285,349 immigrants arrived in the United States. The vast majority landed on the 27 acres of Ellis Island, whose red spires with their bulbous green cupolas had a faintly Byzantine air.

Among those disembarking that year was a ten-year-old Italian boy, named Edward Corsi. He later became the United States Commissioner of Immigration and Naturalization and took charge of the part of American soil on which he first set foot. His book, *In the Shadow of Liberty,* describes his boyish reactions the day of his arrival. He was struck by the fact that American men did not wear beards. Because most Italian men let their whiskers grow, young Corsi thought that American males looked almost like women. Until then it had never occurred to the lad that any language except Italian was spoken. No doubt boys from other foreign lands felt the same kind of surprise. Gazing across the Upper Bay toward the Manhattan skyline, young Corsi pointed and cried, "Mountains! Look at them!" His brother Giuseppe said with a puzzled frown, "They're strange. Why don't they have snow on them?"

Amusing and pathetic scenes were enacted on Ellis Island during this period of immigration's high tide. The buildings and lawns undulated with a variety of colorful peasant costumes. On occasion as many as twenty-five or thirty different peoples were held in detention at the same time. The Dutch and Germans had the largest families. Shawl-draped immigrant women seemed to feel that their most precious possessions were feather pillows and mattresses. It was impossible to provide a menu palatable to persons accustomed to their own native foods. Corsi said, "The Italian cares nothing for the dried fish preferred by the Scandinavian, and the Scandinavian has no use for spaghetti. The Greek wants his food sweetened, and no one can make tea for an Englishman. The basis of all Asiatic and Malay food is rice, which they will mix with almost anything. The Chinese take to other foods but want rice in place of bread."

One ship brought a group of thirty whirling dervishes. These Mohammedan priests belonged to an order given to mystical practices, such as spinning on their toes and howling at the top of their voices. They wore red fezzes, loose-flowing trousers, bright-blue coats, and soft sandals. Their religion forbade them to eat any food over which the shadow of an infidel had passed. To them all the cooks, waiters, and helpers on Ellis Island were infidels, so the dervishes refused to eat. Before they starved themselves to death, however, someone cleverly offered them hard-boiled eggs. It was true that infidels' shadows had passed over the shells of the eggs, but once the polluted shells were removed, the eggs themselves were considered to be free of contamination. The egg-happy dervishes munched their way back to good health.

Perplexed by the diversity of dietary habits and helpless in the face of grafting food contractors, Ellis Island staff members often fed the immigrants little more than prunes and bread. One employee brought out a big pail filled with prunes. Another walked into the mess hall carrying sliced loaves of rye bread. A third plunged a dipper into the pail, slopped prunes onto a big slice of bread, and cried to the bewildered immigrants, "Here! Now go and eat!"

Grafters preyed on immigrants in many ways. Their baggage checks were conned from them by swindlers, who then picked up the luggage and walked away with it. Before departing from Europe, some emigrants were told that the American gold coins they had collected were no good in the United States unless they contained holes. The swindlers who came up with this spurious story then drilled holes and kept the gold dust, which they sold.

Most foreigners arrived with very little money. In 1907 each had to pay a federal immigration tax of $40. Some aliens were reluctant to admit that they had any more money than this, for fear of being robbed. A Greek who claimed to be penniless actually had more than $5,000 on his person. Before ferrying from Ellis Island to Manhattan, the immigrants changed their foreign currency into American dollars and cents, and some money changers cheated them. Poverty-stricken, unfamiliar with the English language, bewildered by their new environment, and intimidated by the bustle and roar of New York, the newcomers landed in the city proper in a state of confusion. At first some managed to eat for only 3 or 4 cents a day. In squalid sections of town they paid as little as $4 a month in rent.

Elderly immigrants usually were held on Ellis Island until a relative or friend called for them. But sometimes the people they counted on had died before their arrival. The stranded old folks wandered about the immigration station, asking anyone who spoke their native tongue, "Have you seen my son? Have you seen my daughter? Do you know him, my Giuseppe? When is he coming for me?"

American ways were puzzling. When 280 gypsies arrived on one ship, doctors found that 48 of their children had the measles. The youngsters were sent to a Brooklyn hospital. A rumor spread among gypsy adults that their sons and daughters had been drowned by doctors. An immigration physician tried to feel the pulse of another gypsy child on Ellis Island. He was attacked by gypsy men, who screamed that he was a murderer. This started a riot, which raged .all night. Even gypsy women pulled off their heavy-soled slippers and flailed away at any doctor or inspector who came within range. The next gypsy child who developed measles was sent to the hospital like the others, but this time his parents were permitted to go along to see for themselves that all the gypsy children were alive and well tended. They brought the news back to the other gypsies, and the disorders ceased.

The English language was puzzling, too. One immigrant tried to ask for a railroad ticket to Detroit, Michigan, but it came out sounding like *Detroit-a-Mich*. The ticket agent thought the alien had called him a dirty Mick and flamed in anger.

Fiorello LaGuardia came back to his home town in 1906 after living and working in Europe many years. He spoke Yiddish, Hungarian, Italian, German, and Serbian-Croatian. Needing a job to work his way through New York University's law school, which he attended at night, LaGuardia got a civil service appointment as an interpreter on Ellis Island for $1,200 a year. With immigrants pouring in at the average rate of 5,000 a day, the Ellis Island staff worked a 7-day week. LaGuardia would rise early in the morning to catch an 8:40 A.M. ferry, returning to Manhattan on the 5:30 P.M. boat. Tenderhearted and sentimental, the swarthy little LaGuardia never became callous to the heartbreaking scenes he witnessed in the immigration station. It galled him to learn that one provision of the law excluded any alien lacking a job and that another provision of the same law barred an immigrant with a job. LaGuardia tried to correct this anomaly by writing letters of protest to Congress.

Some immigrant women were engaged to men who had preceded them to the New World. Many impatient men insisted on marrying before their fiancées were released by immigration officials. It became the duty of Ellis Island interpreters to accompany these couples to City Hall to get married. In those days city aldermen could perform the wedding service. "In the few instances I attended," LaGuardia later said, "the aldermen were drunk. Some of the aldermen would insert into their reading of the marriage ceremony remarks which they considered funny and sometimes used lewd language, much to the amusement of the red-faced, cheap 'tinhorn' politicians who hung around them to watch the so-called fun." *

Who could tell which immigrants would wind up as heroes and which as bums? In 1910 there arrived a hefty black-haired blue-eyed

* From *The Making of an Insurgent, An Autobiography: 1882-1919* by Fiorello H. LaGuardia. Copyright, 1948, by J. B. Lippincott Company. Published by J. B. Lippincott Company.

twenty-year-old youth, born in County Mayo, Ireland. He had $23.35 in his pockets. His first job was running a pushcart. Then he signed on as a coal passer on a steamship plying to South America. Back in New York again, he worked in the firerooms of night boats cruising the Hudson River. Next, he became a hod carrier at $19.25 a week and helped put up the Hotel McAlpin on Broadway between Thirty-third and Thirty-fourth Streets. Later he worked at the Hotel Vanderbilt, at Fourth Avenue and East Thirty-fourth Street, where Alexanders seemed to be the favorite drink. His name was William O'Dwyer, and ultimately he became the mayor of New York.

For many years a New York Central Railroad monopoly had prevented any other railway from entering Manhattan except by tunnel. There was just one catch: No tunnel existed under either the Hudson or the East River. In 1900 directors of the Pennsylvania Railroad authorized an increase of $100,000,000 of stock. At the time no outsider knew that the Pennsylvania planned to buy the Long Island Rail Road, to tunnel under both rivers, and to erect a monumental station near Herald Square on Manhattan's West Side. People began to suspect that something was afoot in 1901, when the Pennsylvania bought several parcels of property in the Tenderloin district.

The railroad had decided to build its new station on a site bounded by Thirty-first and Thirty-third streets and Seventh and Eighth avenues. The 8-acre area contained 500 buildings. Hoping to make a real estate killing, businessmen started buying property in the neighborhood, but at last the Pennsylvania got possession of all the land it needed. Then the railway asked the state legislature to pass a law giving New York City the authority to grant the Pennsylvania a franchise for construction of the tunnels and station. The franchise was granted in 1902.

All 500 buildings were pulled down, and construction began. New Yorkers gaped in amazement at the colossal hole dug in the ground. The sight was so staggering that they compared it with the Panama Canal, under construction at the time. *Metropolitan Magazine* described it as the "great $25,000,000 hole." The project came to more than this, for in 1906 the Pennsylvania granted $35,000,000 in contracts to build the terminal. Less visible, but an equal source of excitement, were the tunnels being hacked out under the Hudson River.

As early as 1850 the idea of boring under the Hudson had been proposed. In 1873 the Hudson River Tunnel Company was incorporated. In 1874 work began at the foot of Fifteenth Street in Jersey City, but the project was quashed after legal action was taken by jealous railroads. Work resumed later, and in 1887 the tunnel extended 1,840 feet from the Jersey shore. With the aid of British capital the tunnel company had pushed the hole a distance of 3,000 feet by 1891. The same year, because of financial difficulties, the tunnel franchise was sold to some New York lawyers. The following year tall lean William Gibbs McAdoo arrived.

A member of a distinguished Georgia family, McAdoo came to New York to practice law. He acquired the franchise to the tunnel enterprise and organized a firm, called the Hudson and Manhattan Company. At first he had trouble collecting capital, but at last he completed not one but two tubes between Jersey City and lower Manhattan. On March 11, 1904, McAdoo donned rubber boots, a raincoat, and wide-brimmed hat and led a party of sixteen men through one of the tunnels from New Jersey to New York. They emerged at Morton Street. McAdoo later became Secretary of the Treasury and a son-in-law of President Woodrow Wilson.

Despite the successful completion of the Hudson and Manhattan tubes, the Pennsylvania Railroad wanted its own tunnels under the river and built them higher upstream, just opposite West Thirty-second Street. From this point on the western shore of Manhattan it was only four blocks due east to the site of the new Pennsylvania Station.

Architects regarded this terminal as one of the great monuments of classic architecture in the United States. It duplicated one of the wonders of ancient Rome, the baths built by Emperor Caracalla in the third century A.D. The vast waiting room consisted of a skylighted concourse with ceilings, 150 feet high, surmounting vaulting arches of lacy steel and glass. All 4 sides of the grandiose building, made of granite and travertine, were lined with 84 Doric columns, each 35 feet high. Richly detailed in solid stone, the Pennsylvania Station was entered through a magnificent portal topped by 6 huge stone eagles, weighing 5,700 pounds apiece. As the New York *Times* once said, this exalted terminal "set the stamp of excellence on the city." On September 8, 1910, trains first began operating on regular schedules in and out of the new Pennsylvania Station.

Chapter 39

━━━◄◆►━━━

COLONEL HOUSE AND
WOODROW WILSON

A TEXAN MOVED to New York in 1910 and soon made the city a
center of international power and diplomatic intrigue. He was a
behind-the-scenes politician, a modest Machiavelli, a little man
whose soft hand was as fast on the draw as some fabled gunslingers.
However, his favorite weapon was words, not revolvers. His name
was Edward M. House.

Born in Texas and the son of a rich man, with Dutch blood flowing in his veins, House attended private schools and Cornell, was fascinated by politics and history, and inherited an income of $25,000 a
year. Never seeking public office for himself, House preferred to remain a hidden manipulator of political figures. He became close

adviser to four Texas governors and one of them gratefully made him an honorary Texas colonel. Throughout the rest of his life he was known as Colonel House, a title that puzzled Prussian officers who met House when he was on a diplomatic mission to Germany.

Having brought the largest state in the Union under his political dominion, House now wanted to play an important role in national politics. He was a Democrat, who believed that his party's next Presidential nominee should be an Eastern liberal. House was a kingmaker in search of a king, a hero worshiper in search of a hero. An unpretentious man, he moved into an unpretentious building in the Murray Hill section of Manhattan at 145 East Thirty-fifth Street. He and his wife merely occupied an apartment. The colonel's moderate-sized study held a Queen Anne desk, a chaise longue, two giant leather chairs, and a wall lined with books.

Back in Texas, Colonel House had become friendly with William Jennings Bryan, an ambitious politician from the Midwest. The Bryan family had left the chilly prairies of Nebraska to winter in the warmer climate of Texas because of their ailing daughter. Looking over Bryan, as he looked over all promising politicians, House was amazed to see "how lacking he was in political sagacity and common sense." House made this judgment before Bryan ran three times as the Democratic Presidential candidate, only to be defeated in 1896, 1900, and 1908. Although Bryan hankered for a fourth chance at the Presidency, he told House that Mayor Gaynor of New York might be able to win for the Democrats.

William Jay Gaynor liked to mislead those who wrote about his early life, but it seems that he was born on a farm in central New York State in 1851. A Catholic, in 1863 he entered the novitiate of De la Salle Institute in New York City and was assigned the name of Brother Adrian Denys. After almost five years in the religious order Gaynor withdrew and abandoned Catholicism. He taught school, worked as a newspaper reporter, studied law, passed his bar examination, and practiced law in Brooklyn. For sixteen years he served as a justice of the New York State supreme court. With the help of Tammany Hall he was elected mayor of New York and took office on January 1, 1910.

Mayor Gaynor was the most cantankerous man ever to rule the city, his temper tantrums making even Peter Stuyvesant and Fiorello LaGuardia look like altar boys. Of average height and slight of build, an inveterate walker who moved with almost feminine grace, Gaynor was a handsome man, with a graying Vandyke beard and sharp eyes under his black eyebrows. He liked children and adored pigs, and while serving as a judge, he once threw an inkwell at a man in open court. Still, Gaynor was of a philosophical bent, read widely in the classics, and concealed his malicious humor behind unsmiling blue eyes.

After taking office as mayor, he gave the back of his hand to Tammany politicians, who had put him there. Concerned only with having his own way and, incidentally, with making this a better city, Gaynor lashed out on every side. During the first 2 months of his administration he saved taxpayers about $700,000 by pulling politicians away from the public trough. He cut other city expenses. He killed boards and bureaus he considered superfluous. One disgusted Tammany brave snarled that Gaynor "did more to break up the Democratic organization than any other man ever has in this city."

Regardless of the roars of the Tammany tiger, the mayor won a reputation as a liberal. Magazine articles declared that Gaynor had the stuff of which Presidents are made. With the perspective granted us by time, we know that this was not true. Gaynor couldn't break through the stalemate of forces surrounding him, never was able to lead the board of estimate, and foolishly placed faith in his naïve police commissioner.

Colonel Edward House looked and listened. Mulling over what Bryan had said about Gaynor and reading laudatory articles about him, House felt that perhaps this righteous reformer was just the man he sought. One of Gaynor's few friends was James Creelman, the celebrated reporter, war correspondent, and editorial writer. In 1910 Creelman was working as associate editor of *Pearson's Magazine* and writing another book. Colonel House, who knew Creelman, asked him for an introduction to Mayor Gaynor. In the early summer of 1910 the three men met for dinner in the Lotus Club, at 556 Fifth Avenue near Forty-fifth Street.

Creelman was a delightful host. A dignified man with a small goatee and a worldly character, who had interviewed Chief Sitting Bull and Count Leo Tolstoy, Creelman ordered the best wine for his guests. The dinner lasted until after midnight. Colonel House was impressed with the mayor. Later he said:

> I had been told that Gaynor was brusque even to rudeness, but I did not find him so in the slightest. He knew perfectly well what

the dinner was for, and he seemed to try to put his best side to the front. . . . He showed a knowledge of public affairs altogether beyond my expectations and greater, indeed, than that of any public man that I at that time knew personally.

Anticipating the Presidential campaign of 1912, Colonel House wooed Mayor Gaynor. He also went back to Texas and induced members of the legislature to invite the New York mayor to address them. A formal invitation was telegraphed to Gaynor. For several days nothing was heard from him. Finally, a reporter on a small Texas newspaper wired Gaynor to ask whether or not he planned to speak to the Texas lawmakers. Gaynor replied that he had heard of no such proposal and had no intention of appearing in Texas. The mayor then sent Creelman a letter saying that anyone who thought he had the Presidency in mind was wrong.

It is difficult to explain Gaynor's behavior. Maybe he really didn't want to become President. Perhaps he indeed wanted this exalted office but felt he couldn't get it. There is even the possibility that Gaynor forsook a try for the Presidency to avenge himself upon William Randolph Hearst. Gaynor and Hearst always fought bitterly. The Hearst papers had published a story saying that Gaynor was going to Texas to address the legislature. Maybe Gaynor chose this way of making a liar out of Hearst. In any event, Colonel House became disenchanted with the mayor, saying, "I wiped Gaynor from my political slate, for I saw he was impossible." Like Diogenes, lantern hunting for a man he could admire, Colonel House continued his search.

Meantime, an attempt was made to assassinate Mayor Gaynor. After having worked for seven months on municipal affairs, Gaynor decided to vacation in Europe. On August 9, 1910, accompanied by his son Rufus, he boarded the S.S. *Kaiser Wilhelm der Grosse* at Hoboken, New Jersey, just across the Hudson from Manhattan. A natty dresser, his outfit topped with a black derby, the mayor stood on deck, chatting with friends, three city commissioners, his corporation counsel, and his male secretary. A New York *World* photographer, William Warnecke, raised his camera to take a picture of the group. At that moment an untidy little man stepped up behind the mayor. This intruder turned out to be James J. Gallagher, who had been fired from his job in the city docks department and who blamed the mayor for his trouble. Gallagher pressed a gun to the back of

Gaynor's neck. He pulled the trigger. The bullet entered behind the mayor's right ear. Gaynor later wrote to his sister:

> My next consciousness was of a terrible metallic roar in my head. It filled my head, which seemed as though it would burst open. It swelled to the highest pitch, and then fell, and then rose again, and so alternated until it subsided into a continuous buzz. It was sickening, but my stomach did not give way. I was meanwhile entirely sightless. I do not think I fell, for when I became conscious I was on my feet. I suppose they saved me from falling, and they were supporting me. My sight gradually returned, so that after a while I could see the deck and the outlines of the crowd around me. I became conscious that I was choking. Blood was coming from my mouth and nose and I tried all I could to swallow it so those around me would not see it. But I found I could not swallow and then knew my throat was hurt. It seemed as though it were dislocated. I struggled to breathe through my mouth, but could not, and thought I was dying of strangulation. I kept thinking all the time the best thing to do. I was not a bit afraid to die if that was God's will of me. I said to myself just as well now as a few years from now. No one who contemplates the immensity of Almighty God, and of His universe and His works, and realizes what an atom he is in it all, can fear to die in this flesh, yea, even though it were true that he is dissolved forever into the infinity of matter and mind from which he came. In some way I happened to close my mouth tight and found I breathed perfectly through my nose. I then believed I could keep from smothering. But I kept choking and my mouth kept opening to cast out the blood. But much of it went down into my stomach.

The *World* photographer, who clicked his camera two or three seconds after the would-be assassin fired, got one of the most notable pictures in journalistic history. Blood gushed down the mayor's beard. More blood mottled his neck and dripped onto the front of his neat suit. At the time the *World*'s city editor was Charles E. Chapin, a brilliant but cynical man, who later murdered his own wife. When Warnecke's print was developed in the *World* office, Chapin grabbed it and exulted: "What a wonderful thing! Look! Blood all over him—and exclusive, too!"

Aboard the liner at Hoboken, "Big Bill" Edwards, the New York street-cleaning commissioner and a former Princeton football player, grabbed Gallagher and held him until the police arrived. The mayor was urged to lie down on the deck but refused. He couldn't bear to have people see him in this horrible condition. He was led to his stateroom and lifted into bed. Because he was choking, they had to prop him up. The ship's doctor washed Gaynor's face and beard and bandaged his wound. An ambulance came to take the mayor to St. Mary's Hospital in Hoboken. He remained there for about three weeks.

When Mayor Gaynor returned to City Hall on October 3, a crowd of 10,000 people gathered to cheer him. Although the mayor looked haggard, he was as crusty as ever. Hearing an officious policeman bellowing at people around his car, Gaynor poked his head out a window and snapped, "None of that, now! None of that!" The next day the mayor resumed his habit of walking from his Brooklyn home across the Brooklyn Bridge to City Hall and then back again in the evening. But surgeons had been unable to extract the bullet from his throat, and he was a sick man the rest of his life. When he didn't want to talk about an unpleasant subject, Gaynor would croak, "Sorry, can't talk today. This fish hook in my throat is bothering me." His temper, always brittle, now shattered at the slightest touch.

Former Mayor George B. McClellan wrote in his memoirs:

> I doubt if Gaynor was ever quite normal, certainly not after he was shot at the base of his brain by a lunatic. I was told by an employee of the Harriman Night and Day Bank that about two o'clock one morning a bearded face appeared at his window, and the owner asked him to cash a check for ten dollars. The employee recognized the mayor and cashed the check. Whereupon the mayor, evidently intending to return the courtesy, said "Wouldn't you like to feel the bullet in my throat? If you will stick your finger into my mouth you will be able to do so." He seemed rather hurt when my informant politely declined to accept his offer. I was told that during the last months of his life Gaynor was in the habit of appearing at the City Hall at all hours of the night, routing out the night watchman, and sitting for hours in his office with his eyes fixed on vacancy.*

The mayor quarreled with nearly everyone. When he couldn't force his iron-willed police commissioner to do his bidding, Gaynor replaced him with Rhinelander Waldo. A hero of the Spanish-American War and a socialite with high ideals, Waldo was so naïve that veteran

---

* From *The Gentleman and the Tiger, The Autobiography of George B. McClellan, Jr.*, edited by Harold C. Syrett. Copyright © 1956 by The New-York Historical Society; copyright © 1956 by Harold C. Syrett. Published by J. B. Lippincott Company.

policemen regarded him as a glorified Boy Scout. Unable to believe that any cop could be corrupt, Waldo was slow in catching onto the nefarious activities of Police Lieutenant Charles Becker. This officer commanded the so-called Strong Arm Squad, charged with suppressing gambling and vice. Becker was as handsome as he was venal. On the sly he became a partner of Herman Rosenthal, an influential underworld figure. After opening one gambling joint after another, only to have them raided by the police, Rosenthal decided to pay protection money by tying in with Lieutenant Becker.

This partnership worked well for a while, but soon Mayor Gaynor and Commissioner Waldo received anonymous complaints about Becker's link with the underworld. The police commissioner habitually referred complaints about cops to the police themselves for investigation. Naturally, they would report that there was nothing to the accusations. Becker's connections with Rosenthal and other crooks were so profitable that he banked about $100,000, although his salary was a mere $2,250. Even Waldo finally became suspicious and ordered Becker to crack down on gambling. To protect himself and to allay suspicion by doing as ordered, Becker made the gesture of raiding one of Rosenthal's gambling dens. Along with two other men, he arrested Rosenthal's nephew. When Rosenthal heard the news, he flushed with anger and asked Becker what the hell he thought he was doing. Becker tried to soothe his furious partner by saying that it was a token raid and by assuring him that his nephew would be released.

The grand jury took the charges seriously, however, and indicted Rosenthal's nephew and his companions. Rosenthal felt that he had been doublecrossed. Eager for revenge, he went to District Attorney Charles Whitman and tried to swear out a citizen's complaint against Becker. The D.A. told the gambler that he didn't have enough evidence to indict the police lieutenant. Given the brush-off by Whitman, Rosenthal told his story all over again to the New York *World*, then in the midst of a gambling exposé. He was taken seriously by Herbert Bayard Swope, one of the *World*'s top reporters. The newspaper published articles that goaded the district attorney into action, and finally Whitman summoned Rosenthal to his office. They agreed that Rosenthal would testify before the grand jury on July 16, 1912.

Becker realized that his vice empire would topple the moment Rosenthal took the witness stand. The officer got in touch with his bagman, a Polish immigrant, named Jacob Rosenschweig, but known as Billiard Ball Jack Rose because he didn't have a hair on his body. Becker ordered Rose to hire some gunmen for $1,000 and have Rosenthal murdered. The bagman had no stomach for this kind of crime, but under pressure from Becker he hired four thugs: Frank Muller, alias Whitey Lewis; Harry Horowitz, alias Gyp the Blood; Louis Rosenberg, alias Leftie Louie; and Frank Ciroficci, alias Dago Frank.

At 2 A.M. on the day Rosenthal was to appear before the grand jury, these hoodlums shot him down on the sidewalk in front of the Metropole Hotel on West Forty-third Street just east of Broadway. Although 7 policemen were within 500 feet of the spot, one of them only 50 feet away, the gunmen escaped in a gray sedan.

Well aware of the enmity between Rosenthal and Lieutenant Becker, other police tried to cover up the crime so that it couldn't be traced to their fellow officer. However, Swope got District Attorney Whitman out of bed within an hour of the shooting, and Whitman launched a thorough investigation of the case. Billiard Ball Jack Rose later swore that he had asked Becker if Becker had seen the corpse. Rose quoted Becker as replying, "Sure! I went to the back room and had a look at him. It was a pleasing sight to me to look at the Jew there. If Whitman had not been there I would have cut his tongue out and hung it somewhere as a warning to other squealers."

When Whitman promised Rose immunity from prosecution, the bagman confessed full details of the crime. The case was the talk of the town. Mayor Gaynor tried to shrug it off by saying:

> The case of Becker did not surprise me at all. Although we had done much to remove grafting and make it impossible in the Police Department, I knew very well that it would in all probability crop out in more places than one. The instance which has cropped out has enabled the degenerate press to characterize the whole force as a band of grafters. But I am certain that the intelligent community still have in mind, and have had in mind all along, what we have done in the way of reform in the Police Department.

Despite the mayor's defiant words, New Yorkers grumbled about this latest evidence of police corruption. The four gunmen and Lieutenant Becker were electrocuted at Sing Sing. The Rosenthal case drove gamblers out of town, made Swope's reputation as a crusading newspaperman, and elevated Whitman to the office of governor of New York State.

While still holding office, Mayor Gaynor died in 1913 aboard a ship a few miles off Liverpool, England. The New York *Sun,* once bitterly hostile toward Gaynor, now mourned that "first and foremost, he was, as no other Mayor ever was, the people's champion, the actual father of the city." The New York *Times* described Gaynor's funeral as the greatest public demonstration since Lincoln's death; this seems highly unlikely.

Gaynor was gone, but Colonel Edward House had found his hero —Woodrow Wilson. After the colonel's disenchantment with Gaynor the Texas politician had considered and rejected others he might promote for the Democratic Presidential nomination. Wilson, like Gaynor, had been elected to office with the help of political bosses and had then declared himself free of them. Now he was governor of New Jersey. Wilson had trimmed his sails in another way, too, by switching from being a conservative before his election to being a progressive after taking the oath of office. As Wilson won national attention by denouncing boss rule and the vested interests, Colonel House began to study his personality and career.

In August, 1911, some prominent Texans launched a Wilson for President campaign. William Jennings Bryan still dominated the national Democratic organization despite his three defeats as a Presidential candidate. Now Bryan, the progressive, told friends that Governor Wilson of New Jersey was making speeches that sounded mighty progressive. Colonel House himself began to believe that Wilson might be just the man the Democrats needed for the 1912 campaign.

Wilson spoke at the Dallas Fair, but Colonel House was in New York at the time and did not hear him. It was just as well. A master strategist, who thought through every tactic, House had not cared to meet Wilson for the first time amid the tumult of a Dallas reception. He preferred a quiet private meeting. Wilson, for his part, had begun to hear about Colonel House, who was represented as a man of great political influence. Furthermore, House was close to Bryan, and Wilson wanted Bryan's approval before announcing for the Democratic nomination. So William F. McCombs, general manager of the Wilson for President movement, asked Colonel House to invite the New Jersey governor to New York to confer with him.

At four o'clock on Friday afternoon, November 24, 1911, Wilson and House met alone in the swanky Gotham Hotel at Fifth Avenue and Fifty-fifth Street. Wilson was fifty-five years old, and House was fifty-three. New Jersey's governor had broad shoulders and a narrow waist, stood half a head taller than Colonel House, wore pince-nez that made his long face look even longer, and had a pointed chin. Despite the flinty features of his clean-shaven face, Wilson broke into a crisp smile when he chose to turn on the charm. His laugh revealed horsy teeth. Virginia-born Wilson spoke in a mellow tenor voice with overtones of a Southern drawl. Colonel House was a meek-looking fellow with sloping shoulders, a receding chin, big ears, and a mustache. His catlike eyes peered in cool calculation over high Mongolian cheekbones. He spoke slowly and huskily. Wilson, when alone with his family, was given to high jinks and did an amusing imitation of a drunk. Colonel House, even in private, was far more reserved than Wilson, indulging only in a thin smile or, at most, a half chuckle.

Here were two men who wanted parallel things. Wilson wanted to become President of the United States. House wanted to serve the man he thought best qualified for the Presidency. For all of the colonel's political cunning he was a progressive, a man of high principle; if Wilson's ideals had not matched his own, he would not have lifted a finger to help. According to one personality study of Wilson, he had a compulsive need for love and adoration, his perfectionist father having left him with a subconscious feeling of inadequacy. House was quick to praise Wilson, who glowed. By a kind of chemical affinity Wilson and House fell into friendship. As John Dos Passos described it: "This pair of middleaged politicians, family men both, were as excited about each other as two schoolgirls developing a crush." Colonel House later said of this first meeting:

> We talked and talked. We knew each other for congenial souls from the very beginning. . . . We exchanged our ideas about the democracies of the world, contrasted the European democracies with the United States, discussed where they differed, which was best in some respects and which in others. . . . I remember we were very urbane. Each gave the other the chance to have his say. . . . The hour flew away. It seemed no time when it was over.

Then Wilson had to leave because he had a date to meet a California Senator. He and House agreed to dine together within a couple of days. Only a few weeks later House said to Wilson, "Governor, isn't it strange that two men who never knew each other before, should think so much alike?" Baring his teeth in a horsy grin, Wilson replied, "My dear fellow, we have known each other all of our lives." Later, in response to a question from a politician, Wilson said, "Mr.

House is my second personality. He is my independent self. His thoughts and mine are one."

Wilson won the Democratic nomination and in 1912 was elected President. The selection of Cabinet members began in Colonel House's New York apartment on November 2. Besides picking most of the men Wilson ultimately appointed to the Cabinet, House's influence also counted heavily in Wilson's selection of ambassadors. Wilson was in and out of House's apartment several times between his election and inauguration. After the President-elect awakened at 8 A.M., House personally served him cereal and 2 raw eggs, into which orange or lemon juice was squeezed. In the evening, after dining in the seclusion of Colonel House's apartment, the telephone lifted off the hook to avoid interruptions, Wilson sometimes read aloud from the works of Keats, Wordsworth, and Matthew Arnold.

The Murray Hill section of Manhattan became the mecca of everyone wanting anything from Woodrow Wilson. They realized not only that House could put them in touch with the President-elect, but that House's recommendations carried great weight. The burgeoning friendship between Wilson and House disturbed some professional politicians. When Senator Thomas P. Gore of Oklahoma was asked what he thought of the colonel, he replied, "Take my word for it, he can walk on dead leaves and make no more noise than a tiger."

After Wilson was sworn in as President, a direct telephone line was set up between the White House and 145 East Thirty-fifth Street in Manhattan. To guarantee the utmost secrecy, Wilson and House communicated in code. The phone would ring in New York. Picking up the receiver, House would hear the President of the United States say, "This is Ajax." Over the phone Wilson called House any of three names—Beverly, Roland, or Bush. The President and his adviser also referred to Cabinet members by aliases plucked from Greek and Roman mythology. Only rarely did Wilson dictate letters to House; most of the time he pecked them out on his own typewriter. And nearly always the President signed himself "Affectionately yours."

Chapter 40

THE TRIANGLE FIRE

CONDITIONS were scandalous in New York's garment industry. Men, women, and children toiled day and night in smelly dingy factories and tenements. State labor laws were inadequate and seldom enforced. Factory inspection was a farce. Liberals fretted especially about working women and children. An 1899 law banning nightwork for women was declared unconstitutional by the New York court of appeals in 1907. The court held that the law deprived women of their "liberty" to work in factories all night or as long as they liked. Mayor Gaynor sputtered that "to such a use indeed did they (the judges) stretch this sacred word *liberty*." Although the International Ladies'

489

Garment Workers Union (I.L.G.W.U.) had been organized in 1900, most bosses tried to keep the labor movement as weak as possible.

One of the city's largest and most reactionary garment-manufacturing firms was the Triangle Waist Company. It was owned by Max Blanck and Isaac Harris, the very prototype of sweatshop bosses. They billed their female employees for needles and other supplies, taxed them for the chairs on which they sat, charged for their clothing lockers, and imposed fines treble the value of goods accidentally spoiled by the girls.

In 1908 Blanck and Harris tried to quell their workers' complaints by setting up a company union. Some rebellious employees, scorning paternalism, considered joining a real union. Behind locked doors and lowered shades about 100 Triangle workers met with officers of the I.L.G.W.U. and of the United Hebrew Trades. A few days later the Triangle company fired several employees suspected of trying to join a bona fide union. Although management claimed that it was compelled to cut the staff because of poor business, it quickly advertised for more employees.

Local 25 of the I.L.G.W.U. then called a strike against the firm for locking out its workers. Blanck and Harris hired thugs to beat up male pickets and employed prostitutes to mingle with female workers on the picket line. The police and courts sided with the Triangle owners. In sentencing one picket, a magistrate cried, "You are on strike against God!" The Women's Trade Union League cabled this remark to George Bernard Shaw, who cabled back: "DELIGHTFUL! MEDIEVAL AMERICA ALWAYS IN THE INTIMATE PERSONAL CONFIDENCE OF THE ALMIGHTY." After rich New York women and socially conscious pastors came out publicly on the side of the strikers, a compromise was reached. But this left the Triangle Waist Company a non-union shop, and many employees still felt bitter toward their bosses.

On March 25, 1911, the weather was raw. It was a Saturday afternoon, and although other shirtwaist plants were closed, the Triangle shop was working full blast. It occupied the top three floors of the ten-story Asch Building, a brick loft at 22 Washington Place near Greene Street, one block east of Washington Square. On the eighth, ninth, and tenth floors more than 600 employees were squeezed back to back and elbow to elbow at sewing machines. Most of them were girls between the ages of thirteen and twenty-three, Jewesses and Italians who lived on the Lower East Side.

At 5 P.M. a bell rang. The girls cut off their machines, ran to the dirty washroom, snatched coats out of lockers, and scurried for the elevators. Just then a mysterious fire broke out in the southeastern corner of the eighth floor. Perhaps it was caused by a burning match or cigarette thoughtlessly tossed into the ankle-deep litter near a sewing machine. With a whoosh and crackle the flame gushed into a flash fire. An updraft of air drew the flames and smoke from the eighth floor toward the roof. In a matter of seconds the upper three floors roared like a funeral pyre.

An immigrant youth, named Louis Waldman, later a Socialist candidate for governor of New York, was reading in the old Astor Library on Lafayette Street three blocks to the east. Roused from his book by the sound of fire engines, Waldman bolted out the door and ran toward the burning building. At the same time strollers from Washington Square swiveled their heads in the direction of the jangling fire bells and then scurried to the scene.

Inside the flaming building, horror was being piled on horror. Like many lofts, this one had no sprinkler system. There was a stand-pipe hose; but the working girls panicked, and the hose was never used. Eighth-floor windows blew out, sprinkling glass slivers onto the sidewalk. Sheets of flame now licked out of glassless windows, only to be sucked into other windows two floors above. A fireman said that the flames almost seemed drawn back inside by a magnet. One terrified elevator man darted out of his car and clattered down a stairway to safety. A passerby, named Joseph Zito, ran inside and took charge of the abandoned elevator. Five times he rammed through a gauntlet of flames to the ninth floor, bringing down twenty-five to thirty girls each trip.

Girls on the eighth floor ran to the stairway exit on the Washington Place side, but the door was locked. Fences of flame cut them off from the elevators. Screaming, praying, coughing, and clawing, they stampeded to windows, leaned out, and tried to gulp fresh air. Other girls, unable to reach the windows and suffocated by smoke, collapsed on sewing machines and burned to death. When the inferno became unbearable, young women at the windows started jumping.

Firemen had responded quickly to the four-alarm fire and cordoned off the block, keeping back ashen-faced spectators, who gazed help-lessly toward the torch in the sky. The firemen were equally helpless. Their extension ladders reached only to the sixth floor. Their hoses threw streams of water only as high as the seventh floor.

Girls were jumping in groups of three, four, and five. The firemen quickly pulled out rope nets, but as a battalion chief later sighed, "Life nets? What good were life nets? The little ones went right through the life nets and the pavement, too. Nobody could hold a life net when those girls from the ninth floor came down." A trio of girls landed on one net, it broke, and the firemen holding its edges were jerked in on the mangled bodies. The sky seemed to rain flesh. Spectators winced at the sound of bodies hitting the ground. Now fire trucks dared not move closer for fear of running over the dying. People standing on the sidewalk twisted damp fingers together as they watched the death of a pair of lovers. Suddenly silhouetted against the glare in a ninth-story window stood a man and a girl. Their clothing was stitched with flames. They kissed. Then, entwining their arms about each other, they stepped into eternity.

In only 10 minutes the holocaust was all over. A total of 141 workers died in the Triangle fire, and of this number, 125 were girls.

Sorrow ran like a river through the Lower East Side and gathered in guilty pools elsewhere in the city. Even in the mansions of the mighty, tenderhearted men and women wept as they read their newspapers. Jewish labor organizations collected a fund for the injured, and most of the city's workmen donated one day's pay to honor the dead. City officials prohibited any public demonstration, but the bereaved made a silent display of their grief by holding a mass funeral. Rain fell the day of the funeral and for more than 5 hours more than 100,000 persons splashed speechlessly through wet streets, following hearses to a common grave in the Mount Zion Cemetery in Maspeth, Queens.

Two days after the fire—and two days too late—the city building department posted a sign on the Asch Building proclaiming it unsafe. About a week after that a protest meeting was held in the Metropolitan Opera House. Rabbi Stephen S. Wise declared "the life of the lowliest worker . . . sacred and inviolable" and urged instant action to avert this kind of tragedy. Redheaded Rose Schneiderman, an organizer in the needle trades, made an inflammatory speech. From all sides of the opera house came shouts of "Down with the capitalistic legislature!" and "Why can't workingmen have their own legislators?" A committee of safety was organized. Henry Moskowitz, a settlement-house worker, introduced a resolution calling on the state legislature to make a thorough investigation of safety conditions in factories and to pass new and more stringent laws.

Nine months after the fire Max Blanck and Isaac Harris were tried on charges of manslaughter. The case was heard in the Tombs, a brownstone monstrosity occupying two blocks just north of Foley Square. The attorney for the proprietors was Max D. Steuer, a soft-voiced Tammany brave, who later served a long list of notorious clients. On the bench sat Justice Thomas Crain, another Tammany stalwart. In effect, he directed a verdict of acquittal, and the jurors took only 100 minutes to pronounce the defendants not guilty. On December 28, 1911, a New York *Evening Mail* columnist, named Franklin P. Adams, wrote in his diary: "Reading that Mr. Harris and Mr. Blanck are not to suffer at all for their so dreadful negligence I am grieved, and at odds with them that did acquit them, albeit my heart is soft as any melon."

Less melonlike was the reaction of working families that had lost loved ones. The day the verdict was handed down, hundreds of grieving relatives gathered outside the Tombs. Blanck and Harris, guarded by five cops, tried to sneak out of the building by the Leonard Street exit. They were spotted. A howl of fury smashed through the air. David Weiner, a young man whose seventeen-year-old sister had perished in the fire, charged her bosses, shaking his fist and shrilling, "Not guilty? Not guilty? It was murder! Murder!" He screamed and wept and finally collapsed and had to be taken to a hospital. One clothing worker wrote in his autobiography: "For half a year I was unable to enjoy the taste of food. Through those days and nights, I had no rest neither in the shop nor at home. Day and night I saw their forms, living and dead."

On March 29, 1911, the State Capitol Building at Albany caught fire and caused more than $5,000,000 damages. It was one thing for upstate lawmakers to read what had happened in New York City four days earlier. It was quite another thing to see for themselves the angry glare of flames. A state factory investigating commission was organized. It consisted of two state senators, three assemblymen, and four citizens appointed by the state government. The commission was granted broad powers of investigation, and it sat for sixteen months. State Senator Robert F. Wagner, father of the city's later mayor, Robert F. Wagner, Jr., was elected chairman. State Assemblyman Alfred E. Smith was named vice-chairman. Like-minded in their liberal outlook, the German immigrant and the Irish boy who grew up on the streets of New York tackled the problem fearlessly and effectively.

Monumental reforms flowed from the Triangle fire. New York State's entire labor code was rewritten, becoming the best of any state in the nation. Labor unions, so long ignored and repressed, began to come into their own. Some historians pinpoint this tragedy and its consequences as the genesis of the New Deal.

At the turn of the century New York's public libraries did not compare with those of Boston, Cleveland, Minneapolis, and Cincinnati. However, the city fathers were remedying this situation.

At the urging of Andrew H. Green and others, in 1895 three private libraries were consolidated—on paper. One was the Astor Library, bequeathed by John Jacob Astor, who had died in 1848. Another was the Lenox Library, put together by a book collector and philanthropist, named James Lenox, who had died in 1880. The third was the Tilden Library, established by Samuel J. Tilden, a corporation lawyer, governor of New York and Democratic Presidential candidate, who had died in 1886.

To bring the three collections together under one roof, it was decided to erect a huge new library building on the west side of Fifth Avenue between Fortieth and Forty-second streets. At the time the reservoir still occupied the site, which in 1884 had been named Bryant Park in honor of poet William Cullen Bryant. The city agreed to provide the land, to build and equip the new library, and to maintain it. On the other hand, trustees of the newly created New York Public Library, Astor, Lenox and Tilden Foundations—its full name —promised to establish a free circulating branch and a public library and reading room. Andrew Carnegie donated $5,000,000 to the project.

The reservoir was torn down, and construction of the new building began in 1902. The architects were John Merven Carrère and Thomas Hastings. They built an enormous marble palace, costing more than $9,000,000. Incorporated into the structure was marble from Vermont, Tennessee, Greece, Italy, France, Germany, and Belgium. According to present-day architects, the building probably comes nearer than any other in America to the realization of Beaux-Arts design at its best, and they call it a joyous creation.

The wonderful new library was dedicated on May 23, 1911. Library directors and trustees, together with civic dignitaries, marched, two by two, past 600 invited guests to a platform erected in the central portico of the library's Fifth Avenue entrance. Bringing up the rear were William Howard Taft, the portly President of the United States, and ninety-three-year-old John Bigelow, editor, author, diplomat, and president of the library's board of trustees. Bigelow had fretted that he wouldn't live long enough to take part in this ceremony, and when he spoke, his voice was so weak that he couldn't be heard more than two feet away. President Taft summed up the occasion best of all when he said, "This day crowns a work of national importance."

Indeed it did. Apart from the 80 branch libraries later developed, the New York Public Library on Fifth Avenue became the most widely used research library in the Western world, visited by 3,000,000 persons a year. It contains the world's largest reading room. With its 4,500,000 volumes and bound pamphlets, it ranks third in the nation, exceeded only by the Library of Congress and Harvard University. Its 80 miles of bookshelves contain data in 3,000 languages and about 50 centuries of human wisdom and folly. Its 800-member staff answers 10,000 questions a day.

Two stone lions flank the library's Fifth Avenue entrance. According to New York folklore, these kingly beasts only roar when a virgin passes.

Another notable structure that took shape about this time was the Woolworth Building, erected by round-faced Napoleon-worshiping Frank W. Woolworth, the ten-cent-store tycoon. He envied the Metropolitan Life Insurance Building, which in 1908 was the tallest skyscraper in town. It stood at Madison Avenue and East Twenty-fourth Street, its tower soared fifty stories heavenward, and it contained four clocks with faces larger than those of Big Ben in London's Houses of Parliament.

Determined to let no one surpass him, the department store magnate hired an engineer just to measure the Metropolitan Building. From street level to the tip of its ornate peak the skyscraper loomed 701 feet 3 inches high. Woolworth then ordered architect Cass Gilbert to design a structure that would dwarf the Metropolitan. The site chosen for Woolworth's masterpiece was Broadway between Barclay Street on the south and Park Place on the north. At the time the land was occupied by a 6-story building. Woolworth told his architect to model his new building after the Houses of Parliament, so Gilbert designed in the Gothic style. The building's terra-cotta façade was so elaborately ornamented, so delicate and lacelike in effect, so studded with gargoyles, and so beautiful that it resembled a cathedral more than an office building. In fact, it came to be called the Cathedral of Commerce. One of the hod carriers who helped build it was William O'Dwyer.

The finished structure rose 60 stories, or 792 feet above Broadway. It cost Woolworth $13,500,000, which he paid in cash. This was no strain for the chain-store owner; in 1913 his 684 stores did a business of more than $66,000,000. The new skyscraper was opened on April 24, 1913. Woolworth invited 900 guests to honor Cass Gilbert at a banquet held on the twenty-seventh floor. Woolworth's private office, modeled after a room in one of Napoleon's palaces, contained a life-size bronze bust of Napoleon, one of Napoleon's clocks, and a painting of Napoleon seated in his coronation robes. Woolworth exulted because he now owned the tallest skyscraper in the world. It attracted 300,000 visitors every year until the Empire State Building was completed. Frank Woolworth once received a postcard from the Pacific coast addressed simply: "The Highest Building in the World," and while traveling in Europe, he gleefully noticed that a trade paper symbolized all America with a photograph of his building, not even bothering to name it.

The day the Woolworth Building opened, President Woodrow Wilson sat in the White House and pressed a button that turned on 80,000 light bulbs in the new skyscraper. Despite the glow, lights dimmed elsewhere in the world with the approach of war.

Chapter 41

THE LEAGUE OF NATIONS
OPENS ON BROADWAY

KAISER WILHELM II, the last emperor of Germany, said long afterward, "The visit of Colonel House to Berlin and London in the spring of 1914 almost prevented the World War." President Wilson had sent his man from Manhattan to Europe in the hope of bringing about an understanding between Germany and England, which were rasping one another raw. On June 1, 1914, Colonel House was given a private audience by the Kaiser at Potsdam. House later wrote:

> I found that he had all the versatility of (Theodore) Roosevelt with something more of charm, something less of force. He has

what to me is a disagreeable habit of bringing his face very close to one when he talks most earnestly. His English is clear and well chosen and, though he talks vehemently, yet he is too much the gentleman to monopolize the conversation. It was give-and-take all the way through.

The Colonel was left with the impression that the Kaiser did not want war. House felt that Wilhelm, by trying a bluff, had put himself in a situation from which he could not back down.

New Yorkers were surprised when they picked up the New York *Times* of June 28, 1914, and read this headline:

HEIR TO AUSTRIA'S THRONE IS SLAIN
WITH HIS WIFE BY A BOSNIAN YOUTH
TO AVENGE SEIZURE OF HIS COUNTRY

Psychologically unprepared for war, New York's citizens tended to shrug off the assassination at Sarajevo. They thronged to movie houses to see the latest episode of *The Perils of Pauline,* a serial in which actress Pearl White was often left dangling from a cliff—in actuality, the New Jersey Palisades, where much of the action was filmed. Europe had had no general war for ninety-nine years, or ever since the end of the struggle against Napoleon in 1815, so it seemed unlikely that the continent could now be ravaged by a new war.

Regardless of wishful thinking, events in Europe developed quickly. Austria sent Serbia an ultimatum. Serbia gave in to most of Austria's demands. European stock exchanges collapsed. Despite peace efforts, Austria declared war on Serbia. Herbert Hoover said in his memoirs: "It is a curious commentary on a civilization in process of being blown up that so well informed a newspaper as the *New York Times* from July 1st to July 22nd carried no alarming European news on the front page." An Austrian force attacked Belgrade. Russia, France, and Germany mobilized. A British fleet sailed under sealed orders. Germany ordered Russia to end its mobilization. The balance of power had been upset, and chaos was replacing order.

On July 31 the New York Stock Exchange closed. Two days later Secretary of the Treasury William G. McAdoo hurried from Washington to New York at the urgent request of Wall Street bankers. Among other pressing problems, $77,000,000 worth of New York City's bonds and notes were held in Europe. McAdoo and his wife were met at Pennsylvania Station by harried financiers. She later wrote: "I was startled by their white faces and trembling voices. Could these be America's great men?"

German troops goose-stepped into Luxembourg and demanded free passage across Belgium. Great Britain demanded that Germany observe Belgian neutrality. Germany refused. England then declared war on Germany. So did France. Here in neutral America, here in the port of New York, ships of the warring nations were strung out from Ellis Island to Tottenville, so close that crew members could exchange scowls and hard words.

Sixty-three days before the Sarajevo assassination that triggered World War I, an attempt had been made to assassinate New York's new mayor. This was tall, long-legged, brown-eyed John Purroy Mitchel. As president of the board of aldermen, Mitchel had served as acting mayor during Mayor Gaynor's recuperation from his bullet wound, and after Gaynor died, the administration of city affairs fell on Mitchel. On November 4, 1913, Mitchel was elected mayor in his own right. A Democrat, Mitchel was the candidate of the Republicans and the Fusion party, which resented, among other things, Gaynor's attitude toward the Becker case.

Taking office at the age of thirty-four, Mitchel became the youngest mayor in the city's history. At noon on Friday, April 17, 1914, Mitchel started to leave City Hall to go to lunch. With him were Frank Polk, the corporation counsel; Arthur Woods, the police commissioner; and George V. Mullan, the tax commissioner. An elderly man stepped up to the mayor and fired at him point-blank. The bullet grazed the mayor's ear and slammed into Polk's left cheek, lodging under the tongue. The corporation counsel's wound was painful but not critical, and he quickly recovered. The attacker was seized. Mayor Mitchel walked beside his assailant as the small group of excited men crossed City Hall Park and entered a nearby police station.

The would-be killer was identified as Michael P. Mahoney, a psychotic with imagined grievances against the city administration. He was sent to an insane asylum. When the public read about this assassination attempt, it also learned for the first time that Mayor Mitchel always carried a revolver for his own protection.

Next to LaGuardia, Mayor Mitchel gave New York the best government it has ever known. Brilliant, well educated, and honest, Mitchel did his work extremely well. His election as a Fusion candidate was one of Tammany Hall's most decisive defeats. Theodore Roosevelt said that Mitchel had "given us as nearly an ideal administration . . . as I have seen in my lifetime, or as I have heard of since New York became a big city." Oswald Garrison Villard, president of the New York *Evening Post,* wrote of Mitchel's regime: "Never was the fire department so well handled, never were the city's charities so well administered, nor its finances grappled with upon such a sound and far-sighted basis. . . . Under him the schools progressed wonderfully, while prisons were carried on with some semblance of scientific and humanitarian management." The gangs that had terrorized the city for nearly a century were broken up, Police Commissioner Woods declaring that "the gangster and the gunman are practically extinct."

For all of Mayor Mitchel's accomplishments he lacked tact and sometimes seemed downright unfair. When State Senator Robert F. Wagner tried to delay the federal government's acquisition of property needed for coastal defense, Mitchel attacked him as "the gentleman from Prussia." The remark antagonized New Yorkers of German birth or descent. Himself a Catholic, Mitchel also incurred the enmity of Catholics by insisting that the city had the right to examine the books of Catholic charities subsidized by the city.

The outbreak of World War I intensified unemployment in New York, and young Harry Hopkins was named executive secretary of the city's board of child welfare. Iowa-born Hopkins was now launched on the career that reached a climax when he became to Franklin D. Roosevelt what Colonel House was to Woodrow Wilson.

New York's large German population worried officials who favored England, France, and Russia. On August 1, 1914, when Germany declared war on Russia and the Kaiser made a rousing speech from the balcony of his Berlin palace, a German-American newspaper called the *New Yorker Herold* printed the story under this headline: "ALL GERMAN HEARTS BEAT HIGHER TODAY." William Randolph Hearst owned a New York German-language periodical, called the *Deutsches Journal.* He opposed any help to the Allies. The Germans praised Hearst in the Berlin *Vossische Zeitung,* saying that "he has exposed the selfishness of England and her campaign of abuse against Germany, and has preached justice for the Central Powers." Federal officials scanned Hearst's papers for sedition, a Secret Service agent infiltrated Hearst's home disguised as a butler, and a woman in a restaurant hissed, *"Boche!"* at him. Hearst is said to have bowed toward her and murmured, "You're quite right, madame, it is all bosh." Still, Hearst newspapers were banned in England, Canada, and France.

Some men living in New York were reservists in the German army, and they paraded the streets with German flags. Occasionally they brawled with New Yorkers of British and French descent who displayed flags of their mother countries. Mayor Mitchel finally banned all foreign flags. President Wilson officially proclaimed the neutrality of the United States and called on all Americans to remain impartial in thought and action, but there was little neutrality. Colonel House believed that "civilization itself" could not afford to see the British "go down in the war," and he preached preparedness to Wilson; but the President hesitated.

In 1914 the private banking firm of J. P. Morgan & Company moved into a new gray five-story building at 23 Wall Street. Soon after the outbreak of the European war Henry P. Davidson, a Morgan partner, telephoned the State Department in Washington and asked for a ruling on loans to belligerent governments. Secretary of State William Jennings Bryan told President Wilson that "money is the worst of all contrabands because it commands everything else." The State Department told the House of Morgan that it had no objections to loans to neutrals, but that "loans by American bankers to any foreign nation which is at war are inconsistent with the true spirit of neutrality." Yet at the same time the State Department sanctioned unlimited sales of munitions to all nations.

On September 10, 1915, a joint English-French commission arrived in New York, hoping to float an Allied war loan in America. More than a year had passed since the State Department forbade American bankers to lend money to belligerent nations. Ties between the United States and the Allies had grown closer. Thomas W. Lamont, another Morgan partner, admitted many years later: "Our firm never for one moment had been neutral; we didn't know how to be. From the very start we did everything we could to contribute to the cause of the Allies." The Morgan bank now was allowed to sign a contract for a loan of $500,000,000 to be floated by 61 New York banks. Obviously, America had abandoned strict neutrality. Before the war ended, the House of Morgan bought $3,000,000,000 in war supplies for the Allies and realized a commission of 1 percent, or $30,000,000

In 1915 a German submarine sank the *Lusitania* 10 miles off the coast of Ireland. Among the passengers were 188 Americans, 114 of whom lost their lives. The day after the disaster the largest crowds since the outbreak of war gathered in front of New York newspaper

offices to read about the *Lusitania* on bulletin boards. Many spectators cried that America should declare war on Germany. Frank
Munsey, the newspaper magnate, telephoned from his New York
office to Jay Edwin Murphy, managing editor of his Washington
Times. "Has Wilson declared war yet?" Munsey shouted. "No, Mr.
Munsey." Furiously, Munsey screamed, "Tell him to declare war
against Germany at once!" Here in New York, as elsewhere in America, the sinking of the *Lusitania* did much to destroy the considerable
pro-German sentiment which had existed during the earlier part of
the war. When the French composer Saint-Saëns arrived in New
York, he was welcomed at the pier by, among others, a Wagnerian
diva. The old man shrank from her in horror, crying, "No! No! Away!
You are a German!"

Now the United States stepped up the shipment of war matériel to
the Allies. The most important spot in this nation for the transfer of
munitions to Allied ships was Black Tom, a mile-long peninsula jutting into the Hudson River from Jersey City just behind the Statue of
Liberty. Originally an island, Black Tom had been connected to the
Jersey shore by a fill about 150 feet wide. Freight cars were nosed
along a network of tracks to piers, where their supplies could be
unloaded onto barges for transfer to waiting vessels in the harbor.
The night of July 30, 1916, 2,000,000 pounds of explosives were
stored in the railway cars, on piers, and in barges tied alongside docks.

At 2:08 A.M. the New York area was rocked by a mighty explosion. All 2,000,000 pounds of munitions erupted in a series of blasts
that demolished the Black Tom terminal. New York skyscrapers and
apartment houses quivered. People were thrown out of bed. Bridges
trembled. Half the windows in the Customhouse were shattered. In
the nearby Aquarium all the skylights were smashed, but the fish
tanks remained intact. Every window was broken in the House of
Morgan, and a total of $1,000,000 worth of damage was done to
windowpanes throughout the Wall Street area. In Brooklyn and as
far north as Forty-second Street in Manhattan, windows shattered
into glassy splinters. Damage estimated at $45,000,000 was done
within a radius of 25 miles, and the shock was felt as far away as
Pennsylvania, Maryland, and Connecticut. For more than 3 hours
shrapnel and shells burst through the heavens like skyrockets.

Surprisingly, only 7 lives were lost. Damage at Black Tom itself
came to $20,000,000. New Jersey clapped an embargo on the transit
of munitions through the state, but this ban remained in effect only

10 days. Most people regarded the disaster as an accident. The theory was not accepted by businessmen who suffered financial loss. For the next 14 years investigators conducted a worldwide hunt for the German agents they believed responsible for the blast. However, in 1930 the Mixed Claims Commission sitting at The Hague ruled that it had not been established beyond a reasonable doubt that Black Tom was the work of German saboteurs.

Nevertheless, New York had become undercover headquarters for a gigantic ring of German saboteurs and spies. This was financed in part by Count Johann von Bernstorff, the German ambassador to the United States, who brought $150,000,000 in German treasury notes to this city and deposited them in the Chase National Bank. Perhaps the favorite rendezvous for German agents was a four-story brownstone, at 123 West Fifteenth Street. This old-fashioned dwelling, with its big dining room and its wine cellar, was rented by Martha Held, who called herself Martha Gordon. A handsome buxom woman, with dark-blue eyes and glossy black hair, she herself did no spying but provided a haven for secret operatives. So many of them skulked in and out of her home at all hours of the night that neighbors whispered that she ran a bawdyhouse. This gossip probably suited her because it kept snoopers away. Bombs and dynamite were stored in her place, and the destruction of ships and munitions and factories was discussed in guttural German accents over beer and wine.

Colonel House learned that one German agent in New York was involved in a plot to kill President Wilson. By a series of notes to Germany the President caused that nation to restrict its U-boat attacks awhile, and largely because of his skillful diplomacy and the slogan "He Kept Us Out of the War," Wilson won the Democratic nomination and in 1916 ran for the Presidency a second time.

His Republican opponent was Charles Evans Hughes, Associate Justice of the United States Supreme Court. The November election was so close that Hughes fell asleep in the Astor Hotel thinking that he was the next President, only to awaken the following morning to learn that Wilson had been reelected. New York newspapers actually published extras bearing huge portraits of "The President-Elect— Charles Evans Hughes." Tammany, dominated by Irish Catholics who were angered because Wilson had not helped Irish rebels, did little, if anything, to keep him in the White House. A straitlaced Presbyterian, Wilson considered New York "rotten to the core."

When Germany notified the United States that it was going to resume unrestricted warfare, the President asked Congress to arm American merchant ships. The Senate refused, but Wilson armed them by executive order. New Yorkers braced themselves for the worst. A cavalry force began guarding the city's water supply, and other soldiers patrolled the East River and its bridges. James W. Gerard, the American ambassador to Germany, was recalled and happened to be in New York on the evening of April 2, 1917. He went to the Metropolitan Opera House for a performance of De Koven's *The Canterbury Pilgrims*. Between acts he heard newsboys shouting on the streets outside that the President had asked Congress to declare war on Germany.

Gerard darted for a phone and called Herbert Bayard Swope of the *World,* who told him that the news was indeed true. Just as Gerard hung up the receiver, an opera company director passed by. Excitedly, Gerard broke the news and demanded that the director do something—"order the news read from the stage, for example, and have *The Star-Spangled Banner* played." The director replied coolly, "No, the opera company is neutral." Shocked and angered, Gerard hurried back to his private box, shouted the news to the audience, and called for a cheer for President Wilson. Startled by this announcement, the opera-goers sat in silence a moment and then broke into cheers. On its own initiative the orchestra swung into the national anthem. Some people in the audience were still yelling and applauding when the curtain went up on the last act to reveal, among others, a German singer, named Margarete Ober, who played the Wife of Bath. It was obvious to all that she was nervous. About two minutes later she fainted and had to be carried off stage; the opera finished without her.

On April 6, 1917, Congress voted for war, and the President signed a resolution declaring that hostilities existed between the United States and Germany. At 5 A.M. that day Dudley Field Malone, collector of the port of New York, got a crucial phone call from Washington. Word also was flashed to the army installation on Governors Island. In port at the time were eighteen German ships, five of them anchored in the Hudson just off West 135th Street.

When Malone gave the signal, 600 waiting customs agents seized the vessels. In the anemic light of dawn Malone, accompanied by a group of his men, boarded the *Vaterland,* one of the world's largest passenger ships. At the top of the gangway he was met by Commodore Hans Ruser, who knew Malone. They bowed and exchanged wispy smiles. The German officer said sadly, "We are ready." Down came the flag of Germany, and up went the flag of the United States on this and the other German vessels thus interned. It was the first act of war.

The Twenty-second United States Infantry had slept on its arms awaiting the call. Army tugs nosed against Governors Island, took aboard the soldiers, and then posted them on piers throughout the city. A total of 1,200 German sailors and 325 naval officers were arrested and sent to Ellis Island. A company of American soldiers marched through the Hudson tubes to Hoboken, where they seized piers of the North German Lloyd and Hamburg-American lines, placing part of the Hoboken waterfront under martial law. About 200 Germans were rounded up in saloons and boardinghouses of the Hoboken dock area and interned on Ellis Island. New York City Police Commissioner Woods had organized 12,000 of his policemen into what he called "a fighting force." Now he threw guards around all bridges and filled 180 trucks with machine gunners and sharpshooters ready to put down any attempted demonstration. After all, the city still held many German army reservists.

A sunken steel net was stretched across the Narrows to prevent U-boats from sneaking into the Upper Bay. At the outbreak of war the United States ranked only ninth among the nations of the world in total tonnage of oceangoing vessels. New York now became the principal port for movement of cargo and shipment of troops, a total of 1,656,000 doughboys sailing from here for France. Before long German submarines sowed mines around Sandy Hook in the path of outbound ships, so 16 tugs were outfitted as minesweepers. Working in pairs, they found and exploded floating mines, which might have taken hundreds of lives and sunk thousands of tons of shipping.

Intolerance swept New York like a plague. A statue symbolizing Germany was one of twelve figures decorating the sixth-floor façade of the Customhouse just south of Bowling Green. A sculptor was hired to chip the imperial eagle from the breastplate of this Valkyrie. A Brooklyn pastor cried that "German soldiers are sneaking, sniveling cowards!" Dachshunds, a breed of dog well liked by Germans, were kicked on the sidewalks of New York and renamed liberty pups. Sauerkraut became liberty cabbage. German measles were called liberty measles. German-language lessons were banned in city schools. The Bank of Germany at First Avenue and Seventy-fourth Street changed its name to the Bank of Europe.

Theodore Roosevelt demanded that the German-American press be muzzled. Assistant Secretary of the Navy Franklin D. Roosevelt urged the translation of a book about German atrocities—most of which later were proved untrue. Telephone wiretapping, first used in New York in 1895, was resumed on a large scale in 1917. The federal government set up a huge switchboard in the Customhouse, tapped the lines of hundreds of aliens, kept relays of stenographers taking notes on private conversations, and nabbed many enemies.

However senseless and cruel some of these acts may seem in retrospect, there was a very real danger of subversion and sabotage. Colonel House wrote President Wilson: "Attempts will likely be made to blow up waterworks, electric light and gas plants, subways and bridges in cities like New York. . . . Police Commissioner Woods tells me he has definitely located a building in New York in which two shipments of arms have been stored by Germans." Mark Sullivan said: "Five German spies, taking up points of strategy and acting simultaneously, could paralyze the city of New York." Mysterious fires broke out along the Brooklyn waterfront, fire bombs were found in ships heading for Europe, and in the first 7 months of the war more than $18,000,000 worth of food supplies was burned in the United States by German sympathizers. It must be added in all fairness, though, that only a few aliens interfered with our war effort.

After Herbert Hoover was appointed the nation's food administrator, the all-out effort to conserve food was called Hooverizing. New York's vacant land and some small parks were turned into vegetable gardens. No meat was served on Tuesdays. The Hotel Association of New York City gave Hoover a plan that called for adulterating wheat bread with cheaper flour and holding rolls to one ounce or less. Oscar of the Waldorf prodded his chefs into inventing desserts to be made without eggs, butter, or white sugar, and a recipe for War Cake à la Waldorf was distributed throughout the country.

Employment rose, and office space became scarce as industrial contractors poured into the city. The largest armory in America was erected in the west Bronx. Ten two-story buildings were constructed on Wards Island to serve as a military hospital. More than seventy structures and a temporary railroad system were installed on Governors Island. Schoolchildren collected fruit pits and nutshells for use in making gas masks, besides gathering twenty-five tons of clothing for the children of Belgium and France. And Broadway became a rehearsal hall for the League of Nations.

Colonel House was intimate with many of the most powerful men on earth, but the man who attracted him most, next to Woodrow Wilson, was Sir Edward Grey. A high-minded statesman, sincere and experienced, Sir Edward was Great Britain's Secretary for Foreign Affairs. He and House soon discovered that they thought alike. Sir Edward believed that war might have been averted if the nations of the world had been organized into some kind of permanent international conference. As early as 1915, in a letter to the colonel, Sir Edward had used the phrase "League of Nations." In later letters and conferences with Sir Edward, House agreed that an association of nations was needed to preserve the future peace. Looking forward to the years after this unfortunate war, the colonel transmitted Sir Edward's idea to Woodrow Wilson. On May 27, 1916, in a major address the President first announced his belief in the establishment of such a league, saying that "the nations of the world must in some way band themselves. . . . " In the summer of 1917 the President suggested that Colonel House organize a group of experts to draft a constitution for a League of Nations.

Since these men would concern themselves with postwar problems, they were wary of letting the Germans hear about the project, lest they think that the United States was considering surrender. Work therefore went forward in absolute secrecy. The League was given the noncommittal name of the Inquiry. Colonel House named his brother-in-law head of the organization; this was Dr. Sidney E. Mezes, president of the College of the City of New York. Walter Lippmann was made executive secretary of the Inquiry. A native New Yorker and an editor of the *New Republic,* Lippmann had gone to Washington to help Secretary of War Newton D. Baker handle labor problems connected with war production. Only twenty-seven years old, Lippmann was brilliant and capable.

The State Department played no part in this project. The Inquiry's expenses were met by private funds available to President Wilson. Colonel House and his associates recruited a small staff of specialists from academic circles and held their first meetings in the New York Public Library. But because of the lack of space and the fear that they might attract attention there, the new group soon moved its headquarters. Among the recruits was Dr. Isaiah Bowman, director of the American Geographical Society, the nation's oldest such organization. It occupied a building on Broadway between 155th and 156th streets, and this is where the Inquiry really buckled down to work.

The nearly 150 scholars brought into the group included geographers, territorial experts, specialists on colonial possessions, historians, ethnographers, cartographers, economists, political scientists, and the like. Reading, writing, conferring, checking references, and blowing dust off ancient atlases, these dedicated men avoided any major conflict with the State Department and managed to keep their work a secret from the press. In their collective wisdom they compiled a suggested outline for a permanent association of nations. This, they hoped, would guarantee the territorial integrity and political independence of its members, ban the manufacture of munitions by private enterprise, and otherwise enforce disarmament. Their original draft consisted of twenty-three articles, which House offered to President Wilson. The President approved all but five. Wilson dropped the proposed international court but retained the suggested secretariat and an assembly of delegates. Thus did the League of Nations first take shape on upper Broadway in New York City.

Colonel House became suspicious of another New Yorker who had won the President's respect. This was Bernard M. Baruch, a handsome long-legged Wall Streeter, who camouflaged his lightning-quick mind behind an easygoing manner. He made a fortune in the stock market and bluntly identified himself as a speculator. But Baruch's definition of a speculator was "one who thinks and plans for a future event—and acts before it occurs." In 1912 he had met Wilson for the first time in New York's Plaza Hotel. Like Colonel House's, Baruch's life was changed from that moment on. He said reverently, "I have met one of the great men of the world." As war deepened, Baruch was often seen at the White House, reporters noting his air of self-assurance, his high stiff collar, and the costly stickpin in his tie.

Baruch believed that "if you understand raw materials, you understand the politics of the world." Baruch knew raw materials. He understood the sources of supply, production, and prices. Wilson appointed him chairman of the War Industries Board, thus bestowing on him perhaps the greatest power ever held by any American except a President. Granted the authority to mobilize industry and manpower, Baruch was expected to convert the entire nation into one huge factory. Henry Ford, during his anti-Semitic period, called Baruch "the most powerful man in the world." Colonel House distrusted Baruch because of his Wall Street background and put a spy on his trail. The secret agent found nothing suspicious in his behavior; indeed he came to like Baruch so much that he finally confessed that he had been hired to watch him.

To conserve coal, the federal government ordered all big cities to cut down on the use of electric signs. Secretary of the Navy Josephus Daniels later wrote:

> New York responded with such howls and denunciations as can hardly be described . . . in some respects New York is more set in its provincialism than any "hick" town in America. Smaller cities obeyed the order to do without the White Way at night because of the exigency of war. Not New York. It raised such a row that coal operators doubled their energies to furnish enough coal so that the White Way could again blaze brightly and let New York City turn night into day.

New York was anything but a hick town. In 1917, for the first time ever, it contained more motor vehicles than horses. That watershed of a year the city had 114,717 cars of various kinds and only 108,743 horses. New York's last 2-horse streetcar made its final trip down Broadway on July 26, 1917.

In the municipal election of 1917 Mayor Mitchel's talent for making enemies caused him trouble. Standing for reelection, he lost the Republican primary and ran on the Fusion ticket alone. His Tammany Hall rival for mayor was John F. Hylan.

A ponderous man lacking wit, warmth, or wisdom, Hylan was called Red Mike because of his red hair and mustache. Although he was only a mediocre lawyer, he had served as a Kings County judge. Hearst backed Hylan for mayor because both favored municipal ownership and operation of rapid transit and because Hearst knew that he could control Hylan. The campaign was vicious. Mitchel and other Fusionists tried to smear Hylan as pro-German, but Hylan himself was almost forgotten in the attack on Hearst, the so-called spokesman of the Kaiser. Bumbling empty-headed Hylan won, however, and Woodrow Wilson murmured, "How is it possible for the greatest city in the world to place such a man in high office?" Once again Tammany Hall sat in the saddle.

The defeated Mitchel enlisted in the army and was commissioned a major in the air service. He suffered from excruciating headaches, which may have been caused by an Indian poison that had got into his system when he was traveling in the wilds of Peru. The attacks would leave him temporarily blind. "If I get a real bad headache

while up in the clouds," he told a friend, "it will be all over with me."
On July 6, 1918, Major John Purroy Mitchel fell 500 feet from his
single-seater scout plane and was killed at Camp Gerstner, Lake
Charles, Louisiana. An investigation proved that his safety belt had
been unfastened.

As other gallant youths spilled their blood in strange places with
unpronounceable names, a horror as great as war itself visited New
York City. This was the flu epidemic.

Influenza is an Italian word meaning influence. An acute infectious
disease, it was called influenza because it was first believed to be
caused by the influence of some mysterious agency. This was before
the discovery of the filterable virus. In September, 1918, the flu was
brought to the eastern seaboard by sick people disembarking from
transatlantic liners. Americans and others called it Spanish influenza,
but there is no proof that it originated in Spain. At first the disease
was the subject of feeble jokes, such as this: "I had a little bird named
'Enza.' I opened the window and in-flu-enza."

Franklin D. Roosevelt didn't regard the illness as a jest. On
September 19 the handsome Assistant Secretary of the Navy landed
in New York after a two-month tour of overseas naval bases and the
front lines. Stricken with the flu, he was carried off the transport
Leviathan and driven by ambulance to his mother's home at 47 East
Sixty-fifth Street.

The onset of sickness was rapid. A victim felt chilly and weak,
suffered pains in his eyes or ears or head or back, complained of
dizziness, coughed, clutched his throat because it felt sore, and in a
few hours was prostrated. Anyone in close contact with a flu patient
could expect to be stricken within the next few hours or days, so
quickly did the plague spread.

After the first few cases of influenza had been diagnosed in New
York, Dr. Royal S. Copeland, city health commissioner, declared,
"The city is in no danger of an epidemic." He was wrong. More and
more New Yorkers sickened and died from the flu. Incoming ships
were fumigated. It was too late. The death toll in the city quickly
climbed to more than 800 persons within 24 hours. Some hysterical
people claimed that the disease had been sent here deliberately by the
Germans, possibly by U-boats. Hospitals filled up, overflowed, and
turned away patients. Doctors urged everyone to stay home. So many
staff members at Bellevue Hospital succumbed that a few doctors

suggested the place be closed, a proposal voted down by the trustees. Nurses dragged about their duties, eyes black-ringed with fatigue.

Two thousand telephone operators, about one-quarter of the city's staff, were stricken. Municipal services slowed down as transit workers, garbage collectors, firemen, and policemen failed to report for work. Cops lucky enough to stay on their feet directed traffic wearing masks over their faces. Children enjoyed the cheesecloth masks their mothers fitted over their faces but gagged on poultices made of garlic and camphor. City welfare workers were pressed into unfamiliar jobs such as carrying stretchers, scrubbing floors, and digging graves.

A worried Mayor Hylan told city engineers to plan the excavation of many graves. He said he would punish any doctor who overcharged, but apparently few did. To be sure, some undertakers gave special consideration to the rich, and in one tenement a corpse was not removed for four days. By contrast, a certain prostitute gave such tender care as a volunteer nurse that she was praised by patients and authorities alike.

As the epidemic mounted, business firms, cultural institutions, and places of entertainment closed down. From September to November, 1918, the city's hubbub was hushed. The flu killed more New Yorkers than any plague in the city's history. In relative numbers, however, it was by no means the most deadly epidemic. In 1832, 1849, 1854, and 1866, when the population was smaller, cholera killed proportionately more.

The final death toll from the flu epidemic of 1918 was New York City, 12,562; New York State, 20,000; the United States, 500,000; and the entire world, 21,000,000. The disaster struck a heavy blow at New York's insurance firms. They paid more money to the beneficiaries of flu victims than they did to survivors of soldiers killed in battle during World War I.

About the time the plague waned, the war itself came to an end. When the United Press wrongly reported on November 7, 1918, that an armistice had been signed, New Yorkers celebrated wildly. Elderly brokers danced in Wall Street, J. P. Morgan threw ticker tape out of his office window, strangers hugged one another, pushcart peddlers gave free candy to children, girls kissed the first uniformed men they saw, and a French general was carried triumphantly up Fifth Avenue. A roll of toilet paper tossed from the Waldorf-Astoria landed in the lap of a dowager, and motion-picture star Mary Pickford looked and listened as Italian tenor Enrico Caruso stepped onto a balcony of the Hotel Knickerbocker and sang "The Star-Spangled Banner" to the multitudes massed in Times Square. When the real armistice was announced on November 11, much the same scenes were reenacted.

America emerged from World War I as a creditor nation and thus the strongest country on earth. New York superseded London as the world's foremost financial mart, and Wall Street became the pinpoint of power the globe around.

Chapter 42

WALL STREET IS BOMBED

WHEN THE DOUGHBOYS got back to New York, they were feted and petted and soon forgotten. Shedding their uniforms for civilian clothes, the veterans began asking themselves, "What price glory?" which became the title of a fine Broadway play. People were tired. They felt that it was time for fun and games. Between 1919 and 1929 a change in emotional weather swept over the country. After spilling so much blood and offering up sacrifices that seemed to count for little, with the overthrow of traditions and conventions, many people wallowed in a vacuum of cynicism and intellectual anarchy. Now they threw themselves wildly into the Jazz Age, also called the Lawless Decade, the Era of Wonderful Nonsense, and the Roaring Twenties.

The cost of living in New York City had risen 79 percent between 1914 and 1919. A depression set in. The federal government bought fewer goods that it had during the war. There was a sharp drop in domestic purchasing power, which had been partly financed by federal money. Private bankers curtailed loans. Interest rates rose. In 1919 the average worker had an income of only $1,144. President Wilson addressed a joint session of Congress about the high cost of living. As New Yorkers suffered from a housing shortage, Henry Clay Frick died and left a $17,000,000 mansion filled with $30,000,000 worth of art treasures. Strikes flared across the nation. When New York's streetcar workers walked off the job, people were amazed to see Broadway trolleys armed with bulletproof screens to protect motormen still on the job. The city also endured strikes by dress- and waistmakers, cloak- and suitmakers, engineers and firemen, American Railway Express drivers, cigarmakers, longshoremen, printers, subway employees—and actors.

On August 7, 1919, New York's actors and actresses walked off the boards, as Actors' Equity Association struck against the high-handed methods of theatrical producers. The public and press supported the performers. They were led by Frank Bacon, a character actor and playwright. Opposed to Bacon was George M. Cohan, actor, playwright, songwriter, dancer, and one-half of the producing team of Cohan and Harris. He hastily organized a rival union called the Actors' Fidelity League, which sided with the producers. Life-long friendships broke up. There were street brawls and arrests and speeches and suits and countersuits. About 250 chorus girls staged a rally on Wall Street. Comedian Ed Wynn performed stunts at street corners. Ethel Barrymore, John Drew, Al Jolson, and Marie Dressler addressed the performers. Tallulah Bankhead, then only sixteen years old, coaxed her father out of $100, which she donated to the strikers. On September 7, Equity won the strike and has since remained the undisputed spokesman for legitimate actors.

During the war an alarming tendency to suppress civil liberties had developed; it was born of fear of sabotage and espionage. Now the federal government overreacted and indulged in some of the very tyrannical acts it condemned. In 1919 a reactionary lawyer named A. Mitchell Palmer was appointed U.S. Attorney General. At the time President Wilson was a very sick man and out of touch with affairs. Left pretty much on his own, Palmer launched a reign of terror.

At 2 A.M. on April 29, 1919, Charles Caplan, a clerk in the

parcel post division of the New York Post Office, was on his way home when he read a newspaper story. This told about a Negro servant who worked for Senator Thomas R. Hardwick in Atlanta, Georgia. She had opened a package addressed to the Senator, and a bomb inside it blew off her hands. Before this happened, Senator Hardwick had urged the restriction of immigration as a means of keeping Bolshevism out of America. The news story described the Atlanta package as being about six inches long and three inches wide, wrapped in brown paper, and marked with the return address of the Gimbel Brothers' department store in New York City. Now this struck a chord in the mind of the postal clerk. Suddenly he remembered.

Changing trains, he hurried back to the post office and found what he was looking for. He had put sixteen brown-wrapped packages on a shelf, because they didn't have enough postage. One was intended for Attorney General Palmer, another for J. P. Morgan; all, in fact, were addressed to highly placed federal officials and capitalists. Each bore the deceptive Gimbel label. Caplan notified his superior, who called the police. The packages were taken to a nearby firehouse, gingerly unwrapped, and found to contain bombs. Besides these sixteen packages, twenty others had been mailed elsewhere in the nation. Fortunately, none of the intended victims was injured. Officials never discovered the identity of the person or persons who mailed the bombs.

Another unsolved mystery resulted in a monumental tragedy. Late in the morning of Thursday, September 16, 1920, all seemed to be business as usual at the corner of Wall Street and Broad Street; which narrows into Nassau Street at this spot. The southeastern corner was occupied by the House of Morgan. The southwestern corner held the New York Stock Exchange and a fenced-in hole where a twenty-two story addition to the exchange was about to be erected. On the northwestern corner stood the thirty-nine-story Bankers Trust Company Building with its pyramided peak. The northeastern corner was occupied by the Subtreasury Building.

One block west, at the head of Wall Street, the Trinity Church clock began chiming the noon hour. Clerks and brokers, messengers and telegraphers prepared to leave for lunch. Hundreds of persons already strolled the streets. Up Wall Street from the east came a brown wagon covered with canvas. Drawn by an old dark-bay horse, it stopped at Wall and Nassau streets. The driver tossed his reins across the horse's back, jumped to the pavement, and walked away. As the twelfth bong of the Trinity clock reverberated through the autumn air, horse and wagon vanished in a tremendous explosion.

Eyewitnesses told different accounts. Some said that the blast gave off a bluish white glare. Others described it as a white ball of fire emitting acrid yellow flames that changed color, spat tongues of green flame, and soared skyward in a pillar of thick brown smoke. Higher and higher soared the smoke, darkening from brown to black and flattening mushroomlike above nearby skyscrapers. Awnings burst into flames a dozen floors above the street. The roar of the explosion bounced from building to building like a cannonball rolling free in the hold of a foundering ship. Iron fragments zinged through the air. They gashed pedestrians' arms and smashed legs and crushed skulls. The shower of metal was followed by a shower of glass, cascading onto the pavement. The blast knocked out windowpanes within a half-mile radius. A man walking along John Street, five blocks north, was felled by a four-inch length of pipe crashing on the base of his neck.

Like the eye of a hurricane, an ominous hush followed the first roar. Then people screamed. Fatally stricken girls stiffened, sagged, and slumped to the pavement. Blood seeped from them and spread fanlike over the concrete. Up from the street leaped a fountain of flame that clawed the façades of buildings on both sides of Wall Street. Desks caught fire. Officeworkers suddenly found their hair flaming torches. People in offices as high as the sixth floor were badly burned.

Among those who died in the explosion was Edward Sweet, a millionaire who once owned the famous Sweet's seafood restaurant at Fulton and South streets; all they ever found of him was one finger with his ring still on it. On Bloody Thursday 35 persons were killed, and 130 others injured. Property losses amounted to almost $3,000,000. The House of Morgan suffered the worst damage, and Junius Spencer Morgan, a grandson of J. Pierpont Morgan, sustained a slight gash on one hand. Apart from young Morgan, no other important Wall Street figure was hurt. Despite a protracted and far-flung investigation, the perpetrators of this crime were never discovered.

Prohibition was scheduled to go into effect at midnight on January 16, 1920. New York's weather that night was bitterly cold, the temperature sinking to six degrees above zero. In saloons, bars, cafés, restaurants, and supper clubs all over town the dry era was ushered in on a melancholy binge. Waiters dressed as pallbearers carried coffins. Some establishments had mailed black-bordered invitations to patrons to take part in "Last rites and ceremonies attending the departure of our spirited friend, John Barleycorn."

In one elegant café two golden slippers were filled with champagne and passed from table to table. The owner of a chili house on Forty-first Street pondered the idea of eluding Prohibition by serving booze in teacups. Pandhandlers prospered with a standardized whine: "Give a guy a quarter for a last drink." Bat Masterson, the fabled gunfighter from Dodge City, Kansas, now employed by the New York *Morning Telegraph,* finished writing a column about a prizefight, walked to a nearby bar, and sadly ordered a cup of tea. Elsewhere in the city a famous madam, named Polly Adler, scoffed, "They might as well try to dry up the Atlantic with a post office blotter."

She was right. Before Prohibition a man could get a drink in 15,000 places in town, but soon thereafter 32,000 illegal New York establishments sold liquor. There weren't enough federal Prohibition agents, many were inefficient, and some were downright corrupt. Stanley Walker wrote: "It was a common sight in certain New York speakeasies to see a group of agents enter a place at noon, remain until almost midnight, eating and drinking, and then leave without paying the bill." The venal agents kept up the price of illegal spirits. Some took protection money and raided other operators refusing to pay off.

Izzy Einstein was a postal clerk when Prohibition began. He lived in a $14-a-month flat on the Lower East Side and was the neighborhood cutup. Forty years old and balding, Izzy stood only 5 feet 5 inches tall and weighed 225 pounds. He had a huge cantaloupe head perched on a pumpkin-fat body. For all of his love of the ridiculous, Izzy was an intelligent man, who could speak English, Yiddish, German, Polish, and Hungarian; could make himself understood in French, Italian, and Russian; and even knew a few Chinese phrases. Bored with his post office job, he asked the chief enforcement agent of the Southern District of New York for a position as a Prohibition agent. The official was dubious, but Izzy convinced him that "this Prohibition business needs a new type of people that can't be spotted so easy." He got his gold badge.

The fat man showed up at a Brooklyn speakeasy, knocked on the door, and announced, "I'm a Prohibition agent. I just got appointed." The doorman grinned and let him inside. The bartender poured a whiskey, and Izzy quaffed it. This was the wrong technique, for it provided no evidence. When Izzy grabbed for the bottle, the bartender became frightened, scooped it off the bar, and ran out the back door. After this fiasco Izzy changed his tactics. In his vest pocket he hid a tiny funnel connected to a rubber hose that led to a flat bottle secreted in his vest lining. From that time forward, when Izzy was served a drink, he would take a sip and then pour the rest into the funnel while the bartender was making change.

After a few weeks Izzy talked his friend Moe Smith into joining him. Moe, who also liked to clown, weighed more than Izzy but was a couple of inches taller. Moe turned his little cigar store over to a relative and teamed up with Izzy. They were a spectacular success from the start.

They wore disguises. They used offbeat approaches. They carried objects tending to allay suspicion. They never looked like Prohibition agents. Izzy disguised himself as a longshoreman, Park Avenue dude, poultry salesman, and football player and even blackened his face with burnt cork to resemble a Negro. Who could suspect a little fat man lugging a pailful of dill pickles or a pitcherful of milk, carrying a fishing rod, or burdened with a violin or trombone? He pinched so many bootleggers and blind pig operators that his picture was displayed in bars all over town.

Izzy was more imaginative than Moe, but they made an unbeatable team. Izzy never carried a gun, and Moe, who sometimes did, fired it only twice. They timed their raids for the convenience of reporters and newspaper photographers, winning reams of publicity. Columnist O. O. McIntyre declared that Izzy had "become as famous in New York as the Woolworth building." For more than five years newspaper readers chuckled over the antics of the two rolypoly agents.

They were the best Prohibition agents in the service. They confiscated 5,000,000 bottles of liquor, worth $15,000,000, and thousands of gallons of booze in kegs and barrels, as well as in hundreds of stills and breweries. They made 4,392 arrests, of which more than 95 percent resulted in convictions. Despite this phenomenal record, federal officials were annoyed by their burlesque performances, and in 1925 they were dismissed "for the good of the service." The *Tribune* said: "They never made Prohibition much more of a joke than it has been made by some of the serious-minded Prohibition officers." In 1962 Izzy Einstein and Moe Smith were the inspiration for a Broadway musical comedy called *Nowhere to Go But Up.*

Prohibition closed many restaurants which had depended on the sale of liquor to make a profit. The respectable oases were replaced by speakeasies, nightclubs, and clip joints. With a new type of customer frequenting such resorts, Café Society was born. Socially prominent young men and women now rubbed elbows with criminals, for most speakeasies fell under the control of gangsters.

Greenwich Village started to become an artists' colony in the first decade of the twentieth century. One winter night in 1916 a group of tipsy Villagers climbed to the top of the Washington Arch on the northern side of Washington Square to shoot off a cap pistol and proclaim Greenwich Village an independent republic. By the end of the war the Village was populated mainly by Italians, who were annoyed by the antics of writers and painters, but the influx of bohemians kept increasing because rents were low.

This Manhattan enclave, with its old-world atmosphere, became the mecca for many young people from all parts of America who rebelled against their parents and the materialistic values of the day. College graduates and nonconformists headed for the Village to create or talk about the creation of artistic masterpieces. A hard core of talented people made the Village the center of America's literary movement, but surrounding them was a lunatic fringe. Men wore their hair long, girls wore their hair short, and some wore their morals thin. Poets debated whether love was sex or vice versified.

One of the most romantic figures in Greenwich Village was Edna St. Vincent Millay. Born in Rockland, Maine, in 1892, she moved to the Village after graduating from Vassar. Her first book of poetry was published in 1917, and in 1923 she won a Pulitzer Prize, for poetry. Carl Van Doren wrote: "Rarely since Sappho has a woman written as outspokenly as this." Burton Rascoe called her "one of the few poets who have been able to breathe life into the sonnet since Shakespeare." Another critic said that next to Elizabeth Barrett Browning, she was the supreme mistress of sonnets.

A small woman with a wraithlike figure, Miss Millay had bobbed chestnut hair shot with glints of bronze and copper, a long and graceful neck, a fey smile, a snub nose spattered with freckles, and bright-green eyes. Edmund Wilson, one of many men who fell in love with her, wrote that "her eyes had the bird-lidded look that I recognized as typically Irish." Edna St. Vincent Millay stimulated men and women alike. Restless and neurotic, she boasted about burning her candle at both ends. For a while she lived in the city's narrowest house, a three-story structure at 75½ Bedford Street. It was only nine and a half feet wide and thirty feet deep.

One of her friends was Eugene O'Neill, the playwright. O'Neill was born in 1888 in the heart of New York's theatrical district in the Barrett House, on the northeastern corner of Broadway and Forty-second Street. He was the younger son of James O'Neill, a popular melodramatic actor. An unhappy and rebellious young man, Eugene was expelled from Princeton, prospected for gold in Honduras, worked as an ordinary seaman, drifted aimlessly for years, endured a bout with tuberculosis, and began writing plays.

During his Greenwich Village days he hung out at a dive, called the Hell Hole, located at Sixth Avenue and Fourth Street. A heavy drinker, O'Neill became a favorite of an Irish gang, called the Hudson Dusters, who made the Hell Hole their headquarters. It was from this place that O'Neill drew most of the character for his famous play *The Iceman Cometh*. The Iceman was Death. O'Neill, like Edna St. Vincent Millay, wrote much about death. Morose and silent, smiling sardonically and never laughing aloud, the mustached O'Neill was a handsome black Irishman, who attracted women. "I'm all Irish!" he often cried. Nothing shocked him. His big brown eyes shifted quickly from softness to savagery, for if Millay was a candle burning at both ends, Eugene O'Neill was a live volcano, seething, boiling, bubbling, and then overflowing with searing dramas. In 1936 he won the Nobel Prize for literature, and he was awarded the Pulitzer Prize four times, the last time posthumously. In their definitive biography of him, Arthur and Barbara Gelb wrote that O'Neill became, "except for Shakespeare and possibly Shaw, the world's most widely translated and produced dramatist."

A great wave of Negroes from Southern states and Caribbean islands had washed into the city during the war. In 1910 the 90,000 Negroes in New York represented less than 2 percent of the population. By 1920 their numbers had increased to 150,000, or about 3 percent. Before the end of the 1920's the Negro population more than doubled, leaping to 327,000. Most of them wound up in Harlem, which became a city within a city and the Negro capital of the world.

"Nigger Heaven," as Negroes themselves called Harlem, lay in the northeastern corner of Manhattan. Its approximate boundaries were Central Park and 110th Street on the south, the East River on the east, the Harlem River on the northeast, 168th Street on the north, and Amsterdam Avenue and Morningside Park on the west. Many were unable to find jobs, and there was no such thing as public relief. Hard pressed to find dwellings as well, the Negroes lived jammed together in this black ghetto. Some held rent parties, also called whist parties or dances, to raise money for rent. These affairs were publicized by cards such as the one saying: "We got yellow girls, we've got black and tan—Will you have a good time?—YEAH MAN!" A welcome was extended to anyone, Negro or white, who had cash to spend. Some white people considered the rent parties more amusing than nightclubs.

It became commonplace for whites out on the town to say late in the evening, "Let's go uptown for yardbird and strings." Yardbird was Harlem's vernacular for fried chicken, and strings were spaghetti. This food—together with steaming chitterlings, good fried fish, and bad bootleg booze—could be enjoyed at low cost at the rent parties, and the impromptu singing and dancing often went on until dawn.

White New Yorkers and visitors also flocked to Harlem's famous nightclubs, such as the Cotton Club and Connie's Inn. There they drank illicit whiskey, listened to the blues, and watched some of the greatest talent in the world. Harlem catered to the ofay, the secret Negro word for the white man—foe—in pig Latin. Anyone with enough money could find anything he wanted—girls, liquor, narcotics, perversion. As composer Duke Ellington later said, "That part of Harlem was degrading and humiliating to both Negroes and whites." Considering the fact that many Negroes masked their hatred of white people behind smiles and that most Harlem hot spots fell into the hands of mobsters, there was amazingly little violence. Decorum was demanded in all of Harlem's big nightclubs, but in small cellar joints and private apartments anything was likely to happen.

Negroes knew that they were unwelcome in other parts of the city, most held menial jobs, and only the exceptional individual could claw his way out of this crippling environment. About 1925 Harlem's literary renaissance began. A group of talented young writers depicted Negro life with such skill and honesty that they won the admiration of literary critics.

In 1920 Harlem elected its first Negro alderman, an independent Republican, named George Harris, and ever since then Harlem has been represented on the board of aldermen. More than politicians, however, the one man who gave the Negro a sense of his own dignity was a pure black man, named Marcus Garvey.

Born in Jamaica in 1887, intelligent but unschooled, a newspaper writer in Jamaica and Costa Rica, short chunky mustached Garvey came to Harlem in 1917. The next year he began publishing a weekly, called the *Negro World,* in which he urged Negro unity, nationalism, and the resettlement of Negroes in Africa. He appealed to racial pride at a time when Negroes felt that they had little cause to hold up their heads. A skilled orator, clever organizer, and shrewd psychologist, Garvey touched off the first real mass movement among American Negroes.

He asked the League of Nations for permission to settle a colony in Africa and entered into discussions with Liberia. Unable to negotiate the return of American Negroes to Africa, Garvey organized the Universal African Legion, the Black Eagle Flying Corps, and the Universal Black Cross Nurses to force white people out of that continent. Establishing the African Orthodox Church and promising a utopia under the African sun, Garvey became the uncrowned dictator of an imaginary black empire. Some Negroes hailed him as God.

Between 1919 and 1921 Garvey collected $10,000,000. In 1923 he claimed 6,000,000 followers. This was an exaggeration, but even his critics admitted that 500,000 Negroes had pledged blind loyalty to him. Garvey set up two steamship companies and bought three seagoing ships in the name of his Universal Negro Improvement Association. He intended to man the vessels with Negro crews and sail from the United States to Africa and the West Indies. In 1923 he was found guilty of using the mails to defraud in raising money for his steamship lines and was sent to the federal penitentiary at Atlanta for five years. In 1927 President Calvin Coolidge pardoned him but had him deported as an undesirable alien. Marcus Garvey, who had touched both glory and shame, died in London in 1940.

Chapter 43

THE WALL STREET CRASH

JAMES J. WALKER was born on June 19, 1881, in a flat at 110 Leroy Street in Greenwich Village. From boyhood he was steeped in Tammany politics; his Irish-born father had been a Tammany alderman, assemblyman, and leader of the old Ninth Ward. Jimmy Walker was reared in a nice house, went to a parochial school, never attended college, played professional baseball, acted in amateur theatricals, learned to play the piano, and yearned to compose popular songs.

He went to work for a music publishing house in 1908 and wrote the lyrics for "Will You Love Me in December as You Do in May?" which earned him more than $10,000 in the next 30 years. Then, bowing to his father's wishes, Walker abandoned his career on Tin

Pan Alley and entered politics. In 1912 he was elected to the New York state assembly. Later he was sent to the state senate, where he became Democratic floor leader.

"I really was moving against my own desires most of the time, and the inner conflicts were great," Walker told his friend Gene Fowler. The ambivalence left Jimmy Walker a neurotic, who feared crowds and cars, felt uneasy in elevators, shrank from slaps on the back, perspired at night, and had hands always cold to the touch and sometimes clammy. He camouflaged his tensions behind a façade of gaiety and charm. A skinny fellow who weighed only 125 pounds during periods of especial strain, Walker stood 5 feet 8½ inches tall, had a flat belly, had practically no hips, and tried to disguise his string-bean appearance by wearing suits that emphasized the breadth of his shoulders.

Considering himself a fashion plate, but always dressed in ultra-Broadway style, Walker designed his own clothes and owned hundreds of custom-made ties. He was a close friend of actors, who taught him the theatrical trick of using his left hand to pick his handkerchief from the left-hand pocket of his jacket, instead of crossing his right hand over his chest. He lighted denicotinized cigarettes with a monogrammed gold lighter. His lean face, sharp nose, and flashing grin gave him a foxlike look. He parted his brown hair on the left. His flushed cheeks gave rise to remarks about his drinking habits, but although Jimmy Walker imbibed, his florid complexion was part of his heritage. He scorned Prohibition, declaring "this measure was born in hypocrisy and there it will die."

During his early Albany years he shared a hotel room with Al Smith, whom he admired. Smith, a devout Catholic and a man of moderate habits, worried about Walker's playboy tendencies. But the quick-witted Walker, despite his frivolity, racked up a good record during his fourteen years in the state legislature. Typically, he married a pretty chorus girl, and typically, he was more than two hours late for his wedding.

With the approach of the 1925 mayoralty election Mayor Hylan let it be known he was eager to serve a third term. However, most citizens had had their fill of the bumbling and bewildered Hylan. Tammany Hall opposed Hylan because it was tired of Hearst's attempts to run the city from his California estate. Governor Al Smith, too, was disenchanted with Red Mike. A Walker for mayor boom was launched by some of Jimmy's Broadway friends, and Smith somewhat reluctantly agreed to Walker's candidacy. Hylan shouted that Walker intended to make New York an open city for gangsters, thieves, prostitutes, and dope peddlers, but Walker defeated Hylan in the Democratic primary. In the citywide election Walker easily beat his Republican rival, a fountain-pen manufacturer, named Frank D. Waterman.

Jimmy Walker took office on January 1, 1926, as the city and nation basked in prosperity. Approaching the dais to be sworn in, he bowed to his wife and relatives and to the Tammany bigwigs, who were much in evidence. During the campaign Walker had said time and again that because Tammany Hall had created him he would never forget it. On the dais stood a radio microphone, and Jimmy Walker became the first mayor of New York whose inaugural ceremony was broadcast. While he was speaking, a woman fainted nearby. Walker rushed to her side and asked for a glass of water, which he put to her lips. People listening to the broadcast were puzzled by the sudden silence at City Hall, and within thirty seconds hundreds telephoned to ask if the new mayor had been assassinated. There was a sigh of relief when Walker returned to the microphone and finished his address.

After the formalities were over, Mayor Walker strode jauntily into the mayor's office in the west wing of City Hall. He gazed at the Colonial desk that had become his. He eyed the mellow furnishings. Catching sight of a portrait of the Marquis de Lafayette hanging over the mantelpiece, Walker arched his eyebrows and pretended to speak to it: "If I may borrow a phrase, I wish to announce, 'Lafayette, we are here.' " The playboy had become the leader of a metropolis of nearly 6,000,000 citizens. He had never held any administrative position in the city government. He admitted that he knew nothing about many of the city's problems. To City Hall reporters he confessed, "I've read not more than fifteen books from cover to cover." When they asked how he had managed to amass so much information, he replied, "What little I know, I have learned by ear."

In those days City Hall was covered mainly by hack reporters. They adored Walker because he shot craps with them and always made good copy. They let him hobble them by insisting that most of his remarks be off the record. When serious matters were debated by the board of estimate, Walker won headlines with glittering wisecracks while the issues of the day went largely unnoticed. Never arising before 10 A.M. and sometimes suffering hangovers, Walker's charm often wore thin when he had to buckle down to city business. He would scold a citizen for taking one minute more than the allotted five minutes to discuss a proposed measure and then would keep sweating crowds waiting in board chambers while he dallied an hour and a half over lunch. Savage and coarse at times, Walker shouted down many an unfortunate person who aroused his ire. Once a man interrupted the mayor by shouting, "Liar!" Walker snapped, "Now that you have identified yourself, we shall proceed."

Jimmy's churlish behavior, loyalty to Tammany, and willingness to appoint political hacks did not dim the affection most people felt for their debonair mayor. He didn't mind being dubbed the late mayor because of his tardiness. He actually enjoyed being called the nightclub mayor. He was, as Gene Fowler said in *Beau James,* "a man of rainbow charm." Douglas Gilbert wrote in the *World-Telegram*: "New York wore James J. Walker in its lapel, and he returned the compliment." He had a twinkle in his eyes and a quip for every visiting celebrity—such as aviator Charles Lindbergh, channel-swimming Gertrude Ederle, and Queen Marie of Rumania —who reached City Hall after riding up Broadway amid the soft hail of ticker tape.

Tammany tightened its grip on the city as Walker neglected the serious side of his job. Reviving frauds common during Boss Tweed days, politicians and criminals teamed up, favors were sold, and the municipal corporation inched toward bankruptcy. In this blithe era nobody worked very hard—least of all the city magistrates whose court sessions averaged only 3 hours and 11 minutes a day. During his first 2 years in office Walker took 7 vacations for a total of 143 days, visiting London, Paris, Berlin, Bermuda, Canada, Havana, Hollywood, San Francisco, Atlanta, Florida, Louisville, Houston, and Rome. Stopping in the Italian capital in 1927, Mayor Walker had a half-hour audience with Benito Mussolini as a movie crew recorded the scene.

Walker gave pleasure, but he took freely as well. In 1929 his salary was boosted from $25,000 to $40,000—almost three times that of a member of the President's Cabinet. When LaGuardia attacked Walker for this, Walker flashed his boyish smile and joked, "That's cheap! Think what it would cost if I worked full time." He lived ever more extravagantly and sank into debt. Once he said, "If I earn a million dollars this year, by the end of the year I'd have spent one million, ten thousand dollars." To high-living free-spending New Yorkers, Jimmy Walker became a symbol of their way of life. They reelected him mayor in 1929. One week before the election the stock market felt its first tremor. Soon were heard the first rumblings of a great judicial scandal. Walker had been riding high, wide, and handsome. Now he was riding for a fall.

In the late 1920's a segment of America had become one vast permanent floating crap game. Waiters and plumbers, motormen and grocers, seamstresses and chauffeurs, actors and writers—at least 1,000,000 Americans—gambled in the stock market. They bet on whether stock prices would rise or fall in a short period of time. They were more interested in the stock market pages than in the sports pages of newspapers. The little man had discovered that he could speculate in securities with borrowed money by buying on margin. The big man in the know seemed to encourage this speculation.

In 1928 President Coolidge said, "No Congress of the United States ever assembled, on surveying the state of the Union, has met with a more pleasing prospect than that which appears at the present time." Secretary of Commerce Herbert Hoover prophesied that "with the policies of the last eight years we shall soon with the help of God be in sight of the day when poverty will be banished from this nation." Irving T. Bush, owner of the Bush Terminal in Brooklyn, declared that "we are only at the beginning of a period that will go down in history as a golden age." Bernard Baruch said that "the economic condition of the world seems on the verge of a great forward movement."

New York City alone had more automobiles than all of Europe. Fifth Avenue's opulence was rivaled only by Park Avenue, where apartment rentals of $40,000 were not uncommon. Between 1919 and 1929 land values here increased by 75 percent. Real estate taxes provided about four-fifths of the city's revenue in 1928. National productivity increased; the output per wage earner grew 43 percent between 1919 and 1929. During the same period the use of telephones doubled, 1 out of every 3 American homes owned a radio, electrical goods sold as fast as they could be made, and there was an average of 1 auto for every 5½ Americans.

The other side of the coin was less bright. Of the nation's wealth 90 percent was held by 13 percent of its citizens. Installment buying had increased, and buy-now-pay-later had become an accepted way of life. Corporations and investment trusts lent carelessly to stockbrokers for speculative purposes. There was an overproduction of capital goods.

People were convinced that prosperity was eternal. Wall Street branch houses increased. A New York actress converted her Park Avenue apartment into an office and played the stock market by telephone. A broker's valet made nearly $250,000. Brokers' offices were so crowded that it was difficult for a customer to find a spot to watch the posted quotations. Columnist Franklin P. Adams saw three famous artists in a restaurant and walked up, hoping to engage them in an intellectual discussion, and found the trio discussing the Federal Reserve Bank. Alexander Woollcott, the drama critic and author, got "hot tips on the market from big shots." Comedian Groucho Marx took tips on investments from such diverse authorities as Bernard Baruch and a theatrical wardrobe woman.

Then came Thursday, October 24, 1929, remembered as Black Thursday. The New York Stock Exchange opened at 10 A.M. with prices steady. United States Steel was quoted at 205½, a point or two above the previous closing. For a few minutes all prices remained firm. Then brokers began unloading margin accounts, which their customers no longer could cover. Selling started with the roaring confusion of a river breaking through a dam. Nearly everybody wanted to sell, and almost nobody wanted to buy. All seemed to be getting out. By 11 A.M. the market had degenerated into a mad scramble of sales, and by 11:30 A.M. panic had set in.

Edward H. H. Simmons, president of the exchange, was on vacation. Responsibility fell upon the shoulders of the exchange's vice-president, thirty-nine-year-old Richard Whitney. The son of a Boston banker, educated at Groton and Harvard, and married to the widow of a son of Mrs. William K. Vanderbilt, Whitney was a power on Wall Street. He owned a 495-acre gentleman's farm in New Jersey, a town house on Manhattan's East Side, 8 automobiles, 47 suits, 12 walking sticks, and 4 pink coats for fox hunting.

The selling wave was so gigantic that ticker tapes ran far behind transactions. A time lag of up to thirty minutes ensued between prices quoted on the floor of the exchange and those on the ticker tape. As a result, all was confusion and uncertainty and worry. Among those watching this mad scene was Winston Churchill, Britain's former Chancellor of the Exchequeur. He and the others heard a false rumor that eleven speculators had committed suicide. A crowd standing in Wall Street gazed apprehensively at a workman on the roof of a building, convinced that he was preparing to jump. There were untrue reports that the exchanges in Buffalo and Chicago had closed. Police Commissioner Grover Whalen sent a police detail to Wall Street to maintain order.

At noon, five of the nation's most influential bankers slipped into the House of Morgan. J. P. Morgan was in Europe, so they conferred with Thomas W. Lamont, senior partner of the firm. The vast wealth of the House of Morgan aside, these titans commanded more than $6,000,000,000 in banking reserves. Each chipped in millions of dollars to form a pool to buy stocks in order to create confidence in the market. Lamont later said that they did not try to hold prices at any given level but simply made enough purchases to restore order to the trading operation. Chosen to act for them was Richard Whitney, floor trader for the Morgans.

At 12:30 P.M. the exchange closed its visitors' gallery. At 1:30 P.M. Whitney walked onto the floor of the exchange and pushed his way past shouting men toward trading post No. 2, where U.S. Steel was handled. The vast hall hushed briefly as brokers watched him and then filled again with a buzz of excited voices. Whitney held a slip of paper in one hand. He called out: "Two hundred five for Steel!" He was offering to buy 10,000 shares of U.S. Steel at 205 when the current bids were several points lower. Only 200 shares were available at 193½, but Whitney's gesture impressed brokers and customers and revived their courage. Then, moving with studied nonchalance, Whitney visited other trading posts, offering to buy from $20,000,000 to $30,000,000 worth of stock. His maneuver checked the selling wave, vanquished fear, and led many speculators to reinvest, lest they miss out on the new advance. It also gave some big and conservative operators time to unload. Prices boomed again.

When trading ended at 3 P.M., U.S. Steel closed at 206. Montgomery Ward, which had opened at 83 and fallen to 50, shot back up to 74. An astonishing total of 12,894,650 shares changed hands that day. The New York *Times* called it "the most disastrous decline in the biggest and broadest stock market of history." Not until 8:07 P.M. did the tardy tickers stop chattering prices from the exchange floor. That night Wall Street buildings were honeycombed with lights as brokers and clerks struggled out of an avalanche of paper work.

Brokers wired customers to ask for more margin. The Marx Brothers, natives of New York City, were playing in a show in Pittsburgh. Harpo Marx's broker telegraphed him: "FORCED TO SELL

ALL HOLDINGS UNLESS RECEIVE CHECK FOR $15,000 TO COVER MARGINS." The harp-playing comedian managed to get the sum and sent it to his broker. The next morning Harpo got a similar request. Then a third. The last wire read: "SEND $10,000 IN 24 HOURS OR FACE FINANCIAL RUIN AND DAMAGING SUITS STOP MUST HAVE $10,000 REGARDLESS WHETHER I CAN SELL YOUR HOLDINGS." By this time Harpo's holdings had shrunk to $1 per share, he had borrowed all he could, and he had liquidated every asset he owned. Once worth $250,000 on paper, Harpo was almost penniless. His brother Groucho was completely wiped out.

In the next few days, despite reassuring words from President Hoover and others, prices continued to fall. The *Commercial and Financial Chronicle,* taking a realistic view, said that "the present week has witnessed the greatest stock-market catastrophe of all the ages." On November 13 prices sank to a low for 1929. The disaster blew into thin air $30,000,000,000 worth of supposed values. As Frederick Lewis Allen later pointed out, this was "a sum almost as great as the entire cost to the United States of its participation in the World War, and nearly twice as great as the entire national debt."

No one man was responsible for the crash. The get-rich-quick mania had afflicted almost everybody. About 9,000,000 savings accounts were wiped out, 85,000 businesses went to the wall, 5,000 banks failed, agriculture hit bottom, and national income was cut in half. New York and all America suffered the biggest jolt since the Civil War. In 1929, according to John Kenneth Galbraith, there began "the most momentous economic occurrence in the history of the United States, the ordeal of the Great Depression."

Chapter 44

THE GREAT DEPRESSION

POLLY ADLER, who ran the most famous bordello in town, noticed a curious change brought about by the depression. Most of her clients were, or had been, rich, and now they visited her place not so much for sex as for liquor. They got drunk on champagne costing $30 a bottle and beer costing $1 a glass and behaved like madmen. One man kept muttering that he used to control Wall Street but didn't know now whether he could pay the next month's rent. Another said that he came back night after night because a whorehouse was the only place where he could cry without being ashamed.

Bernard Baruch stood rigidly in his Madison Avenue office and murmured to a *Times* reporter: "In the presence of too much food,

people are starving. Surrounded by vacant houses, they are homeless. And standing before unused bales of wool and cotton, they are
dressed in rags." At the Canterbury School in New Milford, Connecticut, thirteen-year-old John Fitzgerald Kennedy wrote his father:
"Please send me the *Literary Digest,* because I did not know about
the Market Slump until a long time after, or a paper. Please send me
some golf balls. . . ."

New York City nearly went under financially. Because property
owners were unable to pay taxes, city revenues declined. Expenses,
however, continued to mount. The city had to borrow on anticipated
tax collections, piling up a public debt almost equal to that of the
forty-eight states combined. As a result, city credit suffered.

As unemployment rose, hopeless men stared at smokeless chimneys. Manufacturing firms quit the city, leaving fewer plants in operation than at any time since 1899. Bryant Park, behind the New
York Public Library, degenerated into a weed-filled jungle. Construction of the Triborough Bridge was stopped for lack of funds. Work
halted on a fashionable new hotel, named the Hampshire House, at
150 Central Park South. The city's taxicabs decreased from 28,000
to 13,000, and some hackdrivers made only $20 a week. Saleswomen
in some Woolworth stores were paid $10.80 a week, and others got
as little as $7.

To help homeowners, the state legislature declared a moratorium
on foreclosures if the interest on mortgages and taxes were paid.
But many people were too poor to pay even these and lost their
homes. In the Sunnyside area of middle Queens eviction notices were
fought by collective action. Doors were barricaded with barbed wire
and sandbags. Householders bombarded sheriffs with pepper and
flour. More than 60 percent of Sunnyside's homeowners lost their
houses through foreclosure. Families began doubling up in houses
and apartments.

The homeless slept under bridges, in railroad terminals, on subways, in missions, and in municipal shelters. By buying one drink,
a man could sleep on sawdust in a cheap speakeasy. The unemployed
also lived in parks, someone saying that "ten-cent men sleep under
thousand-dollar trees." A young Ph.D. camped for eight months in
Morningside Park. Another man loaded all his worldly goods into
a baby buggy and sought refuge in Central Park. Each night he
lowered the buggy's dashboard, put down the seat in the back,

crawled in, covered himself with a rubber sheet, pulled the buggy's hood over his head, and fell asleep.

College graduates suffered, along with the uneducated. Professional men slept in subways, while Queens County politicians rode around in Pierce-Arrows. Although Hollywood ignored the depression as long as possible, it finally faced up to the ugly problem. A movie called *One More Spring* depicted actor Warner Baxter as a penniless producer roasting a partridge in his makeshift home in Central Park. Sallow-cheeked men sold apples in the streets. New York became accustomed to the sight of the breadline, which Heywood Broun described as "the worm that walks like a man."

When the weather was bad, many children failed to attend school because they lacked warm clothing and shoes. Those who did go could not pay attention to lessons because they suffered from malnutrition. Groucho Marx said that he knew things were bad when "the pigeons started feeding the people in Central Park." In 1931 four New York hospitals reported ninety-five deaths from starvation. The Welfare Council told about a family in the Brownsville section of Brooklyn:

> Family reported starving by neighbors. Investigator found five small children at home while mother was out looking for vegetables under pushcarts. Family had moved into one room. Father sleeping at Municipal Lodging House because he could get more to eat there than at home and frequently brought food home from there in pockets for children and wife. Only other food they had for weeks came from pushcarts.

The depression hit rock bottom in December, 1932. Nearly one of every four employable New Yorkers was jobless. The song "Brother, Can You Spare a Dime?" became a byword. Men with elbows poking out of sleeves asked one another ruefully, "Got change for a match?" Charles M. Schwab, a steel company president living in a seventy-five-room mansion on Riverside Drive, confessed, "I'm afraid. Every man is afraid." Carl Van Doren, the brilliant editor, historian, and critic, later wrote: "I had no systematic thoughts but I had recurrent dreams. One dream, rather, in several forms. It was a dream of fear. . . ."

There was much talk of suicide—some of it sad, some cynical. A favorite joke concerned a hotel clerk who asked guests if they

wanted a room for sleeping or jumping. A total of 1,595 New Yorkers killed themselves in 1932—the highest number since 1900.

Harlem suffered more than any other section of the city. Negro
men who worked as casual laborers and colored female domestics
soon found themselves unemployed. Negroes lucky enough to find
jobs were paid less than whites but charged more than whites in
rentals. Knowing that their tenants could not move to other neighborhoods, Harlem landlords were quick to raise rents. As a result, there
were wholesale evictions. To help pay for their apartments, some
Negroes took in lodgers, which produced appalling overcrowding.

Cheated and cramped, jobless and hopeless, many Negroes tried
to escape reality by drinking, buying "love potions," consulting for-
tune-tellers, burning incense to destroy "evil spirits," purchasing
dream books, and playing the numbers game. Lottery tickets sold
for as little as a penny and paid off at 540 to 1. A banker for one of
Harlem's big policy games, a Negress who called herself Mme. St.
Clair, enjoyed an income of $250,000 a year and a private body-
guard. One of Harlem's best-known purveyors of "love potions"
was a man who styled himself High John the Conqueror.

The greatest of all these charlatans was Father Divine. Although
his origin is shrouded in mystery, he is thought to have been born
in Georgia about 1877 and named George Baker. After growing up,
he drifted to Baltimore, where he worked as a handyman. Sometime
during this period he decided to become a minister and started calling himself the Reverend M. J. Divine. Then he headed farther north,
settling in Sayville, Long Island.

Squat, only about five feet tall, bald as a balloon, with a flashing
grin and sparkling eyes, Father Divine had a magnetic personality.
His preaching was so rhythmical that it hypnotized ignorant people.
Seeking something greater than themselves, they drank in nonsense
such as: "It is personifiable and repersonifiably metaphysicalization-
ally reproducible—" Besides being a spellbinder, Father Divine was
a shrewd organizer and manipulator. He attracted disciples and be-
witched them into giving him their earnings. With this money he
founded cooperatives where all true believers could live in peace
and comfort. "Peace" was the slogan. His followers, called "angels,"
regarded him as God, and when they got together they chanted, "He
has the world in a jug and the stopper in his hand." In 1931 the
Sayville police arrested him for maintaining a public nuisance. A

judge sentenced him to a year in jail, but the conviction was reversed.

In the pit of the depression, Father Divine arrived in Harlem, where he established the first of his many "heavens." Unemployed Negroes turned in growing numbers to his promise of security and dignity. No other Negro since Marcus Garvey had attracted such a large following. Forbidding his disciples to accept public relief and providing living quarters and food with the money supplied by employed believers, Father Divine became a power. The trademark of his movement was the banquet. Devotees would sit down to the table at his most important "heaven," located at 152 West 126th Street, and feast on twenty kinds of meat, five salads, eleven relishes, fifteen kinds of bread, six desserts, six different beverages, and cheeses and cakes "as big as automobile tires." For all this each disciple paid only fifteen cents.

Father Divine demanded that his "angels" give up sex, tobacco, alcohol, and their money, but in those hard times this didn't seem too much to surrender. Husbands and wives slept in separate dormitories for only two dollars a week. Those joining the movement sacrificed their names and took others, such as Angel Flash, Blessed Mary Love, Peaceful Dove, Love Note, and Gladness Darling. In spite of the fun poked at them, they made good workers and were rarely involved with the police.

While Father Divine tackled the depression in his own self-rewarding way, others began questioning the worth of an economic and political system that could result in such mass misery. The dean of the Harvard Business School admitted, "Capitalism is on trial and on the issue of this trial may depend the whole future of Western civilization." Heywood Broun, a syndicated columnist for the Scripps-Howard newspapers, became a Socialist, but this was too tepid a change for those who wanted deeds, not words. In 1932 John Dos Passos wrote: "Becoming a Socialist right now would have just about the same effect on anybody as drinking a bottle of near-beer." Wherever the unemployed looked, they seemed to see Communists in action—taking part in jobless demonstrations, leading strikes, suffering beatings, going to jail, and sometimes being killed. Granville Hicks later wrote: "What impressed us about American Communists was their absolute devotion to the cause. We didn't like them very well, but they did get results." Besides, the Communists glorified the poor and in those days nearly everyone was poor. Clifford Odets, who wanted to become a playwright, was trying to live on ten cents a day. In 1935 he joined the Communist party but resigned eight months later because its leaders tried to regiment his writing.

The American Communist party increased the number of its members. They were organized into three categories of clubs—community clubs, shop clubs, and industrial clubs. Above the clubs were sections and state organizations. The area embraced by a club or section depended on the density of membership. New York had city, county, and section groups. Because this was a vast city, a local club might embrace only a neighborhood, whereas in a small town there might be only one club in the entire community.

In the Coney Island area of Brooklyn there were several clubs. They were known collectively as the Coney Island section. This, in turn, was part of the boroughwide Brooklyn organization. As David A. Shannon wrote in *The Decline of American Communism*: "In some parts of New York there were enough party members in one apartment building to constitute a club. Isadore Begun, Bronx county chairman, gloated over one building in which there were ten members: 'Just think, if you want to call a meeting all you have to do is knock on the steam pipe.' "

Russian periodicals exaggerated the American depression. A Moscow paper published pictures of holes dug in Broadway by repairmen, the captions declaring that the pits were caused by "bombings" and "riots." The Third International, a worldwide organization set up by the Bolsheviks with the aim of conquering the world, ordered that March 6, 1930, be observed as International Unemployment Day. According to Benjamin Gitlow, an American Communist official who quit the party, the Comintern commanded the comrades to provoke police. The Soviet plan was to touch off bloody riots in an attempt to prove that capitalistic nations were oppressing the workers.

Grover Whalen was police commissioner of New York in 1930. His intelligence squad reported that 100,000 postcards had been mailed to Communists and sympathizers in the New York area, summoning them to a rally at noon on March 6 in Union Square—sometimes known as Red Square because Communist orators harangued crowds there. Whalen had little patience wtih radicals. According to Socialists Norman Thomas and Paul Blanshard, he said publicly that Communists, "these enemies of society, were to be driven out of New York regardless of their constitutional rights."

Whalen asked William Z. Foster, Robert Minor, and Israel Amter to come to Police Headquarters to confer. Foster was the nation's No. 1 Communist, Minor was editor of the *Daily Worker,* and Amter was a local Communist organizer. Whalen told them that under a city ordinance it was necessary to obtain a permit three days in advance of any outdoor meeting. Having been ordered by Moscow to antagonize American officials, the Communist leaders snarled that they did not respect the laws of the United States, of New York State, or of New York City. Curtly they refused to apply for a permit for the Union Square rally. Then they turned on their heels and strode out of Whalen's office. He later wrote: "I doubt if any police commissioner has ever been more openly defied."

The biggest Communist demonstration in the history of New York City was held on Thursday, March 6, 1930. It was a clear and windless day. By 10 A.M. a crowd had begun to gather in Union Square. Police spies within Communist ranks had told Whalen that there were exactly 9,567 Communist party members in New York City. They provided the hard core of the Union Square crowd, which was reinforced by thousands of sympathizers and curiosity seekers.

The dapper Whalen wore a dark overcoat and light homburg. He set up emergency headquarters in a garden house inside the square. A wall three feet high surrounded the park. Whalen did not interfere with newspaper photographers and silent movie cameramen, but he forbade picture taking by photographers for the new talking pictures. Whalen later explained: "I saw no reason for perpetuating treasonable utterances, and I don't mean to engage in censorship. But why glorify these people?"

Ever more overcoated men and women thronged into Union Square. By noon, according to Whalen, more than 100,000 people had congregated in and around the square. New York *Times* reporters estimated the size of the crowd at 35,000. Five speakers' platforms had been erected in the center of the park, and diehard Communists clustered around them. These party members carried placards declaring that they wanted no charity, protesting evictions of the jobless, and insisting that public buildings be used to house the unemployed.

Congestion became so great at subway entrances near the square that Whalen arranged for all subway trains on the line to skip the stations between Brooklyn Bridge and Grand Central. Just before the rally started, he ordered Foster, Minor, and Amter brought to his temporary office. Accompanying the three Red leaders were a Negro sailor and a white soldier. The five men announced that they constituted a committee of workers, soldiers, and sailors. Trying to control his Irish temper, Whalen said that although their meeting was illegal (since they had failed to get a permit), he would let it go on, provided that it ended promptly at 1 P.M. Again the Communist leaders stamped out.

As they dived back into the massed throng in the square, a Soviet flag was run up on a flagpole over the Stars and Stripes. Police told the Communists to reverse the sequence, declaring that no one would be allowed to speak until Old Glory fluttered over the Soviet banner. The flags were reversed. Then five Communist orators climbed onto the portable stands and began haranguing the multitude about "Whalen's cossacks" and their "brutality."

All of Manhattan's daily newspapers had censured the police for the way they had handled an earlier demonstration in City Hall Park. Now Whalen stood on the porch of the garden house in Union Square and heard himself denounced again and again. One speaker urged that when the rally broke up, everyone should march once more to City Hall to demand that Mayor Walker remove Whalen as police commissioner.

Whalen wasn't concerned about his job, but this was a turn of events he hadn't anticipated. Now he called for reinforcements to prevent a march on the seat of city government. Soon more than 300 patrolmen, detectives, mounted cops, and motorcycle policemen were gathered in and around Union Square. Also summoned to the scene were firemen under orders to turn fire hoses on demonstrators if they got out of hand.

The time was now 12:50 P.M. The temperature stood at 50 degrees. With everything in readiness, Whalen told police officers to bring the five Red leaders back to his temporary headquarters. The commissioner then told the quintet to break up the rally in exactly 10 minutes. They reviled Whalen. He offered to send Foster and a Communist committee to City Hall in his own car to present Mayor Walker with whatever grievance or petition they wished. The Communists spurned the compromise.

Foster and his cohorts turned their backs on Whalen and again plunged into the crowd. Foster jumped onto a stand and exhorted the tens of thousands to march down Broadway to City Hall. Then he and his lieutenants faded from the scene, found a taxicab, and drove to City Hall to await the throng.

Two thousand disciplined Communists moved west out of Union Square and turned south on Broadway. A squad of mounted police advanced, maneuvering their horses in an attempt to disperse the marchers. A police emergency truck drove into Broadway and stopped in the middle of the street to serve as a barrier. Hundreds of cops and detectives, swinging nightsticks and blackjacks and bare fists, now rushed into the marching columns, flailing about on all sides and chasing many Communists into side streets.

Some marchers fought back. According to the *Times*: "This only served to spur the police, whose attack carried behind it the force of an avalanche." A *World* reporter saw a patrolman hold one girl while another cop crashed his blackjack into her face three times. Francis Rufus Bellamy, editor of the sedate magazine *Outlook,* watched from an office window as a dozen plainclothesmen and uniform cops beat and kicked two unarmed men until they nearly fainted. Women screamed. Men shouted. Blood began to trickle down faces. Soon a score of men sprawled on the ground.

After fifteen minutes of spectacular fighting the riot was over. Later that afternoon the five Communist leaders were arrested outside City Hall. The soldier and sailor were freed; but Foster, Minor, and Amter were arraigned upon Whalen's testimony, convicted of inciting to riot, and sentenced to three years in jail.

By provoking the police, all too eager to crack skulls, the Communists had incited the riot they sought. It was the worst disorder New York had seen in many years. More than a score of people, including 4 policemen, had been severely injured, and 100 others had suffered assorted cuts and bruises.

Although Red leaders blamed Whalen, an undiplomatic statement was issued by Herbert Benjamin, secretary of the local Communist party. Benjamin called the riot "a great success." He described the demonstrations in Union Square and elsewhere in the world as the prelude to the "overthrow of capitalism and the establishment of a revolutionary workers' and farmers' government."

Chapter 45

THE JIMMY WALKER SCANDALS

IN THE GATHERING gloom of the depression, Mayor Jimmy Walker gleamed like a soap bubble. Empty, colorful, tossed by the breeze of every impulse, he floated toward the pinprick of reckoning. Preferring pleasure to power, he abdicated his responsibilities to the new Tammany boss, John F. Curry, and Tammany now fastened itself like an octopus on the city, as it had in the days of Boss Tweed. It controlled the mayor, all city departments, the courts, and every prosecuting agency within the five boroughs.

Tammany relatives were put on city payrolls, while their unemployed neighbors had to go on relief. Businessmen paid tribute for services due them under the law. The granting of franchises became a political football and a common source of graft. Politicians allied themselves with criminals. Cops took bribes, beat up prisoners, framed innocents, terrorized the law-abiding. Much of Tammany's power lay in its concern for lawbreakers. By seeing to it that they stayed out of jail, Tammany won the gratitude, votes, and money of crooks of all kinds. A Bronx Democratic district leader admitted that this "is the way we make Democrats." Of the 514 persons arrested in gambling raids during a 2-year period, only 5 were held for the court of special sessions.

Judgeships were bought and sold. The city had three kinds of criminal courts—magistrates' courts, the court of special sessions, and county courts. County court judges were elected. In the other two kinds of court a man seeking to become a judge paid a bribe of from $10,000 to $50,000, thus won Boss Curry's recommendation, and received his appointment from the mayor.

Political hacks piled up incredible fortunes. Thomas M. Farley, sheriff of New York County and a Tammany sachem, earned only $8,500 a year but accumulated nearly $400,000 in 6 years. During the six years John Theofel served as Democratic leader of Queens, his net worth increased from $28,650 to $201,300. James J. McCormick, a Manhattan Democratic district leader and deputy city clerk, deposited his $384,788 in plunder in 30 different bank accounts.

At last decent citizens began to grumble about the way the city was run. LaGuardia accused Magistrate Albert H. Vitale of borrowing $19,500 from gambler Arnold Rothstein. Then Vitale was given a testimonial dinner by a group that included underworld figures like the notorious Ciro Terranova, known as the Artichoke King because of his grip on the artichoke business. The Association of the Bar of the City of New York petitioned the appellate division of the state supreme court for Vitale's removal. He was taken off the bench after he admitted borrowing from Rothstein and after it was disclosed that during his four years as magistrate he had accumulated $165,000 on a total salary of only $48,000.

Next, a witness testified that Magistrate George F. Ewald had paid $10,000 to a Tammany leader for his appointment. Ewald was tried, but the indictment against him was quashed when a jury disagreed. Nonetheless, Ewald resigned, telling a reporter, "I was a respected man until I got mixed up with that pack of thieves that hangs out in Tammany Hall. They ruined me."

The New York Bar then asked Governor Franklin D. Roosevelt

to probe charges of corruption in the appointment of magistrates. Roosevelt pointed out that the governor lacked the power to remove magistrates. However, he asked the appellate division of the first judicial department, comprising Manhattan and the Bronx, to investigate the magistrates' courts. Such was the start of the most widespread probe of the city since Boss Tweed's death. It developed into three separate probes: (1) an investigation of the magistrates' courts; (2) an investigation of the competency of District Attorney Thomas Crain; and (3) an inquiry into the entire city government.

Samuel Seabury, a righteous man, was picked as referee of the first investigation. Born in New York in 1873, Seabury was graduated from the New York Law School, admitted to the bar, and elected a justice of the city court of New York, then a justice of the state supreme court, and finally an associate justice of the state court of appeals. In 1916 he resigned from the bench to run unsuccessfully for governor of New York on the Democratic ticket.

Seabury was an anti-Tammany Democrat. After his defeat he practiced law at 120 Broadway and prospered. He lived in a six-story mansion at 154 East Sixty-third Street and was chauffeured around town in a green Lincoln. He was a handsome man with a big face, a florid complexion, and dark eyebrows that contrasted sharply with his white hair, and he wore pince-nez glasses and a high starched collar. He played chess, doted on genealogy, read political philosophy, put together a large library, and smoked a pipe. When he was a judge, his decrees were highly regarded for their literary excellence, as well as their legalistic reasoning.

The probe of the magistrates' courts began in September, 1930. Only the fifty magistrates in Manhattan and the Bronx were affected; those in the other three boroughs were outside the jurisdiction of the first judicial department. As referee, Seabury had no power to initiate criminal actions; he could only make recommendations. However, he wisely planned to use the lever of public opinion. Aware that he was taking on a Tammany tiger with unsheathed claws, Seabury assembled a staff of young attorneys less likely to be corrupt than older lawyers because they had fewer political contacts.

Seabury and his men questioned the magistrates in private. The next step was to ask them to repeat their testimony in public. This touched off a wave of resignations. One magistrate left the bench with the excuse that he suffered arthritis in one finger. Another quickly fled from the state. Two magistrates were removed by the appellate division. Seabury revealed that most magistrates had been appointed for services rendered, and he added, "This evidence presents a situation which is a scandal and a disgrace, as well as a menace, to the city of New York."

By now almost everyone knew of Jimmy Walker's extramarital affair with an actress, named Betty Compton. One day they went sailing on a private yacht off Montauk Point. When a storm arose, the mayor became seasick, so they put ashore at Montauk. Nearby was a gambling casino. Miss Compton begged Walker to let her visit the place, and with a weary shrug he acquiesced. As they entered, the manager was careful not to use the mayor's full name, merely saying, "Good evening, Mr. W. What is your pleasure?" Walker replied, "I haven't any pleasure. I'm still seasick, but"—gesturing toward his actress friend, he added—"Miss C. would be pleased to play hazard." Walker watched as she won almost $2,000.

Just before midnight some burly men burst into the gambling room. One bellowed, "Stand where you are, everybody! This is a raid!" The Suffolk County sheriff had picked that night to crack down on gambling joints. Miss Compton gasped as she saw Walker vanish through a door leading to the kitchen. When she tried to follow, an officer stopped her. With other patrons she was taken into temporary custody and led through the kitchen to the outdoors. Seated at a kitchen table was Mayor Walker, wearing a waiter's apron and eating beans. At the sight of her lover in this thin disguise, she exploded, "Jim, are you going to let these farmers—" A deputy sheriff growled at her, "Come on, lady! Tell it to the judge." Walker, who didn't even lift his eyes, went on eating beans. A few hours later Miss Compton was released and made a beeline for the yacht. Walker was calmly sitting on deck. After glaring at him awhile, she finally cried, "Why did you desert me? You and your beans!" Walker apologized, saying, "It might be a good idea if I didn't tempt fate at this moment by showing up in a rural hoosegow."

The second phase of the Seabury investigation was a long look at District Attorney Crain, a Tammany wheelhorse who often let people indicted for major crimes plead guilty to misdemeanors. After studying Crain's record, Seabury reported to Roosevelt that the district attorney wasn't corrupt—he was just incompetent. Crain was not removed from office.

While probing the magistrates, Seabury put on the stand a man he called "a witness without parallel in the history of American jurisprudence. This was Chile Mapocha Acuna, a stool pigeon who did dirty work for the police vice squad. Acuna was so depraved that he became known as the Human Spittoona. At the behest of corrupt cops, he helped frame innocent women as prostitutes. The details were so sordid that Seabury asked ladies to leave the courtroom before Acuna told his story.

The stool pigeon would wait until a doctor left his office and then enter it posing as a patient. When the doctor's nurse approached him, he would put some money in a conspicuous spot and take off his clothes. Naturally, the startled nurse would protest. At just this moment in would dash police to arrest the nurse for prostitution. This was just one of the many filthy tricks used by Acuna. Seabury asked if he could identify any vice squad officers who had hired him, and Acuna pointed an accusing finger at twenty-eight policemen. The new police commissioner, Edward P. Mulrooney, immediately suspended every cop identified by Acuna and other stool pigeons. Mayor Walker told reporters that he was "more or less shocked by the reports of the framing of innocent women."

The Reverend John Haynes Holmes and Rabbi Stephen S. Wise, acting for the City Affairs Committee, now drew up a document charging the mayor with ignoring corruption, appointing unworthy officials, and failing to administer the city government properly. They handed the indictment to Governor Roosevelt in his mother's Manhattan home. The governor, who wanted Tammany support to further his political career, received them coolly and lectured them half an hour. But the 4,000-word document contained 10 specific charges that Roosevelt could not dismiss out of hand. He forwarded it to Walker, who then sent a 15,000-word reply to the governor. Walker called the City Affairs Committee "an annex of the Socialist party" and characterized Holmes as "a leader in a group of agitators and Soviet sympathizers." Roosevelt told committee members that there was insufficient evidence to remove the mayor.

The Republican-ruled state legislature, however, refused to let the Democratic governor protect the city's Democratic mayor. On March 23, 1931, state legislators called for the appointment of a committee for "the investigation of the departments of the government of the City of New York." Roosevelt approved a $250,000 appropriation. Named chairman of the new committee was Samuel H. Hofstadter, a Republican who had defeated a Tammany candidate for the office of state senator. The committee consisted of five Republicans and four Democrats. They named Seabury as their counsel, and now began the third and most crucial probe.

Seabury's assistants bored into the underground of Walker's life by examining his income tax returns, bank deposits, savings accounts, brokerage statements, real estate records, and other pertinent papers. They failed to find any solid clue to the mayor's wealth until a Chase National Bank teller suggested that they search for letters of credit. The investigators then made out a subpoena for letters of credit, got no help from the bank, threatened its president, and finally took possession of Walker's letters-of-credit record. When this was shown to Seabury, he cried, "This is the fatal blow to Tammany Hall! It is the first time in the history of New York that a mayor is caught taking money with his actual receipts for the bribe."

All the pieces now fell into place. A group of politicians and businessmen had maintained a slush fund for the mayor in exchange for favors. Whenever they communicated with one another, they used a secret code, in which the term "boyfriend" signified Walker.

One plotter was a Wall Street broker, who had invested in a big taxicab corporation. He had said he was going to "take the mayor in" on some oil stocks. Although Walker put up no money, one of the broker's friends appeared at City Hall and gave the mayor an envelope containing $26,535 in alleged profits.

Another conspirator was John A. Hastings, a Democratic state senator from Brooklyn, who had become friendly with Walker when both had served in Albany. After Walker had become mayor, Hastings went on the payrolls of several firms, including some that operated taxis in Manhattan. About this time trolleys were giving way to buses, so Hastings and some Ohio manufacturers organized the Equitable Coach Company, asked for bus franchises in New York, and sought control of all the city's surface transportation. The Equitable people paid for one of Walker's European vacations.

Still another Walker crony was Paul Block, who owned the Brooklyn *Standard-Union* and eight other newspapers. Block was associated with Hastings in a chemical firm that hoped to produce tile for the city's subway stations. Block opened a joint brokerage account for Walker and himself, using the initials "P. B." and "J. J. W." Walker never contributed a cent to the dual account, but in two years he received $246,693 from it.

The mayor's principal go-between and bagman was an accountant, named Russell T. Sherwood. Soon after Walker took office as mayor,

Sherwood opened an investment trustee account in a large brokerage firm, and in the next 5½ years he deposited nearly $1,000,000 for Walker, of which $750,000 was in cash. The secret joint account was kept in a brokerage house because if the money had been put in a bank, the name of the depositor and the existence of the fund would have become known. When Seabury began closing in on Sherwood, the mayor's bagman took off for Mexico, rather than testify.

Now Walker himself was ordered to appear before the Hofstadter committee. The morning of May 24, 1932, he prepared for his public ordeal. At the time Walker was living in the Mayfair House at Park Avenue and Sixty-fifth Street. His valet helped him don a blue ensemble: light-blue shirt, dark-blue tie, double-breasted blue suit, and matching blue handkerchief. Walker kidded: "Little Boy Blue is about to blow his horn—or his top." Jauntily he walked out of the hotel and into a group of waiting reporters. One asked if anyone had advised him about the testimony he was to give. A grin splitting his foxy face, Walker replied, "There are three things a man must do alone—be born, die, and testify." Then he stepped into a limousine and told the chauffeur, "Drive carefully. We don't want to get a ticket." The car purred south toward the new nine-story State Office Building, on the northeastern corner of Foley Square.

The hearing was scheduled to begin at 11 A.M., but at 8:30 an attendant had opened the hearing room doors prematurely. Within seconds all 340 seats were occupied, and about 400 standees crowded inside the relatively small chamber. These early birds were infuriated when they were told that the only persons allowed inside were holders of passes signed by Chairman Hofstadter. Ordered out, they refused to move. Police reserves were called, and the intruders were pushed out into the warm May sunshine. Perhaps 5,000 persons clotted the sidewalks about the building when the mayor's limousine pulled up at 10:45 A.M. They cheered Walker, who grinned and touched a thin finger to his light gray fedora. There were shouts: "Good luck, Jimmy!" and "Attaboy, Jimmy!" and "You tell 'em, Jimmy!" He clasped his hands over his head like a triumphant prizefighter. Then he walked inside, strode through a marble foyer, and took an elevator to an upper floor.

When Walker entered the hearing room, he was greeted again with cheers and applause. Senator Hofstadter banged a gavel and warned spectators that they would be ousted if they interrupted the proceedings. At 11 A.M. the senator turned to Judge Samuel Seabury, who wore a gray suit, white starched shirt, and conservative dark tie. "Judge Seabury," said the senator, "the committee is ready, if you are." Seabury turned to Walker and asked courteously, "Mr. Mayor, will you be good enough to take the stand?" Walker stepped briskly into the witness chair and sat with one hand dangling gracefully over the oaken rail.

One of Seabury's associates, warning the judge about Walker's legendary charm, had advised, "Don't look him straight in the eye when he's on the stand. He has an uncanny ability to stare you down." Seabury took this advice. During his examination of the mayor he stood to one side and faced him as little as necessary. Their exchanges were like a duel between a jack-in-the-box and an adding machine.

Seabury stuck to facts—grim and revealing facts. Walker fought back with wisecracks and tart answers, stalled for time to reflect by asking for more details, interrupted Seabury's questions, made speeches, feigned indignation, shed crocodile tears, insisted that questions were so complex that he couldn't trust his memory, announced that the answers were in the record anyway, and asked the judge to repeat his questions. Refusing to be hoodwinked, Seabury turned his back on the witness and told the stenographer to read back the questions. The committee's minority Democratic members tried to protect the mayor by objecting repeatedly to questions and by heckling Seabury. Chairman Hofstadter practically wore out his right arm banging the gavel to restore order. Seabury was relentless. Using the evidence amassed by his assistants over the previous seven months, he tripped up Walker time after time and forced him to make damaging admissions. The judge got into the record a series of confessions, whose import was lost on Walker's admirers. After the second and final day of the mayor's appearance, roses were strewed in his path as he strode out of the State Office Building.

But a few days later at Yankee Stadium the mayor was booed. New Yorkers began to understand that their erstwhile pet was an ersatz mayor, able to play the role of Beau Brummell only because he was subsidized by rich and conniving men seeking favors at the expense of taxpayers.

On June 8, 1932, Seabury sent Governor Roosevelt fifteen charges against Walker, the first one declaring that Walker had "failed properly to execute the duties which, as Mayor of the City of New York, it was incumbent upon him to discharge." Seabury urged the Democratic governor to dismiss a Democratic mayor backed by Tammany

Hall at a time when the Democratic national convention was only a few weeks away. Roosevelt wanted the Democratic presidential nomination and felt that he needed Tammany support to get it. He was very much on the spot. In his Hyde Park home the governor turned to Raymond Moley and mused aloud, "How would it be if I let the little mayor off with a hell of a reprimand?" Before Moley could reply, Roosevelt jerked up his great chin and snapped, "No! That would be weak!"

Now the scene shifted to Albany. In twelve sessions held in the State Capitol Building Roosevelt sat as judge in a hearing to determine if Walker should be deposed. Like Seabury, the governor quickly learned how difficult it was to get a straight answer from the playboy mayor. Before the Albany hearings began, Roosevelt conferred with Felix Frankfurter, then a Harvard law professor. Frankfurter later said, "I worked out with Roosevelt the legal theory on which Jimmy Walker had to go—the theory being that when a public official has acquired money during the time that he was in public office, the presumption of wrongdoing lies there unless he can explain why he suddenly came into money that he couldn't have got merely through his salary."

There was a break in the Albany hearings so that Walker could return to New York to attend his brother's funeral. The mayor met in the Hotel Plaza with a dozen or more Tammany leaders, including Al Smith. When Walker asked Smith for his opinion, Smith said, "Jim, you're through. You must resign for the good of the party." The evening of September 1, 1932, Walker sent the city clerk this statement: "I hereby resign as Mayor of the City of New York, the same to take effect immediately."

Walker then issued an angry statement calling Roosevelt "unfair" and his hearings "un-American," and in the late afternoon of September 2 he sailed for Europe. The Jimmy Walker era was over. The bubble had burst.

Chapter 46

FIORELLO LAGUARDIA BECOMES MAYOR

JIMMY WALKER'S duties as mayor were taken over temporarily by the president of the board of aldermen, Joseph V. McKee. Then a special election was held in November, 1932, to select a man to serve the rest of Walker's unexpired term. Boss Curry picked John P. O'Brien as the Tammany candidate, and O'Brien won. A former surrogate of New York County, O'Brien was so gauche that his enemies called him the wild bull of the china shop. He once referred to Einstein as "Albert Weinstein." When a reporter asked the Tammany-controlled mayor the name of his new police commissioner, he replied, "I don't know. I haven't got the word yet."

In the regular election of 1933 three candidates vied for mayor.

The Democrats were split, O'Brien running as the Tammany candidate and McKee running as an independent Democrat. Fiorello H. LaGuardia, a Republican in name only, was the choice of the Republican and City Fusion parties. It was a vicious campaign besmirched with violence. LaGuardia charged that McKee was antiSemitic, and McKee declared that LaGuardia was "a Communist at heart." LaGuardia promised to destroy the Tammany system of bosses and machine politics and replace them with nonpartisan government by experts. New Yorkers were weary of Tammany domination, shocked by the Walker scandals, and sobered by the depression. Between them O'Brien and McKee won more votes than LaGuardia, but he was elected.

The evening of December 31, 1933, LaGuardia and leaders of his reform coalition gathered in the second-floor library of Judge Samuel Seabury's town house. The host and most male guests were in tuxedos, but LaGuardia wore a business suit. At midnight a black-robed state supreme court justice swore him into office, thus ending sixteen years of Tammany rule. LaGuardia then turned to his wife and kissed her while Seabury cried, "Now we have a mayor of New York!" A minute later LaGuardia picked up a telephone and ordered the arrest of Charles "Lucky" Luciano, the most notorious gangster in town.

Now the "Little Flower" held the office he had sought three times. With cyclonic energy he threw himself into the job, dictating to relays of secretaries up to twelve hours a day and dashing here and there in the city to see conditions firsthand. Only about five feet tall, the new mayor was sensitive about his height. He had a chunky body, a round face, black hair, dark and burning eyes, a swarthy complexion, and eyebrows that met over the bridge of his nose. His full lower lip pushed out petulantly whenever he was crossed. He bounced about on short legs and walked with a choppy gait. Indifferent to clothes, he wore rumpled suits and never quite got his tie firmly tucked into the V of his collar. He was an exuberant Latin, who spoke in a high-pitched voice and waved his hands as he talked. He knew all about gutter politics, yet genuinely cared about the welfare of the people. Trigger-fast at repartee, a master of the crushing retort, he pounded lecterns and often shouted until his voice broke. No intellectual, he saw life in blacks and whites. A liberal, he distrusted big business and pronounced the word "rich" as though it nauseated him. He was irascible, stubborn, autocratic, impatient, belligerent, opinionated, and overbearing. He was charming, warmhearted, generous, and loving. He adored children, enjoyed parties, smoked a cigar or corncob pipe, was a talented mimic, played chess, and blew the cornet.

Although this was LaGuardia's first administrative job, he knew city government inside and out. It pained him to delegate power, but he nonetheless surrounded himself with as distinguished a group of city officials as could be found in the world. These departmental heads developed an infectious esprit de corps, despite the polished bone the mayor kept in a jeweler's box. Whenever a commissioner pulled a *boner*, LaGuardia presented this symbol to him with ceremonious irony.

When LaGuardia took office, city finances were chaotic, crime was rampant, housing was a mess, and soon the city's unemployed equaled the entire population of upstate Buffalo. The new mayor preferred welfare to economy, although he restored the city's credit rating. He was friendly with the new President, Franklin D. Roosevelt, obtained vast sums of New Deal money for city relief and used them well. LaGuardia built more public projects than any other mayor in the city's history.

Municipal parks had been deteriorating for a decade, and the mayor chose an exceedingly able man, Robert Moses, to renovate and beautify them. Park Commissioner Moses said, "We aim to rebuild New York, saving what is durable, what is salvageable, and what is genuinely historical, and substituting progress for obsolescence." In the Central Park Zoo the lions' cages were so flimsy that animal keepers carried shotguns to protect children if the beasts escaped. The park itself teemed with rats, and in a single week Moses's exterminators killed more than 200,000 of them. In 2 years Moses increased recreational facilities by about 35 percent. With parks and playgrounds multiplying at incredible speed, Moses snapped at the sanitation commissioner for piling garbage cans along a certain park. The commissioner asked plaintively, How were his men to know when they set down garbage cans that there would be a new park beside them the next day?

At the beginning of the depression poor people were dependent on private charity and local government, but neither could cope with the worsening situation. New York was hit harder than any other American city because of its size. In 1931, when Walker was mayor, the city had launched its own relief program, issuing bonds to pay the cost. Mayor O'Brien had met relief needs mainly by borrowing. La-

Guardia, who wanted to put relief on a pay-as-you-go basis, received authority from the state to finance relief from current revenues. This meant that he had to find new taxes.

Although LaGuardia had opposed sales taxes while he was a member of Congress, as mayor he imposed a 2 percent sales tax, a 3 percent utility tax, and a gross business tax of 0.1 percent to meet the city's share of relief costs. The state and federal governments contributed 75 percent of the city's relief burden. Between 1933 and 1939 the United States spent more than $1,000,000,000 for relief in New York City. The peak came in March, 1936, when 1,550,000 men, women, and children in the city, or nearly 20 percent of the total population, got some form of public assistance.

The phrase "work relief" was avoided at first; relief projects were called emergency work. Officials couldn't decide whether it was work being performed or relief being dispensed. At last they faced up to the grim fact that relief was intended to keep people from starving and to boost their morale with jobs that made them feel useful. Nonetheless, there was much sneering about leafraking and loafing on the job. The efficiency-minded Moses once snapped, "The official who promises one hundred percent efficiency is taking the public for a ride!" But Moses was softhearted. After a fishing trip with friends off Long Island, he cleaned 500 flounders and gave them to the poor.

In those dark days little girls played a game called Going on Relief. One youngster would take the part of a relief worker. She would question her friends about their families; whereupon the other little girls displayed their dolls and told sad stories about how many children they had to support. Small boys, for their part, took up another game, which they called Picketing. Carrying crude signs, marching back and forth, and hooting at "scabs," they reenacted labor clashes they had seen or heard about from their fathers.

A building boom had begun before the stock market crash, and now many of these projects continued, providing jobs for workers who had not been hired for public construction. Some new structures were finished before LaGuardia took office. The 102-story Empire State Building, the world's tallest skyscraper, opened on May 1, 1931, on the site of the old Waldorf-Astoria Hotel. Will Durant, the historian, once wrote that "the Empire State Building is as sublime as Chartres Cathedral." On October 1, 1931, a new Waldorf-Astoria opened on the block bounded by Park and Lexington Avenues and Forty-ninth and Fiftieth streets. Then came the city's most important single architectural project—Rockefeller Center. This city within a city was erected by John D. Rockefeller, Jr., on the west side of Fifth Avenue between West Forty-eighth and West Fifty-first streets. He employed 75,000 men for 10 years. The tallest peak in this sierra of skyscrapers was the 70-story Radio Corporation of America Building, completed in May, 1933. The *New York City Guide,* written by talented relief workers, declared, "In its architecture Rockefeller Center stands as distinctly for New York as the Louvre stands for Paris."

The construction industry and labor unions, like many other businesses and institutions, had become infested with racketeers. When Prohibition ended, bootleggers and gangsters tried to find a new way to make a dishonest dollar, so they muscled their way into control of a wide range of enterprises, such as restaurants, theaters, bakeries, the garment trade, loan sharking, prostitution, and all forms of gambling. They forced honest businessmen and labor leaders to pay them so-called protection money under fear of reprisals. After the racketeers had taken over a firm or entire industry, they fixed prices, as is done by cartels. Protection money and price boosts were passed along to consumers, already hard pressed to make ends meet.

LaGuardia, who had promised to rid the city of crooks, improved the police department, tried to make honest men of cops, cracked down on gamblers, and smashed slot machines and pinball machines. His crime-busting record was exceeded, however, by that of Thomas E. Dewey. Born in Michigan, Dewey had received a law degree from Columbia University, entered a Manhattan law firm, and had become Chief Assistant United States Attorney for the Southern District of New York. In 1935 Governor Herbert H. Lehman appointed Dewey a special prosecutor and told him to run racketeers out of town.

Various gangs throughout the country had put aside their differences and organized themselves into a national syndicate. The eastern division, headquartered in New York, was known as the Big Six. Francesco Castiglia, better known as Frank Costello, was in charge of the division's gambling. Lucky Luciano headed the prostitution and narcotics rackets. Arthur Flegenheimer, called Dutch Schultz, controlled the restaurants and the Harlem policy banks. Joseph Doto, whose alias was Joey Adonis, ruled the bail bond racket and Brooklyn waterfront. Louis "Lepke" Buchalter and Jacob "Gurrah" Shapiro dominated the industrial and labor extortions. Benjamin "Bugsy" Siegel and Meyer Lansky were strong-arm enforcers.

When Dewey probed the restaurant racket, Dutch Schultz began worrying. When Dewey looked into the policy racket, Schultz banged a table with his fist and screamed, "Dewey's gotta go! He has gotta be hit in the head!" But with criminals now organized in a cartel, Schultz couldn't act alone. Ranking East Coast gangsters held a summit meeting in New York to discuss Dewey's assassination. Most were against the overt act; one mobster argued that if they killed Dewey, federal agents might take up where he left off and chase the syndicate out of the country. Syndicate directors voted to let Dewey live. However, they soon heard that the furious Dutchman was going to take Dewey by himself. To protect their interests, they had Dutch Schultz murdered.

Dewey's investigators found damaging evidence about James J. "Jimmy" Hines, a Tammany leader who acted as the principal link between the underworld and Tammany Hall. Hines had protected Schultz's policy racket and guarded the interests of a host of other criminals. Dewey got an indictment from a grand jury, and Hines was sent to Sing Sing. Dewey also masterminded the arrest and conviction of Lucky Luciano on a charge of compulsory prostitution. During his two years as special prosecutor, Dewey obtained seventy-two convictions out of seventy-three indictments.

A girl living in Jackson Heights read in her history book that George Washington had been sworn in as the first President of the United States in 1789. The year 1939 would mark the 150th anniversary of the historic event, and the youngster thought that the city should celebrate by staging a world's fair. The city fathers and civic leaders agreed. Various sections of each borough wanted the fair, but the arguments ended when Park Commissioner Moses refused to cooperate unless Flushing Meadow was selected. The meadow had served as a city dump the last quarter century, and Moses hoped to use a temporary fair to create a permanent park. Groundbreaking ceremonies were held in 1936, and the two-year fair opened in 1939.

It was the greatest world's fair ever held up to that time, attracting a total of nearly 45,000,000 visitors and costing $157,000,000, but it was a financial failure. New York had not had a world's fair since 1853, when the city's population had stood at 581,018. In 1939 New York was a metropolis of 7,434,346 persons. This was more than the combined populations of Arizona, Colorado, Delaware, the District of Columbia, Idaho, Maine, Montana, Nevada, New Hampshire, New

Mexico, North Dakota, Rhode Island, Utah, Vermont, and Wyoming —plus all the foreign-born white males of Oklahoma. More people lived in New York City than in Australia or Bulgaria or Peru or Greece or Sweden or Morocco.

The day the fair opened, Mayor LaGuardia said, "May I point to one exhibit that I hope all visitors will note, and that is the city of New York itself." He had cause to be proud of the city and of himself as well. He was completely honest. He was the best mayor New York ever had. He served longer than any mayor since Richard Varick, who held office from 1789 to 1801. Not since Mayor Mitchel's time had any city administration been so vigorous. He instituted more reforms than any mayor of any city at any time in the nation's history. He improved and expanded municipal services, secured the adoption of a new city charter, reformed the civil service, attacked the slum problem, bettered housing conditions, resumed the construction of schools, unified the subway systems, stimulated cultural affairs, made the city an aviation center, and opened the nation's first free port. He cleaned up the magistrates' courts. He abolished the Tammany-controlled board of aldermen and established a city council elected by proportional representation. Grateful New Yorkers reelected him in 1937 and again in 1941.

The Japanese had put up a lovely pavilion at the World's Fair. Modeled after an ancient Shinto shrine, it included a dainty garden with reflecting pools, tiny waterfalls, and dwarf evergreen trees. One part of the pavilion was dedicated to the long friendship between Japan and the United States. At a dinner held on the eve of Japan Day ceremonies at the fair the Japanese ambassador to this country had hissed politely and assured the guests that Japan intended to stay out of the European war, which had begun in 1939, and "to keep the war out of Asia."

Ah, so? On December 7, 1941, two Japanese envoys had an appointment to see Secretary of State Cordell Hull in Washington. This was a Sunday, and here in New York the weather was mild. A White House switchboard operator opened emergency lines to Washington offices of the United Press, Associated Press, and International News Service. "This is the White House," she said. "Stand by for a conference call."

Arthur DeGreve was almost alone in the U.P.'s Washington office that Sunday afternoon. Muscles tensed, he crushed the phone against his ear. Then came a simultaneous flash from the White House to the

three wire services. DeGreve scribbled notes on copy paper. The tele- ·
types, as Joe Alex Morris explained in *Deadline Every Minute,* had
not yet been readied for the Sunday night report. DeGreve hung up
the phone to the White House and grabbed another. He called the
international headquarters of the United Press on the twelfth floor of
the New York Daily News Building, at 220 East Forty-second Street
in Manhattan. Phil Newsom took the call.

"This is DeGreve in Washington—Flash!—White House an-
nounces Japanese bombing of Oahu!"

"Bombing what?"

"Oahu, dammit! Oahu!"

"Spell it, for Pete's sake!"

"*O-A-H-U*—wahoo! We've got a war on our hands!"

Chapter 47

NAZIS PLAN TO BOMB NEW YORK

LAGUARDIA had called Hitler a "perverted maniac." A little later Hermann Goering, the Nazi minister of aviation, ordered the German aircraft industry to produce planes capable of carrying five-ton bombs to New York to "stop somewhat the mouths of the arrogant people over there." Goering's experts also made a special map of lower Manhattan, painting a bull's-eye at the corner of the Bowery and Delancey Street. Concentric rings drawn around the dot showed zones of primary and secondary damage. This map, later captured by the Allies, proved that Goering hoped to inflict destruction as far north as Rockefeller Center and as far south as Governors Island.

Just before noon on December 9, 1941, an alarm sounded at the

Air Defense Command located at Mitchel Field, twenty-eight miles east of New York. A siren shrilled like an anguished nightingale, while under it could be heard the bullfrog warble of a foghorn. In the staff building, officers looked up with puzzled frowns. They jumped out of chairs, rushed to windows, and stared out. Soon they had the word: enemy planes approaching the east coast. A major snatched up a phone on his desk. Oddly, he *whispered* his order: "Load the B-25's with thirty- and fifty-caliber machine guns."

The B-25's were medium Martin bombers. Their racks were emptied of bombs, and guns were installed. Then up zoomed the bombers. Up, too, flitted Aircobras, cannons snouting from their black muzzles. In less than 20 minutes 280 planes gashed the sky over New York and the Atlantic seaboard. Mitchel was at war. But the warning about enemy aircraft had been false, just as London's first air raid alert had been an error. Later a pilot sat in a hangar at Mitchel Field and told how it felt to defend New York. Lieutenant Lennon Blackman said slowly, "It's kind of hard to explain. You sit in your plane and look down, and you feel kind of warm at the people below you. It's New York you feel."

Although the city never was bombed, it took no chances. Its very magnitude made it so complex that it was as sensitive as a Swiss watch, and the problem of defending it was staggering. Defense measures struck grisly undertones. The fire department sent three battalion chiefs to London to see how incendiary bombs were handled. New Yorkers were told what to do in the event of a gas attack. Temporary morgues were set up here and there in the city, and volunteers were taught how to dispose of bodies. A local funeral director bought radio time to suggest, "You never know when to expect bad news, so be prepared. Buy a family lot."

London had evacuated most of its youngsters, and New York learned from this experience. More than 1,000,000 identification tags were made for New York's public and parochial schoolchildren, and an evacuation camp was built for them at New Milford, Connecticut. Fortunately, the camp never had to be used. But air raid drills were held in the city's schools, and little boys and girls stretched face down on the floor while teachers read aloud to them.

When German submarines began attacking American ships near the Atlantic seaboard, sight-seers were barred from the Woolworth Building tower, which provided a clear view of the harbor. Because U-boat crews could see silhouettes of vessels against the glow of the city's lights, blackouts were ordered. In Foley Square the thirty-two story Federal Building had a pyramidal roof covered with gold leaf; because this glinted on moonlit nights, black paint was daubed onto it. The torch atop the Statue of Liberty was turned off. No longer did the electric bulletin board around the Times Tower flash the news of the day. Air raid wardens patrolled the streets and bellowed up at apartment windows lacking black window shades.

Television, becoming popular just when war began, was used to train the wardens and the police. Pedestrians were kept off East River bridges so that explosives couldn't be dropped onto passing ships. Subway lockers were bolted shut to prevent anyone from placing time bombs in them. Nazi saboteurs were caught before they could blow up the Hell Gate railroad bridge over the East River or disrupt the city's water supply by blasting holes in its Westchester County reservoirs. Fourteen members of a German spy ring were convicted in a Brooklyn court of espionage and failure to register as German agents. Nazi propaganda was disseminated by a Nazi agent, whose luxurious apartment at 305 Riverside Drive was decorated with a portrait of Hitler.

As war's tempo increased, LaGuardia became so overburdened with work that his performance as mayor began to fall off. In addition to trying to run the nation's largest city, he served as director of the Office of Civilian Defense (with the right to attend Cabinet meetings) and as chairman of the American section of the Joint Permanent Defense Board. His duties forced him to commute between New York and Washington. In the national capital he had an apartment in the Dupont Circle apartment building. In New York he lived with his wife and two adopted children in a modest apartment at 1274 5th Avenue, between 108th and 109th streets. Like all previous New York mayors, he lived in a place of his own choosing and paid his own household expenses.

This seemed unfair to certain municipal officials, who now proposed that the city buy and maintain an official residence for La-Guardia and the mayors who would succeed him. They favored the Charles M. Schwab palace on Riverside Drive between Seventy-third and Seventy-fourth streets, a seventy-five-room French château that was considered one of the most impressive mansions in the world. A man of simple tastes, LaGuardia squeaked, "What! Me in *that!*" He preferred Gracie Mansion on the shore of the East River in Carl Schurz Park on East End Avenue just off East Eighty-eighth Street.

This fine old house stood on a point of land called Horn's Hook, for the village of Hoorn in Holland. A fort dating from the American Revolution was a landmark there until 1794, when the property was bought by Archibald Gracie, a wealthy merchant born in Scotland. He tore down the fort, and about 1799 he built a sixteen-room wooden house in the Federal style, with verandas running around three sides. Among the famous guests entertained in Gracie Mansion were John Quincy Adams, James Fenimore Cooper, Washington Irving, John Jacob Astor, Alexander Hamilton, and Louis Philippe, who later became king of France.

In 1891 the city acquired the property, and in 1927 the white frame house was restored by the park department and opened as a museum. Remodeled in 1942, it then became the official residence of New York's mayors. LaGuardia was secretly glad to move away from his apartment on upper Fifth Avenue. The champion of minority groups, he nonetheless worried about the safety of his children as Negroes and Puerto Ricans began infiltrating the neighborhood.

New York played a major role in the national war effort, its industrial firms and cultural institutions converting to defense production and military techniques. In the New York Public Library, for example, a Japanese naval code was broken. American intelligence officers had learned that this code was based on a certain Mexico City directory of a certain year. However, not a single copy of this book was left in Mexico. In all the Allied world, as a matter of fact, the only extant copy was in the New York Public Library, whose collection of city directories and telephone books was unequaled.

Individual New Yorkers did their part. George Hyde, to name one, worked secretly in the basement of his home at 552 Third Avenue, in Brooklyn. Born in Germany, Hyde had designed machine guns for the Kaiser's army during World War I. By the time he came to the United States in 1926, he was one of the world's great gunsmiths. When army officers planned to land American troops in Europe during World War II, they realized that the M1 (Garand) rifle was too heavy for beach landings and too light in firepower. They asked Hyde to invent a lightweight, rugged, fully automatic weapon that would function well under the harsh conditions expected on the Normandy beaches.

Hyde went to work. Remembering a toy gun he had seen as a boy in Germany, he designed and hand-tooled a prototype of the M3 submachine gun. It was ready for testing only 4 weeks after he got the assignment. It weighed just 8 pounds, was completely automatic, shot .45 ball cartridges 1,760 yards, and was spectacularly successful. The invasion of France was delayed several weeks while Hyde's new "grease-gun" went into production. More than 8,000,000 of these weapons proved effective in the D-day landings and in action on Pacific islands.

One of New York's most important contributions to the war was made by Columbia University scientists. They learned that German physicists in Berlin apparently had split an atom by bombarding uranium with slow neutrons made of radioactive materials. The news aroused Dr. John R. Dunning, an associate professor of physics at Columbia, and Italian-born Dr. Enrico Fermi, who had recently been made a physics professor at the university. They deduced that when the Germans split the atom, a vast amount of energy was released. They also theorized that the two fragments of the atom had been pushed apart at great speed by the mutually repulsive force of their positive charges. Both were eager to test the theory, but Fermi had to leave for Washington.

Deciding to go ahead with the experiment, Dunning enlisted the help of two assistants. At seven o'clock on the cold and windy evening of January 25, 1939, the three scientists met secretly in Columbia's cyclotron laboratory in the basement of the Pupin Physics Laboratories. This twelve-story red-brick building, topped by a green bronze astronomical dome, stood on the southeastern corner of Broadway and West 120th Street. Working in muted excitement, the physicists set up their equipment and began the test.

At the critical moment they watched a round oscilloscope. Green lines suddenly shot toward the top of the screen, leaped high and ever higher, and finally skyrocketed out of their field of vision. The test was a success. They had split a uranium atom into two parts, each part consisting of 100,000,000 electron volts, the greatest amount of atomic energy ever liberated on earth. Dunning quickly calculated that 1 pound of uranium 235 could yield as much energy as 5,000,000 pounds of coal.

Thus, on a New York City campus, for the first time in the New World, an atom was split. Bending over his laboratory notebook, Dunning scribbled eleven prophetic words: "Believe we have observed a new phenomenon of far reaching consequences." Years later he mused, "That night I was pretty well convinced this was the beginning of a new age."

Columbia physicists now asked themselves this question, Was it possible to set up a nuclear chain reaction? A couple of two-man teams began independent experiments on the campus to try to find the answer. Fermi headed one team. Hungarian-born Dr. Leo Szilard was in charge of the other. Working separately, but simultaneously, they proved that the enormous energy released by the fission of uranium could be used to make a bomb. And what a bomb! It would contain a million times more energy *per pound* than any known explosive.

Dr. George B. Pegram, physics professor and dean of graduate faculties at Columbia, had closely watched these experiments. Although he wasn't quite sure that an atomic bomb could be made, he felt it was his duty to report to the federal government. He wrote a historic letter to Admiral S. C. Hooper in the Office of the Chief of Naval Operations in Washington. This was the very first contact between the scientific world and the United States government about atomic energy. For the next few months, however, federal officials did nothing.

Albert Einstein agreed to alert President Roosevelt to this great potential by writing him a personal letter, that began: "Sir: Some recent work by E. Fermi and L. Szilard, which has been communicated to me in manuscript, leads me to expect that the element uranium may be turned into a new and important source of energy in the immediate future. . . ." This letter was handed to the President by Alexander Sachs of New York, vice-president of the Lehman Corporation in Wall Street and a friend of Szilard's. After brief hesitation Roosevelt said, "This requires action."

Columbia physicists were already building the world's first atomic furnace, or pile, on the seventh floor of the Pupin Building. On January 20, 1940, the first federal *grant* for atomic energy research was awarded to Columbia. It was a mere $6,000. The following November the first federal *contract* for such work went to the university. This time the Columbia scientists got $40,000. Such was the genesis of the supersecret program first named the Manhattan Engineering District and later called merely the Manhattan Project. Its purpose was to make an atomic bomb before the Nazis did.

By the summer of 1941 the scientists needed more space, so they moved their equipment out of the Pupin Building and into the basement of the nearby Schermerhorn Building. Tons of uranium oxide and graphite were used. Both substances are black, and soon the physicists looked like coal miners. Their backs ached from lugging around 50- and 100-pound cans of uranium and handling graphite bricks. Dean Pegram suggested that they use Columbia football players for this manual labor. The scientists were delighted. They hired a dozen husky youths who hadn't the faintest idea that they were taking part in one of the greatest scientific experiments in the annals of mankind.

The atomic furnace began to outgrow its new quarters in the Schermerhorn basement. Federal officials conducted a quiet search for more space and found it at the University of Chicago. Transported from New York to Chicago, early in 1942, was every piece of portable atomic research equipment. In a transformed squash court at the University of Chicago on December 2, 1942, Fermi produced the world's first self-sustaining nuclear chain reaction. He was still employed by Columbia University.

In those days the most important source of uranium ore was the Shinkolobwe mine in the Belgian Congo. The mine was owned by the Union Minière du Haut-Katanga. Its managing director was Edgar Edouard Sengier. In 1938 Sengier had visited London. While in the office of Lord Stonehaven, a director of the Union Minière board, he was asked to meet secretly with Sir Henry Tizard, the famous British physicist. Sir Henry told Sengier that German scientists might be able to make an atomic bomb from uranium. He cautioned Sengier not to let any of his ore fall into German hands. A few days later several French scientists asked for Sengier's help in constructing an atomic bomb in the Sahara Desert. He agreed, but the outbreak of World War II in September, 1939, ended this project before it began.

A month later Sengier left his Brussels home and came to New York. He took command of his company's office on Broad Street and stayed in New York throughout the war. Alerted to the value of the uranium ore in the Congo mine, Sengier made a big decision. On his own initiative, he ordered 1,250 tons of this ore shipped from the Belgian Congo to New York. Stored in 2,000 steel drums, the precious cargo arrived here in September and October, 1940. It was stashed away in a secret warehouse on Staten Island.

Sengier then told American officials what he had done. The State Department wanted to rush his deadly ore to Fort Knox. But, as John Gunther has said, "because of various confusions" nearly two years passed before the United States government "acted to take advantage of Sengier's foresight and perspicacity."

On September 23, 1942, Brigadier General Leslie R. Groves assumed command of the Manhattan Project. That very day he discussed with Lieutenant Colonel K. D. Nichols the necessity of getting an adequate supply of uranium ore. They knew that Sengier was the man to see. However, neither was aware that Sengier already had talked to federal officials.

Nichols visited Sengier in his Broad Street office and said that the United States must obtain some of his ore from Africa. Sengier listened and said nothing. Piqued by the failure of government agents to act, Sengier let Nichols talk himself out. Then he told the astounded colonel that tons of this ore lay in a Staten Island warehouse. A contract was scrawled on yellow scratch paper and signed by Sengier, and the United States had a firm promise that it would get all the ore from Staten Island, with more to come from the Belgian Congo.

Sengier lived in a suite in the Hotel Ambassador on Park Avenue. Early in the morning of August 6, 1945, his phone rang. A man's voice suggested that he stay close to his radio that day. At last Sengier heard the flash: An American bomber had dropped an atomic bomb on Hiroshima.

The war in Europe had ended the previous May 7. By now the news ticker around the Times Tower was operating again, and crowds gathered day after day to watch it. A replica of the Statue of Liberty loomed high on a traffic island in the middle of Times Square. One-third the size of the original and made of white plaster, the statue had been used to promote war bond sales. Nearly half a million people thronged the square at 7 P.M. on Tuesday, August 14, 1945, when the *Times* flashed official word from President Truman that the Japanese had surrendered.

The war was over. A total of 891,923 men and women from New York City had donned uniforms to serve their country. Of this number, 16,106 were killed in action, died of wounds, died of injuries, died non-battle deaths, or were reported missing.

Chapter 48

WILLIAM O'DWYER SWEATS

WILLIAM O'DWYER was born July 11, 1890, in a cottage in Bohola, County Mayo, Ireland. Both his parents were teachers, a fact which helps explain his love of learning. He studied for the priesthood in Spain, quickly learned Spanish, changed his mind about taking orders, and decided to try his luck in America. In 1910 he landed in New York, a husky and ambitious twenty-year-old.

He held a variety of jobs over the next seven years and then became a policeman. Once, while wading into a gang of roistering sailors, he slipped in snow and was beaten to a pulp. Another time he shot and accidentally killed a drink-crazed man who pulled a gun on him. During his eight years on the force O'Dwyer was out of uniform most of the time, for he chauffeured a police inspector and served as plainclothesman. During off-hours he studied at the Fordham University Law School, passed the state bar examination, and was transferred to the police department's legal bureau.

In 1925 O'Dwyer resigned from the force to become a clerk in a law office. The next year he opened his own law office on Court Street in Brooklyn. For extra income he worked as a sports promotor, bringing Irish soccer teams to New York. This brought him into contact with Mrs. William Randolph Hearst, who wanted Irish teams for her milk fund benefits. Through her he met Joseph V. McKee, then president of the board of aldermen. When Jimmy Walker resigned and McKee became acting mayor, one of the first persons to appear at City Hall and offer congratulations was Bill O'Dwyer, who had become active in Democratic clubhouse politics. The young attorney said, "Joe, I'd sorta like to be a magistrate." On December 7, 1932, O'Dwyer entered public life as a city magistrate.

He got off to a good start and took an especial interest in juvenile delinquents. When LaGuardia became mayor, he made O'Dwyer presiding judge of an experimental adolescent court in Brooklyn. Now the squarely built, black-haired, blue-eyed Irishman received ever more requests to speak at civic functions. In 1937 Governor Lehman appointed O'Dwyer to the unexpired term of judge in the county court of Brooklyn. When this interim service ended, he won election to a full fourteen-year term. Instead of remaining on the bench, however, he was elected district attorney of Brooklyn after promising to rid it of crime. Years earlier one of his brothers had been killed by a thug during a restaurant holdup, and Bill O'Dwyer had declared himself an enemy of all criminals.

As previously noted, the nation's underworld had merged into a crime syndicate, whose members called it the Combination. It had no supreme boss but was ruled by a board of directors. In its table of organization, power descended from these directors to vice-presidents to top gangsters to lesser mobsters. Each syndicate-controlled mob was known as a troop. Troop members were called punks. The directors dictated what kinds of crime the various gangs might engage in and parceled out geographical areas for their operations.

Now and then some rash mob leader or punk tried to open up in forbidden territory or keep more than his allotted share of the take. If the offender was important, he was tried in a kangaroo court; found guilty, he was summarily executed. Lesser offenders were tracked down and killed by syndicate assassins.

A group of hoodlums from the southern part of Brooklyn, long a spawning ground for vice, proved so efficient at assassinations that they became the syndicate's official firing squad and did their dirty work the length and breadth of the land. Their overlord was Joe Adonis, a director of the Combination. His chief executioner was Albert Anastasia, who took part in almost thirty killings, was arrested for murder five times, was twice tried for homicide, but nonetheless continued to strut around Brooklyn a free man. Anastasia's right-hand man was Abe "Kid Twist" Reles, who had a hand in fourteen murders, was arrested forty-two times, but was convicted on only seven occasions—for assault, petit larceny, parole violation, disorderly conduct, and juvenile delinquency.

A reporter called the entire syndicate Murder, Inc., and the catchy title caught on in newspapers and magazines. However, it did not accurately describe the Combination, which preferred profits to murder. Board members sternly forbade murder for personal reasons. Assassinations were ordered only for business reasons. And only the Brooklyn executioners truly qualified for the title of Murder, Inc.

Most syndicate directors were Italian, and as their fortunes rose, the influence of Irish politicians fell. Mayor LaGuardia was making good his promise to wipe out Tammany Hall. From 1934 to 1949 Tammany was headed by one weak boss after another, and its decline was symbolized by the sale of the Tammany Hall building in 1943. Italian vice lords saw their opportunity. They had money. Tammany was falling apart. The syndicate gave campaign funds to Tammany politicians and thus won control of them. In the past the underworld had bought protection. Now it bossed the bosses.

When Bill O'Dwyer ran for district attorney, he promised not to take orders from party bosses, but of his first forty appointments, thirty-three came from lists supplied by Democratic district leaders. When he took office in 1940, John H. Amen, a special prosecutor, was investigating the six Brooklyn waterfront racketeering unions controlled by Albert Anastasia. O'Dwyer now launched his own probe of Anastasia. Amen suspended his investigation and gave all his records to O'Dwyer. Two weeks later O'Dwyer dropped his probe of Anastasia and never reopened it. He said that he was too busy with murder cases.

Early in 1940 Kid Twist Reles was arrested for the 1933 murder of a small-time hoodlum. In an effort to save himself, Reles offered to tell all he knew about Murder, Inc. O'Dwyer and his assistant, Burton B. Turkus, agreed to strike a bargain with Reles, promising him leniency if he would name names. Reles eagerly gushed names and facts and figures, his confessions wearing out relays of secretaries. He talked about 1,000 homicides in every corner of the United States, spelled out details of 85 murders in Brooklyn alone, and implicated every mob in the Combination.

Using this information, O'Dwyer prosecuted dozens of hoodlums and sent four to the electric chair. He soon won the reputation of a great gang buster, but none of the syndicate's six board members was prosecuted—except for Bugsy Siegel, who was indicted in California. O'Dwyer produced Reles before a California grand jury but refused to allow him to testify at Siegel's trial.

While confessing, Reles said truthfully that he had taken his orders from Anastasia. He declared that he had been with Anastasia when details of a murder were being planned. Curiously, O'Dwyer didn't even seek an indictment against Anastasia. Reles knew that the syndicate knew he was confessing and would try to kill him. For twenty months the singing gangster was guarded by Acting Captain Frank C. Bals of the New York police department, a close friend of O'Dwyer's, and by six other cops.

Reles was locked alone in a room at one end of a corridor of the Half Moon Hotel at Coney Island, and once an hour a policeman would stroll down the hall to look in at him. About 7 A.M. on November 12, 1941, Reles' body was found on a balcony 5 floors below his room. Dangling against the hotel wall was a sheet. O'Dwyer, who knew that Reles was terrified of gang retribution, said that he had fallen to his death while trying to escape.

That same month O'Dwyer ran for mayor of New York, only to be beaten by LaGuardia. On Pearl Harbor Day, less than a month after Reles' death, O'Dwyer telegraphed President Roosevelt to offer his services in the national emergency. He was commissioned a major, took a leave of absence as district attorney, and two years later rose to the rank of brigadier general.

While O'Dwyer was away, criminals consolidated their hold on Tammany Hall. Frank Costello, one of the most important board members of the syndicate, became friendly with district leaders and handed out money where it would do him the most good. Using his influence with these leaders, Costello helped make Michael J. Kennedy the boss of Tammany Hall in 1942. Kennedy, in turn, helped Costello's good friend, Thomas A. Aurelio, win the Democratic nomination for justice of the state supreme court. New York District Attorney Frank Hogan had ordered his men to tap telephone wires leading into Costello's seven-room penthouse at 115 Central Park West, and they overheard Aurelio thank Costello for the nomination. Hogan released the shocking revelation to newspapers, but Aurelio nevertheless was elected a justice.

When O'Dwyer got out of the army, he ran for mayor again. Opposing him were Jonah Goldstein, the Republican candidate, and Newbold Morris, who ran at the head of a No Deal ticket launched with LaGuardia's endorsement. Morris described the O'Dwyer regime in Brooklyn as "a rotten mess." Goldstein startled New Yorkers by accusing O'Dwyer of visiting Costello's penthouse during the war. In spite of all this, O'Dwyer won easily.

Then the triumphant Irishman dropped into City Hall to pay his respects to LaGuardia. The dumpy little mayor jumped up, grabbed O'Dwyer's left arm, and laughingly pushed him into his own chair, shrieking, "Now you'll have a perpetual headache!" On January 1, 1946, O'Dwyer was sworn in as mayor, and Fusion government came to an end.

LaGuardia was a sick man, but he nonetheless served as director general of the United Nations Relief and Rehabilitation Administration, discussing its affairs with Stalin, Tito of Yugoslavia, and the Pope. Not surprisingly, he became embroiled in several controversies and finally resigned when he could not get a $400,000,000 food fund he demanded. LaGuardia turned out a column for the newspaper *PM,* wrote editorials that were used as advertisements by a furniture store, broadcast his opinions on national affairs for *Liberty* magazine until he was fired for "reckless and irresponsible statements," and sold milk via radio by airing his views on city affairs. At last he entered a hospital for an operation but failed to recover. On September 20, 1947, riddled with cancer, the greatest mayor in the history of New York died in his sleep.

As LaGuardia had predicted, O'Dwyer suffered a perpetual headache. A tugboat strike paralyzed the port, caused a fuel shortage, and frightened the new mayor into declaring an emergency, which almost resulted in panic. War veterans complained about the difficulty of finding a place to live. There was a smallpox scare in 1947, and

6,350,000 New Yorkers were vaccinated. O'Dwyer couldn't even see all his department heads every day because there were so many of them. Finally, his rugged Irish frame bending under his burdens, the mayor was hospitalized for a fortnight, suffering "almost complete nervous and physical exhaustion."

Many years later O'Dwyer told Philip Hamburger of *The New Yorker* magazine, "There were times when I was mayor when I wanted to jump. . . . You know, the city's too big. It's too big for one government. . . . You would look out over the city from some high place above it, and you would say to yourself, 'Good Jesus, it's too much for me!' . . ."

In 1949 O'Dwyer hesitated about running for reelection but finally entered the race. This time his only major opponent was Newbold Morris, who now had the endorsement of the Republican, Liberal, and Fusion parties. Morris warned the voters that if New York were to be saved from "plunder and corruption," O'Dwyer must not be reelected. In spite of this, Bill O'Dwyer trounced him at the polls.

Before taking office a second time, O'Dwyer flew to Florida for a rest. He also took this opportunity to marry Sloan Simpson, a beautiful model. His first wife had died. Like O'Dwyer, Miss Simpson was a Catholic and had been married before, but because the Catholic Church had never recognized the validity of her marriage, she was free to wed again. New York reporters flew to Stuart, Florida, to watch the fifty-nine-year-old mayor and the thirty-three-year-old model join hands in wedlock. O'Dwyer came back to Manhattan to be sworn in as mayor for the second time on January 1, 1950, and twelve days later returned to Florida, suffering from nervous exhaustion and a virus infection.

All his previous municipal headaches throbbed faintly by contrast with the Harry Gross scandal, which now rocked the city. The Gross case began in September, 1949, when Ed Reid, a Brooklyn *Eagle* reporter, overheard a man say at a bar, "A new boss has taken over the bookie joints in town. Guy called Mr. G. They say he was put in business by three top coppers." Reid began digging. He thought it curious that thus far in 1949 not a single bookmaker had been sent to jail from gambler's court in Brooklyn. He found there were 4,000 bookies in the entire city. One had been arrested 50 times in 12 years but had never served a day in jail. It became increasingly clear that bookies were buying police protection. Reid wrote an 8-article exposé that began running in the *Eagle* in December, 1949. It touched off one of the greatest shake-ups in the history of the police department.

Miles F. McDonald, the Brooklyn district attorney, and his assistant, Julius Helfand, launched a probe of gambling and police corruption. They used forty young policemen fresh out of the police academy, reasoning that the rookies had not had time to establish friendships in the force or to become a part of the corrupt system. Of course, veteran policemen soon realized the department was being investigated. Among the old-timers called in for questioning was Captain John G. Flynn, who later shot himself to death in a Brooklyn police station.

O'Dwyer resented McDonald's probe. Although the mayor didn't denounce it publicly, he let word get around that he disliked the idea. Once he offered to help McDonald, but the Brooklyn district attorney said he could work better alone. O'Dwyer now expressed his resentment by making a public display at Flynn's funeral.

Unofficial word filtered through the police department that the mayor wanted as many cops as possible to take part in the ceremony. More than 6,000 policemen, one-third of the entire force, marched in a silent demonstration against McDonald's probe. They were led to the church by the mayor and his appointee, Police Commissioner William P. O'Brien. Referring to the policeman who had killed himself, O'Dwyer said, "Nobody had the guts to say he was a clean man, but six thousand policemen walked by his children to tell them so. I am not opposed to the gambling investigation in Brooklyn. I have aided it when asked. But I am opposed to witch-hunts and the war of nerves made popular by Hitler!" Newspapers denounced the demonstration as a farce, and O'Dwyer squirmed.

He was taken off the hook by Edward J. Flynn, Democratic boss of the Bronx and a national Democratic committeeman. Flynn hurried to Washington and conferred with President Truman. Soon it was announced that the President had nominated O'Dwyer as the new American ambassador to Mexico. In February the mayor had declared, "As God is my judge, I shall serve the four years to which I was elected." In August he announced his imminent departure for Mexico, saying, "My reasons for going are good. Although I am in no position to say what they are now, when the true story is told you will understand."

Columnist Robert Ruark wrote:

> If I were O'Dwyer I wouldn't have let myself be chased out of New York with anything short of a submachinegun until my term expired. The departure looks a touch peculiar. . . . Did he jump or was he pushed? Was it heart trouble, cop trouble, gambling trouble or the firm foot of Democratic Boss Ed Flynn, whose state ticket would profit by having a mayor to elect this fall? Or was it a combination of all? Whatever it was, Bill's subjects don't like the smell. . . .

Before resigning, O'Dwyer handed out $125,000 in raises to his close friends on the city payroll. To James J. Moran—the first deputy fire commissioner who was known as the mayor's alter ego—went a $15,000-a-year lifetime appointment as a commissioner of the city's water supply board. Moran was later convicted of conspiracy and extortion for heading a shakedown racket involving fire department permits for fuel-oil installations.

On September 2, 1950, O'Dwyer sent the city clerk this note: "Dear Sir: I hereby resign as Mayor of the City of New York. . . . Very truly yours, William O'Dwyer."

Thirteen days later Harry Gross was arrested. The flashy young gambler said to the arresting officers, "I gotta hunch there're going to be a lot of worried people in the city soon." This was a Gross understatement. He masterminded a bookmaking ring extending from Brooklyn to other nearby counties, bribed policemen up and down the line, handled more than $20,000,000 a year, and made an annual net profit of $2,000,000.

He said that in 1945 and again in 1949 he had contributed $20,000 toward O'Dwyer's campaign expenses. He said that he paid these sums to James J. Moran and accused Moran of soliciting funds for O'Dwyer from all the bookies in town. Later it was disclosed that when O'Dwyer had been in the army, Moran had handled his personal finances. Gross also said Moran had invited him to a gathering to meet O'Dwyer, but Gross had been unable to attend because he was sick. Gross declared that the mayor had met with seven or eight of the city's leading bookmakers.

When Gross's confession was made public, more than a dozen civic and political groups demanded that O'Dwyer be recalled from Mexico, but the new ambassador wrote that he was busy with "highly secret, restricted matters." Police Commissioner O'Brien, for his part, charged that the Brooklyn gambling probe was inspired by Communists. This was at a time when Communists were attacking the Brooklyn prosecutors as "Fascists." The investigation O'Dwyer had denounced as a "witch-hunt" now boiled over like a witch's stew.

Some policemen were corrupt, and O'Dwyer had failed to do much about this situation. The F.B.I. no longer trusted crime statistics compiled by the New York police department. O'Brien resigned under pressure, as did his two top aides. Nearly 200 police were implicated in the investigation, more than 100 resigned, many were dismissed from the force, and a few were convicted of taking graft. Harry Gross was sent to jail for 12 years.

The Gross case helped set the stage for New York sessions of the Kefauver Committee. On May 10, 1950, Vice-President Alben Barkley organized the Senate Crime Committee, which soon came to be called the Kefauver Committee for its chairman, Democratic Senator Estes Kefauver of Tennessee. The committee, which embarrassed Democrats in Washington and New York alike, consisted mainly of Democrats. It focused on the infiltration of criminals into politics and business and held sessions in many cities across the land.

In the spring of 1951, the Kefauver Committee came to New York. Forty-nine witnesses were heard in private sessions, and forty testified at open hearings. They were gangsters, politicians, public officials and law enforcement officers. Of the eighty-nine witnesses, by far the most important were William O'Dwyer and Frank Costello.

The first open hearing of the Kefauver Committee began on the morning of March 12, 1951, in a third-floor courtroom of the Federal Building on Foley Square. The room had a lofty ceiling, tall narrow windows, blue velvet drapes, and marble walls. With a thump of his gavel, Senator Kefauver launched one of the most unusual spectacles ever seen in New York. Actually, it was seen far beyond the confines of this city because the committee allowed the open hearings to be televised.

Frank Costello had been described in newspapers as "the Prime Minister of the Underworld," so his appearance in the courtroom caused a sensation. He stared around the brilliantly lighted chamber with slit-eyed arrogance and mumbled, "A damn moom pitcher set!" Of medium height, with a short neck and wide shoulders, Costello was proud of the deep tan on his narrow forehead, carrot-big nose, and heavily lined face. His attorney objected to T.V. cameras on his client's face; but nothing was said about keeping the lens off the rest of his person, so millions watched in fascination as his fingers diddled with papers or poured water into a glass.

He was questioned by Rudolph Halley, chief counsel to the committee. Costello emphatically denied that he was a leader of a national crime syndicate and insisted that he was only a businessman. But, according to the subsequent Kefauver report: "There is no question that he has been a strong and evil influence in New York politics. . . . Costello reached the height of his power in New York politics when he unquestionably had complete domination over Tammany Hall. . . . His sinister influence is still strong in the councils of the Democratic Party organization of New York County." Hugo Rogers, the boss of Tammany Hall from July, 1948, to July, 1949, told the Kefauver probers in a private session, "If Costello wanted me, he would send for me."

Rogers had been succeeded by Carmine De Sapio, the first man of Italian descent ever to become Tammany boss. Costello admitted that he knew De Sapio very well. Costello also said that he knew leaders, co-leaders, or both in at least ten of the sixteen districts in Manhattan. Asked how he was able to influence them, Costello said, "I know them, know them well, and maybe they got a little confidence in me." Interestingly, he had entertained James J. Moran, who was O'Dwyer's confidant. Also interesting was Costello's friendship with shirt manufacturer Irving Sherman, another O'Dwyer favorite. After committee members trapped Costello in a lie, he walked out on them, returned the next day, refused to answer further questions, and walked out a second time. The Kefauver report said that Costello's testimony reeked of perjury, and he was sent to prison for contempt of the Senate.

O'Dwyer flew from Mexico City to New York and appeared before the committee on March 19, 1951. So many people wanted to see him in person that extra chairs were brought into the courtroom, and standees squeezed into every empty space. Erect of bearing, his face more rutted than ever, his broad black eyebrows emphasized by his whitening hair, Bill O'Dwyer, wearing a pinstripe suit, was an affable Irishman who turned on the charm. He received permission to make an opening statement. Gesturing toward microphones on the table before him, O'Dwyer said, "I need these mikes to talk to the people." Then, twiddling a paper clip in stubby fingers, he launched into a rambling account of his life and his accomplishments as mayor.

O'Dwyer said that he had worked hard to bring the United Nations headquarters to New York. He had reorganized and improved the welfare department, created a traffic department, established a smoke control bureau, made progress in city planning, and given city employees a pay raise. Although it was politically dangerous to do so, he had raised the subway fare from five to ten cents. He had created a division of labor relations to help prevent strikes. He had set up a management survey committee to look into the city's management needs. The Kefauver Committee later declared that "unquestionably he accomplished many noteworthy achievements." Its report added, "Certainly it would be unfair to give the impression that the matters in which this committee is interested give anything like a complete picture of O'Dwyer's accomplishments in public office."

Senator Charles W. Tobey of New Hampshire, who wore a green eyeshade and spoke with a twang, finally interrupted O'Dwyer's monologue. The Republican Senator wanted to pin the Democratic witness down to cases. This was the start of a searing cross-examination, which lasted two days.

Did O'Dwyer agree that Costello was a sinister influence in Tammany Hall? Yes. Hadn't O'Dwyer told a 1945 grand jury that he wouldn't be surprised to learn that his good friend Irving Sherman was a collector for Costello? Yes. Hadn't Sherman helped in his 1945 campaign? Yes. While O'Dwyer was in the army, hadn't he kept in touch with Sherman by long-distance phone from all over the country? Yes. What did Sherman want from O'Dwyer? Nothing. Hadn't O'Dwyer called McDonald's probe of police corruption a "witch-hunt"? Yes, but that was because O'Dwyer regretted that a few grafters on the police force might be considered typical of the 18,000 men in uniform. Had O'Dwyer talked with McDonald before making his "witch-hunt" remark? No, because O'Dwyer was so certain that the police department was clean that he couldn't believe the things McDonald's probe was disclosing. From the witness stand O'Dwyer admitted that later events proved McDonald was right and said that he had apologized to McDonald. Then O'Dwyer agreed that bookmaking was rampant during his administration? Yes. And wasn't it true that widespread bookmaking couldn't exist without police protection? Yes.

Had O'Dwyer ever visited Costello's apartment? A gasp went up from the television audience across the land as the former mayor of New York admitted that he had indeed called on a board member of the Combination. Then O'Dwyer told this story: In 1942 he was a major in the army air force attached to air procurement. He was ordered to keep Wright Field, in Dayton, Ohio, clean. O'Dwyer said that an anonymous letter to the district attorney's office in Brooklyn charged certain clothing frauds at Wright Field by a Joe Baker. This letter also said that Baker was a friend of Costello. O'Dwyer testified that he had asked Irving Sherman to arrange a meeting with Costello. Why hadn't O'Dwyer invited Costello to his army office? O'Dwyer said that he was then "no longer a district attorney with a fistful of subpoenas, but just a little major or maybe a lieutenant colonel." Accompanied by James J. Moran, O'Dwyer went to Costello's apartment on Central Park West. (Moran testified before the Kefauver Committee that it was he who made this appointment and that he did it through Michael J. Kennedy, then the boss of Tammany Hall.)

O'Dwyer disclosed that among those present in Costello's home were Irving Sherman; Bert Stand, secretary of Tammany Hall; and Mike Kennedy. O'Dwyer said that the presence of the boss of Tammany Hall in Costello's apartment made such a strong impression on him that he never forgot it. Did O'Dwyer ever announce that he had seen the Tammany boss there? No. Had O'Dwyer ever helped Kennedy after Kennedy had been deposed as Tammany boss in 1944? Yes, O'Dwyer supported Kennedy in 1948 in a leadership fight on Manhattan's West Side. Had O'Dwyer ever said publicly that he himself had visited Costello? No. In the army file on the Joe Baker case was there any mention of O'Dwyer's meeting with Costello? No. What happened to the case? O'Dwyer testified that Costello said he knew a Joe Baker but didn't know whether this Joe Baker had any interest in air force contracts. Did O'Dwyer try to find Baker? No. Did he ask anyone else to do so? No. Was Baker ever barred from Wright Field? No.

Committee members made no secret of their belief that O'Dwyer had called on Costello to discuss politics. By now O'Dwyer was shifting uneasily in the witness chair and mopping his brow. The committee established that Frank Bals was a close friend of O'Dwyer. Bals had been O'Dwyer's chief investigator when O'Dwyer had been Brooklyn district attorney. After O'Dwyer first became mayor, he made Bals seventh deputy police commissioner. Then Bals was put in charge of the six cops guarding Reles.

Bals had testified before the Kefauver Committee. He tried to explain Reles' death by saying the prisoner was playing a joke on his guards. Bals said that Reles wanted to climb out of his hotel window, reach the ground, reenter the hotel, climb back upstairs, and confound his guards. When he was asked how Reles could have made his preparations without the cops hearing anything, Bals said that all of them must have fallen asleep.

O'Dwyer now admitted that Bals' story was nonsense. Then how did O'Dwyer explain Reles' death? O'Dwyer said that he thought Reles was trying to escape. The theory failed to convince the committee because at another point O'Dwyer said Reles was afraid of being killed by the syndicate. Well, who *was* responsible for the loss of O'Dwyer's most important witness against Albert Anastasia? O'Dwyer said that it was pure negligence by the cops guarding Reles. What happened to them? They were demoted. But hadn't O'Dwyer said in public that they were blameless? Yes. What happened to Bals? O'Dwyer promoted him.

Did O'Dwyer know John P. Crane, president of Local 94 of the International Association of Fire Fighters? Yes. Had Crane ever handed O'Dwyer any campaign contributions? No.

Then Crane took the witness stand. He said that in the 1949 mayoralty campaign he donated money for O'Dwyer's candidacy. Why? Well, city firemen needed the mayor's goodwill. To whom did Crane give this money? Crane testified that he gave $55,000 to James J. Moran. Crane also said that he himself went to Gracie Mansion and met O'Dwyer alone on the porch. Crane said that he then handed O'Dwyer an envelope containing $10,000 in cash.

O'Dwyer, appearing before a grand jury when the Kefauver Committee was through with him, denied meeting Crane at Gracie Mansion and denied receiving cash or any contributions from Crane. In its report the committee said that it did not have "sufficient evidence to form a conclusion concerning the transactions alleged by Crane to have occurred." But the report added:

> A single pattern of conduct emerges from O'Dwyer's official activities in regard to gambling and water-front rackets, murders, and police corruption, from his days as district attorney through his term as mayor. No matter what the motivation of his choice, action or inaction, it often seemed to result favorably for men suspected of being high up in the rackets. . . .

After publication of the Kefauver report, O'Dwyer declared that its charges against him were "fantastic." He went back to Mexico and resumed his duties as ambassador. When reporters asked if he planned to resign, he answered, "No!" *Newsweek* magazine said:

> True, the Kefauver committee hadn't actually proven anything against the ambassador, but, politically that was a minor matter. His own admissions had been enough to make him an embarrassment. The President was faced with demands for his recall, and while he evidently planned to ignore them, the President's aides knew they weren't doing the Administration any good. The irony was that Democrats had been primarily responsible for the Administration's troubles.

In 1952 O'Dwyer did resign as ambassador but remained in Mexico City to practice law. In 1961 he came back to Manhattan, stepped into a cab, and asked what would be worth seeing or doing in town. The driver, who failed to recognize O'Dwyer, suggested a ride around the island on a Circle Line boat. O'Dwyer said that he had done that years ago, and as the boat passed Gracie Mansion he had seen the mayor on the lawn.

The cabbie asked, "Who was the mayor you saw on the Gracie Mansion lawn, mister?" O'Dwyer replied, "O'Dwyer." The hackie exploded, "That crook! That thief!" When O'Dwyer finished his one-dollar ride, he tipped the cabdriver fifty cents and said quietly, "I'm O'Dwyer. I don't find a bit of fault with you for not liking me. Many people exposed to the press feel like you do. But I have never been charged with a crime, let alone convicted."

Chapter 49

ROBERT F. WAGNER'S ADMINISTRATION

BEFORE WILLIAM O'DWYER resigned as head of the city government, he had created a mayor's committee on Puerto Rican affairs. Only one of its fifty-one members was a Puerto Rican, and a critic described the committee as a handy and painless device that passed manifestoes and proved its use as a harmless propaganda group.

The influx of Puerto Ricans into the city was the latest of a series of mass migrations filling the sidewalks of New York with people of alien cultures. However, this migration was different because the new-comers were already United States citizens, because most arrived by airplane, and because they settled down in a city that had become a quasi-welfare state.

Puerto Rico, an island about two and a half times the size of Long Island, lies in the Caribbean 1,600 miles southeast of New York. Although the name means rich port in Spanish, it was far from rich, for it had few natural resources. Its high birthrate resulted in great population density, which resulted in acute poverty, which resulted in a mass exodus. The outpouring of Puerto Ricans became a torrent after World War II, and most of those who came to the mainland in search of jobs settled in New York City. It needed their labor and had a reputation for comparative freedom from prejudice. However, in 1947 newspapers and magazines began publishing articles about what they called the Puerto Rican problem.

As had always happened in the history of New York, the new immigrants were despised by some of the minority groups whose ancestors had suffered discrimination when they landed here decades earlier. Some Negroes resented the fact that Puerto Ricans competed with them for jobs and low-cost housing. Some Jewish cabdrivers and Irish bartenders, forgetting insults heaped on their fathers and grandfathers, growled that the Puerto Ricans were taking over the city. Because from one-fifth to one-fourth of Puerto Ricans were Negroes, some New Yorkers feared that the city's racial balance would be upset. They begrudged the welfare assistance given the Puerto Ricans and complained about the added strain put on the school system.

Many studious Puerto Rican boys and girls bent over books in their crowded and cluttered apartments, but their application was unseen by the man on the street. One drunken Puerto Rican man or a single Puerto Rican prostitute evoked comments about all Puerto Ricans. Cultured and educated Puerto Ricans lamented that "people have a stereotype about us." Chief Magistrate John M. Murtagh agreed, saying, "Don't forget—in our time we Irish gave New York a few headaches, too." But New Yorkers did forget, and they also failed to realize that Puerto Rican *adults* never banded together into gangs, as had the rowdies and criminals of other immigrant groups.

Because of the new wave of immigration and because of the higher birthrates of Puerto Ricans and Negroes, 800,000 white middle-class New Yorkers fled to the suburbs. The exodus deprived the city of some of its best civic leaders, taxpayers, producers, and consumers. Their places were taken by people less concerned about civic affairs, less educated and skilled, paying fewer taxes, and needing more municipal services, such as relief.

In 1953, the year the Puerto Rican immigration reached its peak,

Robert F. Wagner, Jr., was elected mayor of New York. The son of a German-born father and an Irish-American mother, he entered this world on April 20, 1910, in an apartment house on the northeastern corner of Eighty-seventh Street and Lexington Avenue in the Yorkville section of Manhattan. He almost died minutes after his birth, recovered, grew in strength, and was christened with Tammany district leader Mike Cosgrove serving as his godfather.

Because his real father was a liberal member of Tammany and a successful politician, young Wagner absorbed political lore from childhood. He worked as a page boy for the New York state senate, went with his father to Woodrow Wilson's summer home in New Jersey, traveled with the elder Wagner on upstate political campaigns, and moved to Washington when his father was elected a United States Senator.

After attending public and parochial schools in Manhattan, Bob Wagner enrolled in the fashionable Taft School in Connecticut. Then he entered Yale, where he had "a hell of a good time," as a friend remembered it, but also gave studious attention to economics and international relations. He spent a year at the Harvard School of Business Administration and one summer at the School of International Relations in Geneva, Switzerland, where he took a course under Socialist Clement Attlee. In 1937 he was graduated from the Yale Law School.

Later that year, with the help of Tammany Hall, he was elected a state assemblyman from Yorkville. It was only natural for Tammany to advance Senator Wagner's bright son, and for the next twenty-four years Bob Wagner remained a party regular. Two weeks after the United States entered World War II, he resigned from the legislature to enter the air force. He spent more than two years in Europe, planning bombing raids and handling judge-advocate duties, and returned in 1945 as a lieutenant colonel with six battle stars and a Croix de Guerre. A bomb blast in England left him totally deaf in his left ear.

In the immediate postwar period Wagner quickly climbed the political ladder—again with Tammany backing. He served successively as city tax commissioner, commissioner of housing and buildings, chairman of the city planning commission, and president of the borough of Manhattan. He rarely stayed in one office long enough to get the feel of it because Tammany kept grooming him for bigger things.

After O'Dwyer resigned in 1950, his duties as mayor were taken over by Vincent R. Impellitteri, president of the city council. Then, in a special election, Sicilian-born Impellitteri was elected mayor to fill out the last three years of O'Dwyer's second term. In the regular election of 1953, Robert F. Wagner, Jr., was elected the 102d mayor of New York City and soon dropped the "Jr." from his name.

Mayor Wagner stood 5 feet 8 inches tall and weighed between 150 and 155 pounds, depending, in part, on whether he could resist eating corn on the cob, which he relished. He had black hair, brown eyes, a splayed nose, and turtle-tight lips and looked nervous and harried most of the time. One reporter said he had the air of "an unloved Airedale." The colorblind mayor let his wife choose his ties and paid scant attention to clothing, except for shoes; he enjoyed wearing loafers with tassels. He had a good memory for names and faces, kept the common touch despite his Ivy League background, and was so ready to listen to people seeking his attention that he was almost always late for appointments. A patient man, he never yelled and seldom swore, although his ears reddened when he became angry. He worked hard at his job and during emergencies would go without sleep for more than a day. Adept at reading speeches, he tended to ramble during television interviews.

Because of Wagner's colorless public image, his consummate skill as a politician sometimes was forgotten. One of his political foes said, "Wagner just doesn't have anything—except the votes on election day." In 1953 he was reelected mayor with the support of two of the five Democratic county organizations in the city. He kept Tammany hacks out of top policy-making jobs but let political considerations influence lesser appointments. Tammany leaders, who wanted patronage up and down the line, turned on Wagner in the 1957 primary, but he won the Democratic nomination against the opposition of all five Democratic county organizations and went on to win the election itself.

His first two administrations were stained by a series of scandals, whose existence Wagner was slow to acknowledge, but none of the mud splashed high enough to splatter him. He matured on the job, his performance as mayor improving with each successive term. He established the office of city administrator, strengthened the city planning commission, emphasized education and overhauled the board of education, increased the size of the police force, improved the lot of city employees, served as prime mover in rezoning the city, played a major role in the creation of the City University, and was patient and generally effective in mediating some major labor disputes.

Wagner also helped put through a new city charter granting him more power than any other mayor in the city's history, but he did not choose to become a dictator. A politician to his fingertips, he lacked the instinct to close these fingers over the jugular vein of an enemy. He seemed hesitant to tangle with Robert Moses, who was known for his superlative mind and imperious ways. Wagner was intelligent, but not brilliant. There were times when the mayor also seemed to quail before blustering Michael J. Quill, who headed the subway workers union and occasionally threatened to halt all trains unless his demands were met.

Wagner was good at formulating plans and programs but often failed to implement them. Sometimes he vacillated when firmness was needed. He always remembered his father's advice: "When in doubt—don't." On the other hand, he ignored LaGuardia's warning that it is impossible to be both a good fellow and a good mayor. He tarried over hard decisions and muddled his way through several crises. Wagner once said defensively:

> You have to rule by compromise in this city or you will have constant fighting and get nothing done. I know there are some people who don't think I'm forceful enough. What they don't realize is that you just don't pick up the ball and run with it. You have to look where you're going first. Everything isn't black and white. You have to sit back, consider all sides, and think about it for a while. Some people like the dramatic. I'm just not built that way. I've been around long enough to know that the dramatic doesn't really work.

This last remark is not necessarily true. LaGuardia was both dramatic and effective. But each mayor has his own approach to a position considered the most difficult in the nation except for the Presidency itself.

Wagner was sensitive to the Puerto Rican immigration. In 1955 the New York City commission on intergroup relations (C.O.I.R.) was established. Dr. Alfred J. Marrow, who served awhile as the chairman of C.O.I.R., wrote that its creation "marked the most comprehensive attempt yet made at achieving the goal of positive intergroup relations through healthy democratic participation via the avenues of education, law and social therapy." In 1957 Wagner appointed a Puerto

Rican to the post of city magistrate. The next year New York City passed the first law in the nation banning discrimination in *private* housing because of color or creed.

By 1964 Puerto Rico's standard of living had improved so much that migration into New York had ceased to be a problem. In fact, reverse migration set in—that is, more Puerto Ricans returned to their island than entered New York. Nevertheless, this city was left with more than 700,000 Puerto Ricans, and Spanish became the city's second language.

The so-called Puerto Rican problem coincided with the Negro revolution. After the U.S. Supreme Court decided in 1954 that racial segregation in public schools violated the Constitution, American Negroes launched the most massive effort in their long history to win full civil rights. At first the struggle was waged mainly in the South. White New Yorkers, sitting before television sets, winced at the sight of Southern police breaking up Negro demonstrations with dogs, fire hoses, and electric cattle prods. Although New York was not a paradise for minority groups, it was far ahead of other American cities in the number and scope of its laws protecting the rights of all citizens. As the Negro revolution gained impetus, New York itself became a trouble spot.

Hundreds of civil rights demonstrations erupted here in 1963, with more pickets on the march than ever before in the city's annals. Defying the platitude that "you can't fight City Hall," thousands now tried to do so. Negro leaders protested what they called the undercurrent of racism here and elsewhere in the North. Negroes and Puerto Ricans complained that they were not given a fair share of jobs in the construction industry. By marching, picketing, parading, carrying placards, shouting slogans, singing, lying down in front of trucks, and signing petitions, demonstrators tried to halt $2,500,-000,000 in state and city construction projects until more jobs went to Negroes and Puerto Ricans.

A liberal like his father, Mayor Wagner said, "Dissent and protest have always held a cherished, if controversial, place in American government and life. . . . Protest marchers and picketing demonstrations have been employed by many groups in support of many different objectives. . . . The country owes much to those who focused our attention on the pressing need." Despite the mayor's liberalism, civil rights pickets staged sit-ins outside his City Hall office. Wagner put up with them for forty-four days; but then his patience wore thin, and he ordered them ousted. Three policemen were hurt in the melee that followed. Negroes complained time and again of police brutality and demanded that a board of civilians review charges filed against cops.

Generations of Negro and white pupils had sat in classrooms together in New York City, which had legally ended school segregation in 1900. Now some militant Negroes demanded total and instant integration. But to achieve absolute racial balance in classrooms seemed an impossibility. In predominantly Negro neighborhoods there naturally were more Negro than white pupils in local classrooms. Some Negroes insisted that children be sent by bus to distant schools to achieve a more even distribution of the races. Many white mothers objected for a variety of reasons, including the greater danger of traffic accidents during longer bus rides. The board of education tried to satisfy Negroes and whites alike but succeeded only in further antagonizing both.

Communication seemed to break down between all dissenting groups and the city administration. Teachers were assaulted in schools, policemen were attacked on the streets, the crime rate rose, violence increased in subways, business and industry reassessed their employment policies, rookie cops were trained to be patient and impartial, and by August, 1963, civil rights demonstrations were costing the city $15,000 a day in overtime pay to policemen. Negro and Puerto Rican mothers demanded that something be done to kill the rats biting their children. Negro tenants launched a rent strike against their slumlords, who did little, if anything, to keep apartment buildings in good condition. Honorable landlords lamented that although they spent thousands of dollars to improve their property, hooligans quickly broke windows and defaced walls.

Negro leaders indignantly denied a newspaper report that teen-age Harlem gangs were being trained in karate and judo for the purpose of killing any stray white person found there. Roy Wilkins, executive secretary of the National Association for the Advancement of Colored People, publicly lashed out at "teen-age Negro hoodlums" whose violence, he said, "was undercutting and wrecking gains made by hundreds of Negro and white youngsters."

New Yorkers lived in a climate of fear. All the white middle-class residents of an apartment building at 226 East Third Street moved out because of Puerto Rican threats against the landlord. The fear of violence in a forty-block area of Manhattan's upper West Side caused many residents to "seal themselves in at night," according to the Fund for the Republic. In fact, one man characterized this part of Manhattan as a combat zone. Quasi-vigilante groups were formed here and there in the city to help make streets and homes safer.

Some citizens called for decentralization of city government, a development that worried Mayor Wagner. He protested that many community groups "want to assume the functions of the government themselves." Then he asked rhetorically, "Who shall decide whether the viewpoint of the neighborhood or the viewpoint of the central government of the city shall prevail? If it is morally right for the local view to prevail in one case, on what basis shall it be denied in another?"

Civil rights agitators schemed to attract worldwide attention to their various causes by inciting trouble at the opening of the new World's Fair here in the city. After a secret meeting in a Harlem tenement some of these leaders issued a statement denouncing "discrimination practiced by the power structure of the city." Other civil rights spokesmen threatened to stall cars and thus snarl traffic on highways leading to the exposition ground in Flushing Meadow. They announced that they would use nonviolent combat teams to halt railroad traffic to the site. The mayor denounced these tactics and ordered a heavy concentration of policemen to take up positions in and around the fair.

When the exposition opened on the rainy morning of April 22, 1964, it was only about 85 percent complete, 15 pavilions and 3 amusement area shows still being unfinished. Despite public apprehension, the threatened auto stall-in failed. Traffic was slowed up briefly, but motorists found it easy that first day to get to the fair by private car. However, subway trains were delayed by activists, who jerked emergency cords, held train doors open, and sat down on the platforms at subway stations. This led to scuffling between police and demonstrators, with some heads being cracked.

The worst disorders took place at the fair itself. Led by officials of the Congress of Racial Equality, hundreds of chanting and shouting men and women staged lie-in and sit-in demonstrations at exhibits and pavilions. Cries of "Freedom now!" and "Jim Crow must go!" drowned out Mayor Wagner's opening remarks and served as a harsh counterpoint to the main speech by the heavily guarded President of the United States, Lyndon B. Johnson. Before the day ended,

10 persons were injured and 109 were arrested. The demonstrators did succeed in attracting attention—unfavorable attention.

Despite a few other incidents in the days and weeks that followed, the fair settled down and attracted visitors from all over the world. The most popular exhibit, which drew 29,000,000 sight-seers through its doors, was the General Motors Pavilion with its slanting canopy 110 feet high. Taking a "ride into the future," guests sat down in plastic contour chairs equipped with speakers that provided an explanation of everything to be seen. The seats moved along a track that dipped and climbed through the two floors of the exhibit hall. Visitors, from the comfort of these chairs in motion, looked at sets depicting a trip to the moon and life under the ice, under the water, in a jungle, and in a desert.

The 1964-65 New York World's Fair was the first billion-dollar exposition in history. Its theme was man's achievements in an expanding universe, and its purpose was to promote peace through understanding. However, a variety of controversies, besides the civil rights demonstrations, brought the fair bad publicity, and total attendance was only 51,000,000 instead of the 70,000,000 that had been predicted. Investors lost money.

The morning of July 16, 1964, a group of Negro boys were lounging on East Seventy-sixth Street in the Yorkville section of Manhattan. An apartment house superintendent, who was watering his flowers, turned his hose on them—either accidentally or intentionally. They attacked him. Their leader, fifteen-year-old James Powell, went after the man with a knife, according to the police. The boy's friends later said that he didn't even own a knife. In any event, the ruckus attracted Thomas Gilligan, an off-duty police lieutenant. The police report said that Gilligan ordered the lad to drop the knife, fired a warning shot when he refused to obey, was slashed by Powell, then fired twice more, and killed the youngster.

Negro leaders flared in rage, demanding to know why an experienced police officer had to shoot a boy much smaller than himself. The next day 200 Negro boys and girls staged an orderly 4-hour demonstration in Yorkville to protest the shooting, and in separate incidents 2 white men were attacked by roving bands of Negro youths. The people of Harlem seethed in fury.

Harlem was ripe for an explosion. It was nearly 3 times more crowded than the rest of the city. Within its 3½ square miles lived more than 232,000 persons, of whom 94 percent were Negroes. Half of Harlem's buildings were officially classed as "deteriorating" or "dilapidated." Harlem's landlords got $50 to $74 a month for 1-room flats that rented for only $30 to $49 in white slums. Infant mortality was nearly twice that in the rest of New York.

Every fourth Negro man was without work. Nearly one-fourth of Harlem's people were on welfare. Their families having been torn apart by white slave traders in the past, Negroes lacked a tradition of family stability. Only half of Harlem's children lived with both parents. Negro boys lagged behind in their studies, and more than half who entered high school quit before graduating. Harlem's juvenile delinquency rate was almost 2½ times as great as in the rest of the city. Narcotics were used at a rate 8 times that prevailing elsewhere in New York. Harlem's murder rate was 600 percent higher than the city's. A Harlem woman declared, "This is the jungle—the very heart of it." James Baldwin, the brilliant Negro writer, said, "The most dangerous creation of any society is that man who has nothing to lose."

Harlem erupted on Saturday, July 18, 1964. It was a hot and humid night. Workers for the Congress of Racial Equality set up a blue kitchen chair and a small American flag at 125th Street and 7th Avenue, which was the Times Square of Harlem. One speaker after another climbed onto the chair to shrill angrily about the killing of James Powell. More and more Negro spectators crowded closer to hear: "James Powell was shot because he was black. . . . It is time to let the Man know that if he does something to us, we are going to do something back. . . ."

A minister exhorted everyone to march to the 123d Street Police Station, a couple of blocks away, to demand that Police Lieutenant Gilligan be arrested for murder. The people moved off in the direction of the precinct house, picking up reinforcements and swelling from a crowd into a roiling mob. "Killer cops!" screamed the Negroes. "Murderers!" Policemen tried to seal off approaches to the station, but the enraged multitude bulled past the barricades and clashed with the cops.

Hoodlums, skulking across the roofs of tenements, threw bricks and bottles and garbage-can covers onto the streets below. Homemade Molotov cocktail bombs hit the pavement and burst into flames five feet high. Screaming thousands thrashed back and forth in the heart of Harlem, fighting policemen, assaulting white people, menacing reporters, and smashing windows. Helmeted policemen clubbed them. The mob refused an order to break up and go home. Now police officers gave the order to fire over their heads. Cops also squeezed off warning shots above the roof-scampering hooligans. It was a full-scale riot, in which the police never lost control of the streets. Gunfire hiccuped throughout the rest of this sad and sour night, but reason did not return with the dawn.

Between July 18 and July 23 violence rocked both Harlem and the Bedford-Stuyvesant section of Brooklyn. One person was killed, and 140 persons were seriously injured. A total of 520 persons were arrested. Perhaps no more than 1 percent of the city's Negro population was directly involved in the riots.

President Johnson ordered 200 F.B.I. agents to investigate, declaring, "American citizens have a right to protection of life and limb —whether driving along a highway in Georgia, a road in Mississippi, or a street in New York City." Mayor Wagner was in Europe at the time, and Paul R. Screvane, president of the city council, was serving as acting mayor. Screvane said that the disorders were incited partly by "fringe groups including the Communist party." Two months later, however, the F.B.I. reported that there was "no systematic planning or organization" behind these riots in New York and eight other Northern cities.

The F.B.I. concluded that the riots were not basically racial. Instead, it announced, "a common characteristic of the riots was a senseless attack on all constituted authority without purpose or reason." The F.B.I. said further that "the Communist Party U.S.A. does not appear to have officially instigated these riots, though its members were observed taking part" in some of them. In 1965 an admitted Communist was convicted of conspiring to riot and of advocating the overthrow of the state of New York. He had been arrested soon after the Harlem riot.

Mayor Wagner cut short his visit to Europe and flew back to New York. The evening of July 22, 1964, he was driven to a studio in Liederkranz Hall, at 111 East Fifty-eighth Street, to address New Yorkers by television. Looking solemn and drawn, Wagner said:

> Law and order are the Negro's best friend—make no mistake about that. The opposite of law and order is mob rule, and that is the way of the Ku Klux Klan, the night riders and the lynch mobs. Let me also state, in very plain language, that illegal acts,

including defiance of, or attacks upon the police, whose mission it is to enforce law and order, will not be condoned or tolerated by me at any time. . . . The nation and the world have their eyes on New York. The racists in the South and North certainly do. Minority groups everywhere do. Africa and Asia do. Indeed, all the world is watching us. . . .

Some people sadly wagged their heads and said that the city was sick, that it was trying to destroy itself, that it was too huge and complex to be governed, and that its problems were too difficult to be solved. Undeniably, the problems were staggering, and they seemed to worsen with each passing day. There was violence on the streets, in the subways, and in the lobbies of apartment buildings. The gulf between rich and poor increased. Welfare cases mounted. Automation threw people out of work. Manufacturing firms moved out of the city. Unemployed boys lolled about the streets, looking for trouble. Dope addiction increased. Decent housing was inadequate. Traffic jams strained tempers. Commuter service declined. Sometimes there were delays in getting patients into hospitals. The city's budget rose. The quality of education and racial balance in schools fretted thoughtful people. Courts were jammed with backlogs of civil cases. Air pollution edged toward lethal levels. Water too was polluted and becoming ever more scarce. Piers rotted, and the port got an ever smaller share of the nation's oceanborne foreign trade.

Trying to govern a city in crisis visably aged Mayor Wagner, who finally decided he had had enough. When he announced that he did not plan to run for a fourth term, he set the stage for an exciting and significant mayoralty campaign in 1965.

Three candidates vied for what Robert Moses called the "preposterous, impossible job" of being mayor of New York City. Abraham Beame, the colorless city comptroller, ran as the candidate of the city's Democratic machine. William F. Buckley, Jr., the tart-tongued editor of the *National Review,* ran as the candidate of the Conservative party, with the avowed purpose of taking votes away from the third candidate. This was John V. Lindsay, a maverick Republican, who won the endorsement of the Republican, Liberal, and Independent Citizens parties.

Lindsay said, "You hear a lot of people say that the city is too big to be governed by one man. I don't agree with that at all." Political observers gave him a scant chance of winning in a city where registered Democrats had a seven to two edge. Lindsay was up against a rich and entrenched Democratic machine, and right-wing members of his own Republican party opposed him.

A liberal Congressman who had helped draft the 1964 civil rights bill, Lindsay announced, "I am a Republican, but New York City must have an independent, nonpartisan government." His campaign literature quoted John F. Kennedy: "Sometimes party loyalty asks too much." Lindsay all but disowned his own party, disdained the help of regular Republicans, relied heavily on volunteer workers, opened storefront offices throughout the city, averaged only 4 hours of sleep the last part of the campaign, and traveled nearly 7,000 miles visiting every corner of New York. But Lindsay posters boasted: "He's fresh while every one else is tired."

Lindsay was only forty-three years old, having been born on November 24, 1921, in a modest West Side apartment. After he attended a private school in Manhattan, he was graduated in 1940 from St. Paul's School in New Hampshire. He next took an accelerated course at Yale and then entered the navy, taking part in the invasion of Sicily and participating in landings on various Pacific islands. In 1946 he was discharged as a full lieutenant with five battle stars.

Following the war he earned a degree from the Yale Law School. After working briefly as a bank clerk, he signed up with a top Manhattan law firm and within five years became a full partner. A superb trial lawyer, he won praise from Supreme Court Justice Felix Frankfurter. Ever since returning to the city after the war, Lindsay had been active in Manhattan politics, and in 1958 he was elected to Congress from Manhattan's Seventeenth Congressional District, called the Silk Stocking District because it included the fashionable Upper East Side. During his seven years in the House of Congress he racked up a voting record more liberal than that of many Democrats.

By the time Lindsay ran for mayor, he was married and the father of four children. He was a strikingly handsome man—even better looking than John F. Kennedy, with whom he was favorably compared. Broad-shouldered and narrow-waisted, Lindsay stood six feet three and had wavy light-brown hair, blue eyes, and a flashing smile. He was ambitious and earnest, vigorous and eloquent, and had an appetite for command. He blamed the city's decline on Mayor Wagner and hammered away at "machine men" and the "backroom, clubhouse hacks."

In a major political upset, Lindsay won the 1965 election by a narrow margin. His triumph was an intensely personal one. Richard Nixon, the former Republican Vice-President, said, "It is a Lindsay rather than a Republican victory." Shortly before being sworn in as the 103d mayor of New York City on January 1, 1966, Lindsay said, "I plan to give New York the most hard-working, the most dedicated and, I hope, the most exciting administration this city has ever seen."

Chapter 50

"THIS CITY IS THE CENTER
OF THE UNIVERSE"

NEW YORK is one of man's greatest achievements. There never has been another city like it. Only superlatives can express its magnitude, power, and renown.

New York is the capital of the world because it contains the headquarters of the United Nations. It is the best known city on earth. It is the wealthiest city of modern times. Its influence is felt in every corner of this planet. It is the world's greatest cultural center and creative force. It has the world's largest educational system. It is the greatest tourist attraction in the world. It is the biggest and busiest manufacturing city in the world, Robert F. Wagner once saying that New Yorkers "make more, sell more, buy more, eat more and

enjoy more than the citizens of any other city in the world." It is
the financial capital of the world. It is headquarters for most of the
biggest corporations in existence. It is the communications capital of
the world. It is the entertainment capital of the world. It has more
churches than any other city in the world. Its government is the
largest in the United States, except for the federal government. Its
police force is larger than the standing armies of many foreign nations. Its subway system is the most heavily traveled passenger railroad in the world. Its harbor is bigger than the world's next six
largest harbors put together.

During its relatively brief existence New York has been the inspiration for, or has served as the background of, countless books, movies,
plays, photographs, poems, music, paintings, and sculptures.

New York's almost 8,000,000 residents make it the third most
populous city on earth, Tokyo being first and London second. However, the New York metropolitan region contains the greatest concentration of human beings on this globe. More than 16,000,000
persons live within this region, which includes the 5 counties of New
York City, 7 other counties in New York State, 9 counties in eastern
New Jersey, and 1 county in Connecticut. New York is no longer just
a city, but the nucleus of a vast metropolitan area sprawling along the
Atlantic seaboard.

Because of its size, New York is like a gigantic magnifying glass
that enlarges human emotions and behavior. Depending on the
viewer and his attitudes and what he wants to see, New York is
evil or benign, steeped in ignorance or mellow with wisdom. To the
gregarious it offers companionship, and on the shy it bestows isolation almost as absolute as that of the desert or the ocean. At one
and the same time it is cruel and indifferent, kind and concerned.
New Yorkers can turn their backs on murder committed under their
apartment windows and then go out of their way to help strangers
board the right subway train. Because newspapers and television
focus on the unusual and bizarre, good people living quiet lives seldom get into the news. As Robert F. Wagner has said of New York:
"It is a city of love and compassion and hundreds of thousands of
unsung and uncelebrated acts of charity and kindness and heroism
every minute of every hour and every hour of every day."

Hoodlums terrorize the subways—but serenity may be found by
sitting on a bench behind Grant's Tomb and gazing up the Hudson
at a riverscape so majestic that it hushes the heart. Dope addicts

steal goods to sustain their habit—but at sundown the claret-stained façade of the Empire State Building looks like Mount Everest seen through rose-colored glasses. Police sirens chill the spine—but from a helicopter on a clear night the city's lights resemble diamonds scattered upon black velvet. Voodoo rituals are held in secret cellars —but Fifth Avenue is promenaded by women so beautiful and elegant that they look like Aphrodites in buttons and bows.

Down through the years people have been attracted to and repelled by New York. Too huge and powerful to be ignored, the city stirs extreme opinions. Here are some of them:

Robert F. Wagner: "This city is the center of the universe." *Raymond L. Bruckberger:* "A fabulous, strange, disturbing city, where the man outside a group must feel more alone than anyone else on earth." *E. B. White:* "To date New York has shown nothing but progress. Hopefully we wait the first signs of decadence—partial decadence being the only condition under which anybody can exist with any degree of grace or civility."

Robert Moses: "New York notoriously lacks citizen leadership and is hard to arouse." *James Huneker:* "Many years ago I learned to discount the hurry and flurry of New York. We are no busier than Bridgeport or Jersey City, but we pretend we are. It is necessary for our municipal vanity to squeeze and jam and rush and crush." *Ambrose Bierce:* "New York is cocaine, opium, hashish." *Günter Grass:* "Here you have everything—all of Europe and America, and people of all nations and colors."

Billy Graham: "New York is a crime-ridden city. . . . Immorality is rampant." *Alec Waugh:* "New York has been a magnet drawing to itself from East, North, South, West, from every state of the Union and from every European country, the restless, the dissatisfied and the ambitious, who have demanded more from life than the circumstances of their birth offered them." *Simeon Strunsky:* "New York has more hermits than will be found in all the forests, mountains and deserts of the United States."

R. L. Duffus: "New York is a sort of anthology of urban civilization. The song that any city sings she sings. All that anybody can seek for that can be housed in steel and cement is here, and with it, never lost in all the city's drabness, respect for the striving, combative beauty-loving spirit of man." *Carl Van Doren:* "Confusion rose around me and poured over me. . . . My mind could not help me by thinking. It too was panic, spun in a vortex of sensations. There is no reason in a nightmare. Over and over I said to myself: This is New York, where I thought life would be large and free. This is New York, and I am a stranger in a nightmare."

John Mansfield: "New York City, in herself . . . a gladness, that romantic, beautiful, exciting city, the queen of all romance cities, with such sparkle in her air and in her people." *Henry Miller:* "New York has a trip-hammer vitality which drives you insane with restlessness, if you have no inner stabilizer." *Sidney Hook:* "Educationally New York is to the United States what Paris is to France. . . . Whoever seeks intellectual stimulation will find it in America's first city."

Irvin S. Cobb: "There is this to be said for New York City. It is the one densely inhabited locality—with the possible exception of Hell —that has absolutely not a trace of local pride." *John Lardner:* "The beauty of New York neighbors is that they can be acquired slowly, carefully, and selectively." *Henry James:* "The very sign of its energy is that it doesn't believe in itself; it fails to succeed, even at the cost of millions, in persuading you that it does."

William Makepeace Thackeray: "Nobody is quiet here, no more am I. The rush and restlessness pleases me, and I like, for a little, the dash of the stream. I am not received as a god, which I like, too." *Aubrey Menen:* "The true New Yorker does not really seek information about the outside world. He feels that if anything is not in New York it is not likely to be interesting." *John Jay Chapman:* "The present in New York is so powerful that the past is lost."

Raymond Loewy: "New York is simply a distillation of the entire United States, the most of everything, the conclusive proof that there is an American civilization. New York is casual, intellectual, subtle, effective and devastatingly witty. But her sophisticated appearance is the thinnest of veneers. Beneath it there is power, virility, determination and a sense of destiny." *Frank Lloyd Wright:* "This man-trap of gigantic dimensions, devouring manhood, denies in its affected riot of personality any individuality whatsoever."

Walt Whitman: "An appreciative and perceptive study of the current humanity of New York gives the directest proof yet of successful democracy, and of the solution of that paradox, the eligibility of the free and fully developed individual with the paramount aggregate." *Christopher Morley:* "Truly the magic of her spell can never be exacted. She changes too rapidly, day by day. Realism, as they call it, can never catch the boundaries of her pearly beauty. She needs a mystic."

Max Murray: "The New Yorker says that he could live nowhere but in New York. He says it with a touch of pride. A scientist once discovered a frog alive in the solid rock, and when he took it out the frog died." *P. G. Wodehouse:* "To say that New York came up to its advance billing would be the baldest of understatements. Being there was like being in heaven without going to all the bother and expense of dying." *Edward Fisher Brown:* "Under maximum traffic conditions, a lion's roar would have difficulty in making itself heard on the streets of New York."

Margot Asquith: "I have never seen a modern town comparable to New York. The color of the stone and lightness of the air would put vitality into a corpse." *Alexander Klein:* "There are some who say with passion that the only real advantage of living in New York is that all its residents ascend to heaven directly after their deaths, having served their full term in purgatory right on Manhattan Island." *Cyril Connolly:* "If Paris is the perfect setting for a romance, New York is the perfect city in which to get over one, to get over anything."

George Jean Nathan: "The New Yorker, by and large, leads a life that is no more artificial, when you come to look at it closely, than the life led by the average country town hick. . . . Both are dolts." *Heywood Broun:* "The plain fact of the matter is that New York is much too good for New Yorkers. Complete appreciation will come only when some Vesuvius has laid it low and posterity is forced to dig down into the dust to bring to light the buried treasure."

Perhaps the main characteristic of the twentieth century is the rapidity of change, and this pace is faster in New York than anywhere else on earth. Always the unfinished city, New York tears down and builds anew with scant reverence for ancient landmarks, although steps are now being taken to save these monuments. Generally ignorant of the city's history, New Yorkers are less concerned with the past than with the present and the future.

Sir Patrick Geddes was a Scottish sociologist and town planner, who in 1913 drew up a scheme of city development. According to him, a large city goes through five stages during its rise and fall. First, there is the Polis, the young city. This develops into the Metropolis, a large but healthy city. In turn, this swells into the Megalopolis, an unhealthy, oversized city with a tendency toward megalomania. Next, said Sir Patrick, comes the Parasitopolis, the parasitic city which drains an entire country of its lifeblood. Lastly, there is the Pathopolis, the diseased, shrinking and dying city. If one accepts Sir Patrick's theory of the growth and decay of a city, New York now seems to be a Megalopolis beginning to turn into a Parasitopolis.

Oswald Spengler, the German philosopher and historian, agreed that the life of a city follows an inevitable pattern. Spengler wrote: "The stone colossus of the cosmopolitan city appears at the end of the life span of each great culture. Man, the cultural being, emotionally formed by the land, is taken possession of by his own creation—the city; he is being made its creature, its executive organ, and finally its victim."

Arnold Toynbee, the British historian, disagreed with Sir Patrick and Spengler. Toynbee denied that there was any parallel between the development of a culture and the birth, maturation, and death of an organism. Wolf Schneider, the German author of *Babylon Is Everywhere,* said: "Unless one is entranced by a system, one cannot presume, after a survey of over 7000 years of city history, to make rules concerning the duration of a city's life or the decline of cities. Babylon was leveled four times and each time it rose again."

Whatever the fate of New York, it continues to present charming vignettes. Early one evening, for example, a small crowd gathered at West End Avenue and Ninety-first Street. A little Negro boy stood on the second-floor terrace of a five-story building. He was making bubbles. Into a bowl of soapy water he dipped a plastic gadget shaped like a gutless tennis racquet, then lifted this wand, and with quick strokes sent bubbles into the air. Some were as big as basketballs.

A writer and his wife stopped to watch. So did a Puerto Rican delivery boy and a father and mother with their two children. A young crew-cut man and a couple of girls who looked like coeds climbed out a window onto a nearby balcony for a better view. If the Negro lad noticed the spectators, he gave no sign of it. Solemn-eyed, he went about his business—which was to touch this world with beauty.

The history of New York is the story of battles and riots, immortal men and great achievements, but the bubbleboy also was a part of that history. No yelping pack of reporters and photographers recorded the moment, for they concentrate on conflict, and this was serenity.

Around the world had gone the word that New York seethed with danger, but in this autumn gloaming, one bubble after another swung gently toward heaven and then winked to extinction. And before each bubble burst, for a few gleaming seconds it reflected the city, its streets, trees, houses, and smiling faces.

Perhaps those who watched might have agreed with Paul Morand, a French writer, who said of New York: "If the planet grows cold, this city will nevertheless have been mankind's warmest moment."

Selected Bibliography

Abbott, Wilbur C., *New York in the American Revolution.* New York, Scribner's, 1929.

Adams, Franklin P., *The Diary of Our Own Samuel Pepys, 1911-1934.* New York, Simon and Schuster, 1935. 2 vols.

Adams, James Truslow, *The March of Democracy.* New York, Scribner's, 1933. 2 vols.

———— ed., *Dictionary of American History.* New York, Scribner's, 1940. 7 vols.

Allen, Frederick Lewis, *Only Yesterday: An Informal History of the Nineteen-Twenties.* New York, Harper, 1931.

———— *Since Yesterday: The Nineteen-Thirties in America.* New York, Harper, 1939.

———— *The Great Pierpont Morgan.* New York, Harper, 1949.

———— *The Big Change.* New York, Harper, 1952.

Americana Annual. New York, Americana Corporation, 1923-1964. 42 vols.

AMORY, CLEVELAND, ed. in chief, *International Celebrity Register.* New York, Celebrity Register, 1959.

―――― *Who Killed Society?* New York, Harper, 1960.

ANGLE, PAUL M., *The American Reader.* New York, Rand McNally, 1958.

ARM, WALTER, *Pay-Off.* New York, Appleton-Century-Crofts, 1951.

Army Almanac. Harrisburg, Stackpole, 1959.

ASBURY, HERBERT, *The Gangs of New York.* New York, Garden City Publishing, 1927.

―――― *The Great Illusion, An Informal History of Prohibition.* New York, Doubleday, 1950.

BALES, WILLIAM ALAN, *Tiger in the Streets.* New York, Dodd, Mead, 1962.

BARKER, CHARLES ALBRO, *Henry George.* New York, Oxford University Press, 1955.

BARNHART, CLARENCE L., and HALSEY, WILLIAM D., eds., *The New Century Cyclopedia of Names.* New York, Appleton-Century-Crofts, 1954. 3 vols.

BATES, ERNEST SUTHERLAND, *The Story of Congress, 1789-1935.* New York, Harper, 1936.

BEALES, CARLETON, *Brass-Knuckle Crusade, The Great Know-Nothing Conspiracy: 1820-1860.* New York, Hastings House, 1960.

BEARD, CHARLES A., and MARY R., *The Rise of American Civilization.* New York, Macmillan, 1930.

―――― *America in Midpassage.* New York, Macmillan, 1939.

―――― *A Basic History of the United States.* New York, Garden City Publishing, 1944.

BELL, H. C. F., *Woodrow Wilson and the People.* New York, Doubleday Doran, 1945.

BERGER, MEYER, *The Eight Million.* New York, Simon and Schuster, 1942.

―――― *The Story of The New York Times, 1851-1951.* New York, Simon and Schuster, 1951.

―――― *Meyer Berger's New York.* New York, Random House, 1953.

BISHOP, JOSEPH BUCKLIN, *A Chronicle of One Hundred & Fifty Years: The Chamber of Commerce of the State of New York, 1768-1918.* New York, Scribner's, 1918.

BLUM, JOHN M., *Joe Tumulty and the Wilson Era.* Boston, Houghton Mifflin, 1951.

BOATNER, MARK MAYO, III, *The Civil War Dictionary.* New York, David McKay, 1959.

BONNER, WILLIAM THOMPSON, *New York: The World's Metropolis, 1623-1924.* New York, Polk, 1924.

BOOTH, MARY LOUISE, *History of the City of New York.* New York, W. R. C. Clark & Meeker, 1859.

BOTKIN, B. A., ed., *Sidewalks of America*. New York, Bobbs-Merrill, 1954.
—— *New York City Folklore*. New York, Random House, 1956.
BOWEN, CATHERINE DRINKER, and VON MECK, BARBARA, *"Beloved Friend," The Story of Tchaikowsky and Nadejda von Meck*. New York, Random House, 1937.
BRANDON, WILLIAM, *The American Heritage Book of Indians*. New York, American Heritage, 1961.
BRIDGWATER, WILLIAM, and SHERWOOD, ELIZABETH J., eds., *Columbia Encyclopedia*. New York, Columbia University Press, 1952.
Britannica Book of the Year. Chicago, Encyclopaedia Britannica, 1938-1964. 27 vols.
BRITT, GEORGE, *Forty Years—Forty Millions: The Career of Frank A. Munsey*. New York, Farrar & Rinehart, 1935.
Brooklyn Daily Eagle Almanac, 1905.
BROOKS, VAN WYCK, *The World of Washington Irving*. New York, Dutton, 1944.
—— *The Times of Melville and Whitman*. New York, Dutton, 1947.
—— *The Confident Years: 1885-1915*. New York, Dutton, 1952.
The Brown Book: Biographical Record of Public Officials of the City of New York for 1898-1899. New York, Martin B. Brown, 1899.
BROWN, HENRY COLLINS, *In the Golden Nineties*. Hastings-on-Hudson, Valentine's, 1928.
—— *Brownstone Fronts and Sarotoga Trunks*. New York, Dutton, 1935.
—— ed., *Valentine's Manual of Old New York*. New York, Valentine's, various years.
BRYCE, JAMES, *The American Commonwealth*. New York, Macmillan, 1914. 2 vols.
BURKE, W. J., and HOWE, WILL D., *American Authors and Books, 1640-1940*. New York, Gramercy, 1943.
BURLINGAME, ROGER, *March of the Iron Men: A Social History of Union Through Invention*. New York, Scribner's, 1938.
—— *The American Conscience*. New York, Knopf, 1957.
BURNHAM, ALAN, ed., *New York Landmarks*. Middletown, Conn., Weslyan University Press, 1963.
BURTON, KATHERINE, *The Dream Lives Forever: The Story of St. Patrick's Cathedral*. New York, Longmans, Green, 1960.

Cambridge Modern History. London, Macmillan, 1902. 14 vols.
CANBY, HENRY SEIDEL, *Walt Whitman, An American*. Boston, Houghton Mifflin, 1943.
CARLSON, OLIVER, *Brisbane: A Candid Biography*. New York, Stackpole, 1937.
CARMER, CARL, *The Hudson*. New York, Rinehart, 1939.
CARRUTH, GORTON, and ASSOCIATES, eds., *Encyclopedia of American Facts and Dates*. New York, Crowell, 1956.

CHAPIN, ANNA ALICE, *Greenwich Village.* New York, Dodd, Mead, 1917.

CHITWOOD, OLIVER PERRY, *A History of Colonial America.* New York, Harper, 1948.

CHURCHILL, ALLEN, *Park Row.* New York, Rinehart, 1958.

———— *The Improper Bohemians: Greenwich Village in Its Heyday.* New York, Dutton, 1959.

———— *The Year the World Went Mad.* New York, Crowell, 1960.

———— *The Great White Way.* New York, Dutton, 1962.

CHURCHILL, WINSTON S., *A History of the English-Speaking Peoples.* New York, Dodd, Mead, 1958. 4 vols.

Civil List and Forms of Government of the Colony and State of New York. Albany, Weed, Parsons, 1870.

CLAPP, MARGARET, *Forgotten First Citizen: John Bigelow.* Boston, Little, Brown, 1947.

Climate and Man, Yearbook of Agriculture. Washington, U.S. Department of Agriculture, 1941.

COIT, MARGARET L., *Mr. Baruch.* Boston, Houghton Mifflin, 1957.

COLLINS, FREDERICK L., *Money Town.* New York, Putnam's, 1946.

COMMAGER, HENRY STEELE, ed., *The Blue and the Gray: The Story of the Civil War as Told by Participants.* New York, Bobbs Merrill, 1950.

COMMAGER, HENRY STEELE, and MORRIS, RICHARD B., eds., *The Spirit of 'Seventy-Six: The Story of the American Revolution as Told by Participants.* New York, Bobbs-Merrill, 1958. 2 vols.

Concise Dictionary of American Biography. New York, Scribner's, 1964.

COON, HORACE, *Columbia: Colossus on the Hudson.* New York, Dutton, 1947.

COOPER, KENT, *Kent Cooper and the Associated Press, An Autobiography.* New York, Random House, 1959.

COOPER, PAGE, *The Bellevue Story.* New York, Crowell, 1948.

CORSI, EDWARD, *In the Shadow of Liberty, The Chronicle of Ellis Island.* New York, Macmillan, 1935.

CRANE, MILTON, ed., *Sins of New York.* New York, Grosset & Dunlap, 1947.

CRANSTON, RUTH, *The Story of Woodrow Wilson.* New York, Simon and Schuster, 1945.

CROCKETT, ALBERT STEVENS, *When James Gordon Bennett Was Caliph of Bagdad.* New York, Funk & Wagnalls, 1926.

CRONON, EDMUND DAVID, *Black Moses, The Story of Marcus Garvey.* Madison, University of Wisconsin Press, 1955.

CUNEO, ERNEST, *Life With Fiorello.* New York, Macmillan, 1955.

DALEY, ROBERT, *The World Beneath the City.* New York, Lippincott, 1959.

DANFORTH, HAROLD R., and HORAN, JAMES D., *The D.A.'s Man.* New York, Crown, 1957.

DANGERFIELD, GEORGE, *Chancellor Robert R. Livingston of New York, 1746-1813.* New York, Harcourt Brace, 1960.

DAN GOLENPAUL ASSOCIATES, *Information Please Almanac.* New York, McGraw-Hill, various years.

DANIELS, JOSEPHUS, *The Wilson Era.* Chapel Hill, University of North Carolina Press, 1946.

DAVIS, ELMER, *History of The New York Times, 1851-1921.* New York, The New York *Times*, 1921.

DAY, DONALD, ed., *Woodrow Wilson's Own Story.* Boston, Little, Brown, 1952.

DESMOND, ALICE CURTIS, *Martha Washington, Our First Lady.* New York, Dodd, Mead, 1942.

DE VOE, THOMAS F., *The Market Book*, Vol. 1. New York, printed for the author, 1862.

DEWITT, J. DOYLE, *America Goes to the Polls.* Hartford, Conn., Travelers Insurance Companies, 1960.

DICKENS, CHARLES, *American Notes.* New York, Crowell.

DIX, MORGAN, ed., *A History of the Parish of Trinity Church in the City of New York*, Vol. II. New York, Putnam's, 1898.

The Documentary History of the State of New-York, arranged under direction of Christopher Morgan, Secretary of State, Vol. III. Albany, Weed, Parsons, 1850.

DOS PASSOS, JOHN, *Mr. Wilson's War.* New York, Doubleday, 1962.

DRAPER, THEODORE, *The Roots of American Communism.* New York, Viking, 1957.

DUNSHEE, KENNETH HOLCOMB, *As You Pass By.* New York, Hastings House, 1952.

EARLE, ALICE MORSE, *Colonial Days in Old New York.* Port Washington, Friedman, 1962.

ELLIS, DAVID M., FROST, JAMES A., SYRETT, HAROLD C., and CARMAN, HARRY J., *A Short History of New York State.* Ithaca, Cornell University Press, 1957.

ELLIS, EDWARD ROBB, *Briefly I Tarry.* An unpublished journal.

Encyclopedia Americana. New York, Americana Corporation, 1952. 30 vols.

Encyclopaedia Britannica, 11th ed. New York, University Press, 1910. 28 vols.

EWEN, David, *Panorama of American Popular Music.* Englewood Cliffs, Prentice-Hall, 1957.

FARLEY, MOST REV. JOHN M., *History of St. Patrick's Cathedral.* New York, Society for the Propagation of the Faith, 1908.

FAULKNER, HAROLD U., *The Decline of Laissez Faire, 1897-1917.* New York, Rinehart, 1951.

FEDER, SID, and TURKUS, BURTON B., *Murder, Inc.* New York, Farrar, Straus & Cudahy, 1951.

FEDERAL WRITERS' PROJECT OF THE WORKS PROGRESS ADMINISTRATION FOR THE CITY OF NEW YORK, *A Maritime History of New York.* New York, Doubleday Doran, 1941.

—— FOR THE STATE OF CONNECTICUT, *Connecticut, A Guide to Its Roads, Lore, and People.* Boston, Houghton Mifflin, 1938.

—— FOR THE STATE OF DELAWARE, *Delaware, A Guide to the First State.* New York, Viking, 1938.

—— FOR MASSACHUSETTS, *Massachusetts, A Guide to Its Places and People.* Boston, Houghton Mifflin, 1937.

—— FOR THE STATE OF NEW JERSEY, *New Jersey, A Guide to Its Present and Past.* New York, Hastings House, 1939.

—— IN NEW YORK CITY, *New York Learns.* New York, Barrows, 1939.

FIELD, CARTER, *Bernard Baruch, Park Bench Statesman.* New York, McGraw-Hill, 1944.

THE FIFTH AVENUE ASSOCIATION, *Fifty Years on Fifth.* New York, International Press, 1957.

FINEGAN, JAMES E., *Tammany at Bay.* New York, Dodd, Mead, 1933.

FISKE, JOHN, *The Dutch and Quaker Colonies in America.* New York, Houghton Mifflin, 1899. 2 vols.

—— *The American Revolution.* Boston, Houghton Mifflin, 1902. 2 vols.

Five Borough Street Guide to New York City. New York, Geographia Map Co., 1962.

FLEISCHMAN, HARRY, *Norman Thomas, A Biography.* New York, Norton, 1964.

FLICK, ALEXANDER C., ed., *History of the State of New York.* New York, Friedman, 1962. 10 vols.

FLYNN, EDWARD J., *You're the Boss.* New York, Viking, 1947.

FORBES, B. C., *Men Who Are Making America.* New York, Forbes, 1917.

FOSDICK, RAYMOND B., *John D. Rockefeller, Jr.* New York, Harper, 1956.

FOWLER, GENE, *Beau James: The Life and Times of Jimmy Walker.* New York, Viking, 1949.

FRANKLIN, JOHN HOPE, *From Slavery to Freedom: A History of American Negroes.* New York, Knopf, 1956.

FREEDLEY, GEORGE, and REEVES, JOHN A., *A History of the Theatre.* New York, Crown, 1955.

FREEMAN, ANDREW A., *Abraham Lincoln Goes to New York.* New York, Coward-McCann, 1960.

FREEMAN, DOUGLAS SOUTHALL, *George Washington, Leader of the Revolution,* Vol. IV. New York, Scribner's, 1951.

FURNAS, J. C., *Goodbye to Uncle Tom.* New York, Sloane, 1956.

—— *The Road to Harpers Ferry.* New York, Sloane, 1959.

GALBRAITH, JOHN KENNETH, *The Great Crash, 1929.* Boston, Houghton Mifflin, 1955.

GARRETT, CHARLES, *The LaGuardia Years.* New Brunswick, Rutgers University Press, 1961.

GAUVREAU, EMILE, *My Last Million Readers.* New York, Dutton, 1951.

GELB, ARTHUR, and BARBARA, *O'Neill.* New York, Harper & Row, 1960.

GEORGE, ALEXANDER L., and JULIETTE L., *Woodrow Wilson and Colonel House.* New York, Day, 1956.

GILBERT, DOUGLAS, *American Vaudeville.* New York, Whittlesey House, 1940.

GILDER, RODMAN, *The Battery.* Boston, Houghton Mifflin, 1936.

GITLOW, BENJAMIN, *I Confess: The Truth About American Communism.* New York, Dutton, 1940.

GLAZER, NATHAN, and MOYNIHAN, DANIEL PATRICK, *Beyond the Melting Pot.* Cambridge, M.I.T. Press and Harvard University Press, 1963.

Going to the Fair: A Preview of the New York World's Fair 1939. New York, Sun Dial, 1939.

GOLDMAN, ERIC F. *The Crucial Decade: America, 1945-1955.* New York, Knopf, 1956.

GORDON, MITCHELL, *Sick Cities.* New York, Macmillan, 1963.

GRAHAM, FRANK, *Al Smith, American.* New York, Putnam's, 1945.

GRAMLING, OLIVER, *AP: The Story of News.* New York, Farrar and Rinehart, 1940.

GREEN, ABEL, and LAURIE, JOE, JR., *Show Biz From Vaude to Video.* New York, Holt, 1951.

GRODINSKY, JULIUS, *Jay Gould, His Business Career.* Philadelphia, University of Pennsylvania Press, 1957.

GROVES, LESLIE R., *Now It Can Be Told: The Story of the Manhattan Project.* New York, Harper, 1962.

THE GUILDS' COMMITTEE FOR FEDERAL WRITERS' PUBLICATIONS, *Almanac for New Yorkers 1939.* New York, Modern Age, 1938.

———— *The Italians of New York.* New York, Random House, 1938.

———— *New York Panorama.* New York, Random House, 1938.

———— *New York City Guide.* New York, Random House, 1939.

GUNTHER, JOHN, *Inside U.S.A.,* rev. ed. New York, Harper, 1951.

———— *Inside Africa.* New York, Harper, 1953.

HACKER, LOUIS M., *Alexander Hamilton in the American Tradition.* New York, McGraw-Hill, 1957.

HALE, WILLIAM HARLAN, *Horace Greeley: Voice of the People.* New York, Harper, 1950.

HALSEY, FRANCIS WHITING, *The Literary Digest History of the World War.* New York, Funk & Wagnalls, New York, 1920. 10 vols.

HAMBURGER, PHILIP, *Mayor Watching and Other Pleasures.* New York, Rinehart, 1947.

Hammond's Ambassador World Atlas. Maplewood, N.J., Hammond, 1957.

HANDLIN, OSCAR, *The Uprooted.* Boston, Little, Brown, 1951.

———— *The Newcomers: Negroes and Puerto Ricans in a Changing Metropolis.* New York, Doubleday, 1962.

HANSON, EARL PARKER, *Puerto Rico: Land of Wonders*. New York, Knopf, 1960.

HAPGOOD, NORMAN, and MOSKOWITZ, HENRY, *Up From the City Streets: Alfred E. Smith*. New York, Harcourt Brace, 1927.

HARBAUGH, WILLIAM HENRY, *Power and Responsibility: The Life and Times of Theodore Roosevelt*. New York, Farrar, Straus and Cudahy, 1961.

HARLOW, ALVIN F., *The Road of the Century: The Story of the New York Central*. New York, Creative Age, 1947.

Harper's Encyclopaedia of United States History. New York, Harper, 1901. 10 vols.

HARRIS, SARA, *Father Divine: Holy Husband*. New York, Doubleday, 1953.

HART, JAMES D., *Oxford Companion to American Literature*. New York, Oxford University Press, 1948.

HARTNOLL, PHYLLIS, ed., *The Oxford Companion to the Theatre*. London, Oxford University Press, 1951.

HAWKINS, STUART, *New York, New York*. New York, Wilfred Funk, 1957.

HEILBRONER, ROBERT L., *The Quest for Wealth*. New York, Simon and Schuster, 1956.

HELLMAN, GEOFFREY T., *Mrs. de Peyster's Parties*. New York, Macmillan, 1963.

HERALD TRIBUNE STAFF, *New York City in Crisis*. New York, David McKay, 1965.

HIBBEN, PAXTON, *Henry Ward Beecher: An American Portrait*. New York, Doran, 1927.

HICKS, GRANVILLE, *Where We Came Out*. New York, Viking, 1954.

HIGHAM, JOHN, *Strangers in the Land: Patterns of American Nativism, 1860-1925*. New Brunswick, Rutgers University Press, 1955.

HIRSCH, MARK DAVID, *William C. Whitney*. New York, Dodd, Mead, 1948.

Historical Statistics of the United States, 1789-1945. Washington, Bureau of the Census, 1949.

A History of Columbia University: 1754-1904. New York, Columbia University Press and Macmillan, 1904.

HOEHLING, A. A., *The Great Epidemic: When the Spanish Influenza Struck*. Boston, Little, Brown, 1961.

HOFFMAN, FREDERICK J., *The Twenties: American Writing in the Postwar Decade*. New York, Viking, 1949.

HOLBROOK, STEWART H., *The Story of American Railroads*. New York, Crown, 1947.

—— *The Age of the Moguls*. New York, Doubleday, 1954.

HOOVER, HERBERT, *The Memoirs of Herbert Hoover: Years of Adventure, 1874-1920*. New York, Macmillan, 1951.

—— *The Memoirs of Herbert Hoover: The Cabinet and the Presidency, 1920-1933*. New York, Macmillan, 1952.

HORAN, JAMES D., *The Desperate Years: A Pictorial History of the Thirties*. New York, Crown, 1962.
How the Dutch Came to Manhattan. A colonial monograph. New York, Herrick, 1897.
HOWE, IRVING, and COSER, LEWIS, *The American Communist Party*. New York, Praeger, 1962.
HOWE, QUINCY, *A World History of Our Own Times*. New York, Simon and Schuster, 1953. 2 vols.
HOYT, EDWIN P., *The Vanderbilts and Their Fortunes*. New York, Doubleday, 1962.

The Intimate Papers of Colonel House, arranged by Charles Seymour. Boston, Houghton Mifflin, 1926.

JAMES, RIAN, *All About New York*. New York, Day, 1931.
JENKINS, JOHN S., *Lives of the Governors of the State of New York*. Auburn, Derby and Miller, 1951.
JENKINS, STEPHEN, *The Greatest Street in the World*. New York, Putnam's, 1911.
────── *The Story of the Bronx: From the Purchase Made by the Dutch From the Indians in 1639 to the Present Day*. New York, Putnam's, 1912.
JERNEGAN, MARCUS WILSON, *The American Colonies, 1492-1750*. New York, Ungar, 1929.
JOHNSON, GERALD W., *An Honorable Titan: A Biographical Study of Adolph S. Ochs*. New York, Harper, 1946.
JOHNSON, JAMES WELDON, *Black Manhattan*. New York, Knopf, 1930.
JOSEPHSON, MATTHEW, *The Robber Barons*. New York, Harcourt, Brace, 1934.
────── *The Politicos, 1865-1896*. New York, Harcourt, Brace, 1938.
────── *Edison, A Biography*. New York, McGraw-Hill, 1959.

KANE, JOSEPH NATHAN, *Facts About the Presidents*. New York, Wilson, 1959.
────── *Famous First Facts*. New York, Wilson, 1964.
KATCHER, LEO, *The Big Bankroll: The Life and Times of Arnold Rothstein*. New York, Harper, 1958.
Kefauver Crime Committee's Third Interim Report. New York, Arco, 1951.
KELLER, HELEN REX, *The Dictionary of Dates*. New York, Macmillan, 1934. 2 vols.
KIERAN, JOHN, *A Natural History of New York City*. Boston, Houghton Mifflin, 1959.
KING, MOSES, *Notable New Yorkers—1896-1899*. New York, Bartlett, 1899.
KLEIN, ALEXANDER, ed., *The Empire City: A Treasury of New York*. New York, Rinehart, 1955.
KOENIG, LOUIS W., *The Invisible Presidency*. New York, Rinehart, 1960.

KORNGOLD, RALPH, *Two Friends of Man: The Story of William Lloyd Garrison and Wendell Phillips and Their Relationship With Abraham Lincoln.* Boston, Little, Brown, 1950.

KOUWENHOVEN, JOHN A., *The Columbia Historical Portrait of New York.* New York, Doubleday, 1953.

———— ed., *The New York Guidebook.* New York, Dell, 1964.

KRAMER, DALE, *Heywood Broun.* New York, Current Books, 1949.

KREYMBORG, ALFRED, *A History of American Poetry.* New York, Coward-McCann, 1929.

LADER, LAWRENCE, *The Bold Brahmins: New England's War Against Slavery (1831-1863).* New York, Dutton, 1961.

LAGUARDIA, FIORELLO H., *The Making of an Insurgent, An Autobiography: 1882-1919.* New York, Lippincott, 1948.

LAMB, MARTHA J., *History of the City of New York.* New York, Barnes, 1877, 1880. 2 vols.

LANCASTER, BRUCE, *From Lexington to Liberty: The Story of the American Revolution.* New York, Doubleday, 1955.

LANDAU, HENRY, *The Enemy Within: The Inside Story of German Sabotage in America.* New York, Putnam's, 1937.

LANG, DANIEL, *From Hiroshima to the Moon.* New York, Simon and Schuster, 1959.

LANGER, WILLIAM L., ed., *An Encyclopedia of World History.* Boston, Houghton Mifflin, 1940.

LAURENCE, WILLIAM L., *Dawn Over Zero: The Story of the Atomic Bomb.* New York, Knopf, 1947.

LAURIE, JOE, JR., *Vaudeville: From the Honky-Tonks to the Palace.* New York, Holt, 1953.

LEE, ALFRED MCCLUNG, *The Daily Newspaper in America.* New York, Macmillan, 1937.

LEECH, MARGARET, *In the Days of McKinley.* New York, Harper, 1959.

LEIGHTON, ISABEL, ed., *The Aspirin Age: 1919-1941.* New York, Simon and Schuster, 1949.

LENT, HENRY B., *The Waldorf-Astoria.* New York, Hotel Waldorf-Astoria Corp., 1934.

LESCOHIER, DON D., and BRANDEIS, ELIZABETH, *History of Labor in the United States, 1896-1932,* Vol. III. New York, Macmillan, 1935.

LEVINSON, LEONARD LOUIS, *Wall Street: A Pictorial History.* New York, Ziff-Davis, 1961.

Life magazine.

LIMPUS, LOWELL M., *History of the New York Fire Department.* New York, Dutton, 1940.

Lincoln Library of Essential Information. Buffalo, Frontier Press, 1955.

LODGE, HENRY CABOT, *Alexander Hamilton.* Boston, Houghton Mifflin, 1882.

———— *A Short History of the English Colonies in America,* rev. ed. New York, Harper, 1881.

THE LONG ISLAND ASSOCIATION, *Long Island: The Sunrise Homeland, 1636-1950.* Williston Park, N.Y., Colonial Press, 1950.

LONG, J. C., *George III.* Boston, Little, Brown, 1960.

LORD, WALTER, *The Good Years: From 1900 to the First World War.* New York, Harper, 1960.

LOSSING, BENSON J., *History of New York City.* New York, Perine, 1884.

LOWI, THEODORE J., *At the Pleasure of the Mayor.* New York, Free Press of Glencoe, 1964.

LUNDBERG, FERDINAND, *Imperial Hearst: A Social Biography.* New York, Modern Library, 1936.

———— *America's 60 Families.* New York, Vanguard, 1937.

LUTHIN, REINHARD H., *American Demagogues: Twentieth Century.* Boston, Beacon, 1954.

LYNCH, DENIS TILDEN, *"Boss" Tweed: The Story of a Grim Generation.* New York, Blue Ribbon, 1927.

———— *Grover Cleveland: A Man Four-Square.* New York, Liveright, 1932.

LYNES, RUSSELL, *The Tastemakers.* New York, Harper, 1949.

LYON, PETER, *Success Story: The Life and Times of S. S. McClure.* New York, Scribner's, 1963.

LYONS, EUGENE, *The Red Decade.* New York, Bobbs-Merrill, 1941.

McCABE, JAMES D., *New York by Sunlight and Gaslight.* New York, Union, 1883.

McCARTHY, JAMES REMINGTON, with RUTHERFORD, JOHN, *Peacock Alley: The Romance of the Waldorf-Astoria.* New York, Harper, 1931.

McCULLOGH, ESTHER MORGAN, ed., *As I Pass, O Manhattan.* North Bennington, Vt., Coley Taylor, 1956.

McCULLOUGH, EDO, *Good Old Coney Island.* New York, Scribner's, 1957.

McELROY, ROBERT, *Grover Cleveland: The Man and the Statesman.* New York, Harper, 1923. 2 vols.

McKELVEY, BLAKE, *The Urbanization of America, 1860-1915.* New Brunswick, N.J., Rutgers University Press, 1963.

McMASTER, JOHN BACH, *A History of the People of the United States.* New York, Appleton, 1913. 8 vols.

MACK, EDWARD C., *Peter Cooper: Citizen of New York.* New York, Duell, Sloan and Pearce, 1949.

MAHONEY, TOM, *The Great Merchants.* New York, Harper, 1955.

MANN, ARTHUR, *LaGuardia: A Fighter Against His Times, 1882-1933.* Philadelphia, Lippincott, 1959.

"Manna-hatin": The Story of New York. New York, Manhattan Co., 1929.

Manual for the Use of the Legislature of the State of New York. Various years.

MARROW, ALFRED J., *Changing Patterns of Prejudice.* Philadelphia, Chilton, 1962.

MARTIN, MICHAEL, and GELBER, LEONARD, *The New Dictionary of American History*. New York, Philosophical Library, 1952.

MARX, HARPO, *Harpo Speaks!* New York, Geis, 1961.

MAURICE, ARTHUR BARTLETT, *The New York of the Novelists*. New York, Dodd, Mead, 1915.

———— *Fifth Avenue*. New York, Dodd, Mead, 1918.

MAYER, GRACE M., *Once Upon a City*. New York, Macmillan, 1958.

Mayor Gaynor's Letters and Speeches. New York, Greaves, 1913.

MAZUR, PAUL M., *American Prosperity: Its Causes and Consequences*. New York, Viking, 1928.

MEHLING, HAROLD, *The Scandalous Scamps*. New York, Holt, 1956.

MENKE, FRANK G., *The New Encyclopedia of Sports*. New York, Barnes, 1944.

Messages and Papers of the Presidents. Washington, Bureau of National Literature, 1912. 11 vols.

MIERS, EARL SCHENCK, ed., *The American Story: From Columbus to the Atom*. New York, Channel Press, 1956.

MILLER, JOHN C., *Origins of the American Revolution*. Boston, Little, Brown, 1943.

MILLETT, JOHN D., *The Works Progress Administration in New York City*. Chicago, Public Administration Service, 1938.

MILLIS, WALTER, *The Martial Spirit*. Cambridge, Mass., Literary Guild of America, 1931.

———— *Road to War: America 1914-1917*. Boston, Houghton Mifflin, 1935.

MITCHELL, BROADUS, *Depression Decade, 1929-1941*. New York, Rinehart, 1947.

———— *Alexander Hamilton: Youth to Maturity, 1755-1788*. New York, Macmillan, 1957.

MITGANG, HERBERT, *The Man Who Rode the Tiger: The Life and Times of Judge Samuel Seabury*. New York, Lippincott, 1963.

MONAGHAN, FRANK, and LOWENTHAL, MARVIN, *This Was New York: The Nation's Capital in 1789*. New York, Doubleday, Doran, 1943.

MOODY, RICHARD, *The Astor Place Riot*. Bloomington, Indiana University Press, 1958.

MORAN, EUGENE F., and REID, LOUIS, *Tugboat: The Moran Story*. New York, Scribner's, 1956.

MORRIS, CHARLES, ed., *Makers of New York*. Philadelphia, Hamersly, 1895.

MORRIS, JOE ALEX, *What a Year!—The Colorful Story of 1929*. New York, Harper, 1956.

———— *Deadline Every Minute: The Story of the United Press*. New York, Doubleday, 1957.

———— *Nelson Rockefeller: A Biography*. New York, Harper, 1960.

MORRIS, LLOYD, *Postscript to Yesterday*. New York, Random House, 1947.

———— *Not So Long Ago*. New York, Random House, 1949.

———— *Incredible New York.* New York, Random House, 1951.

———— *Curtain Time: The Story of the American Theater.* New York, Random House, 1953.

MORRIS, RICHARD B., *Fair Trial.* New York, Knopf, 1952.

———— ed., *Encyclopedia of American History.* New York, Harper, 1953.

———— ed., *Alexander Hamilton and the Founding of the Nation.* New York, Dial, 1957.

MOSES, ROBERT, *Working for the People: Promise and Performance in Public Service.* New York, Harper, 1956.

MOTT, FRANK LUTHER, *A History of American Magazines, 1741-1850.* Cambridge: Harvard University Press, 1930. 4 vols.

MUMFORD, LEWIS, *Herman Melville.* New York, Harcourt Brace, 1929.

———— *The City in History.* New York, Harcourt Brace & World, 1961.

MURPHY, MARY ELLEN, MURPHY, MARK, and WELD, RALPH FOSTER, eds., *A Treasury of Brooklyn.* New York, Sloane, 1949.

MYERS, GUSTAVUS, *The History of Tammany Hall.* New York, published by the author, 1901.

———— *History of the Great American Fortunes.* New York, Modern Library, 1936.

———— *History of Bigotry in the United States, 1872-1942.* New York, Random House, 1943.

MYERS, WILLIAM STARR, and NEWTON, WALTER H., *The Hoover Administration.* New York, Scribner's, 1936.

NEUFELD, ERNEST, ed., *The Renascence of City Hall.* New York, New York City Department of Public Works, 1956.

NEVINS, ALLAN, *Grover Cleveland: A Study in Courage.* New York, Dodd, Mead, 1932.

———— *Abram S. Hewitt: With Some Account of Peter Cooper.* New York, Harper, 1935.

———— *The Emergency of Lincoln.* New York, Scribner's, 1950. 2 vols.

———— *Study in Power: John D. Rockefeller, Industrialist and Philanthropist.* New York, Scribner's, 1953. 2 vols.

———— *Herbert H. Lehman and His Era.* New York, Scribner's, 1963.

NEVINS, ALLAN, and HILL, FRANK ERNEST, *Ford: Expansion and Challenge, 1915-1933.* New York, Scribner's, 1957.

NEVINS, ALLAN, and KROUT, JOHN A., eds., *The Greater City: New York, 1898-1948.* New York, Columbia University Press, 1948.

NEVINS, ALLAN, and THOMAS, MILTON HALSEY, eds., *The Diary of George Templeton Strong.* New York, Macmillan, 1952. 4 vols.

Newsweek magazine.

New York *Herald Tribune.*

NEW YORK STATE HISTORICAL ASSOCIATION, *New York: A Guide to the Empire State.* New York, Oxford University Press, 1940.

New York *Times.*

New York *World-Telegram and Sun.*

NILES, BLAIR, *Martha's Husband, An Informal Portrait of George Washington.* New York, McGraw-Hill, 1951.

OBERHOLTZER, ELLIS PAXON, *A History of the United States Since the Civil War, 1865-1872.* New York, Macmillan, 1922. 2 vols.
O'BRIEN, FRANK M., *The Story of The Sun, New York, 1833-1928.* New York, Appleton, 1928.
O'CONNOR, HARVEY, *The Astors.* New York, Knopf, 1941.
O'CONNOR, RICHARD, *Hell's Kitchen.* New York, Lippincott, 1958.
————— *Courtroom Warrior: The Combative Career of William Travers Jerome.* Boston, Little, Brown, 1963.
Official Guide, New York World's Fair 1964-1965. New York, Time Incorporated, 1964.
Official Guide Book: The World's Fair of 1940 in New York. New York, Rogers, Kellogg, Stillson, 1940.
OLDER, MRS. FREMONT, *William Randolph Hearst, American.* New York, Appleton-Century, 1936.

PARKER, ROBERT ALLERTON, *The Incredible Messiah: The Deification of Father Divine.* Boston, Little, Brown, 1937.
PARKES, HENRY BAMFORD, *The American Experience.* New York, Knopf, 1947.
PARRINGTON, VERNON LOUIS, *Main Currents in American Thought.* New York, Harcourt Brace, 1927.
PAULI, HERTHA, and ASHTON, E. B., *I Lift My Lamp.* New York, Appleton-Century-Crofts, 1948.
PERINE, EDWARD TEN BROECK, *Here's to Broadway!* New York, Putnam's, 1930.
PFEFFER, LEO, *Church, State, and Freedom.* Boston, Beacon, 1953.
Pictorial History of the Second World War. New York, Wise, 1944. 5 vols.
PIERCE, CARL HORTON, *New Harlem.* New York, New Harlem Publishing, 1903.
PILAT, OLIVER, and RANSON, JO, *Sodom by the Sea: An Affectionate History of Coney Island.* New York, Doubleday Doran, 1941.
PINE, JOHN B., ed., *Seal and Flag of the City of New York.* New York, Putnam's, 1915.
PLEASANTS, SAMUEL AUGUSTUS, *Fernando Wood of New York.* New York, Columbia University Press, 1948.
POSTAL, BERNARD, and KOPPMAN, LIONEL, *Jewish Landmarks in New York.* New York, Hill and Wang, 1964.
POTTER, GEORGE, *To the Golden Door: The Story of the Irish in Ireland and America.* Boston, Little, Brown, 1960.
POUND, ARTHUR, *The Golden Earth.* New York, Macmillan, 1935.
PRESTON, JOHN HYDE, *Revolution 1776.* New York, Harcourt Brace, 1933.
PRINGLE, HENRY F., *Theodore Roosevelt.* New York, Harcourt Brace, 1931.
PUTNAM, CARLETON, *Theodore Roosevelt: The Formative Years, 1858-1886,* Vol. 1. New York, Scribner's, 1958.

RACHLIS, EUGENE, and MARQUSEE, JOHN E., *The Land Lords*. New York, Random House, 1963.

RAMSAYE, TERRY, *A Million and One Nights: A History of the Motion Picture*. New York, Simon and Schuster, 1926.

RANKIN, REBECCA, ed., *New York Advancing*. New York, Municipal Reference Library, 1945.

——— *Guide to the Municipal Government of the City of New York*. New York, Record Press, 1950.

REDMAN, ALVIN, *The House of Hanover*. New York, Coward-McCann, 1960.

REID, ED, *The Shame of New York*. New York, Random House, 1953.

Revolutionary Radicalism, Report of the Joint Legislative Committee Investigating Seditious Activities, Vol. I. Albany, Lyon, 1920.

RIDER, FREMONT, ed., *Rider's New York City*. New York, Holt, 1923.

RIIS, JACOB A., *The Making of an American*. New York, Macmillan, 1901.

——— *How the Other Half Lives: Studies Among the Tenements of New York*. New York, Sagamore Press, 1957.

RIKER, JAMES, *History of Harlem*. New York, New Harlem Publishing, 1904.

RISCHIN, MOSES, *The Promised City*. Cambridge, Harvard University Press, 1962.

RODGERS, CLEVELAND, *Robert Moses: Builder for Democracy*. New York, Holt, 1952.

RODGERS, CLEVELAND, and RANKIN, REBECCA B., *New York: The World's Capital City*. New York, Harper, 1948.

ROOSEVELT, THEODORE, *An Autobiography*. New York, Scribner's, 1926.

——— *The Rough Riders*. New York, Scribner's, 1926.

ROOT, JONATHAN, *One Night in July: The True Story of the Rosenthal-Becker Murder Case*. New York, Coward-McCann, 1961.

ROSS, ISHBEL, *Ladies of the Press*. New York, Harper, 1936.

ROSSITER, CLINTON, *Seedtime of the Republic*. New York, Harcourt Brace, 1953.

ROWAN, RICHARD WILMER, *The Story of Secret Service*. New York, Doubleday Doran, 1937.

RUSSELL, CHARLES EDWARD, *From Sandy Hook to 62°*. New York, Century, 1929.

SANDBURG, CARL, *Abraham Lincoln*. New York, Harcourt Brace, 1939. 6 vols.

SATTERLEE, HERBERT L., *J. Pierpont Morgan, An Intimate Portrait*. New York, Macmillan, 1940.

SAVELLE, MAX, *Seeds of Liberty*. New York, Knopf, 1948.

SAYRE, WALLACE S., and KAUFMAN, HERBERT, *Governing New York City*. New York, Russell Sage Foundation, 1960.

SCHACHNER, NATHAN, *Thomas Jefferson, A Biography*. New York, Appleton-Century-Crofts, 1951. 2 vols.

SCHLESINGER, ARTHUR M., JR., *The Crisis of the Old Order, 1919-1933*. Boston, Houghton Mifflin, 1957.
—— *The Coming of the New Deal*. Boston, Houghton Mifflin, 1958.
—— *The Politics of Upheaval*. Boston, Houghton Mifflin, 1960.
SCHNEIDER, WOLF, *Babylon Is Everywhere*. New York, McGraw-Hill, 1963.
SCHRIFTGIESSER, KARL, *Oscar of the Waldorf*. New York, Dutton, 1943.
SCHULTZ, EARL, and SIMMONS, WALTER, *Offices in the Sky*. New York, Bobbs-Merrill, 1959.
SEITZ, DON C., *Joseph Pulitzer, His Life and Letters*. New York, Simon and Schuster, 1924.
SELDES, GEORGE, *Freedom of the Press*. New York, Bobbs-Merrill, 1935.
—— *Lords of the Press*. New York, Blue Ribbon Books, 1938.
SELTZER, LEON E., ed., *Columbia Lippincott Gazetteer of the World*. New York, Columbia University Press, 1952.
SHANNON, DAVID A., *The Socialist Party of America*. New York, Macmillan, 1955.
—— *The Decline of American Communism*. New York, Harcourt Brace, 1959.
—— ed., *The Great Depression*. Englewood Cliffs, N.J., Prentice-Hall, 1960.
SHANNON, FRED A., *The Farmer's Last Frontier, 1860-1897*. New York, Farrar & Rinehart, 1945.
SHANNON, WILLIAM V., *The American Irish*. New York, Macmillan, 1963.
SHERWIN, OSCAR, *Prophet of Liberty, The Life and Times of Wendell Phillips*. New York, Bookman Associates, 1958.
SHERWOOD, ROBERT E., *Roosevelt and Hopkins*, rev. ed. New York, Harper, 1950.
SINGLETON, ESTHER, *Social New York Under the Georges, 1714-1776*. New York, Appleton, 1902.
SMITH, ALFRED E., *Up to Now, An Autobiography*. New York, Viking, 1929.
SMITH, ARTHUR D. HOWDEN, *John Jacob Astor: Landlord of New York*. New York, Blue Ribbon Books, 1929.
SMITH, MORTIMER, *William Jay Gaynor: Mayor of New York*. Chicago, Regnery, 1951.
SNYDER, LOUIS L., and MORRIS, RICHARD B., eds., *A Treasury of Great Reporting*. New York, Simon and Schuster, 1949.
SONDERN, FREDERIC, JR., *Brotherhood of Evil: The Mafia*. New York, Farrar, Straus and Cudahy, 1959.
SOULE, GEORGE, *Prosperity Decade, 1917-1929*. New York, Rinehart, 1947.
SPILLER, ROBERT E., THORP, WILLARD, JOHNSON, THOMAS H., and CANBY, HENRY SEIDEL, eds., *Literary History of the United States*. New York, Macmillan, 1953.
SQUIER, GEORGE O., *Telling the World*. Baltimore, Williams & Wilkins, 1933.

STARR, JOHN, *Hospital City.* New York, Crown, 1957.

STEARNS, HAROLD E., ed., *America Now.* New York, Scribner's, 1938.

STEBBINS, HOMER ADOLPH, *A Political History of the State of New York, 1865-1869.* New York, Columbia University, 1913.

STEFFENS, LINCOLN, *The Autobiography of Lincoln Steffens.* New York, Harcourt Brace, 1931.

STEINMAN, DAVID B., *The Builders of the Bridge, The Story of John Roebling and His Son.* New York, Harcourt Brace, 1945.

STEINMAN, DAVID B., and WATSON, SARA RUTH, *Bridges and Their Builders.* New York, Putnam's, 1941.

STEINMEYER, HENRY G., *Staten Island 1524-1898.* New York, Staten Island Historical Society, 1950.

STEUER, ARON, *Max D. Steuer: Trial Lawyer.* New York, Random House, 1950.

STILL, BAYRD, *Mirror for Gotham.* New York, New York University Press, 1956.

STIMPSON, GEORGE, *A Book About American History.* New York, Harper, 1950.

STODDARD, HENRY LUTHER, *Horace Greeley: Printer, Editor, Crusader.* New York, Putnam's, 1946.

STOKES, ANSON PHELPS, *Church and State in the United States.* New York, Harper, 1950. 3 vols.

STOKES, I. N. PHELPS, ed., *Iconography of Manhattan Island.* New York, Robert H. Dodd, 1928. 6 vols.

STONE, IRVING, *They Also Ran.* New York, Doubleday Doran, 1945.

STRUIK, DIRK J., *Yankee Science in the Making.* Boston, Little, Brown, 1948.

SULLIVAN, MARK, *Our Times.* New York, Scribner's, 1935. 6 vols.

SWANBERG, W. A., *Jim Fisk: The Career of an Improbable Rascal.* New York, Scribner's, 1959.

———— *First Blood: The Story of Fort Sumter.* London, Longmans, 1960.

———— *Citizen Hearst.* New York, Scribner's, 1961.

SWIGGETT, HOWARD, *The Great Man, George Washington as a Human Being.* New York, Doubleday, 1953.

SYLVESTER, ROBERT, *No Cover Charge: A Backward Look at the Night Clubs.* New York, Dial, 1956.

SYRETT, HAROLD C., ed., *The Gentleman and the Tiger, The Autobiography of George B. McClellan, Jr.* Philadelphia, Lippincott, 1956.

TALESE, GAY, *New York: A Serendipiter's Journey.* New York, Harper, 1961.

TAYLOR, GEORGE ROGERS, *The Transportation Revolution, 1815-1860.* New York, Rinehart, 1951.

TEBBEL, JOHN, *The Life and Good Times of William Randolph Hearst.* New York, Dutton, 1952.

THOMAS, LOWELL, *History as You Heard It.* New York, Doubleday, 1957.

THOMAS, NORMAN, and BLANSHARD, PAUL, *What's the Matter With New York*. New York, Macmillan, 1932.

THOMPSON, CRAIG, and RAYMOND, ALLEN, *Gang Rule in New York*. New York, Dial, 1940.

Time magazine.

TUCKER, GLENN, *Poltroons and Patriots: A Popular Account of the War of 1812*. New York, Bobbs-Merrill, 1954. 2 vols.

TUCKERMAN, BAYARD, ed., *The Diary of Philip Hone*. New York, Dodd, Mead, 1889. 2 vols.

TULLY, ANDREW, *Era of Elegance*. New York, Funk & Wagnalls, 1947.

TUMULTY, JOSEPH P., *Woodrow Wilson as I Know Him*. New York, Doubleday Page, 1921.

UNTERMEYER, LOUIS, *Makers of the Modern World*. New York, Simon and Schuster, 1955.

U. S. News and World Report magazine.

VALENTINE, D. T., ed., *Manual of the Corporation of the City of New York*. New York, McSpedon & Baker, various years.

VAN DOREN, CARL, *Benjamin Franklin*. New York, Viking, 1938.

VAN DUSEN, ALBERT E., *Connecticut*. New York, Random House, 1961.

VAN DYKE, JOHN C., *The New New York*. New York, Macmillan, 1909.

VAN RENSSELAER, MRS. SCHUYLER, *History of the City of New York*. New York, Macmillan, 1909. 2 vols.

VERRILL, A. HYATT, *The American Indian*. New York, Appleton, 1927.

VILLARD, OSWALD GARRISON, *The Disappearing Daily*. New York, Knopf, 1944.

VOSS, CARL HERMANN, *Rabbi and Minister, The Friendship of Stephen S. Wise and John Haynes Holmes*. Cleveland, World, 1964.

WAKEFIELD, DAN, *Island in the City: Puerto Ricans in New York*. New York, Houghton Mifflin, 1957.

WALDMAN, LOUIS, *Labor Lawyer*. New York, Dutton, 1944.

WALKER, STANLEY, *The Night Club Era*. New York, Stokes, 1933.

———— *Mrs. Astor's Horse*. New York, Stokes, 1935.

WALTON, FRANK L., *Tomahawks to Textiles: The Fabulous Story of Worth Street*. New York, Appleton-Century-Crofts, 1953.

WARD, CHRISTOPHER, *The War of the Revolution*, John Richard Alden, ed. New York, Macmillan, 1952. 2 vols.

WARSHOW, ROBERT IRVING, *The Story of Wall Street*. New York, Greenberg, 1929.

WEITENKAMPF, FRANK, *Manhattan Kaleidoscope*. New York, Scribner's, 1947.

WELD, RALPH FOSTER, *Brooklyn Is America*. New York, Columbia University Press, 1950.

WERNER, M. R., *Barnum*. New York, Garden City Publishing, 1927.

———— *Tammany Hall*. New York, Garden City Publishing, 1928.

———— *It Happened in New York*. New York, Coward-McCann, 1957.

Werstein, Irving, *The Blizzard of '88*. New York, Crowell, 1960.

Wertenbaker, Thomas Jefferson, *Father Knickerbocker Rebels*. New York, Scribner's, 1948.

Whalen, Grover, *Mr. New York, Autobiography*. New York, Putnam's, 1955.

Whitaker's Almanac. London, Whitaker & Sons, Ltd., various years.

White, William Allen, *A Puritan in Babylon: The Story of Calvin Coolidge*. New York, Macmillan, 1938.

Who Was Who in America, 1897-1942. Chicago, Marquis, 1943.

Who's Who in America. Chicago, Marquis, various years.

Wiley, Bell Irvin, *The Life of Johnny Reb: The Common Soldier of the Confederacy*. New York, Bobbs-Merrill, 1943.

——— *The Life of Billy Yank: The Common Soldier of the Union*. New York, Bobbs-Merrill, 1951.

Williams, Sherman, *New York's Part in History*. New York, Appleton, 1915.

Williams, Stanley T., *The Life of Washington Irving*. New York, Oxford University Press, 1935. 2 vols.

Wilson, Edmund, *The American Earthquake, A Documentary of the Twenties and Thirties*. New York, Doubleday, 1958.

——— *The Shores of Light, A Literary Chronicle of the Twenties and Thirties*. New York, Random House, 1952.

——— *Classics and Commercials, A Literary Chronicle of the Forties*. New York, Farrar, Straus, 1950.

Wilson, Forrest, *Crusader in Crinoline: The Life of Harriet Beecher Stowe*. New York, Lippincott, 1941.

Wilson, James Grant, ed., *Memorial History of the City of New York*. New York, New-York History Co., 1892. 4 vols.

Wilson, James Harrison, *The Life of Charles A. Dana*. New York, Harper, 1907.

Wilson, Rufus Rockwell, *New York: Old & New*. Philadelphia, Lippincott, 1902. 2 vols.

Wilson, Rufus Rockwell, with Wilson, Otilie Erickson, *New York in Literature*. Elmira, N.Y., Primavera, 1947.

Winkler, Cecelia, ed., *Statistical Guide for New York City*. New York, Department of Commerce and Industrial Development, New York City, various years.

Winkler, John K., *Incredible Carnegie*. New York, Vanguard, 1931.

——— *Morgan the Magnificent*. New York, Doubleday Doran, 1932.

Woodward, W. E., *George Washington, The Image and the Man*. New York, Liveright, 1926.

Worden, Helen, *Here Is New York*. New York, Doubleday Doran, 1939.

World Almanac. New York, New York World-Telegram and Sun, various years.

Zink, Harold, *City Bosses in the United States: A Study of Twenty Municipal Bosses*. North Carolina, Duke University Press, 1930.

Index

619